10

Florence B. Houlding

EUROPE with pictures

Copenhagen

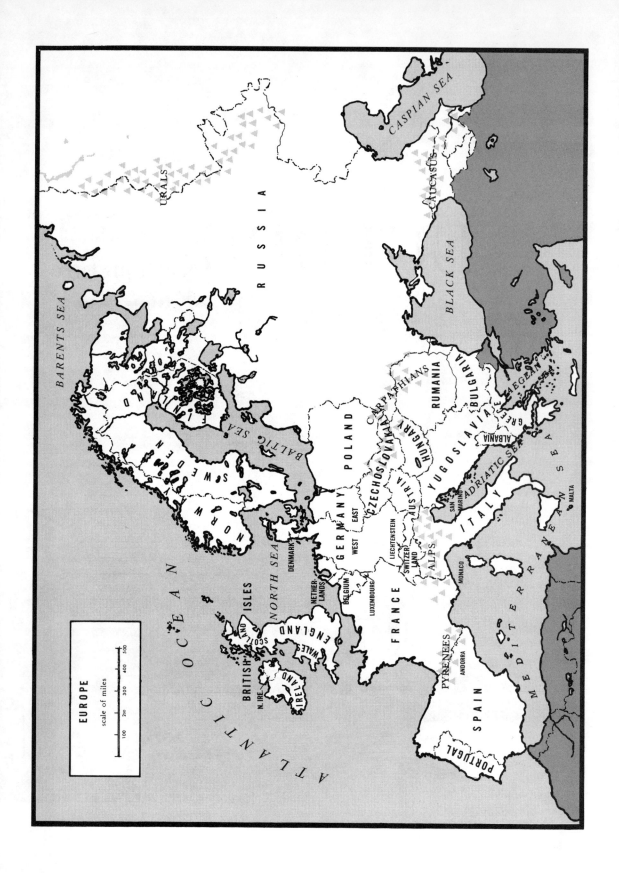

EUROPE
scale of miles

100 200 300 400 500

BARENTS SEA

ATLANTIC OCEAN

URALS

RUSSIA

CASPIAN SEA

CAUCASUS

BLACK SEA

AEGEAN

FINLAND

BALTIC SEA

SWEDEN

NORWAY

NORTH SEA

DENMARK

BRITISH ISLES

SCOTLAND

N. IRE.

IRELAND

WALES

ENGLAND

NETHER-
LANDS

BELGIUM

LUXEMBOURG

GERMANY

WEST

EAST

POLAND

CZECHOSLOVAKIA

CARPATHIANS

AUSTRIA

HUNGARY

RUMANIA

YUGOSLAVIA

BULGARIA

ALBANIA

GREECE

ADRIATIC SEA

SAN
MARINO

ITALY

LIECHTENSTEIN

SWITZER-
LAND

ALPS

FRANCE

MONACO

PYRENEES

ANDORRA

SPAIN

PORTUGAL

MALTA

MEDITERRANEAN SEA

EUROPE

with pictures

Bellver Castle, near Palma, Mallorca.

A tour of the 29 countries

STERLING
PUBLISHING CO., INC. NEW YORK

Oak Tree Press Co., Ltd.
Distributed by WARD LOCK, Ltd., London & Sydney

PLAN OF THIS BOOK

THIS BOOK PRESENTS the countries of Europe (other than Iceland and Turkey), arranged in a roughly slalom-like pattern beginning in the British Isles, then swinging north through Scandinavia to Russia, looping back along the Baltic to the Atlantic coast, then down along the Mediterranean, up through Central Europe, and down again to Greece and the Balkans. (The very small countries—Monaco, etc.—are not included in this plan, but are grouped together at the end.) The "slalom" permits the reader to progress gradually from one distinct geographical or cultural zone into another, by passing through transitional areas. It avoids categories such as "Central" and "Western," which are not always easy to delimit. Is Switzerland, for example, Central, Western or Southern?

The emphasis of this book is on places and people, and their history. Governmental structures and economic activities, while far from being slighted, are covered less fully.

Much of the material in this book has been excerpted from the following books of which Sterling Publishing Co. Inc. 419 Park Avenue South, New York 10016, is the copyright owner:
England—in Pictures, Copyright 1970, 1969, 1965
Scotland—in Pictures, Copyright 1968, 1964, 1963
Wales—in Pictures, Copyright 1969, 1967, 1966
Ireland—in Pictures, Copyright 1970, 1969, 1967, 1964, 1962
Denmark—in Pictures, Copyright 1969, 1966, 1961
Norway—in Pictures, Copyright 1967
Sweden—in Pictures, Copyright 1969, 1967
Finland—in Pictures, Copyright 1969, 1968, 1966, 1963
Russia—in Pictures, Copyright 1970, 1967, 1966
Poland—in Pictures, Copyright 1969
West Germany—in Pictures, Copyright 1967
Berlin—East and West—in Pictures, Copyright 1969, 1965, 1962
Holland—in Pictures, Copyright 1970, 1967, 1963
Belgium and Luxembourg—in Pictures, Copyright 1970, 1966
France—in Pictures, Copyright 1970, 1969, 1965
Switzerland—in Pictures, Copyright 1968, 1966, 1964, 1961
Spain—in Pictures, Copyright 1968, 1964, 1962
Portugal—in Pictures, Copyright 1969, 1966, 1965
Italy—in Pictures, Copyright 1967, 1966
Austria—in Pictures, Copyright 1970, 1964
Czechoslovakia—in Pictures, Copyright 1969
Hungary—in Pictures, Copyright 1970
Yugoslavia—in Pictures, Copyright 1970, 1968, 1963
Greece—in Pictures, Copyright 1968, 1967, 1965, 1962
Bulgaria—in Pictures, Copyright 1970
Rumania—in Pictures, Copyright 1970

CONTENTS

ENGLAND 7	
The Land 7	
History 19	
Government 37	
The People 43	
The Economy 49	
SCOTLAND 55	
The Land 55	
History 59	
The People 70	
The Economy 81	
WALES 83	
The Land and its History . . . 83	
The People 92	
IRELAND 97	
The Land 97	
History 101	
Government 122	
The People 125	
The Economy 135	
DENMARK 141	
The Land 141	
History 145	
Government 152	
The People 155	
The Economy 171	
NORWAY 175	
The Land 175	
History 189	
Government 199	
The Economy 202	
The People 205	
SWEDEN 217	
History 217	
The Land 227	
The Economy 234	
The People 238	
FINLAND 249	
The Land 249	
History 251	
Government 261	
The People 263	
Economy and Industry . . . 274	
RUSSIA 277	
The Land 277	
History 291	
Government 310	
The People 313	
The Economy 322	
POLAND 325	
The Land 325	
History 337	
Government 345	
The People 347	
The Economy 354	
WEST GERMANY 359	
History 359	
Government 367	
The Land 370	
The Economy 384	
The People 389	
BERLIN 401	
The Area 401	
History 407	
The Future 424	
HOLLAND 425	
The Land 425	
History and Government . . . 443	
The People 449	
Industry and Economy 467	
BELGIUM AND LUXEMBOURG . . . 477	
The Land 477	
History 486	
The People 497	
The Economy 515	

FRANCE 517	
The Land 519	
History 531	
Government 543	
The Economy 547	
The People 550	
SWITZERLAND 569	
History 569	
Government 571	
The Land 574	
The People 587	
The Economy 597	
Tourism 606	
SPAIN 613	
The Land 613	
History 619	
Government 630	
The People 635	
The Economy 648	
PORTUGAL 653	
The Land 653	
History 661	
The People 674	
The Economy 681	
ITALY 689	
The Land 689	
History 703	
Government 713	
The Economy 715	
The People 723	
The Arts 735	
AUSTRIA 741	
History 741	
The Land 754	
Government and Economy . . . 766	
The People 769	
CZECHOSLOVAKIA 775	
The Land 776	
History 782	
The People 794	
Industry 801	
HUNGARY 803	
The Land 803	
History 814	
Government 828	
The People 829	
The Economy 836	
YUGOSLAVIA 843	
History 843	
The People 851	
The Land 860	
The Economy 866	
GREECE 875	
The Land 877	
History 883	
The People 897	
Art 907	
The Economy 911	
BULGARIA 916	
The Land 917	
History 925	
The People 931	
The Economy 935	
RUMANIA 936	
The Land 937	
History 943	
The People 948	
The Economy 953	
ALBANIA 955	
MINOR STATES	
Andorra 957	
Liechtenstein 958	
Malta 959	
Monaco 959	
San Marino 960	

6 ■ ENGLAND

ENGLAND

Named Bath on account of its six springs where baths were built by the ancient Romans, this cathedral city in Somersetshire has as fine an appearance today as any in England. A variety of levels provide commanding sites for fine and regular streets, crescents and public buildings. The Pulteney Bridge over the River Avon is as crowded with shops and houses as in 1770, when it was built.

THE LAND

GEOGRAPHICAL SETTING

England covers the southern and largest portion of the island of Great Britain. With a total area of 50,337 square miles, England greatly exceeds each of the other parts of Great Britain in size. Scotland, which shares England's northern boundary, has an area of only 29,795 square miles while Wales, England's only land boundary on the west, possesses an area of barely 8,000 square miles.

The island of Britain is situated just north of the European continent, the southeast of England being the closest part of the island to

Europe. At Dover the English Channel, separating England from France, narrows to a width of only 21 miles (the Strait of Dover). As one travels up the east coast of England, Europe is never very far away. Belgium, Holland, Germany, Denmark, and Norway are all ranged across the North Sea. The most distant of these nations is Norway, about 400 miles from England at its closest point. England is very conveniently situated in respect to Europe, especially since the advent of aircraft as an important means of international transportation. The following air distances (in miles)

The skyline of modern London is dominated by the General Post Office Tower. The tallest building in Britain—620 feet—it has a revolving restaurant and serves as a station for transmitting and receiving telephone conversations by micro-wave radio.

View of Birling Gap and Seven Sisters chalk cliffs, Eastbourne, Sussex. The Gap was formerly a popular haunt of smugglers.

from London to several European capitals show that England is right on Europe's doorstep: Paris—215, Berlin—593, Amsterdam—231, Oslo—722, Copenhagen—609, Rome—908, Madrid—775.

On England's west, across the narrow Irish Sea is Ireland. At one point in the North Channel just over 20 miles separate the islands of Britain and Ireland. The small self-governing Isle of Man in the Irish Sea is practically a dependency of the United Kingdom, but is not strictly part of England.

The Channel Islands, off the northwest coast of France, belong to Great Britain but have their own laws. Total land area of the islands is only 75 square miles, Jersey and Guernsey being the largest and most heavily populated. Dairy cattle of famed Jersey and Guernsey types were named after the islands where they were first bred. New Jersey, one of the 50 United States, likewise takes its name from the island of Jersey.

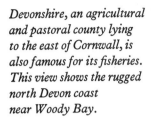
Devonshire, an agricultural and pastoral county lying to the east of Cornwall, is also famous for its fisheries. This view shows the rugged north Devon coast near Woody Bay.

The Isle of Wight, located along the English Channel, between the great southern English port cities of Portsmouth and Southampton, is the largest island off the coast of England. Administratively it is part of Hampshire.

England is roughly triangular in shape. Within this relatively small triangle, an amazing diversity of landscapes can be found. Perhaps the most striking natural feature is the nearness of all parts of the country to the sea. No place in England is more than 75 miles from the sea. The distance across the southern part of England (the base of the triangle), from Land's End at the tip of Cornwall in the west to South Foreland in the east, is 316 miles. From South Foreland to Berwick-on-Tweed, England's northernmost town, the distance is 348 miles. However, the sides of the triangle are by no means smooth. England has a long, irregular coastline of some 1,835 miles with the Irish Sea to the west, the English Channel to the south, and the North Sea on the east. The entire coastline is characterized by deep indentations of the sea, particularly on the west coast. In a number of places the land drops off abruptly into the sea in the form of rugged cliffs, such as those

Ponies roam Hampshire's New Forest. Motorists must drive with care through the forest, for the ponies often cross roads without paying attention to oncoming cars. Many of the ponies are friendly, but there is a fine for feeding them.

York is one of northern England's most important cities. The Romans built here a fortress known as Eboracum in A.D. 71, of which many relics remain. In the 13th century, the city was surrounded with this 2½-mile-long wall. The York Minster is Britain's largest and perhaps grandest cathedral, and was completed in 1472. The city played an important rôle in the intermittent thirty-year struggle (1455-85) between the noble houses of York and Lancaster known as the Wars of the Roses.

found along the coast of Cornwall, and the world-famous "white cliffs of Dover."

England's closeness to the sea and rise to world power have had much to do with one another. The irregular coastline has provided the country with many fine natural anchorages for ships and has been an indispensable aid in the development of a strong merchant marine and navy. England's position just off the northern shores of Europe enabled it to assume a leading rôle in international trade and commerce, particularly with North America.

It should never be forgotten that the sea has been England's most valuable ally in protecting the country from invaders. Referring to England and the waters around it, Shakespeare called his homeland:

"... This precious stone set in the silver sea,
Which serves it in the office of a wall
Or as a moat defensive to a house,
Against the envy of less happier lands . . ."
(*Richard II*, II.1)

Since the time of the Norman conquest in 1066, no one has successfully invaded England. It was on the seas about England that Drake and Hawkins destroyed the Spanish Armada in 1588 before the Spaniards could land troops on English soil. Adolf Hitler's Nazi armies conquered France with ease in 1940, but the German dictator was never able to unleash his troops on England because the Royal Air Force defeated the German air force in the Battle of Britain and in so doing prevented Hitler from launching an invasion across the English Channel.

TOPOGRAPHY

English topography is diverse but falls into two general divisions: the predominantly mountainous terrain of the northern and western parts of the country and the lower-lying areas of the southeastern part. The term "mountainous" may be misleading, for English mountains cannot compare with the Alps or Himalayas. England's highest peak, Scafell, located in the Lake District of northwest England, has an altitude of only 3,210 feet. Yet, many English mountains, especially in the Lake District, are far more rugged than their modest size would lead one to believe. Rocky, barren summits rising sharply above long, narrow lakes have captured the imagination of such poets as Wordsworth and have attracted many an English mountaineer seeking practice for more difficult climbs in other parts of the world.

The Pennine uplands region of northern England includes a group of hills running in a north-south direction. They have been worn down by hundreds of centuries of erosion, and the highest of the Pennines, the Peak, has an elevation of only 2,088 feet. The Pennines may be thought of as England's backbone. Although the upland areas themselves are sparsely settled, many cities and towns are located along the edges of the hilly area close by deposits of iron and coal which are found on the flanks of the Pennines. These mineral deposits, especially coal, were a primary factor in England's meteoric rise to world leadership in industrial production during the 19th century. Among the important industrial cities adjacent to the Pennines are Leeds, Nottingham, Bradford, Manchester, and Sheffield (the last being famous for its high-quality steel and cutlery).

England's southwestern peninsula, including the counties of Devon, Cornwall, and part of Somerset form yet another area of hilly terrain. England's best-known moors (large, desolate tracts of land covered by heath and similar types of vegetation), Dartmoor and Exmoor, are situated here. The region has a mild climate and heavy rainfall. Livestock-raising is carried on by the few people who dwell on the moors. Most of the inhabitants of the southwest live in the towns along the coast which include the port city of Plymouth. Alternating hard and soft rock along the south coast of Cornwall and Devon has been worn away by the constant beating of the sea where the softer portions are exposed so that the harder rock remains where it was and the sea occupies former soft-rock areas. As a result, many excellent natural ports of varying size have been formed over the ages.

The majority of the English, including the residents of Greater London, live in the lowland plains of southeastern England. Birmingham, second largest city in England, and

The Little Harbour Lighthouse guides Cornish sailors to a safe anchorage. Penzance, Cornwall's most important town for both business and pleasure, is on the left.

Where the South Downs meet the English Channel at Beachy Head in Sussex, chalk cliffs tower above the 142-foot high Beachy Head Lighthouse, which warns ships in the Channel to keep their distance.

Coventry are located in the western part of this area. This is by no means a table-flat expanse, but few hills rise over 600 feet in elevation. The most prominent surface features of the land are alternating ridges and valleys. Many of the ridges are composed of chalk, a form of pure white limestone. At one time millions of years ago, a layer of chalk covered all of the south-eastern portion of England, but erosion has left the ridges, which radiate from the chalk plateau of Salisbury Plain in southern England like spokes of a wheel. In the south, many of these spokes are called "downs." The meeting of the North Downs with the English Channel has produced the well known white cliffs at Dover which can be seen from France, 21 miles away, on a clear day. Farther to the north, in Yorkshire and Lincolnshire, the chalk deposits are termed "wolds." The chalk country is thinly inhabited, and most of the downs are covered with grasses and clumps of beech trees which make the chalky areas suitable for grazing flocks of sheep.

The valleys are fertile. Most of them consist of clay and also of débris left by the sheets of ice that covered most of England during the Ice Age. Many small farming towns are clustered in the valleys.

London is located in a large basin of clay and gravel between two of the chalk ridges fanning out from Salisbury Plain.

Most of England's east coast is flat and slopes gently into the North Sea. At one time, millions of years ago, the present shallow bed of the North Sea formed a land bridge to the European continent. The fenlands, consisting of parts of the counties of Norfolk, Lincoln, and Cambridge, are a region of low-lying marshes. Many of the fens have been reclaimed from the sea by the building of dikes and canals to facilitate drainage. As a result, several parts of the fenlands are now below sea level—and make fine soil for the growing of wheat, vegetables, and sugar beets.

England has many rivers, but because Britain is a small island no river is very long. The Thames is the longest, extending for some 209 miles—if allowance is made for its windings. Many events important in English history have occurred on the banks of the River Thames as it follows its course to the sea through Oxford, Windsor and London. It was

The mists of night settle over Wyndham Place, London, as a "bobby" patrols the street. Members of the Metropolitan Police Force, organized in 1829, acquired their nickname from the founder of the force, Sir Robert Peel. They carry no firearms under normal circumstances.

Derwentwater in Cumberland is one of the loveliest of the 15 lakes in the Lake District of north-western England. Dense woods and barren mountain crags form a scenic background to the lake.

at Runnymede, a meadow 20 miles upstream from London, that King John signed the Magna Carta on June 15, 1215. This famous document ended the absolute power of English monarchs and gave legal rights to the barons (but not the common people) of the Kingdom.

Other important English rivers are the Severn and its tributaries, the two Avons (Shakespeare was born at Stratford-upon-Avon on the northern Avon; the busy port of Bristol is located on the southern Avon), the Mersey (on which the port of Liverpool is located), the Tyne, the Humber, and the Tees.

CLIMATE

Many people are quick to characterize England as a land of rain and fog. While it does rain a lot and there is sometimes fog in England, the sun comes out too. However, the most important factor in English climate is often overlooked by critics. This feature is the lack of extremes in English weather. Winters are not normally characterized by bone-chilling cold, nor do the English swelter under broiling heat during the summer months. Hurricanes, tornadoes, and similar disasters are unknown.

The English climate is determined by three major influences. The first of these is the North Atlantic drift, the great current of warm water that bathes the shores of Western Europe. The North Atlantic drift is a continuation of the Gulf Stream, a river-within-an-ocean that originates in the Gulf of Mexico.

Prevailing winds blowing from the southwest are a second important factor in English climate. These winds are warmed by their passage over the waters of the North Atlantic drift and provide England with a moderately warm climate. The importance of the drift to England can easily be seen by comparing its climate with that of other parts of the world in a similarly high latitude. Southern Canada, for instance, experiences harsh, long winters. Most Canadian ports are ice-locked for several months during the winter; English ports remain open for shipping the year round.

The third factor in English climate is the nearness to the sea of all parts of the country. This prevents the winds that blow in from the Atlantic from cooling off very much while passing over the land. It also places England in the path of considerable moisture—in the form of rain and fog (and some snow in the winter).

Western England receives the greatest amount of precipitation since it is exposed to the prevailing southwesterly winds which are laden with moisture and often carry storms born in the Atlantic. The higher elevations of western England are another reason for the heavier precipitation of the region. Some parts of the Lake District have an annual rainfall of over

60 inches. As one travels eastward towards the North Sea and into the low-lying areas, rainfall decreases. Average annual rainfall in the region about the mouth of the Thames falls below 25 inches. Although October is generally the wettest month for most of England, precipitation is fairly evenly distributed through the year.

In the winter, cold, dry air from Europe often pushes its way across the North Sea and gives England, particularly the eastern portion of the country, clear, cold days with periods of below-freezing temperatures. Thus western England, during the winter, has more rain and warmer temperatures than the eastern portion of the country. In summer, however, a large mass of warm, dry air over the Atlantic Ocean (termed "the Azores high") frequently reaches as far north as England and brings good weather. The

eastern part of the country generally has damper and hotter summers than western England. In July, London's mean temperature is 64°F. For England as a whole, the July mean temperature is 62°F. while in January it is 40°F.

England is not the best place to sunbathe. The sun is visible for only about one-third of all daylight hours on the average. The remainder of the time it is hidden by clouds and mists. The number of hours of sunshine in England varies between 1,200 and 1,700 annually.

In the cities, industrial smoke and fumes sometimes mix with fog to produce "smog." Smog is annoying to humans, and in extreme cases, such as the London "killer" smogs (fortunately of very infrequent occurrence), has been known to be responsible for deaths.

Almost all English towns have a high street, a main road stretching from one end of the town to the other and lined with shops. This is the High Street of Dorking, Surrey, a market town and dormitory of London, located at the edge of the North Downs. Dorking was the home of Thomas Malthus, the political economist who wrote on the relationship of population growth to food and other resources, and of George Meredith, the 19th-century novelist, who is buried there.

The fox hunt is on. Hounds sniff the ground in order to find and follow the scent of the quarry. Although fox hunting on horseback with a pack of dogs existed in the 18th century, it developed, not as a sport, but as a means of reducing the lamb-killing foxes. The modern hunt began in the 19th century and was popularized by Hugo Meynell, the "Father of the English Chase."

FLORA AND FAUNA

The demands of man have had a drastic impact on England's natural vegetation and wildlife. Forests now cover only about 5 per cent of the English countryside. Most remaining forests were preserved by kings and wealthy landowners for hunting and other diversions. Oak, beech, and other hardwoods are the dominant trees in English forests. In the 20th century the government has been undertaking an extensive project to replace many of England's vanished woodlands by planting millions of new, young trees. Although man has cut down most of England's forests, this has had little effect on the moorlands, and these vast tracts of bleak-looking scrub vegetation growing in upland areas have changed little over the centuries. In Cornwall (England's "Riviera"—although there is much less sunshine there than on the French Riviera) the mild year-round climate allows the outdoor growth of palms and yucca plants, an amazing occurrence when one considers that Cornwall is farther north than the city of Winnipeg in Canada.

England's wildlife has suffered much the same fate as its woodlands. By the end of the Middle Ages, the brown bear, wolf, and beaver had all been exterminated. The larger animals still remaining in England—deer and fox for instance—have survived because they have been "protected" by wealthy huntsmen who understandably require animals to hunt if their sport is to continue. Many Englishmen question whether the unrelenting chase of one unfortunate fox or deer by scores of mounted hunters and hunting dogs is a sport at all. Private game preserves of the wealthy have always been an attraction for unofficial hunters (i.e. poachers). As a youth, William Shakespeare is said to have fled Stratford after having been revealed as a deer poacher and threatened with prosecution.

Many types of smaller animals still thrive. Among these are the badger, otter, weasel,

Apart from their commercial importance, canals have their recreational uses. Here, a pleasure boat cruises down the Grand Union Canal. The first modern English canal was built in 1761 to carry coal.

and rabbit. English bird watchers are kept busy keeping track of several hundred species of birds that either live in or migrate to England during a part of the year. The draining of the fens has deprived many birds of their homes.

Fresh-water trout and salmon attract many anglers eager for excitement and tasty dining. Izaak Walton's *The Compleat Angler, or the Contemplative Man's Recreation* which was first published in 1653 is considered the definitive work on the subject. While many Englishmen fish for pleasure, others make their living catching mackerel, haddock, herring, and other species of sea fish which abound in the waters around Britain.

NATURAL RESOURCES

English mineral deposits have been worked since ancient times. Cornish tin deposits and lead deposits in other parts of the country attracted many Phoenician traders. A need for these valuable minerals was one of the reasons for the Roman conquest of England in 55-54 B.C. Production of tin, lead, zinc, and other mineral ores was carried on at many small

Although only a small percentage of the English population are farmers, the food supply for England is now half home-grown. This has been made possible by a high degree of mechanization and improved agricultural methods which now produce the highest yield per acre in the world.

The Clifton Suspension Bridge spans the River Avon at Bristol. Designed by Isambard Kingdom Brunel in 1831, the 702-foot span was not completed until 1864. Brunel was also the designer of the first steamship to make regular trans-Atlantic voyages, the "Great Western."

mines scattered over the countryside. England was the world's greatest producer of tin ore until near the end of the 19th century. Iron mines also provided needed raw material for the great Industrial Revolution of the 19th century. But, the mining of most English minerals was carried on on a small, inefficient scale. The demands of mass production of the modern era and the opening of large-scale mining operations in other parts of the world (often under the guidance of English investors and technicians) forced most English mining enterprises to close down—with one major exception.

The major exception is coal. England sits on top of a virtual treasure chest of this valuable mineral—enough to last at least 500 years if current estimates are correct. There is coal in Durham and Northumberland in the north and in Kent in the south. The coal itself runs in seams which range in thickness from a few inches to more than 30 feet. At some coastal mines, tunnels have been dug several miles out under the sea in order to follow workable coal seams.

In various parts of England several non-metallic substances are mined. The fine clay of Cornwall provides the raw material for the world-famous English chinaware. Chalk excavated from the Downs is used in the production of cement. Gypsum, salt, fluor-spar, building stone, and other materials also find their commercial uses. Although a few minor discoveries of oil have been made in England, almost all petroleum used must be imported from abroad. However, the recent discovery of what may be the world's largest natural gas field in nearby Holland has sparked off a search of the North Sea and surrounding land areas by the countries concerned, and there is hope of discovering new and large deposits of natural gas and oil in England or off its shores.

Pigeons and political demonstrations are common sights in Trafalgar Square, which commemorates Nelson's great naval victory over the French. The National Gallery, housing many of the nation's art treasures, and St. Martin-in-the-Fields Church can be seen in the background.

The natural wealth of Cornwall lies underground and in the seas surrounding the county; a popular Cornish toast is "fish, tin and copper." Here is a view of the mouth of the River Fowey. Cornwall is one of the most popular holiday areas in Britain.

Industrial smoke and traffic jams are all but unknown on the Isle of Man as one can see in this peaceful setting at Laxey. The insignia on the building at the right is the "three-legs" triquetra, the arms of the island.

Stonehenge, situated on Salisbury Plain near Amesbury in Wiltshire, is England's most famous prehistoric monument. Its stones, arranged in 2 concentric circles, are 13 to 28 feet high. Of unknown origin or purpose and more than 3,500 years old, Stonehenge was for many centuries a place of pilgrimage. There is some speculation that it might have been erected by Druids as a sun dial.

HISTORY

Discoveries of ancient bones, tools, and dwelling places by archæologists make it clear that men have lived in England since long before the beginning of recorded history. The early inhabitants of Britain passed through periods known as the Old and New Stone Ages. Later, as their culture developed and they learned to extract metals from the soil and fashion tools and objects from them, came the Bronze and Iron Ages.

About 600 B.C. the Celts, a Central European people, began migrating to the British Isles and mixing with the native people. There were several waves of Celtic immigrants. The Gaels were the first and they were later followed by the Brythons (after whom Britain is named).

Under the Celts, England flourished. The Celts were organized along tribal lines, and the tribes often fought one another. Trade was important, and tin, mined in England, found a ready market in Europe. The Celts were divided into three large castes: the Druids (priests), the warriors, and the common people. The Druids supervised what scanty education there was, settled disputes, and, most important of all, conducted Celtic religious ceremonies which included worship in oak groves, the oak tree and the mistletoe being sacred to them. There were also human sacrifices to please the gods on occasion.

In 55 B.C. Julius Caesar, the Roman conqueror of Gaul (France), crossed the English Channel and staged a short raid on Kent in south-east England, but he soon returned to Gaul. Caesar came back to England in 54 B.C. with a large army. He marched inland to the vicinity of what is now London, defeated the Celtic tribes in the area and forced them to pay tribute. However, Caesar soon withdrew his Roman legions and returned once again to Gaul.

The Romans left Britain alone until A.D. 43 when the Emperor Claudius ordered the con-

Archaeologists excavating the old Roman town of Corstopitum, about 21 miles west of Newcastle-upon-Tyne, uncovered this large granary. Corstopitum, founded by Agricola about A.D. 80, had a forum, a main street, a six-sided public fountain, and centrally heated homes. The town was an important military outpost.

quest and occupation of the island. By A.D. 61 the Romans had subdued most of England. However, Roman attempts to conquer what is now Scotland failed. The Emperor Hadrian had to order the construction of a 77-mile-long wall across northern England from the Solway to the Tyne (built A.D. 122-28) to keep out invaders from the north.

Rome helped to develop England's economy and expand trade. Roads were built, connecting the fortified cities, to make it easier for the Roman legions to move about the country, and this aided commerce. London became England's commercial, military and political capital during the Roman era.

The Roman occupation did not leave nearly as great an imprint on England as it did on other countries, such as France. Although Latin words

found their way into the local English languages and Christianity was introduced, most of the Roman cultural influence was wiped out by an invasion of Britain by semi-barbarian Teutonic tribes from northern Europe following the withdrawal of the Roman legions in A.D. 401.

During the 5th century A.D. these Teutonic tribes—the Angles, Saxons, and Jutes—began coming to the British Isles both as settlers and as pirates. According to legend, a Celtic ruler named Vortigern hired two Jute pirate chiefs, Horsa and Hengist, to protect his land from the warlike Picts and Scots living in the north. Unfortunately for Vortigern, the Jute chiefs liked England so much that they decided to take over his lands.

Most of the Celtic inhabitants of England migrated westward to Cornwall, Wales and Cumberland as the invaders moved in from the east. After a period of turmoil, seven separate Teutonic kingdoms arose. They were Kent, Northumbria, East Anglia, Mercia, Wessex (West Saxons), Sussex (South Saxons), and Essex (East Saxons).

In 597, St. Augustine, a Catholic missionary sent by Pope Gregory I from Rome, came to Kent and converted the ruler, King Ethelbert. The Kentish capital of Canterbury soon became the point from which Catholicism began spreading over most of England. A Celtic Christian Church, also existed in 7th-century England, but at the Synod of Whitby held in 664 Catholicism gained the preference, thus uniting England more closely with the European countries.

Under King Egbert, Wessex rose to prominence, and briefly, in 829, all England was united under one ruler.

England soon had to face a new danger. The Danes (Vikings), pagan Scandinavian adventur-ers, began landing along the English coast and raiding many towns, including Winchester and York. The first landings came in 793 and less than a century later, in 871, the Danes were powerful enough to launch an attack on the Kingdom of Wessex. King Alfred the Great finally checked the Danish advance at the battle of Edington in 878. By the Treaty of Wedmore in 886, the Danes agreed to become Christians and to live in an area of eastern England north of the Thames and south of the Tees.

The Danes were not satisfied with their lot, however, and fighting continued in fits and starts. In order to buy peace, the English collected a special tax, known as the *Danegeld*, and used the money to bribe the Danes or raise an army for defence. Danegeld money saved London when the city was attacked in 994 by Sweyn Forkbeard, the Danish king, and Olaf I, the Norwegian ruler. The English naturally resented the Danish

To prevent bands of tribesmen from the Scottish Highlands from raiding Roman England, the Emperor Hadrian ordered the building of a 73-mile-long wall across the northern part of the country. First built of turf about A.D. *122, the wall was later partly rebuilt with stone and represented the high-water mark of the Roman conquest. The Romans patrolled the entire length of the wall from forts and watch-towers. This is a view of the wall looking eastward from Cuddy's Crag, Northumberland.*

intruders, and in 1002 King Ethelred II inspired a massacre of Danes living in England. Sweyn Forkbeard retaliated by conquering England and his son, Canute, ruled England from 1016 to 1035. Sons of Canute ruled England until 1042 when Edward the Confessor, a son of King Ethelred II, became ruler of the country. After Edward's death in 1066, his brother-in-law, Harold II, became king.

William the Conqueror built the Tower of London in 1078 to impress upon Saxon Londoners the strength of Norman authority. However, the Tower has gained its chief notoriety from the many famous political prisoners (including Sir Walter Raleigh, Mary Queen of Scots, and Lady Jane Grey), who have been confined within its walls and some executed here.

THE NORMAN ERA, 1066-1153

1066—William, duke of Normandy (France), claims the English throne and invades England. He defeats army of the English ruler, Harold, at battle of Hastings and has himself crowned King of England.
1066-71—William (The Conqueror) puts down opposition to his rule. William seizes large amounts of land from his enemies and divides them up amongst his trusted friends. French becomes language of the royal court and nobility; English remains language of common people.

1085-6—Domesday Book, compiled by order of king, lists land holdings, economic resources, customs, and other data about England during Norman era. (Domesday Book has been used as late as the 20th century to settle arguments concerning property ownership.)
1087—William the Conqueror dies in France. His son, William II, succeeds him.
1087-1100—King William oppresses people by levying heavy taxes.
1100—William II killed by arrow while hunting. Henry, another son of William the Conqueror, seizes throne.
1100—King Henry issues Charter of Liberties.
1107—Compromise of Bec ends dispute between the Church and the Crown.
1135—Henry I dies and is succeeded by nephew, Stephen.
1139—Rival claimants to throne invade England, and period of civil war follows.
1153—Treaty of Wallingford ends civil war. Henry of Anjou made heir to throne.

It was in Canterbury Cathedral in Kent that Archbishop Thomas à Becket was murdered in 1170 while at prayer, by four knights presumably encouraged by King Henry II. Becket was made a saint three years later, and in 1220 his remains were enshrined behind the altar. Canterbury became a goal of pilgrims from all parts of Europe until Henry VIII's break with the Church of Rome three centuries later. Here is the north choir aisle, facing east.

THE PLANTAGENETS 1154-1398

1154—French-born Henry of Anjou becomes first Plantagenet king of England. King's domains include much of what is now modern France.

1155—Thomas à Becket made Chancellor. Appointed Archbishop of Canterbury in 1162.

1164—Constitutions of Clarendon increase authority of king at expense of Pope. Becket opposes Constitutions.

1166—Assize of Clarendon. Grand jury made a regular part of the English judicial system.

1170—Becket murdered in Canterbury Cathedral.

1189—Henry II dies two days after being forced to recognize his rebellious son, Richard (the "lion-hearted"), as heir to throne. Richard immediately begins preparations for crusade to Holy Land to rescue it from Moslems.

1192—Richard concludes truce with Moslems in Holy Land. . . . Richard captured and held for ransom by Duke of Austria on his return trip.

1194—Heavy taxation pays Richard's ransom. Richard returns briefly to England and crushes rebellion inspired by his brother, John.

1199—Richard dies from arrow wound received in battle. John becomes king.

1204—Normandy and many other English possessions in France captured by French king, Philip II.

1205-13—King John feuds with Pope over choice of new Archbishop of Canterbury.

1208—Pope Innocent III places England under papal interdict (prohibition).

1209—King John excommunicated by Pope.

1213—Threatened with French invasion, King John gives in to Pope and promises to become his vassal.

1215—The barons, discontented with King John's harsh rule and heavy taxation, force him to sign *Magna Carta* (Great Charter) at Runnymede.

1216—King John dies and his 9-year-old son (Henry III) becomes king with government in hands of a regency.

1217—French army, which had landed in England at invitation of barons hostile to John, is defeated and returns to France.

1227—Henry assumes full powers of rule; regency ended.

1258—The Great Council (Parliament) of barons and church leaders meets at Oxford and demands a greater share in the government—demands known as Provisions of Oxford.

1263-65—Barons war against king (who had disregarded the Provisions with papal permission).

1264—Barons defeat and capture King Henry at battle of Lewes.

1265—Simon de Montfort, leader of baronial

The choir of Durham Cathedral, which stands impressively on a hilltop overlooking the town. Construction of the cathedral began in 1093, and additions were still being made as late as 1500.

party, summons Model Parliament, composed of knights from shires and representatives from cities and towns in addition to usual barons and clergy. . . . Henry's son, Edward, escapes from captivity, raises an army, and defeats barons at Evesham. De Montfort killed in battle; Henry resumes rule.

1272—Henry III dies and is succeeded by Edward.

1277-82—English forces conquer Wales.

1279—Statue of Mortmain: restrictions placed on property transactions involving Church.

1290—Jews expelled from England. (Re-admitted by Oliver Cromwell in 17th century.)

1294-1302—War with France. Scots and French make alliance (1294).

1295—Model Parliament meets.

1307—Edward I dies; his son becomes Edward II.

1311—Parliament meets and demands more control over operations of government.

1312—Gaveston, king's closest adviser, executed by Earl of Warwick.

1314—Robert Bruce, king of Scots, defeats King Edward at Bannockburn, assuring Scottish independence.

The ruins of a 12th-century Cistercian abbey, Tintern Abbey on the River Wey in Monmouthshire. In William Wordsworth's poem, "Lines Composed a Few Miles above Tintern Abbey," he wrote: "The sounding cataract / Haunted me like a passion; the tall rock, / The mountain, and the deep and gloomy wood, / Their colours and their forms, were then to me / An appetite; a feeling and a love . . ."

1322—Parliament asserts its right to approve or disapprove all laws (Statute of York).

1327—Edward II deposed by wife, Queen Isabella, and her lover, Roger de Mortimer, who rule in place of the young Edward III. . . . Edward II imprisoned and murdered.

1330—Edward III assumes control of government. . . . Mortimer executed.

1337—Beginning of Hundred Years' War with France.

1340—Geoffrey Chaucer born.

1346—Battle of Crécy. English army, using long-bows and cannons, destroys much larger French army, composed of knights clad in coats-of-mail and using mediæval battle tactics.

1347—English capture Calais on French coast.

1348-49—Black Death (plague) strikes England. One-third of population dies in less than year. National economy badly affected by plague.

1356—Battle of Poitiers. Black Prince, son of Edward III, defeats French. John II, French king, captured and held for large ransom.

1360—Treaty of Brétigny brings Hundred Years' War to temporary halt

1362—English language ordered used in all courts of law.

1369-96—Fresh fighting breaks out between England and France. French recapture most of land previously lost to English.

1376—The Good Parliament. Crown officials impeached for first time by a Parliament.

1377—Edward III dies. Richard II, son of Black Prince, ascends throne.

1381—Unsuccessful peasants' revolt led by Wat Tyler and Jack Straw.

THE HOUSES OF LANCASTER AND YORK AND WARS OF THE ROSES, 1399-1484

1399—Henry (Bolingbroke), exiled son of John of Gaunt, duke of Lancaster, invades England and captures Richard II. Parliament deposes Richard, and Bolingbroke crowned King Henry IV.

1403 and 1405—Henry defeats Percys (family from northern England) and Welsh under Owen Glendower who had rebelled against Lancastrian rule.

1413—Henry IV dies, succeeded by his son, Henry V.

1414—Rebellion by Lollards, heretical religious sect, thwarted.

1415—King Henry revives Hundred Years' War and invades France, taking advantage of un-settled conditions in that country. At battle of Agincourt, English archers and foot soldiers, outnumbered 3 to 1 by French, rout enemy,

King Richard II gazes solemnly from a wall of Westminster Abbey. In his hands he holds the orb and sceptre, symbols of royal authority. The unpopular Richard was deposed in 1399 and died shortly thereafter. He is entombed in the Abbey.

proving disadvantage of using troops clad in heavy and burdensome coats-of-arms and mail.

1417-19—Successful English campaigns in France. French sue for peace.

1420—Treaty of Troyes. Henry to marry daughter of insane French king, Charles VI, and to become king of France on Charles' death.

1422—Henry V dies while attempting to put down French revolt. His infant son succeeds him as Henry VI.

1422-37—England and English possessions in France governed by regents, the king's uncles.

1429—French army, led by Joan of Arc, saves Orleans from English.

1431—Joan of Arc burned at stake by English on charge of witchcraft.

1445—Henry marries Margaret of Anjou, niece of Charles VII, French king crowned at urging of Joan of Arc.

1450—French begin final campaign to expel English troops.

1453—English possessions in France reduced to Calais, bringing Hundred Years' War to end.... Constantinople captured by Turks.

1454—Richard, Duke of York, appointed Pro-tector of England during period of mental illness suffered by Henry VI.

1455—King Henry recovers his reason; Richard dismissed; War of Roses between the Houses of Lancaster and York breaks out.

1460—Richard of York killed in battle after initial triumphs.

1461—Edward, son of Richard of York, defeats Lancastrians at Towton and assumes title of King Edward IV. Henry VI flees to Scotland.

1470—Earl of Warwick, architect of the Yorkist triumph, engineers return to throne of Henry VI after breaking with Edward IV.

1471—Yorkists defeat Lancastrian forces at battles of Barnet and Tewkesbury. Warwick killed; Edward king once again. Henry VI dies in Tower of London under mysterious circumstances.

1471-83—Period of personal rule by Edward IV.

1483—Edward dies and his young son (Edward V) becomes king at age of 12. Richard, Duke of Gloucester ("Crouchback"), king's uncle and his "protector," soon has Edward deposed and murdered in the Tower of London (along with younger brother). Richard has himself crowned King Richard III.

THE TUDORS, 1485-1602

1485—Henry Tudor's troops defeat army of Richard III at Bosworth Field. Richard III killed in battle and Henry crowned Henry VII.

1486—King Henry helps end Lancaster-York feud by marrying Elizabeth, daughter of Edward IV.

1492—Treaty of Etaples with France. English claims to Brittany dropped in return for in-

Richard III (left), last of the Yorkists, reigned briefly, 1483-1485, after having usurped the throne from his nephew. Following Richard's defeat and death at Bosworth, Henry Tudor (right) assumed the crown as Henry VII.

After Henry VIII divorced Catherine of Aragon, he was excommunicated from the Roman Catholic Church, so he installed himself as head of the church in England. When their Catholic daughter ascended the throne, she sought to restore papal authority, and as a result of the religious persecutions that ensued, won the name "Bloody Mary."

demnity of £159,000. . . . Columbus' first voyage across Atlantic, discovers West Indies.

1497—The Cabots, sailing west to discover new route to China, discover North American coast.

1509—Henry VII dies; his son succeeds to throne as Henry VIII. . . . Henry marries Catherine of Aragon, widow of his elder brother (later mother of Queen Mary).

1512-13—War with France.

1513—English destroy Scottish army at Flodden Field.

1515—Thomas Wolsey named Lord Chancellor and Cardinal.

1521—Henry gains title "Defender of the Faith" for writing a pamphlet attacking Martin Luther.

1529—Wolsey dismissed for failing to obtain order from Pope Leo X ending Henry's marriage to Catherine of Aragon.

1533—Henry marries Anne Boleyn (later mother of Elizabeth I). . . . Marriage to Catherine declared invalid by Thomas Cranmer, Archbishop of Canterbury.

1534—Payments to Pope stopped. Act of Supremacy makes king supreme head of Church of England and completes break with Rome.

1535—Sir Thomas More beheaded for refusing to recognize Henry as head of church.

1536—Seizures of Catholic monasteries begun by king. New lands and incomes from them parcelled out to friends of crown. . . . Anne Boleyn beheaded. Henry marries Jane Seymour, who becomes mother of Edward VI, dies in 1537.

1538-47—Wars with Scotland and France.

1541—Henry takes added title of King of Ireland. . . . Catherine Howard, Henry's fifth wife, beheaded.

1547—Henry VIII dies; his 9-year-old son ascends throne as Edward VI.

1547-53—Because of Edward's tender age, Dukes of Somerset (until 1549) and Northumberland (until 1553) rule.

1549 and 1552—Books of Common Prayer issued by Church of England. . . . Other Protestant sects active during Edward's reign.

1553—Edward VI dies. Northumberland's attempt to make Lady Jane Grey queen fails, and Catherine of Aragon's daughter, Mary, a Catholic, becomes queen.

1553-58—Protestant laws repealed, England becomes a nominally Catholic country once again. About 300 Protestants burned at the stake for heresy, giving Mary nickname "Bloody Mary."

1558—England loses Calais, its last French possession. . . . Mary dies and Anne Boleyn's daughter, Elizabeth I, becomes queen.

1559—Act of Supremacy restores monarch as head of (Anglican) Church of England. Pro-Catholic legislation passed during Mary's reign repealed.

The powerful Cardinal Wolsey (left), adviser and close friend of Henry VIII, died a broken man accused of high treason and was succeeded as chief adviser to Henry by his protégé, Thomas Cromwell (right).

1564—William Shakespeare born.

1570—Pope excommunicates Elizabeth.

1571—Royal Exchange founded.

1572-3—Francis Drake stages raids against Spanish in Caribbean Sea.

1577-80—Drake raids Spanish possessions along Pacific coast of Americas and continues westward around globe, first Englishman to do so.

1585—Elizabeth sends troops to help Dutch drive Spanish from Netherlands.

1587—Mary Queen of Scots beheaded for involvement in plot to assassinate Elizabeth.

1588—Spanish Armada defeated.

1598 and 1601—Poor Laws passed to provide care for needy and jobs for unemployed.

1600—East India Company chartered by crown to trade in Orient.

Hampton Court Palace was built by Henry VIII's loyal public servant, Cardinal Thomas Wolsey. Later, King Henry, jealous of Wolsey's money and power, had the Cardinal "present" this palace, largest in England, to him. At Hampton Court, located on the Thames 15 miles from London, tourists can see the tennis court where Henry played and the lawn where he wrestled.

THE STUART ERA AND THE COMMONWEALTH, 1603-1687

1603—Elizabeth I dies; James I (James VI of Scotland), son of Mary Queen of Scots, becomes king.

1604—Peace treaty ends war with Spain. . . . Parliament's Apology denies that kings have divine right to rule as they please.

1605—Gunpowder Plot to blow up King and Parliament uncovered. Guy Fawkes and others executed.

1607—Jamestown, first permanent English settlement in North America, founded.

1611—King James version of Bible published.

1616—Lord Chief Justice Edward Coke, leading advocate of supremacy of common law over king, removed from office.

1618—Sir Walter Raleigh beheaded to please king's new friend—Spain.

1621—Lord Chancellor Francis Bacon impeached.

1625—James I dies, succeeded by son, Charles I.

1628—Parliament's Petition of Right again denies king entitled to any arbitrary powers.

1629-40—King Charles dismisses Parliament and rules England with aid of personal advisers.

1640—Long Parliament meets, passes more anti-royalist legislation.

1642—Civil war breaks out between King Charles and royalist supporters (Cavaliers) and Puritan-dominated Parliament and its supporters (Roundheads). . . . Isaac Newton born.

1645—Led by Cromwell and Fairfax, Roundhead armies defeat royalist forces at Marston Moor and Naseby.

1646-48—Period of truce. Bargaining between king and various political and religious groups.

1648—Renewed fighting. Rump Parliament, purged of all opposition members, votes to have King Charles tried on a charge of high treason.

1649—Charles I convicted of treason and beheaded.

1649-53—The Commonwealth formed. Puritan minority rules England. Strict temperance laws passed, Anglican church disestablished.

1653—Oliver Cromwell made Lord Protector.

1658—Oliver Cromwell dies; his son Richard Cromwell becomes Lord Protector.

1659—Richard Cromwell dismissed as Lord Protector.

1660—Restoration of Stuarts. Charles II, son of the executed Charles I, becomes king.

1661-65—Parliament passes "Clarendon Code," re-establishing supremacy of Anglican church.

1665—Great Plague strikes England, thousands die.

1665-67—War with Holland (one of three during 17th century).

1666—Fire destroys much of London.

1667-73—Unpopular Cabal (Clifford, Arlington, Buckingham, Ashley, and Lauderdale) advises king on policy matters.

1670—Secret treaty between Charles II and Louis XIV of France. Charles promised £200,000 to turn Catholic.

1673—Test Act: All officeholders required to be members of Anglican church.

1678—False "Popish Plot" causes anti-Catholic hysteria in England.

George Villiers, first Duke of Buckingham, and his family. Minister to two kings, James I and Charles I, he was blamed for the wars with Spain and France and assassinated on the eve of embarking for La Rochelle.

London was a thriving city when this engraving, now in the Guildhall Library, was made by Wenzel Hollar in 1647. Nineteen years afterwards, the Great Fire, which began at the king's baker's in Pudding Lane, and burned for five days, destroyed 89 churches, 13,200 houses, and 400 streets.

1679—Parliament passes Habeas Corpus Act.
1683—Rye House Plot to assassinate King Charles and his brother James miscarries. Several innocent people executed.
1685—King Charles II dies (converted to Catholicism shortly before death). James II, a Catholic, brother of Charles ascends throne.
1685-87—James II antagonizes Anglican majority by giving Catholics prominent government positions, flouting Parliament's wishes, and undermining Anglican church.

An almost inevitable bloody clash between monarchy and Parliament took place during the Stuart era. Stuart kings (and others before them) avowed that they had a "divine right" to rule as they saw fit since they were kings "by grace of God." Parliament, on the other hand, maintained that as a body elected by the country, it had the right to pass whatever laws it wants, regardless of the opinions of kings.

Religious controversy also added to the problems of the age. England had become a primarily Protestant country by the beginning of the 17th century. The Anglican church, of which the reigning monarch was (and still is) the head, enjoyed a privileged position. Members of other Protestant sects in England were persecuted by unfair (although not particularly severe) laws. All Protestants were suspicious of Catholics who were also persecuted. Tolerance of religion was notably absent in 17th-century England, but fortunately the intolerance did not lead to the wholesale bloodshed that occurred in other European countries during the same period.

The outcome of the turmoil was the end of rule by the Stuarts and the discarding of the divine right theory. However, the monarchy was not abolished (as it had been during the one period of Puritan rule, 1649-1660). Instead, Parliament became the real ruler of England, and the sovereign, although still active in government affairs, had his powers greatly diminished and limited by law.

During the 17th century, English commerce at home and overseas expanded greatly. Many colonies were founded, especially in North America. Some, such as Maryland, Massachusetts, and Pennsylvania were settled by groups of Englishmen seeking a place to worship in peace. Others were strictly commercial ventures. Colonies provided the mother country with raw materials and proved good markets for English-manufactured products.

1688-1713

1688—James II issues new declarations threatening established Church of England. . . . Leading Englishmen invite William of Orange, ruler of Netherlands and son-in-law of James II, to save the country. . . . William lands in England; James II flees.
1689—William and his wife Mary, both Protestants, accept crown as joint rulers after agreeing to Bill of Rights drawn up by Parliament. . . . War of Palatinate begins.
1694—Queen Mary dies; William rules alone . . . Bank of England founded.
1697—Treaty of Ryswick ends war with France.
1701—Act of Settlement establishes a succession to throne of sovereigns belonging to Church of England.
1701-13—War of Spanish Succession: England, Holland, and Austria against France.
1702—Death of King William; his sister-in-law, Anne, becomes queen.
1704—John Churchill, Duke of Marlborough, defeats French in Battle of Blenheim.
1707—Act of Union unites England and Scotland.
1713—Treaty of Utrecht ends war of Spanish Succession. England gains Gibraltar, Minorca,

new territories in North America, and limited trade rights with Spanish colonies in South America.

James II (left) was overthrown by William of Orange as a result of his Catholic policy. John Churchill (right), first Duke of Marlborough and ancestor of Winston Churchill, supported William against James in the Glorious Revolution of 1688.

The hasty departure of James II marked the exit of England's last Catholic sovereign. An important step in the growth of Parliament's power soon followed. This was the Bill of Rights drawn up by Parliament and assented to by William of Orange as a condition for his becoming king. The Bill of Rights guaranteed Englishmen liberties such as the rights of petition and habeas corpus, which could not legally be taken away by the king. The English Bill of Rights has had a great influence on the constitutions of many other lands, including the United States.

England continued to expand overseas during this period, and the American colonies prospered. In the continuing European power struggles, England made its weight felt. At home, tolerance of minorities and of responsible criticism increased.

THE HANOVERIAN ERA, 1714-1789

1714—Queen Anne dies; George I, Elector of Hanover (Germany) and great-grandson of James I, becomes king.
1718—Quadruple Alliance: England, Holland, France, and Austria. . . . English fleet defeats the Spanish off Cape Passaro.
1721-42—Robert Walpole, most influential member of government, becomes England's first real prime minister.
1727—George I dies, succeeded by son, George II.

1739—War of Jenkins' Ear with Spain.
1740-48—War of the Austrian Succession: England, Hanover, and Austria against France, Spain, and Prussia.
1746—Battle of Culloden Moor. Army of Charles Stuart ("Bonnie Prince Charlie") the pretender to the throne, defeated in last battle to take place on British soil.
1748—Peace of Aix-la-Chapelle restores prewar territorial conditions for the most part.
1756-63—Seven Years War: England, Hanover, and Prussia against Austria, France, Russia, and several pro-Austrian German states (known as French and Indian War in North America).
1757—Battle of Plassey in India establishes English dominance in subcontinent. . . . William Pitt the Elder dominant figure in government (until 1761).
1759—English defeat French at Quebec.
1760—George II dies; grandson George III, becomes king.
1763—Treaty of Paris ends Seven Years War. England gains Canada and other territories from France. English dominance in North America and India assured.
1764—James Watt develops improved version of steam engine (patented 1769, commercial production begun in 1774). . . . Spinning jenny invented by James Hargreaves.
1765—Stamp Act passed by Parliament; American colonists protest.
1766—Stamp Act repealed by Parliament.
1769—Richard Arkwright patents improved method for yarn manufacture.

George I (left) first British sovereign of the House of Hanover, was not well received in England. His Germanic ways and his failure to learn English alienated him from the people. (Right) William Pitt (the Elder), first Earl of Chatham, was known as the "Great Commoner" by the people because of his eloquent demands for electoral reforms while Prime Minister and for his belief in civil liberties.

This is Sulgrave Manor in Northamptonshire, George Washington's family's home. In 1914, it was presented to the George Washington-Sulgrave Institution and has been restored, refurnished and made into a Washington Museum.

1773—Boston Tea Party: American colonists dressed as Indians dump English tea overboard as protest against English tea tax.
1775-83—American Revolution.
1775—Fighting breaks out between colonists and English troops in Massachusetts. . . . George Washington made commander of American army.
1776—The 13 American colonies declare independence from England.
1777—English army under Burgoyne captured at Saratoga by an American force. France encouraged to aid American cause.
1781—American and French armies and French navy co-operate to capture General Cornwallis' English army at Yorktown, Virginia.
1782—Admiral Rodney destroys French fleet in fierce battle off island of Dominica in Caribbean, re-asserting English control of the seas.
1783—Treaty of Paris. England recognizes independence of United States of America. William Pitt the Younger becomes Prime Minister at age 24.
1785—Edmund Cartwright patents power loom.
1788—Group of English convicts settled in Australia.

With the death of Queen Anne, the throne passed to the Elector of the German state of Hanover who became George I. Both George I and his son George II were more interested in their German domains than in Great Britain. In fact, George I spoke German his entire life and never bothered to learn English. The governing of the nation was left primarily in the hands of Parliament giving rise to one of the most important features of modern British government, the Cabinet system.

The country continued to develop a strong national spirit. Opposition to government policy, which in previous times had frequently taken to violence, took a more peaceful turn. There were many violent speeches in Parliament, but almost all opponents of the government used only legal methods to voice their discontent.

Eighteenth-century England was the seedbed of the Industrial Revolution. English inventors developed the machinery necessary for mass

George III (left) appointed 24-year-old William Pitt (the Younger) his Prime Minister. George's reign, marked by long periods of insanity, allowed Pitt to gain almost complete control of the government.

production of manufactured goods. The prosperous and growing merchant class provided the capital necessary to build new factories. England's stable and progressive political structure greatly aided the infancy of modern capitalism, while the growing number of colonies in all parts of the world provided ready markets for textiles, iron products, and other manufactured goods and cheap sources for raw materials.

The loss of the American colonies was chiefly caused by the stubbornness and pride of George III and his ministers who refused to satisfy the colonists' demands of "no taxation without representation" and other requests for the same rights as Englishmen. Many Englishmen, especially Pitt the Elder and the Whig Party, opposed the reckless policy which led to the American Revolution, but they did not have political power at the time.

1789-1836

1789—Paris mob storms Bastille, French Revolution begins. . . . George Washington elected first President of U.S.A.
1793—New French Republic declares war on England and other European powers.

Commanded by Horatio Nelson, the British fleet defeated the combined French and Spanish fleets in 1805 at the battle of Trafalgar, near Gibraltar. This memorable victory ended Napoleon's challenge to English naval supremacy. Nelson, however, was mortally wounded at the height of the battle. This painting by J. M. W. Turner is in the Tate Gallery, London.

Henry John Temple, 3rd Viscount Palmerston, served as Secretary at War, Foreign Secretary and Prime Minister between 1809 and 1865. A forceful statesman and a liberal-minded Tory, he effectively opposed injustice and oppression. Palmerston's attitude to the American Civil War was officially neutral, but his sympathies were with the South.

1796—Edward Jenner discovers smallpox vaccine.
1797—Financial crisis brought on by war with France. . . . After Austria makes peace with Napoleon, Britain is left to fight France alone.
1798—Admiral Horatio Nelson destroys French fleet at Battle of Nile, ending French threat in Middle East. . . . Uprising in Ireland.
1799—Napoleon becomes First Consul of France.
1800—Parliamentary union of Great Britain and Ireland.
1801—Nelson defeats Danish navy at Copenhagen.
1802—Treaty of Amiens between Britain and France; an unsuccessful attempt to restore peace to Europe.
1804—New wars with France break out. . . . Pitt once more Prime Minister.
1805—Nelson killed at Trafalgar in England's greatest naval victory—combined French-Spanish fleet destroyed.
1806—Pitt dies. Napoleon declares Great Britain in state of blockade.
1808-14—Peninsular War. Wellington directs British troops in successful campaigns to drive French armies from Spain.
1811—George III insane; Prince of Wales (later George IV) becomes regent.
1812—U.S.A. declares war on England because of English interference with American shipping.
1814—Napoleon defeated, exiled to Elba. . . . Congress of Vienna, attended by representatives of all great European powers, draws boundaries of post-Napoleonic Europe.
1815—Napoleon escapes from Elba, returns to France, regroups his armies but is defeated at Waterloo by Wellington and exiled to St. Helena, British island in South Atlantic. . . . Parliament passes Corn Law to keep up domestic grain prices by placing high tariffs on imported grains. . . . Treaty of Ghent ends war with U.S.
1819—Domestic discontent over political and economic conditions. . . . Peterloo massacre and the repressive "six acts."
1820—George III dies; George IV becomes king.
1823—Britain recognizes independence of Spain's former Latin American colonies. (British fleet provides "teeth" for U.S. Monroe Doctrine.)
1827—British fleet helps defeat Turkish navy at Navarino, assuring independence of Greece.
1829—Long overdue Catholic Relief bill enables Catholics to be seated in Parliament.
1830—George IV dies; William IV ("sailor king") ascends throne.
1831-32—Reform bill finally enacted over strong opposition. Distribution of seats in Parliament altered to give better representation to growing cities and to eliminate "rotten" boroughs.
1831-37—Many new reforms; although most do not improve the lot of the lower classes.

The period of the French wars was a time of great change in England. With the introduction of the steam engine, spinning jenny, and other new inventions in manufacturing industries, the Industrial Revolution began to take hold in England. Mass production became a reality. The population began to grow rapidly because of generally healthier living conditions (the elimination of smallpox epidemics, for example). The English fleet dominated the seas, allowing the country to control overseas markets and sources of raw materials. The Napoleonic wars created new markets for manufactured goods, and London became the financial capital of the world. However, the new era produced some serious problems. The new machines destroyed the livelihood of hand craftsmen. Workers for new factories were crowded into city slums. Wartime

Traditions live on in England. Here, the Governor of the Tower of London inspects the Yeomen Warders. The Warders, more often called Beefeaters, are charged with the defence of the Tower and care of prisoners. Of course, there is little danger now of an enemy attack and no prisoners have been kept since Rudolf Hess, the Nazi leader who parachuted into Britain, was jailed there during World War II.

inflation raised the cost of living. Heavy new taxes were levied to pay for the cost of the wars. After the conclusion of the Napoleonic wars, agitation for social reform increased. England came perilously close to open revolution in the 1830's before badly needed reform measures were taken.

VICTORIAN ENGLAND, 1837-1900

1837—William IV dies; Victoria becomes queen at the age of 18.
1837-40's—The Chartist Movement: workers demand universal suffrage and other electoral reforms. No demands met at the time.
1838-46—League agitate for repeal of Corn Law. Prime Minister sacrifices political career by successfully urging repeal of Corn Laws (1846).
1840—War with China over opium trade. Hong Kong ceded to Britain (1842).
1848—Revolutions break out in many European countries in protest against undemocratic governments; England remains undisturbed by violence.

1850-60—Second war with China. Chinese government forced to make further concessions to Britain and other Western powers.
1851—Great Exhibition in London, first large international trade fair.
1853-56—Crimean War. Britain, France, and Turkey against Russia. Charge of Light Brigade. Florence Nightingale distinguishes herself by caring for wounded soldiers.
1857—Native troops mutiny against British in India.
1858—British government assumes direct control over India, replacing British East India Company.
1861—Civil war breaks out in United States. . . . Supplies of American cotton for English textile mills cut off, causing economic hardship in England. . . . Prince Albert, consort of Queen Victoria, dies.
1867—Electoral reform nearly doubles number of men eligible to vote. . . . Canada becomes first self-governing dominion in British Empire.
1870—School attendance of children between the ages of 5 and 13 made compulsory.
1872—American claims for damages caused by

Alabama and other English-built Confederate sea raiders during Civil War settled by peaceful arbitration. Britain pays U.S. $15.5 million in damages.

1875—Controlling interest in Suez Canal purchased by British government.

1876—Queen Victoria given title "Empress of India."

1878—Congress of Berlin: Turkey safeguarded against Russian encroachment; Mediterranean island of Cyprus given to Britain.

1884-85—New electoral reforms triple number of eligible voters and provide for fairer distribution of seats in Commons.

1885—General Gordon's army annihilated by Dervishes at Khartoum in Sudan after heroic stand.

1888—Local Government Act provides for elected county councils, another important step in growth of democracy.

1893—Labour Party founded.

1895—Jameson raid into Transvaal in South Africa antagonizes Boers (settlers of Dutch ancestry).

1898—General Kitchener defeats Dervishes at Omdurman in Sudan and avenges Gordon.

1899-1902—Boer War. Britain conquers Transvaal and defeats Boers after hard fighting.

Britain's Unknown Soldier of World War I was buried in Westminster Abbey on November 11, 1920. Less than 19 years later, the nation found itself engaged in an even greater war. Plaques in the floor of the Abbey mark the graves of political leaders, writers and scientists, as well as warriors.

The Victorian age saw Britain become the world's most powerful nation. At home, the production of iron and steel, coal, textiles, and a wide variety of manufactured goods grew rapidly. Overseas, Britain became the leading commercial and imperial power. India, Malaya, South Africa, and many other territories, large and small, scattered over the face of the globe became part of the Empire. The popular statement "The sun never sets on the British Empire" was quite literally true.

The 19th century was also a time of great social upheaval. The cities grew rapidly and so did problems arising from poor living and working conditions. However, new laws eliminated some of the worst abuses suffered by the working class. Meanwhile a new class, the capitalists, came into being and reduced the importance of the landed aristocracy. Politically, democratic government developed in a steady and orderly fashion. There were no violent revolutions in England like those in several other European countries. Peel, Palmerston, Disraeli, and Gladstone were among the leading political figures of the age. By the turn of the century, the modern-day Conservative, Liberal, and Labour Parties had all become firmly established. Many Britons also distinguished themselves in the arts and sciences—Tennyson, Dickens, Darwin, Mill, and Maxwell.

1901-18

1901—Queen Victoria dies after a reign of 63 years; Edward VII ascends the throne.

1902—Anglo-Japanese Treaty (a defensive alliance).

1904—Entente Cordiale with France settles outstanding differences between the two nations and makes them allies.

1906—The "Dreadnought," most powerful warship built up to that time, launched, demonstrating Britain's naval might.

1908—Government old age pension scheme introduced.

1910—King Edward VII dies; George V becomes King.

1911—New law reduces powers of House of Lords to interfere with legislative acts of House of Commons.

1914—World War I begins. Britain enters war as ally of France and Russia after German troops invade neutral Belgium.

George V, grandson of Victoria, and grandfather of Elizabeth II, abandoned all his German titles in 1916, after the outbreak of World War I, changing the name of the royal house from Saxe-Coburg-Gotha to Windsor.

1915—Coalition war-time cabinet with members from all parties instituted.

1917—United States enters war on the side of Allies (now including Italy). . . . Bolshevik revolution; Russia withdraws from war.

1918—War ended by armistice . . . . Women are given the vote.

During these years the pace of social and political change grew more rapid. The trade union movement (and Labour Party) expanded, and Parliament passed much social legislation aimed at improving the lot of workers and retired persons. Women demonstrated frequently demanding the right to vote, which was finally granted in 1918.

In 1914 came the greatest war the world had yet seen. It was the outcome of a half-century-long arms race carried on by the larger European nations. Hostilities were touched off by the assassination of the Austrian Archduke Franz Ferdinand in Sarajevo, Serbia (present-day Yugoslavia), by a young Serbian nationalist.

Entangling systems of alliances and secret treaties drew the nations of Europe into war one after another, following Austria-Hungary's declaration of war on Serbia.

World War I did not have the glory (real or imagined) that surrounded previous wars. The rival armies settled down to year after year of dirty trench warfare complete with poison gas attacks. The United States' entry into the war in 1917 finally tipped the scales for Britain, France, and the Western Allies. World War I cost Britain over 812,000 killed and more than $2\frac{1}{2}$ million in total casualties. Commerce and shipping were disrupted, and the national debt rose more than ten-fold.

1919-45

1919—Peace Conference at Versailles settles claims arising from World War I: Germany forced to pay heavy indemnities to victorious European nations; League of Nations set up; Britain gains most of Germany's African colonies and former Turkish domains in Middle East including Palestine. . . . Violence in Ireland as Irish nationalists wage campaign of terror to gain independence from England. Equally violent methods used by English-organized emergency constabulary force called "black and tans."

1920-21—Post-war economic depression causes unemployment and strikes.

1922—Southern Ireland becomes self-governing dominion, ending England's centuries-old "Irish problem". . . . Coalition government ends.

1924—First Labour Party government (with Liberal Party support).

1926—Poor working conditions in coal mines and general unemployment lead to nationwide strike, paralyzing country for week.

1928—Important new social legislation affecting local government, education, and pension schemes . . . Britain and other nations sign Kellogg-Briand Pact outlawing war as means of settling international disputes. . . . Alexander Fleming discovers penicillin.

1929—World economic depression causes severe unemployment in England.

1931—New Conservative-dominated coalition government formed by Ramsay MacDonald of badly split Labour Party. . . . Statute of Westminster recognizes equality and independence of dominions of British Empire.

1932—Britain adopts protective tariffs on imports, ending nation's historic policy of free trade.

1933—Adolf Hitler comes to power in Germany.

1935—Stanley Baldwin, Conservative, becomes

A Supermarine Spitfire prepares to take off from a cowfield airstrip. Outnumbered Royal Air Force pilots flying Spitfire and Hurricane fighter aircraft were guided to the attacking German planes by English radar stations. Of the victory of R.A.F. pilots in the Battle of Britain, Winston Churchill said: "Never in the field of human conflict was so much owed by so many to so few."

Prime Minister and leader of coalition government.

1936—George V dies, son Edward VIII king, but abdicates to marry American woman: his brother ascends throne as George VI.

1937—New taxes aid expanded re-armament scheme.

1938—Prime Minister Neville Chamberlain returns from Munich conference with Hitler (after ceding German dictator part of Czechoslovakia) and declares agreement means "peace in our time," but Churchill, Eden, and others attack policy of appeasing Nazi Germany.

1939—German aggression in Europe continues. Britain and France guarantee security of Poland. Germany invades Poland Sept. 1, Britain declares war Sept. 3.

1940—Europe overrun by German armies; Britain, now under leadership of Winston Churchill, left alone to fight Germans. . . . Outnumbered pilots of Royal Air Force fight off the German Luftwaffe in skies above Britain. . . . London and other cities heavily bombed.

1941—Germany attacks Soviet Union, which becomes ally of Britain in war against Nazis. . . . Japan launches surprise attacks on British and American possessions in Pacific. U.S. enters World War II.

1942—Singapore falls to Japanese. . . . General Montgomery turns back Rommel's German army at battle of El Alamein, Egypt. . . . Anglo-American invasion of French North Africa.

1943—Allied landings in Italy.

1944—Allied invasion of Normandy. Final push to conquer Germany begun.

1945—Founding of the United Nations. . . . Germany surrenders. . . . Labour Party defeats Winston Churchill's Conservatives in election. . . . Japan surrenders.

England emerged from World War I with diminished power. World leadership passed to the U.S., which, however, failed to exercise its new role, preferring instead to remain isolated from world affairs. This attitude of the U.S. doomed the League of Nations, predecessor of the United Nations.

The war had many important social effects: The traditional class system was badly shaken. The rise of the Labour Party signalled the end of government as an exclusive preserve for "gentlemen." Trade unions grew in size and pressed their demands for better wages and working conditions by staging frequent strikes. Unstable postwar economic conditions caused large-scale unemployment. Emergency government measures to improve conditions became necessary.

In foreign affairs, attempts were made, through treaties, to secure a lasting peace and to prevent any nation from touching off a new world conflict. However, when Japanese, German, and Italian aggression became a fact of life in the '30's none of the democratic nations took effective steps to safeguard endangered countries. The U.S. remained in isolation while Britain and France followed a policy of appeasing Hitler and his Italian allies. The price for such a foolish policy was World War II, the second global conflict in less than 21 years.

1946-65

England faced serious domestic and international challenges after the end of World War II. With Germany defeated and Europe devastated, the Soviet Union attempted to bring Western Europe into the Communist orbit. This plan was thwarted by the prompt action of the United States and Britain in countering the Russians' aggressive moves. A major turning point in the "cold war" struggle was the Berlin airlift of 1948-49 when the Western allies, faced with a Soviet blockade of land routes to the city, supplied Berlin by air and eventually forced the Russians to give in to Western demands for land access to the city. Britain is one of the most important members of the Western alliance and is a charter member of NATO, founded in 1949 to defend Western Europe against a Communist attack. British troops fought on the side of the United Nations during the Korean War which broke out in 1950.

At home, the new Labour Party Government was faced with the problem of repairing the damage done to the economy by World War II. With the help of massive aid and loans from the U.S.A., England rebuilt its war-torn industries. At the same time, Parliament passed a series of far-reaching laws nationalizing many of the most important industries, such as coal mining, railways, electricity, and even the Bank of England. Comprehensive social welfare laws were also enacted.

World War II's end also saw the unleashing of the force of nationalism throughout the British Commonwealth. British colonial possessions in Africa, Asia, and the Americas were swept by native movements—some peaceful, others violent—demanding independence from the mother country. India and Pakistan, both formed from the former British India, gained independence in 1947. Ghana, the former Gold Coast, became independent in 1957, the first of Britain's African colonies to do so. Many other former colonies have been granted their independence and most

Wearing a steel helmet and with cigar firmly planted, Prime Minister Winston Churchill watches an aerial battle between German and British aircraft in August, 1940, during the Battle of Britain.

have chosen to remain members of the British Commonwealth; however, they retain their right to govern themselves as they please and to leave the Commonwealth at any time.

As a result of the national elections held in 1951, the Conservative Party under the leadership of Winston Churchill regained control of the Government. Most of the important measures enacted during the period of Labour Party rule were retained, and Britain embarked on a course of prosperity which turned the unhappy war and post-war years into merely an unpleasant memory. In 1955, Winston Churchill resigned as Prime Minister and was followed in office by Anthony Eden. However, the Eden government did not long survive the Suez crisis of 1956 which included an invasion of Egypt by British, French, and Israeli troops after the Egyptian government seized the Suez Canal. In 1957, Harold Macmillan, another Conservative, became Prime Minister and led his party to a third consecutive victory in the 1959 elections. In 1963, Mr. Macmillan resigned and was succeeded by Sir Alec Douglas-Home. Following the general election of 1964, a Labour Government under Harold Wilson came to power. In 1970, the Conservatives were returned to office, with Edward Heath as Prime Minister.

Buckingham Palace is named after the mansion built by the Duke of Buckingham in 1703 and later purchased by King George III. British monarchs since Queen Victoria have made the palace their London residence. Many additions have been made to the original structure, and the palace now contains 602 rooms. The Changing of the Guard ceremony held in front of the palace attracts many tourists during the summer months.

During sessions of the House of Lords, the Speaker of the House, the Lord Chancellor (who is also head of the judiciary), sits on the "woolsack," a broad, red-covered ottoman. When making political speeches, the Lord Chancellor moves a few feet away from the woolsack.

Queen Elizabeth awaits the Trooping the Colour parade marking her official birthday. Her Majesty's actual birthday is on April 21, but is officially celebrated in June. Since titles and other awards are traditionally bestowed on the monarch's birthday, the celebration is held on a date considerably removed from January 1, the other official date for distributing awards of merit.

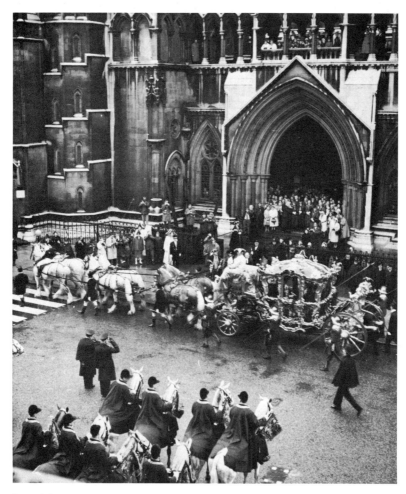

One of the great November ceremonies in London is the arrival at the Guildhall of the new Lord Mayor in his three-ton golden coach. Picturesque pikemen escort him in the long, public procession which highlights the Lord Mayor's Show.

GOVERNMENT

People often refer to the English Constitution. This can be misleading, for there is no *written* constitution. Instead, the name encompasses the various acts of Parliament through the centuries, together with the traditional common law (based on custom and prior decisions in law courts rather than legislative acts). In theory, Parliament has the right to pass any law it chooses, but, in practice, no Parliament would dare pass a law needlessly abridging the civil rights of Englishmen. Centuries of tradition and dedication to the rights of man have made the English Constitution stronger than most of its written counterparts.

The Speaker's Chair in the House of Commons with the Clerks' Table in front. At the right rear are the benches for the Opposition Party. The Government benches cannot be seen here. The present chamber, opened in 1950, replaced its predecessor which was destroyed by German bombs in 1941. Photographs cannot be taken while Parliament is in session.

PARLIAMENT

England is governed by the Queen (or King) and Parliament. However, for approximately the last 250 years, the British monarch has had little political power. Parliament (particularly the Cabinet) has become the seat of government, although the sovereign still plays a symbolical role. For instance, all acts of Parliament must receive the Royal Assent before becoming law. The last time a British monarch vetoed an act of Parliament was in 1707. Many appointments to government office are made by the monarch with the "advice" of the Prime Minister whose suggestions in such matters are never rejected.

Parliament (from the French word *parler*, to speak) began during England's feudal era when kings summoned the barons to discuss matters such as taxes. The deposing of James II (1688) is usually considered the turning point in the struggle for supremacy between King and Parliament. During the 19th and 20th centuries, extensive schemes to reform Parliament have been carried out.

The democratically elected Commons is the more powerful of the two houses, Commons and Lords. It has 630 members: 511 for England, 71 for Scotland, 36 for Wales, and 12 for Northern Ireland. Members retain their seats for the life of the Parliament to which they are elected. By law, no Parliament may last more than five years. Elections are held at shorter intervals if the Government (i.e., the political party in power) cannot gain a vote of confidence (approval of a majority of members present). Religious discrimination for election to Parliament no longer exists, and virtually all Britons over the age of 21 are entitled to vote in elections for the House of Commons.

Members of the House of Lords (over 1,000) hold office by virtue of their titles and neither receive a salary nor stand for election. Many are

The Chapel of the Royal Naval College at Greenwich. Originally opened as a hospital for seamen in 1705, the building was converted to student use in 1869. Greenwich was also the home of the world-famous Royal Observatory from 1675 to 1946. Through it "passes" the Greenwich Meridian from which all longitudes in the world are reckoned.

Looking much like the average English family, Queen Elizabeth, Prince Philip and their children, Princess Anne and Princes Charles, Andrew and Edward, stroll on the grounds of Home Park, Windsor.

highly qualified to debate bills because of careers in civil, church, and military service. Less than one-quarter of the peers eligible to take seats in the House of Lords actually do so. One of the functions of the House of Lords is to act as Britain's highest court of appeal. The Lords cannot prevent a bill passed by the Commons from becoming law, but can delay certain legislation for up to one year.

THE CABINET

The Cabinet is the executive arm of government and is headed by the Prime Minister who is ordinarily the leader of the majority party in the House of Commons. Cabinet ministers come from both houses of Parliament. Unlike the United States, where the executive branch is independent of the legislature, the British

Every year Horse Guards and Life Guards, known collectively as the Household Cavalry, take part in a musical ride held in Windsor Great Park. Windsor Castle, seen in the background, has been a royal residence for over 800 years.

The Central Criminal Court, popularly known as the Old Bailey, acts as the Court of Assize for the judgment of criminal cases in London and parts of the surrounding counties. Many famous trials have taken place here. This scene is from the film "British Justice"—photographs are forbidden during real trials.

Cabinet is responsible to the House of Commons. If a majority of Commons disapprove of Cabinet measures, the Government falls and the Prime Minister and the members of his Cabinet must resign. The sovereign then calls on the leader of the Opposition to form a new Government, or new Parliamentary elections may be ordered.

THE CABINET
(In order of precedence)

Prime Minister
First Secretary of State and Minister for Economic Affairs
Foreign Secretary
Lord President of the Council and Leader of the House
Lord Chancellor
Chancellor of the Exchequer
Secretary for Defence
Home Secretary
Secretary for Commonwealth Relations
Secretary for Scotland
Secretary for Wales

Colonial Secretary
President of the Board of Trade
Lord Privy Seal
Secretary of Education and Science
Minister of Housing and Local Government
Chancellor of the Duchy of Lancaster
Minister of Labour
Minister of Technology
Minister of Agriculture, Fisheries and Food
Minister of Power
Minister of Transport
Minister of Overseas Development

King's Road, Chelsea, is one of the liveliest streets in one of the most picturesque quarters of London. Here the younger generation throngs the shops and coffee houses, wearing the miniskirts, trouser suits and new hair styles which started in Carnaby Street in another section of London, and are now sweeping the world.

THE PEOPLE

By far the greatest number of the people of the United Kingdom live in England. At the time of the 1961 census, England had a population of 43,430,972. The total population of the United Kingdom—England, Wales, Scotland, and Northern Ireland—was 52,675,094. Although England has a large population and a relatively small land area, the English tend to live in cities, and Greater London with a population in excess of 8,000,000 is one of the largest cities in the world. England's population density of 790 inhabitants per square mile is not far below Holland's 918 persons per square mile and makes countries like the United States (50 per square mile) appear sparsely inhabited

by way of comparison. However, owing to the large urban population, there are still many areas in England—the Lake District in Cumberland and the moors in Devon, for example—that are lightly settled.

Greater London is, of course, the largest city in England. Birmingham, second largest, has a population of just over one million. Other important cities include Liverpool, Manchester, Leeds, Newcastle-upon-Tyne, Bristol, and Nottingham.

During the past three centuries, England has experienced emigrations and immigrations of fairly considerable proportions. Many Englishmen have left and still do leave their native land

Blackpool, in Lancashire, on the Irish Sea, is one of the largest and most popular seaside resorts in England. Its 7-mile promenade is lined with gardens, swimming pools, an amusement park and several piers. The town itself sprang up and expanded rapidly in the 19th and 20th centuries as a result of the Industrial Revolution.

The English afternoon tea is a world-famous custom and every town and hamlet in England has its tea shops. This shop is in Marlborough, Wiltshire, where the body of Merlin, the great court magician of Arthurian legend, is purported to lie under a mound in the grounds of Marlborough College.

to seek a new life elsewhere. In the 17th and 18th centuries, many people left England for the North American colonies in order to practise their religious faith without interference. Later waves of migrants left their homeland to seek better economic opportunities abroad. In recent years, upwards of 100,000 Englishmen have been leaving annually to start new lives elsewhere, mainly in Australia, New Zealand, Canada, and the United States. At the same time many people have been migrating to England. Many arrived as refugees from other parts of Europe, while others came from Pakistan, India and the West Indies. The latter now number 1,000,000, and their presence has caused racial tension in many urban areas.

Englishmen who have migrated overseas have taken their language, customs, and culture with them. Time and local circumstances have altered many things, but countries such as Australia, New Zealand, and even the United States all have a heritage of common tradition with England. By the same token, immigrants have also enriched the "Anglo-Saxon" culture.

Every year the costermongers (vendors from barrows) of London traditionally choose a Pearly King and Queen to represent the separate districts of the city. Here the Pearly King and Queen of Hampstead, northwest London, drive in the Van Parade in Regent's Park. Their Edwardian-style clothes are covered with thousands of mother-of-pearl buttons.

Symbolic of free speech in England is Speakers' Corner in Hyde Park. Here people of all sorts come to voice their opinions or grievances. They must be prepared to put up with constant heckling from the audience. Speakers must observe only four rules: No collections may be taken, no racing tips given, no commercial advertising, and no sound amplifiers used.

LANGUAGE AND LITERATURE

During the time of Queen Elizabeth I, English was the mother tongue of barely 5,000,000 people, all of whom lived in relative isolation. The English-speaking population in the middle of the 20th century now numbers nearly 300,000,000, and the language has become the most important tongue for international trade and diplomacy. Undoubtedly, political and economic reasons (the rise of the United States and the colonial expansion of England, for example) have been largely responsible for this rapid growth. English is, after the Mandarin dialect of Chinese, spoken by more people than any other language on earth. Even though English is the youngest of the world's major languages, it has the largest vocabulary of any—about 800,000 words.

The English language has its roots in the Teutonic (Germanic) language spoken by the tribes of Angles, Saxons, and Jutes who overran England during the 5th and 6th centuries. Even today, many English words have cognates —words descended from a common source—in German and Dutch. A good example is the word "house" which in German is *haus* and in Dutch, *huis*.

English is usually divided into three stages of development: Old English, from the times of the earliest written records to about 1100; Middle English, from about 1100 to the last decades of the 15th century; and Modern English. Throughout its history, English has distinguished itself by its capacity to adopt

In spite of his tremendous output of plays, comparatively little is known about Shakespeare himself—including what he really looked like. This bust shows one version of his appearance.

words from other languages. These new words came (and still come) from the languages that English-speaking people came in contact with. Latin and French, the tongue of the Norman conquerors, have had the greatest effect on English of any foreign languages.

England has produced an uncommonly large number of famous writers and poets. The first English writer to achieve lasting distinction was Geoffrey Chaucer, author of the *Canterbury Tales* and other works, who wrote in the Middle English of the 14th century. In 1477, William Caxton put into operation England's first printing press. The Renaissance

On the banks of the River Avon at Stratford, the town where Shakespeare was born, the Royal Shakespeare Theatre was opened in 1932. Since then, the annual Shakespeare Festival has seen the production of his best-liked plays and also some that had not been performed since his death in 1616.

Anne Brontë, the youngest of the Brontë sisters, is buried at St. Mary's Church at Scarborough, Yorkshire. Her two novels, "Agnes Grey" and "The Tenant of Wildfell Hall," were overshadowed by those of her sisters, Emily and Charlotte, and she remains better known today for her verse and hymns.

spread to England at about the beginning of the 16th century and stimulated interest in scholarship and literature. The Elizabethan age (the latter part of the 16th century) is generally considered one of the high points in the history of the world's literature. William Shakespeare,

Fleet Street, the hub of London's newspaper district, suffered extensive damage from air raids during World War II.

the outstanding literary figure of the age, is considered the greatest playwright of all time. In the next century, English literature was further enriched by the varied contributions of Francis Bacon, the poetry of John Milton, the spicy Restoration comedies of William Congreve, and the philosophical writings of Thomas Hobbes and John Locke, to name but a few of the noted authors of the period.

The 18th century brought the sharp satire of Jonathan Swift in *Gulliver's Travels* and other books. Henry Fielding, author of *Tom Jones,*

No, the photographer has not burst in upon a startled English family; this is a scene from a comedy show "The Reluctant Peer" at the Duchess Theatre. London theatres are known for the quality of their presentations—light-hearted and serious.

was among the first of the modern novelists. Dr. Samuel Johnson compiled the first complete dictionary of English and was the central figure in a brilliant literary circle of the time. The late 18th and early 19th centuries were noted for the romantic poets Wordsworth and Coleridge, and later, Byron, Keats, and Shelley. Among many prominent 19th century novelists were Jane Austen, Sir Walter Scott, Charles Dickens, George Eliot (Mary Ann Evans), and Thomas Hardy. Robert Browning and Alfred Tennyson were poets of the later 19th century. English literature in the 20th century has already benefitted from the writings of Irish-born George Bernard Shaw and James Joyce, Aldous Huxley, and many others.

Professional football, with keen competition between teams and with many leagues, probably attracts the greatest popular following of all English sports. In this game, the Burnley goalkeeper leaps high to make a save on a shot by a Tottenham Hotspur forward.

The batsman tenses in expectation of the hard, leather-covered cricket ball. He must prevent the ball from striking the wicket—the three upright stakes set in the ground. Thousands of cricket matches are played on village greens and sports grounds during the summer months.

While not drawing the same large following as cricket or football (soccer), polo has been played in England since 1869. Here players from the Ancient Mariners and Cheshire teams manoeuvre for position with mallets held ready to strike the ball. The Duke of Edinburgh is a keen polo player, and has done much to popularize the game.

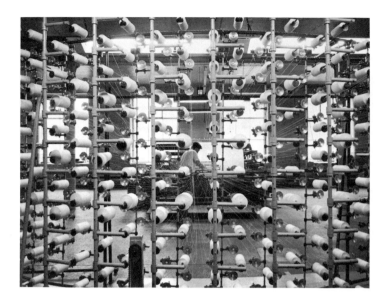

A century ago workers toiled many hours each day for low wages. Today, laws, trade unions, and enlightened management have vastly improved the worker's lot. New machines, such as this creel which winds worsted thread, have greatly increased the speed of production.

THE ECONOMY

England, seedbed of the Industrial Revolution that swept the world in the 19th century, remains one of the world's major manufacturing nations. A predominantly agricultural nation of 12,000,000 at the close of the 18th century, Britain had tripled its population and become the hub of the greatest commercial and political empire ever at the opening of the 20th century. However, English industrial prosperity rested on a few important products, such as textiles, coal, and heavy machinery. During the 1840's, for example, textiles made up two-thirds of all British exports. Such dependence on a few important industrial products caused serious problems in England after World War I. Traditional markets for British goods disappeared, causing widespread unemployment and discontent.

The current industrial prosperity of England did not begin until after the close of World War II. With its own resources and with the aid of large loans and grants from the United States and Canada, England rebuilt its industries along more modern lines. As a result, England has a greater variety of thriving industries than at any previous time. Unemployment is no longer a serious problem.

Industrial complexes dot the English countryside. Certain areas are traditionally noted for their concentrations of various types of industry. For instance, Lancashire is famous for its textile industry and the Midlands for the production of machinery, coal, motor cars, and chemicals. In recent times, regional industrial distinctions have become less clear as more and more new factories are built in the different parts of the country.

Trade unions, progressive social legislation by Parliament, and enlightened management have all improved the lot of English factory workers who once worked long hours under dangerous and unhealthy conditions for extremely low wages. These abuses, which led a German refugee named Karl Marx to forecast the doom

London, the largest port in the world and the most important in the Common-wealth, is located on the River Thames about 40 miles from its mouth. Because of variations in the river level caused by the tides, "wet" docks with lock gates have been constructed to accommodate ships. At the Royal Victoria Docks, a freighter is discharging its cargo of grain.

of the capitalist system, have been almost entirely eliminated. The English are enjoying a prosperity which they have never before known. Television sets can now be found in almost every home, and the number of motor-cars on the road increases annually causing head-aches for traffic planners.

England has remained at the forefront of world scientific research. British chemists have been responsible for the discovery of several of the synthetic "miracle" fibres that have revolutionized the textile industry. A variety of wonder drugs (including penicillin) and plastics have also been developed in English laboratories along with many other products which have been responsible for the

rapid progress in science in the 20th century. Britain has also been a pioneer in the peaceful uses of atomic energy. The first power station in the world to use atomic energy to produce large amounts of electricity for domestic con-sumption went into operation in 1956 at Calder Hall, Cumberland, and many more have already been built or are planned for the future.

FOREIGN TRADE

Foreign trade is vital to England's livelihood. With a large population, small land area, and few natural resources (coal is a major exception), the country must depend on foreign trade to supply the raw materials for English factories

The Queen Elizabeth 2, Britain's new super-liner, sails down the Clyde for the first time under her own power. The 963-foot, 65,000-ton ship is the most powerful twin-screw passenger liner in the world.

London's famed Covent Garden, long the site of the largest wholesale fruit, vegetable and flower market in the United Kingdom, is to be the site of a new complex of offices. When the new buildings are completed in 1971, the market will have been moved to another part of the city.

and to provide a market for the sale of the thousands of types of manufactured goods produced by English industries.

The English economy is extremely sensitive to fluctuations in world trade. In order to maintain a high standard of living, England must be able to pay for imports (which include one-half of the food needed to feed the population). There are several "invisible" ways that England also pays for imports. Among these are the profits earned by extensive English investments in other countries, monies spent by the two million tourists who visit Britain annually, and the profits of the British merchant shipping fleet which is one of the world's largest.

Formerly, the empire provided a ready-made market for exports. However, many former colonies have greatly reduced their purchases of British-made goods since gaining their independence. They have done this not out of dis-

The "Junella" is England's first all-refrigerated stern trawler. Electronic navigation equipment, a large refrigerated cargo space, and other modern mechanical devices allow the "Junella" to cruise far from her home port of Hull in search of fish.

The old London of low buildings is gradually being crowded in, as more and more skyscrapers are built. Here is the tall Centre Point Building at the junction of Oxford Street and Tottenham Court Road.

like for their former colonial master but because they have developed their own industries and in addition can often obtain better trading terms with other nations which are more "natural" trading partners. England has come to realize that as a part of Europe it must look to the Continental nations for a great share of future trade. In order to protect its commercial and historical links with other member nations of the Commonwealth, Britain turned down membership of the European Common Market in 1957. Instead, Britain helped to create the rival European Free Trade Association (1959). A bid by Britain to join the Common Market was vetoed by France in 1962, in part because of British reluctance to abandon special economic ties with Commonwealth nations and price supports for British farmers. Australia, New Zealand, and other Commonwealth nations were heartened by this happening. Later bids to join the Common Market were blocked by France, and, in 1967, the British pound was devalued by 14 per cent, in order to meet the export-import gap.

AGRICULTURE

Although only a small fraction of the total population (about 2 per cent) are engaged in agriculture, the yields of English farms and pastures are high. Scientific farming methods include use of tractors and other modern machinery. As a result, Britain now produces half the food needed to feed itself as compared with one-third just before the outbreak of World War II.

Wheat, barley, oats, and potatoes are the most important crops grown. Sheep (a source of both wool and mutton—the best-liked English meat), cattle and pigs, are the most numerous types of livestock.

English farms are intensively cultivated. They must produce far more food per acre than farmlands in much less densely populated areas, such as America. Here, liquid fertilizer is applied to the soil from a Hovertruck, a wheel-less English-designed vehicle which can support 75 per cent of its weight on a cushion of air.

Coal provided much of the energy that made the Industrial Revolution possible. Modern machinery has somewhat eased the miner's job. Here, a begrimed miner controls a trepanner as it cuts its way through a coal seam in a Nottinghamshire colliery.

FINANCE

London is one of the world's financial capitals. At the heart of England's free enterprise system is the London Stock Exchange where millions of shares are traded daily. There are also exchanges in several other cities but the London Exchange is the most important. London is also the headquarters of many prominent international banking and insurance concerns which deal in foreign shares, insurance, and bonds and handle English investments in other countries. The crippling cost of two world wars has reduced the rate of English overseas investments while foreign investment in English industries and real estate has been increasing.

The central feature of Government finance is the Bank of England, founded under a royal charter as a private company in 1694 to provide loans to the Government and nationalized in 1946 by act of Parliament. The Bank of England is the country's national bank, carries out Government monetary policies, and acts as the "banker's bank" for privately owned banks and other Commonwealth nations. Paper currency in circulation is issued by the Bank. The monetary unit, the pound(£) sterling (equivalent to about $2.40 in 1970), is divided into 20 shillings (s.), and each shilling into 12 pence (d.). In 1968 a decimal coinage was simultaneously introduced, to replace the old scale fully by 1971, with the pound equal to 100 pence or 10 shillings.

The motor age has crowded English highways—many dating from Roman times—beyond their capacity. To relieve congestion and speed intercity commerce, the government is undertaking the construction of an extensive network of controlled-access motorways. The M.4 motorway, whose London end is seen here, connects the capital with Bristol and southern Wales.

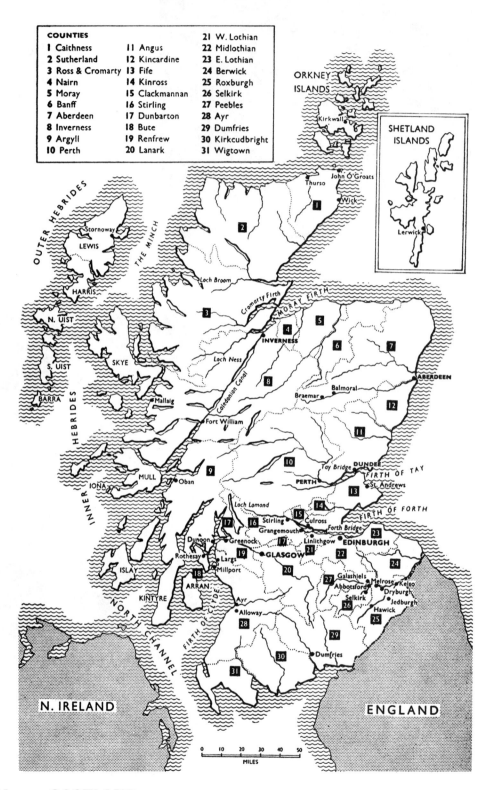

COUNTIES

1 Caithness	11 Angus	21 W. Lothian
2 Sutherland	12 Kincardine	22 Midlothian
3 Ross & Cromarty	13 Fife	23 E. Lothian
4 Nairn	14 Kinross	24 Berwick
5 Moray	15 Clackmannan	25 Roxburgh
6 Banff	16 Stirling	26 Selkirk
7 Aberdeen	17 Dunbarton	27 Peebles
8 Inverness	18 Bute	28 Ayr
9 Argyll	19 Renfrew	29 Dumfries
10 Perth	20 Lanark	30 Kirkcudbright
		31 Wigtown

ORKNEY ISLANDS

Kirkwall

SHETLAND ISLANDS

Lerwick

John O'Groats
Thurso
Wick

1

2

OUTER HEBRIDES

Stornoway
LEWIS

THE MINCH

HARRIS

N. UIST

SKYE

S. UIST

BARRA

Loch Broom

Cromarty Firth

MORAY FIRTH

3

4
INVERNESS

5

6

7

Loch Ness

Balmoral

Braemar

ABERDEEN

8

12

HEBRIDES

Mallaig

Coledonian Canal

Fort William

INNER HEBRIDES

IONA

MULL

Oban

9

11

10

Tay Bridge

DUNDEE

FIRTH OF TAY

St. Andrews

PERTH

13

Loch Lomond

14

15

Stirling

Culross

16

Grangemouth

Forth Bridge

FIRTH OF FORTH

23

17

Dunoon

Greenock

17

Linlithgow

EDINBURGH

Rothesay

Largs

19

GLASGOW

21

22

Millport

18

ARRAN

KINTYRE

20

27

Galashiels

Abbotsford

Melrose

Kelso

24

Dryburgh

Selkirk

Jedburgh

26

Hawick

25

Ayr

Alloway

28

29

ISLAY

NORTH CHANNEL

FIRTH OF CLYDE

30

Dumfries

31

N. IRELAND

ENGLAND

0 10 20 30 40 50
MILES

SCOTLAND

THE LAND

Scotland is a land of rugged mountain-masses (some of them 4,000 feet high), deep glens, many lakes from large Loch Lomond (24 miles long) to small mountain pools (called Lochans) and many swift rivers flowing through wide estuaries to the sea. Scotland, the most northern of the countries that comprise Great Britain, has about 2,300 miles of broken coastline, facing the Atlantic Ocean on the west and north, and the North Sea on the east. Some 800 islands lie off these shores. On its southern border, Scotland meets England across a long, lonely stretch of hills and moors. Geologically, Scotland is divided into three main regions: the Northern Highlands, the Central Lowlands and the Southern Uplands.

Scotland's coastline is so indented by the sea that the mainland covers an area of only 29,795 square miles and few places are more than 40 miles from the sea. Its maximum length (running from northeast Duncansby Head, south-southeast to the Mull of Galloway), is only 274 miles, and at its widest is 154 miles (from Applecross to Buchan Ness).

The Northern Highlands are westward extentions of the Scandinavian mountains and, like them, are a rugged mass of ancient crystalline rocks. Many summits, practically treeless and bare, rise to over 4,000 feet above sea level, and bogs and heather cover the base of the rocky slopes. From sea to sea, the region is subdivided by Glenmore or the Great Glen of Scotland, a steep-sided valley. On the west, the coast is essentially one of bold, rocky headlands deeply grooved by inlets of the sea, while on the east it forms a sloping, narrow but practically continuous coastal plain.

The Central Lowlands are a low-lying belt. They occupy a *graben* valley, a portion of the earth's crust bounded on at least two sides by faults—shifts in the terrain—that have moved downward, and separate the Highlands from the Southern Uplands. Settling of sedimentary rocks and coal beds in this valley saved it from the erosion to which the two bordering sections were exposed. A level topography, fertile soil, and deposits of coal and iron, make this middle area like the meat in a sandwich—the richest part of Scotland.

Coolin Hills, on the Isle of Skye, are typical of the rugged mountains in the Hebrides.

The lochs are one of the main geographical features of Scotland. This is dream-like Loch Shiel with Prince Charlie's Monument standing on the near shore.

RIVERS AND LAKES

Most of Scotland's bigger rivers flow to the east to drain into the North Sea. The largest of these are the Tweed, Tay, Forth, Don, Dee and Spey. In the south, the rivers flow about equally to east or west. Among the rivers flowing westward to the Atlantic is the well-known Clyde, running through Glasgow, and carrying a great amount of traffic from that city where its channel has been dredged and deepened.

Scotland is dotted with innumerable lakes or *lochs*, besides Loch Lomond. Generally long and narrow in shape, they often look like expansions of rivers. Popular lochs are the Tay, Shin, Awe and Maree, but all have been eclipsed by the fame of Loch Ness and its fabulous water monster. Loch Katrine, though quite small, is noted for its beauty. It is surrounded by lovely glens of silver birches, green oaks, mountain crags and a luxuriant growth of ferns, flowers and mosses.

Loch Morlich, Inverness-shire, lies in the middle of Glenmore Forest, east of Aviemore. A flourishing herd of reindeer, imported from Sweden, make their home in the forest.

56 ■ SCOTLAND

CLIMATE

Scotland's climate is as variable as its geography. Heavy mists rolling off the rivers can be suddenly dispersed by gentle zephyrs blowing through the Highlands. Although winters can generally be described as raw, the west coast benefits from the warm currents of the Gulf Stream, which winds up and across the Atlantic from the Caribbean, and enjoys warmer weather than may be expected in so northerly a country. Winds from the west, however, bring heavier rains to the high western border, while the east coast, lying in the lee of the mountains, is considerably drier but colder. Summer temperatures are comfortable, rarely going above 59°, which is about 4° higher than the average summer day in England.

WILD LIFE AND GARDENS

Rarely is so great a medley of flora and fauna to be found in so small an area. The variety of bird life is an ornithologist's dream. Hundreds of species from the small swallow to the majestic golden eagle thrive in Scotland. Rugged granite cliffs in the southwest house a multitude of gannets, gulls, and the "clown" puffins. The Island of Handa is a bird sanctuary where kittiwakes nest in such large numbers that their cries can be heard over the booming surf. Migrant birds from Iceland and Greenland stop here, and geese particularly are abundant. To many a traveller reaching the lonely Borderland from England, the first sounds of Scotland are apt to be the song of a lark or the curious mournful note of a curlew far off in the distant moors.

Common animal species are the Atlantic grey seal, wild red deer, wildcat, otter, foxes, and also a scattering of mountain and brown hares. Owing to their early isolation, the islands boast some rare species, notably the field and bank voles. Runs of salmon and sea trout are found in most rivers; trout streams fill many mountain hollows and *lochs* hold many distinct species of trout.

Fishing for trout on the River Tweed. Notice how far out one hip-booted fisherman stands in this shallow stretch of the upper river.

Edinburgh, capital of Scotland, is said to be one of the loveliest cities in the world. Dominating the city is the Castle, perched on a rock that rises 270 feet from the gardens below. Elegant shops, hotels and restaurants line Princes Street, opposite. The Gothic spire in the foreground commemorates the author, Sir Walter Scott.

The same area as seen from Edinburgh Castle. In the distance is the Port of Leith and the Firth of Forth (a wide-mouthed river) leading to the North Sea. In the foreground are the Royal Scottish Academy and the National Gallery.

HISTORY

The earliest records of Scotland date from the years A.D. 78 to 84 at the time when the Roman general, Julius Agricola, completed the conquest of Britain and headed north. To his amazement he found that his forces were unable to subdue the wild tribesmen from the Highlands. As a precautionary measure, Agricola built a line of forts across the narrow neck of Scotland between the Firths of Clyde and Forth, between what is roughly now Glasgow and Falkirk. Behind this line he could retreat. Later on, during the Roman occupation of northern Britain (that lasted until A.D. 410), the Emperor Hadrian added another wall between the River Tyne and Solway Firth.

Although the Romans are said to have named the unconquered natives of the north, Caledonians, this name is more likely Celtic in origin, meaning either "men of the woods" or "men of the thistle." Today the thistle is the national emblem of Scotland and is used in heraldic devices along with the English rose and the Irish shamrock.

Another name for the Caledonians was Picts, a Latin word meaning "painted men." All the time the Romans occupied Caledonia, they could not repress them. In A.D. 208 the Roman Emperor Severus attempted to subdue them. For three years the Romans and Picts fought. The battles ended in a defeat for the Romans. After the emperor died, in 211, the Roman legions withdrew from the north country but did not leave England for another 200 years.

Peace, however, did not come to Scotland. Instead, new waves of conquerors besieged the area from all sides. Norsemen invaded the islands—the Orkneys, the Shetlands and the Hebrides. About the year 500, the Irish cast covetous eyes on the Pict territory and began sending in invading expeditions. These invaders were the first men called Scots. They landed along the west coast of Caledonia and gradually drove the Picts to the east.

A full three centuries of turmoil and strife followed before the heads of the warring

Iona, a small island in the Hebrides, is one of Scotland's most hallowed spots. St. Columba, most famous of the early missionaries who brought Christianity to Scotland, landed here 14 centuries ago. This tiny cathedral, one of the many restored buildings on the island, dates from the 13th century.

Glamis Castle in Angus was the scene of the murder of King Duncan in Shakespeare's "Macbeth," and is today the home of the Earls of Strathmore. Princess Margaret, granddaughter of the 14th Earl, was born here in 1930. Glamis Castle owes many of its picturesque features to the first Earl of Strathmore, who supervised the building of the clusters of turrets, bartizans and "extinguisher" roofs.

factions—the Picts and the Scots—decided that unity was more rewarding than war. Aycha IV, King of the Scots, married the sister of the King of the Picts and this was the first step toward unification of Scotland. In 844 the last resistance to unification was eliminated when the grandson of this marriage, Kenneth MacAlpin, defeated Wrad, the last of the Pictish kings.

But the Scots and the Picts were not the only groups that populated the area, for there were the Britons and the Angles as well. From continual conflicts between the four kingdoms, the Scots gained the most and eventually took over leadership. These four peoples eventually fused into modern Scotland. The introduction of Christianity (Catholicism) from Ireland did much to stoke the small flame of unity. On the Scottish island of Iona in 563, a Celtic saint named Columba had founded a monastery. This became the focal point of missionary enterprise all through northern Britain. Despite fierce family feuds among the reigning monarchs, Christianity made headway.

South-eastern Scotland, The Lothians, was still part of the Danish Kingdom of Northumbria, but in 1018 Malcolm II, descendant of Kenneth MacAlpin, defeated the Northumbrians and Scottish rule was extended as far as the Tweed. After his death he was succeeded by his grandson, Duncan, whose own death at the hands of Macbeth in 1040 is the subject of Shakespeare's great dramatic tragedy. Macbeth, the usurper, reigned with great ability until 1057, when as playreaders know, he was defeated at the famous battle of Dunsinane, near Perth, by Duncan's son, Malcolm III, and later slain at Lumphanan.

LINKS WITH THE SAXONS AND NORMANS

While in exile, Malcolm III had spent much time at the cultured and ecclesiastical court of Edward the Confessor in London. After the Battle of Hastings in 1066 when the Normans conquered England, Edgar the Atheling, the Saxon claimant to the English throne, took refuge at the court of Malcolm III. Thus, for the first time, Scotland was brought into direct contact with a more advanced way of life. In 1070 Malcolm III married Edgar's sister, Margaret, who was later to become St. Margaret. This union brought about the settlement of many Saxons in Scotland and led to the adoption of the English language.

In 1100 Henry I of England married Margaret's daughter, Matilda, thus uniting the royal blood of Saxons and Normans and drawing Scotland into still closer association with England. Despite these growing ties, the Scottish kings had continual hopes of securing the northern English counties by war or family inheritance. They did not succeed. In 1138, David I of Scotland invaded Northumberland

Dryburgh Abbey, Berwickshire, was founded in 1150, and sacked by the English invaders in 1322 and 1385. The Earl of Hertford completely destroyed it in 1544. Its ruins were presented to the nation by Lord Glenconner in 1919.

Melrose Abbey, Roxburghshire, was founded in 1136 by King David I. Like many of the border abbeys, it was often sacked during English invasions.

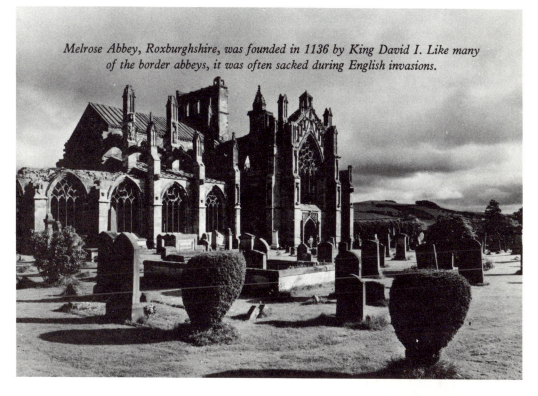

Looking out over the city of Glasgow from Gilmour Hill, with the Glasgow University Reading Room and Wellington Church in the foreground.

to try to annex it. He was defeated at the Battle of the Standard, but despite this he made King Stephen of England cede Northumberland to him. Fifteen years later his successor, Malcolm IV, was forced to hand it back to England.

The Scottish kings did, however, obtain estates in England through marriage or inheritance. This made them English noblemen, and as such they had to pledge fidelity for these lands to the English king. This was to bring great trouble on Scotland in the future.

FEUDAL DEPENDENCY

From 1165 to 1214, William the Lion, so called because his shield bore the red lion of Scotland, attempting to throw off Scotland's ties with England, inaugurated an alliance with France. Throughout Scottish history, alliances with the French, traditional enemies of the English at the time, were often entered into. With his eyes on Northumberland as usual, William invaded England, but was captured at Alnwick in 1174, and was forced to accept the Treaty of Falaise, under which Scotland became a feudal dependency of England. However, 14 years later, Scotland was released from its pact by Richard Coeur de

Lion (the Lion Hearted); he sold the rights back which William the Lion had signed away, to obtain funds he needed for his third Crusade.

NATIONAL DEVELOPMENT

During the reign of Alexander III (1249-86) Scotland made great strides in its national development. Alexander defeated the invading forces of the king of Norway, who was thus forced to hand over the Hebrides. The Orkney and Shetland Islands were recovered 200 years later from the Danes, in default of the unpaid dowry of Anne of Denmark when she was married to James III.

When Alexander III was killed by a fall from his horse in 1286, he left no heirs. His two sons and daughter died before him and his only living descendant was his daughter's infant child, Margaret, whose father was Eric of Norway. Two distant relatives were John Balliol and Robert Bruce. The Scots were thus faced by a choice between a baby girl queen, daughter of a foreign sovereign, and a civil war between two Scottish claimants. The nobles decided that the former was the lesser of two evils and appointed guardians to conduct the government in the name of Margaret. The Bruce party began to raise a rebellion but Edward I of England, a great-uncle of the baby queen, intervened to secure her crown. The long peace with England, adoption of English speech, manners, and institutions made it natural for him to offer and for the Scots to accept a guarantee of the succession of the Little Maid.

At this point, disaster struck. Within two months the Maid of Norway died on her way to Scotland and civil war broke out between the Bruces and the Balliols, each party wishing to secure Edward's support. Bruce was the stronger but Edward was jealous of his strength and threw his support to Balliol in the hopes of making Scotland once more a vassal kingdom of England. When Balliol realized what Edward was doing, he rebelled against his sponsor and made an alliance with the French. Edward, at war with the French, with various domestic quarrels at hand, and a rebellion in Wales, still was able to assemble a powerful army to battle Scotland. The Scots resisted stubbornly but the country was divided. The Bruces denied

support to Balliol and Edward easily defeated the Scottish army and made a triumphal march through Scotland in 1296.

The Scots at once found a new leader in Sir William Wallace. Within a year, Wallace as commander of the army, routed the English army of occupation at Stirling Bridge. Wallace ruled in the capacity of guardian for John Balliol but his rule did not last long. Before a year was up, Edward, relieved of both domestic and foreign anxieties, led an army into Scotland and defeated Wallace who escaped but resigned his office. By now the spirit of resistance had been thoroughly awakened in the Scots. New guardians were appointed, including Robert Bruce, the future Robert I and the grandson of the previous Bruce. Edward, summoned to London by fresh domestic complications had to leave Scotland unconquered. He returned, however, in 1303 and captured Stirling Castle the following summer. In 1305 Wallace was captured and put to a cruel death as a traitor. The story of Wallace's betrayal, his conviction

Inverness Castle, Inverness-shire, in the capital of the Highlands, still stands majestically. The castle where Macbeth lived, in this same locality, was razed to the ground in the 11th century by Malcolm, who avenged his father Duncan's murder by slaying Macbeth.

Stirling Castle was erected to command the bridges over the Forth. The Castle almost seems to be part of the rocky cliff upon which it was built. Note the height of the walls and the small windows in the left side of the Castle.

as an outlaw and traitor after a mock trial, and his beheading are remembered by every Scottish schoolboy today.

Scotland was restless. Edward believed he had a conquered country but Robert Bruce and John Comyn, a nephew of Balliol, each wanted the throne. At a meeting between the two there was a quarrel and Bruce stabbed Comyn. Bruce was crowned king in 1306 at Scone but he had made no preparations for resistance against Edward and he was defeated at Methven near Perth. He spent the following winters as a fugitive—his adventures are described in Sir Walter Scott's *Lord of the Isles* and *Tales of a Grandfather*. Later Bruce was to prove himself a great national leader. In spite of a Papal excommunication, the clergy supported the new monarch-in-exile. The Scots were determined after the death of Wallace to fight the English to the end. Bruce won a victory at Loudoun in Ayrshire. Soon afterwards, Edward I died and his successor abandoned the campaign. The delay at first seemed disastrous for the English but Bruce's stabbing of Comyn had resulted in

an English party being created in Scotland by nobles who were unswervingly for English interests. Robert Bruce as King Robert I between 1307 and 1314 crushed Edward II's followers, expelled English garrisons from Scottish castles, and with the help of his brother Edward and of the "Black" Douglas, a Border Noble, inflicted great damage by raids on the northern counties of England. Then Edward II made a serious effort to invade Scotland. He suffered at Bannockburn the greatest disaster the English army had ever sustained. In 1328 England finally acknowledged the independence of the kingdom of Scotland once more.

Disaster overcame the Scots again in the following year when King Robert died, leaving as his heir a son, David II, a child of five. In accordance with the provision of the Treaty of Northampton in 1328 (which had made Scotland independent), David had been married to Joanna, daughter of Edward II. Edward III had succeeded to the throne when his father had been murdered by his mother and her paramour, Mortimer. Thus, England had a strong king and Scotland a weak one. The disinherited Scots who had gone to England to live after Comyn's death, now urged Edward to strike back and he did. Using Balliol, an heir of the previous Balliol, as the leader of his army, he got revenge for the defeat at Bannockburn and crowned Balliol as Edward I of Scotland at Scone in 1332. Scotland once more became a vassal kingdom. However, Balliol never established himself as king and tides of battle turned back and forth. Young David II was brought back from France, and fighting and negotiations with England went on until he died in 1371. The nephew who succeeded him, Robert II, was the first monarch of the House of Stuart.

Robert II, after an uneventful reign, was succeeded by Robert III, a lame old man. The old king was alarmed when his heir,

This imposing monument, just off Princes Street, Edinburgh, surrounds the figure of Scotland's great writer, Sir Walter Scott.

Rothesay, was killed in a bitter feud with The Regent, Albany (an event told in Scott's *Fair Maid of Perth*); he therefore sent his remaining son, Prince James, to be educated in France. The boy was captured by the English at sea and Robert III died when the news reached him. James I, held captive in England for 18 years, received an excellent education there and acquired interest in settling the affairs of his country. On returning to Scotland, he tried to curb the warlike acts of the nobles but he was murdered in 1437. The House of Douglas and other Scottish families were gaining so much strength that they were a danger to government. The next king, James II, broke the power of the Douglases in battle; but his successor, James III, suffered two rebellions by his barons. The barons were alarmed by his feeble rule and poor conduct of public affairs, and in the second revolt his son James sided with them. The king was defeated and killed.

James IV was the first able and strenuous ruler to gain complete control over the Scottish parliament. He built a great navy, encouraged his captains to challenge English seamen and hoped to make Scotland count in European politics. However, this prosperous era ended when James crossed the English border with a strong army but was defeated and killed in the battle of Flodden Field in 1513. Henry VIII was the English ruler. The whole of Scotland, lords and vassals alike, fought in this tragic battle. Standing in their traditional *schiltrons*, or squares of spearmen, they were no match for the arrows and axes of the English infantry and the final onslaught of the English cavalry.

CONFLICT OF TWO QUEENS

James IV left an 18-month old infant, James V. The Queen Mother, Margaret Tudor, was barred from the regency and a French uncle became regent. When James V came of age, he proved capable as well as popular. However, his uncle, Henry VIII, was too strong for him. Refusing to denounce the Catholic Church as Henry VIII had done, James V married two

Bedroom of Mary Queen of Scots.

French wives, one after the other. He refused to meet his uncle Henry and finally Henry invaded Scotland. James V, broken in health and spirit, died a week after the birth of his daughter and only legitimate heir, Mary Stuart, known as Queen of Scots.

Henry VIII used the situation to wean Scotland from the Catholic Church and from its alliance with France. He arranged a marriage for his heir, afterward Edward VI, to the infant Scottish queen but the conditions were so unacceptable that the regents repudiated the marriage treaty. Thus, at 6 years of age, the girl queen was sent to France with the idea of marrying the heir to the French throne. When the French made peace with England in 1550, they helped the Scots to recover their territory and French soldiers remained on Scottish soil. Arran, who had been regent during the early years, now resigned in favor of Mary of Guise, mother of Mary Stuart. The young Mary then married the dauphin of France with the intention of bringing about a stronger alliance, and with Scotland becoming a province of France.

Then in 1547, Henry VIII died. His daughter, the Roman Catholic Mary Tudor, in turn died in 1558, and was succeeded by her half-sister, Elizabeth. Mary Stuart claimed the throne as the rightful successor. The following year the husband of Mary Stuart became Francis II of France. The Franco-Catholic-Scottish menace was too real and pressing to be overlooked by Elizabeth, and she began an intrigue with Scottish reformers to unseat Mary or at least prevent her from gaining the throne of England. Mary of Guise died in 1560 and Francis II died very shortly afterwards. Mary Stuart, therefore, widowed at the age of 18, returned to Scotland to face a highly dramatic situation in a country that was torn by conflicting interests.

At this time John Knox was leading the rise of Protestantism and Mary Stuart was a Catholic. In Scotland she found no wise or loyal advisers and what is more important, she was practically a stranger in her own country. Meanwhile, Elizabeth in England was fast becoming a skilled political thinker. Elizabeth was both jealous and fearful that Mary in the near future might ally herself again with a strong foreign king.

Mary in Scotland, meanwhile, was too busy with personal affairs to counteract Elizabeth's intrigues. She chose to marry her cousin, Lord Darnley, who stood next to herself in the English succession. Since Darnley was a Catholic, this gravely offended the Scottish Protestants. Mary's position became even more precarious when, after she seemed to tire of Darnley because of his arrogance and presumptions, Darnley was killed in a mysterious explosion at Kirk-of-Field. The chief conspirator was found to be the Earl of Bothwell, one of Mary's close advisers whom she soon chose as her third husband. The nobles took up arms against the queen and she surrendered to them at Carberry Hill in 1567. Mary was at first imprisoned in Edinburgh Castle and then moved to Lochleven Castle. Asked to consent to a divorce from Bothwell, she refused and was forced to abdicate. Her infant son became king with Moray, her half-brother, as regent. She escaped from Lochleven within a year and went to England where she sought the protection of Queen Elizabeth.

Elizabeth knew that it would be foolhardy to allow Mary any freedom in England. Uneasy about Mary's earlier challenge to the crown, Elizabeth imprisoned her. Mary lost any hope of liberation after the discovery of a plot in which Mary was to marry the Duke of Norfolk and, with the help of the Catholics, take over the English throne. For 19 years, Mary Stuart was imprisoned and finally executed in 1586 after another conspiracy against Elizabeth's life had been brought to light.

UNION OF THE TWO CROWNS

Meanwhile the capture of Edinburgh Castle in 1573 had destroyed the last resistance of Mary's supporters and established Presbyterian Protestantism in Scotland. The Presbyterian leaders began to claim that they were independent of the civil power, and the young King James VI waged a continual campaign against them, and another campaign to succeed Elizabeth on the English throne. He was victorious in both campaigns and succeeded to the

This is the house in Edinburgh where it is said John Knox, Scotland's great religious reformer, died in 1572.

English throne in 1603. As king of both nations, James continued his conflict with the Kirk. His new prestige as James I of England brought the nobles into line. By the time of his death in 1625, he had gradually converted Scotland into a mere dependency of the Crown, and effectively destroyed Presbyterianism for the time being although he had authorized a revised edition of the Bible in English and fifty revisers had spent seven years doing the work. The King James Authorized Version was published in 1611.

James's policies were further followed by his son, Charles I (1625-49). He, however, pushed this thinking to such extremes that he provoked a national revolt and thus brought about his own downfall. The attempt of Archbishop Laud in 1637 to impose the English Prayer Book on Scotland led to armed resistance. In 1643, the Scots signed the famous Solemn League and Covenant with English Parliamentarians who were resisting Charles I. By this, the Scots and the Parliamentarians agreed to have Presbyterianism as the only form of church government in the two countries. But in England power passed from Parliament to the magnifi-

Gate of the Palace of Holyrood House, official residence of the Queen when in Edinburgh. Parts of the Palace are open to the public. The name derives from Holy Rood, the cross of ivory, ebony and silver which had belonged to King David I's mother and which he gave in 1128 into the Abbot's care. The Abbey of Holyrood is still standing too.

cent New Model army of Cromwell, and they were determined not to have Presbyterianism as the only religion. In 1646, the defeated Charles surrendered to the Scots, who handed him over to Parliament. Then, seeing that Parliament was powerless against Cromwell, they invaded England in support of Presbyterianism, and were crushed by Cromwell at Preston in 1648.

The execution of Charles the following year turned the Scots against the English Parliament. They proclaimed Charles II king. Cromwell promptly defeated them at Dunbar, and again at Worcester. For the next nine years Scotland was under military occupation.

The history of Scotland parallels that of England from this point on. When Charles II was restored to the throne, he attempted to invoke the civil and ecclesiastical policy of James VI. This brought about two rebellions, both of which were crushed. When James II of England, a declared Roman Catholic took the throne, he was bitterly opposed by Scottish Presbyterian forces. In 1689, English Parliamentary leaders forced James to abdicate. The English throne was offered to William and Mary and a convention in Scotland made a similar declaration.

William's reign, 1689-1702, was continually beset by difficulties. In the first session of a Scottish Parliament that sat under William, episcopacy was abolished. In the second parliament, Presbyterianism replaced it as the established Church of Scotland.

The final and lasting union of Scotland with England was confirmed during the reign of Queen Anne in 1702-14. Anne grudgingly agreed to an Act of Security that gave Scotland a voice in the succession to the throne and also gave recognition to the need for commercial opportunities within the growing British Empire.

THE ACT OF UNION

After prolonged discussion, the Scottish and English parliaments finally came to terms in 1706 and an Act of Union was passed in 1707 which allowed Scottish laws and procedures to remain unchanged but abolished the Scottish Parliament. By the end of the 18th century, peace finally settled in Scotland.

At Scotland's oldest university, St. Andrews (above), students in their traditional scarlet capes cross the yard near the cloisters.

At the University of Aberdeen (below), a Nigerian student mixes with Scottish-born students. In the background is the King's College Chapel and Library.

Down Princes Street, Edinburgh, come the pipers on their way to the gathering of the clans at Murray-field. The sights and sounds never fail to thrill the spectators.

THE PEOPLE

Considerable emigration from Scotland as early as the 17th century has spread some knowledge —and notions— about Scottish people to all parts of the world. A characteristic reserve and slow acceptance of strangers, often mistaken for dourness, combine with a warm nature and intense loyalty. The thriftiness of a plain people, that enabled them to survive a harsh and severe existence, frequently is lampooned as stinginess. To this absurdity, the Scots respond with their own laughter and ready wit.

Recognized everywhere is the lilting inflection and stressed *r* of their speech, along with the many variations with which they have adapted English as their national language. In fact, even the accent varies according to region so that it can be as locally pinpointed as, for example, the Berwickshire versus the Midlothian accent.

London-style English filtered north from England about the 15th century and *Inglis* replaced *Scottis* as the national tongue, with many regional distinctions and traces of Norse and Gaelic. To this day English accents can be heard in the far reaches of the Highlands, except for their pronunciation of "b" as "p" and "j" as "ch." Around the Rhinns of Galloway, the speech follows the brogue of Ireland. Gaelic is the general language in the Hebrides. Most place names in the Orkneys are Norse, bearing testimony to the early influence and settlements of the Scandinavians in Scotland.

About two-thirds of a population estimated at 5,190,850 in 1966 are concentrated in the industrialized central region, where they dwell mostly in cities. Glasgow, with over a million people, is the largest city and has been the focal point of industrial life in Scotland, while Edinburgh, the capital and second largest with over 460,000 inhabitants, is the literary and artistic seat. An old and friendly rivalry exists between these two, but it is generally conceded that Edinburgh is truly the more beautiful, and Glasgow the more commercially enterprising.

In size, Aberdeen (185,000) follows, then Dundee and Paisley.

A secondary but much smaller concentration of people is found along the southwestern and eastern coasts. Throughout the rest of the land, which is about nine-tenths of Scotland, the population density averages less than one person per square mile. The average density of population of the whole Kingdom is 174 persons per square mile.

Kilted soldiers of military bands playing at a Highland Gathering. How many differences in costume can you see? Notice that the man on the right has the Tartan Plaid pinned to his left shoulder in true tradition.

CUSTOMS AND SOCIAL LIFE

July is the holiday month in Scotland. Festivals are numerous during the second and third weeks. There are mass exoduses from the cities, such as Glasgow's *doon the*

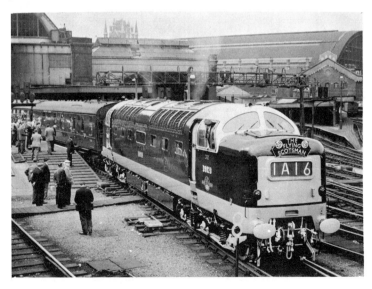

The Flying Scotsman express train has left London for Edinburgh at the same hour of 10 A:M. for 100 years, except for a wartime break, when it left at 9.30. In 1862 it covered the 393 miles in 10½ hours. Today its 374 passengers travel the distance in 6 hours.

Tossing the caber is a contest of strength at the Braemar Games.

A "braw lad and lass" lead the common riding in Galashiels on the English border. This traditional custom, marking the boundaries of a burgh, is a June event in many of the Lowland counties.

Dance contests at the Braemar Games are not restricted to girls. These boys score points for grace, poise and exactness in following a standard set of steps and movements.

water (down the river Clyde to the nearby seaside resorts). Highland dancing is an essential feature of the numerous *gatherings* (or festivals) which take place during the summer months. In the famous Gathering at Galashiels, a custom of the Border counties, a cavalcade of horsemen and horsewomen ride around the local boundaries to "establish" them for the coming year. One of the greatest events is the Royal Highland Gathering at Braemar, Aberdeenshire. In all the glory of their clan tartans, the participants in traditional kilts compete in various contests to the *skirl* of the bagpipes. Traditional competitive events include *tossing the caber* (the roughly trimmed trunk of a young tree), and *throwing the hammer*

(a device that resembles a cannonball on a stick). Highland flings and reels vie in speed, grace and agility with the fascinating sword dances. Points are awarded for performance and adherence to the traditional steps.

The hammer throw at the Braemar Games is different from the Olympic event. The usual wire is replaced by a stiff shaft with the ball (hammer) firmly anchored on the end. If you look closely in the left background you will see that a dance contest is going on at the same time.

The Searchlight Tattoo at the Castle is part of the Edinburgh Festival each August. Visitors from all over the world attend, and internationally famous artists in music, dance and drama are invited to perform.

"Piping in the Haggis" is a carefully observed ceremony at Scottish functions, particularly Robbie Burns Night and St. Andrew's Night. Led by the bagpipers, the chefs proudly carry trays bearing what has been called Scotland's secret weapon—a concoction of the sheep's innards. Burns dedicated an ode to this unusual national delicacy.

When the annual Edinburgh Festival of Music and Drama opens, the Lord Provost of Edinburgh and City officials walk in procession to St. Giles' Cathedral, decked in their robes of office as seen here, and carrying age-old symbols of authority.

For three weeks in August and September, Edinburgh is the scene of one of the greatest of all festivals of the arts. The brilliant finale is the Edinburgh Tattoo. This military display is remarkable for the vast number of kilted clansmen passing in review before the Castle, the swirling of batons and kilts, and the wild volume of the bagpipes. As midnight approaches, the lights in the Castle are dimmed one by one until only one turret remains floodlit. There on the dot of midnight, a lone piper fills the air with the strains of *Lights Out* and the vast castle goes dark.

Kilts are thought to have evolved from the dress of the early Celts, and have been worn in the Highlands for centuries. The original full kilt was a large 15-foot length of Tartan plaid that the wearer spread on the ground, tucked into pleats, then lay down on; he then belted it about himself and pinned the upper part to his left shoulder. The little kilt of today, the *feile beag*, only extends from the waist to the knee. Over the years the designs became the insignia of the different clans. The hairy *sporran* that hangs from the waist is a pouch; there are no pockets in a kilt.

Apart from public events and competitions, social life, especially among the middle income groups, revolves to a large extent around church associations and their various "socials." It has only been since World War I that entertainment such as theatres, night clubs, radio and dance halls, and the cinema have become regular parts of the scene for the average Scot.

In the kitchen the Scottish housewife considers herself a plain cook. Yet the writer H. V. Morton claims, "Scotland is the best place in the world to take an appetite." Scottish culinary art excels in the rich "stick to the ribs" soups, of which *cockie leekie* has been exported all over the world; roast grouse, pheasant, mutton and beef—none more famed than that of Aberdeen-Angus cattle; and of course, *haggis*, scones, porridge (oatmeal) and

St. Giles' Cathedral, Edinburgh, has famous stained glass windows that tell the stories of battles and historical events. St. Giles is of unknown date; the pillars supporting the tower are said to date back to Norman times (1120, or thereabouts).

collops (small slices of bacon or meat). Haggis is a veritable institution, nationally prepared to commemorate Robbie Burns Day (January 25) and other occasions—a pudding of sheep hearts, liver, etc., minced with suet and oatmeal and boiled in the bladder of a sheep. (It has been called Scotland's other secret weapon, second only to the bagpipes.)

CULTURE

The feeling of bridging the gap of centuries in Scotland is more than an illusion. In the capital city, in Edinburgh Castle which crouches like a guardian lion on the steep cliff that is its foundation stone, St. Margaret died in 1093. The Castle and Holyroodhouse still fulfil their function as military headquarters and royal residence. St. Giles' Church and many other important old buildings still stand in The Royal Mile, Edinburgh's main artery in the old Stuart days. Princes Street, running straight through the city with shops on one side and gardens on the other, marks the frontier of the New Town created 200 years ago by Georgian architects. To these stately vistas flocked the élite of Georgian and Regency society, so distinguished for their scholarship and literary achievements that the city became known as "the northern Athens." Classical monuments on Carlton Hill, reminiscent of the Acropolis, add to the similarity. At the castle is Mons Meg, the 15th-century cannon that fired a salute to Mary Queen of Scots when she became engaged to the dauphin of France 400 years ago. Here too are the Regalia of Scotland, including the medieval crown worn by sovereigns before the union of the kingdoms.

This statue in Ayr memorializes Robert Burns, Scotland's most famous poet. Many interesting items belonging to Burns can be seen in a visit to the museum which adjoins the Burns Cottage.

Abbotsford, the home of Sir Walter Scott in Roxburghshire, was built by the writer in 1815-23 in a style of architecture that is now called "Abbotsford Gothic."

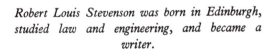

Robert Louis Stevenson was born in Edinburgh, studied law and engineering, and became a writer.

The most famous golf course in the world, St. Andrews Old Course is open to any golfer who pays the green fees. The Old Course has a name for each hole. This picture shows the 18th green, which is called Tom Morris after the famous father and son. "Young Tommy" won the British Open Championship four times in succession before his tragic death at the age of 24. St. Andrews is where the official rules of the game are made and interpreted.

There are so many golf courses in Scotland that tourist guidebooks are often unable to list all of them. This is King's Hame, the 18th hole of King's Course, with the first tee in the background, at Gleneagles Hotel, Perthshire.

SPORTS

While the battle of Langside was still raging, Mary Queen of Scots sought diversion by having her retainers play a game of football. Sports have flourished through political upheavals no matter what the outcome, and in the face of severe economic restrictions. Curling, football and golf began in Scotland, at least in the standardized forms used universally today. The earliest record of golf is contained in a statute of James II of Scotland. "Golf be utterly cryit doune and nocht usyt," he ordered, because golf was being played at the expense of archery and other exercises vital to the protection of the realm. Played in Scotland for more than 5 centuries, golf has evolved slowly from a pastime brought back by soldiers from Flanders, to today's form of progress about the course with a variety of clubs.

Yachting in Scottish waters is gaining in popularity, particularly in the idyllic seaside resort of Oban on the west coast. To the east over the Devil's Elbow Pass to the valley of the River Dee where stands Balmoral, the shooter and fisherman find an all-in-one paradise—a salmon river, grouse moors and deer forests. Just over the Cairngorm Mountains is another great salmon river, the Spey. Grouse shooting in Scotland is a regal sport, with helpers flushing the birds towards the shooters.

In the Highlands somewhere near Inverness, this expert rock climber is nearing the top of his journey. In the background is Craig-a-chalamain, 2,600 feet above sea level. The climber has come from Glenmore Lodge, where many Scottish sportsmen spend their holidays.

This is not a castle, but a Youth Hostel at Auchendennan on Loch Lomond. Open throughout the year, the hostel provides lodging for 300 young people at a time. In a year, as many as 24,000 hostellers come from 34 nations. This hostel was built in 1860.

Curling has been Scotland's winter sport for over 400 years—ever since it was first brought to the country by Flemish merchants in the 15th or 16th century.

The game of curling is played by propelling stones along the ice toward a target circle about 35 yards distant. The object is to get as close as possible to the target, or to knock away or block one's opponent's stones. The stones are circular and highly polished, with fixed handles. The ice is swept with brooms to remove particles of snow and leave a smooth, fast surface. The players have to wear rubber-soled shoes to prevent slipping. These two curlers are brushing away the loose ice from in front of their stones on historic Loch Leven, Kinross. Six inches of ice is needed to support the great weight of the players, stones and spectators.

Many of the sporting activities of the Scottish Council of Physical Recreation are based on the Speyside resorts, particularly winter sports. The first chair-lift, however, was opened in Glencoe, west of Speyside. Ben Nevis, Britain's highest mountain, is a great challenge for climbers as well as for tourists exploring the western Highlands, the most romantic region in Scotland.

Skiing above the clouds in Scotland.

Shipbuilding has been the major industry of Glasgow for generations. The city fathers today are diversifying but still the shipyards of the River Clyde continue to provide the major employment for residents. Both ships in the foreground were assembled from large prefabricated units. On the right is a passenger and transport ferry being completed for Canada and next to it is a general cargo and passenger ship being built for the Norwegian Bergen Line.

THE ECONOMY

Scotland's economy has been moving steadily towards diversification ever since the depression of the 20's. At that time the heavy industries on which Scotland had relied to an excessive extent from the onset of the Industrial Revolution, were shut down. The success of the recovery since then is evident in significant social changes, higher wages and increased leisure time. Attendance at cultural and entertainment media is growing. Clubs and societies are sprouting. Purchases of such luxuries as television sets and cars are booming. However, there still is a long road to hoe before Scotland attains the peak prosperity of the rest of the Western world.

Grazing near the shores of Loch Fyne, Argyll, are these hardy Highland cattle whose thick shaggy coats enable them to withstand the cold winters of the Scottish mountains. They provide excellent beef.

The crofter, or tenant farmer, who lives in this cottage pays land rent in cash. It is then up to him and his family to make the farm succeed. Many farms are located in isolated areas and outside help is not plentiful.

82 ■ SCOTLAND

WALES

Skerrid Fawr, or Holy Mountain, a hill near Abergavenny, has a notch in it, attributed to an "earthquake that shook the world" at the Crucifixion. In the foreground are some black-faced Welsh sheep.

THE LAND AND ITS HISTORY

THE PRINCIPALITY OF WALES with the border county of Monmouthshire has a land area of 8,006 square miles. The boundary with England is a north-south line which deviates little from longitude 3° West.

Cymru, or Wales, is a country of mountains and valleys. The greater part of it consists of a plateau of old rocks surrounded by narrow plains. This plateau is deeply carved by rivers:

the Dee, Clwyd, Conway, Teifi, Towy, Tawe, Usk, Wye and the Severn.

The uplands are principally sandstone and slate with patches of granite. To the south are the great coal fields from which the principal wealth of the country has come.

In fact, South Wales is one country and North Wales another, with the usual rivalry between them born of their physical differences.

IRISH SEA

WALES

IF THE BRITISH ISLES are represented as a seated goat with Scotland as the shoulders and head, England as the body and legs, Wales must be the stomach. The seated goat holding Ireland in its arms faces the Atlantic, which is fitting, since the influence of Britain has been across the seas rather than over the Continent at its back.

While England's British cousins—Ireland, Scotland and Wales—have at various times wanted to break away, Wales, being closest to England, would find the separation difficult, since the lives of the two countries have been mingled so long. There can hardly be a single township in all England without its Welsh draper, its Welsh dairyman or its Welsh schoolmaster.

Yet "Wild Wales" as George Borrow, the great 19th century traveller called it, is completely individual, and one step across the border from England shows the difference.

SOUTH WALES

South Wales with its coal fields stretches along the Bristol Channel from Monmouthshire across Glamorgan to Carmarthen. Here the black of coal dust prevails, and behind the docks of Newport, Cardiff and Port Talbot grows a forest of factory chimneys among mountainous slag heaps, pit-head gear and miles of railway lines where coal is hauled down the grimy valleys to the sea.

GLAMORGAN

In Glamorgan's soft coal measures, more than half the population of all Wales is concentrated. The narrow valleys of the Taff, the Rhymney and the Rhondda rivers behind Cardiff are covered with colliery towns, Ebbw Vale, Pontypool, Tredegar, Pontypridd and Aberdare, all seeming to be linked by an endless street, since there is no space on the steep hillsides for the towns to spread out.

Cardiff, busy and cosmopolitan, with its splendid Civic Centre and its international port on Tiger Bay is the hub of these valleys and the principal city of Wales. King Arthur's legendary Camelot was not far off and it was from Cardiff that Sir Lancelot took ship when he sailed away into the mist. South Wales is a land of sharp contrasts. Only a few miles from Cardiff lies Caerphilly Castle, built by the Normans at the strategic junction of the valleys. This magnificent ruin is, after Windsor, the second largest castle in the British Isles. The town of Caerphilly is celebrated for its cheese.

To the west of Cardiff between the mountains and the sea is the fertile Vale of Glamorgan. For centuries the Welsh have praised the beauty of this vale where the art of thatching is still handed on from father to son. Gaels, Danes, Normans and Flemish settlers all landed on these sandy beaches, and orders of monks founded their abbeys in the Vale. Llantwit Major was one of the earliest Christian settlements in Wales and by the fourth century there was a thriving university attached to it. Legend has it that a band of Irish raided Llantwit, sacked the abbey and took Patrick, the abbot, back to Ireland as a trophy. Patrick, it is said, turned the tables, converted his kidnappers, and became the patron saint of Ireland.

It is hard to take many steps in Wales without being reminded of its stirring history. At St.

Caerphilly Castle, the largest in Wales, is in Glamorgan, and like Pisa, has its leaning tower.

An aerial view of the Cardiff Docks which serve the heavy steel manufacturing industry in that city, as well as coal. During the reign of Elizabeth I, the port of Cardiff was notorious as a pirate refuge.

Llandaff Cathedral in Cardiff has the figure of Christ sculptured by Jacob Epstein above the aisle.

Mumbles, overlooking Swansea Bay, while retaining its pleasant fishing village air, is one of the leading seaside resorts of South Wales.

Athan in the Vale the eleventh century Normans planted orchards and vineyards to provide fruit and wine for William the Conqueror's household.

In the present century it was from St. Athan aerodrome that some young R.A.F. pilots of the Battle of Britain took off to fight a different invader.

The seaport of Swansea marks the end of the industrial region, and beyond its metal works and foundries is an unspoilt place of woods and beaches—the Gower Peninsula with a pocket of English-speaking people and English place names, a pattern that is repeated in other parts of Wales. Gower, important in ancient days, was guarded by several castles, all of them now in ruins. A mile from Reynoldston stands an enormous cromlech, a prehistoric pillar, known as Arthur's Stone. It is said locally that at night it comes down to the sea to quench its thirst. When smuggling was profitable, a great deal of contraband was brought to the caves of Gower in small boats.

Princess Street runs through Swansea's new shopping area. Often called the metallurgical capital of Wales, the seaport town is important for its manufacture of tin-plate and zinc. Swansea, because of its reliance upon the metal industry and its refined oil exporting facilities did not suffer as greatly as many coal-dependent areas during the depression of the 1920's and 1930's.

NORTH WALES

The mist rolls in over the summit of Snowdon. Comprising five ridges that extend from Cardigan Bay to Beaumaris Bay, Snowdon is surrounded by lovely valleys, streams and lakes.

In the north is a different Wales. When the Welsh first came down from their mountains to raid England they were stopped by the River Severn in the south and the Dee in the north, but between these rivers was a gap through which they could sweep. One of the Saxon kings, Offa of Mercia, in 779 built an earth rampart along this gap for a hundred miles. Some of it still exists and a Welshman to this day will speak of crossing Offa's Dyke.

The northern gateway into Wales is through the ancient city of Chester on the Dee with its well-preserved Roman amphitheatre.

An old house in Aberconway, North Wales, has been restored by the National Trust. The trace of crossed beams can be seen on the upper storey underneath the plaster.

High above the green fields of Merioneth stands 13th-century Harlech Castle, built by Edward I. The old fortress is in an excellent state of preservation.

Of the more than 100 stone castles in Wales, Harlech, in Merionethshire, is closest to the Welsh heart. Harlech Castle stands on a promontory overlooking the Irish Sea, and Edward I thought he had built so solidly that the castle would never be taken. The Welsh under Dafydd ap Ifan ap Eynion were holding it in 1468 against the Yorkists, and Dafydd, when summoned to surrender, replied:

"I held a castle in France until every old woman in Wales talked of it and I will hold this Welsh castle until every old woman in France talks of it!" His words still ring down the centuries in Ceiriog's stirring battle song "Men of Harlech."

At Llanbedr, south of Harlech, begins the long line of stone steps which climbs upwards for two miles and whose purpose is still a mystery. Inland among Merioneth's mountains is Lake Bala.

The road drops down to Dinas Mawddwy, a small slate-quarrying village in Merionethshire. Situated at the junction of the Rivers Dovey and Cerist, it is much frequented by fishermen after salmon and trout.

BRIEF HISTORY OF WALES

Pre-history	Before the Celtic people came in the late Bronze Age, the country was inhabited by people of the Iberian race.
Roman Times	1st century A.D. Julius Frontinus conquered the Silures in South Wales and Agricola subdued the Ordovices in Central Wales. Romans built a string of forts along the border after conquering the part of Britain later to become England. Wales not really Romanized as other parts of Britain, accounting in part for retention of Welsh tongue.
4th Century	Arrival of Christianity in *Britannia Secundia* (as Wales was then called) brought by monks from Ireland.
5th Century	Following abandonment of Britain by the Romans, conflicts arose between the Britons and the Gaels, the two principal language groups, with Britons prevailing.
A.D. 664	Council of Whitby brought Welsh Christians into relations with the Church of Rome.
844–877	Rhodri the Great, Prince of Gwynedd, checked Viking advances.
910–950	Reign of Howel the Good, "King of all the Welsh!" His code of law was considered the finest achievement of mediaeval Wales.
10th Century	Welsh wars with the Saxons.
1039–1063	Gryffydd ap Llewelyn unified all Wales.
1072–1093	The Normans invaded and annexed Glamorgan. Welsh chieftains along the border adopted English ways. One Welsh noble was signatory of the Magna Carta (1215).
1272–1307	Reign of Edward I of England. With the death of Prince Llewelyn, Edward made his own son Prince of Wales, establishing the title as that of the male heir to throne of England.
1399	Increased use of English resented by the Welsh who rebelled against Henry IV (Bolingbroke) under Owen Glendower.
1415	The revolt finally quelled and Glendower becomes a fugitive, having refused amnesty, until his death soon after. Punitive laws put into effect in Wales.
1485	Henry Tudor ascends the English throne with Welsh military support.
1536	Act of Union with England with English system of law and land tenure.
1542	Monmouth formally annexed to England.
1830	English circuit courts extended into Wales.

The Roman amphitheatre at Caerleon in Monmouthshire was built about A.D. 75 and for nearly 300 years it was the fortress of the Roman Second Legion. According to legend it was later the capital of King Arthur and it was to Caerleon that Tennyson came to get atmosphere for his poem "The Idylls of the King."

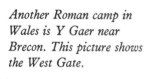

Another Roman camp in Wales is Y Gaer near Brecon. This picture shows the West Gate.

WALES ■ **91**

Welsh a love of learning which is one of their most striking traits.

In Wales, it is noticeable that the few Welsh surnames like Lloyd, Owen, Davis, Thomas, Williams, Jones, have to stretch a long way. In a small village where there are many Jones's, it becomes necessary to say Jones, the Baker; Jones, the Fish; and Jones, the Railway, to distinguish them. The undertaker would be Jones, the Death.

The Welsh love to sing, love to play their harps and love to talk, and many of them talk in their old Celtic tongue, Brythonic. The revival of the Welsh language in the last few years has led to a new feeling of nationalism. It is spoken now by 25 per cent of the people.

All the Welsh, however, are not bards. Beyond the thousands of coal miners and dairy farmers are all those living quiet lives in remote villages, many of them faithful chapel-goers. The Calvinistic Methodist Church has built chapels all over Wales.

Bishop William Morgan, when he translated the Bible into Welsh in 1588, not only laid the cornerstone for modern Welsh but helped to implant in the Welsh their love of learning.

THE PEOPLE

LANGUAGE AND NAMES

Bishop William Morgan's masterly translation of the Bible into Welsh in 1588 laid the foundation of modern Welsh. In the following years the Welsh Bible became the great textbook of the people, spreading across the country by way of Griffith Jones's famous "Circulating School" and through the Sunday Schools. It played a significant part in the moulding of the national character, stimulating interest in religious and moral issues and implanting in the

Methodist preacher William Williams, circa 1800, started an Evangelical Revival, one of whose aims was the preservation of the Welsh language. But for this movement Welsh might have become nearly as extinct as Irish became in the 19th century.

Fine Welsh collies are waiting their turn at an international sheepdog trial. These delightful black and white dogs usually have a white tip to their tail and are considered an invaluable help in efficient shepherding in Wales.

Easy does it! A new climber gets to the top at Capel Curig. Such peaks are occasionally shrouded in clouds as can be seen in the distance.

Young rock climbers can hire their most precious possession—boots. These two boys are off on a seven-day adventure, a rock-climbing course.

Sheep dipping to clean the wool and prevent skin disease comes before clipping.

This fourstand cold reduction tandem mill is capable of rolling at finishing speeds of 4,000 feet per minute. It is powered by motors with a total of 23,000 h.p.

Great skill is required to clip by hand without leaving patchy and rough spots.

The Trawsfynydd atomic power station in Merionethshire, operating at 500,000 kilowatts, is second in power in the world only to the new 1,180,000-kilowatt plant at Anglesey.

Nuclear power stations are operating at Trawsfynydd in Merionethshire and Wylfa in Anglesey. Anglesey, it will be remembered, was called Mona, the Mother of Wales, because of her bountiful cornfields, and perhaps it is fitting that the largest atomic power station is sited here.

The motto of Wales is Y Ddraig Goch Ddyry Cychwyn—The Red Dragon Sets the Standard.

> Av I dir Môn, cr dwr Menai,
> Tros y traeth, ond aros trai.
> "I will go to the land of Mona, notwithstanding the water of the Menai, across the sand, without waiting for the ebb."
> *A couplet written by the 17th-century bard Robert Lleiaf ("the least of the Roberts")*

Sheep graze peacefully on the Pembroke shore against a background of the island bird sanctuary of Skomer.

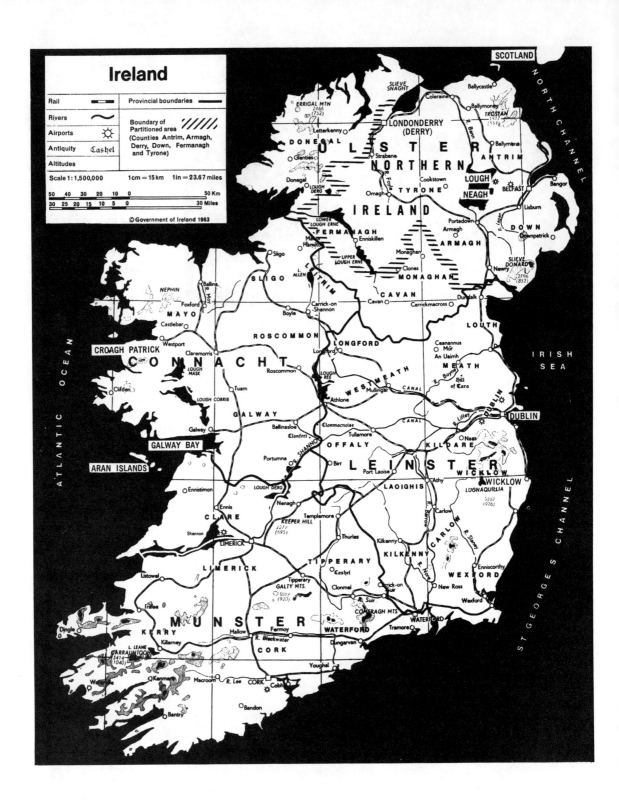

Ireland

Rail	▭▭	Provincial boundaries	▬▬
Rivers	～	Boundary of Partitioned area	▨
Airports	☼	(Counties Antrim, Armagh, Derry, Down, Fermanagh and Tyrone)	
Antiquity	Cashel		
Altitudes			

Scale 1 : 1,500,000   1cm = 15km   1in = 23.67 miles

50 40 30 20 10 0 ———————— 50 Km
30 25 20 15 10 5 0 ———————— 30 Miles

© Government of Ireland 1963

SCOTLAND

NORTH CHANNEL

SLIEVE SNAGHT

ERRIGAL MTN 2466 (752)

Ballycastle

Coleraine
Ballymoney
TROSTAN 1817 (554)

Letterkenny

DONEGAL

ULSTER

NORTHERN

Ballymena

ANTRIM

Glenties

Omagh
Foyle
TYRONE

Cookstown

LOUGH NEAGH ☼

BELFAST

Bangor

Donegal

LOUGH DERG

IRELAND

Portadown
Armagh

R. Lagan
LISBURN

DOWN

Downpatrick

LOWER LOUGH ERNE

FERMANAGH

Manor Hamilton

Enniskillen

Clones

Monaghan

MONAGHAN

ARMAGH

Newry
SLIEVE DONARD 2796 (852)

Sligo

UPPER LOUGH ERNE

L. ALLEN

LEITRIM

CAVAN

Cavan

Carrickmacross

Dundalk

NEPHIN 2646

Ballina

R. Moy

SLIGO

Carrick-on-Shannon

LONGFORD

LOUTH

Foxford

MAYO

Boyle

ROSCOMMON

Ceanannus Mór
An Uaimh

MEATH

Castlebar

Longford

WESTMEATH

IRISH SEA

Westport

CROAGH PATRICK

CONNACHT

LOUGH MASK

Claremorris

Roscommon

LOUGH REE

Mullingar

CANAL

R. Boyne
Hill of Tara

Tuam

Clifden

LOUGH CORRIB

Athlone

Clonmacnoise

Tullamore

CANAL

R. Liffey

DUBLIN

DUBLIN

GALWAY

Ballinasloe

OFFALY

KILDARE

Nass

Galway

Clonfert

SHANNON

Athy

ATLANTIC OCEAN

GALWAY BAY

Portumna

Birr

Port Laoise

LEINSTER

WICKLOW

WICKLOW
LUGNAQUILLIA 3039 (926)

ARAN ISLANDS

LOUGH DERG

LAOIGHIS

Ennistimon

Nenagh

Carlow

R. Barrow

Ennis

Templemore

KEEPER HILL 2279 (695)

Kilkenny

CARLOW

R. Slaney

CLARE

Thurles

KILKENNY

Enniscorthy

Shannon ☼

LIMERICK

TIPPERARY

R. Nore

WEXFORD

Listowel

LIMERICK

Tipperary
Cashel

Clonmel

Carrick-on-Suir

New Ross

Wexford

GALTY MTS. 3018 (920)

Tralee

Dingle

MUNSTER

Mallow

Farmoy

R. Suir

COMERAGH MTS.

WATERFORD

WATERFORD

Tramore

KERRY

Killarney

R. Blackwater

WATERFORD

Dungarvan

L. LEANE
CARRAUNTOOHIL 3414 (1040)

CORK

Youghal

Kenmare

Macroom

R. Lee

CORK
Cobh ☼

ST GEORGES CHANNEL

Bandon

96 ■ IRELAND

IRELAND

THE LAND

The "Emerald Isle" is well named, for heavy rainfall encourages deep green vegetation along Ireland's wild seacoast and in the countless little inland glens or valleys. The fertile central plain is ringed, more or less, by gently rolling mountains, beyond which are soft heath-covered moors. The scenery of the west coast has a striking grandeur. Rocky, windswept mountains jut into the sea; steep cliffs rise above tiny islands and in many places the coastal mountains are cut up by inlets from the sea. The interior is marked by many twisting rivers, some of which spill into the sea, while others give rise to deep, shimmering lakes. The land has the same fierce, untamed quality which, for centuries, has characterized the people.

Ireland is an island. Bounded on two sides by the Atlantic Ocean, it is as close as $13\frac{1}{2}$ miles to the Scottish coast on the northeast, and only 50 to 70 miles across the Irish Sea from England on the east.

Most of the island is occupied by the Republic of Ireland (formerly Eire) and the rest by Northern Ireland (Ulster), which is part of the United Kingdom. The whole island is small—not even as large as Iceland. Some 360 miles long and 180 miles wide, it covers 32,000 square miles. Of this, Northern Ireland, which resembles Scotland geologically in its hill formations and coal deposits, spreads over 5,242 square miles in the northeast corner of the island. The North's coastline is 245 miles long, and its southern frontier is almost as long. The dividing line twists and twines across the face of the map to follow the county borders that separate the two regions.

Although the southern part of Ireland has many natural ports, Northern Ireland, with a rocky, inaccessible coastline with lofty cliffs, has only three ports large enough for ocean-going vessels: Belfast, Larne and Londonderry.

Coursing through mountains, towns and villages is Ireland's River Shannon, renowned in song and story, the longest river in the British Isles. Extending over 230 miles and covering one fifth of the country, it forms many important lakes, such as Lough Allen, Lough Ree, and Lough Dearg. In Northern Ireland, Lough Neagh, not a part of the Shannon, is the largest lake in the British Isles.

The name Ulster is used interchangeably with Northern Ireland, since the ancient kingdom of Ulster occupied most of that area. But technically Ulster consists of nine counties, three of which are in the Irish Republic, and the other six in Northern Ireland. The county division of Ireland has been preserved in modern times, but it is many centuries since the old grouping into provinces has had any political significance. Besides Ulster, there are Munster (six counties); Leinster (twelve counties); and Connacht (five counties). Originally Meath, now a part of Leinster, was a separate province, making five provinces in days of old. So the Irish word for province, *cuige*, means a fifth part.

Most of Ireland is a central plain, a stretch of hilly, rugged land, made up mostly of limestone and covered with bog and glacial deposits of sand and clay. Where the Shannon flows, the central plain is extremely fertile. The plain is almost completely ringed in by low mountains, or highlands, rising up around the coastal rim,

Against the backdrop of the Mourne Mountains in Northern Ireland, a shepherd and his black-faced sheep cross the stone bridge near Tullyree, County Down.

With caravans like those used by itinerant tinkers, tourists in the south travel leisurely on sparsely trafficked roads.

and these are picturesque but barren for the most part.

In the north are four mountain ranges, the Donegals, the Sperrins, the Antrims and the Mournes. Along the east coast lie the Dublin and Wicklow ranges, the former near the country's capital city. In the south, running east to west, are several other ranges with typically Irish names: the Comeraghs, the Knockmealdowns, the Galtees, the Mullagheirks and the Macgillycuddy Reeks. Ireland's highest mountain is Carrantuohill in Macgillycuddy Reeks, 3,400 feet above sea level. Completing the circle in the west are the Connemaras, the Nephins and the Ox mountains.

(Below) On the north Antrim coast in Northern Ireland is the Giant's Causeway. According to folklore, it was built by an Irish giant, Finn MacCool, in order to cross over to Scotland to fight a rival Scottish giant. Geologists, however, believe the odd formation is a result of molten lava going through a process of rapid cooling which caused the lava to crack into these strange formations.

CLIMATE

Ireland has a temperate climate with a relatively small range of temperature and no extremes of hot or cold. The country's nearness to the sea helps to make its winters mild and summers cool. The prevailing wind blows from the southwest and passes over the Atlantic Ocean; this wind also helps to moderate the temperature throughout the year. Moisture from the ocean gives Ireland a plentiful rainfall at all seasons and, as a result, this agricultural land rarely suffers from drought. The soil is rich and fertile, especially in the river valleys; however, much of the surface is bogland. These bogs are marshy areas created by heavy rainfall and insufficient drainage, which cause decayed vegetation. This builds up into steadily increasing layers of spongy matter called "peat" which is dried and used as fuel by the people, but is not fertile when left in the fields.

Although many Irish bogs have been cleared of peat and are used for growing potatoes, they make a considerable amount of Ireland's land unsuitable for farming. Nevertheless, most of the soil is excellent for farming and cattle raising.

(Above) The Upper Lake, surrounded by mountains and luxuriant woods, is one of the three main lakes of Killarney in County Kerry.

(Left) Because of its mild, moist climate, Ireland's central plain has the richest soil in the country. Dairy farming is the chief occupation. Here is a panoramic view of the plain in County Tipperary, its fields symmetrically divided by carefully tended hedgerows.

Birr Castle, in the Irish Midlands, was the scene of fierce sieges during the 16th and 17th centuries. Later, it became famous for the observatory built there by one of the Earls of Rosse. It is currently the home of the Countess of Rosse; her son (the former Anthony Armstrong-Jones) and his wife, Princess Margaret, spend many quiet holidays at this historic site.

HISTORY

EARLY HISTORY TO 1601

The history of Ireland is sad, valiant, and courageous. It is peopled by heroes majestic in body and spirit, and by heroes small yet unconquerable. Its history goes back to prehistoric times and is accented by invasions, massacres, starvation, defeats and persecution. But underlying the centuries of trouble runs a strong, bright thread that weaves its people together and strengthens them time and time again. This is the thread of liberty. For twelve centuries the Irish fought and died to win their liberty until, finally, in 1937, stronger and more confident than ever before, they won their independence from Great Britain.

Ancient writings tell how the three sons of Mileadh of Spain came to Ireland about

350 B.C. and conquered the land from the Tuatha De Danann, a race gifted in magic, who then retired to the mountains, to intervene from time to time in the affairs of the people of Mileadh, rather in the manner of the Greek gods.

Archaeologists, on the other hand, tell us that several primitive peoples reached the island before the arrival, about 600 B.C., of the advanced Celts, whose iron weapons swept all before them. Some Celts seem to have come by way of Britain, others directly from the Continent, where they held sway from Spain to Hungary. Best known of them are the Gauls of France, thanks to such Roman historians as Julius Caesar.

The Romans called the Irish Celts *Scotti* and Ireland *Hibernia*, while the Irish called the island *Eriu* (Erin) and themselves *Goídil* (Gael). The Gaels were not a united people, being split into many petty kingdoms, but they shared a common culture. Celtic society was influenced strongly by the Druids, a priesthood claiming special knowledge of the gods and life and death, who advised the chiefs in war and peace. Our knowledge of the Druids comes mainly from Roman accounts of Gaul and Britain, but it seems clear that the practices of the Druids of Ireland were essentially similar, and this is borne out by numerous references to the priests in the old Irish sagas.

The Celts brought not only their religion

(Below) One of the most ancient and historic sites is Ireland's Rock of Cashel in County Tipperary, seat of the Munster kings from about 370 A.D. to 1101. This aerial view shows the buildings on the Rock, including a 10th-century round tower, Cormac's Chapel, the Cathedral and the Hall of Vicars Choral. In the lower right foreground is St. Patrick's Cross.

(Above) The unique form of writing on this ancient stone, an Ogham stone, dates back to the first centuries of Christianity. The inscription, carved in lines up to five in number, gives the name of an unidentified hero and his ancestors.

but also their own highly refined society in which historians and poets were equal to kings, and the practice of law reached moral and artistic heights. Their Brehon Law Code continued to be the law of most of Ireland until the 16th century and, in general, it protected the poor and weak from the rich and strong.

Constant wars prevented acceptance of a single king until Conn of Connacht was made the first High King or *Ard-Ri* of Ireland sometime in the 3rd century. The Race of Conn lasted for eight centuries and reached the height of its expansion under the greatest ruler of Conn, Niall of the Nine Hostages, who reigned from A.D. 380 to 405. It was an age when the Roman Empire was crumbling in Britain. The Irish made constant raiding expeditions to Britain and settled there in large numbers. Probably because of its isolation from Western Europe, Ireland escaped occupation even though the Romans occupied England for almost 400 years.

(Right) In the ancient realm of Tara, King Laoghaire, the Queen and Princess awaited the coming of St. Patrick although they had been warned by the Druids that the light of the "Resurrection" of the new religion "if not quenched now, will burn forever and consume Tara." These players portray the three royal characters in the "Pageant of St. Patrick."

Round towers, such as this in County Galway, were built near monasteries to warn of approaching raiders. Often the church treasures were stored here until the danger was past.

The Age of Saint Patrick and

The Viking Invasions

Niall made conquests as far away as Gaul where his soldiers swept Gauls of Roman citizenship into slavery. Among the captives was the 16-year-old son of a Roman-British official, later to be known as St. Patrick, the Patron Saint of Ireland. His birth is dated at about 390 A.D., and he died about 461 A.D. With the advent of St. Patrick, Irish history is based more firmly on fact than on a combination of legend and fact.

Patrick was sold as a slave in about 405 A.D. and herded swine in Antrim, Ireland, until his escape six years later to France and Britain. There he spent long years learning the prin-

ciples of Roman Catholicism, ultimately becoming a priest. In 432 A.D. he returned to Ireland to found the Catholic Church there. The Irish love of mysticism, as evidenced by the Druid's influence, and their love of knowledge, were channelled into an acceptance of St. Patrick's Christian teachings. He brought with him a knowledge of Latin and taught the people to read and write so that they could follow the prayers and Gospels. Ireland became the main base of Latin learning; schools and monasteries were founded to which thousands of European scholars flocked. Many returned to Europe as missionaries.

For three and a half centuries from the time of St. Patrick, Ireland was free from foreign interference. While the rest of Western Europe was in chaos because of the destruction of the

Roman Empire by barbarian tribes, Ireland enjoyed the golden years of its culture. The Church taught every subject—Latin, geometry and astronomy—as well as religion. Gaelic literature had its beginnings in this period, and music, too, became a popular expression of the Irish.

But the end of the 8th century brought the Viking invaders. These sea raiders, Norsemen and Danes, descended upon Ireland year after year, murdering and plundering but many of them eventually settled on the coast, founding the cities of Dublin, Cork, Limerick, and Waterford. The Vikings were finally defeated by one of the great heroes of Ireland, Brian Boru, who became King in the 10th century. Many of the defeated Vikings fled home by sea, but many more remained in Ireland to become Christianized and to merge into the Irish scene. The Norse invasions led to a shift of power from the inland areas to the coast, and to the beginning of medieval town life in Ireland— previously the Irish lived mostly in pastoral communities scattered over the interior.

(Above) Muireadach's Cross in Monasterboice of County Louth is one of the high crosses still standing from the early Christian period. Its surface is ornamented with sculptured panels of scriptural scenes, human and animal figures and symbolic carvings.

(Right) This huge granite statue of St. Patrick stands on the summit of a hill in Saul, County Down, where the Patron Saint of Ireland allegedly landed in the year 432 A.D., and began his mission of converting the islanders to his religion. To explain the Christian concept of deity, the "Trinity," he used the three loops of the "seamar trefoil," or shamrock, which became Ireland's national emblem. Down through the ages, every March 17th is, in his name, the day of the "wearing of the green" shamrock (or ties, et al.) for the Irish all over the world.

(*Above*) *The ivy-clad ruins of Boyle Abbey in County Roscommon, dating back to 1161.*

(*Above*) *St. Finbarr's Cathedral on the River Lee in County Cork stands on the site he founded in the 6th century.*

St. Patrick's Purgatory on lonely Lough (lake) Derg in Donegal, in the north of Ireland. Here pilgrims fast on dry bread and black tea, and go barefoot all day.

The Norman Conquest

and English Rule: 1170-1601

It was a century and a half before the next invasion—the Norman invasion under Henry II of England. The Normans were professional fighters with superior weapons. The Irish kings, who would not unite, were no match for them. The people resisted fiercely, but were untrained and disorganized.

England's power in Ireland rose and fell. Hard fighting by the Irish, who came to include many Gaelicised Normans, limited England's rule to the settlement around Dublin called "the Pale."

No English king until Henry VIII wanted to add "King of Ireland" to his title, for the English regarded the Irish as "wild," and inferior. They called them the "*mere* Irish." When Henry VIII (1509-1547) ascended the English throne, he adopted an active policy as King of Ireland and later proceeded to impose his Protestant religion on the country. During the course of this religious Reformation, abbeys were wrecked and churches looted of their treasures.

During Henry's reign, however, no real effort was made to enforce the conversion of Ireland to Protestantism. Under Edward VI (1547-1553), the English government issued an edict to establish that religion officially in Ireland. Furthermore, a number of the Irish chiefs were deprived of their lands, their followers sharing in their ruin, and English speculators settled them with English tenants. This was known as the "plantation" system. It continued under Mary Tudor and later under Elizabeth I, who also instituted massacres. Warfare with the English dragged on for fifty years although the chiefs of Ireland, such as the O'Neills, waged heroic battles.

Again and again, Hugh O'Neill of Tyrone attacked Elizabeth's English troops, but his army lacked the necessary artillery to rout them. O'Neill appealed to Spain for help; but when the fleet of Philip III came, the Spanish commander insisted on waging battle prematurely. The Gaelic and Spanish forces were defeated in the Battle of Kinsale in December, 1601, and the fate of Ireland was decided. At least temporarily it had lost its fight for independence. All of its liberties were abolished, and with them, old traditions disappeared. The historians, the poets, the *brehons*, or law-makers, were stilled.

Carrickfergus Castle in the background of this port near Belfast witnessed America's first naval victory in 1778 when John Paul Jones' ship "Ranger" defeated the British vessel "Drake" during the American Revolutionary War.

THE STRUGGLE AGAINST ENGLAND:

1603-1800

During the reign of James I his government encouraged a large-scale immigration of English and Scottish settlers into the ravaged and depopulated province of Ulster. This thriving settlement grew and was the nucleus of the modern Northern Ireland. In 1641 the Irish again rose in revolt, at first with great success.

But in 1649 soldier-politician Oliver Cromwell, with an army of 20,000 men landed in Dublin as Lord Lieutenant and General for the Parliament of England. In a raid known as "Cromwell's Curse" he massacred the townspeople and soldiers alike, and laid waste to the country. Finally, in 1652, the Irish forces submitted to overwhelming odds. A year later Cromwell became Lord Protector of the Commonwealth, and even more Irish land passed into England's hands. Cromwell's death in 1658 released Ireland somewhat from the grip of his inhumane treatment.

During the reigns of Charles II and James II, called the Restoration, some of the injustices imposed upon the Irish people were offset. Then, in 1698, during the reign of William of Orange, a Protestant, the Irish Protestant Parliament passed the first of the hated Penal Laws which increased religious persecution. Catholics were barred from buying land, from trade and professions, education and voting. The Catholic peasants lived in the most miserable conditions in all Europe. The Penal Laws had been created to force the Catholics from Ireland; instead, they served to unite the Irish both spiritually and nationally.

From 1714 to 1760, Ireland had very little political history, but social and economic conditions were terrible. Almost alone, the bitter and brilliant pen of Jonathan Swift championed the Irish. Swift's hatred of injustice and human misery inspired his classic satire in the form of a children's book, "Gulliver's Travels" which appeared in 1726. The bad conditions of life caused many thousands of Protestants from Ulster to emigrate during the century to the American colonies, where they formed an important

Champion of Irish political rights in the 18th century, one of the greatest satirists in the English language, Jonathan Swift led Ireland's literary fight for independence from England. In 1701 he travelled to London to fight directly in the English political arena for the remittance of England's taxes on the earnings of the Irish clergy. For his efforts on behalf of the clergy and all the oppressed people of Ireland, he was rewarded in 1713 with the deanship of St. Patrick's Cathedral in Dublin. During his lifetime, he was one of the most popular and beloved men in Ireland. In his later years he suffered severe ill health. Before his death in 1745 he had gone completely insane.

In St. Patrick's Cathedral, Dublin, shown here, is the epitaph Swift (dean there from 1713 to 1745) wrote for himself: "He lies where furious indignation can no longer rend his heart."

segment in the population. Dissatisfaction in Ireland was again ready to explode into rebellion by the time the Hanoverian (German) George III ascended the English throne in 1760.

When, in 1776, England was engaged in the American Revolutionary War, Ireland took steps that proved extremely important later. Since Irish Catholics were ineligible for the army, and since the Irish Protestant army was being used in America, Ireland was left virtually undefended. This situation gave the Irish an excuse to raise the Irish Volunteers. England, finding the 40,000 Volunteers too strong to ignore, gave in to Ireland's request for an independent Parliament. At the insistence of Henry Flood, an Irish Protestant political leader, the Renunciation Act was passed in 1783, acknowledging the right of the legislative independence of the Irish nation.

For the next ten years, Ireland enjoyed political and religious freedom from a war-weary England, and a period of prosperity that revived the Irish spirit. It found expression in poetry, literature and scholarship.

However, the Irish were still far from free; political unrest continued. The French Revolution stirred a young lawyer from County Kildare, Theobald Wolfe Tone, into establishing the Society of United Irishmen at Belfast in 1791. The organization soon became revolutionary and five years later, Tone sought aid from France. But bad weather forced a French fleet of 43 ships carrying 15,000 armed soldiers to return to France. The ill-fated Rebellion of 1798 was savagely put down by the English. Wolfe Tone died by his own hand as a prisoner of the Crown.

Union with Britain was almost inevitable now. In June, 1800, the Irish Parliament passed the Act of Union transferring legislative power to Westminster. William Pitt, the British Prime Minister, had wished to see this change associated with a restoration of full political rights to Roman Catholics. Disappointed in this, he resigned.

Village statesman talked with looks profound,
While news much older than their ale went round.

(*Left*) *In the turbulent days of the 18th century, Irishmen met to air their political views in such picturesque public places as "The Three Pigeons Inn" in Westmeath Hamlet, County Roscommon, Connacht. In this copy of an old drawing is a quotation from Oliver Goldsmith's poem, "Deserted Village"—written as a protest against Britain's land policy and the impoverishment of the peasant farmers.*

(*Below*) *O'Connell Street in Dublin was named after Daniel O'Connell who fought and won Catholic emancipation in 1829. Dublin, which means "Dark Pool" in Gaelic, is situated where the River Liffey (lower right) enters Dublin Bay.*

THE INDEPENDENCE MOVEMENT: 1800-1922

Catholic Emancipation was soon taken up by a young Irish barrister, Daniel O'Connell. Because of his tireless efforts, resulting in a near-Civil War, the Catholic Emancipation Act was signed by George IV in 1829. O'Connell next turned his talents to the repeal of the Act of the Union. This "uncrowned King of Ireland," as O'Connell was called, brought new spirit and patriotic passion to the Irish. But when the English arrested him for sedition and sentenced him to prison for a year, he lost his power of leadership. Disheartened, he died in 1847. With his death the repeal movement was greatly weakened. Many Young Irelanders, former members of O'Connell's Repeal Party, fled to America and France to organize resistance groups.

The Great Famine

Half of Ireland's 8,000,000 people were wretchedly poor, almost entirely dependent upon the potato for their existence. When the blight, caused by a fungus disease, hit Ireland in 1845, a terrible famine occurred which lasted for four years. About one million Irish lay dead from starvation or disease. Another million left the country, taking with them fever and pestilence. Many died on the ships they had hoped would take them to a more humane way of life. Others reached countries, such as the United States, only to die in hospital rooms. By 1881, the population of 8,000,000 had shrunk to 5,000,000.

The renowned Bells of Shandon ring from the giant "pepper box" steeple of St. Anne's in County Cork in the Province of Munster. This is one of Ireland's most renowned churches. After long and bitter battles, the Roman Catholics in Ireland finally won the right to practice their religion in 1829 when England's Duke of Wellington introduced the Emancipation Act. Previously, Daniel O'Connell had refused to accept England's proposal that such emancipation be granted only with the stipulation that the English government would have veto power over the appointments of Irish Catholic Bishops.

(Above) Gone is the devastation of the blight of 1845 from Southern Ireland! Its abundant potato crops now yield more than enough for local consumption. Here packers at Ballina, County Mayo, are sorting and bagging seed potatoes for marketing.

The Fenian Brotherhood

Now the Irish looked to the United States where in 1858 John O'Mahoney, a native Irish patriot, had formed a secret society called the Fenian Brotherhood, whose purpose was to obtain Ireland's complete political independence from England. A similar movement was founded in Dublin. (The Fenians derived their name from the "Fianna" of Irish legend who repelled invaders from the Irish coasts about 200 A.D.) In March, 1867, there was an armed uprising by the Fenians in Ireland. Although the English managed to suppress it, they themselves became awakened to their nation's wrongs against the Irish. A new ally for Ireland appeared in the English Liberal party, Prime Minister William Gladstone. He became a lifelong friend of the Irish by sponsoring legislation to end the special status of the Anglican Church in Ireland and to give tenant farmers greater security of tenure in their land and some help in becoming owners of their farms.

Potatoes are still a staple item of the Irish diet. Here are the richly productive rows of the potato crop on a modern farm—a vast change from the land devastated by the blight of the 1840's. Today there are almost 40,000 small farmers in Southern Ireland earning a peaceful living from their land.

This monument to Charles Stewart Parnell in the heart of Dublin City is inscribed with his words, "No man has a right to fix the boundary to the march of a nation. No man has a right to say to his country, thus far shalt thou go and no further. We have never attempted to fix the ne plus ultra to the progress of Ireland's nationhood and we never shall."

Charles Parnell and the Home Rule Movement

At about this time, 1870, another great leader emerged from the dominant Protestant group in Ireland. Charles Stewart Parnell, son of a country gentleman and an American mother, was elected at the age of 29 to the British House of Commons. Three years later he became the head of the Irish Nationalist

Harvesting hay on their farm in County Kerry, Province of Munster, these farmers are the beneficiaries of Parnell's and Davitt's efforts to turn the land over to families who had cultivated it for generations. (In Munster, the southernmost and largest province in Ireland, one goes from barren highlands or mountains to low-lying fertile plains; County Kerry averages over 80 inches of rain annually—the reason for the brilliant green grass of the "Emerald Isle.")

Party in the British Parliament, and made a separate Parliament in Ireland his foremost aim.

To the Irish people, Parnell was "the Chief," a name going back to their Gaelic past. By uniting the Land issue (to return Irish land to Irish ownership) and the Home Rule issue, Parnell won the personal devotion of the common people. Essentially, the Home Rule issue meant that Ireland was to manage its internal affairs, leaving to Great Britain control over trade, the army and navy, and foreign policy.

Among Parnell's supporters was Michael Davitt, whose life work was improving the lot of the small farmer. These two men combined their efforts in the Land League to help the farmers gain ownership of the land they farmed and to bring down high rents. They encouraged the tenant farmers to pay no rent at all unless the landlords reduced it. They also advocated the "boycott" of any tenant who took over the farm of an evicted tenant. The people carried the boycott idea even further. They also boycotted the offending landlord and anyone who gave any kind of service to the boycotted people. The name came from Captain Boycott, a land agent, who was hated because he refused to take the lower rents offered. The captain himself was the first person to be boycotted.

Parnell's greatest triumph was the so-called

(Right) On display in the library of Trinity College, Dublin, is the Book of Kells which dates back 1,200 years. Oriental and Egyptian influences may be seen in the intricate illustrations of the Book. Much of the art work, such as this of the Virgin and Child, has retained its original brilliance.

(Lower right) The Book of Kells is a hand-illuminated manuscript of the four Gospels of the New Testament.

Gladstone Act of 1881 which reduced the rents by 20 per cent and provided for another reduction in fifteen years. The "Land War" was now almost over.

Suddenly and dramatically, Parnell, the adored hero of the Irish people was cast off and stripped of his leadership, when he became involved in a divorce case. Both Prime Minister Gladstone and the Roman Catholic bishops of Ireland denounced him, and the majority of the Irish people followed the anti-Parnellites. Parnell's efforts to recover his lost leadership resulted in a physical breakdown and his death in 1891. The second "uncrowned King of Ireland" was dead at the age of 45.

*The Custom House, on the banks of Dublin's
River Liffey, ranks as one of the noblest buildings
in the world. Built in the 18th century, it was
burned to a shell in 1921 during the Irish rebellion,
then magnificently restored.*

Scottish bagpipers? No, they are as Irish as the beloved Irish airs they play in this Pipe-Band Championship held each June in Dublin. A musical instrument of great antiquity, the bagpipes in olden days resounded throughout the countryside—a call to arms and battle as well as to the merriment of native dances and flings.

The "Sinn Fein" Movement

In 1899 journalist Arthur Griffith founded the *Sinn Fein* organization, whose name meant "We Ourselves." Sinn Fein sponsored passive resistance to British rule and the withdrawal of Irish members from the British Parliament.

In 1903, an act was passed which gave a bonus to landlords for selling their land to their tenants. Centuries of struggle finally enabled the Irish tenants to become the owners of their farms. The rule of landlords was dead.

Now there remained the bitter problem of Home Rule. Though desired throughout the south, this was strongly opposed in Ulster where it was felt that the province's economic, social and religious affinities were with Britain, and that all Ireland would suffer by secession from the United Kingdom. Nevertheless against bitter opposition from the Tories, a Liberal government under H. H. Asquith as Prime Minister succeeded in carrying through a Home Rule Bill which became law in 1914.

The outbreak of World War I, however changed the whole situation. Home Rule enforcement was suspended until the war ended, and Ireland remained under the Act of the Union until 1919.

About 160,000 Irish Volunteers enlisted in the British Army. The Sinn Feiners, however, preferred supporting any enemy of England; about 12,000 of them, under the Irish Republican Brotherhood, or IRB, trained themselves as a military force. Eamon de Valera, later to become Prime Minister of Eire, was one of the group's commanders.

Planned by the IRB and inspired by Sinn Fein, a revolution occurred on Easter Monday, 1916. The General Post Office and other buildings in Dublin were seized by about 1,000 men, and the Irish Republic was proclaimed. But a large British force was landed and after a bombardment of four days, the main body of rebels surrendered. Fifteen of the leaders were executed, Eamon de Valera escaping the death penalty because of his American citizenship at the time. During the momentous days when these executions were taking place, public opinion came out strongly in support of Sinn Fein. This backing grew, and Sinn Fein candidates won an overwhelming victory at the general election in 1918.

The Sinn Feiners set up an Irish legislature, or *Dail Eireann*, in Dublin in January, 1919. The *Dail* claimed the right to legislate for all of Ireland and proclaimed the Irish Free State, or *Saorstat na hEireann*. De Valera, who helped to shape the *Dail*, was elected its President. Arthur Griffith, the founder of Sinn Fein, was elected vice-president.

Shortly after de Valera organized the Dail cabinet, Ireland again became the scene of violence. David Lloyd George, Britain's Prime Minister, retaliated by sending troops

(*Above*) Thirty miles from Galway lie the three Aran Islands, home of the rugged, individualistic fishermen whom dramatist J. M. Synge immortalized in "Riders to the Sea" and "The Aran Islands." These islanders speak Gaelic and still spin and weave their own clothing.

(*Left*) Browsing through a book barrow on a busy street in Dublin provides many reminders of the great heroes who fought with arms and the great writers who wielded words to oust all kinds of foreign suppression of their national rights.

Eamon de Valera . . .
President of the Assembly
of the League of Nations in
1938 . . . President of the
Republic of Ireland . . .
Irish patriot, statesman and
courageous leader of his
countrymen to unqualified
independence. In 1951 his
Fianna Fail was the largest
political party in "Dail
Eireann," the House of
Representatives, where it
controlled almost half the
seats.

as well as a special police force called Black-and-Tans because of the khaki coats they wore over dark suits. Ireland was the scene of murder, rioting, looting and burning of homes, for these were the acts of revenge taken by the Black-and-Tans against the guerilla warfare of the Sinn Feiners, known then as the Irish Republican Army. Finally, in 1921, under Lloyd George's threat of "immediate and terrible war," Arthur Griffith and Michael Collins signed a treaty providing for an Irish Free State with dominion status. Meanwhile, an altered Home Rule Bill of 1920 gave Ulster limited self-government and freedom to decide to stay in the U.K. or secede with the Free State. It chose the former.

CIVIL WAR—TO THE PRESENT

The extreme Republicans embarked upon a tide of terrorism and destruction in opposition to the establishment of the Irish Free State as their government. For fourteen months a bitter, devastating civil war raged among Irishmen. During these months of fighting, two more great leaders of the Irish nation died. In August, 1922, Arthur Griffith succumbed to a stroke. In the same month, Michael Collins, who had headed the provisional government set up to carry out the treaty, was assassinated by members of the IRA. A little-known fighter for Irish liberty was then made temporary head of the government—William Thomas Cosgrave,

IRELAND ■ 119

Scene of the civil warfare that broke out between the anti-Treaty and pro-Treaty Irish forces in 1922, the Four Courts Building in Dublin was almost completely destroyed during the fighting and later restored as seen here.

a veteran of Irish uprisings at 42 years of age.

By 1926 the Republicans were divided into two factions. Those who accepted the Irish Free State believed in a gradual weakening of the bonds with England, and were known as the Conservatives. But the new group under de Valera took the name *Fianna Fail*, or Warriors of Destiny, after a legendary band of patriots. When many of the Fianna Fail candidates were elected to the *Dail*, the group became for the first time a real national legislature of the Free State.

In 1932 Ireland held its most important general election under the Free State. De Valera's party won, defeating Cosgrave's government.

The Establishment of Eire

When King Edward VIII abdicated from the throne of England in December, 1936, and there was a change of kings, de Valera saw his long-awaited chance to give Ireland a new constitution and at the same time to try to set up a republic for *all* Ireland. His second goal did not materialize because of Ulster's opposition. Nevertheless, in December, 1937, a new constitution was adopted. The Gaelic name of Ireland, *Eire*, replaced Irish Free State. No mention was made of the king, the empire, or the oath of allegiance, even though Eire was to remain a member of the British Commonwealth. De Valera became Prime

Minister and the Gaelic scholar, Dr. Douglas Hyde, a Protestant, became President.

When World War II broke out in 1939, Eire quickly declared its neutrality, enforcing a strict censorship of news and forbidding all stories that might be construed as unfriendly to any of the foreign powers. Northern Ireland, on the other hand, was deeply involved in the war and in defence of the Atlantic approaches.

The Republic of Ireland

In 1948, de Valera was voted out of power and John A. Costello was elected Prime Minister. He at once demanded and received complete independence for Southern Ireland from Great Britain. On April 18, 1949, Eire's elected Parliament officially declared it to be the Republic of Ireland. Ulster, or Northern Ireland, remained an integral part of the United Kingdom.

In 1955, the independent nation, the Republic of Ireland, became a member of the United Nations.

In 1969 Northern Ireland was torn by rioting between Catholics and extremist Protestants. The Catholics claimed that they were denied full civil rights and equality under the law. Militant Protestants attacked Catholic demonstrators and the British sent in troops to maintain order. The political system of Northern Ireland was seriously challenged.

(Below) Taken on April 18, 1949, this picture commemorates the eventful day on which the Republic of Ireland Act became official. This Act supplanted the External Relations Act of 1936, thus severing the last political tie with England. These troops are passing the saluting base at the General Post Office in Dublin.

Captain Terence O'Neill, descendant of an ancient Irish noble family, was Prime Minister of Northern Ireland from 1963 until 1969.

Robert Briscoe, an active member of de Valera's "Fianna Fail" political party, was twice Lord Mayor of Dublin in Southern Ireland.

THE GOVERNMENT

"In the name of the Most Holy Trinity, from Whom is all authority and to Whom, as our final end, all actions both of men and States must be referred . . . We, the people of Eire, do hereby adopt, enact, and give to ourselves this Constitution."

So begins the Constitution adopted July, 1937, that declares Eire to be a sovereign, independent, democratic state.

The Irish, language, or Gaelic, is the first official tongue, and English the second. The government of Eire is set up on a democratic principle, much like that of the United States. The head of the state is the President (*Uachtaran na hEireann*), who is elected by the direct vote of the people. He holds office for 7 years and is eligible for re-election only once.

Parliament consists of the President of

Ireland and two Houses: the House of Representatives (*Dail Eireann*) and the Senate (*Seanad Eireann*). The *Dail* has 147 members elected by the voters on the system of proportional representation. *Seanad Eireann* is composed of 60 members, of whom 11 are nominated by the *Taoiseach* (Prime Minister) and 49 are elected: 3 by the University of Dublin, 3 by the National University of Ireland, and 43 from five panels of persons who represent various fields such as culture, literature, art, education, agriculture, trade unions, industry and commerce, public administration and social services.

The President appoints 7 to 15 members who constitute the government. These men are responsible to the *Dail*, and they are under the leadership of the Prime Minister, who has been appointed by the President on the nomination of the *Dail*.

The President is advised by a 7-member Council of State (we would call it a "cabinet") that is made up of former prime ministers, chief justices, chairmen of the *Dail* and of the *Seanad*, or other persons appointed by the President.

Included in the Constitution is a strong definition of the sanctity of marriage (there is no law that provides for divorce in Eire), provisions for the personal rights of its citizens, the free exercise of all religions, and the guarantee of education for all children.

NORTHERN IRELAND

Northern Ireland is a distinct province within the United Kingdom and has a small Parliament of its own to which certain powers have been delegated by the U.K.

Its territory consists of the counties of

A view of the Dublin quays along the River Liffey. The historic city is ideally situated as a trading port, metropolis and holiday site.

Great progress has been made in Northern Ireland to provide houses at economical rents. The small house (left) is typical of those built for the elderly, the larger homes for families with children.

Antrim, Armagh, Down, Fermanagh, Londonderry and Tyrone and the county boroughs of Belfast and Londonderry. Twelve members are elected to the British House of Commons, 4 of whom represent the Borough of Belfast; the others are county members.

NORTHERN IRELAND GOVERNMENT

The powers of the Parliament of Northern Ireland are delegated to it by the U.K. Parliament. They include control of social services, education, internal trade and lower courts of justice. Matters relating to the Crown, international relations, defence and other questions affecting the United Kingdom are dealt with by the British Parliament. The Northern Ireland Parliament deals with all domestic affairs.

Executive power is vested in the Governor on behalf of the Queen and is carried out through Ministries which are responsible to

Parliament. The Parliament of Northern Ireland consists of a House of Commons of 52 members elected by popular vote, and a Senate, or upper house, of 26 members, 24 elected by the House of Commons under a system of proportional representation. The House of Commons has a maximum life of 5 years, and a senator holds office for 8 years. The Prime Minister of Northern Ireland is head of a cabinet of 8 ministers, of whom the majority are in the House of Commons.

The principal government departments are the Ministries of Finance, Home Affairs, Labour and National Insurance, Education, Agriculture, Commerce, and Health and Local Government, all closely following the British pattern of organization. People in Northern Ireland pay the same taxes and customs duties as those living in Great Britain and use the same coinage. Northern Ireland has the same status as any part of England, Scotland or Wales.

Morning delivery in old Dublin starts the new day.

THE PEOPLE

The people of Ireland are warm and friendly, calm and unhurried, dry in their wit and strong individualists. While most of the working population of the Republic of Ireland is engaged in agriculture, forestry and fishing (about 420,000), the majority of the workers of Northern Ireland are employed in manufacturing.

Although 95 per cent of Eire's 2,834,000 people are Roman Catholics, the remaining 5 per cent, made up of Protestants and about 4,000 Jews, are a welcome part of Irish life. A

(Left) The actors shown here are Abbey Theatre players peforming a scene from J. M. Synge's "Playboy of the Western World." Opened in 1904, this theatre received international fame soon after with the premiere of this modern play. Abbey players, touring the world, are "sell-outs" everywhere.

(Right) This Sunday morning bird market in Dublin attracts a large audience.

(Below) Pubs such as this confirm Eire's reputation as "Ireland of the Welcomes."

recent example was the election of Robert Briscoe, a Jew, to the post of Lord Mayor of Dublin in the 1950's and again in 1961.

Of Ulster's population of nearly 1,500,000, two-thirds are Protestant (mostly Church of Ireland, Methodist and Presbyterian), and one-third are Roman Catholic. There is a Jewish

(*Right*) *Folk-dancing is an integral part of Irish social life. These Aran Islanders are dancing "Cross Roads," especially popular in the southern and western rural districts.*

(*Left*) *Throughout the towns and cities of Ireland, the traditional fiddler plays for market-day shoppers.*

(*Below*) *Irish hearts are gay and Irish eyes are smiling as these youngsters dance to the rhythmic lilt of an Irish tune.*

population of only about 1,500. Over half a million people live in the capital city of Belfast (almost as many as in Dublin), and over one-third of a million in the adjoining counties of Antrim and Down. There are ten other towns with a population of more than 10,000, and Londonderry boasts some 51,000 inhabitants. While the population density is

Queen's University in Belfast, Northern Ireland, was founded in 1845 and received its charter as a university in 1908. It includes Magee University College, Londonderry.

generally lighter in the Republic, the heaviest concentration is in Dublin, the capital city, and in the outlying cities and towns.

There are many newspapers to keep the lively Irish well informed. Northern Ireland has three daily morning papers, one evening paper and 46 weeklies. There are no Sunday papers. In the Republic of Ireland there are also four morning newspapers, three evening and three Sunday papers, in addition to about 44 weeklies.

EDUCATION

School is compulsory in Eire for children of ages 6 to 14. There are 475 national, or state-aided, primary schools where tuition is free. Special emphasis is on the Irish language, Gaelic, both as a subject for regular students and as a means of teaching for some 13,000 men and women teachers. All teacher-training courses are given in Irish.

Bantry House, at the head of Bantry Bay in County Cork, contains an impressive collection of art treasures, including tapestries reputed to have belonged to Marie Antoinette.

Brendan Behan (1923-1964) wrote boisterous plays such as "The Hostage" and "The Quare Fellow."

CULTURE

One of the most fascinating things about the Irish is their need for expression. We immediately think of their passion for conversation, discussion, friendly (and not-so-friendly) debate, or of James Joyce, Sean O'Casey, or W. B. Yeats writing about modern Ireland. But even in ancient Ireland, when there was no writing, there were poets, bards and historians.

When the Celtic tribes from Europe invaded and conquered Ireland after 600 B.C., they brought with them an advanced society. Historians and poets lived in ease. Although the person of a king was not sacred, that of a poet was. Since there was no writing at that time, the historians had to memorize thousands of years of history and the poets had to master 350 kinds of metre. Rhyme, which didn't appear in England until the 8th century, had been used by the Celts much earlier.

In later years, sculpture, music and Gaelic literature were highly developed. Monks applied their skills to writing and to the illumination of manuscripts such as the world-renowned Book of Kells.

Spells, incantations, prayers, poems; tales of love, death and destruction; romances, sagas, epics, patriotic outpourings—these are some of the literary forms that Irish poets and prose writers have used through the centuries. One of the most famous epics in world literature is the "Ulster Cycle," dating back to about the 8th century. One tale from it, "The Death of Deirdre," is still a familiar story to the common people of Ireland.

It is remarkable that a nation no bigger than the Emerald Isle has consistently given the world monuments of literary genius. Modern Ireland has produced James Joyce, who through *Ulysses*, *Finnegans Wake*, and *The Portrait of the Artist as a Young Man* has had a tremendous influence on the writers of the 20th century. His *Ulysses* covered in minute detail 24 hours of a man's life in Dublin, including everything he thought.

Poet and playwright, William Butler Yeats is the century's greatest lyric poet writing in English. In 1923 he received the Nobel Prize in Literature.

Plays of Irish peasant life written by J. M. Synge have become world renowned, especially his *Riders to the Sea* and *Playboy of the Western World*. George Bernard Shaw, although an

(*Above*) George Bernard Shaw was the outspoken, individualistic and highly successful author of such plays as "Pygmalion," "Man and Superman." His death in England in 1950 at 95 years ended a prolific literary career.

(*Left*) Shaw was born in this simple brick house on Synge Street, Dublin, in July, 1856.

(Right) One of Eire's best-known arts, finished Waterford crystal, is displayed here in old diamond and strawberry cuttings as well as in contemporary designs.

The linen industry in Northern Ireland has existed for over 2½ centuries. It was introduced mainly by the French Protestant refugees escaping from the religious persecutions of Louis XIV. Here is a linen tablecloth being made the modern way—by machine. Irish linens like this will find their way into homes all over the world.

Irishman, spent most of his life in England and wrote for the stage about English society and social problems; he always retained his Irish wit. Sean O'Casey is another dramatist who has contributed greatly to Irish literature, with *Juno and the Paycock* and *The Plough and the Stars.* The famous Abbey Theatre, begun in 1904, in Dublin attracted top actors, including Arthur Sinclair, Sara Allgood, and Barry Fitzgerald who went out to fame in Hollywood; Lady Augusta Gregory, a playwright herself, with Yeats and Synge, had organized the theatre.

These and other writers will continue to tell the story of Ireland, that controversial island whose people have the "gift of the gab" and the genius for expression.

In rounding out the picture, we must not forget handicrafts. For centuries, the Irish have shown extraordinary skill and artistry, especially in linen and tweed weaving and in making Waterford crystal glass. The oldest candle-making firm in Europe, Rathborne, is in its 469th year of production. Translucent Belleek china has been treasured by families for generations because of its purity of design and the quality of its workmanship. In all phases of craftsmanship, the Irish hand has been guided by the past and embodies in its work a skill and pride that have made it world famous.

The art of carving in wood has been practised in Ireland since the earliest of times. This craft demands an unusual delicacy of execution: the sculptor must painstakingly prepare his wood, and then carve with a light hand to preserve the pattern of the grain, an ornamental feature of great decorative importance to the appearance of the finished object. The entire design must often be adapted to the direction of the grain. Oak is frequently employed, although birch and ash are also used by the carvers.

SPORTS

Ireland is a country of sportsmen. Whether they be doers or watchers, their sporting interests cover horseracing, golf, fishing, hunting, hurling, soccer, rugby, Gaelic football and greyhound racing, plus other less exerting sports.

Irish horses—born, bred and trained on native soil rich in limestone—have proved to

Hurling has been a national sport in Ireland for untold years. As in football, each team attempts to drive the ball through its opponent's goal posts but, while the ball may be caught by hand, it must be played to the goal with a 3-foot, hockey-like stick. Fields are 140 yards long, 80 yards wide.

(Above) Leaping through the hedge at the Punchestown Steeplechase races is this thoroughbred and his rider. Horse racing is a popular national sport.

Hunting ranks with racing as a popular sport in Ireland. This is the Ward Union Hunt Club, County Meath, starting with their hounds on a stag hunt.

be outstanding competitors in the classic racing events at home and abroad. Horseracing is one of the main features of Irish sports, with particular interest paid to the Irish Derby, St. Leger, the Guineas, and the Irish Grand National races. The Dublin Horse Show attracts thousands of natives and tourists each year in August to watch the magnificent jumping competitions.

Golf is another popular sport, with over 200 courses that are kept in top-notch condition year-round—thanks to the mild climate of the country. Again, various championships and tournaments including the Irish Hospitals' 72-hole tournament keep interest high.

Ireland's lakes, streams and rivers provide more than 900 square miles of fresh water abounding in fish. There are salmon, brown trout, pike and perch. Coastline fishing yields salmon, sea trout and bass, and blue shark. Irishmen are fond of hunting and shooting also.

Important events of rural social life are agricultural shows, ploughing competitions, and open-air carnivals or *feis* where traditional songs, music and folk dances make gay entertainment.

(Right) These cattle have just taken the prizes at the annual Dublin Spring Show.

(Below) An outstanding sporting event, the Dublin Horse Show attracts thousands of spectators each August.

The first turf-fired electricity generating station, this Portarlington power plant is in Laoighis. The 120,000 tons of turf (foreground) burned annually is harvested by machine, although all small farmers harvest turf by hand.

THE ECONOMY

Although Ireland is primarily agricultural, there is an industrial revolution taking place in the north and south today that should prove as exciting and as important economically as its past revolutions proved politically.

INDUSTRY

Long noted for its exports of beef, cattle and dairy products, the Republic is fast becoming a country where industrial export is taking on a new meaning. The government is faced with the economic problem of raising the standard of living, providing work for 6,000 youths who leave their farms each year to seek work in cities and at the same time of stemming the serious problem of emigration, which has been at the rate of about 40,000 each year since 1956. Since producing goods for export provides the best solution to all these problems, the government has instituted a campaign to encourage the building of manufacturing plants by both Irish and foreign firms. All firms are offered outright non-repayable cash grants, 10-year tax exemptions on export profits and a supply of low cost labour to "set up shop."

Nearly all the new plants being built to serve export markets are the result of foreign investment. Since 1958, about 100 new industries have been attracted from the United States, Britain, Germany, the Netherlands, Japan, Belgium and Canada. During 1960 industrial development was estimated at £23,000,000 and in 1961 another 70 firms went into operation. Exports are expected to reach a high of £170,000,000 as compared to £130,000,000 in 1959, when there was a marked increase of 38 per cent over 1958 and 58 per cent over 1956.

Britain is the largest buyer of Eire's goods, taking 75 per cent of the total exports in 1959, or over £93,000,000 worth.

(Above) This Jacquard loom, named after its French inventor of the 18th century, automatically weaves a fine damask cloth. The pattern for the material is controlled by the holes punched in the cards (upper right).

(Below)
Over-all view of Shannon shows the new housing estate for technicians and workers in the foreground with part of the Industrial Estate in the middle and the Airport terminal and runways in the background. Behind the Airport buildings is the River Shannon.

(*Above*) *As in the 1700's, Waterford Crystal is entirely a product of the skilled artisan—handblown, hand-cut, and hand-polished. This prized art has been handed down from generation to generation.*

(*Below*) *Inside the Japanese "Sony" transistor factory in the Shannon Free Airport industrial zone.*

Ireland began exporting goods as far back as 1200 A.D. when Irish woollen fabrics were much in demand throughout the European continent. Irish linen dates back to the 17th century, and Irish whiskey was first mentioned in ancient records kept in 1405. Even today, Waterford crystal is a treasured addition to homes and museums throughout the world. An antique Waterford chandelier hangs in Independence Hall in Philadelphia; fourteen hang in historic St. Paul's Chapel in New York. Also, there is exporting of blends of Irish tea, oatmeal, hams, bacon, and Belleek translucent china. Irish thoroughbred horses are sent all over the world, as is Irish stout.

Moreover, the Republic exports canned meat, fruits and vegetables, and dairy products; recent additions to the list of Irish exports are women's fashionable apparel, textile yarns, knitwear, leather and shoes, ropes and twines, electrical equipment and cables, carpets, steel materials and assembled motor-cars.

The Republic will switch to a decimal coinage system in 1971.

Industry in Ulster

Foremost among the industries of Northern Ireland are textiles and engineering. The linen industry, aided by the climate, grew over the centuries until the spinning, weaving and finishing of Irish linen and other textiles employs almost 50,000 people. The area is also making and using a wide variety of the newest synthetic fibres.

In shipbuilding, Belfast ranks fourth among the leaders of the United Kingdom in tonnage of ships launched. Included in the wide range of engineering equipment made in Northern Ireland are giant industrial fans, electric generating plant, electronic computers and textile machinery. Other products include aircraft, radios, car tyres, cigarettes, bacon, canned fruit and vegetables and whiskey.

The Government is pursuing a vigorous policy of industrial development, including the provision of ready-to-use factories on new factory estates and the offer of substantial non-repayable cash grants. This policy has been successful in attracting over 170 new firms to Northern Ireland in the post-war years.

The reputation of Belfast as a great shipbuilding city is evidenced in the construction of the 45,000-ton liner Canberra. Costing £15,000,000 and built to carry 2,250 passengers, this luxury vessel now voyages between Britain, Australia, New Zealand and the west coast of the United States. Turbo-electric propelled with a docking propeller to enable her to move sideways, she travels at a speed of 27½ knots. Part of her aluminium superstructure is seen here, gleaming in the winter sun. At left is her bow contour plate rising above the promenade deck.

Turf from the shallow mountain bogs in Connemara, County Galway, cut by hand, is widely used as household fuel.

AGRICULTURE

Though the Republic is taking giant steps forward in its industrial expansion, agriculture is still of primary importance to the national economy. It supports a work force of 395,000 male workers, most of whom are small farmers. The farming pattern varies from small subsistence farms (on which the farmer raises only enough to feed his own family), to efficient commercial farms producing grain, milk and meat at lower costs than in any other country.

Since 85 per cent of farmland is in pasture, the government is helping to increase the farm output by providing lime and fertilizers which improve grass, and thereby raise the quality of beef—the dominant Irish farm product. Beef is responsible for 60 per cent of total agricultural exports. Milk accounts for 32 per cent of total farm production and 12 per cent of agricultural exports. With better grass for farming and better strains of cows, milk production has a great potential and offers the farmer higher income than beef production.

Farming is also one of the major industries of Northern Ireland, with over 65,000 small farms in operation at the present time. A typical commercial farm unit comprises between 20 and 50 acres of crops and grass mainly devoted to the production of livestock and livestock products. These account for about 85% of the value of produce sold from farms and include cattle, pigs, eggs and milk. The main crops are barley, oats, potatoes and grass. Apart from the export of seed potatoes, almost all the surplus output of Northern Ireland agriculture is shipped to Great Britain.

Production and marketing are strongly influenced by the fact that, with minor exceptions, the system of price guarantees and other forms of assistance available to farmers in Great Britain apply also to farmers in Northern Ireland.

(Below) The northern flax fields are a lovely sight in late spring and early summer with their tinting of a light and delicate shade of green. Here the flax, from which linen is made, is being dried in stacks after being softened in water.

NATURAL RESOURCES

Ireland's natural resources are not abundant; in fact, they are so scarce they lack economic value. However, some metals are mined in the South and further surveying is in progress. Its history of coal mining goes back 200 years. Ulster imports coal and steel from Great Britain which is only 13 miles away at the nearest point. There are some highly profitable fisheries, commercial quarrying of limestone and granite, and salt deposits in Northern Ireland.

In both sections of Ireland, timber plantations are being steadily developed on land that is substandard for agriculture but suitable for forestry. Both the Governments, seeing excellent possibilities in such a project, included forestry in their plans for economic expansion. The current planting rates are 50,000 acres per annum in the South, 5,000 in the North.

These economic measures are Ireland's new frontier, one that promises its people the prosperity and living standards long denied them by a long history of economic stagnation and civil unrest.

DENMARK

THE LAND

It comes as a surprise to many to realize that the kingdom of Denmark is not self-contained, but is scattered in the North and Baltic Seas. The land consists of the peninsula of Jutland, which separates the North Sea from the Baltic, and some 500 islands—about 100 of which are inhabited. These islands provide wonderful natural facilities for shipping and fishing. The total area of the country is 16,619 square miles. It is a low-lying country, the highest point being 570 feet above sea level. Southernmost of the Scandinavian countries, its only land boundary is with Germany, which adjoins the Danish mainland of Jutland on the south. The Strait of Skagerrak separates it from Norway on the north, and the Strait of Kattegat divides it from Sweden on the east.

The most notable islands are Zealand, Fünen and Falster. Copenhagen, the largest city and capital, is on Zealand, and is the only European capital situated on an island. Denmark is truly a land of bridges, for these connect many of its islands. Other parts of the country are united by ferries and coastal ships—and since no Dane lives more than about 30 or 40 miles from the coast, Jutland is easily accessible from any of the main islands. In summer, modern passenger ships provide quick transportation between Copenhagen, the "Paris of Scandinavia," and large Jutland towns. Every 24 hours these ships make two 7-hour trips.

Denmark also has two overseas possessions. One is Greenland, the largest island in the world, located between Canada and Iceland and lying almost entirely within the Arctic Circle. It measures 840,000 square miles, but almost seven-eighths of Greenland consists of barren mountains, covered with ice as thick as 8,000 feet in some places. The other overseas possession is the Faroes, a group of 19 volcanic islands (18 of which are inhabited) in the Atlantic, northwest of Scotland.

Denmark, "the field of the Danes," is very aptly named, for it is a land of small farms. These constitute about 75 per cent of the country. The panorama of the land is peaceful and harmonious, with its undulating green fields neatly squared, and its abundance of serene lakes reflecting the myriad handsome beech trees. (Approximately 10 per cent of Denmark is taken up by forests, planted to hold down the soil of the heaths by combatting strong winds.)

The land itself presents few sharp contrasts. The western regions of Jutland are composed of stretches of sand, where vigorous grasses have been planted to keep the land from being washed away by the sea. Here on the hills by the shores are large circular mounds—remnants of days long past; these are the burial mounds of ancient chieftains from the Viking Age. Beyond the sand hills, the land is flat. Once this area was a barren, wind-swept heath covering a large portion of Jutland, but today it is almost entirely cultivated. One of the oldest towns of Denmark, located on Jutland, is Ribe, a small, dike-protected village renowned for its many storks. But despite the abundance in nearby marshes of frogs and lizards on which storks feed, these comical birds are slowly diminishing in number. During winter storks migrate to South Africa, where, unfortunately many are killed.

Fünen, the most charming of the Danish islands, is shaped somewhat like a heart, set protectively between two arms of the sea called

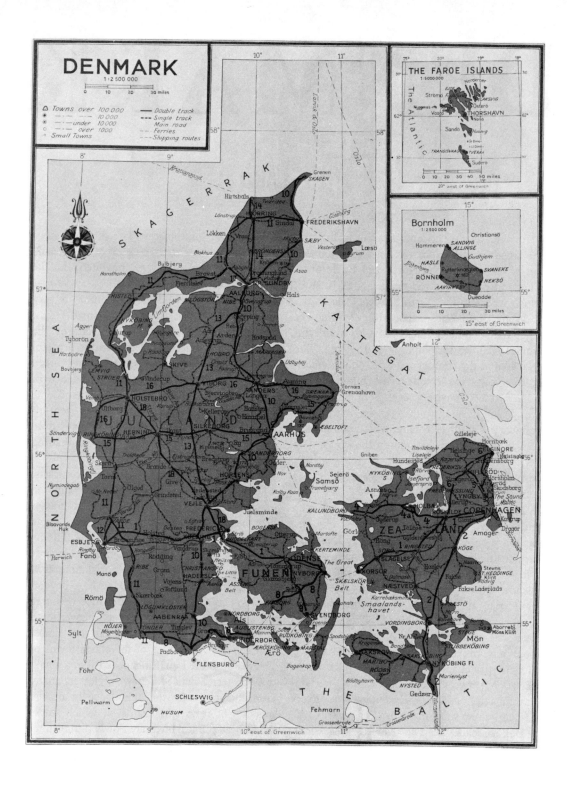

Agricultural Denmark, the supplier of quality foods to the western world, is serene and attractive. Although farming is an ancient occupation, today the fields and farms are cultivated according to efficient, modern methods.

the Little Belt and the Great Belt. It is sheltered by Zealand on the east, and Jutland on the west and northwest. The provincial capital of Fünen is Odense, Denmark's third largest city and the birthplace of her beloved storyteller, Hans Christian Andersen. In the southwest, above a blue fjord—a narrow inlet of the sea nestling between high rocks—and just below gently rolling green hills—sometimes referred to as the "Fünen Alps"—is the picturesque resort Faaborg, an old town that has been sketched hundreds of times by visiting artists.

On the island of Möen, steep, snow-white cliffs reach upward, and all over the kingdom, the rivers of the different islands wind through vast beech woods and into beautiful, serene fjords.

CLIMATE

Unlike the landscape where there are few striking extremes, the Danish climate varies greatly. The winters may be surprisingly mild, although rather grey and cloudy, or the seas and fjords may be completely covered with ice, making travel difficult. But with cold winds blowing off the northern ice in winter, the temperature usually drops to freezing and sometimes below for about 100 frosty days.

In summer, the average temperature is about 61°—mild and temperate. Danes go swimming from May to September, although the water would probably seem a bit chilly to others. The sun shines for a total of about 2 months each year and there is often a soft drizzling rain to keep the fields green and the streets glistening.

Twilight nights, sometimes called "white nights," start on May 8 and end on August 8. During this period the light of the "Midnight Sun" shines around the clock above the Arctic Circle and brightens even the southernmost parts of Scandinavia far into the night, covering everything with a soft, misty haze. The Danes celebrate this spectacle on Midsummer's Eve, June 23rd, by building bonfires in the cool summer evenings. And sun-worshippers crowd the hillsides on Whitsunday (the seventh Sunday after Easter) to see the sun come up, just 3 hours after midnight.

Above: Ferries play an important part in Denmark's transportation system. There are 23 ferries operated by the Danish State Railway plus a number of private ones, some connecting islands within Denmark, and others making trips to Sweden and Germany. Scandinavians do not have to show passports to travel between their own countries.

Left: In the past it was troublesome to cover long distances because the traveller had to change several times between train and ferry. Now, however, there are bridges connecting the larger islands as well as Jutland and Fünen. This is the Storstrom Bridge between Zealand and the island of Falster.

Entrance to Christiansborg Palace

HISTORY

Strange as it seems, idyllic, unmilitary, peaceful Denmark was once a vast and powerful empire that included England and Norway within its domain. During certain periods between the 11th and 15th centuries, Denmark ruled over an area twice as large as that of any kingdom in Europe.

This rise to power started in the Viking Age, a 300-year period beginning in the 9th century, in which all the Scandinavian countries have common roots. The Danish and Norwegian Vikings conquered England, controlled the North Sea, created small kingdoms in Ireland, established colonies in Normandy, and sailed the coasts of western Europe, defeating power after power. Meanwhile, the Swedish Vikings were spreading through Russia and down to the Caspian and Black Seas. Vikings even reached America 500 years before Columbus. The causes of their many raids are obscure, but overpopulation is known to be one of them. Although these Vikings were primarily seamen and shipbuilders, pirates, adventurers and traders, they mastered the arts of colonization and government, too.

Denmark is the oldest nation in the world

today with a government nominally ruled by a king or queen. Nobody knows exactly how long ago the kingdom was formed, but Gorm the Old is the first sovereign about whom there are any facts. It is not known where or when he was born, or when he ascended the throne, but there are records of his death around 950. Gorm and his wife, Thyra Danebrod, are buried at Jellinge in Jutland where their son, Harold Bluetooth, erected stone monuments in their memory. One of the stones bears a carved picture of the crucifixion and claims that Gorm made Denmark and Norway Christian countries. Ansgar, a French monk, had appeared in Denmark in 826. He was the first to preach the Christian religion to the Danes. Previously, they had worshipped pagan gods, the most important being Odin, Freya and Thor.

Christianity did not end the raids of the Vikings. Although Harold Bluetooth accepted it, he continued his raids along with his son, Sweyn Forkbeard. Together they attacked England many times, in 994 besieging London with some 90 ships. Sweyn also partitioned parts of Norway.

It remained for Sweyn's son, Canute II, later known as "the Great," to consolidate the lands won by his father and grandfather. By 1016 he had conquered all of England, which was governed by Danish kings until 1042, and by 1028 he had become the ruler of Norway as well. Canute the Great, a wise militarist, diplomat and administrator, was readily accepted both by the English and by the Norwegians. He was a sincere Christian, and while in England, sent many bishops back to strengthen

This replica of a sturdy yet graceful Viking ship is taking part in the annual Viking Festival at Frederikssund. Many actual relics of these ships are still found along the coast. The Danish National Museum is preparing to raise seven such ships, sunk 1,000 years ago and recently discovered almost intact in Roskilde Fjord, Zealand.

Christiansborg Palace in Copenhagen houses the parliament, the ministry of foreign affairs, the supreme court and the royal reception rooms. In the foreground is a statue of Bishop Absalon who founded Copenhagen on this spot in 1166.

the church in Denmark. Once consolidated, Canute's kingdom prospered in peace. However, after his death England and Norway became separated from the Danish kingdom, Norway, however, only temporarily. Perhaps one of Denmark's greatest kings, Canute was, oddly, buried in England's Winchester Cathedral. The empire he had created crumbled within a few short years.

There is a folk-tale about Canute. One day he ordered his servants to carry him in his royal chair and robes to the edge of the beach in England. As he sat there, the tide began to come in and the waves threatened to wet his robes. In all his majesty, he rose and pointing at the beach commanded the tide to "rise thus far and no farther." Of course, the tide rose and wet his feet, proving that he was not all-powerful.

Although the rulers who followed King Canute the Great tried to build up the Danish kingdom, it was not until the reign of Valdemar I, beginning in 1157, that Denmark became a civilized country, consolidated internally. Cities were founded, churches built and much of the land cleared of forests, giving agriculture a chance to develop. Valdemar I is the only Danish sovereign besides Canute II to bear the title of "Great." But he would not have achieved all that he did without the help of one of the great personalities of the Middle Ages—Bishop Absalon. Valdemar had spent most of his childhood on Absalon's father's estate on Zealand, and so they were close friends. Since Absalon had studied theology in Paris, his knowledge of the outside world was invaluable to Denmark. Together Absalon and Valdemar set out to restore the country that had been wracked by civil wars and oppressed by unjust taxation. To stimulate prosperity and to build a loyal army, Valdemar permitted any Dane who could fully equip himself for military service at his own expense to become a noble, therefore exempt from paying taxes on his estate.

Absalon attended to military affairs as well as to those of the Church. He warred successfully against the Wends, the people of eastern Germany who were continually plaguing the Danes. Then he founded Copenhagen in 1166 as a coastal fortress, strengthened the defences of the east coast, levied taxes for the building of ships, and added to Denmark's holdings parts of northern Germany. Education spread, churches and monasteries appeared by the scores and half the cities of present-day Denmark sprang up. With the help of Absalon, Valdemar the Great ruled in peace for 25 years.

The next 400 years, however, were characterized by frequent changes of national boundaries, by chaos caused by a struggle for supremacy among the royalty, the nobility and the Church and by an external struggle between the Scandinavian countries and the states of present-day Germany. Disputes over German Holstein and Schleswig plagued Denmark until the late 19th century.

Although Valdemar's second son, Valdemar the Victorious (who ruled from 1202-1241), added to the Danish sovereignty parts of Prussia, Estonia, Pomerania and Holstein, political confusion became rampant after his death. Supported by Holstein, the dukes of Schleswig seized control of their area and attempted to overthrow the Danish kings, simultaneously involved in contests for power with the archbishops of Denmark. The kingdom was bankrupt and without a king for 8 years; it was not until 1340 that order was restored.

In that year, Valdemar IV, a dynamic man filled with love for Denmark, was placed on the throne. To consolidate the kingdom, Valdemar married a princess of Holstein and engaged his 7-year-old daughter to marry the son of the Swedish king. Valdemar further strengthened Denmark by taking Visby, the main trading base of the Hanseatic League, a trade monopoly established by 70 or 80 cities of northern Europe for protection against piracy and foreign competition. The base of Baltic trade was transferred from Visby to Copenhagen where it flourished despite resistance from the German states for more than a century.

Nevertheless, the persistent struggle between the Germans and the Scandinavians over land and trade continued, even through the comparatively peaceful reign of Margaret, the only woman who ever ruled over the Danes.

The ruins of Absalon's fortress, built in the 12th century for defence against pirates, still exist under Christiansborg Palace. Saxo Grammaticus wrote his "Historia Danica" here; Shakespeare later used it as a source for his "Hamlet."

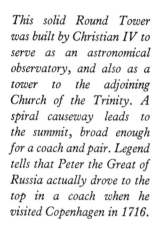

This solid Round Tower was built by Christian IV to serve as an astronomical observatory, and also as a tower to the adjoining Church of the Trinity. A spiral causeway leads to the summit, broad enough for a coach and pair. Legend tells that Peter the Great of Russia actually drove to the top in a coach when he visited Copenhagen in 1716.

Margaret became Queen of Denmark in 1387 after the death of her son Olav V, the grandson of Valdemar IV. A shrewd woman, often compared to Queen Elizabeth I of England, Margaret was a skilled diplomat, managing to reverse many difficult situations to her gain. After her husband the King of Norway died, she became the ruler of that country and, later, of Sweden as well. At their request, she helped the Swedes overthrow their unpopular and incompetent sovereign. Afterwards she called a conference at Kalmar, Sweden, in 1397 to bind the three countries together. Although Norway remained part of Denmark until 1814, Sweden many times attempted to break away and in 1520 was successful. None of the sovereigns who followed Margaret had the power or the shrewdness to hold the Scandinavian empire together.

In 1448 the house of Oldenburg, a former German line from which the present Danish king is descended, came into power with Christian I. He brought the German states of Holstein and Schleswig once more under Danish control. Since his reign, all the Danish kings, except one (King Hans) have taken the name of Christian or Frederik.

During the reigns of Christian II, III and IV, and Frederik I, II and III, the years between 1513 and 1670, war characterized Denmark's history. After the "Blood Bath of Stockholm" conducted by Christian II in 1520, Sweden seceded from the kingdom of Denmark-Norway. Later involving his country in the Thirty Years' War, Christian IV attempted to regain Sweden, but succeeded only in losing part of Norway and leaving Denmark in a state of destruction. Its fleet was ruined, its trade seriously damaged, and the levying of heavy taxes caused rebellion.

These constant wars were a serious setback to the economic and social development of

Christian IV, nicknamed the "Sailor King," always solicitous about the welfare of his seamen, built Nyboder, a row of charming yellow houses near Copenhagen's port. Now, more than three centuries later, retired sailors of the Royal Danish Navy still live in these agreeable clean quarters.

Denmark, for until the disastrous effects of the Thirty Years' War, the kingdom had prospered, partly because the Protestant Reformation had successfully broken the secular power of the Roman Catholic Church. Lutheranism is still the state religion of Denmark. Revenue from the confiscated lands of the Roman Catholic Church enabled the monarchy and the nobility to erect many buildings and to lay the groundwork for economic growth. Although this prosperity was completely destroyed by wars with Sweden and Germany during the reign of Christian IV, Frederik III (1648-1670) did much to restore peace and harmony in his kingdom.

Supported by the Lutheran Church and the newly growing merchant class, King Frederik was able to subdue the nobles and to extract desperately needed taxes from them. In turn, the landowners were empowered to tax the peasants, who still lived in a condition of serfdom. Farmers' sons, by a system of "privileged villeinage" or *Stavnsbaand*, belonged to the owners of the land on which they were born, and their services were sold by one landowner to another with frequency. Although the peasants had small plots of land for their own use, their responsibilities to their landlord were so great that they seldom had time or energy to cultivate their own property.

The year 1800 is a crucial one in Denmark's history, for it marks the beginning of its present-day liberalism and its effort to maintain neutrality in world affairs. In 1800 the abolition of the *Stavnsbaand* became effective. A bank was established to assist farmers in buying their own land. And although Denmark continued to have severe economic problems during most of the 19th century, agriculture has flourished since 1870. Education reforms were introduced in 1841, a radical measure for the times. Led by N.F.S. Grundtvig, who established Denmark's famous Folk High Schools, agricultural workers have steadily gained in economic strength and in political influence.

The 19th century brought still other political and social reforms to Denmark. One of these was freedom of the press. Another was the introduction in 1841 of free compulsory education. The third and perhaps most important measure was political. In 1849 King Frederik VII yielded to the will of the people, particularly expressed by new rebellions in the duchies of Schleswig and Holstein, and accepted a change from absolute to constitutional monarchy.

Today Denmark's social legislation is among the most advanced in the world. Since the basic laws were introduced, a whole structure has been built to provide security for the Danish people. Each year, the government spends 35

All over Denmark many castles are still standing. This is the 115-foot-high Goose Tower of Vordingborg Castle, dating back to the 12th century and to Denmark's struggle for independence of the Hanseatic States. The grounds surrounding the castle have been turned into a botanical garden.

to 40 per cent of its budget on the people's welfare, including health, education and social insurance.

Although Denmark made rapid advances politically, economically and socially during the 19th century, it lost great amounts of land as well as the status of a major European power. It tried desperately to remain neutral during the Napoleonic Wars, but in 1801 Lord Nelson and his fleet sailed into Copenhagen port and opened fire. Against their will, the Danes were drawn into the war, naturally on the side of England's enemy, France. As a result, in 1814 Denmark lost Norway to Sweden, but retained the Faroe Islands, which were a dependency of Norway. Still later, Denmark relinquished Schleswig and Holstein to Prussia, a loss representing one-third of its territory and two-fifths of its people.

Again during World War I, Denmark attempted to remain neutral and afterwards relied on the League of Nations to support its position. Once more, after the weakening of the League in the 1930's, Denmark restated its position of strict neutrality. And once more it was drawn into war against its will. In spite of a nonaggression pact of 1939, Germany attacked Denmark in April, 1940, and occupied the country. This marked the beginning of several years of struggle, during which the Germans increasingly usurped political power, harassed and persecuted the Danes in spite of their original promise not to interfere with Denmark's political sovereignty. Denmark's people retaliated by repeated acts of sabotage and a solid attitude of resistance, but in August, 1943, Germany seized the Danish government.

Denmark was liberated, along with the rest of occupied Europe, in 1945. In 1949 it joined NATO and, today, contributes to the United Nations Emergency Forces.

This statue of Frederik VII, under whom Denmark's absolute monarchy came to an end in 1848, is appropriately silhouetted against the spires of Christiansborg Castle which now houses the "Folketing."

THE GOVERNMENT

In 1848, inspired by the concepts of liberty, equality and fraternity which were the ideals of the French Revolution, the Danes demanded an end to absolute monarchy. A marching delegation advanced on the royal palace and presented their wishes to King Frederik VII. "The King must not drive the nation to the desperation of taking the law in its own hands," the delegation warned.

Without any argument, the King acquiesced to the people's desire that from then on the country would be ruled by their representatives. In accordance with Danish temperament, Denmark's "revolution" was accomplished without bloodshed. On June 5, 1849, a new democratic constitution was drafted. Changes made in 1915 have further extended and strengthened its democratic character.

Today, Denmark's government broadly resembles the British parliamentary system. Like the Queen of England, the Danish King "can do no wrong," but as in Great Britain, he exercises his authority only through his ministers and functions primarily as an adviser. The king has the executive power; the legislative power is vested jointly in the king and in parliament (*Rigsdag*); the judicial power resides with the courts. This means that although parliament can make and pass laws, no new law can take effect unless the king has given it his signature. The one action the king can take independently of parliament is to seek a political leader to form a new government in the event of the current government's resignation. Even this action is taken only after consultation with party leaders. The king is not permitted to declare war or to sign treaties without the approval of the *Rigsdag*.

In one important respect the Danish parliament differs from that of Great Britain. Although it formerly had two houses, today Denmark's parliament only has one chamber, known as the *Folketing*. Parliament is voted into office for a period of 4 years by universal suffrage of everyone 23 years of age and over. The *Folketing* has 179 members, two of which represent the Faroe Islands, and two of which represent Greenland.

Another major difference between the British and Danish forms of government is that Denmark has a multiple- rather than a two-party system. The present government, for example, is a coalition of the Social Democratic Party, the Social Liberal Party, and the Single-Tax Party, the three parties combined having a total of 93 seats out of 179. The largest of these is the Social Democratic Party, with 70 seats. This party derives its main support from wage earners, small tradespeople and farmers.

Because of the multiple-party system, the prime minister has a much harder task staying in office than he would if there were only two parties. When any one of his measures meets

The graceful spires of Rosenborg Palace (in the foreground) seem dwarfed by the surrounding museums—the National Art Gallery, the Mineralogical Museum and (on the left) an observatory. But this gay, rose-colored palace, completed in 1633 by King Christian IV, holds as many treasures as any museum. Its collection of the possessions of Danish kings contains more than 9,900 items. Room after room pours forth a mass of priceless jewels, crowns and even thrones. Perhaps the most magnificent exhibit of all is the tall octagonal case of crown jewels. The treasures of Rosenborg Palace belong to the people of Denmark.

If you walk or cycle through the streets of Copenhagen, you may pass the King and Queen, either taking a walk or pedalling along on bikes. The royal family joins in the pleasant daily life of the capital without fanfare or fuss, and Copenhageners do not spoil this camaraderie by collecting in crowds or making a commotion when royalty appears. Here (from right to left), shortly after the engagement of Princess Margrethe to Count Henri de Monpezat, are Princess Benedikte, King Frederik IX, Queen Ingrid, Princess Margrethe, Count Henri, and members of the Monpezat family.

opposition, the *Folketing* can pass a vote of "no confidence" against him, and he must either resign or demand a new election. In Denmark, a prime minister seldom stays in power the full 4 years.

The Danish monarchy is hereditary. King Frederik's Queen is Ingrid, daughter of the King of Sweden. They have three daughters, and a constitutional revision of June 5, 1953, was especially promulgated, amending the law of succession so that now a woman, Princess Margrethe, the oldest daughter of King Frederik, can succeed to the throne. In 1967, Princess Margrethe married the French Count Henri de Monpezat, who was given the title of Prince Henrik of Denmark.

THE PEOPLE

The Danes are the most cosmopolitan of all Scandinavians, with one-fourth of their 4,800,000 people residing in Copenhagen, the "Paris of Scandinavia." Another fourth live in provincial towns such as Frederiksberg, Aarhus and Odense. The rest of the population is rather evenly distributed throughout the country on farms, forest plantations, and in fishing villages. The density of the population is about 268 people per square mile—much less than in Belgium or Holland.

For the most part, the Danes live up to our concept of them. Most *are* blond, blue- or green-eyed and fair-skinned—but not any more or less so than other Scandinavians. Hamlet was apparently the only "melancholy Dane." The people of Denmark are vigorous and handsome, generous with hospitality and friendship.

Another similarity among Scandinavians is their language. The Danish language is an offshoot of a Germanic group that evolved from the Viking era, but it has remained very close to the other Scandinavian tongues. Danish, Norwegian and Swedish are close enough to each other to be easily understood by speakers of each. And although Finnish belongs to a language group akin to Hungarian, most Finlanders also speak Swedish. English is widely spoken in all of Scandinavia.

The original religion of the Scandinavians is known to us through a work of the early 13th century called the *Younger*, or *Prose Edda*. Although it was intended as a handbook of poetics, this book tells us that the pre-Christian Scandinavians worshipped a family of gods who lived at Asgard, in the middle of the earth, in order to protect the humans they had created from being harmed by a race of evil giants. It is believed that these giants represented the more violent forces of nature. Chief of the Norse gods was Odin, who protected warriors; he was also the wind god, the leader of the souls of the dead and the god of magic and poetry. His wife Frigg, as well as another goddess called Freya, represented love, fertility and beauty. Another important god was Thor, the son of Odin, thought to have been

This table is set with the great variety of dishes included in a Danish "smoerre-broed." This expansive meal is offered aboard the ferry that provides transportation between Zealand and Fünen.

Fireworks light up the sky over the light-silhouetted buildings of Tivoli.

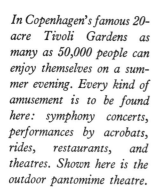

In Copenhagen's famous 20-acre Tivoli Gardens as many as 50,000 people can enjoy themselves on a summer evening. Every kind of amusement is to be found here: symphony concerts, performances by acrobats, rides, restaurants, and theatres. Shown here is the outdoor pantomime theatre.

more highly revered than his father in some parts of Scandinavia. It was his special duty to protect mankind from the fierce giants. Our days of the week come from the names of the Norse gods: for example, Friday from Frigg and Thursday from Thor.

Although Denmark was a Roman Catholic country, like the rest of Europe during the Middle Ages, its people accepted the Protestant Reformation. Today the Evangelical Lutheran Church is the national church of Denmark—the king must be a Lutheran. Ninety-eight per cent of the population belong to this denomination, but other religious communities exist. These include the Swedish Church, the Orthodox Russian congregation, the Church of England, the Roman Catholic Church, the Reformed Church, the Methodist Church and the Jewish community.

Again, there is nothing "melancholy" about Danes. They seem to love life more than any other people in the world. One of their great interests is good food. And there are three basics for a fine meal—*smoerrebroed* (literally meaning "smeared bread"), *snaps* and *snak*. *Smoerrebroed* is the Danish version of a sandwich

—but what a sandwich! It is probably closer to the Swedish smorgasbord. Only one fairly thin slice of bread is used; it is buttered, then laden with smoked salmon, tongue, ham, eggs or cheese, and finally trimmed with herbs and pickles. A *smoerrebroed* is a complete meal. But no meal in Denmark is complete without a bit of strong spirits, and this is where the *snaps* comes in. The *snak*, meaning talk or conversation, follows.

Although the Jutlanders tend to be stolid, the people of Fünen easy-going and the Zealanders quite cosmopolitan because of their close contact with Copenhagen, the one thing that unites all Danes is their love of fun.

It is because of this love of pleasure that Copenhagen is known as one of the gayest cities of Europe. And for pleasure, Copenhagen begins and ends with the Tivoli Gardens, probably the most famous amusement park in the world. It offers everything in the field of entertainment—cabaret shows, dance halls, a pantomime theatre, symphony concerts, ballet, fireworks, games of chance, sideshows and restaurants of every type.

Whether you want simple amusement, a

Left : Only boys between the ages of 10 and 16 can be members of the Tivoli Boy Guard. They are dressed in imitation of the King's Royal Guards, with bushy bearskins and elegant bandoliers. Most of these boys join regular orchestras after the age of 16.

Below: Day or night, Tivoli is always crowded in warm weather. Fountains add to its charm.

Children enjoy a goat cart ride through the Tivoli Gardens.

spin on a merry-go-round or one of many other rides, or more serious cultural entertainment, you will find it at this beautiful park, resplendent at night with its more than 3,000,000 tinted lights, wonderfully scented and gaily colored because of the trees and flowers which grow in abundance along its walks and in its parks. Each day a special guard, composed of large, well-built boys in bearskins, marches through the garden past theatres, concert halls and the Tivoli's 25 restaurants. These range from small cafés where one can relax inexpensively over a cup of coffee and a piece of Danish pastry (here amusingly called "Vienna bread") to the Belle Terrasse, the Tivoli's most elegant restaurant.

This amusement park wonderland is open from May to September and was started more than a century ago by Georg Carstensen. He named it after the Renaissance gardens of Cardinal d'Este in Italy.

As we might guess from the magnificence of the Tivoli, the Danes love celebrations. Among their many holidays is Children's Day, held in May, which consists of shows, fairs, pageants, processions and dancing in the town square. May 4th is Liberation Eve, and candles can be seen glowing in every window to solemnly commemorate Denmark's liberation at the end of World War II.

Unusual as it may seem, the Danes also celebrate the Fourth of July. Theirs is the largest celebration of American independence outside of the United States. The ceremonies are held in Rebild National Park near Aalborg in northern Jutland, a site created by a group of Americans of Danish ancestry in 1912. They

The island of Fanö, off the west coast of Jutland, is famous as an international bathing resort. Many of the island's women still wear picturesque dresses decorated with bright buttons and belts and quaint caps tied with ribbons.

DENMARK ■ 159

North of Copenhagen, along the coast called the "Danish Riviera," lies the large and rustic Deer Park (Dyrehaven), where 2,000 head of red and fallow deer are allowed to roam. This combination park and forest is a popular excursion place for Copenhageners the whole year through. Ermitagen, a small hunting chateau formerly used by the royal family, is located in Dyrehaven. There is also an amusement park and the excellent restaurant (shown here), Peter Liep's House.

bought and deeded the land to the Danish government with a proviso that it be the scene of an annual American Independence Day celebration. The Danes gather there for picnics, song-fests, speeches and concerts every Fourth of July.

The Danes work just as hard as they play. Despite the hardships that followed World War II, Danes have struggled to build their country to its present state of wealth. Now, for example, one-third of all families have telephones, and for 4,000,000 people, there are a million radios.

Over a million and a half of the population work in industry and as craftsmen. Twenty-eight per cent are engaged in agriculture. A nationwide cooperative system has enabled farmers to make a prosperous livelihood. Some farmers own their buildings, but rent the land from the state. In return, the state offers help with land reclamation, aids farmers financially and provides information and training in agricultural techniques. State loans assist the people until they can become independent farmers. Of the 200,000 farmers in Denmark, over 90 per cent own their own land.

Rent and food, the two major expenses of daily living, are low. However, a housing shortage makes it difficult to get an apartment or a house; tenants usually have to meet some sort of requirement, such as having lived in the township for a certain amount of time.

The fondest dream of many Danes is to own their own homes. Although the majority of Danes live in apartments, Danish apartments are modern, pleasant and have plenty of room. Most of them have either a balcony or a terrace. The Dane furnishes his apartment with high quality furniture. He buys it for lifetime use—even to pass on to his children.

For the past two centuries, Denmark has been working towards the elimination of class distinctions, aiming to give all its people more than an even share of the good things in life, providing they are willing to work for them. Men and women have equal legal rights. There is one woman on the Supreme Court, one in the cabinet and 17 women are members of parliament. Women's privileges range from being admitted to holy orders in the Lutheran Church to smoking a man's cigar in public.

The vast majority of Copenhagen's one million population live in apartments, some in modern buildings such as these. Only a small number of inhabitants own their own houses.

THE ARTS

The most popular Danish writers have been those who told whimsical stories with a clever point and perhaps a good moral. The best and the most famous was Hans Christian Andersen, a writer whose works, next to the Bible, have been the most widely translated in the world. *The Little Mermaid*, *The Red Shoes*, and *The Little Matchgirl* are only a few of the never-to-be-forgotten masterpieces that assure Andersen the immortality he so justly merits.

Right: Although Andersen is known mainly for his stories, he also made puppets, wrote plays for his homemade marionette theatre, and excelled in cutting delightful silhouettes out of black paper, such as the "Jumping Jack" pictured here.

Left: Hans Christian Andersen's childhood was marked by poverty and deep unhappiness. His parents quarrelled bitterly, and they were so poor that they slept on a bed made of planks which had previously been used to support coffins in the church. His imagination was Hans' only comfort, and he dreamed up beautiful stories which ever since have enchanted mankind. From his early youth, Andersen loved reading his stories aloud, both to adults and to children. This picture, taken in 1863, shows him surrounded by several rapt young ladies. Andersen died in 1875 at the age of 70.

The Little Mermaid who longed to be human is one of the most famous of Hans Christian Andersen's fairy-tale characters. Now immortalized in bronze, she watches over Copenhagen waters from a little promontory along the shore where children can play all around her.

Other masters of Danish literature are Christian Pedersen, known as the "Father of Danish literature," who translated the Bible during the first half of the 16th century; Ludvig Holberg, born in 1684, whose scathing satire created a new standard for Danish prose; the great historian and educational reformer, Bishop N. F. S. Grundtvig, who founded the Folk High Schools in 1844; and Sören Kierkegaard, born in 1813, whose influence on philosophy makes itself strongly felt today.

Throughout the second half of the 19th century, Danish literature was characterized by a great wave of realistic works. Important writers were Jens Christian Hostrup, Zacharias Nielssen, Jens Peter Jacobsen, Herman Bang, Carl Larsen, Carl Ewald and Henrik Pontoppidan.

The central figure in Danish literature after 1900 is Johannes V. Jensen, who was awarded the Nobel Prize in 1945 for his novel, *The Long Voyage.* Other contemporary writers are the three great B's—Baroness Karen Blixen, who wrote under the name Isak Dinesen and

Right: The most famous contemporary Danish author is the late Baroness Karen Blixen who wrote under the pen name of Isak Dinesen. Each of her books has been highly successful all over the world. Perhaps the best-known are "Seven Gothic Tales" and "Out of Africa," an autobiography which tells of her eighteen years in Africa. In her later years, Isak Dinesen went back to Denmark, living alone in her house situated halfway between Copenhagen and Elsinore. Her major works were written in English, not in Danish!

is probably the best-known Danish writer of this century, H. C. Branner and Karl Bjarnhof—and the lyric poet and novelist, Nis Petersen.

Danish drama dates back to 1722 when the first Danish-speaking theatre was opened in Copenhagen, but the most famous of Denmark's contributions to the theatre world is the Royal Danish Ballet. It was created under the direction of August Bournonville, the ballet master from 1829 to 1879. Under his gifted direction a first-class company was established; it has maintained its status ever since. The company has toured all over the world, and drawn enthusiastic audiences in many countries. The celebrated Royal Danish Ballet and Music

Dancers start their training early for the famous Royal Danish Ballet. They enter the ballet school at the age of 8. Leading roles are cast by seniority, and most dancers are at least 28 years old before being given a starring part. Here, a royal ballet master, Harald Lander, coaches a prima ballerina, Margot Lander, while other dancers look on.

The most famous ballet master of the Royal Danish company was August Bournonville, who wrote 50 original works, more than 10 of which are still performed. The productions of these ballets demand a special technique known as the "Bournonville style." This technique reflects the Danish character, for it expresses lighthearted gaiety and exuberance. Here Flemming Flindt soars through the air in a performance of "Bournonville Cavalcade."

Festival is held annually in Copenhagen at the end of May.

Denmark's largest theatre is the Royal Theatre in Copenhagen. The most modern is the Concert Hall at Tivoli. In addition, the city has 11 other commercial theatres. There are permanent theatres also in Aarhus, Aalborg and Odense. In the provinces are many facilities for the performances of touring companies. A particularly fascinating theatre is the courtyard of Kronborg Castle, Elsinore, the home of Shakespeare's Hamlet. Annual performances of *Hamlet* are held here, given by international

Kirsten Simone and Henning Kronstam appear in a performance of "La Sylphide."

At the Royal Danish Ballet, a ballerina adjusts the headdress of a colleague.

Left: Denmark's greatest composer, Carl Nielsen (1865-1931), was born only a few miles from Odense, Andersen's birthplace. Nielsen's family, like Andersen's, was extremely poor. As a youngster, Carl made his first musical experiment at the age of 4 when he discovered that different sized pieces of wood gave out different tones when struck. Carl's musical education grew when he accompanied his father to weddings where the elder Nielsen supplemented his income as a house painter by playing the fiddle. Carl Nielsen's symphonies reflect the beauty and joy he found in his native countryside, Fünen.

film industry. It is one of the oldest in the world. Since World War II many fine pictures, particularly documentaries, have come from Denmark, some of them winning top awards at international film festivals in various parts of the world.

companies. Kronborg Castle is the most appropriate of all theatres for a production of *Hamlet,* for the story on which Shakespeare's great play is based first appeared in the *Historia Danica* of Saxo Grammaticus, Denmark's first important writer. The tale of "Amleth" appeared in the folklore of Iceland some 200 years before it was recorded by Saxo Grammaticus near the end of the 12th century. Even today in Iceland, "Amlothe" means "fool." In northern Europe the story of Hamlet was so well known and so deeply rooted that it became a myth, but it did not reach England until the 16th century when Shakespeare used it as the basis of his masterpiece.

There is also considerable musical activity in Denmark. The Royal Orchestra is the oldest, having celebrated its 500th year of existence in 1948. The State Radio Symphony Orchestra is the largest in northern Europe.

Denmark's greatest modern composer is Carl Nielsen. Famous contemporary performers include Victor Schioler, Emil Telmnayl, and the late Danish-American opera star, Lauritz Melchior.

No discussion, however brief, of Danish arts would be complete without a word about the

The Royal Theatre of Copenhagen, opened in 1874, has one great advantage over other Danish theatres. By law, it is allowed prior right to produce any foreign play it wishes to stage.

Shown here are handsome examples of Danish porcelain. Characteristic of all Danish handicrafts is a combination of functionalism and grace.

HANDICRAFTS

One excellent way to gain insight into the character of the Danes is to study the handicrafts which have developed during the past 150 years. Simplicity, restraint and elegance are the characteristics of their designs in silver, porcelain, textiles, furniture, ceramics, glass or pewter.

Among the scores of Danish handicrafts that may be purchased abroad, three special ones have achieved international reputations for distinction and quality: Jensen silver, Royal Copenhagen porcelain, and Danish furniture.

The most famous china service produced by the Royal Copenhagen factory is *Flora Danica*. Originally created for Russia's Catherine the Great, the service as a whole displays the botanical wealth of Denmark, each piece being decorated with an exact painting of a flower or plant. Once owned by the Crown, the Royal Copenhagen porcelain factory is now in the hands of private individuals.

Vases of all shapes and sizes, as well as tiles, take form with amazing swiftness under the skilled hands of Danish ceramists. The wares displayed here were made at a ceramic factory in the south of Zealand.

DENMARK ■ 167

Danish glassware, like Danish porcelain, ceramics and stoneware, is internationally appreciated. This glass maker works on an exquisite, delicate vase.

Danish silverware is always associated with Georg Jensen, who established his foundry in 1904. He brought to his craft a sense of symmetry and won international acclaim for the refinement and subtlety of his designs. One of the special charms of his pieces is that he preferred dull tones to the shiny appearance of typically modern silver.

The beauty of Danish furniture gives it a prominent place among the nation's handicrafts. Its hallmark is comfort achieved with clean lines and grace, the special approach to form and space that has brightened countless households. Thanks to the special efforts of a whole group of designers, architects and craftsmen, these home furnishings of functional design and high-quality taste have been placed within the means of the average consumer.

Denmark has contributed to the comfort and beauty of households all over the world, daily reminding us of the ancient island kingdom which has become a peaceful, flourishing nation.

When designed and produced in Denmark, even a wooden chair is a work of art.

Denmark's soccer attracts the same wildly enthusiastic crowds as does soccer in Britain.

SPORTS

Denmark's national sport is soccer, and the defeat of the Danish team by Sweden (Denmark's greatest rival) would plunge the whole country into gloom. The sport has become so popular that 12,000 clubs have sprung up all over the country, with about 457,000 members, of whom 199,000 are active players.

Denmark has also been extremely successful in aquatic sports. The ready access to the sea and to the country's many lakes makes any water sport a natural for the Danes. Rowing, sailing and sculling are top aquatic sports, and Denmark has always been among the leading nations in these sports at the Olympic Games and other international competitions. The achievements of Danish women swimmers are also world famous.

Other sports the Danes enjoy are badminton, tennis, handball, archery, fencing, cycling, and the popular family sport, camping. Golf is also popular, and golf courses can be found in all the major tourist resorts.

July and August are the regatta months, when international contests take place along the Kattegat coast. Many people, even those with moderate incomes, own their own boats.

DENMARK ■ 169

Above: One of the most important annual events is the Livestock and Agricultural Fair at Copenhagen. Here are shown the country's prize farm animals—red Danish dairy cattle, Jutland, Frederiksborg and Belgian horses, and the Danish land race pig (of bacon fame).

One of Denmark's important exports is the working or draught horse. Pictured with his colt is the Jutland, a sturdy animal prized because of his adaptability to various climates and other conditions.

Next to Holland and New Zealand, Denmark stands third as an exporter of cheese. About 12 per cent of all milk delivered to the nation's dairies is used for making a variety of delicious cheeses. Danish "blue" is prized by gourmets everywhere.

THE ECONOMY

The story of Denmark's national economy is an inspiring one, for this small country, poor in natural resources, has nevertheless achieved an impressive level of prosperity.

Only 80 years ago, Denmark's economy was in a critical situation. Its main export then was grain, but increased world competition had brought about a radical drop in prices. Desperately, the Danes searched for a means to survive. With profits from grain-growing wiped out, with only few dairy herds, with no natural resources to fall back on, a nation with less initiative might have given up. But the Danes

set about to show the world that as long as there is no lack of will, there is always a way to do the best with what one has.

The 10th of June, 1882, marks the turning point in Denmark's economy. On that day at Hjedding, a small town in West Jutland, the first cooperative dairy processed the first milk brought in by local farmers. Denmark's cooperative farm program, which enables members to share costs and minimize the risk of loss to each individual, was on its way. After cooperative dairies came cooperative bacon factories, egg cooperatives, and the various

This glistening churn in a typical Danish co-operative dairy produces some of the finest butter in the world.

cooperative export societies with which Denmark has turned the threat of poverty into the prosperity it enjoys today.

AGRICULTURE

What exactly is Denmark's cooperative farm program? It was started by a young man named Stilling Andersen, a farmer living near Hjedding, who urged the local farmers to bring their milk to a central churning station for processing. The creamery was founded on the democratic rule of "one for all and all for one." Each cooperator had one vote regardless of the size of his farm. The advantage, Andersen pointed out, was that the cooperative could afford the most modern machinery and could hire expert agricultural consultants—advantages the individual farmer could never hope to have. Straightaway, the higher quality cooperative butter began commanding a higher price than that produced previously by individual farmers.

News of the dairy spread, and soon the cooperative farm program extended across the land.

As a result, Denmark has become one of the world's largest exporters of agricultural products. Danish butter, cheese, eggs, bacon and hams are known the world over for their high quality. To protect their own interests, the cooperatives see to it that "Made in Denmark" means the product is the very best that can be bought. The blue stamp of "Danish" on an egg, the *lur* symbol of Danish butter, the "Made in Denmark" stamp on a can of ham—all represent the same matchless quality as the name "Jensen" on a piece of silverware. Through cooperatives, the Danes, once faced with economic ruin, have met successfully the competition of much larger and much richer countries.

Danish eggs are marketed cooperatively through the Egg Export Association. Both weighing and grading are done carefully, and a system of stamping each egg makes it possible to identify the farm from which it comes. If a shipment should prove inferior, the producer is immediately warned. These methods of inspection and control have made the blue stamp of "Danish" synonymous with quality.

FISHING

Wherever you may be in Denmark, the sea is never far off. Fishing, therefore, is an important part of the economy. About 20,000 people are employed in the fisheries, and the fishing fleet, totaling 8,000 large and small vessels, brings in an annual catch worth many millions. Fishing is such an integral part of Denmark's way of life that in Copenhagen there is a monument of a fisherwoman dedicated to the women who preside over the city's fish market. This realistic, life-sized statue is called "The Unknown Fisherwoman."

The fish market is one of the major sights of Copenhagen. Here you can see how the fish literally come from the ocean straight to the table. They are brought up the canal in flat-bottomed boats like punts, which are moored side by side to form a series of watery cages where the fish are kept until wanted. The stalls are set up in the open air, and here the fisher-women clean their fish. These women all come from the little fishing village of Skovshoved, a few miles from the capital; they still retain their traditional dress with full dark skirts and wear starched snow-white headdresses. Since national costumes have disappeared from most parts of Denmark, it is very charming to see these women dressed in the manner of their ancestors.

Above: The fish market along the Gammel Strand of Copenhagen retains a touch of charming provincialism. The market is tended by robust women, dressed for sitting outdoors all day. In the buildings on the right are several popular sea food restaurants.

Below: Two young Copenhageners prepare to sail their boats at Nyhavn, where the fishing boats come in.

One of the few Danish manufacturing industries to obtain its raw materials from Denmark itself is the Portland cement industry. The main substances, clay and chalk, are found in enormous quantities along the east coast of northern Jutland, and big cement works have been built there, such as this one at Aalborg. The largest cement rotary kiln in the world is located here and revolves day and night without stopping.

MANUFACTURING

Some 850 of the world's cement factories use special machinery made in Denmark. Danish dairy equipment is sent to Argentina; Danish steam rollers to the Soviet Union; fishing cutters to India; special wood-burning locomotives to Finland; electric dry cells and batteries, head lamps and pocket torches to tropical countries. These products represent only a sample of Denmark's industrial exports, which now account for more than 25 per cent of her total exports. Although Danes have few raw materials of their own, they take those of other countries and turn out finished goods respected throughout the world for their high quality.

OTHER PRODUCTS

On the lighter side of Danish products are three famous beverages: light beer, cherry brandy and *snaps*. The beer is the oldest of the three. Legends tell that the Vikings were especially fond of it and would drink it from the skulls of their enemies during victory celebrations.

Denmark's famous cherry brandy is world-renowned under its trade name Cherry Heering. It dates back to 1818 when a young Copenhagen merchant named Peter Heering was given a recipe for cherry liqueur by the wife of his employer. The formula is still a closely guarded secret and the business is now being carried on by the fifth generation of the Heering family.

The best-known Danish *snaps* is the Aalborg Akvavit, a pure white spirit made from a base of potatoes. More than 11 million gallons of it are produced per year.

This immense burnished copper cauldron is a feature of the Tuborg brewery, where about 3,000 men are employed. At Tuborg also is the largest kettle in northern Europe with a capacity of 345,000 bottles.

The Seven Sisters Mountains, a recurring theme in a symphony of stone and ice, are seen by travellers on the coastal express steamer from Bergen to the North Cape.

THE LAND

JUST AS THE ARTIST'S PALETTE is divided into warm and cool hues, the continent of Europe has been divided into warm and cool regions.

In art, the warm hues—red, yellow, and orange—remind one of warm things such as a hearth fire or the candles on a birthday cake, while the cool colors—blue, green, and violet—make one think of cool things, such as frost on the window pane and the deep, chilly waters of the sea.

In writing about Europe, many historians and men of literature have divided that continent into halves: the warm, friendly lands of the south; and the cool, more reserved countries in the north. They write of a downward movement from North to South—cool to warm, retiring to outgoing, reserved to friendly.

If this is true, and it is a broad generalization, then Norway is surely among the many exceptions to this pattern. From the moment you meet them, you find the Norwegians are a friendly, fun-loving, outgoing people, anxious to know you and eager to make you feel at home in their beautiful country. "Velkommen til Norge! Veldig hyggelig å se deg." "Welcome to Norway. Very good to see you."

These smiling tots are standing on the Arctic Circle. This "polar circle" monument is located near the Arctic Highway on the Saltfjell mountain plateau in north Norway.

from Lindesnes to the Pyrenees. The Arctic Circle divides the country almost in half, and the area above this imaginary line is called "The Land of the Midnight Sun."

BOUNDARIES

Norway is surrounded by water on three sides, and adjoins Sweden, Finland and Russia on the east. The Skagerrak is the body of water lying to the south, extending from the frontier with Sweden to Lindesnes. From there to Stad on the west coast is the North Sea. From Stad all the way up to the North Cape the coastline is bounded by the North Atlantic or the Norwegian Sea. The Barents Sea lies north from the North Cape to the frontier with Russia.

GEOGRAPHICAL POSITION

Norway, a long and slender country, located near the arctic cap of Europe, forms the western and northern part of the Scandinavian peninsula. Parts of the country are as far north as central Greenland. The outlying island of Spitsbergen (Nor. Svalbard) is farther north than the North Magnetic Pole. Norway's southernmost tip lies on the same parallel of latitude as Juneau, Alaska, or Northern Scotland. The country is shaped somewhat like a gourd, broadest in the south, decreasing in width northward like a long slender neck, and widening again slightly in the northernmost county of Finnmark.

On a line from the southernmost to the northernmost points, the country is approximately 1,089 miles long. Distances are great in Norway, and, with the exception of Russia, greater than in any other European country. It is as far from Lindesnes, the southern point, to the North Cape, the northern point, as it is

Imagine fishing by the light of the midnight sun! The fisherman is at Øksfjord in Finnmark, the northernmost province.

The bustling, little fishing port of Svolær, located north of the Arctic Circle in the land of the midnight sun, is watched over by the "Two Lovers," one of the most famous peaks in the Lofoten Isles.

The 1,587-mile-long eastern border of Norway fronts upon Sweden for 1,020 miles, upon Finland for 445 miles, and upon the Soviet Union for 122 miles.

COASTLINE

The Norwegian coastline is one of the most complex in the world. It is approximately 1,650 miles long, not including the many fjords and inlets which account for another 15,350 miles. If the length of the coastline plus the fjords and inlets were added to the coastlines of the larger islands that surround Norway, the total length would be equal to about one half the circumference of the earth.

Norway is famous for its highway construction, especially the switchback roads that lace the mountains. This one zigzags from Hornviken Bay right up to the top of the North Cape mountain plateau, within the Arctic Circle.

the Faeroes, Iceland, and Greenland, and the greater part of the present Swedish, Finnish, and Russian Lapp districts. Today, Norway proper covers an area of 125,064 square miles while the Arctic islands of Svalbard and Jan Mayen, and the Antarctic possessions, Bouvet Island and Peter I Island, encompass an additional area of 24,221 square miles. Norway, therefore, is slightly larger in area than the British Isles or Italy.

SURFACE FEATURES

Because of Norway's great length and geographical position, the surface features of the land vary considerably: from the low-lying and lush countryside of the coastline and the southeast, to the deep narrow fjords and the wooded hills, to the untamed highland plains and the snow-covered mountains lying inland and to the north.

Norway is a mountain plateau interlaced with valleys and fjords, the long narrow fingers of the sea cut into the mountains during the glacial era. The longest fjord is Sognefjord which penetrates 114 miles inland. Only one

AREA

During the Middle Ages, the Kingdom of Norway was considerably larger than it is today. At that time Norway embraced parts of Sweden and Scotland, the Isle of Man and the islands of the Hebrides, Orkney and Shetland,

Highest building in Scandinavia is Fanaråken Lodge in Jotunheimen, the home of the giants. It is 1,547 feet higher than a mile up!

Besseggen is a knife-edge ridge separating Lake Bess from Lake Gjende in Jotunheimen, home of the giants. In the legend dramatized by Henrik Ibsen, daring young Peer Gynt rode wildly astride a reindeer buck to the peak of Besseggen and plunged headlong into the depths of Lake Gjende. This legendary feat is said to have initiated the "Besseggløpet," a foot race held annually in which the runners raced up one side and down the other. The race was stopped several years ago, however, because it proved too dangerous to life and limb.

fifth of the country lies lower than 500 feet above sea level, while in the remaining four fifths the average height is 1,500 feet above sea level as compared with 1,000 feet throughout the rest of Europe. The *vidda*, the undulating highland plateaus, stretch between the valleys and the fjords. These plateaus are covered with typical alpine vegetation and are dotted with many well-stocked lakes.

Lying from west to east, the Dovre Mountains divide the north country from the south. The southern part is divided again from west to east by the north-south Langfjellene. The highest mountain in Norway is Galdhøpiggen, elevation 8,100 feet, while the largest glacier, Jostedalsbreen, covers an area of 315 square miles. Norway's spectacular waterfalls are

The fjords, fingers of the sea that are cut into the Norwegian coastline, are ruggedly beautiful. A spectacular example is the Geirangerfjord.

From a horse-drawn carriage visitors can more fully enjoy the unspoiled, natural scenery and clean, crisp air that surround the Briksdal glacier, a branch of the great Jostedal glacier, largest icefield in Europe. At an average elevation of 6,000 feet, it covers an area of 350 square miles. The ice layer is 1,500 feet thick in certain places.

Lillehammer south almost to the historic village of Eidsvoll, with an area of 141 square miles.

CLIMATE

Despite Norway's location in the extreme north, it has a generally temperate climate, but because of its great length mean temperatures do vary somewhat. On the whole, however, Norway's climate is surprisingly mild, dry, and invigorating. This is caused, to a great extent, by the Gulf Stream and the prevailing southwesterly winds. The Gulf Stream carries warm water from the tropics to the Norwegian coast, keeping most of the ports free from ice during winter.

Precipitation is moderate throughout the country, but heaviest along the west coast, particularly around Bergen. Although the west

found in the western part of the country, the highest being Mardalsfossen with a straight fall of 974 feet.

The longest of the rivers (and there are many) traversing Norway are found in the eastern part of the country. The Glomma is the longest and flows for 380 miles. For the most part, however, the rivers are not this long and those flowing westward are short and swift, forming the impressive waterfalls which help to create Norway's tremendous supply of hydro-electric power.

Because Norway was once completely covered by ice, the country is studded with inland lakes. Most are small, elongated extensions of rivers, but many are among the deepest in Europe. The largest is the magnificent Lake Mjøsa, stretching from the ski resort of

Hardly seen on the edge of the 600-foot-high precipice is Fossli Hotel. It overlooks the spectacular Vøringsfoss waterfall, Norway's most famous, with a direct fall of 597 feet.

NORWAY ■ **181**

Norwegians who enjoy the out-of-doors all year round, find boating a popular summer activity. Almost every family owns a boat. In the quaint little town of Lillesand on the south coast, there seem to be as many boats as houses.

coast climate is typically marine—higher mean temperatures are recorded here than in any other countries situated on the same latitude. The mean temperature for Oslo, located in the South, for January is 24 degrees F. and for July, 63 degrees F. For these same months in Tromsø, situated in the far northern part of the country, the mean temperatures are 26 degrees F. and 54 degrees F. respectively.

CITIES AND TOWNS

In a country with a total population of not quite 4,000,000 inhabitants, it would seem that cities and towns would be few and far between. Generally speaking, this is not the case in

Enjoying a deep view is this adventurous mountain climber standing on the top of the Bride Pinnacle, one of the "Troll" peaks in Romsdal. Groom Pinnacle is to the left and in the distance, enfolded in clouds, is Store Trolltind.

Sitting in the lush park surrounding the Royal Palace one looks over busy Oslo, the capital of Norway. Electric street cars bring shoppers and commuters down past the National Theatre, the Students' Park, and the Parliament. At the left, behind the National Theatre building, is a charming open-air restaurant.

Norway. Although Norway has only one major city, Oslo, there are several smaller ones and the provincial countryside is dotted with charming old towns and villages set in the rolling, wooded hills and nestled in the fertile valleys and lowlands along the fjords and the coastline.

OSLO

Beginning at the Skagerrak, the Oslofjord penetrates almost sixty miles northward into the interior, forming an exceptionally beautiful approach to the capital city, Oslo, lying at the head of the fjord. Oslo was founded over 900 years ago by King Harald Hårdråde. In 1624, the city was rebuilt by King Christian IV and it was renamed Christiania for him. The original name, Oslo, was restored in 1925.

Oslo has a population of almost 500,000 people, but it is one of the largest cities in the world—in terms of square miles. Within the 175-square-mile area of Oslo are miles of virgin forest ideal for overnight camping trips, well stocked lakes that swell the hearts of fishermen, and rivers complete with roaring rapids.

From the Central Railway Station, the main street, Karl Johansgate, runs through the middle of the city, passing the delightful silver shops of David-Andersen and Tostrup, the stately Grand Hotel, the yellow brick Parliament Building, the historic buildings of the University of Oslo, the luxuriant students' park, the imposing National Theatre, and ends at the beautiful gardens of the stately Royal Palace.

Oslo is a city of museums and galleries—the National Gallery, the Munch Museum, the Vigeland Sculpture Park, the open-air Folk Museum and the Norwegian Maritime Museum, to name only a few. Whatever the subject—art, history, sports, sea-faring, folklore, applied arts—Oslo has much of interest to offer the visitor.

The world-famous Vigeland Monolith is the focal point of Frogner Park in Oslo. The 56-foot-high stone includes 121 sculptured human forms. The Monolith is a single block of stone which was transported to Oslo from Iddefjord, a journey which lasted from August, 1926, to February, 1927. The sculptor Gustav Vigeland worked 10 months modelling the Monolith in full scale, and the translation to stone occupied three men for 13 years—1929 to 1942.

BERGEN

The city set among seven mountains, Bergen is second in size to Oslo, with a population of about 116,000 inhabitants, and is almost as old, having been founded some twenty-two years later in 1070. Throughout the centuries, Bergen has suffered many fires and other disasters, but it has remained rich in the tradition of ancient Norwegian culture.

Bergen is a shipping and trading city and the cultural capital of western Norway. It is the seat of a university and several colleges and the home of several museums and galleries, an

The Fløyen funicular railway, a cable-car system, goes almost straight up Mount Fløyen to command a grand view of Bergen. Nestled among seven mountains, Bergen is the gateway to the fjord country.

Tromsø is the famous gateway city to the Arctic, starting point for a series of expeditions to the North Pole. The first church was built in Tromsø over 700 years ago, and township status was granted in 1794. The town limits were greatly enlarged in 1964, and cover no less than 940 square miles with a population of only 33,000. The new bridge which links the island town to the mainland is 3,414 feet long, with a maximum height of 429 feet above sea level. The aerial cableway runs from Tromsdalen to the top of 1,400-foot-high Mount Storsteinen.

Steep mountain slopes rise within the boundaries of Bergen, the city set among seven mountains. Situated on one of these mountainsides, the houses appear to be built on top of each other.

aquarium, a National Theatre, and the annual Bergen Music Festival. As the point of departure for many trips to the spectacular fjords, Bergen is known as the gateway city to Norway's fjord country.

OTHER CITIES AND TOWNS

Older than both Oslo and Bergen, having been founded in 997, Trondheim is Norway's third largest city, with a fast-growing population that is now over 100,000. Important for trade, industry, and shipping, Trondheim is also the seat of the College of Technology and several institutions of science. Trondheim will soon be the home of Norway's third university which at this time is in the planning stage. The famous

Travellers on a coastal steamer debark at Bodø, located at the mouth of the Saltfjord in the north. Bodø is a commercial town of over 12,000 population, a communications hub, and the railhead for the Nordland railway.

Norway's mountain flora offers amateur botanists frequent finds of rare and beautiful flowers, like this Mountain Queen or Saxifraga cotyledon.

FLORA AND FAUNA

With about 2,000 species of plants, Norway is not considered rich in flora, but it is somewhat richer than might be expected from its position so far north. A few of the mountain plants are peculiar to Norway, but most species are found in other countries as well.

The richest vegetation in Norway is found in the southeast part of the country near the Oslofjord and the large lakes such as Mjøsa. Wild berries, including blueberries and cranberries, and mushrooms grow in the forests. Little known outside Scandinavia are the cloudberries, delectable relatives of the blackberry, which are gathered in the mountain areas.

Norwegian forests, which cover approximately one quarter of the land area, abound in fir and pine. These rich forests of the southeast form the basis for the timber and furniture industries. Birch and other deciduous trees are found in many mountain districts.

Because so many families live by the sea, large areas are almost entirely dependent on fisheries. In this country where almost 62 per cent of the land distribution is mountainous,

Nidaros Cathedral in Trondheim is the largest in Scandinavia and is the national religious shrine of Norway.

A number of smaller cities and towns dot the countryside. Stavanger, Kristiansand, Drammen, Skien, Tromsø, and Fredrikstad are in the 30,000 to 80,000 inhabitant class.

Polar bear cubs can be most friendly and cuddly —while they are still very young.

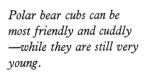

186 ■ NORWAY

The farming districts of Norway would not be complete without mountain goats, which graze peacefully through the hilly, wooded fields. The goats, of exclusive Norwegian origin, are comparatively small, but generally good milkers. Many delicious types of cheeses are produced from their milk.

animal life, particularly life from the sea, is of considerable importance to the economy of the nation.

The bear is almost extinct in Norway. Elk (moose) are found in most of the country except perhaps in the northernmost province of

The Norwegian "fjording" is a docile pony which understands any language— provided it is friendly. It makes an ideal saddle horse for pony-trekking holidays.

Salmon try to jump a waterfall in the Laerdal, one of the best known salmon rivers.

Millions of puffins (Fratercula arctica) nest on the rocks in the Lofoten Isles, northwest of the mainland in the Norwegian Sea. The puffin, a sea bird allied to the auk and the murre, has a deep, compressed bill.

Finnmark, where the reindeer is the most important domestic animal.

Fresh-water fish, particularly trout, are found in almost all of Norway's rivers and lakes. Salmon are caught in the many known "salmon rivers."

May and June are the most beautiful months in Norway's fjord country. Then, the white and red blooms of millions of fruit trees cover the slopes of the towering mountains, which rise above the blue waters of the long, narrow fjords.

*During the Viking Age (*A.D.* 800 to 1050), the Scandinavians sailed westward on many expeditions in small, wooden boats like this one. Vikings of Norwegian descent settled in Iceland and Greenland, and about the year 1000 Leif Ericson is reported to have landed on Vinland on the northeast coast of North America. The Viking ship pictured here on the Hardangerfjord was authentically constructed from ancient relics for use in the Hollywood feature film "The Vikings."*

HISTORY

THE HISTORY OF MAN in Norway is very old, dating back at least some eight to ten thousand years. The coastline has been populated ever since the receding ice of the last glacial period left a rugged and barren shore along which human existence and activity were possible. The earliest settlers were nomadic tribes of hunters and fishermen who migrated from the south leaving traces of their crude existence as far north as the semi-Arctic shores of Finnmark.

The oldest forms of communal government in Norway date from the earliest times. During the early centuries of the Christian era, tribal groups formed small kingdoms in the eastern part of the country. After the year 400, more aggressive tribes came by sea from the south of Norway and settled along the western coast. This forced the small kingdoms of the east to establish commercial exchange with the kingdoms of the west.

A historical Viking drama, performed in the open, is part of the annual Harstad Festival held in the spring of the year. Harstad, in Troms province in northern Norway, is an old fishing and agricultural community located on Hinnøya, the largest island along the coastline.

THE VIKING PERIOD

The years between 800 and 1050 were those of the Viking period during which the name of Norway became known throughout the then civilized world. About A.D. 872 a period of national unification was begun under the leadership of King Harald Haarfagre, Harald the Fair Haired, whose descendents continued to rule the country for about 450 years.

During this age the fierce Vikings sailed westward to raid and plunder and settled in Ireland, Scotland, England, France, the Shetlands, the Orkneys, the Hebrides, the Isle of Man, the Faeroe Islands, and Iceland. From colonies in Iceland, men of Norwegian descent settled in Greenland and in the year 1000, under Leif Ericson, undertook expeditions to an area on the northeastern coast of North America, which they called Vinland. Over-population, superior ships and weapons, strong military organization, and a gusty spirit of adventure, combined to cause this exciting westward movement.

THE MIDDLE AGES

The period of national unification that began during the end of the 9th century under Harald Haarfagre was by no means concluded during his reign. In fact, the various kingdoms of Norway were not consolidated until after the death of King Olav Haraldsson at the battle of Stiklestad in 1030 and his canonization the next year. With his death Christianity emerged officially, leading to the Christian unification of the people and the permanent establishment of the Church throughout the country.

By the middle of the 13th century, Norway found itself totally dependent upon imports for its supplies of grain. By this time, also, the

A unique collection of ancient timbered buildings including this complete farmstead, has been moved intact from the Gudbrandsdal district to the Maihaugen Museum at Lillehammer.

St. Olav, the patron saint of Norway, is depicted in many church murals throughout Scandinavia. During the reign of St. Olav (1015–1030), Norway became a Christian country. Olav was canonized in 1164.

German merchants and craftsmen of the Hanseatic League had secured exceptional commercial privileges in Norway and such importing lay completely in their hands. The need for grain and the dependence upon the Hanse brought a marked economic decline. In addition, the country was ravaged by the Black Death, the bubonic plague which wiped out half of the population.

THE UNION OF KALMAR

Following the economic decline, grave political consequences ensued, and by 1388 the three Scandinavian kingdoms—Denmark, Norway, and Sweden—were united into the Union of Kalmar under the centralized rule of Queen Margaret of Denmark. It was agreed that Margaret would, at the first opportunity, provide the three kingdoms with a king who was to be her nearest relative. In 1389, she proclaimed her infant cousin, Eric of Pomerania, King of Norway and in 1396 homage was also accorded him in Sweden and Denmark. During Eric's minority, Margaret held the office of regent but even after Eric reached the age of majority in 1401 Margaret remained the real ruler of Scandinavia.

This interior is from one of the oldest of the ancient timbered buildings at the Maihaugen Museum in Lillehammer.

NORWAY AND DENMARK UNITED

After many attempts Sweden finally broke away from the Union of Kalmar in 1523, but Norway continued with Denmark under the terms of a treaty drafted in Danish and serving Danish interests. A new era of prosperity emerged as the forests of Norway became an important source of national wealth and as Norwegian shipping expanded. There arose a new class of prosperous townspeople.

The conflicting interests of Norway and Denmark came to the fore during the Napoleonic Wars. Danish hostilities with England brought a demand for a separate Norwegian foreign policy and the Danish alliance with France led to the end of the Danish-Norwegian union in 1814.

At the Norwegian Maritime Museum, near Oslo, visitors may see "Fembøring," ancient Norse fishing boats. Dating back at least 500 years they were widely used until about 50 years ago when motor-powered boats came into general use.

The walls and timbers of this room in the Maihaugen Museum have been decorated with the ancient Norwegian art of "rosemaling" or rose painting. The chest and bench at the right were hand carved centuries ago with similar designs.

NORWAY AND SWEDEN UNITED

On January 14, 1814, by the Peace of Kiel, Norway was ceded to Sweden. Before the war had ended, however, Christian Frederik who was the heir to the Dano-Norwegian throne arrived in Norway as Viceroy. When the Treaty of Kiel was announced, he recognized the sovereignty of the people and agreed to summon a constituent assembly.

THE CONSTITUTION

The assembly met at the little town of Eidsvoll on April 10, 1814, to assume its task of writing a constitution. The Norwegian Constitution was inspired by the American War of Independence and the ideals of the French Revolution. It was modelled after the French Constitution of 1791. On May 17 of that year the Constitutional Law was signed

These beautifully designed tapestries, spinning wheels, and antique hand looms are on display in a weaving room at the Maihaugen open-air Museum at Lillehammer.

Eidsvoll Manor is perhaps the most historical and the best loved building in Norway. It was here that Norway's Constitution was signed on May 17, 1814. The simple yet graceful white wood building is now a museum housing many relics of historical origin.

and Denmark's Christian Frederik was proclaimed king. When Sweden concluded its campaign against Napoleon it demanded the observation of the Kiel treaty and when Norway refused to yield, war with Sweden ensued.

NORWAY AND SWEDEN REUNITED

The war with Sweden was not a long one and an armistice was soon concluded by the Convention of Moss. Under the terms of the Convention, the union of Norway and Sweden was sanctioned by legislation; the Constitutional Law of Eidsvoll was to remain in force; and Christian Frederik was to abdicate and leave the country. Under pressure from Swe-

An enterprising swindler once used this hollow tree as a workshop for making counterfeit coins. He was caught, but his unusual workshop can now be seen at the Maihaugen Museum at Lillehammer.

den, the Swedish-Norwegian union was approved by the first Norwegian Storting on November 4, 1814. Norway was again under the yoke of government by a foreign crown—a condition that would remain until the dawn of the 20th century.

THE UNION IS WEAKENED

During the second half of the 19th century, an internal political transformation took place in Norway. In the Storting two separate political groups were formed: a conservative party supported by the bureaucratic government in power; and a liberal party in definite opposition. The leader of the more powerful opposition party was Johan Sverdrup. In 1884, under the terms of the new Norwegian con-

stitution, the King was obliged to appoint a cabinet with Sverdrup as Prime Minister. Thus the power of the King came to an end and the Storting became the decisive governing body.

This development caused great anxiety in Sweden; the Storting claimed equality for Norway and that demand received increasing support in Norwegian politics.

A KING IS ELECTED

On June 7, 1905, the Norwegian Storting declared the union with Sweden dissolved. In referendum, the people supported the Storting with an overwhelming majority. Under the terms of the new Norwegian Constitution of 1814, division of power lay between royal authority and the representatives of the people, the Storting. Therefore, on November 18,

Akershus Castle in Oslo was built in the 1290's by Haakon Magnusson, King Haakon V. The castle was destroyed by lightning in 1527 and was rebuilt in the 1630's by King Christian IV. Akershus Castle is still used today on formal occasions, particularly when the Norwegian government entertains prominent foreign visitors.

King Haakon VII became the first king of Norway under the present line. He was elected by the Norwegian Parliament on November 18, 1905, a few months after the Parliament had declared Norway a free and independent country.

1905, the Norwegian Storting elected the Danish Prince Carl as King of Norway, King Haakon VII.

From 1905 until World War I, Norway experienced prosperity and increasing industrialism, but accompanied by rising prices, a tendency which was accelerated during the war. In an effort to offset this tendency, the Liberal Party initiated the regulation of prices and rationed foodstuffs. A law for compulsory mediation in workers' disputes was passed in 1916 and the general scope of social legislation was widened. When World War I began, a policy was adopted which maintained Norway's neutrality. This placed a heavy increase on the national debt.

In 1921, there set in a prolonged period of depression which curbed industry and caused much unemployment. This was followed by the international depression of 1929 resulting in

the formation of a Labour Government in 1935. The Labour Government set about the task of reducing unemployment; this resulted in a sizable increase in the national expenditure.

HITLER INVADES NORWAY

When World War II began, Norway again declared neutrality although the sympathy of the people was with the Allied powers. In the early months of 1940, Hitler decided to occupy Norway because he feared that the Allied powers would establish themselves there and because a renegade Norwegian Nazi named Vidkun Quisling had convinced him of the danger of a supposed British occupation of Norway. Should Hitler move against Norway, Quisling offered his full assistance to the Reich. When German forces brutally invaded Norway

Under the leadership of Johan Sverdrup, the Swedish-Norwegian union was greatly weakened during the latter half of the 19th century. Sverdrup was appointed Prime Minister in 1884.

The charming, half-timbered buildings of Frogner Manor, built in the 17th century, are now the home of the Oslo City Museum.

Pernille, named for a character in one of Holberg's plays, is one of the most delightful of the many, popular open-air restaurants in Oslo. In the background is the Royal Palace, situated at the head of Oslo's main street, Karl Johansgate, and commanding a fine view of the city. Between the palace and Pernille is the entrance to the Holmenkolbanen, the electric railway system serving Oslo and its suburbs.

in April, 1940, securing Oslo and several important towns, Quisling became the puppet premier of Norway. His name is now synonymous with traitor.

Norway's forces were weak and had been caught unprepared; however, a strong resistance movement took shape. King Haakon, Crown Prince Olav, and the Storting took refuge in Great Britain from where they directed the rapidly growing resistance movement and undermined Germany's war effort with a scheme of well directed sabotage.

MODERN NORWAY

After the Liberation of Norway in May, 1945, the next ten years were devoted to reconstruction. Long-range investments were made in hydro-electric power plants and heavy industry was encouraged by the government. The program of social reforms begun in the 1930's was carried forward. In general, Norway has enjoyed increased prosperity in the post-war years. Because of the post-war reconstruction effort, many problems concerning housing, education, and transportation have come to the fore and have been dealt with most efficiently. More jobs for more workers and the introduction of automation have increased production in the fisheries and in industries. The increase

Two Atlantic liners of the Norwegian-American Line, the "Bergensfjord" and the "Oslofjord" (lower right) meet in the port of Oslo.

in the number of automobiles by several hundred thousand within the past decade has created a substantial demand for improved highways and road construction. While agricultural production has steadily increased, a rise in "white collar" and service occupations is taking shape at the present time. The military budget has undergone a marked increase, and the successful rebuilding of the Norwegian merchant marine has more than doubled its pre-war tonnage. Today, Norway's merchant fleet is fourth after those of the United States, the United Kingdom, and Liberia.

The first post-war elections in Norway gave a majority in the Storting to the Labour Party and in following elections the party continued to poll over half of the votes cast. The elections of September, 1965, however, brought thirty years of almost unbroken rule by the Labour Party to an end when it lost its control in the Storting to a coalition of four non-Socialist parties.

Rådhuset, the city hall and one of the most impressive buildings in Oslo, serves as the focal point of the city. The foundation stone was laid in 1931 and the building was completed in 1950, the year in which Oslo celebrated its 900-year jubilee. Designed by Arnstein Arneberg and Magnus Poulsson, the building is embellished with the work of many contemporary Norwegian artists. The sculpture in the foreground is by Per Hurum and Emil Lie.

GOVERNMENT

NORWAY is a constitutional and hereditary monarchy with executive power vested in the King and exercised through a prime minister and his cabinet, the Council of State. The Council of State is composed of councillors, who are the heads of the various ministries of the government. The councillors sit in the parliament, or Storting, but they do not vote.

UNIVERSAL SUFFRAGE

The right to vote is accorded to all Norwegian citizens, both men and women, who are over 21 years of age. In 1898, universal suffrage was introduced for men; in 1910, women received the right to vote in municipal elections; and, in 1913, women were first permitted

The home of the Norwegian Parliament, the Storting, was built in Oslo in 1861–66.

of the combined votes. Budget proposals and questions not taking the form of bills are dealt with in joint session; a number of standing committees discuss most questions before they reach the full assembly.

THE KING

Constitutionally, executive power is exercised by the King in Cabinet, and the King must follow the majority of the Cabinet. The King has the right of veto in legislative issues; he is

to vote in Storting elections. The U.S.A. and Iceland preceded Norway in giving the vote to women in local elections, but Norway pioneered the way for women to become eligible for election to the national assembly when the first woman was seated in the Storting in 1911.

Candidates for office must be over 21 years of age and must have resided 10 years in the country, although candidates need not be resident in the constituency in which they stand for election. Substitutes as well as regular members are elected.

THE STORTING

The Storting is elected in September of every fourth year, meets annually in Oslo on the first weekday in October, and remains assembled as long as is necessary. After it is opened, the Storting divides itself into two sections: the Lagting consisting of 38 members and equal to one-quarter of the parliament; and the Odelsting consisting of the remaining members. Bills are first introduced in the Odelsting and, when passed, are sent to the Lagting. The Lagting may return the bill to the Odelsting for further deliberation and if the two still do not agree, a joint session is held and the bill may be passed by a two-thirds majority

King Olav V of Norway, who succeeded his father King Haakon VII in 1957, is much loved and admired by his people. It is not unusual to see the King walking in the streets or visiting the shops of Oslo. On such occasions, the Norwegian people courteously respect the privacy of their sovereign, but often the King, himself, will stop and talk for a few moments. An outstanding athlete, King Olav won an Olympic championship in sailing in 1928.

Trygve Lie is one of Norway's most able statesmen. He became foreign minister of Norway in 1941 and was chosen the first Secretary General of the United Nations in 1946, serving in that capacity until 1953.

the supreme commander of the Norwegian armed forces; and he is the head of the Church of Norway to which he and at least half his Cabinet must belong. The throne is hereditary for male descendants only and passes to the king's eldest son, the Crown Prince.

PRIME MINISTER AND CABINET

The Prime Minister is appointed by the King; according to tradition, it is the duty of the King to appoint to the post the leader of the political party in power. The Prime Minister appoints the Ministers, the heads of the Ministries, who constitute the Cabinet or Council of State. The Ministries are: Foreign Affairs, Commerce and Shipping, Communications, Defence, Family and Consumer Affairs, Municipal and Labour Affairs, Industry, Finance and Customs, Church and Education, Agriculture, Health and Social Affairs, Fisheries, Questions Related to Salaries and Prices, and Justice and Police.

LOCAL ADMINISTRATION

Characteristic of Norwegian public administration is the great extent to which it is based on municipal self-government. Such a highly developed and independent municipal administration can be found in few other countries of the world.

The country is divided into 20 *fylker*, counties or provinces, including the cities of Oslo and Bergen. The fylker are divided into *kommuner*, communities or districts. There are 49 urban districts, *by-kommuner*, and 476 rural districts, *herreds-kommuner*. These local districts are run by community councils elected every fourth year. In each *fylker*, except Oslo and Bergen, there is a county council consisting of members of the community councils.

The striking Norwegian modern design of the Government House in Oslo, completed in 1959, is by architect Erling Viksjø.

Fishing vessels like these, docked in the Lyngenfjord near Tromsø, are a typical sight along the Norwegian coast.

THE ECONOMY

IN THE 19TH CENTURY, the Norwegian economy depended primarily on the basic trades—agriculture, forestry, fishing, and shipping. The timber and ship-building industries are also linked by tradition to the economic development of the country.

Today, particularly after World War II, industry has increased and leads the country's economy. This industrial expansion is based on Norway's abundant, inexpensive water power; on better utilization of natural resources such as fish, timber, ores, and metals; and on general improvement in private purchasing power on the domestic market. Industry accounts for over 25 per cent of Norway's gross national product, which is the total market value of a nation's goods and services before any deductions or allowances are made. In addition to industrial export, revenue derived from the Norwegian merchant fleet helps offset the cost of financing the country's great import surplus.

Norway has a tight manpower market and unemployment is almost non-existent. Some seasonal unemployment does exist, however, particularly during the winter in the building and construction trades. Seasonal trades also include fishing, whaling, agriculture, and forestry. This is because some types of work cannot be carried out during certain seasons. To offset seasonal unemployment, however, it

After the hay is harvested in July, the crop is stacked up in neat rows to dry in the sun. The broad fields and gently rolling hills are typical of the farm lands in the eastern and middle part of the country. Norwegians have their own distinctive style of stacking hay.

is not uncommon for a man to work at more than one trade. But the present trend, aided by increased mechanization, is towards greater year-round specialized employment and less combination of trades.

AGRICULTURE

About 15 per cent of the population is engaged in agriculture, which accounts for just under 5 per cent of the gross national product. Farms are small in Norway—only 20,300 are larger than 25 acres while only about 40 cover more than 250 acres. Only 3.2 per cent of the country's total land area is suitable for farming while only a third of that area is tillable. The remaining two thirds are meadow and grazing land. In livestock production, milk is the main sales product followed by beef,

pork, eggs, and poultry. The primary crops are barley, oats, and potatoes and some fruits and berries. A number of vegetables must be imported to supplement domestic production. Because of the geographic and climatic hardships against which farmers work, agriculture is strongly organized with co-operative purchasing, sales, and processing organizations. Practically all farmers, however, own and work their own farms.

FORESTRY

Just over 20 per cent of the total land area is in productive forests and about two-thirds of this area is owned by farmers. Ownership of the remaining third is divided in about half by government and municipalities and by industry and private enterprise. Forest work is becoming highly mechanized.

Whaling is big business in Norway as this monument in the town of Sandefjord dramatically shows. To help create the fever and excitement of harpooning a whale, the monument revolves in a complete circle every 24 hours.

After whales are killed, the carcasses are hauled on to the deck of the whaling ship for processing and flensing, stripping off the blubber and skin. This carcass, lying on a dock near Tromsø, being butchered for steaks, is approximately 45 feet long.

Folk dancing, in the native costume of one's district, to the tune of the Hardanger fiddle is a popular activity with young and old alike.

THE PEOPLE

LANGUAGE

Norwegian is the language of Norway, but there are two official divisions of the language: *riksmål*, or *bokmål*; and *landsmål*, or New Norwegian. Many Norwegians like to consider riksmål and landsmål as two separate languages, but as the two are so closely related it is simpler to think of them as one. Both have equal status in official use, both are used in the schools, and both are spoken on radio and television broadcasts. Riksmål is used more widely in the urban areas, while landsmål is spoken throughout the rural districts. People who speak and understand one have no difficulty in speaking and understanding the other. In addition, several different dialects are spoken throughout the country.

Although more closely related to Danish and Swedish than to English or German, Norwegian is not generally considered too difficult for a Germanic-speaking person to learn.

Riksmål is closely akin to Danish and was spoken widely in Norway until the end of the 19th century. Landsmål grew out of the various dialects in the country. Opinion is divided in Norway as to whether riksmål and landsmål should be amalgamated quickly or allowed to develop naturally into one common language, *samnorsk*.

The statue of Ludvig Holberg, Norwegian-born dramatist and historian who wrote in Danish, stands beside the National Theatre in Oslo. Flanking Holberg are two characters from his plays.

LITERATURE AND DRAMA

During the Middle Ages the literature of Norway and Iceland was closely linked because the colonists in Iceland were of Norwegian stock. Most of the literature of this time had been composed long before it was written down. Like the old Norse laws, the tales of the ancient Norse gods were passed on orally centuries before they were committed to writing.

The oldest literary works in Norway are the Eddic poems, composed in the 9th and 10th centuries and written down in the first half of the 13th century. The Eddic poems tell of the old Norse gods and reflect the life and times of the people. Next came the Icelandic sagas which dealt with Norse mythology and the early history and life of the medieval period. These sagas had much influence upon the development of national sentiment in Norway.

Ludvig Holberg (1684–1754) was one of the first well known writers of Norwegian birth. He wrote in Danish, however, because during his lifetime Norway was in union with Denmark, and Danish was the tongue of the educated Norwegian. After the union with Denmark was abolished in 1814, Henrik Wergeland (1808–1845) became the leading literary figure in Norway. His romantic poetry earned him the distinction of being acclaimed Norway's greatest poet. His romantic, nationalistic ideas were developed by Bjørnstjerne Bjørnson (1832–1910) and by Henrik Ibsen (1828–1906). Bjørnson took the themes for his books and dramas from Norse history and his style developed into modern realism. Ibsen was more concerned with ethics and the personal conflict of man with social custom and environment.

Knut Hamsun (1859–1952), a Norwegian writer who gained world recognition, was the creator of a new lyrical style in prose. Another well known Norwegian writer is the realistic novelist Sigrid Undset (1882–1949). Bjørnson, Hamsun, and Undset were all awarded the Nobel Prize in literature.

The Norwegian dramatist Henrik Ibsen (1828–1906) is considered the world over one of the outstanding figures in modern theatre. His plays brought a fresh quality to the theatre by presenting natural characters in conflict with social customs and environment; he influenced many writers including G. B. Shaw. Ibsen is best remembered for such plays as "Peer Gynt," "A Doll's House," "Ghosts," "An Enemy of the People," "Hedda Gabler," and "The Master Builder."

The plays of Ibsen and Bjørnson have greatly influenced the development of Norwegian theatre and the personal influence of these two great writers did much to stimulate leadership and instruction in the dramatic arts of the country. The first theatres in Norway were instituted in Oslo and Bergen during the early and mid-19th century. Today there are permanent theatres in Oslo, Bergen, Trondheim, and Stavanger; the rural areas are served by touring shows presented by the permanent theatres. Most theatres receive subsidies from government and municipal funds.

THE PRESS

Of the approximately 159 newspapers in Norway, 82 are dailies. Freedom of the press was established by the Constitution of 1814. Most Norwegian newspapers are politically oriented, but political affiliation does not necessarily affect the circulation size of a newspaper. British and European newspapers may be purchased in most cities throughout the country.

RELIGION

About 96 per cent of the people belong to the National Church of Norway which is Evangelical Lutheran. The Church of Norway is the state church and, by provision of the constitu-

Aftenposten in Oslo is Norway's largest newspaper having two daily editions each with net circulations exceeding 140,000 copies. This Conservative newspaper began in 1860 and moved into its present building when it was completed in 1964.

The interior of the centuries-old Lom Stave Church with its decorative, carved appointments has been executed with a remarkable sense of design and artistic expression.

tion, is endowed by the state. Complete freedom of religion does exist in Norway, however, and all people may worship in accordance with their faith. Membership in various other churches, including Pentecostal, Free Church Lutherans, Methodists, Baptists, and Roman Catholic, totals about 110,000. Norwegian missionaries are active abroad, particularly in Asia and Africa. Norwegian mission organizations have over 900 missionaries in the field serving congregations of about 310,000 members.

Nidaros Cathedral in Trondheim was built in the eleventh century during the reign of King Olav Kyrre. It is the largest cathedral in Scandinavia and the national religious shrine of Norway.

The Stiklestad monument near Trondheim commemorates Norway's Viking King, Olav the Saint, who fell in battle at Stiklestad on July 29, 1030. With the death of Olav and his subsequent canonization, Christianity became permanently established throughout the country.

On display in the Kon-Tiki museum near Oslo is the balsa raft on which the Norwegian explorer Thor Heyerdahl and five companions drifted across the Pacific in 1947 covering a distance of 4,300 miles in 101 days.

MODERN VIKINGS

Like their Viking ancestors, Norwegians are a hearty race and enjoy a keen sense of adventure. Because of Norway's proximity to the sea, exploration has been largely maritime. Although no permanent settlement was established, it is believed that the Vikings touched the mainland of North America about the year A.D. 1000. In 1893, Magnus Andersen and his Norwegian crew demonstrated that such trans-Atlantic navigation was possible with the technology of the Viking period by sailing an exact copy of the Godstad Viking ship from Norway to the United States.

In 1888, Fridtjof Nansen (1861–1930) was the first to cross the Greenland ice cap. He successfully introduced the use of skis in polar travel. Between 1893 and 1896, Nansen made a trans-Arctic expedition in the polar ship, *Fram*. In 1903–06, Roald Amundsen (1872–1928) was the first navigator to take a ship through the Northwest Passage. Amundsen then turned his attention to the South Pole; he was the first to reach the geographic South Pole where he planted the Norwegian flag on December 14,

1911. He early foresaw the coming of aircraft in polar exploration. In 1925, with Lincoln Ellsworth, Amundsen successfully carried out the first extensive aircraft flight over the frozen Polar Ocean.

Thor Heyerdahl (1914–) has contributed much to ethnological research in the Pacific. According to his theory, there exists in Polynesia a sub-stratum of American Indian culture. In 1947, to support this theory, he and five companions drifted across the Pacific in a balsa raft, the *Kon-Tiki*, from Ecuador to Polynesia. The 4,300-mile trip was made in 101 days.

In 1960, author and explorer Helge Ingstad and his wife began searching for the Viking Vinland on North America. For four years they examined the coastlines of Labrador, Newfoundland, and Quebec. On the northernmost tip of Newfoundland, near Lance aux Meadows, they found the remains of an early Norse settlement. This discovery has since been fully acknowledged.

This keen and robust Nordic sense of adventure and exploration exists also among the

Kåre Andersen at left and Bjørn Braaten at right, both from Oslo, load their kayak "Askeladden" with camping gear and provisions for an Eskimo style kayak trip across North America.

Life is not entirely primitive on the Finnmark mountain plateau, home of the nomadic Lapps. This Lapp woman is selecting items in a miniature supermarket in the Lapp village of Karasjok, located a few miles from the Norwegian-Finnish frontier.

youth of Norway today. A striking example is the Eskimo style kayak trek across North America made in 1963 by Bjørn Braaten and Kåre Andersen, two young Oslo men. Their journey from Portland, Oregon, to New Orleans, Louisiana, on the Columbia, Missouri, and Mississippi rivers lasted nine months and embraced over 3,500 miles. Following the Lewis and Clark route in part, they were the first to paddle a kayak from Portland to New Orleans. Their independent resourcefulness is typical of the athletic prowess and spirit of Norwegian youth.

FOOD

The Norwegians are a most active people who work hard and eat well. Throughout Norway the food is delicious—and plentiful, and the *koldtbord,* the cold table similar to the Swedish *smørgasbord,* is the basis for the fine cuisine. The *koldtbord* is usually replete with herring dishes, sliced ham, various cold meats, smoked salmon, sardines, shrimp, cheeses, breads, and salads and may be served for breakfast, lunch, and dinner along with some hot dishes.

Breakfast is somewhat the same throughout the country and will include such items as cheese, bread, jams, sardines, fried or boiled

This is just the "north-east corner" of the giant smørgåsbord served daily for skiers at the Tyin Mountain Hotel in Jotunheimen.

eggs, pan-fried potatoes, and coffee and milk. In the rural areas, the noon meal is called dinner, or *middag*, while the evening meal is like the breakfast *koldtbord* with the addition of a hot dish. For *middag*, hot meat or fish along with vegetables and potato are eaten.

In the cities and towns, the main hot meal is usually taken at night while lunch, or *lunsj*,

The fjords and mountains provide ideal camping grounds for the entire family.

*A street in Oslo is gaily
decorated during the
Christmas season.*

based on the famous *koldtbord*, is served at midday. Popular at lunch time are the delightful
Scandinavian open-faced sandwiches called
smørbrød which are of Danish origin. *Smørbrød*
are made with single slices of bread upon which
are placed pyramids of meat, fish, egg, cheese,
lettuce, and tomato in endless tempting combinations. Norwegian beer is good, and along
with wine and the national strong drink,
aquavit, is served at most meals.

HOLIDAYS

Most Christian holy days are observed in
Norway and the shops and offices are closed on
Maundy Thursday, Good Friday, Easter
Monday, Ascension Day, Whit Monday, and
Christmas Day. As in England, the day after
Christmas, called Boxing Day, is also a holiday.

Norway's national independence holiday is
Constitution Day, the 17th of May. Norwegians

*The Kingdom of Norway and the United States
of America have been allies for many years; in
homage to that bond of friendship across the
Atlantic, Fourth of July celebrations are held
annually in Norway. Here in Sandefjord,
American naval units always arrive on the
Fourth of July for a flag-saluting ceremony.
Celebrations are also held in Oslo.*

feel about the 17th of May as Americans do
about the Fourth of July. The Norwegian
Labour Day is May 1.

During the Christmas season, the mid-winter
festivals are held. The highlight of the summer
season is Midsummer Eve, celebrated on June

Peasant weddings in Norway are still held according to ancient ritual. The festivities include the bridal procession, drinks served by the "kjøgemester" or toast master, playing on the Hardanger fiddle, the wedding feast, and folk dancing led by the bride and groom. Peasant weddings are held in the town of Geilo each year in August; visitors are always welcomed to join in the general merriment.

23. This is the longest day of the year and is a time of great merry-making. Bonfires are lit everywhere, songs are sung, folk dancing is done to the tune of the Hardanger fiddle, and much beer and aquavit is passed around throughout the long and bright midsummer night. Some parties have been known to last throughout the following day as well. Norwegians are a con-vivial people and any excuse provides an opportunity for fun and good fellowship.

This little lass has caught the eye of the soldiers on parade. The occasion is the 17th of May, Constitution Day, which is the national holiday celebrating Norway's independence. The festivities include large processions, elaborate parades, general merry-making, and much good cheer.

SPORTS AND RECREATION

Sports and outdoor life are most important to the average Norwegian as they play an active part in his life. During the summer months most families spend their holidays either in the mountains or along the coastline; at Easter time people in great numbers go from the cities and towns to the mountains for skiing holidays.

Skiing is Norway's national sport. During the winter cross-country skiing through the woodland hills is popular; slalom and downhill are practiced in the mountains during spring. The country is proud of the many Norwegians who have distinguished themselves in skiing. Ski jumping champions include: Birger Ruud, Olympic champion 1932 and 1936; Bjørn Wirkola, World champion 1966; and Toralf Engan, Olympic champion 1964. The champions of cross-country skiing include: Torleif Haug, Olympic champion 1924; and Gjermund Eggen, World champion 1966. In Alpine skiing, Stein Eriksen won an Olympic championship in 1952 and the World championship in 1954.

Skating is popular in Norway during the winter and attracts a large following. During 1910–1920, Oscar Mathiesen became the greatest speed skater in the world and is now a legend in Norway. Among the Norwegians who have won Olympic gold medals in skating are: Ivar Ballangrud, Hjallis Andersen, and Knut

Almost every family in Norway owns a boat and for the young and adventurous it is probably a kayak.

Johannesen. In figure skating, Sonja Henie won three Olympic and ten consecutive World championships from 1927 to 1936. She later became a motion picture actress and appeared in several feature length skating films.

At Tomm Murstad's Ski School for Children in Oslo and throughout the country they start them young. Before reaching school age, many Norwegian youngsters are proficient skiers.

The world's biggest ski meet, Holmenkollen Day, is held in Oslo in March. Top-ranking skiers from all leading winter sports nations compete in ski jumping from the giant Holmenkoll ski jump. The annual event is usually attended by over 100,000 spectators, headed by the Norwegian Royal Family.

Glacier skiing is a popular sport—in summer and winter. Several glaciers provide superb skiing even on the hottest day of summer.

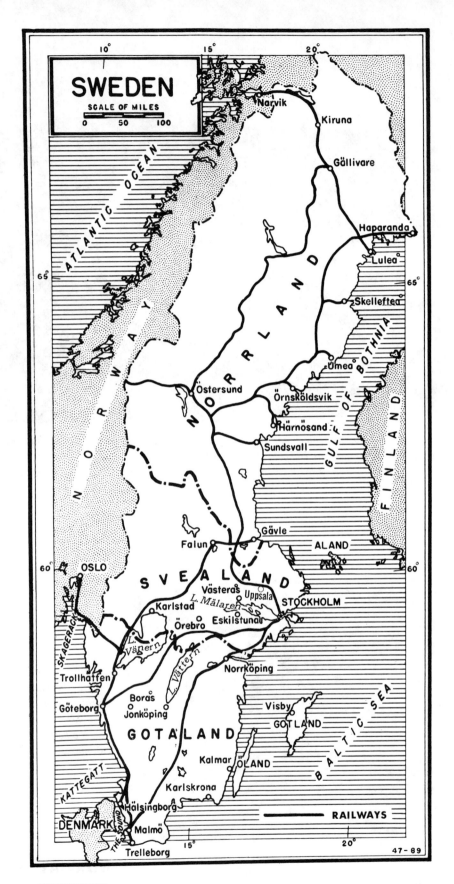

SWEDEN

SCALE OF MILES

0   50   100

ATLANTIC OCEAN

Narvik

Kiruna

Gällivare

Haparanda

Luleå

Skellefteå

Umeå

N O R R L A N D

Östersund

Örnsköldsvik

Härnösand

Sundsvall

GULF OF BOTHNIA

F I N L A N D

N O R W A Y

Gävle

Falun

ÅLAND

OSLO

S V E A L A N D

Västerås

Uppsala

L. Mälaren

STOCKHOLM

Karlstad

Örebro

Eskilstuna

L. Vänern

L. Vättern

SKAGERACK

Norrköping

Trollhätten

Borås

Jönköping

Visby

Göteborg

GOTLAND

G Ö T A L A N D

Kalmar

ÖLAND

B A L T I C   S E A

Karlskrona

KATTEGATT

Hälsingborg

RAILWAYS

DENMARK

THE SOUND

Malmö

Trelleborg

47-89

216 ■ SWEDEN

The Vikings left rune stones like this one in Ostergötland wherever they went. They usually bore terse statements like: "Erik the good conquered his rival Olav Bloodyaxe here and cut down 160 men." Runes are the earliest surviving Swedish writing, dating back to about A.D. 800.

SWEDEN

HISTORY

ABOUT 12,000 B.C. the land that is now Sweden began to emerge from the retreating icecap, and tribes of hunters and fishermen started moving in from the south. The fossil remains of these people indicate that they were of the same Nordic type as modern Scandinavians.

Sometime around 1500 B.C., a native skill at metal handicrafts developed. The beautiful urns, ornaments and weapons which have been found show that the art of working in bronze nearly equalled that of Greece. Such archaeological finds are increasingly filling the great gulfs of unknown history of these early times.

In Roman times the Götar (thought to be a branch of the Goths) inhabited the south of Sweden. In the 5th century A.D., the Goths took part in the great migrations as far south as the Black Sea, coming into contact with the Byzantine and Roman world. Goths returning

to the Baltic brought writing with them. Uppsala, now known as Old Uppsala and a village near modern Uppsala, became the capital of Sweden's other leading tribe, the Svear. A few centuries later, the Uppsala kings ruled both the Götar and the Svear, uniting the country under one crown.

THE VIKING ERA

Soon after A.D. 800, Norsemen became seafarers on a world scale. Each spring, these Vikings (which loosely meant "sea warriors") set out in their long narrow ships, powered by oars and a single square sail, on long expeditions to exchange goods, but killing and plundering if they met with resistance.

The Vikings of Denmark and southwestern Sweden directed their voyages towards Europe, the Norwegian Vikings crossed the Atlantic to

A relic of prehistoric Sweden, this stone tomb, "Hagerdösen," is 5,000 years old. It is on the Isle of Orust north of Göteborg.

Iceland, Greenland, and finally to America, while most of the Swedish Vikings sailed eastward across the Baltic Sea to Russia, whose very name, from *Rus*, applied to Swedes from the Baltic Coast, is supposed to date from the first régime the Vikings set up under their chieftain Rurik.

The ultimate aim of every young Viking voyager was to be a "berserk," that is, to fight without a shirt of mail or a shield, hurling himself into the fray with only a sword as a weapon. Most of our knowledge of these invaders comes from the lands they pillaged so ruthlessly for almost 200 years, since there are few actual Viking records. Consequently, their image has always been one of a brutal, uncivilized people, but in recent years more and more evidence has been unearthed revealing that the Norsemen did indeed have a developed culture, though one vastly different from its contemporaries in other parts of Europe. Their contribution to military and governmental concepts was considerable.

St. Olav, the patron saint of Norway and the subject of church murals all over Scandinavia, was a particularly bloodthirsty warrior. Olav the Big, as he was called, ruled from 1015 to 1030 and converted his subjects to Christianity by the sheer power of the axe. A battle he fought with his own rebellious subjects ended with his being axed himself (as in the painting). There was a total eclipse of the sun at the time, "proving" that Olav's deity was angry. Compared with the misrule of his successor, the reign of Olav rendered him eligible for sainthood in 1164.

218 ■ **SWEDEN**

The Abbey Church at Värnhem, completed in 1250 and recently restored, contains the tombs of 12th- and 13th-century kings.

MIDDLE AGES

During the Viking Age of the 9th and 10th centuries, Christian missionaries under St. Ansgar visited Sweden, but it was not until the end of the 11th century, when the magnificent, gold-hung temple of the Norse gods at Uppsala was levelled to the ground, that Christianity was really accepted. Small Christian churches began to dot the countryside. One of the most famous of Sweden's older temples is the beautiful Abbey Church that Saint Bridget built at Vadstena in the 14th century.

The Hanseatic League, a medieval association of trading towns based mainly in Germany, had by this time extended into Scandinavia. Visby in Gotland was a major city of the League. There were ceremonies, some of them sadistic, for merchants joining the League, and their power in imposing trade monopolies was often absolute.

When the weak King Erik died in 1250, his brother-in-law, the remarkable Birger Jarl, took over control of Sweden, ruling in the name of his son until his death in 1266. He created excellent domestic laws with peace as the keynote: "family peace," "church peace," and "peace in the government." Birger Jarl, the founder of Stockholm, was able to deal decisively with the Hanseatic League, then running rampant over Scandinavia. Instead of letting the League wreck Sweden's economy as it had Norway's, he was able to trade with it, finally establishing a strong central government. Birger Jarl's influence is felt to this day.

The idea of a united Scandinavia gave birth to the Union of Kalmar in 1397 when Denmark, Norway and Sweden agreed to unite. However, the Union was uneasy; power struggles and nationalism nourished by efforts to establish an absolute monarchy, always threatened to upset it. Sweden, fearing Denmark's domination, rebelled and wars followed, although the union between Denmark and Norway lasted until 1814.

Gustavus Adolphus, born in 1594, became king in 1611 and led a tremendous political and military expansion until his death in 1632. He had great personal influence, due in large part to his good education, his strong character and the exceptional assistance of his chancellor of state, Count Axel Oxenstjerna.

Another remarkable man in early Swedish history, mine-owner Engelbrekt Engelbrektsson, led a popular revolt against the Danish Union in 1435. This resulted in the representation of farmers and burghers in parliament, showing that the feudal system had not taken a firm hold in Sweden.

Many obstacles had to be met before national freedom was achieved. Attacks by the Danes penetrated to the very walls of Stockholm in 1471, and in 1520 Christian II of Denmark occupied that capital. That same year, 80 leading noblemen were massacred in the central square, a tragedy known as the "Stockholm Blood Bath."

NATIONAL LIBERTY

Out of this revolt a young nobleman, whose father had been one of the 80 beheaded, emerged to lead a peasant rebellion. Gustavus Vasa, called the "Builder of the Swedish Realm" because he laid the foundations of modern Sweden, drove the Danes out of Sweden in two years. He was elected king in 1523 and began one of the greatest eras in Swedish history. With the Protestant Reformation sweeping Europe, he established a Lutheran state church and placed mining, agriculture and commerce on a sound footing. Gustavus and his three sons, who one after the other succeeded him, were all great builders.

The powerful regent, Birger Jarl, first fortified Stockholm against raiding pirates in 1252, locking off the entrance to Lake Mälaren.

Christina was recognized as queen in 1632, when she was still a minor. Count Axel Oxenstjerna undertook the regency and it was not until 1644 that Christina came of age. Ten years later she abdicated, became a Catholic, and took up residence in Rome, where she died in 1689.

GUSTAVUS ADOLPHUS

Gustavus Adolphus, coming to the throne in 1611 at the age of 17, is sometimes called the "Northern Hurricane." Inheriting from his father three wars—against Denmark, Russia and Poland—he finally concluded them all with treaties. In 1630, his big moment came. The Hapsburg Empire, supporting the Roman Catholic cause, was in deadly conflict with the German Protestants. Fearing that the Hapsburgs might threaten Sweden after their invasion of Denmark, Gustavus Adolphus took the offensive with 16,000 men to rescue Protestantism. He made a victorious march through Leipzig, Nuremberg, Munich and Augsburg. In 1632, his army also won the terrible battle at Lutzen against the imperial army, but the king himself was killed. Gustavus Adolphus has remained, to this day, the Swedes' most highly regarded monarch.

Gustavus Adolphus's daughter, Christina, succeeded her father when she came of age in 1644, and became a zealous, if unpopular, monarch. Seriously interested in the arts and learning, she granted moneys and lands lavishly to artists and scholars whom she liked. In 1654, having been secretly converted to Catholicism, she abdicated and left the country, settling in Rome. She left financial disorder behind her.

On the Swedish throne Christina was succeeded by her cousin, Charles X, who became another great warrior king. Under him Sweden acquired its natural boundaries to the south and southwest, at the expense of Denmark. In 1660, Charles X was succeeded by his son, Charles XI, who devoted himself primarily to administration and finance.

For 80 years Sweden was a great power, but new wars followed under the gallant young monarch Charles XII, and Sweden's star began to set. The king, like Hitler and Napo-

The young Gustavus Eriksson, who became the great King Gustavus I Vasa, rallied the peasants of Dalarna (Delacarlia) in 1520. One province after another came to his support, and he eventually won all of Sweden back from Denmark. He is therefore known as the founder of modern Sweden.

Drottningholm Palace, near Stockholm, had this charming theatre attached to it in 1764–66. It was the scene of much gaiety during the reign of Gustavus III, who himself wrote verse dramas for it and sometimes acted in them. The theatre is still used, as are the original costumes and stage sets. The wings were painted in 1784 by Jacob Mörck.

leon, made the fatal mistake of invading the heart of Russia and in 1709, he was badly defeated in the Battle of Poltava. Charles himself, wounded, escaped to Turkey. Returning to Sweden to fight Denmark with a new army, he was killed, while attacking the Norwegian fortress of Fredrikssten.

Although the Swedish dream of empire was over, a bloodless revolution had vested parliament with greater powers. The country, exhausted by war, found its new leader in Count Arvid Horn. Under his administration, 18th-century Sweden had a quick economic and spiritual recovery which led to a cultural renaissance in natural sciences and literature. Linnaeus, the father of botany, Celsius, who perfected the centigrade thermometer, and Swedenborg, the scientist and mystic, were three of the outstanding men who emerged.

On this wave of the fine arts, Gustavus III ascended the throne in 1771 and became Sweden's most courtly monarch, the "Actor King." He formed the Swedish Academy in imitation of the French, and developed the beautiful Drottningholm Court Theatre for staging plays and operas, but above all, he dreamed of raising Sweden again to a great power. The Russians, he thought, were threatening Finland and hoping to conquer Sweden. When Gustavus had won a great naval battle in 1790, they were forced to sign a peace without territorial change. Two years later, the king was assassinated by some disgruntled officers at a costume ball at the Opera House.

In 1809, Finland, long part of the Swedish realm and closely tied to Sweden politically, culturally, economically and linguistically, was

lost to Russia. The shock to the country was deep. Yet soon after this darkest hour a brilliant new figure appeared.

THE BERNADOTTE ASCENSION

The new leader was Jean Baptiste Bernadotte, who had been one of Napoleon's marshals and was to become the first of the present line of kings. His ascension to the throne came about by the merest fluke.

Gustavus IV Adolphus, the obstinate and unbalanced son of Gustavus III, had a venomous hatred of Napoleon and sided with England against him. After the loss of Finland to Russia, Sweden was in a desperate situation.

The Danes seemed ready to attack from the south and the west, while the Russians were preparing to pounce from the north. In Sweden's anguish, a revolution was raised to

The 14th-century cathedral at Lund boasts this beautiful astronomical clock with jousting knights on top, the four rulers of the winds and the signs of the zodiac. When the clock plays at noon the carved horsemen go into action. Lund is also famous for its open-air museum showing how people have lived since Viking times. ——▶

Jean Baptiste Bernadotte, as King Charles XIV John, founded the present dynasty. A brilliant general in the French Revolution and later one of Napoleon's marshals, Bernadotte was chosen by the Swedish government to succeed the old and childless Charles XIII. This equestrian statue of Charles XIV is one of the popular sights of ◀—— *Stockholm.*

get rid of the monarch, and Colonel Aldersparre marched on Stockholm to arrest him. The king tried to escape and was actually chased throughout the palace before being caught and imprisoned in one of his summer castles.

The aged and childless Charles XIII was temporarily put on the throne while Sweden looked for a new king to found another dynasty. The first choice was Christian August, a Danish prince, who had dreams of restoring the old union of Scandinavia, but shortly after his arrival in Sweden he fell off his horse and died. Many Swedes suspected that Count Hans Axel Fersen, who had gallantly tried to rescue Marie Antoinette from the French guillotine, had caused the "accident." He was unjustly accused and dragged from his carriage by a drunken mob and killed in broad daylight—one of the saddest deeds in Sweden's history.

Skåne or Scania, which gives its name to Scandinavia, is the "Château Country." One of the most exciting of the medieval castles to be seen is Vittskövle, a private fortified stronghold with a moat, watchtower and drawbridge.

The country, obviously sick, needed new blood. Marshal Jean Bernadotte, who had been made Prince of Ponte Corvo by Napoleon, had led the French troops against Denmark and thus became known in Sweden. An enthusiastic lieutenant, Karl Mörner, was so convinced that only Bernadotte could restore the Swedish nation that he rushed to Paris and offered the crown to the former sergeant from Pau. Bernadotte, believing Mörner was Sweden's official emissary, accepted, and Mörner rushed back to give the good news to an astonished parliament. The Swedes had found a new candidate—one whom, so they believed, Napoleon himself was backing.

This misunderstanding pursued its fateful course when Bernadotte sent a French agent to the Swedish court to drop a loaded hint that France would help the destitute Swedes financially. A last-minute decision was made, when indeed Sweden's destiny hung by a thread, and Bernadotte became the real leader of Sweden in the autumn of 1810, when he was adopted by Charles XIII as heir apparent.

Thus began Sweden's present dynasty. Bernadotte soon proved to be an astute and successful ruler. Siding with Napoleon's enemies, he led an army against the Danes, forcing Denmark to cede Norway to Sweden. When the Norwegians balked, Charles John, as Bernadotte was now called, marched his soldiers to the border and forced Norway to capitulate. Norway united with Sweden under one king in a union which lasted until 1905, when it was peaceably dissolved.

In 1818, after the Congress of Vienna which ended the Napoleonic era, Bernadotte was crowned Charles XIV. From this time until the present, Sweden has not gone to war.

MODERN SWEDEN

By the middle of the 19th century, Sweden was again rocked within its borders, this time by the spread of poverty. The old farming economy had slumped and it was a time of general despair and intellectual decline. Large groups of people began leaving for America; yet new forces were at work in Sweden, and the delayed industrial revolution started. Steam-driven sawmills, expanding trade, increased urbanization and better transportation all helped to transform the country. Electoral reforms, the emergence of unions and a redefinition by the Swedes of their rôle in the world were all signs of Sweden's modernization.

August Strindberg, the prolific writer, novelist and playwright, was one of the prime movers in this era. He reacted fiercely against all forms of national complacency and put the people rather than their rulers on the stage. While the country's modernization was not quick enough to stop the drain of Sweden's population to America, the country entered into a period of growing prosperity.

Ever since the mid-1800's, Sweden has been growing more liberal in government and stronger in industrial development. After freedom of the press had been achieved, internal free trade and enfranchisement of the middle class followed. In the early 1900's, the Social Democratic party began its rise, later to become the predominant political entity in Sweden.

Under Gustavus V, king from 1907 until 1950, Sweden's liberalizing and development were continued, and social reforms of a new type began. Universal suffrage for men was introduced in 1909, and in 1913 the long process of welfare legislation began with old-age pension laws. At the same time, the Swedes became more determined to make neutrality the basis of their foreign policy. Sweden did not fight in either World War I or World War II, and is striving at the present time to ensure survival in case of a new war. It has not joined the North Atlantic Treaty Organization, although it is a member of the United Nations and many other international bodies.

Drottningholm, built in 1662–81 in the French style, is open to the public when the Royal Family is not in residence. The interior decor is especially fine, and the impressive park attracts many strollers.

Stockholm's City Hall, St. Clara's Church spire, and the skyscrapers of the Hötorget shopping centre are silhouetted against the darkened sky.

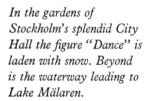

In the gardens of Stockholm's splendid City Hall the figure "Dance" is laden with snow. Beyond is the waterway leading to Lake Mälaren.

The origins of Stockholm are unknown. One Viking saga says that Agne, a warrior king, went off on a raid to Finland where he killed a chieftain and captured his daughter. On his way home he stopped on an island to drink the health of his new bride. Mead flowed freely. Agne fell asleep, and his bride freed her fellow Finnish prisoners, who promptly hanged Agne before sailing home. The shore where they stopped was called Agne Strand and is now part of Old Stockholm.

THE LAND

THE KINGDOM OF SVERIGE occupies nearly 175,000 square miles of the Scandinavian peninsula. Most of the larger rivers of this elongated country flow southeast from the mountainous spine through dense forests of spruce and fir and empty into the Gulf of Bothnia.

Sweden is divided geographically into three regions. Götaland in the south has its shores washed by the warm waters of the Gulf Stream and includes some of the chief ports of Sweden; Svealand, just north of the largest lakes, is called "central" Sweden although it is really within the bottom half of the country. Here Stockholm is located. Norrland covers well over half of Sweden, including mountainous Lapland, and borders on Norway, Finland and the Gulf of Bothnia. Sweden thus presents a wide variety of landscape: the fertile plains of the south, the wooded lake country, the seven-league forests of the north, and, finally, the barren slopes of the Arctic area.

Gripsholm Castle on Lake Mälaren is a three-hour steamer trip from Stockholm. Begun in the 1300's and rebuilt by Gustavus Vasa in 1535, Gripsholm houses a remarkable picture gallery, including the portrait that the sad King Erik XIV sent to Queen Elizabeth of England after his second proposal to her. Upon his dethronement he was held captive in the prison tower. Gustavus III, the "Actor King," built the little theatre attached to the castle. The courtyard is celebrated for its rune stones and the bronze cannon taken centuries ago in the Russian wars.

Iron, wood and water—these three words sum up Sweden's natural wealth. The great rivers, winding down through the massive forests, are harnessed to power stations to supply industry with its greatest resource, cheap electricity.

Since Götaland, Svealand and Norrland are very different in character, we will take them in turn, beginning with Svealand, the cradle of the country.

SVEALAND

Lying between Norrland and Götaland are the heartlands of Sweden. One of the oldest known important settlements is Uppsala, the university town north of Stockholm. Uppsala has witnessed 1,500 years of history, first as a religious capital of the Norsemen, as a political capital, as a Christian see, and then as an educational stronghold. One thousand years have passed since the Vikings made their last sacrifices to Thor, Odin, and Freya, the gods of war, wisdom and domesticity, in a temple hung with gold, and while Uppsala is now the seat of the Lutheran Archbishop of Sweden and of Uppsala University, the political power of the country has moved to Stockholm.

The city of Stockholm, placed on the waters, faces two directions, eastward across the islands of its archipelago to the Baltic Sea and westward over the fresh-water reaches of Lake Mälaren. Where the two meet, sea and lake, is Sweden's capital, "the knot of many waters." It was founded on an island about 1250 by Birger Jarl as a "padlock" to keep the Estonian pirates across the Baltic from raiding Lake Mälaren. The two expressions, "knot of many waters," and "padlock," describe Stockholm's physical appearance and stragetic site. Here the king in his island palace can watch almost every ship that docks nearby. Stockholm, with a population of about 800,000 and another 700,000 in the suburbs, is justly called "Queen of the Waters."

Svealand, with Stockholm guarding the eastern gateway, includes most of the central Lake District. Many of the 100,000 lakes in the country are here, wholly or in part. The three largest are Lake Mälaren, Lake Vättern and Lake Vänern, the third largest lake in Europe.

The picturesque Göta Canal is a 250-mile network of lakes, rivers and canals across the country from Stockholm to Göteborg. It was proposed in 1516 by Bishop Brask, principally to avoid paying the toll that Denmark levied on all shipping passing through the narrow straits between Malmö and Copenhagen. What is now southern Sweden was then part of Denmark and the powerful Danes had complete control of the straits. It was not until 1832, however, that the Göta Canal was completed. Today it is a popular tourist route.

Göteborg (Gothenburg), Sweden's gateway to the West, is a bustling port at the mouth of the Göta River on the Kattegat, the strait leading by way of the North Sea to the Atlantic. Founded in 1619 by Gustavus Adolphus, Göteborg has a population of about 425,000 and a big shipbuilding industry. At that time, the mouth of the Göta River, closely bounded by Norway on one side and Denmark on the other, was Sweden's only outlet to the Atlantic. This precious corridor the king protected still further with a deep moat and a broad canal. A statue of Gustavus Adolphus stands in Göteborg central square as though he still surveyed his handiwork with pride.

Included in discussions of central Sweden is Gotland, an island in the Baltic Sea. Visby, the walled capital of the island, with a history of 40 centuries, is a "city of ruins and roses." Its

Stockholm's white marble Royal Dramatic Theatre houses the top plays. Theatre, opera and ballet are all subsidized by the State, and touring companies carry "Hamlet" and other productions even to the Lapps in the North.

Lund, primarily a university town, was founded nearly 1,000 years ago by King Canute, the Dane who conquered England and Scotland and also ruled most of Scandinavia. The University of Lund has an enrolment of about 7,000.

golden ages were from the 11th to the 14th centuries, during which it was the hub of trade with Russia, Constantinople and the Byzantine Empire.

North of Sweden's great lakes Vättern and Vänern lie the areas of Värmland and Dalarna. Dalarna, where many of the inhabitants still wear traditional costume and fiddlers play music for the Maypole dancers on Midsummer Day, is considered Sweden's most idyllic region. The word *Dalarna* means valleys—the lake and river valleys in the evergreen fir forests.

Falun, the name of both a city and a copper mine, is the heart of Dalarna. Here the oldest company in the world, Stora Kopparbergs Bergslags Aktiebolag, has been in business mining the ore since at least the 13th century, and the riches of the copper mine have financed many imperial adventures over the last 700 years. Falun's ore is also used in producing the

characteristic red paint which covers so many Swedish farmhouses.

GÖTALAND

Götaland, the second large region of Sweden, includes the historic provinces of Skåne and Småland, at the extreme southern tip of the peninsula. There is an old tradition that while the Lord was busy making Skåne, the southern tip of Sweden, into a beautiful garden, the devil sneaked past him and made Småland a harsh, unyielding stretch of country. When the Lord saw what the devil had done, he said philosophically, "Oh, well, it's too late now to change Småland. I'll have to make people to go with it!" A man of Småland, the saying goes, can be put down on a stone island with only an axe in his hand and will turn it into a garden.

Skåne, close to Denmark, *is* really a garden and was for centuries part of the Danish realm.

Not until 1658, when Charles X threatened to attack Copenhagen, did the Swedes force Denmark to give up the historic provinces of Skåne, Halland, Blekinge and Bohuslän.

Many of the people of Halland, with strong Danish ties, still regard Copenhagen as their logical capital and are less ready than other Swedes to accept the dictates of the central government in Stockholm.

Malmö, the third largest city of Sweden, with a population of more than 235,000, faces Copenhagen across the "Oresund" (the Sound), connecting the Kattegat to the Baltic Sea. Now an important port, Malmö, while actually meaning "sandy island" is legendarily named after a miller's daughter who refused a king. In revenge, he had her ground between two millstones (*mäl-mo*, or "ground maiden").

Just as Götenborg remembers Gustavus Adolphus, Malmö has in its central square a fine statue of Charles X, who brought Malmö into Swedish control in 1658.

Ten miles inland is Lund, the archiepiscopal see for all Scandinavia before 1536. King Canute, the Danish king of England, founded the city and called it Londinium Gothorum, to distinguish it from Londinium, the Roman name of the capital of England. The University of Lund has been famous for hundreds of years, and Lund is also an important publishing city.

Kalmar, the magnificent Renaissance castle on the coast of Småland facing the island of Öland, has been called the "lock and key" of Sweden, and it once dominated all the Baltic shipping.

Here at Kalmar the Union was signed in 1397, an attempt to unite all Scandinavia under one ruler. However, after an uneasy period of civil wars, Kalmar fell to the Danes. In 1638, the *Kalmar Nyckel*, a three-masted sailing ship, sailed from Kalmar to North America with settlers who established a colony on the Delaware River.

The Island of Öland is famous for its wind-

Kalmar is a name that rings through Scandinavian history. It was at 12th-century Kalmar Castle that the Kalmar Union was effected in 1397, combining the crowns of Denmark, Sweden and Norway. Sweden left the Union in 1523, and in the 16th and 17th centuries there were numerous sieges by the Danes during their wars with Sweden. The city of Kalmar was destroyed several times, but the castle withstood all attacks.

mills, its rune stones and for the number of its inhabitants who emigrated to the United States during Sweden's "America fever," most of whom, however, returned to Öland. Here, legend has it, the hero Beowulf is buried. The legend of Beowulf was immortalized in the epic written in Old English before A.D. 1000.

In our journeying across Sweden we must use one or two unusual words—*skerries*, the little rock islands scattered along the coast; *fjells* or fells, bare hills; and *bruk*, a small clearing in the woods where some local industry is going on. At Orrefors, an old bottle-works in a clearing in the forest became within a few years one of the greatest names in glass. Through brilliant designers like Simon Gate and Edvard Hald, Orrefors glass is known all over the world.

NORRLAND

The northern highlands, ranging from central Sweden up through the Arctic Circle, are where the real wealth of the country lies—wood, ore, white coal (sawn timber), iron mines and fast flowing water. It is surprising, therefore, that Norrland supports only 17 per cent of the population. The old peasant culture of the river valleys and the coastal regions, deeply rooted in the Middle Ages, survives here together with the older civilization of the nomadic Lapps. In much of Norrland, the sun never sets during the summer.

North of Dalarna are densely wooded areas, and along the coast of the Gulf of Bothnia are several ports, the major cities of northern Sweden. Gävle, at the southern edge of Norr-

Prince Eugen, third son of the late King Gustavus V, was an outstanding painter and collector. Walde-marsudde, his home on one of Stockholm's islands, became a picture gallery and public garden after his death.

Gränna, a small town on the eastern shores of Lake Vättern in Götaland, is set in the heart of some of Sweden's loveliest country.

land, is the oldest and largest city in the upper two-thirds of Sweden. Sundsvall is an important port, while Härnösand and Ümeå are cultural hubs of Norrland. The farther north the port is, the longer it is icebound each year, but Luleå, far into the north, manages to remain an important ore-shipping port.

In every northern river the felled trees lie as plentiful as matchsticks, awaiting the spring thaw to take them miles down to the coastal sawmills. The pounding white water drives the turbines to create electricity, but among the greatest riches of Lapland are the huge iron mountains of Kiruna.

Kiruna, a Lapp word meaning "mountain grouse," is a town of 30,000 inhabitants. The two mountains Kiirunavaara (grouse mountain) and Luossavaara (salmon mountain) produce over 15 million tons of iron ore annually.

While the term "Lapland" refers to a vast territory inhabited by the Lapps that includes parts of Norway, Finland and Russia, the heart of Lapland is in Sweden. The reindeer have long been domesticated and the nomadic Lapps accompany them on their annual migrations between summer grazing on the fjells and winter encampments in the woods.

Surprisingly, the tiny mosquito is the Lapps' best friend. When the reindeer fawns are born in mid-May, the parent reindeer, after eating lichen throughout the long northern winter, are in need of good grass. After three weeks, when the fawn can walk, the summer hatching of mosquitoes drives the herds from the forests in search of the alpine grass their bodies need.

Karesuando, the most northerly Swedish Lapp settlement, consists of a scattered community of wooden dwellings, a Lapp church and a store.

The Three Crowns Flour Mill works far into the night. Modern factories and greater automation help keep Sweden's industries flourishing.

THE ECONOMY

TODAY, Sweden is a great economic power, second only to Britain in the European Free Trade Association. Agriculture has been replaced by industry as the mainstay of Sweden's economy. Since 1900, the industrial capacity of Sweden has multiplied by more than five times, and now only 8 per cent of the workers are still employed in agriculture.

Although 90 per cent of the work force are employed by private companies, Sweden's government participates in many economic activities, as do the co-operatives, which are operated mainly by consumers in the retailing field and by farmers in marketing and purchasing. The state is most active in service indus-

tries, such as rail and bus lines, power, the post office, telephones, radio and television (the latter owned by a subsidiary company of the State alcohol monopoly). The extensive state-owned forests own factories for the manufacture of wooden houses and other wooden goods, competing with privately owned firms. Most state-owned enterprises are *aktiebolag* (joint stock corporations) and are subject to the Swedish Corporations Act. Often having a proportion of private stockholders, they enjoy no privileges over private corporations.

The state has a half-share in SAS, the joint Swedish-Danish-Norwegian airline, and 42 per cent of the electric power in the country is

The glass industry is still dependent upon the skills of individual artisans. Here a master craftsman examines his almost finished crystal bowl.

AGRICULTURE

Only 10 per cent of Sweden's land is arable (compared to 30 per cent in Britain, and 60 per cent in Denmark) and supporting the entire population was for many years a major problem. However, with hard work, expert soil study, upgrading of fertilizers and breeding, crop rotation and mechanization, the problem has been successfully met. Every year more and more people leave the farms for the cities, but every year the yield from agriculture goes up. It is truly remarkable that Sweden has remained self-sufficient agriculturally.

FORESTS AND FOREST PRODUCTS

Three factors are responsible for the healthy state of Sweden's forest industries: rich pine and fir stands; the rivers flowing southeastward down the mountains, which in the past provided cheap transportation for the timber although today most of the logs are hauled by road; and, very important also, excellent conservation measures, such as selective cutting

produced in state plants. The state also owns all the ore deposits in Upper Norrland in the north of the country. Yet free enterprise is maintained as the basis of the system, and relatively few industries have been nationalized.

Iron, wood and water—out of these three resources the Swedes have created their economy. The rich copper mine at Falun which brought the Swedes such wealth is worked out, but the huge new mines discovered in Lapland have replaced it. Even more important and forever being replenished are the forests that cover more than half the country and provide many of Sweden's exports—timber, pulp and paper. The rivers, cascading through the forests, provide electric power for the nation's industries.

Exports are very important, for the money earned from these allows Sweden to import the materials it needs for industry and private use. The traditional liberal trading regulations and low tariffs have helped foreign trade prosper.

New milking machines are tested at an experimental farm.

The forests are Sweden's wealth. The logs are brought to the processing mills by both river and road.

and systematic replanting, which have allowed logging to increase without depleting the forests severely.

In addition to the large lumber industry, the wood is also used to make pulp and paper. Several inventions by Swedish engineers, now spread round the world, helped Sweden establish its importance in these fields many years ago. Especially important is cellulose, or chemical wood pulp, of which Sweden is a leading producer.

Once responsible for one-third of the world's iron output, Sweden was hurt by the discovery of coal as a smelting agent. Yet it has fought to

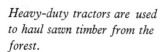

Heavy-duty tractors are used to haul sawn timber from the forest.

An aluminium ingot is re-melted at the Finspong Metal Works. The furnaces there can melt up to ← 100 tons per day.

maintain its importance as a steel producer by turning to high quality steel and exporting the iron ore to other ore-poor countries. The steel is used by Sweden in many of its industries, such as in the manufacture of ball bearings, razor blades and saws. In addition to iron ore, zinc as well as lead and copper are mined in Sweden.

SHIPBUILDING

Sweden has expanded its shipbuilding so much since World War II that it usually ranks among the top three building nations each year, although the industry receives no government subsidy. The majority of the ships are sold to Norway, other major customers being the USSR and Great Britain.

The old economy and the new—the water-power station on the Indalsälven, one of the great power-producing rivers of Sweden. In the foreground a farmer rakes his hay with one horse-power.

Göteborg's economy is largely dependent on the sea. Shipbuilding has been an industry of the city for hundreds of years, and new boats are built for many different countries.

Fiddlers play and the country folk dance in the traditional costume of 1850 Värmland.

THE PEOPLE

THERE ARE IN SWEDEN nearly 8,000,000 people, less than the population of either London or New York, but more than that of Denmark and Norway combined.

A joke about Swedish formality and love of titles is that told of two passengers on a ship, who wishing to speak, but finding no way of knowing each other's status, hit on the idea of addressing each other as "Mr. Steamship Passenger." This is one side of the picture. The other is of a well-balanced people, reserved yet passionate, a tall, sombre, good-looking people with innate good taste that is reflected in their architecture, their design and, above all, in their way of living.

Another insight into the Swedish character is gained by contrasting them with their fellow Scandinavians. The Danes call themselves the French of the Baltic; the Norwegians are wilder and happy-go-lucky; the Finns, from their long struggle for statehood, are stubborn and individualistic; while the Swedes, with Germanic efficiency and orderliness, are really full of enthusiasm once their reserve is pierced. The northern Swedes, however, still-faced and slant-eyed, have something of Mongolian impassivity.

Perhaps the greatest single talent of the Swedes is for organization, for managing to run things as frictionlessly, efficiently and practically as possible despite every difficulty. For instance, in spite of the enormously high wages and taxes industrialists must pay, Sweden can still export successfully and even compete successfully, as they do with the Japanese in shipbuilding. Setbacks and obstacles are immediately met with rationalization.

There are disadvantages to the Swedish passion for orderliness, however. The most characteristic of all Swedish words is said to be *kontrollstyrelse*, which means controlling authority, and the best illustration of this is the enormously elaborate structure of the government, with its ministries, governmental institutes, state departments, commissions, committees, secretariats, inspectorates, and so on. These account in large measure for the heavy burden of the taxpayer. If our two steamship passengers mentioned above found themselves shipwrecked on a desert island, it is highly likely they would immediately set up a kontrollstyrelse in order to rationalize their life together.

EDUCATION AND WELFARE

Sweden has almost no illiteracy—nearly every person can read and write. Responsible for this wonderful record are the compulsory education laws and the great value the Swedish people themselves place on education.

Since 1842, every Swedish child has had to go to school for at least 7 years. Recently, the State School system has introduced the 9-year compulsory school all over the country, aiming to give every child a chance to obtain a higher as well as a primary education. The Ministry of Education has also been moving to make the local provinces responsible for the schools, with the State inspectors as servants, rather than directors, of the schools.

The compulsory 9-year schools take pupils from 7 to 16, while the upper secondary schools, called *gymnasiums*, allow about 25 per cent of the students (at present) to continue their education another three years. It is expected that by 1970 the proportion will rise to at least 30 per cent, and that at least a further 20 per cent will attend continuation schools (*fackskolor*) for two years' general theoretical instruction in semi-industrial or vocational training schools, or full-time courses at vocational schools (*yrkes-skolor*).

These wee folk are not the "little people" the Laplanders say they sometimes see, but pupils at a nursery school.

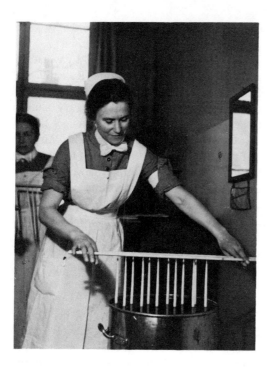

Candle-making for Christmas is not a job but a joy for this nurse. Repeated dipping of the wicks in tallow-grease gives the candles their shape. Candles in Sweden are the best way of lighting up Christmas, which falls close to the dark days of ← the winter solstice.

are special supplements to help needy mothers provide adequately for their children. Largely as a result of this scheme, nearly every child is born in a hospital and the infant mortality rate is among the lowest in the world.

WORKMEN'S COMPENSATION

Every employee in Sweden knows that if he is injured on the job or off, he will receive enough money to preserve the living standard of himself and his family.

CHILD CARE

Sweden feels that its children are especially important and must be taken care of as adequately as possible. Some of the governmental services for their benefit are free medical checkups; free dental care; free school lunches in most schools; scholarships to allow higher education; vocational training for poor children; housing subsidies to the parents so they can provide adequate housing for their family; free vacation travel money for children and

COMPULSORY HEALTH INSURANCE

Since 1955, every citizen has been covered by compulsory health insurance which provides compensation for income lost due to accident or illness and takes care of the total cost of hospital treatment, a large share of the cost of medicine and doctors' bills, and travel expense incurred in serious illness and hospitalization.

UNEMPLOYMENT INSURANCE

The government helps support the unemployment insurance funds of the trade unions and similar organizations, and pays directly the very few unemployed who are not in these groups.

MATERNITY BENEFITS

All pregnant mothers receive free prenatal care, free hospital service at delivery, and cash allowances for some time after delivery. There

Emanuel Swedenborg, one of the great 18th-century intellects, was an engineer, scientist, physicist, geologist, physiologist, philosopher and mystic. Unintentionally, he started a new religious movement which still has adherents, mainly in the United States and England. →

Ivar Kreuger, who was called the "Match King," founded the Swedish Match Company at Jönköping in 1917. His enormous swindles finally brought him to grief—his vast financial empire collapsed and he died by his own hand in 1932.

further severity is imposed. Open prisons, devoid of forbidding bars and resembling large farms, have replaced the old barred institutions to a great extent.

Sweden does not believe in breaking a prisoner's spirit, and a man may, through the work of his hands, make some restitution to whomever he has injured.

RELIGION AND FESTIVALS

Sweden, like the other Scandinavian countries, is overwhelmingly Protestant. The state church, the Church of Sweden, is Evangelical Lutheran. Over 90 per cent of the Swedes are baptized and married by the Church of Sweden, and there are only about 600,000 nonconformists to the prevailing religion—mostly in other branches of Protestantism.

their mother; subsidies for day nurseries and summer camps; and an allowance of about $56 (£23) to mothers for each child under 16. In addition to this government aid, many institutions and industrial corporations provide extensive social benefits for their employees.

PENAL LAWS

On July 1, 1946, a new law went into effect providing that prisoners should always be treated with regard to their dignity as human beings. There has been no execution since 1910 and in 1921 the death penalty was abolished. While half the male prisoners are sentenced to hard work (usually lumbering in the north) no

The Nobel Medals are awarded for eminence in physics, chemistry, physiology and medicine, and literature. The peace prize, when it is warranted, is also awarded. Alfred Nobel, inventor of dynamite, left a fund to provide the prizes named after him. ⟶

Going to church in the lake country of Dalarna often meant going by boat in old times, but now cycles and buses are preferred. On Midsummer Day, however, the old church-boats still put out with the villagers dressed in their finery.

Several of Sweden's biggest festivals are religious in origin. The most elaborate festival is Christmas, which lasts from Christmas Eve to Twelfth Night or even to St. Knut's Day on January 14. On New Year's Eve, the Swedes try to read their fortunes by interpreting the figures produced by molten lead poured into cold water. On New Year's Day everyone visits, and traditionally the governors, bishops and senior officials receive visits from their subordinates.

Lady Day, March 25, is devoted to the Virgin Mary. It falls near the spring equinox, when the day is as long as the night.

Easter brings out small girls with blackened faces astride broomsticks. This phenomenon results from the belief that the witches flew off on Maundy Thursday to confer with the Evil One.

Walpurgis Eve comes on April 30 with bonfire celebrations and a eulogy on the advent of spring, the spirit of the fire marking the sun's return. Walpurgis has survived from Viking times when the warriors held an annual feast to herald the return of spring, lighting bonfires on the hills and banging their sword hilts against their shields to frighten off evil spirits.

All Sweden awaits Midsummer Day with its tall, leaf-decked Maypoles, when everything is decorated with flowers and birch twigs. It is on Midsummer Eve that girls place seven different flowers under their pillows to dream of the man they will marry, hoping that on Midsummer Day, when all the costumes are put on for dancing round the Maypole, they will meet him in the *ringdans* (ring dance) or perhaps in the *långdans* (long dance). It was on Midsummer Day in 1623 that Gustavus Vasa liberated Sweden and entered Stockholm at the head of his troops.

Dag Hammarskjöld, the late Secretary-General of the United Nations, had bought a farm in Skåne to which he planned to retire, but he never reached it. The plane that was taking him to the Congo crashed and he was killed on Sept. 18, 1961.

U Thant paid respects at the grave of Dag Hammarskjöld in Uppsala, the town where the late Secretary-General of the United Nations was educated. The son of a prominent political family, Hammarskjöld entered government service in 1930. As Secretary-General from 1953–1961, he performed a service to the entire world, and he was awarded the Nobel Peace Prize posthumously in 1961.

The Water Lily House is typical of the stimulating architectural designs of modern Sweden. The roof of this house opens to sunlight like the petals of a water lily, but closes by the mere push of a button.

ARTS AND CRAFTS

For a thousand years, Swedish objects have been studied for their artistic values, but it has been in this century that Sweden has enjoyed its greatest influence on arts and crafts.

The beautiful old stone churches dating from before the Middle Ages were not just imitations of architecture in other countries; rather, prototypes were adapted to the Swedish landscape. The castles of the 16th century show the same adaptation, and, remarkably, even modern Swedish architecture, characterized by its simplicity and functional nature, is strongly suited to its Swedish setting. The Swedes think that design in buildings is important, and even the massive new apartment buildings and factories are often architectural gems.

Swedish sculpture has in recent years been identified with Carl Milles, but the wood and stone carvers on Gotland in the Middle Ages

were famous. The old churches of Gotland and the mainland of Sweden are still filled with the beautiful fonts, screens and images by these artists.

The Swedes apply the most lofty principles of beauty and design to even the simplest utensils and furnishings of daily life. With the innate Swedish love of things artistic, it is not surprising to find their greatest strength is in design. Sweden, an isolated and old agricultural country suddenly turned modern in a wave of rapid industrialization, has based clean new lines on the severe foundations of older traditions.

Isolation forced Sweden to develop its own resources (ironmaking, for example, goes back 2000 years) and from this springs the versatile uses of steel, wood, clay and glass. It must be remembered, too, that since Viking times sailors, tradesmen and merchants have brought

ally tried in Great Britain, while shopping centres arose in the United States in response to the acute problems arising from the growing use of private cars. Sweden, also faced with a relatively large number of private cars, found it best to apply town planning ideas to shopping centres and to make them real meeting places for the whole community. The most modern centres comprise not only department stores, supermarkets, and abundant smaller special shops but also public buildings, banks, libraries, theatres and cinemas, medical clinics and "doctors' houses"—where the town's specialists, dentists and general practitioners are all to be found under one roof—and post offices, kindergartens etc. Cars are banned within the centre, all its highways being for pedestrians only.

back goods and ideas to Sweden from all over the world.

Swedish society seldom gave room for feudal grandeur. The granite churches, the manor houses and the farms all have the mark of simplicity, almost of austerity. French influence during the 18th century helped to mellow this, and native art, together with the impulses of rising commerce and industry, have produced "Modern Swedish" design—in glass, ceramics, textiles, furniture, silver and stainless steel.

SHOPPING CENTRES

In connection with Sweden's town and country planning, the new suburban shopping centres have attracted much notice in other countries. Town planning schemes were origin-

An engraved decanter with stopper by the artist Palmquist.

The northern part of Sweden, including much territory within the Arctic Circle, is known as Lapland. The native Lapps are greatly outnumbered by descendants of settlers of the past few hundred years. Here a Lapp lady, on one knee, is milking a doe. Notice the spreading hoofs which prevent the reindeer from sinking through the snow.

LAPLANDERS

The origin of the Lapps, living in the far north of Scandinavia, is still something of a mystery but they are generally believed to have come from central Asia. Although they speak a form of the Finnish language, they are not Finns. They appear to be the first race to have inhabited Norrland. Thirty-four thousand Laplanders, all told, live in Sweden, Norway, Finland and the Kola Peninsula of Russia. Sweden has about 10,000 of them, many of whom are nomads tending their reindeer herds.

While Sweden educates the young Lapp children in nomad schools which follow the herds, the older children must attend "anchored" schools in the forest.

Laplanders are allowed all the reindeer they wish, although a Swede may have no more than 20 in a herd, for the reindeer is the very life-blood of the Lapps. Besides being a very handsome animal, both male and female having large antlers, the reindeer is a draught animal. The flesh provides venison; the doe gives milk which can be made into cheese, the bones make implements; and the skins make warm clothing and tents.

Their skin tents are easily movable and hauled on the boat-like sled (*gieres*) behind their reindeer. Other equipment is the pack-frame (*spagat*), the ski and the lasso. Archaeological finds have established that the Lapps used the ski as far back as the Stone Age. The lasso is also used by the Russian Samoyeds and the American Indians.

The Lapps, nominally Christian, brightly clad in their scarlet, yellow and blue dress, sometimes take their dogs with them into church. "Why shouldn't they come in to talk to God, too?" they ask.

"The Hand of God," sculpted by Carl Milles, is displayed on Lidingö Island near Stockholm. Milles, who died in 1955, was perhaps the most famous Swedish-born artist of the 20th century.

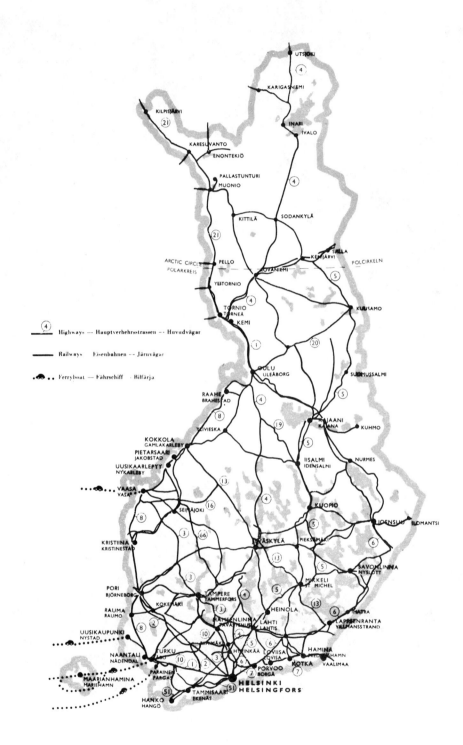

UTSJOKI
④
KARIGASNIEMI
KILPISJÄRVI
㉑
INARI
IVALO
KARESUVANTO
ENONTEKIÖ
PALLASTUNTURI
MUONIO
④
KITTILÄ
SODANKYLÄ
㉑
SALLA
KEMIJÄRVI
ARCTIC CIRCLE
PELLO
POLCIRKELN
POLARKREIS
ROVANIEMI
⑤
YLITORNIO
KUUSAMO
④
TORNIO
TORNEÅ
KEMI

④ Highways — Hauptverkehrsstrassen — Huvudvägar
①
⑳
——— Railways — Eisenbahnen — Järnvägar
OULU
ULEÅBORG
SUOMUSSALMI
••• Ferryboat — Fährschiff — Bilfärja
RAAHE
BRAHESTAD
④
⑧
KAJAANI
KAJANA
KUHMO
KALVIESKA
KOKKOLA
⑲
GAMLAKARLEBY
⑤
PIETARSAARI
JAKOBSTAD
IISALMI
NURMES
UUSIKAARLEPYY
IDENSALMI
NYKARLEBY
⑬
VAASA
VASA
④
KUOPIO
⑯
SEINÄJOKI
JOENSUU ILOMANTSI
⑧
⑤
③
㊏
JYVÄSKYLÄ
PIEKSÄMÄKI
⑥
KRISTIINA
KRISTINESTAD
⑬
SAVONLINNA
NYSLOTT
⑤
③
MIKKELI
ST. MICHEL
PORI
TAMPERE
⑤
BJÖRNEBORG
TAMMERFORS
⑬
⑥
IMATRA
KOKEMÄKI
③
HEINOLA
LAPPEENRANTA
RAUMA
HÄMEENLINNA
LAHTI
VILLMANSSTRAND
RAUMO
TAVASTEHUS
LAHTIS
UUSIKAUPUNKI
⑩
⑧
②
NYSTAD
⑪
④
⑤
HAMINA
TURKU
③
⑤
⑥
FREDRIKSHAMN
ÅBO
HYVINKÄÄ LOVIISA
NAANTALI
⑩
②
③
LOVISA
VAALIMAA
NÅDENDAL
①
PORVOO
KOTKA
⑦
PARAINEN
⑦
BORGÅ
PARGAS
�
HELSINKI
MAARIANHAMINA
HELSINGFORS
MARIEHAMN
�
TAMMISAARI
HANKO
EKENÄS
HANGÖ

248 ■ FINLAND

The Saimaa Lake district with some of Finland's 60,000 lakes.

FINLAND

THE LAND

Finland is the most northerly inhabited country in the world, except for Iceland. About one-third of its total length lies north of the Arctic Circle, where the famous "midnight sun" creates an unusual way of life.

In midsummer in southern Finland (where most of the larger cities are located) daylight lasts 19 hours of each day, but in northern Finland there is constant daylight for all 24 hours of each day for 73 consecutive days! At that same latitude, the 70th parallel, winters are quite another story. Christmas comes in the middle of 51 dreary days of twilight and night. Even in southern Finland there are only 5 hours of daylight during the middle of the winter. People must go to school or work in darkness and return home in darkness too. However, the long winter nights are often made glorious by magnificent displays of the Northern Lights or Aurora Borealis.

CLIMATE

Fortunately for the people of Finland, the Gulf Stream passes near by and general air currents are warm, so the average temperatures are considerably higher than you might expect at such a latitude. In summer, Finland as a whole has an average temperature of 50° Fahrenheit, with a maximum recorded temperature in July of about 90°. The country is snowbound, however, much of the year—5 months in the south and as much as 7 months of the

Along the banks of the river Porvoonjoki are these old storehouses.

year in Lapland, where temperatures in February can go as low as 22° below zero. Because of its relatively milder weather, southern Finland has more rain and snow than the northern part.

AREA

Somewhat smaller than California, but larger in area than the British Isles, Finland is 724 miles from north to south. It touches Norwegian Lapland on the north and northwest, the Soviet Union on the east, the Gulf of Finland on the south, and the Gulf of Bothnia and Sweden on the west. Its longest border is with Russia—some 793 miles. Finland's relationship with Sweden, however, has been closer culturally and politically, especially during the early centuries of its development. The nation still maintains Swedish as one of its two official languages. Part of Finland are the Aland Islands off the southwest coast, one-third of the way across to Stockholm.

In Finnish, Finland is called "Suomi." Both Finland and Suomi are thought to refer to marshes or fens (*suo*, in Finnish), but this has not been proven. About 71 per cent of the total land area (130,165 square miles) is forested. About 16 per cent of the total area is waste land, 9 per cent consists of lakes, and 13 per cent is arable. Inland waters occupy 12,206 square miles. Finland has 60,000 lakes, many with rapids. None of the rivers are large; the Muonio forms a border with Sweden, the Oulujoki is navigable and the Kemi is the third principal river. The surface of the country is mostly tableland, 400 feet to 600 feet above sea level, with very few high elevations. Haltia Mount, 4,344 feet high, in the northwest, is the tallest mountain. Much like the Scandinavian peninsula, Finland's soil consists mainly of moraine deposits left by Ice Age glaciers and the topsoil is usually thin. Along the coast of Bothnia much of the land has been recovered from the sea bottom.

HELSINKI

Helsinki, the beautiful and modern capital of Finland, ranks among the loveliest cities in Europe. Built on a peninsula, the city is surrounded by hundreds of islands, many with beaches. Helsinki is the cultural capital of Finland, as well as a great tourist attraction.

Built in 1475, the Olavinlinna Castle is considered the best preserved castle in northern Europe.

HISTORY

The early history of Finland is cloaked in mystery. Probably the first settlers, a northern segment of the Finno-Ugrian tribes, came from the southern shores of the Gulf of Finland in about A.D. 100. It is likely that some of these people came originally from what is now central and southern Russia, and that another branch of the same group settled in Hungary, where there developed a language similar to the Finnish—the Magyar tongue. The Lapps, who inhabit northern Norway and northern Sweden, have also dwelt in northern Finland for an undeterminable number of centuries.

Finland was then, even more than today, a land of lakes and trees. The first settlers probably had to burn off or cut down some of the forest in order to have fields to till. The weapons, implements and armaments they left behind indicate that they maintained contact with tribes to the south. Historical reference to the *Fenni* is found in the *Germania* of Tacitus, the Roman historian who lived in the first century A.D.

It was not, however, until about A.D. 700 that any homesteads were established in southern Finland. At about this time, the Finns also established relations with the Swedes to the west.

In any event, by the year A.D. 1000, Finland had its own definite culture. That culture is reflected in the *Kalevala*, the Finnish national epic and one of the classics of literature.

The Finns at the beginning believed in pagan gods—in Ukko, god of the air; Tapio, god of the forests; Ahti, god of the water, etc. Crusades were stimulated by the Pope to win the Finnish people from their pagan beliefs and Christianity appeared in Finland in the course of the 11th century.

UNDER SWEDISH RULE

In one of these crusades in 1155, King Erik IX (The Good) of Sweden conquered the Finns. To maintain Christianity, King Erik left English-born Bishop Henry of Upsala in charge

An engraving from the sarcophagus of Bishop Henry shows the saint baptizing the Finns.

at Turku but the Finns reverted to their paganism even though Henry later became their patron saint. In any event, the Catholic Church for the next 300 years held a dominating position in the country. By 1209, when Thomas, another English bishop, took Henry's place, he almost separated Finland from Swedish control and established it as a papal province.

In 1293, the year the Castle of Viborg was built, the Karelians were conquered by Swedish Torkel Knutsen. The castle he built was for centuries the outpost of Swedes and Finns against the Russians.

The Swedes spread civilization and gave the Finns the same civil rights they had. Swedes themselves settled in the Aland Islands and along the southern and western shores of Finland. By the time the 16th century began and the Reformation movement came to Sweden, the Swedish government had consolidated its authority in Finland. At this time a strong national movement developed in Finland, but the country suffered terribly from wars, famine and pestilence. Many Finns fought with the Swedes during the Thirty Years' War, 1618-48, and King Gustavus II of Sweden and his

successors in turn did much for education in Finland.

The Russian Czar, Peter the Great, set out in 1710 to take Finland from Sweden and within six years he had conquered the country. However, King Charles XII of Sweden fought back and many thousands of Finns perished during the fighting. In 1721 by the Treaty of Nystad, the Russians retained only Ingermanland, the whole of Lake Ladoga, Karelia, and the province of Viborg, land they again have today. Sweden was not content, however, and 20 years later tried to reconquer the lost land but suffered disaster. Then again in 1788 war broke out between Sweden and Russia, without any decisive result. Finally, in 1808, Czar Alexander's army invaded Finland without any declaration of war and in 1809, after heavy fighting, Sweden was forced to cede the whole of Finland and the Aland Islands to Russia.

A GRAND DUCHY OF RUSSIA

Strangely enough, Finland was not considered a conquered province and Alexander granted it a free constitution, fundamental laws of its own and semi-independent status as a grand duchy with himself as Grand Duke. Finland had a separate senate and a governor-general. A year or so later, the province of Viborg was reunited with the duchy of Finland. Turku remained the Finnish capital until 1821 when the seat of government was transferred to Helsinki. The diet, which had not met for 56 years, was reconvened in 1863 and a strong pan-Slav movement (an attempt to bring all of the Baltic countries and Russia into alliance) began with the motto, "One law, one church, one tongue."

Politics in Finland at this time saw a rivalry between the Swedish Party, formerly the dominant minority, and the Finnish National Party, which wanted "one tongue" and stronger nationalism for the Finns.

When Czar Nicholas II came to the throne he virtually destroyed the powers of the Finnish Diet in 1899. A new military law ended the separate Finnish army. Russian officials and the Russian language were forced on Finland wherever possible and the Russian governor was given dictatorial powers. The Finns resisted doggedly, but the Russians had a complete system of spies, illegal arrests, banishments, suppression of newspapers and invasions of homes without warrants. Culminating the Finnish struggle was a national strike in November, 1905. After six days of the strike, the Czarist government (which simultaneously had problems in Manchuria and in Russia itself) gave in and restored the laws of 1899. The new Finnish Diet remodelled the constitution, safeguarding freedom of the press, speech, meeting and association—and most important of all, granted full political rights to women for the first time in Europe.

All of this lasted only two years. The Czar changed his mind and insisted on an annual contribution in place of military service. The Finnish Diet was dissolved twice and its social

The Great Church in Helsinki, central cathedral of Evangelical Lutheranism, which is Finland's state religion.

This reconstruction of an old farmhouse at the open-air museum in Helsinki shows the crude tables and furnishings that the old Finns used.

A tremendous room was the King's Hall in the ancient castle of Turku.

reforms killed. The Czar himself did not attempt to rule Finland but the Duma (or Russian Parliament) considered itself alone responsible and competent for ruling in the interest of the Russian Empire. The Duma did make certain reforms—for example, it allowed civil marriages and applied the principle of equal pay for equal work in the teaching profession, in the printing trade, and in the state service. In 1910 it passed several acts which would have meant the virtual end of Finland as a separate entity, but the Finnish Diet refused to pass the laws and dissolved. Judges resigned and high officials left the country either voluntarily or by force.

WORLD WAR TIME

Finland's passive resistance enabled the country to stay out of World War I almost entirely. It escaped invasion, but its merchant marine was bottled up in the Gulf of Bothnia. The Allied blockade caused a steep rise in living expenses, but Finnish industries became prosperous supplying the Russians. At this time the Russians had taken a swing of the pendu-

(Left) Turku today looks like this. The statue is of Per Brahe who was governor-general of Finland in the middle 17th century. He travelled extensively to obtain a clear picture of the country's natural resources and opportunities for development. A great many important administrative reforms were made under his direction and he founded seven towns which are still in existence today. His most important achievement was the founding of Turku University in 1640.

lum back towards pleasing the Finns. They abolished the military tax and merely imposed a 5 per cent tax on property and mortgages. However, Finland naturally feared that if the Russians were victorious in the World War, they would again become oppressive. Some young Finns enlisted to fight on the German side for service only on the Eastern front. When Czar Nicholas II abdicated on March 15, 1917, the Kerensky provisional government took office in Russia and restored the government in Finland. The new diet passed all the laws that

(Right) A modern hero of Finland is Marshal Gustaf Mannerheim who served in the Russian army during the Russo-Japanese War and World War I while Finland was still a grand duchy of Russia. In 1917 when Finland declared its independence, Mannerheim became its regent. In the Winter War of 1939-40 he was commander-in-chief of the Finnish army which surprised the world by holding off the Russians. He again led the Finns in the war of 1941-44 against Russia and served as president of the new republic, 1944-46. This statue in Helsinki was sculpted by Aimo Tukiainen.

FINLAND ■ 255

The Bank of Finland in Helsinki.

had previously been held up by the Czar. Among these laws was one limiting the work-day to eight hours and a total prohibition of alcohol. Thus Finland began prohibition before the United States (and abandoned it in 1932 just before the U.S. did). A food shortage developed because some 40,000 Russian refugees sought sanctuary in Finland, and repeated strikes threatened the existence of the country.

Meanwhile, the Bolsheviks came to power in Russia and the Finns decided to declare their own independence. December 6, 1917 was the day the Finnish declaration of independence was signed. Unpredictable as usual, the new Russian government declared that Finnish independence conformed with their policy. Sweden and other Scandinavian countries acknowledged Finnish independence and France and other nations followed.

During the Russian Revolution the sympathies of the people were not all in the same direction. Finnish workers reinforced by Russians felt closer to Russia and formed what was called the Red Guard which began to overrun the country. A Civic Guard was hurriedly organized by the bourgeois parties under Baron Carl Gustaf Emil Mannerheim, an able former general of the Czar, and this hurriedly improvised army tried to put out the Russian Reds and defeat the Finnish extremists. At the same time the Finns fought a civil war and a war of independence. The Germans sent back some young Finnish troops (Jaegers) who had been training in Germany and they joined with Mannerheim's army. Decisive victories were won even before the arrival of the German expeditionary force.

When the Finnish Diet met in June, 1918, the Socialists had been banned even though they represented 46 per cent of the electorate. This Diet authorized the offering of the crown to a brother-in-law of the Kaiser and he accepted but never came to Finland to take the throne. The Germans were beginning to demand Finnish military assistance, when the Allied offensive in the West diverted Germany's attention and time was gained until the Armistice was signed on November 11, 1918. Mannerheim became Regent and formed a coalition government which led to the establishment of a republic in 1919 under the same constitution that exists today (see Government). In 1920 a peace treaty was signed with Soviet Russia under which Petsamo was ceded to Finland, thus giving the nation an outlet on the Arctic Ocean. Finland was also admitted to the League of Nations and claimed sovereignty over the Aland Islands, a claim that was disputed by Sweden. The League of Nations, however, decided for Finland.

During these years an attempt was made to form a Baltic block with Estonia, Latvia and Poland, but Finland generally rejected it and turned more towards cooperation with Scandinavia.

BETWEEN WARS

Between World Wars I and II, peace generally reigned and democratic procedures solved all problems, such as those of townsmen versus countrymen, property owners versus wage earners, and the Finnish-speaking intelligentsia versus the Swedish-speaking upper class. Fascism never secured a foothold in Finland. Communism, however, flourished in Finland because of its long open border with the U.S.S.R. In 1930, however, anti-Communist laws were passed. The most important reform of this period was splitting up the big estates and bringing new areas into cultivation, so that Finland became a nation of peasant proprietors.

INVASION AGAIN

Relations with the Soviet Union were never good, but Finland did sign a non-aggression pact with Russia in 1932. The treaty, however, did not prevent Soviet Russia from invading Finland in 1939. The Russians (at the time friendly with the Nazis) first demanded some territory which the Finns refused to give and then they launched a military campaign by land, sea and air. Two days later Moscow announced that the People's Government of Finland had been set up. This puppet government consisted

This luxurious manor house called Louhisaari is a museum today.

Built about A.D. 1250 the Hattula Church in the province of Hame still stands and is used today.

wholly of Finnish Communists who had fled to Russia. Once more Field Marshal Mannerheim, now 72, took command of the Finnish forces. The Finns fought so heroically that the Soviets were unable to effect conquest by a "fifth column." Also, the Finns drew promises of aid from Great Britain and France. The League of Nations expelled the Soviet Union from membership as an aggressor. Sympathy for the Finns was widespread throughout the world, but Sweden and Norway remained neutral and the Finns received no practical help. After 105 days of fighting, the Soviet Army managed to break through the Mannerheim Line, and in March, 1940, Finland had to sign a peace treaty in Moscow ceding to the Soviets more than one-tenth of its territory including all of the Karelian Isthmus (by now evacuated), including Lake Ladoga and Viborg, the country's fourth largest city.

Finland in 1940 ceded to Germany the right of transit for Nazi troops through Finnish territory to and from northern Norway, and German troops were in the country at the time Hitler attacked Russia in 1941. This fact alone was enough to prevent Finland's remaining neutral—and so for a third time Mannerheim led the Finns against the Russians. The government, however, refused to be called an ally of Germany, just a "co-belligerent" against Soviet Russia, and refused to participate in operations that served purely Nazi purposes or were influenced by Nazi ideology. Nevertheless, Finland disregarded warnings from the British and

U.S. governments; Great Britain declared war on Finland and the U.S. broke off diplomatic relations.

The Finns tried to secure peace terms from the Soviet Union and withdraw from the war, but Russia insisted on re-establishing the 1940 frontier in Karelia, the return of Petsamo (thus cutting off Finland again from the Arctic Ocean) plus payment of $600 million—£200 million—indemnity, equal to the nation's entire national income for a whole year. These humiliating terms were at first refused, but as the Soviet army forced its way into Karelia and occupied other territory, the Finns changed their minds. Risto Ryti resigned as president and Mannerheim was elected. By the time an armistice was signed in 1944, Finland was able to obtain slightly better terms, having to pay $300 million —£100 million. The agreement required that

(Above) In Lohja Church, built in the 14th century and reconstructed in 1886, the paintings date from 1510-22.

(Left) All over Finland are fascinating interiors of old churches. This one was built in 1304 and the wall paintings date from 1560. The church itself is at Isokyro in western Finland. Note the unusual chandelier.

FINLAND ■ 259

Finland expel the German troops. The Nazis of course were angry about the Finns' succumbing. As they withdrew from northern Finland they burnt everything behind them.

PEACE AND INDEPENDENCE

Although a peace treaty was signed between Finland and the Allies in Paris in 1947, Finland was not without problems. When the Soviet Union annexed Karelia, the inhabitants of that territory (10 per cent of the whole population) had decided to move to what was still Finland and the government was faced with the task of finding housing, employment and even land for more than 400,000 people. The reparations had to be paid and this was even more difficult. Finland had to supply Russia with an enormous quantity of goods at the price level of 1938 and according to certain specifications—one-third to be timber, one-third ships and cables, one-third machinery. Finland lacked the materials, the machinery and the manpower. Nonetheless, by dint of great effort, the country succeeded in meeting its reparations quotas with few exceptions, and by 1952, had completely cleared its debt.

Finland is the only country ever to have been conquered by the Soviets, where democracy has

Modern church architecture can be excitingly unusual, as in this church at Rajamaki.

survived. (It is also amazing that after a century of Russian rule there are no Russian features of note to be found in Finland.) Trade agreements with the Soviet give Russia 14 per cent of Finland's exports today, but more than 2/3 of the foreign trade is with the western European countries. The standard of living in Finland is the same as in Denmark and Norway and somewhat lower than in the richest European country, Sweden.

President during much of the post-war era has been Urho Kekkonen, leader of the Agrarian party. In his own words: "It cannot be in our interest to adopt a policy directed against a Russia which remains a great power. In an era of mechanized warfare a small state cannot stand forever armed to the teeth. As an ally of a great power, Finland would always be the first to be trampled down, and yet she would not have much influence on decisions affecting peace or war. For these reasons, it would be in Finland's national interest to return to a policy of neutrality, while maintaining her close connections with the other Scandinavian nations." This policy of following strict neutrality has been more or less successful in lessening tensions and increasing understanding between Finland and the Soviet Union.

Urho Kekkonen was born in a modest home in a village in the interior. He received his degree as doctor of jurisprudence in 1936, became a member of the board of directors of the Bank of Finland in 1946, and was a member of many governments. He has been prime minister five times, speaker of the house, and president of the republic since 1956.

THE CHURCH

While there is complete freedom of worship in Finland, today more than 93 per cent of the population belong to the Evangelical Lutheran Church. Supreme authority of the church is vested in the government and the president and under the constitution and ecclesiastical laws, the church has a large degree of autonomy. Traditionally, the Archbishop of Turku heads the enlarged Bishops' Conference which has 39 members. The country is divided into eight dioceses, each with a bishop and chapter. One of these is administered in Swedish.

This State Council Building in Helsinki shows classical Greek influence.

GOVERNMENT

Executive power is vested in the president who is chosen for a 6-year term by 300 presidential electors nominated by the citizens. The president has the power of ratifying new laws or withholding his signature. A bill which the president refuses to sign is suspended, but it will come into force if Parliament after a general election passes it without amendment. The president can issue decrees or ordinances provided they do not modify the laws. He can dissolve Parliament, order new elections and conduct foreign affairs through ministers. In fact, all of his powers are exercised through ministers. His decisions have to be taken into the Council of States (the cabinet) which consists of 10 ministers. Besides these ministers it includes two permanent non-political officials, the chancellor and assistant chancellor of justice.

There is a single legislative body, the Eduskunta, which consists of 200 members. These are elected from 12 administrative districts. Both Finnish and Swedish are official languages. (Even street signs appear in both languages in certain cities.)

Both men and women above the age of 21 can vote. Military service is compulsory for men for a minimum period of 240 days. Nor-

Urbo Kekkonen (1900–   ), president of Finland (1956–   ) has guided his nation on a course of strict neutrality.

mally, conscripts must report at the age of 20, but volunteers are accepted at 17.

For all practical purposes, the ministers are appointed to represent the various minority parties in a balance that will allow a coalition to nominate the government.

In Finland there are 8 major parties of which the Center (formerly called the Agrarian) Party has generally been strongest. However, governments have either been coalition or minority governments. Second in strength is the Finnish People's Democratic Union (a leftist party), and almost as strong is the Social Democratic Party, which is roughly equivalent to the British Labour Party. Next in strength is the National Coalition Party (conservative). Smaller parties are the Liberal People's Party and the Swedish People's Party (representing the Swedish-speaking minority) as well as the splinter groups.

The government is committed to a neutral foreign policy. Finland's traditional desire is to stay outside conflicts of interest between the big powers and to maintain good relations with all countries, particularly with adjacent states. In line with this policy, Finland is not a member of NATO. It is, however, a member of the United Nations which it joined in 1955.

Finland feels close to other Scandinavian countries—Denmark, Iceland, Norway and Sweden—all of which are bound together by a common historical, cultural and social background. Under the Nordic Council established in 1952 and joined by Finland in 1955, there is a common manpower market which grants citizens of the member states the right to stay and work in any of the other Scandinavian countries. Citizens of all five countries enjoy practically the same social benefits wherever they may reside. No passports are required by citizens of the member states to travel within the area. Certain joint research and educational institutions are established, especially in the field of atomic research and journalism.

For administrative purposes, the country is divided into provinces and communes. Heading each of the 12 provinces is a provincial government with a governor. The communes are based on local self-government. The Aland Islands, one of the provinces, enjoys a high degree of provincial autonomy. There are three different types of communes: cities, of which there are 43; boroughs, 24; and rural communes, 482. Communes generally rely on salaried experts to manage their affairs rather than elected trustees.

The Ministry of the Interior is responsible for the police, and local forces are assisted by a flying squad.

An interesting judicial sidelight is that the juries in local courts can, by unanimous decision, overrule the judge.

Finland's army, navy, and air force are restricted to duties of an internal character and to defending Finland's frontiers, under the terms of the Paris Peace Treaty of 1947. The treaty also prohibits Finland from possessing, constructing or experimenting with atomic weapons and self-propelled or guided missiles, sea mines, torpedoes, submarines and bombers.

In this small-scale replica of Helsinki's streets, traffic regulations are handled in the same fashion. This playground is part of a residential development.

THE PEOPLE

POPULATION

Total population of Finland (1966) was 4,650,000 of which more than 10 per cent (518,000) live in Helsinki, the largest city and capital. Other large cities are Tampere with 147,000 and Turku, with 146,000 population. The people are evenly divided in their work: 35 per cent of the families receive their support from industry, 31½ per cent from agriculture, and 33 per cent are engaged in commerce and other activities.

LAPLAND

In Finnish Lapland, there are about 170,000 inhabitants but only 2,500 Lapps. The Lapps have their own schools where they are taught in Lapp and Finnish. They are mostly nomads, following and tending their reindeer herds. Every Finnish child knows that Santa Claus lives in Lapland. From there he drives down with his reindeer for Christmas.

In Helsinki High School, these students are studying North America and especially New York City. The writing on the blackboard says that Broadway is 30 kilometres long and the Empire State Building is 108 storeys tall.

LANGUAGE

Finnish is a unique language—it is not Indo-Germanic as is Swedish—its roots derive from the Finno-Ugrian family. Like Estonian and Hungarian (Magyar) and languages of certain other minorities in central Russia, it comes from very ancient peoples who lived before 3000 B.C. However, the Finnish language today has been influenced by Swedish-Teutonic languages. Like Italian, Finnish is an euphonious language with many vowels, and relatively few consonants. Mainly, Finnish is phonetic and pro-nunciation is easy with the stress falling invariably on the first syllable. It has no articles or genders.

The Swedish-speaking minority in Finland are descended from Swedes who immigrated between the 9th and 13th centuries. The number of Swedish-speaking people in Finland has dropped during the last century to about 7 per cent. Until about 1900, Swedish remained the language of administration and culture.

The Lapps speak a language of their own, also from Finno-Ugrian roots.

Modelling figures out of clay is one of the projects of these children in a lower school class. On the wall are examples of their art work.

These silver charms are exact copies of old Finnish ornaments from the Viking Age.

Finnish folk songs originally sung to the accompaniment of native instruments such as the *kantele* are still popular. Finland is very proud of its folk culture and has re-erected as an open-air museum all of the farm buildings on an island called Seurasaari near Helsinki.

A revival of *ryijy* rug weaving began around 1910 and even though the old national costumes went out of general use about that time, modernized costumes were devised, based on the old models, and are often worn today for festivals.

Craftsmen make wood carvings, metal trinkets and *Kalevala* ornaments commercially.

"Kantele" is the Finnish name of this ancient musical instrument, which is plucked by hand. The other object is a wooden drinking vessel.

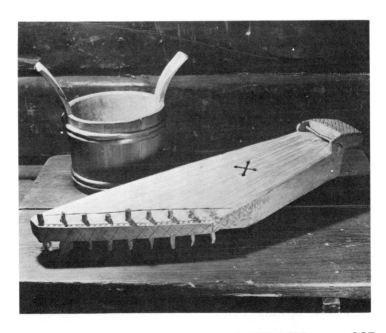

A farmhouse in Finland, such as this old country home, is likely to contain a hand loom and a large open cooking hearth.

Finnish lace-making is a hand operation requiring infinite patience.

Midsummer's Day is celebrated all over Finland with bonfires, an old custom from pagan times to keep the spirits away. Folk dancing goes on all through the night which is interrupted even in southern Finland by only 3 hours of dusk.

LITERATURE

In 1550 an ABC book was published in the Finnish language along with a Finnish version of the New Testament but Finnish literature did not really come alive until the 1860's, inspired by Lonnrot's publication of the *Kalevala*.

Some of the Finnish writers wrote in Swedish —among them J. L. Runeberg, regarded as the country's national poet, and Zachris Topelius, author of historical novels and fairy tales.

Much of the literature is concerned with peasant life. Perhaps the best-known author in English is Mika Waltari, world-famous for his historical novels. His books give a fine

description of middle-class urban life but one or two of his novels have had rural themes. He reached international fame through his historical novels, among which are "The Egyptian" and "The Adventurer" which were best-sellers in the United States and England.

Finland has the largest bookshops in the world. Per capita, more books are purchased in Finland than in any other country.

ARCHITECTURE AND FINE ARTS

While Finland has a great many architectural monuments, churches and castles from mediaeval times, it is only in the present century that Finnish architecture has won fame internationally. Architecture was the first of the arts to free itself from the stodginess of the 19th century. New building materials—concrete, iron and glass—inspired architects to seek forms more readily adaptable to new construction methods. Eliel Saarinen, father of Eero, was the great name of Finnish architecture early in the 20th century. His greatest masterpiece was the Helsinki Railway Station built in 1905-14. He later won second prize in the Chicago Tribune's International Building Competition and his design revolutionized skyscraper construction in America. After he moved to the United States in 1922, he designed buildings for the Cranbrook Foundation in Michigan and he himself became president of the Cranbrook Academy of Art.

Although World War I was a setback to building activities, the 1930's saw new movements springing up in both town and country, especially in rural industrial areas. The Finns

(Left) Modern architectural influences are dominant in the Institute of Commerce in Helsinki. Here we see the entrance.

FINLAND ■ 267

(Left) Hand-made glass processes are employed at the Karhula factory, the biggest in the country. This man is "blowing" the glass at the end of his pipe into a vase shape.

created an art that took advantage of the opportunities offered by industrialization. Schools, hospitals and industrial plants and office buildings have all been constructed in pleasing shapes that provide healthier existences for their dwellers. Imagination in using modern design and lack of ornamentation have been characteristic of the Finns.

Finnish painting has not gained the same international success as architecture. It has deep domestic roots and has been affected by both German and Parisian art. French naturalism came to Finland in the 1880's, but it took on a national tinge influenced by the *Kalevala*. Later, Italian art had its influence and Impressionism came into popularity just before World War I. Finnish painting is generally strong, even brutal. Both Cubism and Surrealism are strongly represented in Finland. Best known perhaps of the Finnish painters is Albert Edelfelt, a portrait painter.

In the 19th century Finnish sculpture was successively neo-classic, naturalistic and realistic. None of the sculptors won a name abroad. Not until World War I did Finland produce a leading sculptor—Waino Aaltonen, who has remained the acknowledged master. From the outset he showed an admirable purity of style. In granite, which is difficult to handle, not to mention marble, his chisel has portrayed lofty idealism and plumbed the depths of the human soul.

Karlervo Kallio has achieved a name in the United States. He is one of the present generation of artists who, with Aaltonen, have produced monumental works which enhance the grandeur of the Finnish urban and rural scenes. Two very recent examples of this monumental sculpture are the statue of K. J. Stahlberg, first President of Finland (unveiled in 1959), by W. Aaltonen and the equestrian statue of Gustaf Mannerheim, Marshal of Finland, by Aimo Tukiainen (unveiled in 1960).

More popular in Europe than America are

Finnish crafts and industrial arts, especially ceramics and glass, which are known for their unusual designs. Finnish ceramic artists enjoy a unique position as they have near-ideal conditions in a large pottery in Helsinki, known for the "most beautiful glazing in the world." Glass artists, too, receive wonderful co-operation from nearby factories, and have raised the level of art in utility glass to an unrivalled magic charm.

Besides the *ryijy* rug, textiles and furniture from Finland have been copied elsewhere in the world. Prizes in international contests are highly regarded in Finland.

The Academy of Finland, founded in 1947, to promote creative work in the arts and sciences is maintained by the state. The salaried members have no duties beyond working in their respective fields and offering guidance to young artists and scientists who show talent.

Among the best-liked 20th century composers is Finland's Jean Sibelius, shown here at Christmas time just a few years before he died on Sept. 20, 1957. His music includes symphonic poems and symphonies all written with great power of expression and imagination.

Finnish craftsmen and artists love to create unusual combinations of flowing design using shallow glass bowls on a veneer table. Tapio Wirkkala has produced this striking effect.

MUSIC

A heritage from olden times in Finland is love of music and singing. A regular feature of life is the music festival, and numerous choirs travel nationally and internationally.

Jean Sibelius typifies Finland to the world at large. He began his career with a symphony based on the *Kalevala*. He continued during the 1890's to compose many works inspired by mythology and national romanticism. His *Finlandia Suite* is internationally famous. It is interesting to remark that his seven symphonies were composed at the time when the symphonic form was supposed to be dead. Besides, he wrote a violin concerto, a string quartet, and composed many songs and incidental music for the theatre.

Looking towards the Olympic Stadium in Helsinki where the 1952 Games were held is this sculptured figure of Paavo Nurmi, Finland's most famous runner. Today a businessman, Nurmi won most of the medium long-distance races in the Olympics of the 1920's and at one time held 24 world records.

SPORTS

In the Stockholm Olympic Games in 1912, Finland first gained prominence by taking first place in wrestling and second place in track and field. From then on through the 1930's Finland was famous for its long-distance runners, especially Paavo Nurmi. Nurmi, known popularly as the Flying Finn, won the 10,000 metre and cross-country races at the Antwerp Olympics in 1920; then he won the 1,500, 3,000, 5,000 metres and cross-country in Paris in 1924; and the 10,000 metres in Amsterdam in 1928. He has held 24 official world records at distances ranging from the mile to the marathon. Now a businessman, Nurmi's statue adorns the entrance to the Olympic Stadium in Helsinki.

When Nurmi declined in the Olympics, Finnish javelin throwers came to the front to break world records. In wrestling, Finland held on to the lead established at the 1912 Olympics and continued to lead the world in long-distance running.

In skiing, the Finns have often taken first and second places in the Winter Olympics, especially in the ski jump. The Finns developed a new aerodynamic style of jumping which has now been adopted by other countries.

All of the people in Finland are given an opportunity to learn skiing at an early age. Since snow is on the ground so much of the time and the lakes are frozen for such a long period, skiing and ice skating are popular with the rank and file.

Finland is very sports-minded. The Finns play a form of ice hockey called *bandy* and have developed a Finnish game called the *pesapallo* which resembles American baseball. The girls play a form that resembles softball. More people take part in ball games, including hockey, than take part in track and field, the second most

(*Left*) *For many months Finland's lakes are frozen over but this does not prevent the enterprising Finn from enjoying his winter fishing.*

popular sport, or in skiing, the third most popular sport.

Sports in Finland are organized under two main athletic sporting associations both of which have a large number of affiliated clubs. They are financed by dividing the profits from a national football pool. Most of the sporting facilities and sports grounds are owned by the communities or by industrial firms.

The popularity of sports is demonstrated by the mass festivals where thousands of people take part in physical training displays in the Helsinki Stadium. Women participate in rhythmic gymnastics. So do the men. In fact, the men won 6 gold, 2 silver and 2 bronze medals for gymnastics at the London Olympics, 1948.

All of the lake sports are popular too: canoeing, rowing, swimming, yachting.

(*Above*) *Snowmen bigger than children can be preserved from the beginning to the end of winter.*

(*Left*) *Hitching up a dog team to a sled is one of the winter sports, even in the city.*

Inside this unpainted wood cabin is a fire for a Finnish sauna bath. In one room, hot stones give off dry heat, raising the temperature to as high as 200 degrees Fahrenheit. Completely nude bathers first enjoy perspiring and beating themselves with moistened birch branches to improve the circulation. When their bodies are thoroughly warmed, they dash outside and either roll in the snow or jump in the lake, which can be seen just past the boat.

THE SAUNA BATH

There are more than half a million saunas in Finland.

The sauna is a special bathhouse which may be a log cabin on the edge of a lake or behind a summer home, or an indoor room in urban dwellings. On the average of once a week, Finns enter the sauna bath for cleansing and relaxation. The sauna is part of their lives — as necessary as food or drink.

The sauna is really not a bath in the sense of a tub or pool. In dry heat caused by stones

272 ■ **FINLAND**

Since ancient times Saturday has been "sauna day." Sauna bathers start young. The higher the bench in the sauna cabin, the hotter the air. Buckets of water are kept near by to soak the birch boughs and water is sometimes thrown on the hot stones to increase the humidity and make the heat more penetrating.

heated over a stove or furnace, the "bather" lies on a high wooden bench, reached by a ladder, until he starts to perspire freely and his body becomes thoroughly warmed. The temperature is usually around 190 to 200 degrees Fahrenheit, but it may go as high as 280 degrees. The body can tolerate far greater dry heat than damp, such as that of a Turkish bath. The sauna is always built or lined with wood, which does not become hot to the touch.

Finns invite guests to their sauna as they would to a meal. They may relax on their benches in silence, or carry on quiet conversation. After about 15 minutes the body starts to perspire, and then it is time to throw a little water on the stones to moisten the air and make it seem hotter. Now the bathers take the leafy birch twigs which have been soaking in the buckets of warm water and beat themselves from head to foot to stimulate circulation. A few minutes later they cool off by plunging into a lake or taking a cool shower. Then they return to the sauna and the cycle starts over again. Finally, the bathers wash off and then lie down to rest in another room, where they slowly cool off until their bodies return to normal temperature.

The Gulf of Bothnia has lovely sandy beaches and although the water is cold in summer, it attracts bathers whose hardy constitutions have been built up by sauna baths. The wooden sheds on the left are not just bathing huts but sauna bath houses.

The lumbering city of Tampere is Finland's second largest. Although these logs have been banded, they are still afloat.

ECONOMY AND INDUSTRY

While agriculture has until very recently occupied most of the people in Finland, industry, including manufacturing and handicrafts, building and construction, has now outpaced agriculture.

Forests provide the base for the national economy and conditions for lumbering are excellent. Trees cover 71 per cent of the total usable land—a higher percentage than in any other country—and their total area is the third largest in Europe (after the Soviet Union and Sweden). Per capita, Finnish growing stock is the greatest in Europe and so is the annual growth. There is no fear that the annual cutting and natural losses will exceed the annual growth.

Pine is the main growing stock, followed by spruce, birch and aspen. These provide valu-

At this sawmill, the logs are trimmed and transformed into planks.

able raw materials for sawmilling, cellulose and paper. Birch is used for plywood and aspen for matches.

The forests are mainly owned by private individuals, generally farmers, who work in the forests in winter themselves.

Crops are not highly developed because of the far northern climate, but wheat, rye, barley, oats, potatoes and sugar beets are grown. In Sweden, 80 per cent of the crops are grown in areas that are farther south than the southernmost parts of Finland.

INDUSTRY

Since World War II, Finland has paid increasing attention to export markets. Besides wood and paper, Finland exports metals and handicraft products. Although the country lacks coal, it has an abundance of water power. A number of new power plants have been constructed, increasing the manufacturing capacity.

Finland ranks high in the production of wood and paper. Producing much more than it can use, it is an important exporter of wood products—sawed timber, plywood, wood pulp, and newsprint. Finland also has a long tradition of manufacturing and exporting prefabricated wooden houses.

The metal-working industry has made great progress since World War II and now includes complete factory plants and equipment which it exports to some extent to the Soviet Union and other countries. For domestic use, the metal-working industry produces tools, farm machinery, dairy plants and machines for woodworking and paper manufacture, locomotives, ships, railway wagons, engines, motors, etc.

In textiles and clothing, the domestic demand is satisfied by Finland's own factories. There is some export too. The same is true in leather and rubber.

Logs of lower quality are pulped and made into paper at a mill where the paper is smoothed on a calendering machine such as this.

From the sawmill, the piles of cut boards go to the timber yards where they are left in the open to season.

Red Square. Moscow, the capital of the USSR, is a truly unique city for it manages to combine the urban with the rural, a perfect blend of the country and a busy, bustling metropolis. It is one of the few cities in the world not yet seriously affected by the problem of air pollution.

RUSSIA

THE LAND

THE NAME RUSSIA was generally used to refer to the land that composed the Russian Empire before 1917, when the Russian Revolution occurred and subsequently led to the establishing of the Union of Soviet Socialist Republics (USSR). Today, outsiders continue to refer to the whole of the USSR as Russia, although within the Soviet Union the name is confined to the largest and most prominent of the USSR's 15 republics—the Russian Soviet Federated Socialist Republic (RSFSR). This republic, containing close to half the total population of the USSR, all but approximately 2,000,000 square miles of the USSR's territory, and many of the nation's most important cities (including the capital, Moscow), is naturally much more familiar to the Western world than are the other, less influential, 14 republics: Estonia, Latvia, Lithuania, Byelorussia, Ukraine and Moldavia, along the Western border; Georgia, Armenia, and Azerbaijan between the Black and Caspian Seas in Transcaucasia; and the Kazakh, Turkmen, Uzbek, Tadzhik and Kirghiz Republics in Central Asia.

Minsk, the capital of Byelorussia, was founded in the beginning of the 11th century, and is one of the cultural hubs of the Soviet Union.

AREA AND POPULATION

The USSR is the largest country in the world. Covering some 8,647,250 square miles, it is over twice as big as China, or the United States (with Hawaii and Alaska) and seven times as large as India. Included within its boundaries is roughly one-sixth of the earth's land area, and its vast bulk extends over two continents: Europe and Asia.

Except in the west, where it borders on Norway, Finland, Poland, Czechoslovakia, Hungary and Rumania, the USSR's boundaries are for the most part formed by natural marine and mountain barriers. Reaching from the Arctic Ocean (in the north) to the Black Sea and the boundaries of Turkey, Iran, Afghanistan, China, Mongolia and Korea (in the south), the USSR extends from its most western point on the shores of the Baltic Sea all the way to the Pacific Ocean. In its most northeastern corner, the USSR is separated from Alaska by the 52-mile-wide Bering Strait.

In the 18th century, Russian geographers created a purely arbitrary separation of Russia into what are today known as European Russia and Asian Russia, using the Ural Mountains as a dividing line. Stretching for 1,300 miles from the Kara Sea in the north to the Caspian Sea in the south, the Ural Mountains are by no means a natural boundary or barrier, since they rise to an altitude of no more than 5,560 feet; even the soil and vegetation on both sides of the Urals are identical. Nevertheless, this geographical separation of the USSR has endured.

The Soviet Union has the third largest population in the world, after China and India. In 1970, the population approximated 241,000,000, with almost half the people widely scattered in rural areas. Throughout the USSR's enormous territory are scattered some 1,763 towns and over 3,255 urban communities, including several cities founded over 1,000 years ago. Ten of these cities have more than 1,000,000 inhabitants: Moscow, 6,466,000; Leningrad, 3,607,000; Kiev, 1,450,000; Tashkent, 1,295,000; Baku, 1,216,000; Kharkov, 1,148,000; Gorky,

The Cathedral of St. Sophia in Kiev is an architectural monument, built about 1037. It is one of the many fine examples of early Russian architecture.

1,140,000; Novosibirsk, 1,079,000; Kuibyshev, 1,000,000; and Sverdlovsk, 1,000,000.

A land of many cultures, the USSR is composed of more than 100 different nationalities and ethnic groups, though three-fourths of the population are Eastern Slavs (Russians, Ukrainians and Byelorussians). Tremendously heavy casualties among the male population in World War II resulted in the present disproportion of 55 females to 45 males for every 100 people.

Like many of the other Baltic cities, Tallin, Estonia, resembles the towns of Western Europe, with its narrow streets and peaked roofs.

*Famous for its shashlyk
and high-speed boats
(better known as "gliders"),
Lake Ritsa in Georgia is
one of the USSR's most
popular vacation resorts.*

Traffic is still feather-light by most western standards, even here on Gorki Street in Moscow. Moscow's streets are enormously wide, and pedestrians cross at some points by means of underpasses. This allows traffic to move at high speeds. Left turns are made in outlined areas in the middle of blocks instead of at intersections.

A camel caravan crosses a fragile bridge over the roaring waters of the Vanch River, high in the Pamir Mountains of Soviet Central Asia.

The Crimea, the most magnificent peninsula of the USSR, can be explored along the "goat paths" of the past.

Gurzuf is one of the most picturesque health resorts on the coast of the Crimean Peninsula. The mountain in the background is called Medved (or Bear) Mountain. Legend has it that a bear came down to the sea for a drink of water and was turned to stone.

This is one of the 20 geysers found on the Kamchatka Peninsula, which has over 60 active volcanoes. It spurts steam and water out of the ground to a height of nearly 300 feet.

TOPOGRAPHY

Despite the popular Western belief that the USSR is for the most part a flat and level land, more than one-third of its territory consists of plateaus and mountain ranges. However, broad plains and lowlands do predominate in the western areas. The land mass west of the Urals and north of the Caucasus Mountains up to the Vistula River is occupied almost entirely by the East European (Russian) Plain, while on the eastern side of the Urals stretches the immense West Siberian Plain. It has often been said that the patience and endurance of the Russian people came from the monotony of the infinite plain and its harsh, severe climate.

Elevations, plateaus and mountains are found primarily in the eastern part of the USSR. Extending eastwards from the Yenisei River to the Lena River, the area of the Central Siberian Plateau alone is equal to half that of Western Europe. Many rugged mountain chains are scattered throughout Far Eastern Siberia. In

Situated on the sub-tropical southern coast of the Crimea, the small village of Yalta grew to become a world-famous seaside resort. In 1945 it was the site of the historic Yalta Conference between Roosevelt, Churchill and Stalin.

the south, the Central Asian deserts border on the Tien Shan and Altai Mountains. The Pamir Mountains border on China. Between the Black and Caspian Seas is the tallest peak in all of Europe, Mt. Elbrus (18,481 feet) part of the Caucasus mountain barrier.

VEGETATION ZONES

The land mass of the USSR is divided by latitude into several broad strips, differing from each other in climate, vegetation and soil, as well as in flora and fauna. Also referred to as vegetation zones, they are (north to south): the tundra, the forest, the steppes and the desert.

THE TUNDRA

The tundra, a permafrost (permanently frozen) area stretching along the shores of the Arctic Ocean and the Arctic Islands, is a bleak unforested region of frozen wasteland, sparsely dotted with patches of moss, lichen and occasional bushes and dwarf trees. Its widest point is at the Kara Sea in northern Siberia. On the Kamchatka Peninsula, desolate, gloomy marshes reach southward to a latitude of about 60° N. The few shrubs capable of surviving the fierce climate grow in tangled, protective clusters. Despite the below-freezing temperatures, in the summer the land becomes marshy and swarms with mosquitoes.

THE FOREST

Immediately south of the tundra, covering nearly half the territory of the USSR, sprawls the dense forest zone. Its southern frontiers ex-

Creating fascinating silhouettes against the sand are the "trees on stilted roots" near Lake Baikal's Peschanaya Bay.

Overlooking the beautiful Black Sea is this romantic "Swallows' Nest" castle, built on a sheer cliff in the Crimea.

tend eastward to the Altai Mountains approximately to the line of the cities of Orel, Kiev, and Kazan. Almost every species of tree imaginable grows somewhere in this enormous 4,240,000-square-mile area. There are boundless forests in Siberia, where the chief species are pine, fir and cedar. This is the famous *taiga*, its untrod, virgin forests stretching for hundreds of miles. Further south are the beautiful silver birch, pine, oak, maple, linden, fir, cedar, and spruce trees, so typical of the Russian landscape. Hidden below the picturesque bushes of aromatic wild berries, the floor of the forest displays an unlimited variety of mushrooms, offering the inhabitants an opportunity to go mushroom- and berry-picking, a popular traditional pastime.

THE STEPPES

The steppe zone is preceded by a relatively narrow section of land known as the "forest steppe," where the transition between the forests of the north and the steppes (plains) of the south takes place. In this narrow strip, large masses of forests alternate with great open spaces. Grey forest soil predominates, mixed with the *chernozem* (black earth) which extends far into the steppe zone.

The steppes themselves are ocean-like grass expanses that offer the best natural conditions for agriculture, and this area is referred to as the "breadbasket of the USSR." The rich black earth would ensure unusually high crop yields were it not for poor agricultural management, lack of modern farm equipment, and frequent bad weather. (During World War II, the German occupational forces exported this soil to their own country by the trainloads.)

The steppes are covered by a wide variety of tough feather grasses tall enough to hide a man on horseback. Trees are rare, but tulips, hyacinths, stars of Bethlehem and many other flowers sprinkle the fields of the steppes with an array of hues.

This section of the country has played a vital part in the culture and history of Russia. Poets and writers have found great inspirations in the overpowering vastness of the steppes, often comparing them to the sea, their tranquil surface producing the illusion of waves at the slightest indication of wind. All throughout early history, the Russians lived in constant fear of nomadic invaders crossing the open, unprotected steppes, which provided easy access to the rest of Russia.

THE DESERT

From the southeastern corner of the Russian Plain, on the north shore of the Caspian Sea, a vast desert region extends eastwards, taking in Kazakhstan, Turkmenia, Uzbekistan and western Kirghizia. Though sandy deserts predominate, small areas of stony desert exist as well.

THE SUB-TROPICS

A narrow coastal strip along the Black Sea, including the Crimean Peninsula, does not belong to the four major belts of climate, and its distinctive sub-tropical features are not found anywhere else in the USSR. Its mineral springs are famous for their exceptional cures; the air is fresh, and unusually invigorating. The coastal hills are covered with luxuriant flora. Vines climb up rocky cliffs above the azure sea, while the flamboyant Riviera-like coast is covered with magnolia, eucalyptus, and hibiscus.

The Yashil-Kul Lake in the Pamir Mountains is situated 9,842 feet above sea level. The Pamirs boast the highest (24,390 feet) mountain in all the USSR, Mt. Communism.

The search for food in the frozen wasteland of the tundra occupies most of the reindeer's long day.

Slightly camera-shy, this little sable has a cool retreat which serves as a convenient hiding place.

FAUNA

Polar bears, foxes, lemmings and reindeer roam the icy, windswept tundra. The Soviet Union's vast forests abound in fur-bearing animals (from squirrels to sables, and muskrat to mink), along with brown bears, deer, and wolves. In the Far Eastern areas live tigers, panthers and snow leopards or ounces.

The tall, weaving grasses of the steppes provide great security for small animals such as hamsters, marmots and mice, while the arid desert region is a paradise for lizards, tortoises, snakes, gazelles, antelopes, and barkhan cats. Porcupines and wild boars flourish in the subtropics.

Perhaps the most famous Russian animal is the Borzoi (wolfhound). Formerly dogs of state for the Czars, the elegant, fleet wolfhounds were used to chase and catch wolves on the steppes.

"*Ferocious*" *bears figure prominently in almost all Russian fairy tales. Having a friendly row, these two Moscow zoo tenants do not appear to be homesick for their more natural habitat in the Arctic.*

RIVERS, LAKES AND SEAS

Magnificent and mighty rivers flow on both sides of the Urals, serving the USSR as traffic arteries for barges and boats of every kind. With tributaries too numerous to mention, these broad, slow rivers flow through the enormous plains, providing the farmlands with life-giving moisture. In no other country are there so many inland waterways.

Originating in the marshes, the rivers have been the main roads of Russian history, for

Some believe that Vladimir I. Ulyanov adopted his pen name, Lenin, from this Siberian river, the Lena, after he spent several years in exile in Siberia. Recently, large deposits of diamonds were discovered in Siberia, making the USSR, already rich in minerals, including gold, iron and coal, the leading country in unmined diamond reserves.

Spanning the Moscow River are a number of bridges including the Novo-Arbat Bridge. Against the skyline stands the Ukraine Hotel, an example of the overdecorated, pompous, heavy architecture of the Stalinist period. Now, for the first time, Russian architects have begun to experiment with steel, glass and concrete, with exciting results, promising to make Moscow a much more modern metropolis.

along their banks moved the early tide of Russian colonization. For centuries, the rivers were almost the only means of communication, and even today they serve the USSR well. Early in Russian history, the rivers were connected by means of "portages"—light boats were carried from one waterway to the next.

The Dniester, the Don, the Dnieper, the Volga, the Ob, the Lena, the Yenisei, the Irtysh, the Pechora and the Angara are the chief rivers of the USSR. Today, these rivers are connected by a system of artificial canals which are used for both transportation and irrigation purposes, the most important being the White Sea-Baltic Canal, the Moscow-Volga Canal, the Volga-Don Canal and the Volga-Baltic Waterway.

The Volga, often referred to as "Mother Volga," flows southwards for 2,290 miles and empties into the Caspian Sea. This mighty river

The Nurek hydro-electric station in Tadzhikistan is the construction site for a dam which will be over 900 feet high. It will form a man-made sea on the river Vakhsh.

The Kremlin, a fortress in mediæval times, contains a museum, a treasure house of Russian art and craftsmanship. It encloses within its walls the cultural, religious and the political history of Russia.

has for centuries captured the hearts of the Russians, and although many of the rivers are spoken of affectionately by the people, the Volga is most commemorated in songs, poems and legends.

Among the USSR's many lakes is Lake Baikal in Siberia, the deepest lake in the world and the largest in Asia and Europe. Situated east of the Volga River is the famous salt-water lake, Baskunchak, better known as "Russia's salt-cellar." It is continually fed by many salt springs. Though salt extractions have been carried on for over a century, its reserves of common salt appear to be inexhaustible. According to Soviet scientists, the lake's supply of salt could last the world for more than a thousand years.

Of primary importance is the Baltic Sea, offering ships the shortest route to the Atlantic Ocean. The Caspian Sea, the chief source of the world-renowned beluga caviar, is the largest inland body of water in the world. The USSR has access to many other seas as well. Most of them, however, are covered with ice for a good part of the year, making navigation almost impossible. The ports of Odessa on the Black Sea, Kaliningrad and Klaipeda on the Baltic, and Murmansk on the Arctic Ocean, are the only ports which are not icebound in the winter.

CLIMATE

The climate of European USSR is for the most part "continental," characterized by hot but relatively short summers, and long, extremely cold winters. Accompanied by heavy snowfall and blizzards, the winter months are harsh. There is little time for the farmer to plant and harvest his crop during the brief summer season.

In the southern part of the USSR, the snow cover lasts from 40 to 60 days, while in the extreme northeastern portion of the USSR it may remain for as long as 260 days, often with temperatures of $-5°$ F. and lower. The world's coldest inhabited place is Oymyakon, in Eastern Siberia, where a temperature of $-96°$ F. has been registered. The Purga, an intense blizzard bringing up to 100-mile-per-hour winds mixed

The USSR spends nearly 15,000,000 rubles annually on the physical education of children alone. Many in Russia do exercises each morning to the instructions on the radio. For a few minutes every day the nation is "all together now, one, two, three . . ." This mountain skating rink is located in Medeo near Alma-Ata.

with snow, blows over the enormous plains of the USSR. On the other hand, the thermometers of Central Asia have been known to register temperatures of 120 to 130° F. during the summer months.

The Crimea's southern coast and Transcaucasia have a sub-tropical climate similar to that of the Mediterranean. This is due not only to the closeness of the sea and the low altitudes, but also to the high mountain barrier in the north, which serves as a wall against the cold air. A truly beautiful region, this was a popular resort area for the Czars and other notables, and was sometimes described as "the Russian Riviera."

NATURAL RESOURCES

Russia would be practically self-sufficient, were it not for the lack of a few raw materials such as rubber, tin and some tropical crops. Since the USSR possesses about one-fifth of the world's forest land, the annual natural increase of its trees is sufficient to meet the timber requirements of every country on earth.

Its numerous rivers make the USSR first in the world in water-power resources. The potential hydro-electric generating capacity amounts to almost 300,000,000 kilowatts.

Astounding reserves of copper and about half the world's supply of iron ore appear to exist in the USSR, while Russian coal resources are superseded only by those of the United States. Estimated to have as much as 60 per cent of the world's total oil, the USSR is also rich in reserves of natural gas.

Other valuable minerals include silver, gold, diamonds, manganese, lead, zinc, salt, nickel, bauxite, tungsten, mercury, and sulphur, plus the widest variety of metals to be found anywhere in the world.

The development of Siberia's resources is a main goal of Russian planners. By 1975, the oil fields of western Siberia are expected to replace those of Baku as Russia's chief petroleum-producing area. Spurring Russia's development of its vast northern Asian region is tension with China, expressed in border clashes in recent years.

Tashkent, the capital of the Uzbek Republic, was founded sometime in the 7th century B.C. *It received its Turkish name (Stone City) in the 12th century* A.D., *and in 1865 was captured by the Russians. Today Novoi Street is the main thoroughfare of Tashkent, with modern buildings rising next to magnificent monuments of the past. Unfortunately, much of the ancient architecture was heavily damaged by the earthquakes of 1966.*

HISTORY

ALTHOUGH IT IS BELIEVED that Russia was inhabited by man as early as the Stone Age, traditionally Russian history is regarded as beginning with the foundation of the Kievan State in A.D. 862. However, according to the records left by the Greek historian, Herodotus, the southern part of Russia (the steppe zone) was inhabited by a people called Scythians in the 5th century B.C. Russia's exposed steppes were an irresistible temptation to potential invaders. Impossible to protect, the steppes were the country's Achilles heel, resulting in much of Russia's turbulent early history.

In the 3rd century B.C., the Scythians were displaced by a distantly related tribe, the Sarmatians, who occupied the vulnerable southern steppe until the 3rd century A.D. After they conquered the Sarmatians in the same century, the German Goths were devastated by a fierce Mongolian tribe of Huns within a few short years. The 6th century brought an invasion by the Turkish Avars; the 7th century brought the powerful Khazars, who conquered the Slavs and settled in the south; and the 8th century saw the establishment of the Bulgars in the Volga region.

Note: Russia followed the Julian calendar up until the Revolution of 1917, and by the 19th century this calendar had fallen behind the Western Gregorian calendar by 13 days. All dates mentioned prior to 1917 are given by the Julian calendar to avoid confusion. Thus, for example, the Bolshevik Revolution occurred on October 25, 1917 according to the Gregorian calendar, rather than November 7. After 1917 the USSR adopted the Gregorian calendar used elsewhere throughout the world.

Armenian history originated in the 9th century B.C. *in the state of Urartu. Recent excavations show that Urartu had a highly advanced agricultural and commercial civilization. Armenia abounds in the most magnificent marble, with varied hues of amber, grey, black with gold veins, and the beautiful tufa. Here is an ancient Kurd cemetery at the foot of the Alagez Mountains in Armenia.*

THE SLAVS

Russia's early recorded history took place in the western part of European Russia. Because only scant information has been preserved, the origin of the so-called Eastern Slavs is still being disputed today, though many historians believe that the Slavs first appeared in the Polish marshes of Galicia. Their ancestors are presumed to have been the Neolithic tribes which inhabited this area several centuries prior to the Christian era. The early Slavs lived scattered throughout the territory in small tribes. Although no one unifying Slavic language existed, the tribal dialects of the Slavs apparently had a common origin. The Eastern Slavs, having somehow managed to survive numerous nomadic invasions, were by the 9th century well established both in the north and south.

THE KHAZARS

Though conquered by the Khazars, the Slavs enjoyed a great deal of freedom under their tolerant domination, and were able to engage in intensive trade with the Eastern Arabs. They had to pay tribute to the Khazars, but the Slavs were allowed to settle wherever they pleased, and they erected many important trade towns, such as Kiev and Novgorod, along the rivers. By connecting the rivers into a north-south route from the Gulf of Finland to the Black Sea, the Eastern Slavs were able to trade with Constantinople. Their flourishing trade soon attracted the attention of the Varangians, Scandinavian warriors and traders, who were also interested in the Greek markets. The Slavs and the Varangians made a mutual trade agreement, the Varangians promising to protect the trade routes.

THE KIEVAN STATE (9th-13th centuries)

Very few records have survived about the founder of the Varangian dynasty, Rurik. According to the chronicles, the people of Novgorod managed to expel the powerful Varangians in 862, only to find almost immediately that they could not do without them. Chaos and instability prevailed—the Slavic tribes, unable to settle their differences, were constantly feuding. To return order to the land, the Slavic tribes invited the Varangians to "come and rule over us and our wide land." Rurik arrived in Novgorod in 862 and established himself there as "ruler." From this time onward, the name Rus was associated with the Eastern Slavs and became the name of the

Kirghizia's "useful" land consists almost entirely of cultivated meadows and pastures. This mountainous region was settled by Mongol Tartars even before the 13th century.

Silhouetted against the open sky are ancient family burial vaults in Kirghizia.

Founded in the 3rd century A.D., Sudak belonged to the Genoese in the Middle Ages. Here they built a fortress so sturdy that it is well preserved to this day.

country. The origin of the word Rus is still being disputed today. Some historians contend that it was the name of one of the Varangian tribes, while others insist that it was used in the southern steppes long before the time of Rurik.

Oleg, the kinsman and successor of Rurik, merged the Eastern Slavs of the north and south into a single Kievan State under the rule of the Varangians, by transferring the capital to Kiev after freeing that territory from its Khazar domination.

Under the rule of Prince Vladimir I (980–1015), a line of strong fortification was built to fend off the ever-increasing attacks by aggressive nomads. Vladimir accepted the Greek Orthodox rite, making Christianity the state religion. Although he frequently resorted to the use of force in order to convert the heathen natives, Prince Vladimir was later made a saint.

Christianity brought with it the cultural influences of Byzantium (Constantinople), then the capital of the declining Roman Empire. The Russians quickly adopted the use of stone rather than wood in the building of churches, following the Greek example. They soon developed a distinctly Russian architectural style, however, and achieved great beauty in icons (portraits, especially of Christ), an art form which also originated in Greece. By the 11th century, Russian local customary law had been codified and the Cyrillic alphabet adopted.

The decline of the Kievan State began with the death of Yaroslav the Wise (1019–54). When first founded, the Kievan State was ruled in succession by one of the princes of the dynasty, and for as long as the family remained small, the power was concentrated. Yaroslav, on the other hand, willed that his realm be divided among his sons. Thereafter, the country became more divided with each new generation, since each prince considered his principality the exclusive property of his family. The political importance and authority of the Kievan Prince declined, shifting from Kiev to the western and northern principalities. In 1169, Kiev itself was besieged and sacked by another Russian, Prince Andrei Bogolubski of Suzdal, who then made the city of Vladimir, on the river Klyazma, the capital of the so-called "grand duchy."

The city of Samarkand dates back to the 4th century B.C. *Destroyed by Alexander the Great in 329* B.C., *and then again by Ghengis Khan in* A.D. *1220, later on it became the capital of Tamerlane's empire. The tomb and palace of Tamerlane are among the many monuments of ancient and mediæval architecture left there. Today it is one of the major cultural and economic cities of Central Asia.*

THE TARTAR INVASION

Kiev's final downfall came with the invasion of the Mongol Tartars from Asia in 1237–40, one of the greatest disasters in all of Russia's history. More than half the population were massacred; the rest either were led into captivity or fled to the forests. Kiev was almost totally destroyed, its churches razed to the ground. The work, the art, and the culture of nearly 300 years went up in smoke. Only Pskov and Novgorod and its northern provinces were spared.

THE TARTAR YOKE (13th-15th centuries)

Khan Batu, the Tartar leader, established the empire of the Golden Horde in the south and east of Russia, on the Volga River. This empire lasted until 1480. For over 200 years the Russian nation was bled white by the Tartars, but the most horrifying aspect of their rule was their periodic attacks upon the Russian people, when whole regions were depopulated overnight.

One of the vital consequences of the Tartar occupation was that the country was divided into two parts, southwestern and northeastern. Thereafter, Russia's economic and political life was focussed in the northeast, with Tver as the political hub. Although still paying taxes to the Golden Horde, the Muscovite princes of the grand duchy of Vladimir regained some of their power and concentrated on unifying their political position.

The beautiful Assumption Cathedral in Karelia, the area adjoining Finland, is one of the finest examples of Russia's early wood architecture. It was erected in the 13th or 14th century, and in spite of its age is still in good condition. Many of the early wooden structures were totally destroyed during the numerous invasions that Karelia suffered.

The Kremlin Palace at the end of the 17th century. The city of Moscow itself and its fortifications have been rebuilt many times because of the frequent, devastating fires that the city suffered.

THE MOSCOW STATE
(12th-17th centuries)

Liberation of Eastern Russia from the Tartars came about with the rise of Moscow. During the 12th and 13th centuries, when the principality of Suzdal-Vladimir was at the height of its power, Moscow was but a tiny fortified village under its jurisdiction. Because the rulers of Vladimir possessed the title of Grand Duke, all the other princes recognized them as their sovereigns.

Moscow grew, for several reasons. It was to Moscow that Metropolitan Peter, the head of the Russian Church, had eventually moved his residence after the fall of Kiev. Also, the location of Moscow at the crossing of the old trade routes was advantageous, for it was in an area not easily accessible to outside attacks by nomads.

During the reign of Dmitri Donskoi (1359–89), Moscow's importance steadily increased. Prince Donskoi's refusal to pay tribute to the Tartars in 1380 resulted in a great battle at Kulikovo Field. Here the Tartars were defeated, and though the Golden Horde was not wiped out, it was sufficiently weakened so that it never was able to raise its head again. By 1480, the Tartar power had completely fallen apart.

The last three decades of the 15th century were years of tremendous expansion for the Moscow State. Ivan III (reign 1462–1505) added four areas, Tver, Novgorod, Rostov and Vyatka, to the grand duchy, thereby ruling one of the biggest territorial states in all of Europe. Under the direction of Ivan III (called Ivan the Great), Moscow gained the appearance of a capital, with beautiful churches and rich, magnificent palaces. In 1493, Ivan III adopted the title of "Sovereign of all Russia." The 16th century was devoted to the difficult task of uniting the country.

IVAN IV, THE TERRIBLE (1533-84)

Under Vasily III, the boyars, who were the upper class nobility, had grown ambitious and they became exceedingly difficult to control. With the advent of Ivan IV to the throne in 1533, an onslaught against the boyars began. Ivan created the "Oprichina," a military police force, with which he exterminated the undesirable elements of the aristocracy, and confiscated the boyars' land holdings, distributing them among his hired assassins.

Conquering the Tartar khanates of Kazan and Astrakhan, Ivan the Terrible added another huge area, the lower and the middle Volga to Russia. The annexation and colonization of Siberia began in the 16th century, after its conqueror, the Cossack Timofeievich Yermak, made a present of the Siberian kingdom to Ivan IV.

In a magnificent ceremony, Ivan IV had himself crowned in 1547 and assumed the title of Czar (Caesar). Much concerned with increasing the prestige of the crown, and realizing that Moscow could not compare with the Western capitals in culture, education or brilliance, Ivan IV sought to improve the economic conditions of the country through trade and closer contact with Europe.

SERFDOM

Theoretically, both the land-owner and the peasant were considered "serfs," each obliged to serve the state in his way, the land-owner by fighting, the peasant by providing for him.

But in time the land-owners came to look upon the peasants as their own personal slaves. Under Ivan IV, as compensation for being deprived of their political influence, the land-owners were given land grants as well as increased rights over the peasants. With pressing military needs, the land-owners began restricting the freedom of the peasants. By the end of the 16th century, the process of turning the peasants into serfs was complete.

Due to Ivan the Terrible's Oprichina, the economic problems, and the enslavement of the peasants, the country entered into "The Time of Troubles"—1584–1613. It was during the beginning of this period that Boris Godunov, a boyar, became regent. In 1598, he was reluctantly elected Czar and was faced immediately with the intrigues and jealousies of other boyar families. He died suddenly in 1605. During this unsettled period, peasant uprisings, civil war, lack of authority, and invasions by Swedes, Poles and Cossacks added to the chaos. Finally, after the Polish armies were driven out, some degree of order was restored. Michael F. Romanov, a boyar, was chosen as the new Czar on February 21, 1613. Thus began the Romanov Dynasty.

Bogdan Z. Khmelnitsky (1593–1657), a Cossack and sovereign of the Ukraine, ended the Ukraine's aspirations for independence by asking for an alliance with Russia against the Poles and swearing allegiance to the Czar in 1654.

THE RUSSIAN EMPIRE

Because Russia was surrounded on three sides by enemies, for centuries its main concern was that of defence, and this served to dictate foreign policy. Despite great territorial gains, the country, lacking a stable military and administrative structure, grew internally weaker.

PETER THE GREAT (1689-1725)

Peter I, who became Czar in 1689, had a dynamic personality. His novel concept of governing the country gave Russia a new political position and prestige among the nations of Europe. Being acutely aware of Russia's deficiencies, and weaknesses, he used the state as a "whip," or driving force, to strengthen and "Westernize" the country and its people. His radical policies provoked strong resistance at home among his subjects, who were accustomed to passive administrations.

Peter I was extremely devoted to his people, but being an impatient man, he drove them, as well as himself, mercilessly. Assuming the title of "Emperor," he proceeded to impose a series of reforms by force on his "idle and ignorant subjects." He was responsible for the creation of a regular army and navy, for improvement in state government departments, and the formation of a Senate and various

The throne of Boris Godunov. Reluctantly elected Czar in 1598, he died in 1605, and was immortalized in the 1869 opera, "Boris Godunov" by Modest P. Musorgsky.

Ministries. The Church was "decapitated" and made a mere governmental department, subordinated directly to the Czar. The fiscal system was revised; education and culture were made compulsory for the children of the nobility; and modern industries, based on European methods, were first introduced into Russia.

Seeking outlets to the sea, Peter acquired Estonia, Livonia, Ingermanland, Finland and areas of Karelia after 20 years of struggle in the Great Northern War. Thus, Peter gained the long-desired access to the Baltic. To symbolize the beginning of a new European era for Russia, in 1703 he erected a city in his own name— St. Petersburg—on the Gulf of Finland, and made it the new capital of Russia.

One of the oldest customs in Russia was that of exchanging eggs at Easter. Here is an example of the delicate workmanship of a crystal egg, designed in 1909 for the royal family.

Catherine the Great, a poor German princess, was married to the Russian heir-apparent, Peter III. Shortly after Peter ascended the throne, he died under very suspicious circumstances. Most historians feel that Catherine was responsible for his untimely departure.

In the next two centuries, Russia increased its territories through the Russo-Turkish Wars while participating actively in the affairs of Europe. Peter's daughter, the Empress Elizabeth (reign 1741–61) allied herself against Prussia in the Seven Years War. However, her nephew and successor Peter III, withdrew Russia from the War. Upon his unexplainable death, his wife, Catherine II, born a German princess, became the new Empress.

CATHERINE THE GREAT (1762-96)

Catherine II, who very much admired Peter the Great, followed his policy of expanding Russia's territories, making the nation a major European power. Among the large new territories she added to Russia were parts of Poland, Byelorussia, the Black Sea shore and the Ukraine west of the Dnieper River. Although under Catherine's "enlightened despotism" Russia's art and culture began to flower, her political reforms served only to consolidate the power of the crown. The privileged classes benefited, at the expense of social reforms.

ALEXANDER I (1801-25)

Under Catherine's successor, Paul I, Russia's eastward expansion reached Alaska and the North American continent. It was during the reign of Alexander I that Russia fought one of its greatest nationalistic wars, throwing back the French under Napoleon in 1812. Russians refer to this as The Patriotic War. With Napoleon's final defeat, the Congress of Vienna peace settlement made Russia and Austria the leading powers in Europe. It was at this time that Alexander I promoted a loose union of states under the name of "The Holy Alliance."

Catherine the Great was a collector of some of the most magnificent carriages in the world. This one, on display in Moscow today, was made in St. Petersburg in 1739.

The notorious Yemilian I. Pugachev claimed to be Peter III and led his followers against Catherine the Great in one of the biggest rebellions ever to shake Russia. His initial victories were short-lived, however, and on January 11, 1775, Catherine had him executed.

NICHOLAS I (1825-55)

An active revolutionary movement had originated in Russia itself, meanwhile. It culminated in the Decembrist Revolt, which was brought on by Alexander's death in 1825. Filled with liberal ideas, the Decembrists dreamed of reforming Russia according to utopian Socialism. At the confused time of the succession, the cry went out for "Konstantin and Constitution." Konstantin was one of Alexander's brothers, and the ignorant soldiers believed that Constitution was Konstantin's wife! The Decembrist revolt was put down, Konstantin abdicated, and Nicholas I came to the throne.

Nicholas felt that revolutions were the result of education and he therefore opened many institutions of higher learning, but, the curriculum was rigidly supervised by the police and by severe censorship. Nicholas gained the reputation of being the most reactionary monarch in all Europe. Russia's reputation suffered greatly during the 19th century because of his enthusiasm for suppressing revolts for other monarchs.

THE REFORMS OF ALEXANDER II (1855-81)

Russia's defeat in the Crimean War (1854–56) against England, Turkey, France and Sardinia exposed to the whole world the complete decadence of the Russian state. Nicholas I, with an army of nearly 1,000,000 men, was unable to crush the 70,000-man army of the enemy.

He was succeeded by Alexander II, who was to be one of the more liberal monarchs of Russia. The new Czar was responsible for the "Abolition of Serfdom," which took place in 1861. Although for some time many of the liberal nobles had advocated this reform, the majority feared that it would ruin the land-owners economically, thus destroying the Crown's chief source of revenue and support. It soon became apparent that the peasant reforms would not live up to expectations, and the land-owners preserved a great deal of their personal power over the fate of the peasants.

In the two years that followed, there were over a thousand peasant disturbances. The government, becoming distrustful of its own reforms, rapidly returned to a reactionary policy. This caused only more unrest among the population, and was followed by the assassination of the Czar "Liberator," Alexander II.

Alexander III (1881–94), who succeeded on his father's assassination, sought to arrest any liberalization, and doggedly strengthened the autocratic regime.

THE END OF THE RUSSIAN EMPIRE

During the tragic era between 1904 and 1917, the Romanov dynasty gradually fell apart and the Russian Empire came to an end. Weak and incompetent, Russia's last Czar, Nicholas II (1894–1917), was easily influenced by reactionary advisors. On their irresponsible advice he involved Russia first in the unpopular and senseless Russo-Japanese War in 1904–05. Defeat in that war strengthened the revolutionary movement which fed on general dissatisfaction within Russia, making revolution possible.

REVOLUTION—1905

A large percentage of the rural population moved to urban areas as Russia became more industrialized. Working under harsh conditions, with long hours and little pay, the workers were naturally receptive to radical ideas.

Nicholas I (1825–55) felt that serfdom was an evil, but considered abolishing it an even greater evil.

On Sunday, January 9, 1905, a crowd of workers gathered in the streets of St. Petersburg. Led by a priest, Georgy A. Gapon, and armed only with icons and pictures of Czar Nicholas II, they marched to the Winter Palace in order to petition the monarch for more democratic reforms to better the lot of the workers. The streets, however, were soon blocked off by police and army units. When the crowd refused to disperse, the soldiers opened fire, killing over 130 persons and wounding several hundred, among them many women and children.

Emperor Paul I was supposedly the son of Catherine the Great and Peter III. There is, however, some doubt as to whether or not Peter III was his parent. After the memoirs of Catherine the Great were made public, Nicholas I, who was the monarch at that time, had all the copies confiscated and burned, for fear that his claim to the throne might be questioned.

Thus was born the first Russian Revolution: a wave of riots, strikes, murders and peasant revolts followed. Russia's heavy losses in the Russo-Japanese War, coupled with the chaos following the "Bloody Sunday," brought forth a general strike forcing the government to grant a limited constitution, with a representative Duma (parliament) to be elected democratically. This meant the beginning of the end of Russia's unlimited autocracy, but even this failed to restore order in the land. It resulted only in the formation of several political parties. Those satisfied with the constitution formed the Octobrist Party; the liberals united into the Constitutional Democratic Party; while the left-wing revolutionaries, who were by no means content, decided to continue their battle for complete social reforms, calling themselves the Social Democrats. The latter organized the first "Soviets" (councils of workers) among the striking workers.

Within a short time, the government arrested the Soviets, and this stopped all insurrections of the Moscow workers. With the restoration of order, the reactionary regime of Nicholas II was reinforced; the short-lived liberties were liquidated. But by now even the most ruthless government methods were unable to turn back a mounting tidal wave of revolution.

WORLD WAR I

As relations with the Kaiser's Germany became worse, Russia was forced into a Triple Entente with England and France, which inevitably drew Russia into World War I.

At the outbreak of World War I, most of the political parties joined in supporting Russia's effort, with the exception of the Bolsheviks, the left wing of the Social Democratic Party. The immense loss of life, suffering, and severe food shortage, both at the front and among civilians, created a "climate" for revolution.

The inept Czar, strongly influenced by his German-born wife, Empress Alexandra Feodorovna, and by her advisor, the sinister monk Gregory Y. Rasputin, as well as the entire cabinet, was soon suspected of secret dealings with Germany. All parties now withdrew their support of the monarchy. Revolutionary terror, strikes, propaganda and assassinations followed,

The Petrograd demonstration by workers and soldiers in 1917, was peaceful until the Provisional Government troops opened fire on the demonstrators.

One of the rare photographs of Vladimir I. Lenin in his Kremlin study, which has been preserved in the exact order that Lenin left it on his death—even the date on the calendar remains the same.

and futile attempts by the government to introduce agrarian reforms came to nothing.

MARXISM-LENINISM

The ideology of the Bolsheviks, later called Communists, was based on the socialist writings of a German, Karl Marx (1818–83). Certain changes were made by the Bolshevik leader and founder of the Russian Communist Party, Vladimir Ilyich Ulyanov who called himself Lenin.

Marxism was one of many schools of socialism which emerged in Western Europe as a result of the misery that accompanied the industrialization of Europe. Forecasting a violent, sudden revolution by the proletariat (working class), Marx urged the workers to seize power and use it for their own benefit. Marx based his theory on three "laws of history." He believed that all human institutions—

from art and religion to society and government—are determined primarily by economic conditions. To him, history was a "dialectic" process, by which he meant a series of struggles between opposing economic groups: the wealthy and the poor. Third, he believed in the inevitability of Communism. He said that the class struggle would result in one final upheaval, making the proletariat victorious over a defeated bourgeois (middle) class.

He predicted the "dictatorship of the proletariat"—a classless society in which the industrial workers would direct all the people. Lenin was Marxism's advocate in Russia, and his small group of Bolsheviks were looking for the right moment to create a revolution in which they could seize power.

REVOLUTION—1917

In February, 1917, the workers of Moscow and Petrograd (St. Petersburg until 1914) went

On the night of November 7, 1917, the Winter Palace, where the Provisional Government was in session, was stormed by the Bolsheviks, along with workers and sailors. Following an intensive battle, the Provisional Government was arrested. Its President, Alexander F. Kerensky, managed to escape, disguised as a woman.

out on strike, demanding higher food rations. The government replied by ordering the soldiers to open fire on the strikers. Mutiny spread in the army like wildfire, and the soldiers refused to fire, joining the ranks of the striking workers. After the fall of Petrograd to the insurgents, the Duma, which Nicholas attempted to dissolve, forced him to abdicate. A temporary Provisional Government was appointed. Nicholas and his family were imprisoned and finally, on July 16, 1918, they were executed in a cellar by the Bolsheviks.

Badly organized for war, and cut off now from its allies, Russia suffered immeasurably. The Provisional Government under Prince Lvov and later under Alexander Kerensky tried in vain to continue the war, only to be met by strong opposition from the soldiers and workers.

On November 6 and 7, 1917, the Bolsheviks, under the leadership of Lenin, seized control of the government with the aid of sailors and workers who stormed the Winter Palace in Petrograd, and captured the key buildings.

A peace treaty was concluded by the Bol-

sheviks at Brest-Litovsk on March 3, 1918. In the bloody Civil War that followed between the so-called White and Red (Bolshevik) forces, the Reds emerged in 1920 as victors. Poland, Lithuania, Latvia and Estonia became independent, and until World War II they formed a "Quarantine Belt" between Soviet Russia and Western Europe.

Lenin moved the government back to Moscow in 1918 and changed the party name from Bolshevik to Communist. By 1922, Russia was reunited with the Ukraine, Byelorussia, and the Transcaucasian (Georgia, Armenia and Azerbaijan) Republics, which had broken away, and officially proclaimed itself the Union of Soviet Socialist Republics or the USSR. In 1924, Uzbekistan and Turkmenia were formed and added to the Union.

Lenin, together with Leon Trotsky and Josef Stalin, his comrades in the Communist party, turned attention to the land, devastated from end to end by years of war and revolution, in an attempt to put the country back on its feet as quickly as possible.

THE RISE OF THE USSR

Russia emerged from the Civil War in a state of collapse unequalled in modern history. The economic system was crumbling. The entire industrial system, burdened by a cumbersome management plan, was coming to a halt. Agriculture was reduced to a level far below the requirements of the nation. And yet, Russia as a nation endured, but at a terrible price of human life and suffering.

Russia pursued an economic policy called "War Communism," as an emergency measure during the course of the Civil War. Under this policy all trade and industry were nationalized by the government, grain and wheat requisitioned by force, and all financial capital confiscated. This resulted in a continuing decline of agriculture and industry, which was rapidly leading the country to total impoverishment. The drought of 1920 and 1921 led to a nationwide famine; 5,000,000 people lost their lives, twice as many as Russia's total casualties in World War I. The death toll would have been higher still had it not been for the assistance of the United States. In August, 1922, the United States fed more than 10,000,000 Russians daily and distributed an enormous quantity of medical supplies.

Public unrest, followed by the insurrection of the Kronstadt garrison, forced Lenin to introduce the New Economic Policy (NEP) in 1921, which allowed for a return to a limited capitalist system, although the basic policy of the Russian Communist party had always called for complete socialism. Private ownership of small business was permitted, private trade restored and the forced collectivization of grain was discontinued. (As a result of NEP, by 1928 the national income of the USSR reached above its pre-war level.) Overwhelmed with practical problems which affected the very existence of the state, and which demanded immediate solutions, the government proceeded first to consolidate Communist power within the country. Basic political plans and procedures were announced and efforts were made in the years 1921–24 to establish them, though without much success.

JOSEF STALIN

Lenin's death in 1924 was followed by a fierce struggle for power between Stalin and Trotsky. This political match was won by Stalin, whose main concern was to strengthen and consolidate Communism in Russia, and by this provide a gradual transformation of the society. He called this "Socialism in One Country." Trotsky, on the other hand, was impatient to realize his ideal of immediate Communist world revolution through what he called the process of "Permanent Revolution." Trotsky was later exiled from the Soviet Union. He settled in Mexico, where he was murdered in 1940.

It was under Stalin that the first Five Year Plan was introduced, when it became apparent that NEP would be inadequate for the country's future economic growth. Gradually the state managed to gain control of all aspects of life from politics to culture, education and public information.

The assassination on December 1, 1934, of Sergei M. Kirov, political leader of Leningrad and one of Stalin's most trusted aides, unleashed a series of purges against thousands of military

"Winter Palace Taken," was painted by Valentin A. Serov (1865–1911), an outstanding artist and a master portrait painter. Most of his work is now housed in Moscow's Tretyakov Gallery and the Hermitage Museum in Leningrad.

The two monuments on the sides of Dorogomilovsky Bridge in Moscow were erected to commemorate those who died defending Moscow against the armies of Napoleon in 1812 in the battle of Borodino. This is how the bridge looked in 1928.

and political leaders, lasting from 1936 to 1938. An alleged plot against Stalin had supposedly been uncovered, involving such Communist leaders as Trotsky and Marshal Mikhail N. Tukhachevsky, and many of Lenin's closest comrades-in-arms, such as Grigory Y. Zinoviev and Lev B. Kamenev. Russia's heavy losses later in World War II were caused in part by the fact that most of the army's best and most experienced leaders had fallen victim to the purges. Some were executed, while others were sent to work camps.

FOREIGN POLICY

Keeping the nation out of war has been the main objective of the Soviet government's foreign policy ever since the 1920's. As the "outcasts" of Europe after World War I, Russia and Germany concluded a co-operation accord at Rapallo, Italy in 1922. Most Soviet leaders realized that any attack against it by a major power was likely to result in complete economic and political destruction of the USSR. Co-operation with Germany continued, despite Hitler's rise to power. When the Western powers failed to invite the USSR to negotiate with Hitler at Munich (1938), the Soviet Union concluded a non-aggression pact with Germany in 1939. Hitler's attack on Poland brought France and England into war with Germany. The USSR temporarily continued its pro-German policy and with Germany partitioned Poland by occupying all its territory up to the Bug River. At the same time, the Soviet Union annexed the Baltic States of Latvia, Lithuania and Estonia, making them into republics of the USSR by 1940. Russia invaded Finland in 1939 and waged war during the bitter winter into 1940. The Finns withstood the attack and obtained a Russian withdrawal after ceding Karelia and allowing the establishment of Russian military bases.

WORLD WAR II

Despite the non-aggression pact with Germany, there were growing signs that Hitler intended to invade the Soviet Union. The USSR grew apprehensive, and with good reason: Germany attacked on June 22, 1941. Kiev fell, as the German armies overran most of the Ukraine and Byelorussia. By 1941 Leningrad was surrounded. During a 29-month siege, some 3,000,000 heroic inhabitants of Leningrad withstood starvation, and more than 600,000 died.

A bitter winter, and a determined Russian counter-offensive saved Moscow. But the city of Stalingrad (later renamed Volgograd) was totally destroyed in 1942–43 during one of the most decisive and agonizing battles in all history. This served as a turning-point of the war, with nearly 330,000 German troops surrendering. Then, with a steady, unyielding offensive, the Soviet troops pushed into Poland and the Balkan Peninsula, liberating as they went. Finally on May 2, 1945, they marched through the streets of Berlin, and five days later, together with the Western Allies, accepted Germany's official surrender. Russia had paid a high price for victory, with a loss of millions and millions of lives.

The USSR declared war on Japan on August 8, 1945. Within a month, the Soviet forces penetrated deeply into Korea and Manchuria before Japan surrendered on September 2, 1945. As a result of the war and Allied agreements at Teheran, Yalta and Potsdam, the USSR gained the following territories: the Kuriles and the southern half of Sakhalin Island from Japan; some additional territory from Finland; and the northern territory of Eastern Prussia from Germany. The areas of the Ukraine and Byelorussia were greatly increased.

Today the Dorogomilovsky Bridge's name has been changed to Borodinsky Bridge. Below the waters of the Moscow River is the world's deepest underground transit station, the Kievskaya-Koltsevaya.

"Socialist Revolution Triumphed!" by B. Ioganson, is one of the few recent (1957) paintings in the government-sponsored Socialist Realism style, which strikingly resembles the style developed in Mexico in the public murals celebrating the revolutionary triumph of the lower classes. The revolutions in both countries took place during the same era.

THE COLD WAR

With the end of World War II, the USSR and the United States emerged as the two leading world powers. However, their co-operation and friendly relationships soon began to cool, and finally deteriorated into the "Cold War." The Western world became apprehensive over the increasing influence of the Soviet Union over Poland, Czechoslovakia, Hungary, Rumania, Bulgaria, Albania and mainland China, fearing the unlimited expansion of Communism. The Soviet Union was equally afraid that the Western powers would surround it. The relationship with the West went from bad to worse, finally erupting into hostilities when the United Nations beat back Communist forces in Korea in 1950–53.

The severity of the Cold War varied. At times Soviet-American relations seemed to warm, as during 1959, when Vice-President Richard Nixon journeyed to the American exhi-

bition in Moscow, or during 1962–63, the last year of President Kennedy's administration.

But there were deep and continuing crises, many of which revolved round West Berlin, which is located far inside the territory of the East German Communist state. During the post-war period, the Russians attempted to blockade Berlin (1948–49), causing the Western Allies to mount a life-saving airlift to the troubled city. On various occasions the USSR threatened to end unilaterally Berlin's status as a city occupied by the wartime allies. On August 13, 1961, the East Germans frightened the West by erecting the notorious Berlin Wall, which sealed off the eastern section of the city from the American, British and French sectors.

Another crisis came in November, 1956, when the Soviet Union rushed troops into Hungary to quell a swelling anti-Communist revolt by Hungarian "Freedom Fighters." A decade later, hostilities again erupted over United States involvement in Vietnam.

THE KHRUSHCHEV ERA (1953-64)

Stalin's death (March 5, 1953) came as such a shock that top government officials warned the people against panic and disorder. "Collective leadership" was proclaimed with Nikita S. Khrushchev becoming the party chief, and Georgi M. Malenkov, the premier. Later Khrushchev assumed both positions after successfully defeating an opposition movement called the Anti-Party Group in 1957 and side-tracking his rivals.

The people of the Soviet Union began to gain more personal freedom and security. Under Khrushchev's leadership, the famous 20th Communist Party Congress ushered in a "de-Stalinization" campaign, and altered Communist theory to permit "peaceful co-existence" of nations with different social systems and the possibility of peaceful transition from "bourgeois democracy" to "Socialism." At the same time it continued a definite economic, diplomatic and psychological offensive abroad, especially in underdeveloped nations. It also startled the world with the launching of the first artificial satellite (or sputnik), on October 4, 1957, and subsequent space launchings of human beings. It alarmed the world with the testing of atomic bombs.

BREZHNEV AND KOSYGIN

The era came to an end on October 15, 1964, when Khrushchev was replaced as head of the Communist Party by Leonid I. Brezhnev and as Premier by Aleksei N. Kosygin, in a peaceful coup. On the domestic front, a new approach to government soon became evident. The government leaders denounced through the press Khrushchev's "subjective and emotional" style of leadership, but reaffirmed previous Soviet policy. They reshuffled power among themselves and called for a return of "collective leadership," in contrast to the one-man rule which had emerged under Khrushchev. The Five Year Plan they announced on February 20, 1966, is considered by most Western observers to be much more realistic than any previous plan in the goals it has set. This may be attributed to the fact that Kosygin himself is an economist. He is viewed by outsiders as a shrewd businessman. Although the Soviet Union is not expected to reduce its heavy industrial output, the future plans of the country include a definite increase in light industry, with a strong emphasis on consumer goods for the purpose of raising the standard of living.

Although Nikita Khrushchev has been ousted from his formerly powerful position, the effects of his policies will be felt for some time to come.

In the background of this view of the Palace Square in Leningrad is the General Staff Building, while the foreground is dominated by the graceful Alexander Column, erected to celebrate the victory of Russia over Napoleon in 1812.

GOVERNMENT

THE COMMUNIST PARTY

THE RULING POLITICAL ORGANIZATION in the USSR is the Communist Party of the Soviet Union (CPSU), the only legal political party in the country. In practice, major Soviet policies issue from its Central Committee, which instructs government and public organizations on how best to develop almost everything from the economy, to mass culture, to the needs of social welfare.

The Central Committee is the reigning body between sessions of the party's Congress which convenes, according to the Party Statutes, once every 4 years. The Congress brings together for a period of about 10 days to 2 weeks some 1,500 top Communists who are elected to represent the party's total membership, which now numbers well over 12,000,000 (out of a population of 241,000,000.) It is the Congress which elects the Central Committee. Thus neither the Soviet people nor the mass of Communist members

The USSR is the most education-conscious country in the world after the United States, but the curriculum is rigidly supervised by the government. Although Russia can boast that there is virtually no uneducated citizen, free speech in public is definitely not encouraged.

have a direct say in its composition or its decisions.

Since the Central Committee is a body of about 300 members, and usually meets only two or three times a year, it, in turn, elects various bodies to direct and execute its policies on a day-to-day basis. These bodies are the Politburo and the Secretariat. The Politburo is composed of about a dozen members who are actively concerned with, and are ultimately responsible to the Central Committee for, developing policy. The Secretariat, also responsible to the Central Committee, is the party's chief executive arm. It is headed by a General Secretary who is, in fact, the Communist Party's chief, and who theoretically sits as an equal among equals on the Politburo.

GOVERNMENTAL ORGANS

Parallel to the Communist Party stands the vast governmental apparatus which conducts the nation's foreign and domestic policies, that is,

the policies developed within the Communist Party.

As in Western countries, the Soviet government may be divided into executive, legislative, and judicial branches whose authority is based on a constitution. The present constitution, which was written under Stalin, was adopted on December 5, 1936. It supplanted the previous constitutions of 1918 and 1924. Under former Premier Khrushchev a commission was established to formulate yet another constitution.

The highest legislative power is theoretically vested in the Supreme Soviet of the USSR, which meets about 10 days to 2 weeks every year to discuss and approve legislation. In practice, it amounts to a rubber stamp parliament and a dignified forum for open discussion of Soviet policies. Its debates are, on the whole, laudatory, although mild criticism is on occasion permissible.

The Supreme Soviet consists of two chambers—the Soviet or Council of the Union and the Soviet or Council of Nationalities. The former represents the interests of the entire Soviet people, while the latter expresses the special interests of the Soviet Union's many nationalities. The 1,400 Deputies of these two chambers are elected by universal suffrage for a period of four years.

It is a joint session of the two Chambers which formally names a Council of Ministers of the USSR, or cabinet, and designates the Chairman of the Council of Ministers or Premier. The Premier and his cabinet form the executive branch of the government.

A similar session names the Supreme Court of the USSR and appoints the country's Procurator General. The Supreme Court justices and the Procurator General head the Soviet judiciary which, of course, comprises an extensive system of lower courts and legal officers.

Since the Supreme Soviet assembles so infrequently, legislative matters which crop up between sessions are handled by a steering committee whose title is The Presidium of the Supreme Soviet. The chairman of this Presidium is deemed to be the chief of state, and his 15 deputies—one from each of the 15 Soviet republics—are considered, in Western terminology, to be Vice-Presidents of the Soviet Union.

Additionally, both chambers of the Supreme Soviet name committees to deal with various aspects of Soviet policy, and these meet from time to time to hold discussions on particularly important issues.

VOTING

Anyone over 18, male or female, can vote, and the minimum age for holding office is 23. Candidates for election may be nominated at factory meetings, collective farm gatherings, from trade unions or any other organization. A candidate need not be a member of the Communist Party, and once nominated he is assured election since he runs on a single slate, unopposed by any other candidate, in his constituency.

Soviet elections are always held on a Sunday and they take on the aura of a national holiday in which 99 per cent or more of the registered voters consistently turn out to cast their ballots for the single candidate. Of course, since the ballot is secret, voters can, and sometimes do, vote against the candidate. But in general, the candidate is elected by a huge proportion of the voters. Thus, in practical terms, the selective process in the Soviet election system ends with the nomination.

THE PRESS

The Soviet press—radio, television, and newspapers—are effectively controlled in the Soviet Union by the party and government authorities. In contrast to the part the press plays in Western democracies, the role of the press in the USSR is to inform the population on a carefully edited basis, to offer "inspired" criticism of social issues, and to mould public opinion to follow official policies.

Interior decorating varies from one region to the next. In northern Russia one can see houses decorated with fancy carvings, stocked with wooden utensils that have not changed in years. In the Ukraine, many houses are whitewashed, embroidered runners are the traditional decoration features, and the stoves are decorated with tiles portraying animals and plants. In the Caucasus and Central Asia, the main adornments consist of sheepskin rugs, beautiful pillows and carpets.

THE PEOPLE

THE PEOPLE of this multi-national country, with their varied traditions and customs, have made great contributions to world culture in ballet, music, literature, theatre and the fine arts. Although Russian is the official language of the country, the Soviet government has encouraged the many different nationalities to retain their heritage and language. Strangely enough, it is from these that some of the finest talent has emerged, despite the fact that only 30 years ago many of these ancient nationalities did not possess a written language.

LIVING CONDITIONS

What are the Russians like? Many foreigners find that the average Russian is quite similar to the average American. Both are hard workers, good providers and attached to their families. Russians display a genuine curiosity towards the foreigner and are known for their hospitality.

Living conditions have vastly improved in recent years, although the lack of consumer goods and living space is still a major problem.

RUSSIA ■ 313

Every town has its market known as the "Rynok." Most of the products there consist of fruits and vegetables. However, it is still quite difficult to buy fruit and vegetables out of season, and even if they are available their prices are exorbitant.

The average family usually has two bread-winners, but the lot of the woman is much harder than that of the man. Although both men and women enjoy professional respect and equality, the woman is still faced with all her household chores after working for 7 hours each day. Frequently the "babushka" (grandmother) helps out. However, there is no feeling of insecurity under the system, because the education of children is free and so is medical care. Therefore, there is no pressure to save money, a great deal of which is spent on food. If a person becomes ill he may receive either all, or at least 75 per cent of, his salary. Life in the rural areas is considerably more difficult, but even there, as industrialization penetrates deep into the country, both culture and living standards are rising rapidly.

Young Russians are especially conscious of modern trends and furnish their homes very simply, but with good taste.

Nearly 7,000,000 pre-school children spend their day in nurseries and kindergartens, and the demand for more nurseries is continually increasing.

YOUTH

Virtually every boy and girl between the ages of 9 and 15 is a member of the Young Pioneers. These groups engage in a wide variety of activities which teach the youngsters to have a healthy respect for work, use their initiative, organize socially useful activities and be happy and courageous. Youngsters have at their disposal thousands of clubs, palaces, stadiums, libraries, and camps. Most of these children later join the Young Communist League, a youth organization which is mainly concerned with the political education of the future citizens of the Communist State. It tries to instill in them the moral principles and ideals of the Communist society.

RELIGION

Most Russians belong to no church, and in fact atheism is strongly advocated by the Communist Party. Of the few who are religious, the denomination with the largest number of adherents is the Russian Orthodox Church. The second largest denomination is Islam; there are also Roman Catholics, Lutherans, Evangelical Baptists, and a number of Jews. Buddhists can be found in many parts of the Asian USSR.

The state does not finance the church in any way, nor is religion taught in schools. The church and clergy have to depend on their own sources of income or on donations from their congregations. The teaching of religious beliefs by the clergy is also limited by the state.

Although many churches and places of worship have been open to the public for some time, the majority of those attending are old men and women. The younger generation has not been brought up to believe in God and therefore tends to view religion with a mixture of cynicism and amazement. However, on big religious holidays there is always a crowd of curiosity-seekers, especially during the beautiful Easter services.

Early introduction to acting teaches and stimulates the children to love and respect the theatre. Plays are produced in 45 languages in the USSR's more than 500 professional theatres.

During the Stalin period Russian women were officially reproached if they attempted to look too feminine, because they were "wasting valuable time." Today, although it may cost half her monthly salary, the woman living in a large city will sport the latest spike-heeled shoes or an elegant Italian knit suit. Here is the interior of GUM, Moscow's State Department Store.

Chess is a popular national pastime and both young and old play the game with great enthusiasm. The world's leading chess players are usually Russian.

Ballet star Rudolf Nureyev took a record 89 curtain calls with Dame Margot Fonteyn in the Vienna State Opera House in one of Nureyev's first appearances after his defection from the USSR. Russia has produced many of the world's best ballet dancers, and some of the loveliest and most enduring ballet music. The Bolshoi ballet plays to a full house, whether in Russia or on tour throughout the world.

MUSIC

Although Peter the Great and Catherine the Great brought European music to Russia in the 18th century, the real father of Russian music was Michael I. Glinka (1804–57). He was the first to use folk and even Oriental elements in his works, which were not mere imitations of Western music. Subsequently Alexander Borodin, the prolific Nikolai Rimsky-Korsakov, Modest Musorgsky, and Peter I. Tchaikovsky (1840–93) developed some of the world's best-loved music.

LITERATURE

Despite the fact that Russian literature did not appear on the European scene until the middle of the 19th century, its tradition is quite long, dating back to the 11th century. However, the first really exciting literary figure was Russia's greatest poet, Alexander S. Pushkin (1799–1837). Deeply imbued with the spirit of classicism, he had a literary genius that managed to withstand the test of time. He was the first to fuse together successfully the spoken and the literary languages, which up to that time had

The great Russian painter, Ilya E. Repin, with his family. Among his famous canvases are "Ivan the Terrible Kills His Son Ivan" and the exuberant "Zaporozdzy Cossacks."

been totally different. He is the author of *Boris Godunov*, Russia's first national drama, and *Eugene Onegin*, one of the greatest verse novels.

Another great writer of the 19th century was Fyodor M. Dostoyevsky (1822–81), whose novels explored different stages in the development of psychology and philosophy, uncovering the hidden nature of man. Some of his best-known novels are: *The Brothers Karamazov, The Idiot*, and *Crime and Punishment*. Ivan S. Turgenev (1813–83) devoted much attention to the description of nature and the peasants. Later he concentrated on Russia's social conditions and changes, and was the first Russian writer to become acclaimed in the West. A member of the school of realism, Count Leo N. Tolstoy (1828–1910) is rightly considered to be the greatest Russian novelist of the 19th century. In his world-renowned novels *War and Peace* and *Anna Karenina*, Tolstoy not only recaptured "reality" most convincingly, but showed great insight into the human heart and mind. A fascinating writer with great universal appeal was Anton P. Chekhov (1860–1904), whose short stories and plays enjoy a great deal of popularity.

The Soviet period is enriched by the overpowering figure of Maxim Gorky (whose real name was Aleksei M. Peshkov) (1868–1936), often called the "father of Soviet literature." Although he started as an Impressionist, his later attraction for minute detail earned him the title of "the greatest master of Socialist Realism," a style created under Stalin's inspiration in the late Twenties. In practice it called for works which would serve to educate and instill party viewpoints in a mass audience. In literature this meant that it had to be socialist in content and realistic in form. Michael A. Sholokhov's great epic, *And Quiet Flows the Don*, amazing in its broad grasp of life, dramatic intensity, and the

Alexander S. Pushkin, whose black-skinned grandfather was an Ethiopian page of Peter the Great, is considered the father of Russian poetry and a master of prose and drama. Tragically, he died at the age of 38 in a duel.

This exquisite wash bowl and pitcher are the work of a 17th-century craftsman. Many indescribably lovely works of art were the possessions of the rulers of Russia.

simple and honest portrayal of its complex characters, won the Nobel Prize for Literature in 1965.

Poetry as an art form has had the most freedom of all artistic expressions in the USSR. The futurist poet Vladimir V. Mayakovsky (1893–1930) attained the highest poetic skill of the century, leaving a strong imprint on the work of his disciples. Among other Russian poets are Anna A. Akhmatova (1888–1966) and the late Boris L. Pasternak (1890–1960), whose novel, *Dr. Zhivago*, angered Soviet officialdom because of its deeply critical passages, and who was pressured to reject the Nobel Prize for Literature in 1958. Current poets include Andrei A. Voznesensky, Yevgeny A. Yevtushenko, and Bella A. Akhmadullina.

ART

Russian art is virtually unknown in the West, with the exception of the beautiful icons. After Russia's conversion to Christianity, iconography was almost the only form of painting Russia knew, up to the 16th century. Russian classicism developed under the guidance of Catherine the Great and many fine painters emerged at that time. The reign of Czar Nicholas I brought with it the development of Romantic painting.

The movement that followed was that of Russian Impressionism which lasted until 1920. Soon, however, it was replaced by a new group which called itself "Mir Iskusstva," formed by Serge P. Diaghilev, Alexander N. Benois, and Leon N. Bakst. They believed in "art for art's

These exquisite gold filigree medallions, with garnets and enamel, were found in the 19th century, and are the rarest discovery of Russia's early art form.

Wearing his traditional costume, a teacher engages in the ancient art of archery. Almost everyone in Russia engages in some form of sports activity.

"Kuresh" is a national wrestling game of Kirghizia. Every republic has its own particular sport, reflecting a variety of cultural influences.

Soccer is the number one form of sports entertainment, with nearly 15,000,000 spectators a year filing into the grandstands.

One of the most exciting sports to watch is the daring motorcycle race on ice.

This is the main arena of the Lenin Stadium in Moscow. The pride and joy of sports-loving Muscovites, it is pointed out to tourists as one of the seven wonders of the modern world.

sake" and quickly formed ties with the West. During the Soviet period the style of Socialist Realism was officially adopted. This called for the creation of a "positive hero" and resulted in a great deal of portrait painting.

Today, Russia has become more exposed to modern, Western art. For the past few years, young artists have produced many fine paintings, most of which are abstract and non-objective, showing an amazing freedom of expression and vitality. Though many of them have not been officially exhibited and do not earn the approval of the USSR's Artists Union, these paintings are slowly emerging from the "closets," and can be seen. Some of the leading figures are Yury Vasilyev, Dmitri Krasnopevtsev, and Ilya Glazunov.

SPORTS

The people of the USSR are ardent sport enthusiasts and if they do not participate in a sports activity themselves, they readily enjoy being spectators.

Although officially there are no professional sports in the USSR, most of the athletes cannot really consider themselves amateurs either. Their training is severe, demanding much time and energy, and a great deal of assistance comes from the government, both financial and moral. In fact, many of the leading athletes want to be called professionals, because they feel this would be a much more realistic appraisal. The most popular sport is soccer and both young and old fill the grandstands when there is a match.

Since 1952 Soviet sportsmen have participated in the Olympic Games, coming away every time with some of the gold medals after setting new records. Russia's women athletes are considered the best in the world. All in all, nearly 5,000,000 people participate in light athletics, 4,000,000 play volleyball, almost 4,000,000 ski, more than 3,000,000 enjoy football and about 1,000,000 are gymnasts.

This house in Leningrad is being constructed from top to bottom, after the framework has gone up. Each section has been prefabricated, complete with space for wiring and pipes, before being lifted into place. The electricians and plumbers need only to connect the sections together after all are hoisted into position. It is easier to thread wires and pipes downward, and that is why the Russian workers start at the top.

THE ECONOMY

AFTER THE REVOLUTION of 1917, all private enterprise was abolished in the USSR, although the Communists met strong initial resistance. Today all the land, minerals, waters, banks, factories, mines, large agricultural enterprises, and most of the dwellings are State property, theoretically belonging to all the people collectively. Although a person may own a house, the land on which it is built belongs to the State. Since there is no private enterprise, in the Soviet Union all workers are employed by the government.

Today the country is operated on a basis of a planned economy. This enables the men who are in charge of production to concentrate a particular factory on one objective or to change it if necessary to another type of manufacture— something which is not done so easily in other nations. The current Five Year Plan was preceded by seven others. The first was put into operation in 1928, under Stalin, when it became obvious that NEP was delaying the formation of a state-operated, socialist economy. During the first three Five Year Plans, heavy industry and production of vitally needed equipment and raw materials were tremendously accelerated, resulting in a fantastic growth of both agriculture and industry in a few short years.

In the fourth Five Year Plan (1946–50) industrial production surpassed the pre-war level, although agriculture continued to suffer from lack of incentive among the peasants. The fifth Five Year Plan continued to stress heavy industry, but did increase consumer goods slightly. Replacing the over-estimated sixth Five Year Plan (1956–60) was the ambitious Seven Year Plan (1959–65), which called for accelerated housing construction, industrial output and a 40 per cent increase in the standard of living.

THE FIVE YEAR PLAN OF 1966-70

Announced in February, 1966, the blueprint of the eighth Five Year Plan stressed priority to consumer goods and emphasized agricultural production. The Soviet government had in effect promised its citizens better food and clothing, higher income (or lower prices), and more motor-cars and apartments by 1970; in short, a better material life.

However, Russia entered 1970, the last year of the 1966 Plan, with a slowed-down, rather than an expanding, economy. Housing was far more available, and television and radio sets abundant—but furniture, motor cars, and good clothing were hard to come by. Foreign observers blamed the slow-down on the failure of management to keep up with technological change.

World-renowned for its squirrel, muskrat, sable, silver fox, mink and Persian lamb, the USSR ranks first in the world in the variety, quantity and value of its furs.

AGRICULTURE

With the introduction of the first Five Year Plan in 1928, collective farms were ruthlessly introduced throughout the country. With the land owned by the State, all smaller farms were forcibly collectivized and were then worked by the peasants together. In these farms the peasants have collective ownership of the basic means of production such as farm buildings, draught animals, livestock and farm machinery.

In recent years, Soviet agriculture has suffered numerous setbacks, largely due to harsh weather conditions. These forced the Kremlin to buy enormous quantities of grain abroad, particularly from the United States and Canada. However, other difficulties exist in the Soviet farming system which make for yields far below the potential. The greatest problems are a lack of widespread mechanization, and a lack of chemical fertilizers. Further, the previous organization of farm workers was inefficient and offered little incentive. Current changes in working conditions are aimed at overcoming these drawbacks. In March, 1965, Brezhnev announced a vast plan to invest very heavily over the next five years in agriculture, and generally ease the financial situation with more generous credits. The Soviet government, revising working conditions on the collective farms, has decided to introduce a guaranteed monthly wage for farmers. This went into effect on July 1, 1966, and replaces an earlier system of payment for the amount of work produced and its quality. Last year, pensions were also introduced for the first time for collective farmers. The Soviet Union also has State Farms, which are state-operated and state-owned. The peasants do not own any part of these farms and are paid strictly in cash. In the countryside, an agricultural tax is collected on incomes from personal products grown on the small private plots allocated to each collective farmer.

Land, like all natural wealth, is considered state property, belonging to all the people. Agriculture, however, has for years been the weakest area of the USSR's economy. With modern methods and machinery the Soviet Union expects to secure better crops in the near future. Now, for the first time, the collective farm worker has been guaranteed a wage equivalent to that of a factory worker. This was done in the hope of luring and holding skilled workers, who often prefer to live in the city.

INDUSTRY

The USSR accounts for over 20 per cent of the total world industrial production, which puts it in second place after the United States. Its main output is in heavy industry, mainly electrification, mechanization and automation of the economy. The USSR is the first in Europe and second in the world in the production of electric power. Until recently, coal dominated the Soviet Union's fuel balance, but because oil and natural gas are more expedient and far more convenient to use, the USSR has now emphasized priority in oil and gas extraction and processing. Under the long term plan (1961–80), gas output is to increase nearly 14 to 15 times and oil five times.

A large-scale chemical industry is rapidly being built up—the USSR stands second in the world already in its output of chemical products. A great deal has been done in the automation of production, and the possibilities for further automation and mechanization are endless. If workers are displaced, the State simply moves them to other jobs.

WORKING CONDITIONS

The average working week in the USSR is a little under 40 hours, with 36 hours for all persons working under unusually difficult conditions. Wages depend on the worker's qualifications, as well as on the conditions under which he has to perform his job. Bonuses are given for over-fulfilling the quota, or if the finished product has in some way been improved by the worker—as well as for long years of service.

Women have full equality with men in almost any profession. They are often seen working as street cleaners, steam-roller operators and in steel mills. Expectant mothers are granted 3 months' paid leave when their child is about to be born. Almost all factories and offices have their own nurseries for the care of the children of the female employees. The rigorous climate, lack of conveniences and hard work often age Russians more than their counterparts in the wealthier capitalistic countries. The retirement age in the Soviet Union is 60 for men, 55 for women. If a person does not wish to retire, he may continue to work on salary.

POLAND

The Vistula River goes right in through the "Stare Miasto" ("the Old Town") in Warsaw.

THE LAND

GEOGRAPHICALLY, Poland is situated in about the middle of the European continent, its outline being somewhat like a distorted circle. With an area of 120,733 square miles, Poland ranks seventh in size in Europe. Its land area was considerably greater before World War II —approximately 150,470 square miles. In compensation for the 69,860 square miles ceded to the Soviet Union in 1945, Poland received some 40,000 square miles of German territory. This was all east of the Odra-Nysa line, and comprised Silesia, Pomerania, West Prussia and part of East Prussia. This arrangement has not been fully recognized by Western nations, however. In other words, Poland's boundaries after the war were almost literally pushed from east to west giving Russia more land and taking away some of Germany.

Poland is bounded on the north by the Baltic Sea and the Soviet Union, on the east by the Soviet Union, on the south by Czechoslovakia, and on the west by East Germany. Poland today has approximately the same amount of land area as the state of New Mexico, and is slightly larger than Italy.

Poland's frontiers extend for 2,197 miles, 1,872 on land, and 325 miles along the coast of the Baltic Sea. Poland has a common border with the Soviet Union of 772 miles; with Czechoslovakia for 814; and with East Germany for 286 miles.

TOPOGRAPHY

Poland's landscape is predominantly a series of plains with 97 per cent of the country's area

Szczecin (Stettin), one of the oldest cities in western Pomerania, is beautifully located on the River Ina. In recent years over 12,000 dwelling units have been constructed in the Szczecin district.

The Square of the Three Crosses is one of the most beautiful places in Warsaw. St. Alexander's Church, a replica of the Roman Pantheon, which stands in the middle, was built originally in the 19th century. All the buildings around St. Alexander's were rebuilt in the early 1950's.

situated below an altitude of 1,640 feet. In fact the Poles from the earliest times were known as "Polanie," meaning "plainsmen." However, there are also many areas rich in picturesque forests, mountains and lakes. The highest point in Poland is the Rysy, a peak in the Tatra Mountains, standing at 7,950 feet above sea level.

Geographically, Poland can be divided into three major regions crossing the country in three generally latitudinally parallel zones. In the north is a low-lying plain, a segment of the great North European Plain. It rises gradually southward into the second, or central region, which includes the low, rolling hills of Upper Silesia. South of Silesia are the

The High Tatras in southern Poland make an ideal locale for skiing, tobogganing and a variety of other winter sports. In the west Tatras alone there are nearly 100 miles of ski trails.

mountains of the Sudetes in the west and the Carpathians in the east, which together form Poland's border with Czechoslovakia. The High Tatras form a part of the Carpathian mountain system and only in the High Tatras can the Poles participate in any genuine Alpine sports, such as skiing and mountain climbing.

Poland's longest river is the Vistula, 664 miles long. The major rivers sweep across the three major regions: the Vistula with its tributaries drains more than half of Poland, and the Odra with its tributaries drains much of western Poland. A small area in southern Poland drains to the Danube and to the Dnestr.

A ride on the Dunajec River through the picturesque Pieniny Mountains provides unforgettable moments for tourists who come to Poland.

Spruce trees are covered with snow during the long winter months in Glodowka, near Zakopane, in Poland's southern mountain region.

The largest lake of Poland is the Sniardwy, covering 36 square miles. In the voivodship (province) of Olsztyn are the most lakes—over 10 per cent of its total area (compared with an average of one per cent for the whole country).

The low-lying Baltic coast is indented by the Stettin Lagoon, the Gulf of Danzig, and the Vistula Lagoon. Szczecin (Stettin), Gdynia, and Gdansk (Danzig) are the chief ports along this generally sparsely inundated coast.

CLIMATE

Poland is situated in a zone of transitional climate, right between the cool, dry continental climate of eastern Europe and the warmer, moist oceanic climate of western Europe. Consequently, the climate is generally known for its variability of weather. It is possible to distinguish six seasons instead of the traditional four: early spring, spring, summer, autumn, early winter, and winter.

The mean summer temperature is 62.6 degrees F., and the mean winter temperature 26.6 degrees F. Absolute maximum temperature was reached at Pruszkow on July 29, 1921, with 104.4 degrees, and the absolute minimum at Zywiec, February 10, 1929, with minus 41.1 degrees F.

The greatest number of sunny days occur in May through July. Most frequent sunshine and highest temperatures prevail along the seacoast between Darlowo and Rozewie, in the south on the Sudetes slopes, and in northern Wielkopolska (Greater Poland) in the western part of the country.

NATURAL RESOURCES

Poland is rich in minerals, though as a result of World War II it lost many of its oil wells and deposits of potassium salts. However, it gained enormous deposits of high-grade coal, zinc, and lead, and valuable iron ore fields in Silesia.

*The picturesque valley of
the River San, near the
town of Lesko, in
southeastern Poland.*

Poland now ranks sixth in the world in hard coal deposits (estimated at 86,000,000,000 tons). The richest deposits of hard coal are found in Upper Silesia. Deposits of brown coal (lignite), an important fuel for the power industry (40,000,000,000 tons) are located mostly in southwestern and central Poland.

During the 1956-59 period, several series of discoveries of rich deposits of natural gas were made in southeastern Poland, and copper-ore deposits, estimated as the largest in Europe, were uncovered in western Poland.

Sulphur deposits, discovered in central Poland in 1953, and rock salt deposits in southern and central Poland (estimated at 11,000,000,000 tons) are among the world's richest.

Numerous mineral springs should also be listed among Poland's natural resources. Poland has over 30 fully-equipped modern spas, chiefly in the southern part of the country.

FLORA AND FAUNA

Plants and animals of Poland are typical of the moderate climate zone in Central Europe. Virtually all of modern Poland was originally forested. Although major inroads were made into the forest areas during the Middle Ages and subsequent centuries, Poland is still a well-wooded land, with forest regions covering at least 26 per cent of the total area. The only significant area of primeval or virgin woods is the Bialowieza Forest, a large park in the northeastern section of the country, near Bialystok, at the Russian frontier. Almost three quarters of Poland's forests are evergreens, chiefly pine and spruce. In the southern region, leaf-bearing trees are more common, including ash, poplar, willow, birch, beech, elm, oak, and alder.

The Bialowieza Forest is inhabited by bison, elks, lynx, bears, tarpans (wild ponies), foxes, deer and other animals.

In the mountain ranges of the Bieszczady, wild boar, wolves, mountain deer and other animals still roam free. In the rocky, Alpine landscape of the Tatra National Park one can find eagles, marmots, chamois (goats) and bears, and among plants, the edelweiss, the stone pine, and rare species of numerous other plants.

The clear waters of the lakes and rivers of northern Poland abound in various kinds of fish and wild fowl, including such rare species as cormorants, black storks and wild swans.

Rare species of plants and animals have been placed under special protection in the national parks (of which there are 12 at present) and in nature reserves (over 450). Because they contain so many of the curiosities of nature, and because of their great scenic value, the national parks are now major tourist attractions.

New office buildings and apartment houses in downtown Warsaw make this one of Europe's most attractive capital cities. The circular building in the foreground is the headquarters for PEKAO, Poland's foreign trade agency.

CITIES

WARSAW

The capital and largest city, Warsaw, is located in the middle of the country, on both banks of the Vistula, 715 miles southwest of Moscow, 320 miles east of Berlin. Founded in the 13th century in the dukedom of Masovia, Warsaw became an important trading point in the Middle Ages. After the union of Poland and Lithuania, Warsaw grew even more important, and the seat of government was transferred there in 1596 from Krakow.

The Palace of Staszic and its statue of Polish Astronomer Nicolaus Copernicus is a Warsaw landmark.

The Palace of Culture (left), the tallest structure in Warsaw and the rest of Poland, is in Soviet architectural style. The library on the main floor houses many hundreds of books on technical subjects written in English.

Most of the city's historic buildings along the Royal Axis parallel to the Vistula River have been beautifully and faithfully reconstructed according to their original designs. The northern end of this axis is the old city ("Stare Miasto") with the medieval Market Square as the core. The reconstructed Gothic Cathedral of St. John, the seat of the Roman Catholic Primate of Poland, is situated between the Market Square and the ruins of the Royal Castle. The middle of the Axis consists of two avenues where most of the palaces of the nobility of the past three centuries were located. Lazienki Park, with its 18th-century Summer Palace of Poland's last king, lies at the southern end of the axis.

WROCLAW

Wroclaw, formerly known as Breslau when it was the capital of German Lower Silesia,

This part of Wroclaw was almost entirely rebuilt after World War II.

Suburban sections have grown around Wroclaw during the past 15 years. These apartment houses are under construction in Gajewice just outside the city.

was turned back to Poland by the Potsdam Conference of 1945. In the closing days of World War II, Wroclaw withstood an 84-day siege against the Russians and gave in only after the German surrender. The city's main section was nearly 75 per cent destroyed.

Wroclaw lies approximately 200 miles southwest of Warsaw on both banks of the Odra River. An important Polish town during the Piast Dynasty, Wroclaw has been a Roman Catholic bishopric since the middle of the 11th century.

In 1945, liberated Wroclaw, the chief city of Silesia, was returned to Poland. Known as Breslau when it belonged to Germany during World War II, it was 70 per cent destroyed. The reconstruction, which took more than a decade, was a painful process. Shown here is the main building of Wroclaw University.

After World War II, Lublin developed rapidly as an industrial area. Over 20,000 apartment dwelling units were constructed.

When completed, Katowice's downtown section will be as modern as any city's in Europe. Katowice, in south central Poland, together with five other Silesian cities, Sosnowiec, Gliwice, Bytom, Zabrze, and Chorzow, compose the Silesian Industrial Region.

"Trojmiasto," the "Three Towns," is the name applied to three closely connected cities on the Baltic Sea, Gdansk, Sopot and Gdynia. One of the most recently established and attractive quarters of Trojmiasto is "Przymorze"—"Seashore." Construction of the quarter commenced in 1959 and by 1963 there were already 7,000 people living there. By the end of 1972 the population of Przymorze will be at least 60,000. Shown here is the new quarter as it looked at the beginning of construction.

After World War II, most of the historic buildings were carefully reconstructed according to original designs. These buildings include the cathedral of St. John the Baptist, the Protestant church of St. Elizabeth, and the Gothic City Hall.

KRAKOW

Krakow, capital of Poland from the 12th century to 1596, is situated 155 miles southwest of Warsaw in a broad valley on the left bank of the Vistula where it meets the Rudawa River. Founded in the 9th century, Krakow became the country's commercial and cultural hub during the Middle Ages. Called "the Polish Rome," Krakow has been the seat of a Roman Catholic bishopric since the 10th century. (The Jagellonian University founded there in 1364 is Poland's oldest university.)

The Royal Wawel Castle, one of the city's main points of interest, contains the tombs of many Polish kings and a museum that has attracted tourists from the world over.

Krakow escaped destruction during World War II, though it suffered many acts of terror at the hands of the Nazi occupiers.

GDANSK

Gdansk, one of Poland's most historic cities, was founded as a fishing village in about 970. Located on the left bank of the Vistula, three miles from the Baltic, Gdansk became Poland's leading port and gained membership as a city in the Hanseatic League in 1361. In the 16th and 17th centuries, Gdansk was the central point of Poland's international trade.

The city came under Prussian rule during the partitions of Poland, and in 1919, the Allies, attempting to give Poland an outlet to the sea, made Gdansk (then known as Danzig) a "free city." Poland was given access to the city by a corridor some 20 to 90 miles wide which separated Germany from East Prussia. Poland's refusal to give in to Hitler's demand for a German corridor across the Polish corridor was one incident that brought on World War II.

Gdansk suffered great destruction during the war when the population dropped from 250,000 to 118,000. As in Warsaw, the historic buildings, representing Gothic, Renaissance and Baroque architecture, were restored to their original forms.

POLAND ■ **335**

Gdansk has four universities and colleges, a philharmonic orchestra, two legitimate theatres, and other cultural attractions. The city is again Poland's leading seaport.

POZNAN

Poznan, located in western Poland on both banks of the Warta River, 175 miles west of Warsaw, has a turbulent history stretching back for more than 1,000 years. A Roman Catholic bishopric was formed there in the 10th century and the Polish kings lived in Poznan until 1296. Poznan fell under Prussian rule during the partitions and suffered in the struggle between Germany and Russia during World War II.

The city today is Poland's leading manufacturer of agricultural equipment.

LODZ

Lodz, Poland's second largest city with a population of 750,000, is situated 82 miles southwest of Warsaw by rail in the country's central region. The city's growth was rapid: the population, which was only 50,000 in 1872, reached 672,000 in 1939. During this period the textile industry in Lodz became one of the most extensive in all of Europe. Before World War I, the city was the focal point for a myriad of Polish worker and socialist movements.

For years Lodz has been known as Poland's "Problem City" because of inadequate housing, air pollution, traffic congestion and related urban ills. However, recent urban redevelopment schemes have met with some success and the city for the first time is developing a cultural life.

All the historic buildings in Gdansk were carefully reconstructed according to their original designs after World War II. Here the statue of Neptune can be seen in front of a government building.

Malbork, Europe's largest Gothic castle, was originally constructed in the 13-15th centuries, though many additions have been made since that time. Malbork was used as a fortress by many Polish kings, and for a long period coins of gold and silver were minted there.

HISTORY

WHILE POLAND celebrated its millennium (1,000-year anniversary) as a Christian state in 1966, its history actually stretches back into the deep mists of antiquity. In Roman times, the name of the region where Poland is now situated was called Sarmatia. Specifically, Sarmatia was the land mass lying between the Vistula and Volga rivers. In fact, one of Rome's earliest commemorative coins was a bronze piece marking the victory by Roman legions over German and Polish tribes in 180 A.D.

Ancient tribes roamed Polish soil as long ago as 500-1000 B.C. These tribes left behind a great number of objects, including tin rings which were used as currency. Tin was the primary metal utilized in these rough pieces of money along with a number of alloys.

However, Poland as a nation did not emerge until the 10th century. It was Prince Mieszko I (Miecislas), the dominant political figure in the 960-992 period, who unified the many small principalities into a nation. Mieszko, the founder of the Piast Dynasty, by 963 was successful in imposing his rule over an area extending from the Odra to the Vistula Rivers. This date is often used to mark the official beginning of Poland's history.

Prince Mieszko made the final decision to have Poland become Christian in 965 when he married Dabrowka, a Christian princess of Bohemia. He was baptized at the time of the marriage, and in the following year, he invited missionaries from Prague to convert Poland. Wishing to gain the protection of Pope John

The Nicolaus Copernicus monument can be seen against the background of the Town Hall Tower in the city of Torun, the birthplace of the great scientist. Copernicus (1473-1543) proved that the sun and not the earth is the focal point of our solar system.

XV, Mieszko drew up in 985 a document ceding his lands to the Holy See under a feudal over-lordship.

Eventually, Christian Poland constituted Europe's eastern fortress against the pagan Tartars, and later the Turks.

For purposes of convenience the history of Poland may be outlined according to seven distinct periods: (1) Dynasty of Piast, 960-1382. (2) Dynasty of Jagellon, 1386-1572. (3) The Crown Elective, 1573-1795. (4) Period of Foreign Rule, 1795-1918. (5) Republic of Poland, 1918-39. (6) German Occupation, 1939-45. (7) The People's Democracy, 1945 to the present.

The long Piast Dynasty may itself be divided into four separate periods: (a) Princes and Dukes of Poland, 960-1034, (b) Period of Anarchy, 1034-1138. (c) The Seniorate, Dukes of Krakow and Princes of Poland, 1138-1290. (d) Kings of Poland, 1290-1382. During the 1382-86 period, there was an interregnum (span of time without a ruler).

THE MONARCHY

Outstanding among Poland's many rulers were the following:

Boleslav I son of Mieszko I, succeeded his father in 992 as ruler of Poland. One of the outstanding Polish leaders, he firmly established his country as an independent kingdom. Boleslav V, "The Chaste," reigned for 52 years (1227-79), longer than any other Polish ruler. In his reign Tartar invasions from the east resulted in the devastation of large sections of the country.

Under Casimir III, "The Great," (1333-70), the national revival of Poland was culminated. His achievements included a reformed judiciary and a currency based upon the Western pattern.

During the period of the Jagellonian Dynasty (1386-1572), Poland reached its greatest heights —politically, militarily, and culturally. Sigismund I, "The Great," became King of Poland in 1506 and reigned for the next 42 years. Sigismund, known as Poland's first modern ruler, married an Italian princess, who brought the art and architecture of the Italian Renaissance to the court at Krakow.

The kings of Poland were elected after the end of the Jagellonian Dynasty. This did not mean that the people voted—only the nobles did. John III Sobieski, elected King of Poland

School children from throughout Poland frequently visit the Lazienki Palace, the former residence of Polish kings, in Warsaw.

The Warsaw "Barbican" ("City Wall") is one of the three historical monuments of its type still preserved in Europe. The wall and towers were originally built in the middle of the 16th century by the Venetian architect, Jan Baptysta. It is a tradition and custom for young artists to exhibit their works on the walls of the Barbican.

in 1674, proved to be one of the truly heroic figures in the country's thousand-year history. He turned back the Turkish penetration of Europe and defeated their forces at the very gates of Vienna.

Stanislaus II Augustus Poniatowski was elected King in 1764 under pressure from both Russia and Prussia. He was the last King of Poland. During his troubled reign of 31 years, plans were made for the partition of Poland by Russia, Prussia and Austria. Three partitions were effected—in 1772, 1793 and 1795. At the final partition, each of the three powers helped itself to a piece of Poland, and Poland ceased to exist as a sovereign nation until after the close of World War I.

"Nowe Miasto" ("New City") in Warsaw as it appeared before World War II. In the 1920's and 1930's, Warsaw ranked as one of the great cities of culture in Europe.

PERIOD OF FOREIGN RULE, 1795-1918

Hopes for a free Poland came with the Napoleonic Wars. Polish patriots joined Napoleon's armies in an effort to free themselves from the partitioners. But the lights of liberty only flickered—Napoleon, in return for military support, had promised to reconstruct an independent Poland, but accomplished little. The Congress of Vienna made Krakow a free city, but this was only a temporary arrangement. Austria took the crown land of Galicia; Prussia occupied Posen (Poznan), West Prussia and Warmia: and Russia claimed most of eastern Poland, Lithuania, Livonia and Courland. The three powers remained pretty well entrenched for over 120 years, with Russia the predominant occupying power, holding at least 75 per cent of the territory.

Throughout much of the 19th century the Poles staged one insurrection after another as they attempted to regain their freedom. The revolutionaries kept alive the national aspirations for an independent statehood. Poland's cause was supported by democrats, liberals and revolutionaries of many countries around the world. The first few words of the Polish national anthem, composed in 1797, proclaim the Poles' faith poignantly and succinctly: "Poland has not yet perished so long as we live . . ."

Some of the most significant insurrections include:

1830-31—Polish patriots began revolt against Russian rule at Warsaw on November 29, 1830, but the insurrection was crushed by troops from Russia's regular army.

1846—Krakow Insurrection against the Hapsburg rule. Peasant uprising in Galicia under leadership of Jakub Szela. Within two years serfdom was abolished in Galicia.

1848—Wielkopolska (Poznan region). Insurrection against Prussia.

1863-64—National uprising led by patriots from Warsaw. After two years of guerrilla warfare, the movement was crushed by the army of Czar Alexander II. In retaliation, Alexander increased his permanent military forces within the country and imposed a variety of economic restrictions.

1905-07—Series of revolutionary struggles by Poles against Czarism, especially in central Poland; armed uprising by workers in Lodz.

REPUBLIC OF POLAND, 1918-39

The long period of partition ended with World War I, and Poland in 1918 once again became a sovereign nation, a republic.

Poland was invaded by Austrian and German armies in the fall of 1914. The combined Austro-German forces were opposed by the Russians, who promised the Poles an autonomous government under the Czar if they would aid Russia now. Before they could decide, General Paul von Hindenburg took Warsaw in the summer of 1915. The Russians were driven from the country, but as they retreated they burned and wrecked the Polish cities, towns and villages so that no food or equipment would remain for the invaders.

The independence of Poland was proclaimed on November 9, 1918, after a Constituent Assembly had been established. The presidency of the Assembly was held by Ignace Jan Paderewski (1860-1941), the noted pianist, who had been largely instrumental in obtaining Allied recognition of Poland's independence. Recognition of Poland as an independent state was one of United States President Woodrow Wilson's famous 14 Points. It was secured at the Treaty of Versailles in 1919.

However a new outbreak of fighting occurred. In 1919 Poland attacked Russia which had been taken over by a Communist government in

The City Hall of Warsaw before World War II. By 1944, this majestic building was a heap of rubble.

November, 1917. In turn Poland was invaded in 1920 by Russian forces, which were turned back with French aid near Warsaw. The Treaty of Riga, October, 1920, concluded hostilities and, at the expense of Russia, increased Poland's territory by nearly one-third.

General Joseph Pilsudski was the hero of the war against Russia and by now ranked as the most powerful political figure in the country. He was Head of State in 1919-22, and continued to exercise great influence over the political spectrum while Stanislaw Wojciechowski served as president in 1922-26. However, after much political bickering, Pilsudski (now a Marshal) staged a military *coup d'etat* on May 12, 1926, and until his death in 1935 acted as a virtual dictator.

In April, 1935, a new constitution was introduced, a constitution designed to increase greatly the power of the president, and to curtail the rights of both the political parties and the parliament. The constitution was not supported by the main political parties, nor was it popular with the general populace. The controversy surrounding the April, 1935, constitution dominated the political scene in Poland until the outbreak of war in 1939.

GERMAN OCCUPATION, 1939-45

World War II began when Nazi Germany attacked Poland without formal declaration of war on September 1, 1939. The Russians from the east attacked Poland almost simultaneously. Though the Poles fought valiantly, the overwhelming might of German military power on the ground and in the air brought the uneven battle to an end in less than four weeks. On September 27, all resistance ceased, and on the following day Germany and Russia signed a "Treaty of Friendship and Frontiers" by which they divided Poland between them. This treaty came to an abrupt end when Germany invaded Russia on June 22, 1941. Thus, Poland joined the Russian forces against the Germans.

Poland's casualties during the war ran into the millions and Warsaw, the proud capital, was approximately 90 per cent destroyed. Warsaw's population fell from a 1939 level of more than 1,300,000 to a pitiful 162,000 by the

This is the Grand Theatre ("Teatr Wielki") as it appeared before World War II. During the war this magnificent structure was completely destroyed, but it was rebuilt according to the original plans.

Warsaw lay in ruins, about 90 per cent destroyed at the conclusion of World War II. The population had dropped from 1,300,000 to a mere 162,000. Within a few short years, however, the Polish capital almost literally rose like a phoenix bird from its own ashes.

end of 1944. Under Nazi occupation some 2,000,000 Poles were shipped to Germany as slave workers, and nearly all the country's 3,000,000 Jews were wiped out.

The resistance movement, directed by the Polish government-in-exile in London, was fierce. Free Polish troops fought bravely with the Western Allied armies on the Continent, especially in Italy. Monte Cassino was captured by Polish soldiers on May 18, 1944.

Polish heroism came to the fore under the most trying conditions, particularly in and around Warsaw. The famous Jewish ghetto, in which stubborn resistance against the Nazis was maintained, was completely liquidated in the spring of 1943. When Soviet armies reached the gates of the capital in the summer and late fall of 1944, both the surprisingly well-organized Polish underground army and the Warsaw citizens rose up against their German captors.

When the Poles finally surrendered on October 2, it was only after 63 days of intense fighting. At this time, Adolf Hitler gave the order that the city be completely destroyed, and throughout the remainder of 1944, streets were systematically leveled and buildings destroyed. During these months the loss of life was incalculable.

When Germany was finally defeated in 1945, the Russian army of "liberation" was occupying Poland, and the Polish government-in-exile, which had been recognized by the United States and Great Britain, was in London. The Soviet government backed the claims to leadership of the Communist-oriented Polish Committee of National Liberation at Lublin, to which a few members of the London group had been admitted. Both the U.S. and Great Britain opposed recognition of the Lublin Committee, but they struck a compromise with

From 1939 to 1945 Warsaw lost over 72 per cent of its dwelling units, 90 per cent of its industrial establishment, and over 70 per cent of its schools.

Soviet Premier Stalin when he agreed to let free elections be held in Poland. However, when it came to having international supervision of the elections held in 1947, Stalin refused and the elections were completely dominated by the Communists.

Thus, with no Allied armies in Poland, except for those of Russia, and with the London group many hundreds of miles away, the outcome of the election was never in doubt—the Communists won.

General Wladyslaw Sikorski (who was killed in a plane crash in 1943), Wladyslaw Raczkiewicz and Stanislaw Mikolajczyk had been among the leaders of Poland's government in exile.

The Russians now took claim to nearly 70,000 square miles of territory in eastern Poland, giving Poland as compensation some 40,000 square miles of German territory east of the Odra-Nysa line. The Western powers still have not recognized these arrangements.

The heroes of Warsaw of World War II have been commemorated with a monument erected in Warsaw's Theatre Square. Popularly called the "Warsaw Nike," the statue was designed by the well-known Polish sculptor M. Konieczny.

This modernistic building housing the "Sejm," the Polish Parliament, in Warsaw, was designed by the internationally famous Polish architect, B. Pniewski. Voters elect the 460 deputies in the Sejm to 4-year terms.

GOVERNMENT

THE GOVERNMENT is controlled by the Polish Communist Party, the PZPR. Almost all of the cabinet members and high government officials are party members.

The government structure, which somewhat resembles that of the U.S.S.R., is based on the constitution adopted in 1952. The Parliament (Sejm), which consists of 460 members (one deputy for every 60,000-65,000 people), is declared to be the supreme embodiment of state authority. The Sejm as a body is elected for 4-year terms.

The Sejm elects a 15-member Council of State which exercises certain legislative and executive functions. It also elects a Council of Ministers which performs the principal executive functions and corresponds to "the government" as understood in Western European countries.

The policy direction of the Polish Government is in reality furnished by the Politburo of the PZPR, headed by Wladyslaw Gomulka, First Secretary of the PZPR and also a member of the Council of State.

Local administration in the 22 provinces or voivodships, the 322 counties and the 8,800 rural districts is carried on through elective People's Councils, which are guided by the PZPR at every level.

CIVIL RIGHTS

In the broad field pertaining to the relationship between the state and the citizens, the Constitution guarantees political rights, such as freedom of speech, press, conscience and religion, of association and assembly, privacy of correspondence, and the inviolability of the person and the home. The Constitution also includes a long list of socio-economic rights, such as the right to work, to paid vacations and leaves, to health protection and to aid in case of sickness or incapacity for work, and the right to an education.

However, the Constitution also stipulates quite clearly that all of these rights are to be executed in the interest of the *working class as a*

whole and for the sake of "strengthening the socialist state." According to Marxist-Leninist doctrine, the Communist Party represents the totality of the interests of the working class. So it is the central apparatus of the Polish United Worker's Party which interprets the meaning and the applicability of all these fundamental rights and liberties.

Approximately 1,600,000 people are members of the PZPR. Two other political parties—the United Peasant Party and the Democratic Party—also exist, but they are entirely committed to the support of the PZPR's principles. These parties, together with various mass organizations—the trade unions, league of women, youth organizations, etc.—are organized into a PZPR-led Front of National Unity whose function it is to conduct the régime's campaigning during elections and on other special occasions.

Wladyslaw Gomulka, head of the Polish government, held long and important conversations with Charles de Gaulle when the former President of France paid an official visit to Poland in September 1967.

Lublin, capital of Poland for a brief period after Liberation in World War II, is proud of its modern buildings, including this colony of one-family homes surrounded by flowers and greenery.

THE PEOPLE

POPULATION

WITH 32,200,000 people, Poland ranks 7th in Europe and 17th in the world. Poland's pre-World War II population was higher; in 1939, the estimated figure was given at 35,339,000. At the end of the War, that figure had declined to about 24,000,000.

The Poles, who belong to the western branch of the Slavs, represent a mixture of Nordic, Baltic and Alpine physical types. The Poles proper are the descendants of the ancient Lekhs who flourished along the banks of the Vistula River shortly after the time of Christ.

The country's population is now homogeneous as to national origin with 98 per cent of the people being of Polish extraction. Those persons who are of non-Polish extraction (about 650,000 in number) are mainly Ukrainians, Byelorussians, Germans, Jews, and Gypsies. Density of population is 40 inhabitants per square mile.

Warsaw's population, now about 1,300,000, has returned to the 1939 level. During World War II, the population dipped to an incredibly low figure of 162,000. Once again, Warsaw is the seat of the nation's cultural life. There are 18 colleges and universities there, including the University of Warsaw, Warsaw Polytechnical Institute, and the Polish Academy of Sciences. Often called "the Paris of Eastern Europe," Warsaw has 17 legitimate theatres, 18 museums, the National Philharmonic, The National Museum of Warsaw, and the Grand Opera.

In recent years, the city has greatly expanded its hotel facitilies and inaugurated a new air terminal in the summer of 1969.

FOOD

To the Pole the holiest of all edibles is bread. His petition in his daily prayer has a special meaning for him because so many times the Pole has had to do without it. Famine and wars have been a common occurrence in Eastern Europe. Therefore, a Pole never wastes his bread. He eats the dark, heavier breads for his everyday fare, while his holiday baking calls for a lighter bread made from wheat flour. Every crumb of old bread is used for food.

Polish cooking requires the use of bread crumbs for binding, thickening, lining of baking pans, and garnish. Vegetables *Polonaise* are served with a thick coating of buttered bread crumbs. The bread is dried completely and put through a grinder. The crumbs may be kept indefinitely in a clean brown paper bag, or they may be stored in a glass jar.

The country's speciality dishes are so numerous and so widely popular that Polish cookbooks have been printed in many languages, especially in English, and have enjoyed brisk sales in all parts of the globe.

Among the speciality dishes are the cabbage rolls, or *golabki*. Ground beef and pork, rice, an egg, an onion, along with a variety of spices, are placed into fresh cabbage leaves, and then baked.

Pierogi also rank high in Polish cookery. A *pierog*, or dumpling, is made by placing a filling into rounded dough and then cooking it gently for about 5 to 7 minutes. Fillings may be of cheese, potatoes, sauerkraut, mushrooms, prunes, ripe plums, fresh berries, cooked fruits, apples, or other ingredients.

Soup is an essential course in the Polish dinner menu. Thus, soups in literally scores of varieties are served in the typical home during the course of any given year, among them: *barshch* (borsht), meat stock soup, chicken soup, barley soup, beet green soup, tomato soup, pea soup, dill pickle soup, duck soup, sauerkraut soup, mushroom soup, fish soup, potato soup, cucumber soup, apple soup, blueberry soup, and mixed fruit soup.

Polish-style sausage, or *kielbasa*, has proved to be so popular that recipes for making the several different varieties are now used in

Cooking, baking, sewing and other skills are being taught in a "Farmer's Self-Help School" on a collective farm in Opole.

meat-packing plants almost everywhere in the world. Polish hams constitute one of the country's best export items.

The Polish table is attractively set. In season, not only is there a centerpiece of flowers but various leaves are arranged in mosaic patterns. The sides of the tablecloth are often decorated with leaves in garland effects. Even the most modest homes in Poland are known for the careful serving of meals and the artistic arrangement of table settings.

RELIGION

From the standpoint of religion, Poland is in principle almost a homogeneous country. The overwhelming majority of Poles belong to the Roman Catholic Church—some estimates place the figure as high as 90 per cent of the population. In addition, however, there exist and are active in Poland 28 other churches and

This remarkable church in Zakopane in southern Poland was designed by Stanislaw Witkiewicz-Witkacy, the prominent Polish poet, dramatist and painter. Hiking groups travel many miles to visit this church in the mountains.

religious congregations, mostly Christian, with a total of some 800,000 believers.

All churches and denominational groups are equal before the law, and constitutionally, church and state are separated in Poland. Politically, despite the negative attitude of the Communists to any religion, a tacit agreement, a *modus vivendi*, exists between the Roman Catholic Church and the Gomulka government. While much of the Church's secular property, as well as parochial schools, were not restored after World War II, the Church is free to perform purely religious activities.

Today, the Roman Catholic Church maintains 13,200 churches throughout Poland. Over 500 churches destroyed during the 1939-45 period were rebuilt from their foundations, including 50 churches in Warsaw, 16 in Wroclaw, and 11 in Gdansk. Among those reconstructed from scratch are the huge and historic cathedrals in Warsaw, Gdansk, Wroclaw, Poznan and Kamien Pomorski.

In the spring of every year in each of the Polish university towns the youth festivals, or "juvenalia," are held, and the masquerade is usually one of the highlights. This is the "parade of the masks" at the Old Town in Gdansk.

ART

Contemporary Polish artists draw their inspiration from a rich heritage. Among the 19th century Polish painters, Jan Matejko of Krakow (1838-93) is a giant figure. After the failure of the 1863 insurrection led by the patriots of Warsaw against the Russians, he painted many historical pictures that had profound impact upon the 19th and early 20th century patriots. Two of his most significant paintings are "Battle of Grunwald" and "Sobieski at Vienna." Though his canvases are vast and crowded with figures, they still manage to retain an intensely personal touch. Joseph Chelmonski was a different kind of painter. Considered Poland's finest 19th century realist, he devoted his talent to painting scenes from rural life—peasants in the fields, galloping horses, farmhouses, and the like.

Folk dancers from Podhale, in southern Poland, are performing a mountaineers' dance called the "Zbojnicki." The picturesque costumes, musical instruments and singing all contribute to these unusual performances. Note the boy at the extreme left with the axe . . . the girl in the middle will have to jump over the axe as the boy swings it in a rapid circular motion a few inches off the floor. She cannot afford to miss a step!

MUSIC

Poland's musicians have won world-wide fame with the names of Frederic Chopin, Ignace Paderewski, Karol Szymanowski and Artur Rubinstein being among the most familiar. Among the arts in Poland, music is perhaps the most flourishing in respect to public appeal.

Contemporary musical production has attained new standards of excellence. It is particularly noteworthy that this development is due not only to a few talented individuals, but to a large group of composers of different generations, the youngest being the most numerous. The leading Polish composers include: Grazyna Bacewicz, Tadeusz Baird, Witold Lutoslawski, Krzysztof Penderecki, Kazimierz Serocki, and Boleslaw Szabelski. Works of these composers have been performed not only in Poland, but throughout the world as well. Many have received prizes in international music competition.

There are at present in Poland ten philharmonic orchestras, nine symphony, and three radio symphony orchestras, all of which give a total of some 3,500 concerts annually for audiences of nearly 2,000,000 people. Among the symphony orchestras, two have attained performance standards which place them among the world's best; they are the National Philharmonic Orchestra in Warsaw, directed by Witold Rowicki, and the Great Symphony Orchestra of the Polish Radio in Katowice, directed by Jan Krenz. These two orchestras have toured the world several times, achieving success everywhere.

Polish chamber music societies, like the Warsaw quintet, have also attained standards that are highly appreciated both at home and abroad. The growing number of ensembles playing classical music has also made a valuable contribution to musical life in Poland during the past decade.

The works of Krzysztof Penderecki, the distinguished Polish composer and avant garde musician, are popular all over the world. "Stabat Mater" and "Passion according to St. Luke," which had their world premieres in Munster Cathedral, Germany, in 1966, are generally considered to be his best works.

LITERATURE

Polish literature began its development in Latin in the 10th century and it has flourished steadily for a thousand years. While Latin continued to influence the greatest Polish writers for many centuries, the earliest major works in the Polish language began to appear in the 13th and 14th centuries and were religious in character.

Mikolaj Rey (1505-69) is called "the Father of Polish Literature" because he wrote in Polish exclusively. His satires and short poems were all related to various facets of Polish life, and so also was his most important prose work, *Life of an Honest Man.* The poet Jan Kochanowski (1530-84), the Jesuit preacher Father Piotr Skarga (1536-1612) and Maciej Sarbiewski (1595-1640) were all leading figures in Poland's Golden Age of Literature in the 16th and 17th centuries.

Adam Mickiewicz (1798-1855), the key figure in the Polish romantic movement, is generally considered to be Poland's greatest poet. His *Pan Tadeusz* (1834) stands foremost among heroic epics in modern European literature.

Boleslaw Prus (1845-1912), an outstanding proponent of realism, continually referred to the United States in his works though he never had the opportunity to visit America personally. He praised the values of American democracy, as well as American innovations in industrial and agricultural techniques.

Henryk Sienkiewicz (1846-1916), author of *With Fire and Sword, The Deluge,* and *Quo Vadis,* all memorable historical novels, and Wladyslaw Reymont (1867-1925), author of the four-volume novel, *The Peasants,* are both Nobel Prize winners in literature.

International book fairs held at Warsaw, which often draw as many as 200 publishing companies from around the world, are active affairs.

Since the end of World War II, a great number of new Polish writers have emerged, giving real promise to the country's future in literature. Some of the younger writers and their works are: Marek Nowakowski with a volume of excellent short stories, *Zapis* ("The Score"); Ernest Bryll with a novel, *Jalowiec* ("Juniper") and short stories, *Gorzko, Gorzko* ("Bitter, Bitter"); and Tadeusz Nowak with a novel on contemporary problems in Poland, *Takie Wieksze Wesele* ("A Bigger Wedding").

In Poland there are 41 publishing houses, state-owned or co-operative, with most of them located in Warsaw and Krakow. The Polish publishing houses participate in major book exhibitions and fairs around the world. Poles read widely—there are some 50,000 libraries of various kinds located throughout the country with some 175,000,000 volumes available.

SPORTS AND RECREATION

While soccer (popularly called "football") remains as the most universally-played sport in Poland, it has been in track and field that the country has excelled in international competition. The comment has often been made that track and field continues to be Poland's best "export item." In the past dozen years, Poland's teams have ranked third internationally, behind only the United States and Russia.

Both men and women have achieved high recognition. At the 1966 World Championships in Budapest, Irena Kirszenstein—voted Poland's "Best Sportswoman of 1966"—won the 200-meter dash and the broad jump, placed second in the 100-meter, and ran in the victorious 400-meter relay. In the late 1960's, Jan Werner earned world standing in the 400-meter race. Poland also continues to do well in track and field in the Olympic Games.

Poles are now competing more vigorously in championship automobile racing. For the first time in history, a Pole, Sobieslaw Zasada, captured the title of European Automobile Racing Champion. Polish entrants in recent years have also won numerous medals in European rifle and sabre competition.

The soccer stadium at Chorzow in southern Poland (shown here) can accommodate over 100,000 spectators. Top soccer (football) players are idolized by youngsters and are national heroes. Most large cities have professional teams.

This is a display of Polish agricultural machinery. The label "Made in Poland" is becoming known throughout the world as the country's foreign trade has increased seven fold during the past 30 years.

THE ECONOMY

IN THE decade after 1945, the Polish government nationalized virtually all industry and trade, embarked on a scheme of intensive industrialization, and launched a drive for "collectivization" of the land. By the spring of 1956, some 10 per cent of the country's total arable land had been placed under the collectives, with an additional 13 per cent placed under the state farms.

In Poland, as well as in other Eastern European countries, there are three kinds of farms: state, collective and private. On a state farm, which is the preferred type according to the doctrine of Karl Marx, the land belongs to the state, and the workers are paid fixed salaries. On a collective farm, "members" retain ownership of the land they contributed when they joined. On some collectives, farmers are paid solely on the basis of the amount of land, farm implements and livestock they originally contributed; on others they are paid according to the work performed. On still others, a combination of the two payment systems is utilized.

State farms are intended to serve as examples to the peasantry of the advantages of state ownership of the land. However, in actual practice, state farms in Eastern Europe, as elsewhere in the Communist bloc, operate at heavy losses. Although private farms are generally discriminated against, private holdings—and the small private plots that are allotted to workers on collectives—have been far more productive than state or collective farms in all of Eastern Europe.

The "Batory," named for a 16th-century king, is one of Poland's best known ocean liners. Constructed in Poland, the "Batory" regularly plies the waters between its berth at Gdynia (shown here) and North America, carrying tourists and freight.

The 1956 political upheaval at Poznan included admission by the government of its responsibilities for past errors. It spurred the new Gomulka administration to make extensive revisions in the country's economic policies and planning. These revisions included decentralizing the planning for both the factories and the farms. At present only about 1 per cent of the arable land remains collectivized, and 12 per cent is in state and other public farms. Greater emphasis was placed on raising the population's standard of living through expanded production of consumer goods, including that of small-scale private industry and craft shops.

Poland is making efforts to change the emphasis on exports to the West from food products and raw materials to manufactured goods. About 60 per cent of Poland's foreign trade by value is with other Communist countries and 40 per cent with the West.

The port of Szczecin (formerly known as Stettin), near the Baltic Sea, at night. The Polish merchant marine fleet amounts to nearly 250 vessels, and transports more than 17,000,000 tons of cargo annually.

The Gomulka government is also trying to interest Western European industrial firms to go into joint ventures with Polish manufacturers. This type of co-operation is being sought in the production of cars, television sets, home appliances, etc. For example, television sets made in Warsaw can now be converted for color reception through the use of imported French equipment.

Approximately 35 per cent of Poland's total trade is with the U.S.S.R., which remains the principal supplier of petroleum, iron ore, and other raw materials and the most important customer for Poland's machinery and other industrial products.

Nearly 50 per cent of Poland's workers today are employed in some phase of industry; these workers are primarily engaged in the shipbuilding, chemical, textile, engineering and food processing industries.

As one of Europe's great agricultural nations, Poland has been a leading producer of potatoes, rye, and sugar beets. Other important field crops are wheat, barley, oats, hay, clover, millet, poppyseed, corn and hops. Other significant agricultural products include cabbage, garlic, apples, mulberries, peas and mushrooms.

The lignite mine in Turoszow in the western part of Poland is one of the biggest brown coal mines in the country. Adjacent is a major electrical power station.

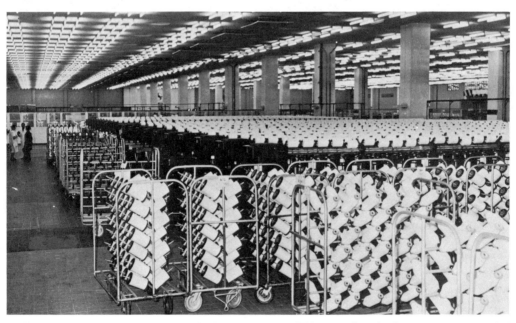

The chemical industry has grown rapidly in recent years. This new plant in Gorzow makes chemical fibre products.

This ultra-modern tire factory in Olsztyn began production in 1967. One of the biggest of its type, this plant is not only a major producer of tires for the Polish car industry, but is expected to become an important exporter of tires and associated rubber products.

A major livestock-producing country, Polish farmers raise many millions of sheep, cattle and hogs. Commercial fish are chiefly herring and cod.

Forestry continues to play an important part in Poland's economy. Coal, lignite, iron ore, zinc, lead, copper and sulphur are the minerals mined.

Warsaw has over 1,500 manufacturing plants with the leading industries being metal processing, the manufacture of machine tools, printing equipment, automobiles, home appliances, and chemicals.

WORKING CONDITIONS

The average work week in Poland is slightly over 40 hours, or $5\frac{1}{2}$ days per week, 8 hours per day. The right to rest and leisure has been guaranteed through the adoption of the normal work week. Overtime (which gives the worker additional compensation) is usually permitted only in exceptional cases, with the consent of the respective trade union. In many trades, working hours have been reduced (in some instances to 36 hours) without any reduction in pay. This relates to jobs particularly onerous or harmful to health, like those in the steel industry, mining, and in certain enterprises in the chemical and printing industries.

Work on Sundays and public holidays is prohibited. Exceptions to this rule are cases when work is indispensable by reason of its social significance or the necessity to meet the everyday needs of the population.

Manual workers are entitled to a vacation of 12 days after one year of employment to 15 days after 3 years and to 30 days after 10 years of employment. White-collar workers acquire the right to a leave of 2 weeks after 6 months and to 30 days leave after one year of employment.

In 1965, the Sejm enacted a comprehensive Law on Work Safety and Hygiene. By the following year, trade union inspectors issued over 250,000 decisions, binding on the management, ordering the removal of defects in general work safety and higher hygiene standards.

The retirement age in Poland is 65 for men, 60 for women. Apart from retirement pensions, all employed persons have the right to disability pensions in the event of partial or complete incapacity for work. All costs in the country's social insurance scheme are borne by the employer, the employee being completely free of contributions. However, the pensions awarded in Poland are generally still so low that many thousands of people cannot afford to leave their regular jobs when they reach retirement age.

FEDERAL REPUBLIC
OF GERMANY

- - Land boundary

358 ■ GERMANY

The "Porta Praetoria," an entrance to a former Roman fortress in Regensburg, East Bavaria. The city was originally a Celtic settlement and later became part of the Roman Empire. This gate was built about A.D. *180*.

WEST GERMANY

HISTORY

EARLY TIMES

When the Romans came to the land that is now Germany in the first century B.C. they found it inhabited by a number of Germanic tribes. In battle after battle, they subdued these barbarians as far as the northern banks of the Rhine, but were halted from further advances at the battle of Teutoberg Forest in A.D. 9. Before the Romans' power declined in the 6th century, they constructed their usual buildings, cities and roads, some ruins of which still stand today.

Later, after the Roman Empire was crushed by tribes from many parts of Asia and Europe, the Emperor Charlemagne ruled all the Germanic tribes of Western Europe.

For almost a thousand years after the death of Charlemagne in 814, the rulers of small kingdoms fought among themselves for power. Foreign rulers with their armies warred back and forth across the territory and there was no one country called Germany.

Martin Luther, a German priest, touched off a religious revolution that greatly changed the Christian world when he hammered his 95 theses to the door of a church in Wittenberg in 1517, protesting some of the practices of the Roman Catholic Church. His reform movement split the church in Germany and created Protestantism everywhere in Europe.

Although Germany, along with the rest of the continent, was devastated by religious warfare in the first half of the 17th century, German Catholics and Protestants live and work together today in peace and harmony.

PRUSSIA AND BISMARCK

The kingdom of Prussia assumed leadership of the German states in the late 1840's and 50's. Prussia had a strong nationalistic feeling for German unity, a well-organized army, and strong leadership in the person of King Wilhelm I of the Hohenzollern family, who took the throne in 1861, and Count Otto von Bismarck Schonhausen, who became chief minister.

Under Bismarck, Prussia marched against Denmark and annexed the provinces of Schleswig and Holstein. Prussia next defeated

Construction of the Charlottenburg Castle on Schlosstrasse in West Berlin was started in 1695 by Sophie Charlotte, the first queen of Prussia. The first floor is in baroque style, the second is used for art exhibitions. In the beautiful rear park are buried King Frederick William III, and other members of the Hohenzollern dynasty. The statue in front by Andreas Schlüter is a monument to the Great Elector (1700).

Austria in the Seven Weeks War of 1866 and established a new North German Confederation with a strong central government. In what amounted to an effort to block Bismarck's growing power, France went to war with Prussia, was defeated in 1871 and lost to its strong enemy the provinces of Alsace and Lorraine.

The new German Empire which evolved from the Franco-Prussian war included the North German Confederation and the South German states of Baden, Wurttemberg, Bavaria, and Hesse-Darmstadt.

Bismarck became Chancellor of the German Empire, which was really a federation. The legislature was constituted of an upper house, or federal council, called the *Bundesrat*, and a lower house, or Imperial Diet, called the *Reichstag*. The king was known by the title *Deutscher Kaiser*, or German Emperor.

A strong nationalism characterized the new Germany. Under Bismarck, the country established colonies in Africa and the Pacific, formed alliances with Austria, Hungary and Italy, created old-age pensions and government insurance for the working class, and established protective tariffs to build industry.

WORLD WAR I

When Wilhelm II ascended the throne in 1888, this marked the beginning of a strong build-up of the Germany Army and Navy to match the continuing growth of the country's industries. Bismarck was summarily dismissed

Til Eulenspiegel, represented here, is one of the great figures in German folklore. A peasant clown who lived in the 15th century, his roguish tricks on the upper class have been re-enacted and retold for centuries. ⟶

Frederick the Great, king of Prussia from 1740 to 1786, was a brilliant leader and made Prussia the greatest power in Europe. A man of many parts— statesman, writer, and musician—he was known as "Old Fritz."

On the Church of St. Nicholas in Kalkar, detail of early architecture depicts David with harp.

Prehistoric pile dwellings on Lake Constance. On the lake's Reichenau peninsula near the city of Konstanz are the earliest traces of culture in Germany.

in 1890, but the course he had set for his country went forward and Germany's mounting strength began to alarm other European powers.

The assassination of the Austrian Archduke Francis Ferdinand at Sarajevo, Serbia (now Yugoslavia), on June 28, 1914, signalled the start of World War I. Following a declaration of war by Austria-Hungary on Serbia, and Russia's protest and mobilization along the frontiers of Germany and Austria, Germany declared war on Russia and France (which was then Russia's ally).

Germany moved quickly into France, marching through neutral Luxembourg and Belgium. Great Britain then declared war on Germany, as a protest to the violation by Germany of neutrality pacts with the two small countries.

Johann Gutenberg's invention of movable type (and hence printing) in the 15th century is one of the greatest of Germany's many contributions to world culture. This is the Gutenberg Museum in Mainz.

British and French forces marshalled along the Marne River and managed to halt the German advance there, after it had swept over northern France and was threatening Paris.

Germany, with its allies—Austria, Hungary, Bulgaria and Turkey—then forced Russia to surrender, but was held from further advances along the French front. Raids by German submarines brought the United States into the war in April, 1917, and the Central European aggressors, surrounded on every side, became exhausted. In an armistice, Germany surrendered to the Western allies on November 11, 1918, marking the end of the German Empire.

Under provisions of the Treaty of Versailles that ended the war, Germany lost all its former colonies, was bound to pay \$33,000,000,000 (nearly £12,000,000,000) in reparations, and to give land to help form Czechoslovakia and Lithuania, as well as to cede territory to France, Poland, Denmark and Belgium.

HITLER AND WORLD WAR II

A republican constitution was drawn up at the east German city of Weimar in 1919, and a new republican type of government established in Germany. But internal dissension, the world's

The interior of a 16th-century Town Hall in Norden, Lower Saxony.

worst inflation, and widespread unemployment plagued the country all through the 1920's. Finally, in 1933, President Paul von Hindenburg, a war hero, appointed an agitator, Adolf Hitler, as Chancellor (Prime Minister) of Germany. The fascistic National Socialists (Nazis), led by Hitler, established a total dictatorship over the stricken country in 1934-35. Hitler called himself the Fuehrer (Leader), abolished the presidency after von Hindenburg's death in 1934, and promulgated laws excluding all German Jews from citizenship, property rights and legal protection.

Anyone opposing the Nazi tyranny was ruthlessly suppressed and persecuted, and Hitler's genocidal policy led eventually to death for approximately six million Jews.

Hitler's next acts were to withdraw his country from the League of Nations, to revive compulsory military training, and to provide a bulwark against France by sending troops to reoccupy the Rhineland in 1936. He also formed the Rome-Berlin axis in that year by allying himself with the Italian dictator Mussolini, and in 1938 he annexed Austria.

Magnificent Neuschwanstein Castle, near Füssen, is one of a number built for King Ludwig II of Bavaria. The ruler's extravagance in the design of this and similar structures may have arisen out of mental illness.

The next of many treaties Hitler signed and eventually disregarded was the peace pact of Munich, September, 1938; the other signatories were Great Britain, France and Italy. By its terms, the British and French consented to Hitler's demands for ceding the Sudetenland in Czechoslovakia to him. The following year he took the rest of Czechoslovakia, absorbed the

A section of the Berlin Wall on Bernauer Street. Restrictions on visiting between the West and East sections of the city have traditionally been relaxed at Christmas.

district of Memel in Lithuania, and then signed a non-aggression pact with Russia.

Next stop on the dictator's timetable of conquest was Poland, which he entered on September 1, 1939, and quickly subdued. Russia, supposedly Germany's ally, at the same time occupied the eastern provinces of Poland. Answering Germany's continuing aggression, France and Great Britain declared war on Hitler on September 3.

In quick succession, Hitler then occupied neutral Denmark, invaded Norway, and conquered The Netherlands, Belgium, and Luxembourg, which were also neutral. By June, 1940, France had surrendered, Italy had entered the war on the German side, and British forces had been forced to withdraw from continental Europe. Instead of following up by an invasion of England, which would have been a death blow, Hitler invaded Russia in the spring of

1941. After fierce fighting through winter weather, the Nazis were eventually halted outside of Leningrad, Moscow, and Stalingrad.

A little later, the United States had entered the war after Japan attacked the naval and air base at Pearl Harbor, Hawaii, on December 7, 1941, and Germany had declared war three days later.

The Allied forces invaded Europe through Normandy, France, in the spring of 1944, following a gradual decline in Germany's fortunes during 1943 and 1944. Hitler is believed to have committed suicide, and on May 7, 1945, Admiral Doenitz, Hitler's successor, agreed to an unconditional surrender.

THE OCCUPATION

After the war Germany was divided into four military zones—occupied by the Americans, the British, the French and the Russians. Berlin, some 110 miles deep in the Russian zone, was itself divided into four occupation sectors.

Austria was declared independent, the industrial Saar basin was given a French economic administration with autonomous status, and the lands Hitler had seized were taken from Germany.

Under the terms of the Potsdam Agreement which ended the war, Russia annexed the northern part of East Prussia, and a new Poland was given administration of the areas east of the Neisse and Oder Rivers.

As the work of dismantling war industries went ahead, Russia moved German factories from its zone on to its own soil. In the meantime, many Nazis were tried and punished at Nuremberg for war crimes.

By this time Russia had indicated that it would block any final peace treaty which would unify Germany. Consequently, France, Great Britain and the United States went ahead independently of Russia to help rebuild West Germany, while the U.S.S.R. rigidly ruled East Germany as a Communist Police state. Among measures taken in West Germany were the issuance in 1948 of a common currency for the three zones. The same currency was issued in the corresponding free zones in Berlin, and this measure helped curtail inflation and the black market.

The currency Russia then issued in its zone was based on a much lower rate of exchange, and this caused problems in Berlin. In a show of force, Russia then blockaded the roads leading from West Germany into West Berlin for 11 months, during which time France, Great Britain and the United States fed West Berlin's two million citizens in their sectors by airlift.

THE FEDERAL REPUBLIC

The growing break between East and West Germany resulted in the formation of two separate governments in 1949. West Germany, under the guidance of the three major western

Rock formations in the Teutoburger Wald (forest).

The Freedom Bell, in the Schöneberg Town Hall in West Berlin, is a replica of the U.S. Liberty Bell. A gift from America to the people of the city, it symbolizes the belief that "all men derive the right of freedom equally from God."

powers, became a federal, parliamentary democracy, achieving full sovereignty under the Paris pact of 1955. This agreement also admitted West Germany into the Western European Union and the North Atlantic Treaty Organization. West Germany's economy, freed and helped by the Allies, recovered with phenomenal speed, and the Federal Republic soon became a leading industrial power.

Two major political parties developed: the Christian Democratic Union and the Social Democratic Party. Konrad Adenauer, leader of the Christian Democrats, became Chancellor in 1949, and he set a policy of alignment with the West which was in the main pursued by his successor of the same party, Ludwig Erhard.

West Germany also joined the Organization for European Economic Co-operation, the Council of Europe, the European Coal and Steel Community, the European Economic Community and the European Atomic Energy Community. It helped form the European Common Market in 1957, in which year the economically important Saar district was returned to West Germany. In 1963, Chancellor Adenauer signed a treaty of mutual co-operation with France.

In the meantime, East Germany had become a Communist totalitarian state governed by the Socialist Unity (Communist) Party. Russia gave full recognition to East Germany in 1955, and the country re-armed and joined the Warsaw Treaty, a Communist-dominated mutual defence pact that includes a number of eastern countries. The West has never recognized East Germany as a sovereign state. The ideological line which divides Soviet-occupied Europe from the rest of the west was aptly termed "the Iron Curtain" by the late Sir Winston Churchill, Prime Minister of Great Britain during World War II and after.

Soviet troops remained in East Germany. In 1961, in another show of strength, the Communists cut off West Berlin from the rest of the city and from East Germany by a "wall" of barbed wire and concrete, increasing the tension between East and West, and emphasizing the increasing difficulties in the path of German unification.

The Communists in East Germany rule by secret police, and thousands of East Germans have fled to west Germany as the years have passed.

In 1966, the government of Ludwig Erhard, which had been losing popularity, was supplanted by a "grand coalition" made up principally of the Christian Democratic party, whose leader, Kurt Georg Kiesinger, became Chancellor, and the Social Democratic party, whose leader, Willy Brandt, Governing Mayor of West Berlin, became Vice Chancellor and Foreign Minister in the new government. Closer alliance with France, while maintaining good relations with America and Britain is the goal.

A German "Rathaus," or city hall, which can perform different administrative functions in city or town governments.

GOVERNMENT

SINCE 1945, Germany has been split into four parts: the Federal Republic, the Berlin territory which is administered by the four powers and, behind the Iron Curtain, the Communist "German Democratic Republic" and the territories of the former German state east of the Oder-Neisse line.

The eastern territories had been settled by Germans from medieval times. After the expulsion of almost 9,000,000 inhabitants between 1944 and 1946, approximately 700,000 Germans remain there. Since no peace treaty has ever been signed relating to these areas, which were recognized internationally as part of the German state in 1937, the issue of what makes up German national territory is still in question.

In 1949, the Federal Republic of Germany with a democratic, freely elected, sovereign government, was created through a federation of the West German States (*Länder*) to include the territory of the three Western Occupation Zones. These are, by descending order of population size: North Rhine-Westphalia, Bavaria, Baden-Württemberg, Lower Saxony, Hesse, Rhineland-Palatinate, Schleswig-Holstein, West Berlin, Hamburg, Saarland, and Bremen.

THE CONSTITUTION

The fundamental rights of individuals are safeguarded even more strongly in the Basic Law of West Germany than in the constitutions of other democratic states. The state is speci-

The "Bundeshaus," or seat of the German parliament, at Bonn. This city on the Rhine has been the capital of the German Federal Republic since 1949.

fically subordinated to the freedom of the individual, and there are legal ways in which a West German citizen can question a decision taken by official authority. Another constitutional guarantee is private property. Personal property can only be restricted for socially beneficial purposes, and then only after adequate compensation.

The Constitution has a generally all-German perspective. It is directed towards ultimate reunification, through peaceful and orderly means, of the various parts of Germany, an issue which has long remained unsettled in German politics. The Constitution is also slanted towards a united Europe, since under it the Federal Republic is specifically enabled to transfer its sovereign power to international institutions on behalf of a peaceful international order.

These functions have already been used:

West Germany is a participant in the European Economic Community and the North Atlantic Treaty Organization.

The national emblems of West Germany are the Federal Flag (black, red and gold) and the Federal coat-of-arms (which shows the black Federal eagle with red beak and claws on a golden escutcheon).

LEGISLATION

The President, elected for a term of five years, is the head of the Federal Republic. The most important instrument of government is the legislature (*Bundestag*) which controls the government and the administration, and is elected for four years by a universal, direct, free, equal and secret ballot. It is made up of 496 deputies, not counting 22 from West Berlin, who exercise only a consultative vote.

The second legislative chamber is the *Bun-*

desrat, created to ensure collaboration between the various states in legislation and administration. The *Bundesrat* has 41 members nominated by the state governments, (not counting four representatives from West Berlin, who also exercise only a consultative vote). All important laws require the consent of the *Bundesrat*, whose chairmanship is assumed by the eleven state presidents in turn.

Much basic political work is performed by the federal government, which through its 19 ministries plays a considerable legislative role, and also sees to the execution of the laws.

One of Germany's great statesmen, Dr. Konrad Adenauer, Federal Chancellor from 1949 to 1963, led the Federal Republic to sovereignty after World War II and forged West Germany's policy of co-operation and friendliness with the Western nations. He was succeeded as Chancellor by Professor Ludwig Erhard.

Willy Brandt, former Governing Mayor of Berlin, Social Democratic party leader, and Foreign Minister under the coalition government headed by Kurt Georg Kiesinger, was elected chancellor of West Germany in 1969. ⟶

Political parties in West Germany represent various shadings of political thought from right to left, the major ones being the Christian Democratic Union, the Social Democratic party and the Free Democratic party; the first two of which are now joined in a coalition.

The Chancellor has one of the most powerful executive offices in the world. He determines the general lines of government policy, which he is, accordingly, responsible for. He can only be replaced by the *Bundestag* if a majority has already agreed on his successor.

The Federal Constitutional Court is independent of all other constitutional organs. It passes on the constitutionality of legislation and on the administration of justice.

The states have the right to pass their own laws, and also have priority in all cultural fields, including education.

STATES

The *Länder*, which are constituent parts of the Federal government, in many ways are similar to the states of the United States. They have individual governments and legislatures, whose political make-up is often quite different from that of the Federal government.

A typical countryside on the Aller River in Lower Saxony near Verden, which has a horse museum and a cathedral.

THE LAND

WEST GERMANY has the shape of a thick pillow slightly crumpled and viewed sideways. A land of great natural beauty, it stretches from the narrowly separated Baltic and North Seas at the southern end of Denmark to the Alpine borders of Switzerland and Austria. To the west, it is bordered by Holland, Belgium, Luxembourg and France. To the east lie East Germany and Czechoslovakia.

A little bit bigger than the United Kingdom, and roughly the size of the American state of Oregon, the Federal Republic is a maximum of 517 miles long from north to south and 281 miles from west to east. Including West Berlin, its total area is 95,744 square miles.

The scenery is so varied that one's first impression on arriving from the south, north or west will always be a different one. In the south are the towering Alps and the foothills of the Black Forest. This part of the country is jewelled with many lakes, large and small.

The characteristic feature of the western part is the fabled and lovely Rhine River and its tributaries. This part of West Germany exhibits great diversity: here are lowlands, cultivated fields and meadows, extensive industrialized areas, vineyards climbing up the slopes of castle-topped hills. To the north is the seacoast,

The Kaiser Wilhelm Memorial Church in West Berlin is next to the octagonal Europa Centre. Parts of the church were destroyed by bombing, but enough of it has been rebuilt so that it can be used. The steeple itself once soared up out of the range of this photograph.

fertile marshlands, and ports with long traditions. Further inland from the sea are heathlands, uplands, and picturesque towns and villages.

It is typical of the Federal Republic that away from the highways and *autobahns* one often finds a highly romantic old-world Germany.

Schleswig-Holstein is the territory between the two seas to the north. The land here is flat, with rich marsh meadows, forests, and plains. The coasts of the Baltic and North Seas are dotted with seaside resorts. In the Bay of Lüebeck, in the east, a dozen of them form a close row, starting with Travemuende. On the North Sea side are Cuxhaven, Buesum, St. Peter-Ording and the North Frisian Islands—the largest being Sylt, with its famous resort of Westerland.

High winds, powerful surf and great changes between high and low tides characterize the North Sea coast. Along the Baltic the climate is milder and more peaceful. In Eastern Frisia, the northwest corner of Germany, vast herds of cattle graze on the marsh meadows, and windmills creak in the fresh breezes. At ebb tide it is possible to hike through the shallows.

Between the Weser and Elbe Rivers the country is crossed by canals navigated by sailing boats. Holstein Switzerland, as the Holstein Lake Plateau is known, is an unusual mixture of glittering inland lakes, gentle hills, and peaceful beech forests.

To the east is the Iron Curtain, dividing East and West Germany. It wanders for 800 miles from the Baltic Sea in the north to the western tip of Czechoslovakia in the south. The border rambles illogically through towns and villages, often separating farmlands from their former owners and close relatives from each other.

TOPOGRAPHY

West Germany is divided into five distinct topographical areas. In the north is the German lowland, stretching from Holland to the East German border. This zone is made up of moors, heath, and the sandy North Sea beaches. The land here has an average elevation of about 1,000 feet, but it gradually rises to the south until it becomes the central German mountains. These rounded, worn-down highlands stretch from the Rhine to the East German borders at altitudes ranging from 3,500 to 5,000 feet.

In the west are a wide valley and a gorge called the Heroic Valley of the Rhine.

The greatest part of southern Germany is made up of plateaus and low mountains averaging about 1,500 feet, including the Odenwald Mountains and the Black Forest.

This area blends gradually into the high wall of the Bavarian Alps, which form the boundary between West Germany, Switzerland and Austria. These mountains average 8,000 to 9,000 feet in height.

WATERWAYS

All of the Federal Republic, except the extreme south, is drained by rivers that flow north into the North Sea. The Rhine is the principal river—537 miles long with two main tributaries, the Moselle and the Main. It empties into the sea in Holland.

The Ems, Weser—formed by confluence of the Fulda and Werra—and Elbe rivers are farther east, and at their estuaries are the ports of Leer, Wesermünde and Hamburg respectively. The Danube in the south is 402 miles long, and it flows from west to east, into Austria and Hungary.

The Lake of Constance, lying along the borders of Switzerland and Austria in the south, with an area of 208 square miles, is the only major lake in West Germany.

Many of West Germany's top tourist and trade events are held in Berlin, some of them in this ultra-modern Congress Hall, built with American funds and named after Benjamin Franklin.

*One of the loveliest tours in Europe is the trip by steamship on the Rhine between Cologne and Mainz.
Weather allows these trips along the most beautiful sections of the river to be conducted only from March
to October.*

*This huge ancient gate, whose walls are removed,
still towers over the small half-timbered houses
around it in the medieval city of Soest.*

*The English Garden, a large natural park, in
Munich, a city that has many lovely vistas.*

GERMANY ■ 373

The market town of Berchtesgaden is where Adolf Hitler while Führer, had a mountaintop castle. Warm winds make spring particularly pleasant here, and the town is surrounded by lakes and the eastern Bavarian Alps.

CLIMATE

Because of a warm sea current near its coasts, West Germany has a climate that is generally mild. January is the coldest month; temperatures during the winter range between 27 and 34 degrees F. at sea level; in the mountains the thermometer generally goes below 21 degrees F. The hottest temperatures in the summer are in the upper Rhine Valley. Summer temperatures generally range from 61 to 70 degrees F. The prevailing winds are from the west bringing rain at any time of year from the North Sea and the Atlantic.

The higher mountains are covered with snow from January to March. The snow often reaches 6 feet in depth at altitudes of 3,300 feet.

Winters are generally rainy in the non-mountainous zones and summers pleasant. There is, however, great variety in the weather from region to region, so that, for instance, when skiing is in full swing in the Alps, the almond trees are blooming on the Bergstrasse in

Berlin. Even on a 200-mile flight from Frankfurt to Munich a great change can sometimes be noted. The seashore has a climate completely different from the climate inland.

FLORA AND FAUNA

One-third of West Germany's forests are beeches, oaks, and other deciduous trees. More evergreens are growing as a result of reforestation schemes. Spruce predominates in the mountains, while larch and pines grow where there is sandy soil. There are many fish in the rivers and in the North Sea. The relatively few wild animals, large and small, are those common to the rest of Middle Europe: bears in the Alps, a growing number of wolves, plus foxes, badgers, otters, moles. Numerous migratory birds cross the Federal Republic.

CITIES AND TOWNS

There are about 25,000 independent townships in the Federal Republic, and most of them have fewer than 2,000 inhabitants. About one-

Mittelberg village in the Allgäu. Snow covers the higher mountains from January to March to a depth between 3 and 6 feet at altitudes of 3,300 feet.

The Black Forest, which lies between Lake Constance and the southwesternmost corner of Germany, consists of rounded mountaintops covered with evergreens. About one-third of the rest of Germany's forests are made up of beeches, oaks and other deciduous trees.

quarter of the population lives in these small villages, while the 52 large cities, aside from West Berlin, contain more than 16,000,000 people. West Berlin, with 2,000,000 people; Hamburg, with almost 2,000,000 people; and Munich, with something over 1,000,000, are the largest. Bonn, temporary seat of the Federal government, has only 144,000 inhabitants. This

Schleswig-Holstein in the north of Germany is a flat region of rich meadows, lakes and sand dunes.

The entrance from Lake Constance to Lindau is on an island and so appears to be floating on water. Lindau has winding narrow streets and old buildings. In the background are the mountains of the Allgäu, Bavaria.

Burgsteinfurth Rathaus (city hall) in Münsterland. This town has one of the old moated castles.

Storks, around which have grown many super-stitions, are allowed to nest on the roofs in Germany. Other native birds are the nightingale, song thrush, warblers, sparrow, falcon, eagle, owl, woodcock, kingfisher, and white heron.

The zoo at the edge of the Tiergarten (Berlin's Central Park), contains one of Europe's most extensive collections of wildlife. Germans traditionally love zoos. Shown here is a Shoebill Stork from northeast Africa.

A guest of the Exotarium (aquarium plus reptiles) in the large zoo in Frankfurt. Small animals native to the Federal Republic include rabbits, hedgehogs, moles, muskrats, lemmings, squirrels, weasels, badgers and martens. Larger animals are foxes, deer, and occasional wolves and brown bears. The chamois is hunted in the Alps.

The old section of Constance, the largest city on the lake of the same name. A good holiday spot, Constance was largely untouched by the war, and its centuries-old buildings still stand. The city, located on the south shore of the lake, is completely surrounded by Swiss territory.

city will continue to serve as the country's provisional capital until the time when Germany can be reunited and Berlin can regain its status as capital.

Many of West Germany's cities were built in medieval times, when in the feudal manner the peasants lived for protection near a knight's castle. They carried on farm work in exchange for protection, and their houses were narrow and set close together.

A number of cities still retain much or all of their medieval character. Others, however, which were destroyed by bombing during World War II, have been rebuilt into attractive, completely modern cities. The recently restored ones still have old quarters where ancient structures still stand, and these romantic sections are often worth visiting. One of these is Stuttgart, a great wine-producing and publishing city, located in the southwest on the Neckar.

The ancient city of Hamburg is the country's largest seaport. A metropolis of international

character, it was severely damaged during World War II, but has been rebuilt in contemporary fashion. Bremen, the northern terminal of the Weser River, is an important port for international freight traffic. It has many cultural treasures and significant buildings. Another busy port is nearby Bremerhaven, also on the Weser. Through it passes a large volume of supplies for the occupying forces.

The division of Germany is particularly reflected in the situation of Berlin. Germany's prewar capital is far to the east and 110 miles behind the Iron Curtain, but is now a divided city—half Western and half Communist-dominated. Agreements signed in 1944 and 1945 between the four former Allied Powers have made it to some extent independent of the Federal Republic and the Federal constitution. Since 1961, the Communist regime has unilaterally declared East Berlin part of the so-called "German Democratic Republic." Berlin's position is further strained in that it is a bone of contention between the Soviet Government and the West.

Russia has been trying since 1958 to turn West Berlin into a so-called "demilitarized free city," which of course would loosen its ties to the West still further, and this has led to numerous crises between the West and the Soviet Union.

Berlin was one of the world's gayest cities before the war, and it still attracts many foreign visitors despite its precarious situation. Many fashionable shops line the major boulevard called the Kurfürstendamm. The city is full of theatres, art galleries, night clubs and cafes, as well as a huge park known as the Tiergarten and a fine zoo.

Just north of the capital on the Rhine, Bonn, is West Germany's industrial heart and the booming cities of Düsseldorf and Essen. The Federal Republic also contains many spas (mineral springs), two of which are at Wiesbaden and Baden-Baden.

Frankfurt-am-Main, east of Wiesbaden, is a lively city that attracts international commerce and industry, with its giant fairgrounds. Largely

A familiar and picturesque sight in many parts of Germany—an ancient castle built on rock. This one is in the Altmühl Valley of southeastern Germany.

Huddled amidst a complex of old buildings in Schlitz, Hesse, is the ancient castle of the town.

The Kiel Canal, one of the many man-made canals in Germany, connects the Baltic and North Seas in Schleswig-Holstein. Since 1950, shipping traffic through the canal has doubled. In 1964, 87,000 ships passed through, transporting a total of 62,000,000 tons.

This stalactite cave in Attendorn, Westphalia, is the largest in Germany.

Frankfurt-am-Main, a major city of industry and commerce, has been largely rebuilt since it was severely bombed during World War II. The cathedral (at the right) miraculously escaped.

Fishing by seine (large net) on the Neckar River, whose valley is famous for its scenic beauty. Freshwater fish in the Federal Republic include sturgeon, trout, pike, perch, and carp.

The lake in the Grunewald, Berlin's largest park. Because the city covers a wide area, the ideal way to see it is by bus and guided tour.

rebuilt after being a principal bombing target during the war, Frankfurt includes a wide variety of restaurants, sights and sports. The Stadtwald (City Forest), in the southern part of the city, contains a huge stadium.

Ancient Nuremberg, in northern Bavaria, also rebuilt, is a toy manufacturing city and a wonderland for children at Christmas time. Here in the Christmas Market piles of toys, ornaments, and Christmas trees are set out.

NATURAL RESOURCES

Although West Germany is highly industrialized, almost 60 per cent of its land is still used for pasture or agriculture, and another 28 per cent is woodland.

The Federal Republic's mineral wealth is made up principally of crude oil, brown coal and, most of all, hard coal. The hard coal deposits in the Ruhr amount to about 65,000,000,000,000 tons, which at the present rate of consumption should last for more than 400 years.

Only 20 per cent of the country's iron ore requirements, however, can be met locally, and coal provides 84 per cent of the over-all energy and power requirements.

Münster, capital of Westphalia, lies between the Weser and Rhine Rivers. A medieval city, it includes among its sights the Prinzipal-Markt (a square) and St. Lamberti Church, shown here. It is a good jumping-off place for visits to the surrounding picturesque Westphalian countryside.

Munich, capital of Bavaria, is a city of art and culture. The Gothic style Town Hall, built in 1867, contains a carousel of figures who perform a dance when noon strikes on the clock just below the steeple above.

The Krupp steel plant at Essen made armaments that contributed heavily to German might in both World Wars. Totally non-military since 1945, Krupp's huge output has been a factor in making Germany the world's third greatest industrial power, and second only to the United States in world trade.

THE ECONOMY

AT THE END OF WORLD WAR II an impoverished Germany lay in ruins. West Germany's rapid economic recovery since 1945 is one of the industrial marvels of the century. One important reason for the revival is that the traditionally energetic Germans, helped by massive economic aid from the United States and other Western nations after 1948, worked without let-up to rebuild their country. Guiding the recovery was Ludwig Erhard, Minister of Economics from 1949 to 1963, and later

Chancellor. By encouraging the incentive to earn and keeping government control to a minimum, Erhard started his country on the road to prosperity and stability.

Steps were taken to lower tariffs and remove restrictions on imports, to create tax advantages for businesses, and to institute currency reform. Whole industries, their factories destroyed during the war or dismantled after it, were rebuilt. West Germany became the third greatest industrial power in the world.

Hamburg, on the Elbe River in the north, is West Germany's largest port. Severely bombed during World War II, it has been almost completely restored. Like Venice, Hamburg is built on piles.

Open-air automatic retailing in West Berlin. The standard of living in the Federal Republic today is among the highest in Europe.

EMPLOYMENT AND INCOME

About 29,000,000 people are gainfully employed in the Federal Republic. Since for many years the number of seasonally unemployed has been less than one per cent, it may be said that for all practical purposes full employment has been achieved. The proportion of breadwinners among women—about 37 per cent—is very high. The law guarantees equality of rights to both sexes, so the same wages are paid for the same work. Almost one quarter of private businesses are owned by women, and nearly two-thirds of the national income comes from working people's wages and salaries, and social service contributions.

INSURANCE AND SOCIAL WELFARE

Social welfare services are of a high order in West Germany. Social insurance is run on a national scale, with individual branches, and membership is compulsory. Approximately every seventh inhabitant of the Federal Republic receives a worker's, office employee's, or miner's pension. Social contributions voluntarily made by industrial employers are growing more and more important. Others assisted by social welfare organizations are the needy, war victims, and those who have suffered material losses.

AGRICULTURE

Soil is generally poor in the Federal Republic, which is not a farming country. Farms average a little less than 20 acres, as against 76 acres in the United Kingdom and 112 in the United States. An effort is being made to improve the agricultural picture by increasing mechanization and consolidating small farms into larger, more efficient units. Production is mostly concentrated on animal products, the most important cultivated crops being oats, wheat and potatoes.

The Volkswagen plant at Wolfsburg has produced millions of cars since World War II. Busy West German industry gets started early in the morning. Workers often get up at 6 and executives are at their desks a short time later.

West Germany grows good potatoes and asparagus, but the grain crops are difficult to raise. To increase farm production, smaller farms are being consolidated into larger, more efficient units, and the Federal government is subsidizing agriculture. Production is still mainly concentrated on animal products.

The richest German agricultural lands were always in the East and are now behind the Iron Curtain. The Federal Republic, nevertheless, manages to produce much of the meat and wheat it needs, and almost 50 per cent of its edible fats.

INDUSTRY

West Germany is a typical industrial country, with more than one-third of its working population employed in factories and mines.

The principal industries are machine manufacturing, electrical goods, textiles, coal mining and chemicals, followed by the food industry and vehicle manufacturing. Machine manufacturing employs the greatest number of persons.

The major industrial areas are the Ruhr, the Rhine-Main region and in South Germany. Within the European Coal and Steel Community, the Federal Republic produces more

than 60 per cent of the hard coal and 46 per cent of the raw steel. Duisburg, on the Rhine, is Europe's largest inland port, and Hamburg and Bremen are among Europe's principal seaports.

"Made in Germany" is a hallmark of quality all over the world. Among the leading export industries are shipbuilding, precision instruments and optical equipment, vehicles, potash and rock salt, and pharmaceutical goods.

HANDICRAFTS AND BUILDING

Handicraft skills, practised in about 740 workshops, are flourishing in West Germany. Crafts are used a great deal for purposes of education and training of apprentices.

Building, partly a craft and partly an industry, was badly needed because of the damage caused by war. So rapidly was this challenge met, however, that from 1949 to 1962 enough new housing was created, at the average rate of nearly one dwelling unit a minute, to house 22,000,000 people, or about 40 per cent of the total population. Public loans have helped to bring rents within the reach of lower income groups.

FOREIGN TRADE

The Federal Republic is second only to the United States and the United Kingdom in volume of imports (DM 70,448,000,000 in 1965), and second only to the United States in world exports. Among its major imports are foodstuffs, raw materials and industrial goods. A valuable export market exists for West Germany's special quality industrial products involving high skills. The Federal Republic has supported lowering of tariffs and freeing of trade which were the original aims of the six-nation Common Market formed in 1958.

The open-air café is the traditional gathering place. A "Gasthaus" or indoor café, is the type of restaurant at which Germans like to gather for an evening of song, beer or wine, and conversation.

An opera performance in West Berlin's new auditorium. German love of opera has always been strong, and the Federal Republic now has about 60 permanent companies.

THE PEOPLE

FOLLOWING THE DEVASTATION of two wars and the division of Germany into two republics, the West German people have turned wholeheartedly and with characteristic energy to the ways of peace and prosperity. A devotion to free enterprise and economic liberalism prevails, with the emphasis on security and keeping the peace. In general, West Germans pursue the ideal of a comfortable, middle-class way of life.

RACIAL MIXTURE

With an average of 600 people to the square mile, the Federal Republic is crowded. Its population numbers about 59,000,000, not counting the non-German NATO forces stationed there and refugees who still escape from the Communist East.

Germans are of mixed racial strains. From about the 1st to the 5th century, Teutonic groups drifted south from the Scandinavian area and intermarried with Latin and Slavic peoples. The two principal types of Germans have been the flaxen-haired, blue-eyed northerners and the brown-eyed, darker-complexioned people of the south. But these regional differences have faded—now you cannot tell where a person comes from by his appearance.

Munich's picturesque "Oktoberfest," which starts annually in September, dates back to 1810 when the wedding of Bavarian Prince Ludwig I to Saxon Princess Theresa ended friction between two powerful domains. The great open-air celebration includes parties, music, and a seemingly endless flow of beer. The essence of Munich, the capital of Bavaria, can be summed up in the words "Stimmung und Gemüt-lichkeit" (good nature and geniality).

A traditional wedding costume in Bavaria. In this area, native costumes are often worn on Sundays and holidays: "Lederhosen" (leather shorts or breeches), and jaunty felt hats for the men, and full-skirted dresses, often with a gaily embroidered apron, for the women.

LANGUAGE AND LITERATURE

The German language derives from the Teuton part of the West Germanic branch of the Indo-European family and is closely related to English. The number of people speaking German in Europe is exceeded only by those speaking Russian.

The literary language of Germany, which developed originally from the language of West German tribes, is called Modern High German. However, this did not become a literary language until the late Middle Ages, and the prevailing spoken tongue was shaped by regional dialects. Literary German became completely free from regional influences only in the late 1700's.

In spoken language, many dialects still exist in Germany. The harsher tone of the North German is much more fashionable among the better-educated, rather than the softer Southern dialects. In prose, particularly in journalism, style tends more and more to be modelled after the shorter, brisker English sentence. Additionally, the Latin alphabet is being substituted for the clumsy Gothic alphabet long characteristic of German printing.

A literature that was distinctly German began to emerge in the 18th century, with a number of poets and dramatists preceding Goethe and the greatest German dramatist, Schiller. Before that the most influential German was Martin Luther, founder of the German Reformation movement, whose influence is still felt in many areas of German society, religion, music and language.

German leaders of the Romantic movement in the 18th century included Jean Paul Friedrich Richter, Ludwig Tieck and August Wilhelm Schlegel, who translated Shakespeare. The brothers Jakob and Wilhelm Grimm are

Günter Grass, an important contemporary novelist, is one of a group of writers who attempt in their work to probe Germany's turbulent past.

The childhood home of Johann Wolfgang von Goethe is in Frankfurt. He is revered throughout the world as a universal genius and major German poet, dramatist and novelist. In addition to influencing the development of the German novel and creating the masterpiece "Faust," he made important scientific discoveries.

famous for their versions of traditional folk and fairy tales, such as "Hansel and Gretel." A statue of the Grimms may be seen in the market place in Hanau.

Other poets, dramatists and novelists of distinction appeared in the 19th century, including the novelists Gustav Freytag and Theodore Storm. In the 20th century, novelists Thomas Mann, Heinrich Mann and Jakob Wassermann became popular.

Over 1,400 privately owned daily newspapers are published in West Germany. The two national channels of West German television present much modern and classic drama, and often explore important issues of the day.

Many picturesque legends, superstitions, and myths still persist in such rural areas of the Federal Republic as the northern heathland, the Odenwald (Odin's Wood), and the Black Forest in the south.

These imposing traditional Alpine headdresses, on display during the Munich "Oktoberfest," keep alive the memory of pre-Christian customs and are designed to exorcise evil spirits.

A beach on the island of Sylt among the North Sea's North Frisian Islands. Beaches on the coast of Schleswig-Holstein facing both the Baltic and North Seas are popular resorts.

The Olympic Stadium in Berlin, as used for the 1936 Games. Sports in cities and tiny villages, are more important than ever due to the shortening of the work week. Soccer is most popular, closely followed by gymnastics.

Bonn University was built in 1717 using materials from old fortifications. New universities and enlargements of old ones are under construction in West Germany, financed by both the individual state and Federal governments.

EDUCATION AND RELIGION

Education is taken very seriously in West Germany, which was a leader in the compulsory education of children. The first eight or nine years of education are compulsory in the Federal Republic, depending on the individual state.

The national government provides financial support for higher education, but does not interfere in the training. People of academic accomplishment, especially professors, are highly regarded. There are 23 universities in the Federal Republic and West Berlin, many vocational and professional schools, and ample facilities for adult education.

About 96 per cent of West Germans are either Roman Catholic or Protestant, with an approximately equal number of each. Religion in West Germany is defined somewhat by geo-graphy, the south, particularly Bavaria, being predominantly Catholic and the north Protestant. Small chapels and churches are numerous in the south, where the great holy days and carnivals are observed. The north, manifesting the Puritan simplicity and lack of ornamentation which was the spirit of the Protestant Reformation, is characterized by plain brick churches with pointed steeples.

The Evangelical (Protestant) Church is an association of 29 regional Lutheran Reformed and United Churches. It is governed by a synod headed by the Bishop of Berlin.

West Germany is divided by Catholics into five provinces. The Archbishops of Cologne and Munich are members of the College of Cardinals in Rome. Some 30,000 Jews, making up 84 congregations have remained in or returned to the Federal Republic.

Winter sports attract thousands of people yearly to the mountains and ice skating rinks. Excellent skiing facilities are available in such areas as the Allgäu, Alps and Black Forest. Accommodations range from simple to sophisticated.

Youth hostels are supported by the Federal Youth Plan. Millions make overnight stops in West Germany's hundreds of hostels, and a high percentage of these are made by foreigners. These inexpensive accommodations provide an ideal way to travel across West Germany.

The public library in Würzburg is an example of German rococo architecture. In general, rococo design prevails in the south and Gothic in the north.

This modern living room is in a student hostel for girls in Bonn. Not content to be the frumpy "Gretchens" of tradition, young German women dress stylishly and attend universities in greatly increasing numbers each year. Women in the Federal Republic are continually entering more and more areas of German professions and industry.

A group of museums and archives in West Berlin's Dahlem district contains an outstanding collection of paintings and other works of art. The city, however, is less important in the world of art than before World War II, as its collections have been scattered to other locations.

ART AND MUSIC

The historical high period of German art occurred for a relatively short time during the Renaissance, in the 15th century. Two great painters of that time were Albrecht Dürer and Hans Holbein the Younger. German art never again achieved world renown until the coming of Expressionism early in the 20th century. Outstanding modern artists include Ernst Ludwig Kirchner, Max Beckman, George Grosz and Emile Nolde.

Germany's contributions to the world of music have been enormous. The Baroque period in the late 16th and 17th century produced Heinrich Schütz, Johann Sebastian Bach and George Friedrich Handel. Christoph Willibald von Gluck came to fame in the 18th century, and the classical period in music was principally influenced by Ludwig van Beethoven. The romantic period brought forth Carl Maria von Weber, and in the 19th century there emerged Felix Mendelssohn-Bartholdy, Robert Schumann, Richard Wagner and Johannes Brahms. Basing his four dramatic "Ring" operas on the medieval epic, the Nibelungenlied, Wagner recounted the adventures of Siegfried, a heroic warrior in both German and Norse mythology.

Musical events are an important part of the German cultural scene, and among them are Bayreuth's Wagnerian Festival and the Wiesbaden May festival of opera and ballet.

Ludwig van Beethoven, born in this house in Bonn, composed some of the finest symphonies and orchestral pieces in musical literature. He is considered the first in the romantic tradition, although his earlier work was in the classic style.

The National Theatre in Munich was rebuilt after being destroyed by bombing in 1943. Performing arts are thriving in West Germany, which has over 200 theatres, heavily subsidized by the Federal government.

A scene from an opera by Richard Strauss performed by the Bavarian State Opera in Munich. Many opera and music festivals are performed yearly in Germany, an outstanding one being the Bayreuth Festival, with original settings by Richard Wagner's grandsons.

GERMANY ■ 397

Richard Wagner, German composer of operas, is considered one of the greatest operatic geniuses of all time. Much of his work was derived from German legends and folklore.

This small house in Marbach, Würtemberg, is the birthplace of Friedrich von Schiller, poet, dramatist, and philosopher. A great idealist, he was a founder of modern German literature.

MEN OF ACHIEVEMENT

Creatively, Germany has greatly enriched Western civilization. Rudolf Diesel developed the oil-fired engine named for him and Count von Zeppelin the first rigid dirigible. Much of the development of the automobile was pioneered by Karl Daimler and Karl Benz. The genius of Albert Einstein, German-born physicist, revolutionized science and led to the development of practical atomic power. The bacteria of tuberculosis and cholera was first isolated by Robert Koch. X-rays were discovered by Wilhelm Roentgen.

Western thought has been influenced by Germans as far back as the 13th century, when the great scholar, naturalist and theologian, Albertus Magnus, lived. Other Germans profoundly affected the intellectual and philosophical development of the West, including Immanuel Kant, Georg Wilhelm Friedrich Hegel, Arthur Schopenhauer, Friedrich Wilhelm Nietzsche, and Heinrich Heine. Later thinkers included Karl Jaspers and Martin Heidegger.

This scene is from the play "Mother Courage and Her Children," by the late Bertold Brecht, one of Germany's greatest modern writers and dramatists.

FOOD

German cuisine is plentiful and hearty. Many warm and cold *wurst* (sausage) dishes appear on menus, one of these being *Wienerwurst* (the American "hot dog"). It is said that a Bavarian emigrant, Charles Feltman, first served hot dogs in his Coney Island restaurant in 1871. *Leberwurst* and *bratwurst* are old specialities in most parts of Germany. Quality hams are a speciality of Westphalia, and a wide range of good food is available in many German cities, from North Sea oysters to roast goose.

German sauerkraut, asparagus and dumplings are renowned. One particularly tasty dish is the potato dumpling (*Kartoffelknödel*). *Spätzle* is a noodle type of delicacy.

West Germany has many bakeries and breweries, both using grain to turn out high-quality products. Two main brewing cities are Munich and Dortmund. Bock beer is available in the spring, and a wheat beer called Weissbier is popular in Berlin. Some of the choicest white wines in the world come from vineyards along the Moselle and Rhine rivers.

Fresh eel, sold by a roadside vendor on the Rhine River, is one of the Federal Republic's great delicacies. Other national dishes: varieties of warm and cold "Wurst" (sausage), "Spargel" (asparagus), sauerkraut, and a great variety of dumplings, especially the hearty potato dumpling ("Kartoffelknödel").

Book publishing is an important industry in West Germany, and the climax of the year is the Frankfurt Book Fair, at which foreign publishers have for some years constituted a full third of the exhibitors.

Many Germans love to camp out during holidays—as at this site in Franconia in the south of the Federal Republic. The tents range from the small two-man size (which can be carried in rucksacks) to some the size of a small house. Most of the campers today own a car or motorcycle.

CUSTOMS AND RECREATION

Germans enjoy travelling, and major cities are connected by a network of four-lane, no-speed-limit Federal highways, called Autobahns. Many of the country's romantic old castles have been converted into good hotels, some luxurious and others offering only the essentials.

The pre-Lenten *Karneval* or *Fasching* is a festive season in the Catholic areas of West Germany. The *Karneval* season in Cologne opens at the 11th minute of the 11th hour of the 11th day of February. In Munich, *Fasching* begins on Epiphany, January 6.

During the *Karneval*, parades, parties and other events reach a peak of excitement near

Lent, and end immediately when that season starts. The citizens of Munich traditionally wash out their empty wallets in the Iser River at the beginning of Lent to show that they held nothing back during the celebration. During July and August, light-hearted wine festivals are held in the Rhineland and along the Moselle River. Many other spectacular festivals are held locally in West Germany to commemorate Easter and Christmas. The Christmas tree as a symbol originated in Germany.

In the Black Forest, the *Karneval* is called *Narrensprung*. During this observance one villager dons a wooden mask with grinning tusks. Called Narro, he carries a broom to sweep away trouble and evil spirits.

ENGLAND—*Windsor Castle has been the main residence of England's monarchs since William the Conqueror. Situated in the attractive town of Windsor, on the River Thames west of London, the vast structure has been enlarged and remodelled by many of England's sovereigns.*

ENGLAND—*Reconstructed gypsy caravans form an exhibit at the home of Shakespeare's mother, Mary Arden, at Wilmcote, Warwickshire. Not far off is Stratford-upon-Avon, where Shakespeare was born and where he died. Also in the area are Kenilworth Castle, known to readers of Sir Walter Scott, and the remains of the Forest of Arden (which may or may not have been the same as the Forest of Arden in Shakespeare's "As You Like It").*

A

SCOTLAND—*Edinburgh Castle, the Acropolis of Scotland's capital, dates in part from the 11th century, replacing a 6th-century fort built by King Edwin of Northumbria. The city of Edinburgh gradually grew up at the base of the 270-foot rocky hill, and in 1437 became Scotland's capital.*

B

WALES—*One of the most splendid Welsh fortresses, Caernarvon Castle was begun by Edward I of England about 1284, after he had conquered Wales. The town of Caernarvon, near the ruins of the Roman city of Segontium, still has its medieval walls. It was Edward I who conferred the title of Prince of Wales on his eldest son, thus originating a custom that has continued to this day in the British Royal family.*

C

IRELAND—*Ross Castle, near Killarney in Ireland's mild and luxuriant southwest, is one of hundreds of castles, manor houses and abbeys, many in ruins, that dot the Irish countryside. Ireland's legendary greenness is due to the ever-present moisture-laden air from the Atlantic.*

NORWAY—*Many old-style farmhouses in Norway have roofs covered with living grass. The girl is wearing traditional folk costume, donned now only for festive occasions.*

D

NORWAY—*The coast is deeply indented by many fjords, really valleys formed long ago by glaciers. Later the land sank, and the sea filled the valleys. Seen here is Lysefjord.*

SWEDEN—*Malmo, a busy port since the Middle Ages, carries on the tradition of the Swede's Viking ancestors, who were among the world's most accomplished seamen.*

FINLAND—*(Above) Few in number, the nomadic Lapps drive their reindeer across the vast snowy wastes of northern Finland, Sweden and Norway in search of forage. The reindeer provides milk and meat, hide, bones and other items for making many objects used by the Lapps. (Below) Helsinki, capital of Finland, is known for its ultra-modern suburbs, wide streets and imposing buildings, and excellent natural port, part of which is seen here.*

RUSSIA—*In medieval Russian cities, the government buildings and churches were usually grouped in a walled city-within-a-city, called a kremlin. Here is part of the Kremlin of Moscow, most famous of these citadels (so famous that it is simply known as The Kremlin), with the Red Square in the foreground.*

RUSSIA—*Leningrad boasts one of the world's great art museums, the Hermitage, originally a palace built by Empress Catherine II.*

G

GERMANY—*A traveller going by boat down the Rhine will see romantic castles and vineyard-covered slopes on both sides of the river, as here at a point above Coblenz.*

GERMANY—*In Munich's famous zoo, youngsters can have a ride in a cart drawn by handsome ponies.*

H

HOLLAND—*(Above, left) Barges ply the peaceful canals, against a background of windmills and lush green fields. (Above, right) Children ride donkeys on one of Holland's many long, sandy beaches on the North Sea.*

HOLLAND—*(Above, left) Old houses with stepped gables line an Amsterdam canal, where children wait to see the bridge open up to let a boat with a mast pass through. (Above, right) Barges, sailboats and even rowboats are berthed together in a canal. With so many waterways, boats are a necessity.*

HOLLAND—*Lakes are numerous—but less numerous than formerly, for many have been filled in to make polders, or areas of reclaimed land.*

BELGIUM—*Bruges with its canals, Gothic towers and Renaissance houses, once rivalled Venice as a commercial hub. Today, along with other old towns of Belgium, it affords a splendid look into the days when Flemish cities were among the glories of Europe.*

BELGIUM—*Every town and region has its distinctive festival, and many include giant figures like these in the annual "Ducasse," held in the town of Ath.*

FRANCE—*At the foot of the Eiffel Tower, straddling the Seine River in Paris stands a small replica of the Statue of Liberty which the United States sent to France as a token of gratitude for the statue by Bartholdi, given to the United States by France in 1884. The white building on the horizon is the famous Church of Sacré Coeur.*

SWITZERLAND—*Mountain climbing is one of many exciting sports in the Alps. Popular though it is today, climbing mountains as a pastime only dates from the middle of the 19th century. The majestic Swiss Alps, which rise to heights of 14,000 feet or more, present an enormous challenge to the climber.*

K

SPAIN—*The Court of the Lions is the most renowned of many courtyards in the Alhambra, a group of magnificent buildings erected by the Moorish kings, on a hill above Granada.*

SPAIN—*Whether you are for or against bullfighting, you can strengthen your arguments greatly by seeing an actual bullfight—and Spain is where to see it.*

L

PORTUGAL—*Street life, with its festivals, cafés, vendors and flowers, is always vivid in Portugal, but even more so when the paving stones are arranged in beautiful mosaic designs, as is the case in many towns.*

ITALY—*The ancient traditions, love of music, and gaiety of spirit so typical of Italy, all come together in Siena's famous "palio" festival.*

M

CZECHOSLOVAKIA—*In Prague, old houses and rows of trees on the Gottwald Embankment overlook the Moldau River.*

YUGOSLAVIA—*(Below) Dubrovnik, on the Adriatic Sea, once known as Ragusa, was an independent republic for centuries and a sea power of importance in the Mediterranean.*

HUNGARY—(*Above*)
*Night falls on the
Danube and the towers
of Budapest's churches
and castles.*

AUSTRIA—*The Gothic spire of St. Stephen's Cathedral rises 450 feet above Vienna, capital of waltzes,
whipped cream and Wienerschnitzel.*

O

GREECE—*The Porch of the Maidens, on the Acropolis, Athens, is a superb example of ancient Greek sculpture as an element of architecture. Dating from the Golden Age of Greek civilization—the 5th century* B.C.—*these caryatids, or columns in the form of female figures, are part of the Erechtheum, a temple sacred to the patron spirits of Athens. The chief patrons were Athena, Poseidon and Erechtheus, the legendary king who founded the city.*

P

Grunewaldsee, a lake in the West's vast woodland.

BERLIN

THE AREA

SURROUNDINGS

In the middle of the flat, sandy plain of Brandenburg lies the city of Berlin, former capital of a large German empire and now the nominal capital of a bitterly divided Germany shrunken by wartime losses.

But few of the world's great cities are so generously endowed with handsome natural surroundings as Berlin. It is fringed by tall groves of fir and oak, and both East and West Berlin have vast forest preserves such as Wuhlheide in the East, and the Grunewald and Tegel forests in the West. More than a dozen

large lakes, clean enough for water sports, are located within the city limits. The Wannsee, Tegelersee, Schlachtensee, Mueggelsee and Weissensee all provide ample room for convenient outings and none is more than a half hour journey by road or rail.

Such is the felicitous location of Berlin that one may find boar and "rehbock," or red deer, in the Grunewald forest only a few minutes from the middle of West Berlin. The 8,400-acre forest was previously a royal hunting preserve belonging to the Hohenzollerns and some of its great oaks, more than 400 years old, are still standing. They are vestiges of a larger stand

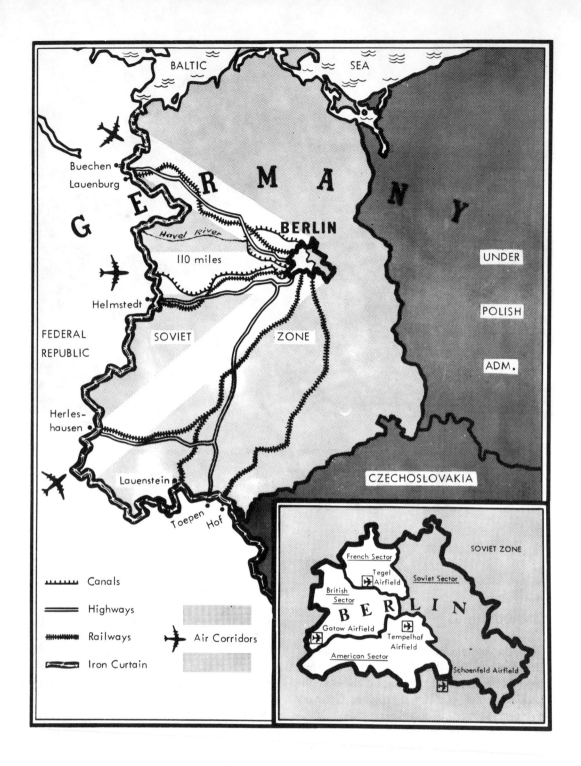

402 ■ BERLIN

that was cut down on orders of Frederick the Great for sale to England as ship timbers. Farther to the west, bathers seek out the fresh waters of the Glienicker See, half of which belongs to East Germany. Here, as in other parts of the city, one can literally drift into Communist territory and some Berliners have done so, with arrest as the consequence. Fortunately for its citizens West Berlin is a spacious place and the feelings of claustrophobia are less than they might be otherwise for persons living in the middle of a Communist country. Yet the Berliners sorely miss the hinterland that used to be accessible to them— the Baltic Sea resorts, the idyllic Spreewald and the fishing lakes that dot the plains of Brandenburg around them. The closest they get to such places now is in a plane flying down one of the Berlin air corridors.

(Below) A West Berlin tourist resort high on the shore of the Wannsee overlooking Pfaueninsel (Peacock Island) in the background. Here the wide waters of the lake are especially suited to boating.

(Above) In East Berlin's Treptow Park, a kindergarten class of youngsters with their teacher view one of the Russian monuments.

CITY DESIGN

The Spree River and its subsidiary canals add still more charm to the heart of Berlin. Thanks to some good planning around the turn of the century, broad boulevards were laid out and factories were discreetly spread among the various boroughs, so that most of the city seems designed more for living than for working. Even the traditional working class districts of Wedding, Neuköelln, Kreuzberg and Prenzlauero Berg have parks and tree-lined streets that would put their counterparts in London, Paris or New York to shame. The trees and water seem to wash clean the air of Berlin, which is renowned for its invigorating quality. "Berliner Luft" (Berlin Air), one of the city's famous songs, boasts of this.

The land is flat, and there are no true skyscrapers in the city. Berlin's plain is about 110 feet above sea level. Virtually all of its "hills" are those made after the war by piling up thousands of tons of rubble from bombed buildings. One of these in West Berlin is affectionately called "Mont Klamott" or Mount Junk. The highest natural point is the 200-foot Kreuzberg in the middle of a park.

(Above) The Spree River, Congress Hall (foreground) and rally before the Reichstag.

A Gropius building, Hansa Quarter, West Berlin.

404 ■ BERLIN

(Right) On Berlin's many lakes and connecting canals, small launches are legion in both parts of the city, but especially in the West. Because West Berliners are encircled by Communist territory, these pleasure boats have become an increasingly popular medium for touring their imprisoned half of the city.

(Below) This striking, modern landscaped "city within a city" housing 2,000 families in West Berlin, was designed by the world-renowned architect Le Corbusier.

(Above) Once elegant Friedrichstrasse in East Berlin was cleared of the war's debris but only partly rebuilt.

(Right) Renamed Stalinallee soon after Communist occupation, this street was completely restored—but strictly for Party members. The first floors house state-owned stores and cafés.

(Below) The end of Potsdamer Platz—in East Berlin.

Brandenburg Gate from inside East Berlin, after restoration in 1958.

HISTORY

Though its origins date back to Slavic fishing settlements in the Dark Ages, Berlin is one of the world's youngest great cities. It has been the German capital only since 1871, when the second German Reich (empire) was established under Kaiser Wilhelm I. Its growth to a population of more than 3,500,000, in an area of 341 square miles, occurred largely in the space of 70 years.

Indeed, the name Berlin has a modern ring, evoking pictures associated with the 20th century: pictures of the proudly strutting troops of Wilhelm II in 1914, of Adolf Hitler in 1939, and now, in the eastern sector of the city, the green-uniformed People's Army soldiers of Walter Ulbricht, the East German Communist chieftain; pictures of revolutions, in 1918 by workers and discontented soldiers against the aristocratic-militarist government, and in 1953 by workers against their "own" Communist régime in East Berlin; pictures of

destruction from the awesome Allied bombing raids and in May 1945 from the cannons of the advancing Red Army; pictures of isolation made vivid by the Allied airlift that broke the Communist-made Berlin Blockade in 1949, and by the Communist wall that cut the sprawling city in half starting in August, 1961.

For that matter, there are few historical landmarks in Berlin that date back before the 17th century—here a palace, there a church—and virtually all of what is now West Berlin was settled and built up during the last 80 years.

Foreigners and Germans alike often overlook the fact that Germany is one of the younger members of the family of nations, younger by almost a hundred years than the United States as a national entity. Before that, Germany comprised a score of feuding principalities, each with its distinctive habits of speech, dress and custom. Though common characteristics like soldiering, authoritarianism and diligence have been traced far back in German history there were few governmental or social traditions that spread throughout this conglomeration of German regions.

While Berlin has served in modern times as a focal point of many activities regarded as typically German, few Germans look on the capital as representative of the country. As the seat of rising Prussian power in the 1860's it was detested in the older German cities that it was soon to dominate. Moreover, Berlin, as the capital and as the first true metropolis of Germany, concentrated the bustling energy and brashness of the Prussians in a big city context. And this, too, was resented in the more serene provincial quarters of Bavaria, Swabia and the Rhineland.

Berlin, with its great government buildings, many crowded shopping areas and broad boulevards was totally unlike other German cities that had grown up in confined medieval traditions. Rather, it was something new, an expression of a modern, fast-developing industrial society.

(Above) Brandenburg Gate from the West—a Communist water cannon truck and barbed wire guard the approach after the border closing.

The Soviet Embassy in East Berlin. Many regard it as the seat of Communist control for all of East Germany.

A Volksarmee (People's Army) company armed with Russian tommyguns march in review before Walter Ulbricht on Marx-Engels Square in East Berlin.

Hitler brought devastation to Berlin, the burning of the Reichstag by his hoodlums, the burning of "non-Aryan" books, and the extinction of the city's exciting cultural life. He built a huge stadium in the western part of the city, vainly hoping to show the world his German supermen in the 1936 Olympic Games, and his architects added scores of long-windowed government buildings to the inner city.

After Hitler's night descended, two men continued to work in the anti-Nazi underground for a time. One was a courier for the illegal Social Democratic Party. His code name was Willy Brandt. The other was secretary of the Communist Party's Berlin-Brandenburg District. His name was Walter Ulbricht. Both men escaped the grip of the Gestapo not to return until 1945—Ulbricht as Stalin's proconsul in the Soviet zone of Germany and Willy Brandt as an exile soon to assume German

(Below) A sports festival in West Berlin's Olympic Stadium. Built by Hitler for the 1936 Olympic games, it seats over 100,000 and is used for sports events and frequent field exhibitions by the West Berlin police.

Bearded Walter Ulbricht (middle) listening to East German factory workers.

(Below) Willy Brandt, who became governing mayor of West Berlin in 1945, was elected chancellor of West Germany in 1969. A Social Democrat, he seeks to improve relations with East Germany.

citizenship again and later to become governing mayor of West Berlin.

The war brought further tragedy. Berlin's Jews, who had contributed so much to its growth as artists, physicians, statesmen and industrialists, were deported to concentration camps. Only a few thousand who could escape abroad or go underground survived.

Then came the bombs—at first the British night raiders retaliating for the attacks on London. Later, the American daylight raids. Finally, the shells of Russian cannon. More than 76,000 tons of bombs were dropped on Berlin, and 40,000 tons of shells ripped into the city. They left an estimated total of 600,000 homes in ruins. The royal palace, the Reich chancellery, the Reichstag, all were shot to pieces. Nearby was the Fuehrer's hide-out, where Hitler committed suicide in the midst of the Soviet siege.

The Tiergarten park, to the west of the Brandenburg Gate, was stripped of its trees for firewood; similarly, the vast Grunewald forest on the southwestern edge of the city. The population, cut by nearly a million, struggled to get food, water and electric current, all of which were in short supply, before and after the war ended on May 8, 1945.

Heavy artillery is brought out in East Berlin's May Day parade. The Western Allies have protested repeatedly without success that such parades violate the four-power statutes governing the city.

Then, on October 20, 1946, the first free election since 1933 was held in Berlin. It was also the last. More than 92 per cent of the eligible Berliners voted. The result was 48.7 per cent for the Social Democrats, 22.2 per cent for the Christian Democratic Union, 19.8 per cent for the Communists, and 9.3 per cent for the Liberal Democratic Party. The Communists never dared allow another all-Berlin election.

In July, 1947, the newly constituted City Council picked Ernst Reuter to be mayor of Greater Berlin. This choice was vetoed by the Soviet members of the Allied Kommandatura, a move which foreshadowed the ultimate division of the city.

The actual split came on an economic issue. These were the days of the black market and inflation, reminiscent of the 1920's. The currency in use was the old Reichsmark, but the Russians in Berlin and other parts of Germany were printing whatever quantities pleased them. A reform was due, yet the Soviet authorities insisted that Berlin and their zone of Germany be considered a single currency unit—with their currency. Negotiations reached a deadlock on June 24, 1948. Next day the Allies ordered issuance of the German Mark of the Bank of German States—the West mark. It has been the legal tender of West Berlin and West Germany ever since.

BERLIN BLOCKADE & THE CITY DIVIDED: 1948-1949

Historians usually date the beginning of the Berlin Blockade from the deadlock. Soviet members had already walked out of the Allied Kommandatura earlier in June. Meanwhile they had begun interfering with access of Allied traffic on the roads, rails and canals to Berlin. The excuse was: "Closed for repairs."

The Western Allies were faced with a dilemma. Their rights, their commitments and their prestige called for a resolute stand in Berlin. But the technical problem seemed insurmountable. West Berlin was entirely dependent on Western supplies of food and fuel. How was it to be transported 110 miles across Soviet-held territory to the isolated city? Gen. Lucius D. Clay, then the United States military governor in Germany and senior commandant in Berlin, argued for a breakthrough by Allied tanks. This idea was vetoed by Pentagon planners who felt the risk of war was too great. Clay's second idea, an airlift, was accepted.

The airlift was an enormous success. It saved the city for the West. It sustained the beleaguered Berliners with minimum rations for nearly a year. It welded a bond between the city and the West that has yet to be broken. There were more than 200,000 flights between June 26, 1948, and May 12, 1949, when the Russians finally lifted the blockade. Altogether,

(*Above*) *Housetop flying was necessary for Airlift pilots landing at Tempelhof Airport, and still is for all daily civilian and military flights to West Berlin over surrounding Communist territory.*

(*Right*) *West Berlin has stockpiled food and fuel to last over six months in the event of another blockade.*

The end of the blockade came when the Russians realized that the airlift was unbeatable and that the Berliners could not be tempted by offers of Eastern rations (only about 4 per cent of the West sector residents went to East Berlin to take advantage of these bribes). It was preceded by "corridor talks" on lifting the blockade at the United Nations between the American delegate, Philip Jessup, and the Soviet delegate, Jakob Malik. On May 12, Mayor Reuter announced, "The technical traffic impediments have been removed since midnight. The attempt to force us to our knees has failed." Five weeks later, at the Foreign Ministers' Conference in Paris, a four-power communiqué was issued stressing the division of Berlin administration and urging normalization of life in the city.

East German armed forces units march in front of the reviewing stand on the site of the old imperial palace. On the left are the ruins of the imperial cathedral, completed in the 1900's.

THE DIVIDED CITY: 1949-1961

Normality never really returned. As a result of efforts by Mayor Reuter, West Berlin became a member state of the Federal Republic of Germany (West Germany) in October, 1950. Though still under the control of the three Western Allies it developed ever-stronger ties with West Germany, particularly economic ties. At this time unemployment was high—300,000 —and aid was badly needed for the reconstruction of the city and for replacement of the industrial plant that had been dismantled and taken away by the Russians as reparations. West Germany provided much of this aid.

Berlin was a divided city in the 1950's. There were separate power systems, and in 1952, after telephone lines between the two halves were cut by the Communists, separate communications were established. Yet in many respects it was a single unit, sharing sewerage systems, waterways, and streets. Thousands of West Berliners worked in East Berlin, and conversely, thousands of East Berliners worked in West Berlin. Perhaps a million Berliners had

relatives living in the opposite sector and visited them regularly.

During the '50's, the Communists gradually imposed more restrictions on the West Berliners, forcing them to pay highway tolls when they travelled to and from West Germany and instituting customs charges for civilian goods moving between the city and the West.

In the Eastern sector of Berlin the Communists were having their own troubles. As a reply to the establishment of the Federal Republic in West Germany they set up the German Democratic Republic in East Germany in September, 1949. Its capital was East Berlin.

This proved to be a bit awkward, for in order to comply with the four-power statutes, East Berlin had to be governed as an entity separate from East Germany, just as West Berlin was governed as an entity separate from West Germany. The solution in each case was to have representatives from the city administrations in the respective state parliaments who did not vote on national legislation. Rather, such laws were submitted and passed separately by the city governments, a practice which prevails today in both East and West Berlin, although the East Berlin administration has practically been absorbed into the East German state. The reason for these niceties was that neither side wanted to give the other an excuse for saying that the four-power arrangement had been violated.

East Berlin Uprising

East Germany, meanwhile, was in poor economic shape. Russian reparations had left its industrial plant stripped to the floor. Now the second and third waves of collectivization began, causing hundreds of thousands of farmers, businessmen, physicians and lawyers to flee west. The people were bitter and disinclined to work hard for small returns. Incentives failed, too, because even with more money there were few goods to be bought. The Communist answer in May 1953 was to raise work quotas in order to increase production. The following month, on June 16, construction workers engaged in building the pompous Stalinallee in East Berlin staged a protest march. Their demands were ignored and on June 17 they marched again. This time they were joined by thousands of other workers all over Berlin and throughout East Germany. They stormed government and party buildings and tore down symbols of the detested Communist regime. The panicky leaders called the Russians, who sent squadrons of tanks rumbling into the cities to put down the revolt. The East Berliners resisted boldly, but their weapons were only rocks, paving stones and rage. The uprising was spontaneous and unprepared and it proved futile against the guns of the Red Army. A wave of arrests followed and a few East Germans were put to death. Nevertheless, though unsuccessful, the revolt forced the Communists to relax their harsh rule for a time in what was called "the new course." But they never altered their plans to communize East Germany completely and to undermine the Allied position in West Berlin.

(Right) An East Berlin family, indistinguishable from West Berliners.

Exodus to West Berlin

The June 17 uprising had many aftereffects. It sent a shock wave through the whole Communist Bloc, for here had been workers who revolted against a "workers' régime," for the first time. It reminded the German Communists and their Russian masters just how fragile their position was. It reminded West Germans and especially the more sensitive West Berliners how close in spirit their imprisoned fellow-Germans felt. And in East Germany it served as a bitter lesson that no matter how strong Western sympathies might be for their plight, they would not provide active support of a rebellion against the Communists. In 1953, more than 300,000 East Germans who had nurtured hopes of eventual liberation and reunification, gave up, packed their bags and fled to West Germany. In the years 1948 to 1961 the number of these refugees swelled to three million, making East Germany the only country in the world to lose population in this period. The continuing flight also caused growing friction on the question of Berlin's future, for virtually all of the refugees escaped by taking a train to the Western sectors. The price was low, and the risks were small since the refugee could mix among hundreds of ordinary Berliner commuters riding between the two sectors.

Scene of the June 17, 1953 revolt—Stalinallee. Renamed Karl Marx Allee after 1961's destalinization, it is called "Rue de Mistake" by Berliners.

East Berlin youngsters in a Sport and Technology Society unit. Their faces perhaps reflect the disdain they feel for this duty. Men, women and children carry arms in the East.

SUMMIT MEETINGS & AFTERMATH: 1961

Berlin was the main subject discussed by Khrushchev and President Kennedy at their Vienna meetings in June 1961. Khrushchev renewed his demands for a rapid settlement, while the President reminded the Soviet leader of Western intentions to hold to their position in West Berlin. Apparently Khrushchev took careful measure of the young American President during this encounter—in particular he noted Mr. Kennedy's emphasis on Allied rights in *West Berlin*. For the late President had made no mention of four-power rights in East Berlin.

There is evidence that Khrushchev took this as a cue, for his next move was to sit down with Walter Ulbricht, who was by this time the chief of the East German government as well as of the ruling Socialist Unity (Communist) Party. Together they drew elaborate plans for sealing the border between East and West Berlin, including a system of "fallbacks" in case Allied resistance should develop.

(*Above*) *After the border closing, the Communists barricaded windows of border houses with wire.*

(*Above*) *Potsdamer Platz after August 13, 1961, looking towards East Berlin. Once the busiest square in Berlin, it is deserted now.*

Communist Mobilization

Their offensive took shape in an atmosphere of mounting tension as the flight of refugees swelled to a thousand a day in late July. Khrushchev and Ulbricht now issued a series of new threats and demands—threats of unilateral action in the German question and demands that the Allies comply with Communist terms for a Berlin settlement. The West responded with declarations and protests. Then, armed with legislation from the East German Volkskammer (parliament) and from the Warsaw Pact (Communist counterpart to NATO) the Communists took action. On the night of August 12, 1961 military units were suddenly called up all across East Germany. A special task force moved into Berlin and in the early hours of August 13, they cordoned off the 80 crossing points between the two sectors and posted guards along the 28-mile intra-city perimeter. Engineer units tore up trolley tracks and paving stones and began rolling out barbed wire.

(*Above*) *The Communists had to wall up the windows, such as these on Bernauerstrasse.*

The slogan at this Communist military parade proclaims the Red goal: "West Berlin will become a demilitarized free city."

East German border guard leaps into West Berlin in August, 1961. More than 500 of his fellow soldiers have followed him.

Western Reaction

There was no Western response, and the stunned West Berliners who went to the border were repulsed by tear gas and water sprayed from high-compression "cannons." The Communists grew bolder. They threw up crude barricades of concrete blocks along the border in the business section. On August 23 they warned the West Berliners to stay 110 yards away from the border on their side. Only then did the Allies take action, moving troops and tanks right up to the line. But nothing was done to stop the expanding wall, not even when the Communists reduced the remaining number of official crossing points from several dozen to only seven, with just one for Allied cars on the Friedrichstrasse.

Rather, the Western response was confined to the sending of an extra American battlegroup of 1,500 men to reinforce the 12,000-man Allied garrison in West Berlin, and the dispatch of Gen. Lucius D. Clay, architect of the airlift, to serve as President Kennedy's special adviser in Berlin.

Escapes Across the Borders

The Communists were almost delirious with the success of their action. They boasted of the 100,000 workers they had gained by stopping the commuting from East to West Berlin, of the sudden halt in the refugee outflow, of the "weakness and inefficiency" of Western leaders. But their claim that they had "reduced tensions" was hollow. For in the following nine months one incident followed another. Bullets whistled as East Berliners made daring escapes across the borders, jumping from high buildings, swimming through frontier waters, squirming through sewer pipes, cutting their way through barbed wire and tunneling underground to West Berlin. More than a score were killed. Meanwhile, the wall grew higher and thicker. In late autumn the East Germans set up dragons' teeth antitank barriers for several miles along the business section of the border, ostensibly to preclude a sudden thrust by the Allies. Gradually they tightened restrictions on remaining movements between the two Berlins. More documents were demand-

(Above) A peek over the wall into East Berlin—a dangerous pastime as Communist trigger fingers have become itchier lately.

(Below) West Berliners with relatives buried in East Berlin must pay their respects across the border.

ed. Travellers were frisked in a humiliating manner. Official Allied vehicles were halted on various pretexts. A climax came when East German border guards held up the car of the senior American diplomatic official in West Berlin, E. Allen Lightner, when he tried to enter East Berlin in late October.

Tanks vs. Tanks

General Clay, who had assumed leadership in the test of will with the Communists, ordered riflemen to escort Mr. Lightner into East Berlin. He followed up by sending a tank unit roaring up to the border barriers on the Friedrichstrasse. At first the Communists were nonplussed. Then, the Russians sent tanks to the border, too. Clay's intention had been to get the Soviet authorities to demonstrate their real responsibility for East Berlin under the four-power agreements, rather than the "sovereign" East German state. Now they had done so, at least in terms of presence. But the face-off of Russian and American tanks muzzle to muzzle caused a war scare in Washington and a retreat was ordered on October 27. Henceforth, the assertion of Western rights to move throughout Berlin without controls was practically abandoned. The wall had done its job.

American infantrymen and West Berlin police stand watch at the critical Friedrichstrasse crossing point on the border between East and West Berlin (foreground). Beyond them are the East German guards and the wall.

The proletarian stress of the Communists' arts is evident in this scene from "The Revision" at the Maxim Gorki Theatre.

CULTURE AND EDUCATION

Citizens sometimes call Berlin, "Spree-Athen"—Athens on the Spree. The allusion is most apt for the neoclassical architecture of the royal museum, Brandenburg Gate and other structures, and perhaps the ancient Pergamon Altar, displayed in East Berlin. In any case, Berliners are proud of the city's cultural life. There are two universities, with more than 20,000 students, in West Berlin and thirteen theatres that draw 11,000 playgoers a year. East Berlin has a university, too, and though Marxist-Leninist dogma has impaired scholarship, a number of first-rate professors still teach there. But it is in theatres that East Berlin really shines. Here is the Theater am Schiffbauerdamm where the works of the late Bertholt Brecht are performed in their brilliant original settings. Here is the Komische Oper, where light opera has achieved new pinnacles of beauty under the direction of the world-famous Walter Felsenstein.

Dress rehearsal of "Aida" at West Berlin's new opera house, directed by Dr. Karl Böhm.

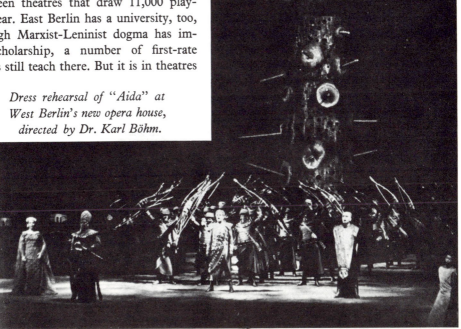

Student councils, such as this one in the West's Ernst Reuter School, were rare before the War.

TEMPERAMENT

It would be easy to claim that the East Berliners are different from West Berliners, and Communist propagandists would like one to think it true. But though the wall split the city it could not split the common heritage and experience of the people. It has been estimated that a third of the Berliners have close relatives living in the opposite sector and these family ties are close. After the barriers went up one could see thousands of Berliners on either side waving to each other, shouting messages and blowing kisses across the concrete and barbed-wire barricades.

If there is any difference between the sectors it is to be found in moods. The West Berliners are bolder, but are anxious about the future. The East Berliners (except for a minority of Communist party members) are bitter and resigned to a future under Soviet rule. These are generalizations, of course, but they certainly apply to the majority of citizens whether they are factory workers, office workers, executives or pensioners. This is perhaps the most striking thing about the Berliners—they think and behave as a unit when it comes to crises. And if Americans or Russians have had any recent doubts about their courage they need only read the statistics of those East Berliners who breached the wall at the risk (and sometimes loss) of their lives. A number have died trying. Several thousand have succeeded in escaping. Many were aided by West Berliners.

Residents in the West's Hansa Quarter relax in the city's special pursuit— the sunshine and Berliner "Luft" (fresh air).

East Berlin's economy has, of course, been completely integrated with that of East Germany. Unlike West Berlin it was not able to turn wartime destruction and reparations to commercial advantage by building new and more competitive plants. Rather, the East sector's industries had to limp along with obsolete or rebuilt equipment. Further hindrances were created by collectivization campaigns, a severe shortage of investment funds and the steady outflow of workers who fled West until the building of the wall. Despite all these handicaps, East Berlin's 1,000 factories made striking recoveries in the post-war years. The main strength has been in the electrical industry which has nearly 60,000 employees—a fourth of the entire East German work force in this branch. But there are also large metal-working and printing plants.

Construction has lagged far behind that in West Berlin, where more than 20,000 apartments are built each year. In East Berlin the figure is about 10,000 new apartments annually. For a time it seemed as if the Communists were halfhearted about engaging in the inevitable "showcase" competition with West Berlin. They built the Stalinallee apartment houses which drew mocking comparisons with West Berlin's glittering Kurfürstendamm. They reconstructed the royal opera house on Unter den Linden and polished up the façades of some government buildings. But by and large East Berlin seemed to go on being a drab and desolate place characterized more by wartime rubble than by new buildings. Actually, construction figures show the Communists poured more into East Berlin than any other city under their control, and now, for the first time, it is beginning to be apparent in new projects along the Alexanderstrasse and Dimitroffstrasse.

A visitor crossing from West to East Berlin is struck by the relative scarcity of automobile traffic in the East, although the East German economy has grown steadily stronger.

(Right) The handsome new zoo in East Berlin was built largely by volunteer workers during their spare time.

The East's houses are built of prefabricated concrete blocks. Construction stopped in 1961 when the blocks were requisitioned for the Wall.

Apprentices start young in Germany. These 16-year-olds are taking a break during construction of apartment houses in East Berlin.

BERLIN ■ 423

*Travellers from West Germany
are greeted by a welcome symbol
after 110 miles of uncertainty on
the East German autobahn. The
name Berlin is believed to be
derived from the word for bear
and possibly commemorates
Albert the Bear, a 12th-century
German ruler.*

THE FUTURE

There is a popular Berlin song with a refrain that goes, "In fifty years it'll all be over." and another that runs, "The islander has hopes quite grand that his island will one day join the mainland." These are the words of the optimist. The pessimist knows that short of nuclear holocaust, the only thing safe to predict about the future of East and West Berlin is that they will go on existing, perhaps even as the German capital. After all, East Berlin has been declared the capital of the German Democratic Republic. Greater Berlin was declared the capital of all Germany in a resolution passed by the West German Bundestag in 1957. More substantial than these declarations are the facts—3,500,000 people, industries, buildings, land and, not the least, traditions.

Of course Berlin's fate is at present in the hands of powers outside Germany. On the Western side its destiny is determined by alterable concepts of rights, commitments, investments and prestige. On the Communist side its destiny is determined by the unalterable concepts of ultimate conquest of the "capitalist" world and by more immediate tactical considerations of what can be gained by harassment and provocation. Both of these conflicting views are currently dominated by the fear of nuclear war. Thus there is the seemingly endless stalemate over Berlin. But it is apparent that a stalemate does not automatically imply a status quo. In Berlin's case it is abundantly clear that the status is anything but "quo"—it changes daily. The direction of the change depends on the will and firmness of the antagonists.

Holland

THE LAND

Why do we call the country Holland when the official name is The Netherlands? When the Dutch themselves speak of "Holland" they normally mean the two provinces (North and South Holland) which contain the nation's three largest cities—Amsterdam, Rotterdam and The Hague. These two of the country's eleven provinces are so important historically and economically that Holland has come to stand for the entire country, The Netherlands, to foreigners.

Netherlands and Holland mean the same thing: low lands. We will see exactly how the Dutch manage to use their low lands, even those beneath the level of the sea. About ten per cent of the land in the tiny, roughly triangular country is or was until recently under water. How it has been rescued from the sea by the ingenious Dutch engineers is a story in itself (and will be described fully in the Polder section). On the north and west are the waters of the North Sea. To the south is Belgium and to the east is West Germany.

Throughout history the land has been flooded by turbulent seas and by erosion of the coast line. For centuries the Dutch have been building dykes to prevent the waves from washing away their land. No point in the whole country is far from the sea.

The Dutch make use of their small land area (now about 12,968 square miles) more efficiently than any other people on earth. With more than 12,661,449 people, Holland has the densest population (974) per square mile of any nation in the world. The surface is almost entirely flat, rising no more than 150 feet above sea level in the west; few rocks are found above the surface except in eastern Holland where heights of 1,000 feet are reached. Coal lies under some of the southern soil, but it is deep (300 to 900 feet); nevertheless, 8,065,000 metric tons are mined annually. Reserves of natural gas which have been found in the northeastern province of Groningen are estimated at 253,629 million cubic feet.

Sand, gravel, clay and salt are abundant, because of the action of the sea in the lowlands. Sand bars lie off most of the coast, broken only by the river deltas, and within the bars are lagoons where peat or marine clay areas have formed. Along the sandy wastes and dunes only stunted grasses, heaths and gorse grow. In fact, some reed grasses are sown to bind the loose sand, and sea asters and sea lavender are cultivated to assist in consolidating the mud flats.

The sand bars prevent the sea from inundating most of the land, but elsewhere artificial barriers (the dykes) have been erected for the same purpose. One of the worst floods in history was that of February 1, 1953, when a large area was submerged. However, all damage was repaired the same year. This disaster led to the planning of the Delta Project.

RIVERS AND PORTS

The rivers in Holland flow in the direction of the general slope of the country from east to west. They are all of international importance in the commerce of Western Europe. The Rhine is the great highway between West Germany and the sea. Entering Holland, it divides into numerous arms, the chief of which are the Waal, Lek and Yssel. Four-fifths of the river trade is carried on the Rhine and Waal, making Rotterdam a Rhine port. The Meuse (Dutch, Maas) joins the Waal, mingling its waters with those of the Rhine. The Scheldt, whose estuary is mainly in the Netherlands, carries ocean vessels to Antwerp in Belgium. Most of southern Holland is laced by a network of these three

Holland

NORTH SEA

FRISIAN ISLANDS

WADDEN SHALLOWS

ENCLOSING DAM

DELFZIJ

GRONINGEN

LEEUWARDEN

GRONINGEN

HARLINGEN

FRIESLAND

ASSEN

DEN HELDER

WIERINGERMEER
POLDER

DRENTE

PETTEN

NORTH

IJSSEL LAKE

NORTH EAST
POLDER

HOLLAND

ALKMAAR

MARKER WAARD
POLDER

EDAM

ZWOLLE

NORTH SEA CANAL

ZAANDAM

LELYSTAD
EAST FLEVOLAND
POLDER

OVERIJSSEL

YMUIDEN

HAARLEM

SOUTH
FLEVOLAND
POLDER

SCHIPHOL
AIRPORT

AMSTERDAM

SOESTDIJK
(ROYAL PALACE)

GELDERLAND

LEYDEN

S-GRAVENHAGE
(THE HAGUE)

SOUTH
HOLLAND

UTRECHT

UTRECHT

WAGENINGEN

ARNHEM

IJSSEL R.

HOEK VAN HOLLAND
(HOOK OF HOLLAND)

DELFT

NEW
WATERWAY

GOUDA

ZESTIENHOVEN
AIRPORT

RHINE CANAL

RHINE R.

"EUROPORT"

PERNIS

ROTTERDAM

LEERDAM

TIEL

NIJMEGEN

WAAL R.

ZEELAND

'S-HERTOGENBOSCH
(BOIS-LE-DUC)

MIDDELBURG

NORTH BRABANT

VLISSINGEN
(FLUSHING)

SCHELDT R.

TILBURG

TERNEUZEN

EINDHOVEN

LIMBURG

MEUSE R.

GERMANY

BELGIUM

MAASTRICHT

In Holland it is not unusual to see a ship steaming past a field of cows above eye level. This canal runs through a dyke that is above sea level, and connects with the North Sea. The ship seen here is on its way to Amsterdam.

rivers and their many branches and deltas, plus long canals to the sea. Amsterdam formerly was a major port on the Zuider Zee, but recent land reclamation projects shut off that bay except for local traffic through a canal from the North Sea to reach that city.

THE CITIES

The capital of Holland is Amsterdam. The name means "dam or dyke of the Amstel," a canalized river that runs through the city to the IJ, which is an arm of the Zuider Zee. It began in the 13th century as a small sea-fishing settlement held by the lords of Amstel and bishops of Utrecht. In 1204 a castle was built there and a little later the dam was built to keep out the sea. In 1482 the town was walled in. During the religious troubles of the 16th century, Amsterdam's prosperity increased as refugees flowed in from Antwerp

The port of Amsterdam has been modernized. It now gives fast service in loading and unloading with the latest lifting machinery.

This aerial view of Amsterdam clearly shows the semi-circular arrangement of the city with its many major and minor canals.

and Brabant. The city did not join other Dutch towns in revolting against Spain until 1578. Then in 1648, it reached further prosperous peaks when Antwerp was ruined by the closing of the Scheldt River under the Treaty of Westphalia. The city has many times held out against invaders by opening the dykes, a device that was successful only temporarily in most cases. It has been occupied by the Prussians, the French and later the Germans again.

Modern Amsterdam has been built to a great extent over bogs. Like Venice, it had to be secured into the clayey soil beneath by the driving of long piles for the foundations of buildings. One of the most picturesque cities of Europe, Amsterdam has four major canals (*singels*) in concentric semi-circles emptying into the IJ, with smaller canals (*grachten*) intersecting the larger ones. As a result, the inner or old city is like a large number of islands.

Motor car traffic is now so heavy that some people have advocated that certain canals be roofed over to provide more streets.

Holland is a country of flowers and there is seldom a home without them. On nearly every street corner in the cities is a little stall selling blooms.

At all times thousands of ships and barges ply their way up and down the Rhine. This wide river empties into the North Sea in Holland, making Rotterdam a Rhine port.

Quite a few of Amsterdam's inhabitants live on barges in the canals. Car traffic runs along the edge of most of the canals.

One of The Hague's loveliest buildings is the Mauritshuis, now a museum, formerly the residence of the Prince of Nassau, Johan Maurits, who built it in 1634.

The Hague is the site of Holland's Parliament and the home of the Permanent Court of International Justice; numerous times it has been the site of peace conferences. In Dutch, the city is called *'s-Gravenhage*, or abbreviated *Den Haag*. As early as the 13th century, when it was little more than a hunting lodge, it was first used as a court of justice, because the count in control made his residence there. Today it has 586,187 inhabitants, compared to Amsterdam's 866,421 and Rotterdam's 723,955. Besides the government buildings and the courts of justice, the city boasts of museums, libraries and churches dating from the Middle Ages.

Rotterdam was founded in feudal times where two castles stood; it is known that in 1299, a count of Holland granted the people of Rotterdam the same rights as the people of Haarlem and Beverwijk. Its location has made it of great importance in ocean trade and it is presently the world's largest port. It suffered a great deal during World War II from a severe bombardment by the Germans before Holland fell in the invasion of 1940.

The Peace Palace in The Hague, home of the Permanent Court of International Justice.

In the heart of The Hague are these parliament buildings surrounding the "Ridderzaal" or Hall of Knights.

The bridge at Nijmegen spans the river Waal. In the foreground, spelled in flowers, is the Latin name for the city, a reminder that Nijmegen was a Roman settlement.

In the 17th century these windmills were used to drain numerous lakes northwest of Amsterdam. Water was pumped into a circular canal behind a dyke which had been built beforehand.

WINDMILLS AND DYKES

No other nation has had the trouble that Holland had in keeping its land from being inundated. Rolling back the sea is the country's national project today and has been for centuries. Some 10,000 years ago, Holland was probably nothing but mud and ooze. When the sea receded a little and left what is now above sea level, it also left the tremendous Zuider Zee like a cavity in a tooth. Much of this bay was covered by shallow water.

The inhabitants of the area were primitive and brave fighters, according to Julius Caesar, but holding back the sea probably never entered their thoughts. The free Frisians from the northern part of Holland were the first known to build mounds along the coast.

The idea of building dykes came in the 8th or 9th century, and with it the Dutch conceived the idea of using the wind to keep the water out. They erected windmills, hundreds of them, that worked 24 hours a day without any effort. The more the gales blew, the more the pumps attached to the windmills worked.

The dunes along the coast of Zeeland, a province which has been entirely reclaimed, are protected from the ravages of the sea by man-made palisades and basalt blocks.

Dykes were smashed and reclaimed lands flooded again in 1953 when a storm sent the North Sea smashing over the Dutchmen's barriers. In the flood areas, work had to begin all over again.

Water that came over or past the dykes and dams was pumped up through a series of levels, each higher than the one before. Finally the water was forced into a network of canals that allowed the water to flow back into the sea at low tide. Some of these canals are high above the surface of cultivated ground.

The windmills caused a problem of their own. During the Middle Ages, the feudal lords carried on endless disputes about who owned the wind, and tried to collect fees from anyone who had a windmill. As late as the 14th century, the baron of Woerden and the bishop of Utrecht quarrelled about the right to collect windmill taxes.

The early windmills worked only when the wind was in the right direction. Later, they were made with turntable tops. Still later, they were put to additional uses—sawing timber, for example.

Today, electric pumping stations assist the more picturesque windmills.

POLDERS

When you think of dykes, your mind pictures them standing guard between land and sea. This is indeed the function of many dykes. Others, as we have seen, serve as dams to separate the sea from what then become inland waters. Still a third use for dykes is to enclose new land or *polders*.

The part of the sea which has been chosen by the engineers to become farmland, is first

No, it's not a mirage. A ship is gliding over the landscape higher than the level of the land because it is passing through the North Sea canal which links Amsterdam to the ocean. This huge canal is about 45 feet deep, between the dykes.

A natural dune is supplemented by a dyke to hold back the North Sea.

surrounded by a double dyke. Two dykes about 100 feet apart are built up from the floor of the sea. Then the space between is filled with sand which is also pumped up from the bottom of the sea. Next, pumps remove the water from the future polder, exposing the muddy land, and then, even before the land is dry, dredgers get busy digging drainage ditches.

Early stage in the construction of a dyke. The dyke profile is being built up by the spouting sand and water under high pressure.

Polder dyke under construction: at (A), the dykes are being built up out of clay from the sea bottom; (B) is a sheet-piling partition being rammed down by machinery to act as a bulwark; (C) is where a brushwood mattress has been constructed and sunk to become part of the dyke; (D) is a hydraulic pump that dredges the sand from the sea bottom and pumps it to the shore between the two dykes; men at (E) finish off the outer slopes with rocky fill; (F) is the finished sand core of the dyke. After the double-dyke encloses a portion of the sea, the area is pumped dry and drained as a polder. Later the land is cultivated.

New dyke under construction in the former Zuider Zee. This so-called ring dyke is to enclose a section of the sea—to be called Flevoland—which will then be pumped dry and thus reclaimed for agriculture. Note in the foreground how boulders are dumped on the willow mat foundation. The cranes in the background are dumping sand in the middle of the dyke, which will then again be covered by layers of willow and boulders, and then by asphalt.

An exciting moment as the enclosing dykes were about to meet in 1931 and the waters of the enclosed area rush out of the only channel left.

The foundations of a dyke underwater are protected by collars of stone and the so-called osiers, shown here. These are very pliable, willowy twigs which are tied in rows of poles with fencing supports. The stones on the barge here will be loaded on to the osiers and the whole thing lowered to cover and protect the portion of the dyke underwater. Then a straw mat covered with rubble will be placed on the top part of the dyke before a layer of loam is put down, on which finally a layer of clay is placed, in which grass is grown. Some dykes are lighter or heavier than others, according to their position in the water. In some cases concrete pillars are built.

Some of the ditches are dug wide enough to serve as shipping canals. Locks are the communicating links between the waters inside and outside the polder, and also between those sections of a polder having different levels.

To reclaim the virgin sea bottom into farmland takes many years, and is accomplished in planned stages, a small area at a time. At first the new land is impassable, but reclamation engineers sow seeds from helicopters. The

Dutchmen at work on the newly-built 56-mile long dyke erected to drain the waters off 133,000 acres of the oval-shaped Eastern Flevoland polder in the Zuider Zee.

(Left) The enclosing dykes met here in 1931, and a monument was erected on the spot. On the one side is the sea, on the other is land drying out. The former island of Wieringen is now part of the mainland of North Holland.

plants develop rapidly, accelerate the drying out of the soil and are easily destroyed once they have served their purpose.

The salt water is sometimes flushed from the drainage canals by fresh water from lakes and rivers.

During the considerable time it takes for the soil to ripen to its maximum usefulness, it is necessary to study the soil and work it with preliminary crops, convert the surface trenches into underground drainage systems, build farm buildings, etc. The government operates the land temporarily, until it can be taken over by farmers.

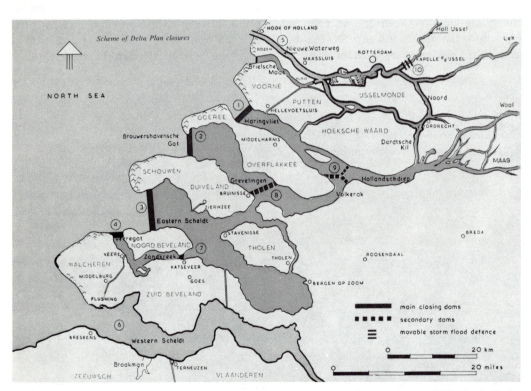

Dams are being constructed to hold back the North Sea in the southwestern part of Holland. Dykes No. 4, No. 7 and No. 8 are ready as well as the bridge project at No. 9. Under construction at present is No. 1.

Before (above) and after (below). Schokland was an island before work began on the Northeast Polder, but after a dyke 30 miles long was closed, the sea began to shrink and the island became the middle of a large open field now completely cultivated.

This is what the Dutch call a chessboard effect in new land just recovered from a polder.

CLIMATE

The weather in Holland is uniform, as the country is so small, but the north and west get most of the fogs coming in from the North Sea. Winds are generally from the west and southwest too bringing gusts of rain. There is a saying, "If you don't like the weather, wait a few minutes." Showers can come as frequently as every half-hour. The temperature usually stays close to 70° in the summertime and 30° in winter, making for comfortable living conditions.

AGRICULTURE

Everywhere in Holland, in homes, stores and offices are cut flowers, for the Dutch are fond of flowers. The most popular in springtime is the tulip, national symbol and most prolific flower in the country. Today Holland grows over 2,000 varieties of tulip, and exports most of them. In actual fact, the tulip did not reach Holland until quite late in its history. It is a native flower of Turkey, where it was named the *tulband* or turban. Austria's ambassador to

In every frozen lake a hole is cut in the ice to ensure a water supply in case of fire. In the distance are skaters and a windmill.

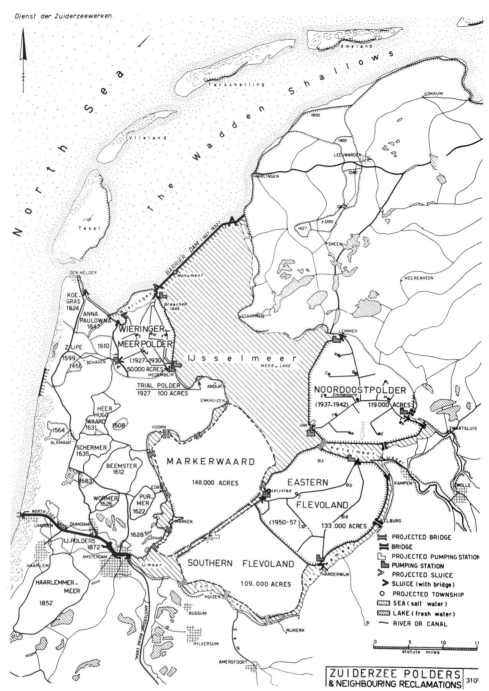

Dienst der Zuiderzeewerken.

N o r t h   S e a

T h e   W a d d e n   S h a l l o w s

Ameland

Terschelling

Vlieland

Texel

DOKKUM

1800

1400

LEEUWARDEN

1260

HARLINGEN

±1200

SNEEK

1427

HEERENVEEN

DEN HELDER

KOE GRAS 1824

ANNA PAULOWNA 1847

BARRIER DAM 1927-1932

Monument

Breached 1945

Wieringer

WIERINGER MEERPOLDER (1927-1930) 50.000 ACRES

IJsselmeer
MEER = LAKE

STAVOREN

LEMMER

HEERENVEEN

ZYPE 1599 1456

SCHAGEN

1610

TRIAL POLDER 1927 100 ACRES

MEDEMBLIK

ANDIJK

ENKHUIZEN

NOORDOOSTPOLDER (1937-1942) 119.000 ACRES

Emmeloord

URK

ZWARTSLUIS

HEER HUGO WAARD 1631

1608

HOORN

1564

ALKMAAR

SCHERMER 1635

BEEMSTER 1612

MARKERWAARD

148.000 ACRES

Ketelmeer

KAMPEN

WOLLE

1683

WORMER 1626

PURMER 1622

EDAM

1628

MARKEN

EASTERN

Lelystad

FLEVOLAND

(1950-57)

133.000 ACRES

ELBURG

NORTH SEA

UMUIDEN

ZAANDAM

IJ.POLDERS 1872

AMSTERDAM

IJmeer

SOUTHERN FLEVOLAND

109.000 ACRES

HARDERWIJK

HAARLEM

HAARLEMMER- MEER

1852

HUIZEN

BUSSUM

NIJKERK

AMSTERDAM RHINE CANAL

HILVERSUM

AMERSFOORT

PROJECTED BRIDGE
BRIDGE
PROJECTED PUMPING STATION
PUMPING STATION
PROJECTED SLUICE
SLUICE (with bridge)
PROJECTED TOWNSHIP
SEA (salt water)
LAKE (fresh water)
RIVER OR CANAL

0   5   10   1
statute miles

ZUIDERZEE POLDERS & NEIGHBOURING RECLAMATIONS 310l

This map of the former Zuider Zee gives a clear idea of how a barrier dam or enclosing dyke cuts off the North Sea waters. Five large polders have been planned for the area and three have already been completed: the Wieringermeer, the Northeast Polder and Eastern Flevoland. Southern Flevoland is now dry and is in the process of being settled. When the project is completed, the total arable land area in the Netherlands will have been increased by 10 per cent. The remainder of the Zuider Zee, now known as the IJssel Lake, will be retained as a fresh-water reservoir. The enclosing dyke was constructed between 1927 and 1932.

Tulips bloom as far as the eye can reach. The bulbs will be part of Holland's major agricultural export crop.

Turkey brought the flower back to Vienna in 1554. There the court gardener of the Hapsburg royal family fell in love with the tulip, and since he was Dutch he introduced it into Holland. During the 17th century, tulips were traded as corporation stocks are today, and people speculated for a time (1634-38) in tulips. The speculators never saw the tulip bulbs they bought and sold, but as many as 10 million guilders changed hands in tulip transactions during a year in a single city of Holland. The speculative fever reached such a pitch that the government had to step in and halt trading.

(Left) Clogs or wooden shoes were originally used in Holland on muddy farms. They are still made by hand by this clog maker. The Dutch name for them is klompen.

HISTORY AND GOVERNMENT

The name Netherlands originally applied to territory that now comprises Holland, Belgium, Luxembourg and part of France. The inhabitants were originally Germanic and Celtic tribes. During Roman times there were three tribes in Holland—the Frisians in the north, the Batavi in the middle, and the Belgae in the south. Caesar himself conquered the Belgae, but the Romans did not subjugate the two other tribes for over 100 years. By the time the Franks (from what is now southern Germany) became a menace in the 3rd century the Batavi, whose land had been an important outpost of the Roman Empire, had become Romanized. But the Frisii allied with the Saxons (from northern Germany) and held a good deal of the seacoast in defiance of the Franks until the time of Charlemagne. The eastern part of the Netherlands was given to Lothair (Lothair's Regnum—or Lorraine) when Charlemagne's kingdom was divided (843) and in 953 it was given to Bruno, archbishop of Cologne. Bruno divided the land again, into Upper and Lower Lorraine, giving Godfrey of Verdun charge of the latter. This territory was far from both French and German seats of government but open to the raids of the Norsemen which continued for 200 years.

In the late Middle Ages the cities of the Netherlands rose to great prosperity, for the seacoast provided a chance to develop a merchant fleet, and some of the cities were practically self-governing republics. As we will see later, the revival of art was second in importance only to the Italian states. The house of Burgundy gained control during this period, but in 1477 the marriage of Mary of Burgundy to Maximilian of Austria put the country under the control of the house of Hapsburg. Charles V, grandson of Maximilian, inherited the Netherlands along with Spain in 1549. At this time Spain was Catholic and the Netherlands were becoming strongly Protestant. Charles, nevertheless, followed a moderate policy in ruling the Netherlands. In 1555 he resigned the sovereignty over the Netherlands to his son Philip II, who was not at all moderate.

Philip had no sympathy with the Netherlands and was extremely oppressive, taking away all civil and religious liberties. When the Dutch rebelled, Philip in 1567 sent the Duke of Alva with troops to curb disturbances in the Netherlands. Alva treated the country as conquered territory and his council sentenced thousands of innocent people to death. He even went so far as to sentence all inhabitants of the Netherlands to die as heretics with a few named exceptions, but this was never carried out, of course.

WILLIAM OF ORANGE

The most important result of Alva's rule was the revolt of the northern, Protestant provinces under William of Orange, starting a struggle which was to last for 80 years. On the sea the Dutch consistently defeated the Spanish, but they suffered severe losses on land. Yet the Dutch showed great courage. The story of Alkmaar is an example. A well-trained force of 16,000 Spaniards besieged this town of 800 inhabitants. The Dutch, however, resorted to their supreme weapon and opened the dykes to flood the countryside, and the Spaniards ran away as swiftly as any poorly trained soldiers. In another instance, the people

Silver coin ("show taler") issued in 1574 commemorating the people who withstood the siege of Leyden. The scene shows the Spaniards fleeing the city.

of Leyden, having withstood a siege for a year, flooded their city so the ships could sail in bringing relief to drive off the Spaniards. In 1573 Alva was recalled and the Duke of Parma took his place. He won the southern, Catholic provinces back to Spain, and in 1579 the seven northern provinces under William of Orange bound themselves together in the Union of Utrecht, thus founding the modern state of the Netherlands. The new state followed a policy of religious toleration which caused many persecuted religious groups to seek refuge there.

The new state suffered a severe blow when William of Orange was assassinated in 1584, but the United Provinces continued their fight for independence under Maurits of Nassau, the son of William and stadtholder (viceroy) of Holland and Zeeland. Maurits led a number of successful campaigns and on the sea the Dutch overwhelmed the Spanish forces. In 1609 Spain signed a 12-year truce, an acknowledgment of the independence of the United Provinces which gave them the right of free trade in the Indies. The Dutch navy at this time became the masters of trade with the East Indies.

In 1621, the 12-year truce was over, and since the Dutch refused to acknowledge allegiance to Spain, Philip IV renewed the war. The Dutch (with the French as allies) carried on a struggle for Flanders (a province now in Belgium), but they were happy to make peace

when Spain started negotiations in 1646. As part of the Treaty of Westphalia in 1648 the "Republic of the Seven United Netherlands" was recognized as a free and sovereign state. The province of Holland now became the real controlling force and, led by Johan de Witt, the Netherlands entered their Golden Age. The Dutch became the leading sea power by defeating the English twice, and the country grew prosperous. The new prosperity brought new problems.

WILLIAM AND MARY

The Netherlands joined with England against France, and Louis XIV did make peace with the Netherlands, but for only four years. During this time he built up arms and in 1672 he moved against the Netherlands. The English took advantage of Louis' move and also attacked the Netherlands, on the sea, in an attempt to regain naval control. The Prince of Orange, the stadtholder of Holland and Zeeland who later became King William III of England, kept the Dutch from having to give in to either country. The immediate threat of the French was ended when Spain joined in

Leyden's city hall.

Like a fairy-tale castle is the 13th-century "De Haar" which fell to ruin and was restored, gardens and all, in 1892.

fighting France on another front. In 1674 the English were weary of fighting the Dutch and returned all the territory they had conquered. By this time the English were anti-French again. The Netherlands' diplomatic position was improved in 1677 by William's marriage to Mary, daughter of the Duke of York. For ten years (1678-88) no fighting occurred in Holland. Then King James II of England was forced to flee his country and the English people asked William and Mary to take the throne, which they did. (William still remained stadtholder in his native country.) When the English began fighting the French in 1688 the Dutch naturally were their allies. By the Treaty of Ryswyk (1697), the Netherlands received a preferential commercial treaty. William remained the King of England and stadtholder in the Netherlands until his death in 1702.

During the 18th century the prosperity declined and peace prevailed. In 1795, however, the stadtholder was overthrown and the Batavian Republic was organized in close alliance with France. In 1806 Napoleon made the country a kingdom under his brother Louis, and in 1810 it became part of the French Empire. In 1813 the French were expelled and the house of Orange was restored. Then in 1815 the Congress of Vienna added Belgium to Holland and created the Kingdom of the Netherlands under the sovereignty of William I, son of the last stadtholder. After fruitless attempts to quell revolts by the Catholic Belgians unhappy as part of a Protestant kingdom, King William I of the Netherlands created the independent Kingdom of Belgium.

William I had trouble in dealing with the Belgians and abdicated. His son became King

This medieval castle, called Muiderslot, once dominated an entrance to the Rhine near Amsterdam, but now the river has been diverted. It served as a prison in 1296 for Count Floris V who was murdered here by his rivals.

William II in 1840. He died in 1849 and was replaced by William III, his son, who ruled until 1890. The new constitutional government, which had become effective just before William III became king, now played an important role. The upper house of the Parliament was chosen by the provinces and the lower house by the people. Political parties also became important during the long reign of William III.

MODERN TIMES

When William III died in 1890 his 10-year-old daughter, Wilhelmina, became Queen, although her mother, Emma, served as regent for ten years. Wilhelmina kept the Netherlands neutral during World War I, but only with great difficulty. The economy was damaged by the stoppage of shipping. The location of the country put it in great danger of being the field of battle between the British and the Germans, and the Dutch had to keep a fully mobilized

army of 450,000 at great expense for the duration of the war.

During World War II it was impossible to keep the country neutral. The Germans invaded in 1940 and the Queen and her ministers escaped to Britain. In addition to the normal damage from military battles, large areas of good land were flooded by the sea when the dykes were cut.

Queen Wilhelmina returned to her country when it was liberated in 1945. Soon after Wilhelmina's golden jubilee she abdicated, and on September 6, 1948, Juliana became Queen.

GOVERNMENT

The Netherlands is a constitutional and hereditary monarchy today. Executive and legislative powers are in the hands of the elected members of the States-General (or Parliament). The First Chamber of Parliament

On Prinsjesdag, the third Tuesday in September, the monarch opens the new session of Parliament. She drives from her palace in The Hague in a "golden coach" drawn by eight horses. Here Queen Juliana is about to alight in front of the Knights' Hall in The Hague.

(or Upper House) with 75 members is elected for 6 years by the provincial states, with half of the body resigning every 3 years. The Second Chamber (or Lower House) consists of 150 deputies and is elected for 4 years, being replaced en bloc. The Lower House can initiate new bills and propose amendments, but the main executive power is exercised by the

The royal family arrives for the opening of the new parliamentary year at the Hall of Knights in The Hague.

Queen Juliana, with the bridge across the IJssel (which is also a storm defence) in the background. When the bulwark is let down, it acts as a dyke.

ministers, headed by the Prime Minister, appointed by the Sovereign. The Prime Minister is the leader of the majority party.

All Dutch men and women of 23 years or older can vote.

The 11 provinces have local governments; these bodies are known collectively as the "Provinciale Staten," presided over by a Royal Commissioner. Each of the 1,014 municipalities in the country has a locally elected Council and a Mayor, appointed by the Crown.

Holland is unique in that its capital is Amsterdam, but the seat of Parliament and the Court is actually at The Hague ('s Gravenhage), some 35 miles away.

Not only is Holland a member of the United Nations and NATO, but it has joined with Belgium and Luxembourg into what is known as the Benelux organization for closer co-operation economically. Benelux is part of the European Common Market which has been gathering in strength in the past few years.

Loss of markets in Indonesia, for import and to some extent for exports, after World War II created grave problems for the government, besides the enormous task of rebuilding after the war's destruction.

The sovereign, Queen Juliana, resides in a country estate "Soestdijk," close to Utrecht and between Amsterdam and The Hague.

THE PEOPLE

The people of Holland are a mixture of many racial elements. Few traces remain of the original Celtic inhabitants. Early settlements were taken over by the Romans, and the Romans mingled with the Batavi to form new strains which persist to this day. Generally the Dutch can be regarded as an independent, democratic people, good businessmen, hard-working and reliable.

SCHOLARS

Holland is famous internationally for its scholars, painters and philosophers. Desiderius Erasmus (1466?-1536) was one of the greatest scholars of the Renaissance and Reformation period. He stimulated the peoples of northern Europe as the chief interpreter of the intellectual movement. As a leader in the humanist movement which made the classics popular again, he translated the works of Aristotle, Plutarch and other Greek and Roman writers. In a somewhat different field, he was important —as a theologian. In pressing for reform, he wanted the primitive simplicity of Christianity to become more important than the ceremonies and dogma of the church, and urged that interpretations in Christianity come from the Bible.

Benedict or Baruch Spinoza (1632-1677) was a great Jewish-Dutch philosopher who suffered want and persecution in his search for truth. He refused to believe in a supernatural deity and based his explanation of God on a more realistic philosophy. This philosophy did not agree with the common thought at the time and he was branded an atheist by the people. The

religious nature of his writing has shown that this was not true. Spinoza tried to find a system to deduce the principles of a moral life by mathematical system. His most important work, *Ethics*, is written mathematically following Euclid, with propositions, proofs, and corollaries.

The people of Rotterdam in the 15th century erected a wooden statue to the scholar, Erasmus, when he was a fellow-citizen. It was destroyed by Spanish troops during the 80-year war. But in 1622, the great Dutch sculptor, De Keyser, completed this new statue, cast in bronze.

Anton van Leeuwenhoek (1632-1723) was the first man to see microbes—he invented the microscope. The lenses he made were small but strongly curved for excellent magnification.

ART

The greatest contribution the Dutch have made to world culture is in the field of painting. Until the middle of the 17th century Flemish painting had been the important art of the Low Countries. At that time the tide changed and art in Holland rose to its peak. Landscape and portraiture were the most important branches of painting for the Dutch painters because of the burghers, who had prospered greatly in commercial trade. They wished to decorate their homes with scenes of their land and to leave portraits to their descendants.

Jacob van Ruysdael (1628 ?-82) is the best-

(Right) Opposite the house where the famous philosopher, Benedict (Baruch) Spinoza, lived in The Hague from 1670 to 1677, is this statue. Born of Portuguese Jewish parents, Spinoza was eventually banished from the Jewish community on account of his "heretic" views. To support himself, he had to earn a living as a polisher of lenses.

450 ■ HOLLAND

*Van Ruysdael, master of the landscape, often
chose windmills for his subjects.*

known landscape painter of that time, and was
one of the first artists to paint landscapes
without people. Little is known about his life
except that he was the son of a Haarlem frame
maker. His scenes of rainy and cloudy days,
with trees and windmills, were handled in
romantic fashion that far surpassed the quality
of his realistic contemporaries.

Frans Hals (1584?-1666) and Rembrandt
(1606-1669) were the most famous guild
(group) portrait painters. The burghers at first
demanded that all the subjects of a guild picture
be dressed alike and be given equal prominence.
Hals, who lived in Haarlem, ended this practice
by showing his groups in the acts of doing
various things, such as conducting a meeting.
His portraits were the first lively ones, appearing
as if they might have been natural rather than
posed. His realistic portraits, generally brighter

*Frans Hals' realistic touch is seen in his "Nurse
and Child," an oil painted fairly early in his
career.*

HOLLAND ■ **451**

Rembrandt's famous oil painting, "The Night-Watch."

than Rembrandt's, showed that he was original and bold.

Rembrandt gained his initial fame with the painting often called "The Night-Watch," which portrays 29 guards in striking dress leaving their quarters. This gigantic picture shows all the guards as life-size. One of the world's greatest artists, Rembrandt was a master of the highlight and near perfect with

Pieter De Hoogh painted the cubical contents of rooms. When he took an outside scene it was usually a lane or courtyard like this—all bricked in.

dark tones and contrasting shades. His people seem often to be raised from the canvas. The figures he painted seem to glow with the moving power of a mighty personality. Among his greatest works are the series of self-portraits, dating from 1629 to 1669 which record every development in his progress as a painter. Rembrandt was also one of the great etchers of all time.

Two Dutch painters of interiors were much alike and very important. Jan Vermeer (1632-75) of Delft and Pieter De Hoogh (1629-81 ?)

Rembrandt van Rijn painted this portrait of himself. He was a master of light and shadow. His home in the middle of Amsterdam is a museum today.

usually painted the same type of scene—what Rodin called "the cubical contents of a room." Vermeer was rediscovered only 100 years ago, and is now considered one of the great Dutch painters. He found his theme in small interior paintings which showed a human figure completely absorbed in his or her activity. He used warm tones and also a warm light which highlighted the objects in the room.

The scenes De Hoogh painted often showed interiors of rooms picturing typical bourgeois

In the Rijksmuseum, a young Dutchman sits enthralled in the presence of Rembrandt's portraits of burgomasters.

Vermeer gave a soft, round look to his women as in "The Lace Maker" shown here. By subtle use of shading he made his characters spring forward from their background.

Self-portrait of the Dutch painter, Vincent van Gogh (before he cut off his ear). Now one of the world's most popular artists, van Gogh was penniless and unknown most of his life and died tragically. His brilliant works are now very valuable.

life, dark rooms with glimpses of light from the outside. His paintings were very precise, and his rooms always followed the exact lines of perspective. De Hoogh's earlier works had a harsh look, but Vermeer's influence on De Hoogh was great, and his later pictures were warmer.

Vincent van Gogh (1853-1890) was born in Holland and started painting rather late in life. He first worked for an art dealer and then as a missionary among miners. In 1882 he moved to The Hague and studied painting. He later moved on to Paris and in two years produced 200 paintings. There he became acquainted with the art of the Impressionists. When he moved to Arles in 1888 his paints brightened and he produced his best works, landscapes, portraits and flowers. His paintings, however, were not popular during his lifetime and brought him no money. He was confined in two asylums for insanity, and suicide cut short his career.

Van Gogh's "Street with Cypresses," a gorgeous painting done in 1890, the last year of his life.

In the middle of Amsterdam is the imposing Rijksmuseum (or State Museum), built in Dutch Renaissance style. It houses many Rembrandt paintings including "The Night-Watch" and others from the Trippenhuis gallery once owned by the (royal) House of Orange and taken by Louis Napoleon.

The recent years have brought appreciation of the power and originality of his art.

DISCOVERERS

The Dutch navigators of the 16th and 17th century opened up many parts of the New World. It was a Dutchman who first sailed around the cape at the southern tip of South America (Magellan had gone through the straits that bear his name) and named it Hoorn for his native town in Holland. A Dutch captain, Abel Tasman, discovered the islands of New Zealand (which he named after the province of Zeeland) and Tasmania in the South Pacific. Dutch whalers were the first or among the first to reach Spitsbergen and Novaya Zembla in the Arctic Circle. The

(Right) Dutch architects can be as modern as any. This is an Adventist church.

The Half-Moon at Yonkers (above) and Henry Hudson (left). "*Toward evening the next day he entered the broad stream and at twilight cast anchor at Yonkers. A strong tidal current placed the stern of his vessel upstream during the night. This event, and the assurances of the natives who flocked to his vessel, in canoes, with oysters and vegetables . . . inspired him with great hope . . . of the long-sought Cathay.*" —HARPER'S NEW YORK MONTHLY MAGAZINE, 1854

Dutch founded Surinam (Dutch Guiana) in South America, and settled the islands of Curacao and Aruba in the West Indies, which are now autonomous parts of the Kingdom of the Netherlands.

The East Indies (now Indonesia) were opened up by Dutch navigators and others hired by the Dutch East India Company, founded in 1602. They settled Java, Sumatra and other islands 57 times as large as the home land. In 1949 the Netherlands East Indies became independent Indonesia.

The Dutch also settled New Amsterdam, which was later to become New York City, but the leader of that expedition was an Englishman, Henry Hudson, hired by the Dutch East India Company to find a passage to China, and it was only by mistake that he got to the area at all. Hudson already had a reputation as a navigator in 1608 when he had a "call" to Amsterdam, where he met famous Dutch map-makers, Hondius and Plancius. He agreed to sail with 20 men in the *Half-Moon* towards the Barents Sea, north of Scandinavia,

Originally an isolated island, Marken continued in ancient tradition, the people dressing strikingly and painting houses gaily. Now Marken is only a few miles from Amsterdam over the dykes, and is a popular tourist spot.

in an effort to find a way through the North Pole area. But, once there, his ship got stuck in the ice, his men became mutinous, and he had to submit to his crew's decision to head for Virginia instead. They were going to find China by sailing up Chesapeake Bay. They stopped at the Faroe Islands (south of Iceland) for water, then made it across the Atlantic toward Newfoundland, where an accident compelled Hudson to put into the Kennebec River in Maine. Sailing further along the coast, he entered New York Bay in 1609, sailed up the Hudson River as far as Albany (150 miles), dealt with the Indians, tried going further and

(Right) This is the ordinary dress of Zeeland women on market day. The basket papoose makes this tandem a bicycle built for three.

On market days on Walcheren Island, the women (and men) wear traditional costumes while at their stalls.

decided that the river did not lead to China, so turned back.

When Hudson returned to Europe, he put in at Dartmouth, England, where his vessel was detained by the government. Hudson and the other Englishmen in his crew were commanded not to leave England but to serve their own country. This Hudson did, later opening the way to northern Canada through Hudson Bay and the Hudson Straits. Nevertheless, his explorations for the Dutch gave Holland an important foothold on America's east coast, the best port in the New World and what was later to become the world's most valuable site, although, alas, the Dutch did not hold on to the territory after 1664.

(Left) Dutch children, following an old custom, tell St. Nicholas what they want—but not for Christmas! They celebrate St. Nicholas Day on December 6th, and presents are given out the evening before. In Holland, Christmas is strictly a religious festival. The St. Nicholas custom was brought by early Dutch colonists to America, where his name was shortened to Santa Claus. Elsewhere, the symbol of Christmas is usually called Father Christmas.

A complete doll-size city, including canals, railroads, ships that move, stores and factories, has been built in the park at Madurodam, just outside The Hague. Here children and their parents can have fun for hours on end.

The miniature town of Madurodam has everything scaled 1/25th of actual size. All of the typical features of the larger Dutch cities are duplicated in this park which is visited annually by about 700,000 people.

The park was established after World War II to help finance a students' sanatorium.

Office workers in Holland may have cars too, but they go to work on their bicycles. There is hardly a Dutchman, woman or child without a bike.

Near The Hague is the largest bathing beach in Holland, a long wide stretch of sand called Scheveningen.

Scheveningen is not pronounced the way it looks. During World War II, it is said that the Dutch caught spies by asking them to pronounce the name of the beach. No non-Dutchman can say it correctly.

Amsterdam's Concertgebouw Orchestra has played in many countries and has had conductors of international fame.

Kralingen was once a town outside of Rotterdam, and now it is completely surrounded by the city. Its old lake and splendid windmill make it popular for sailing, sledding and skating.

EDUCATION

Holland has a few famous and ancient universities. At Leyden, which was governed by the Romans and besieged by the Spaniards in 1572, is a university founded in 1574 by William of Orange as a reward for the heroic defence of 1572. Its scholars (which included Hugo Grotius) raised Leyden University to the height of European fame, a position it maintained until the end of the 18th century. It has emphasized studies in the East Indian languages, ethnology and geography, and has a fine natural history museum, botanical gardens, an observatory and two museums of antiquities. In 1745, the Leyden jar, a device for storing static electricity, was discovered (by accident) by a scholar at the university.

Another university is situated in the moat-surrounded ancient city of Groningen, capital of Holland's northernmost province. There, in the university founded in 1614, is the original copy of Erasmus' New Testament, with marginal annotations made by Martin Luther.

In the picturesque old town of Utrecht, 22 miles south-southeast of Amsterdam, is another university with fine old Gothic cloisters, founded in 1636. The palace built for Louis Bonaparte is now the university's library.

These three and an ancient municipal university in Amsterdam are non-religious institutions. Besides there are two religious universities—in Amsterdam and Nijmegen.

The Deventer town hall built in the 17th century was designed in Westphalian style probably because the city had once belonged to the Hanseatic League. It was here that Erasmus studied. In the town hall itself is housed the Athenaeum Library which dates from the 14th century and contains a large number of types of handwriting.

Holland's three Technological Universities are located in Delft, Eindhoven and Enschede. In addition, there are the Netherlands School of Economics in Rotterdam and the Catholic School of Economics in Tilburg.

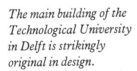

The main building of the Technological University in Delft is strikingly original in design.

A Dutch summer camp with kayaks to sail on the broads (inlets) north of Utrecht.

Skating on frozen canals is a popular winter sport. Participants in the "Tour of the Mills" must sign in at a given number of mills en route.

(Above) A sailboat regatta on a Dutch lake. Many fresh-water lakes have been dammed up.

One of the world's great zoos is Artis in Amsterdam. On this rock surrounded by a moat, the ibexes (or wild goats) live.

HOLLAND ■ **465**

Most popular of all annual sports events in Holland is the soccer match with Belgium which is held in the Feyenoord Stadium in Rotterdam (shown here) in alternate years. There are no less than 425,000 active soccer players in clubs in The Netherlands or 4% of the Dutch population. Not including fishing, chess and draughts, there are 27 registered sports. Soccer is the most popular, followed by gymnastics, with 290,000 participants. Next in order are skating and swimming. Altogether, 10% of the population take part in sports as members of Dutch clubs.

Feet on rear runners, two sleigh riders compete around an icy turn in Friesland.

In Holland, cows have lush grass to feed on, and probably come from pedigree stock— the famous Frisian black and white.

INDUSTRY AND ECONOMY

The Netherlands is strong on agriculture, shipbuilding and international trade while its industry is rapidly expanding. No longer a world power politically, it is an increasingly important participant in international commerce. The port of Rotterdam handles the largest amount of cargo of any in the world.

AGRICULTURE

Dutch farms are generally small, but strong efforts are being undertaken to enlarge their size and to keep their operations efficient. Dutch agriculture is highly diversified.

Dairying is an important pursuit and its products—cheese, butter, condensed milk and milk powder—are traded all over the world.

The Netherlands imports large quantities of grains and other feeds. Together with domestic feed grains and fodder they serve as a raw material for livestock products. Meat products and broilers are shipped to adjacent industrial countries and to other parts of the world.

The Netherlands is not completely self sufficient as far as crop farming is concerned. Yet large quantities of crops, such as potatoes, sugar beets, wheat and feed grains, are produced. An important sector of agriculture includes truck farming and ornamental crops.

The province of Friesland contains 80 co-operative dairies. Here, at a condensery at Leeuwarden, the milk is arriving in a truck. Two stainless steel pipes discharge it in a few minutes into the large receiving vats, and an electric thermometer registers the fresh milk's temperature.

At the condensery's research laboratory, the staff is engaged in the ever-continuing work of improving on quality.

An operator gathers the butter as it comes out of a churner.

Each cheese is given its own container. In Friesland in the 80 co-operative dairies, about 750 million kilos (1,650,000,000 lbs.) of milk are processed annually. Edam and Gouda cheeses are just two of many products.

An operator applies plastic coating to the cheese.

Now the cheeses are ready to go by barge to market.

Fruits also go to market by barge.

Hothouse grapes are grown in this glass-enclosed shed.

470 ■ HOLLAND

Volendam fishermen repairing their nets. Some of the small fishing villages along the former Zuider Zee have died out. In the 17th century the ports along this coast maintained flourishing seaways to Scandinavia, Britain and the Iberian Peninsula.

Dutch flower bulbs are famous all over the world, and so are nursery stock and cut flowers. Large quantities of vegetables and fruits are shipped abroad.

FISHERIES

Traditionally Dutchmen have fished the seas around them. Although herring has been the principal catch since the Middle Ages, Dutch fishermen nowadays land a large variety of seafood. A great part of the catch is exported, either canned, smoked or deep frozen. The number of fishermen is declining, as is the case elsewhere in the world. Various efforts are being undertaken, however, to boost productivity by modernization of the Dutch fishing fleet and improve the marketing of its products.

Women of Scheveningen repair nets for their fishermen husbands.

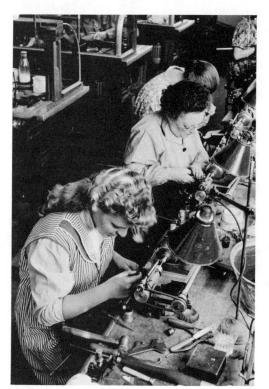

DIAMONDS

Amsterdam is famous for its diamond-finishing industry. Here, highly skilled specialists cleave, cut and polish diamonds for export. Formerly the diamonds came (some still do) from South Africa, which originally had many Dutch settlements. The workers start by sawing the diamonds. The stone is fastened to a cutting machine and kept against an extremely thin phosphorized bronze disc—the saw —which turns vertically. Depending on the size and hardness of the stones, sawing may vary from a few hours to a few days.

After the stones are cut they must be polished into many facets. These workers are operating a polishing disc, a cast iron plate covered with oil and diamond powder. The "brilliant" cut is most popular; it has a total of 58 facets, or faces, 33 in the upper section and 25 on the tapering lower part. It is the expert's function not only to build up the edges and facets, but to see that the facets run the same course as the diamond's grain.

When the port facilities at Rotterdam were destroyed during the war, it gave the city a chance to rebuild in more modern fashion. Rotterdam is not only active today in shipbuilding but is well equipped for cargo transportation in all sizes of vessels. The European river and canal system flows through this port, which is far busier now than ever before.

SHIPPING AND SHIPBUILDING

Holland ranks high among the world's great maritime nations. It has a large ship-building capacity and has 1,297 merchant vessels, the world's eleventh largest fleet. Its many river ports, its strategic location, and its inland shipping routes have all led the Dutch to think of waterways for transportation. River ships and barges number more than 20,000, and navigable rivers and canals are as long as 4,000 miles, compared with only 2,000 miles of railway and 3,000 miles of primary highways.

INDUSTRIES

Compared to other European countries, Holland began its modern industrial development late. By 1900, it still lacked the characteristics of an industrial country, and in the 1920's only a third of its exports were manufactured goods (50% being foodstuffs).

During and after World War I, however, noticeable changes in Holland's industrial structure began. In 1917, for example, at Ymuiden, the basis was laid for a heavy metal industry, with the state-sponsored construction of a processing plant; iron ore was imported and pig iron exported. The blast furnaces which developed from this were later to make Holland the largest exporter of pig iron in the world. A steel plate rolling mill was later added to the blast furnaces. More or less the same thing happened with a nitrogen-fixing plant erected by the coal mining industry.

In the field of consumer goods, an electrical industry began and later grew to a prominent position in the manufacture of appliances. In the 1920's, Holland began to make synthetic fibres. Altogether, about 100 new factories were opened each year in this period.

Since World War II industrial development in the Netherlands has proceeded rapidly with an average annual rise in production of between 6 and 7 per cent. Industrial exports increased from 52 per cent of total exports in 1938 to 75 per cent of total exports in 1966. If agricultural industry, such as bottling and conserving of food products, is included the figure rises to 87 per cent.

A significant factor in this growth has been the encouragement of *foreign businesses*, which have brought to Holland improved technical skills. The first of the new items manufactured in Holland was automobile tires. To this were later added office machines, lift-trucks, oil burners and other heating installations, machine tools, textile machinery, oil extraction equipment, and various textile products. Holland, besides raising its iron and steel production, developed an extensive petrochemical industry and the chemical industry in general was greatly improved.

In spite of these advances, however, Holland has not been without problems in its struggle for industrial and economic improvements. Dismantling and war damage brought its industry to a standstill during the war years. As in other countries, however, reconstruction following the war started industry's wheels turning again, and one of Holland's first postwar factories (automobile tires) opened in 1946. The great demand for goods in the postwar period gave impetus to industrial development—which was helped even further by shortages in other countries—particularly in Germany.

Long-range planning was important, also, to assure continuing industrial expansion and economic stability once the "war shortages" had been satisfied. The population increase and relocation of many people from farming areas made creation of a greater number of industrial jobs essential.

In Rotterdam one of the features of the port is midstream loading and unloading of barges. This is one of 24 dredgers employed in maintaining the port's proper depth.

In this modern Dutch cotton weaving mill only one man is needed to operate between 16 and 48 of the fully-automated looms. By installing more and more such looms, Dutch mills can trim production costs and compete in markets all over the world.

A big boost to Holland's industrial expansion has resulted from the spreading out of its manufacturing sites, away from the congested west. This has been made possible by generally improved communications and transportation, and further encouraged by the government's planning of industrial locations, improvement of residential conditions, and granting of subsidies for industrial building in these areas.

In Rotterdam congestion was relieved in 1968 upon completion of the first section of the city's new underground railway, a marvel of engineering. Boring a tunnel for the trains was not possible in the soft, wet sea-level soil. Pumping the soil dry would have endangered nearby buildings, since the wooden piles upon which they are built will weaken if not kept wet. The problem was solved by digging a temporary canal, at each end of which drydocks were floated. The underground tube was then installed in sections assembled on the drydocks and floated into place. The tunnel thus formed rests on piles, like other structures in the city.

To aid in industrial advances, Holland maintains various research and development agencies.

Scientific research is carried on not only in larger companies, colleges, and universities, but in small concerns as well. Special research institutes (such as the Netherlands Organization for Applied Scientific Research) help the smaller companies that are not equipped to handle research themselves, to study materials and manufacturing processes.

Establishment of the Common Market has left a profound imprint on Dutch industry as a whole. Holland's industrial growth, already healthy, has expanded even further through mergers (such as occurred in the metal, chemical, and textile industries), specialization, and an increase in foreign subsidiaries—all encouraged by the low duty on (or free circulation of) goods afforded by the Common Market.

State participation in financing for industrial growth has been confined to a few financial institutions that help industrial enterprises which are unable to raise funds through the usual channels. Financing in other cases has been carried out, for the most part, from retained profits.

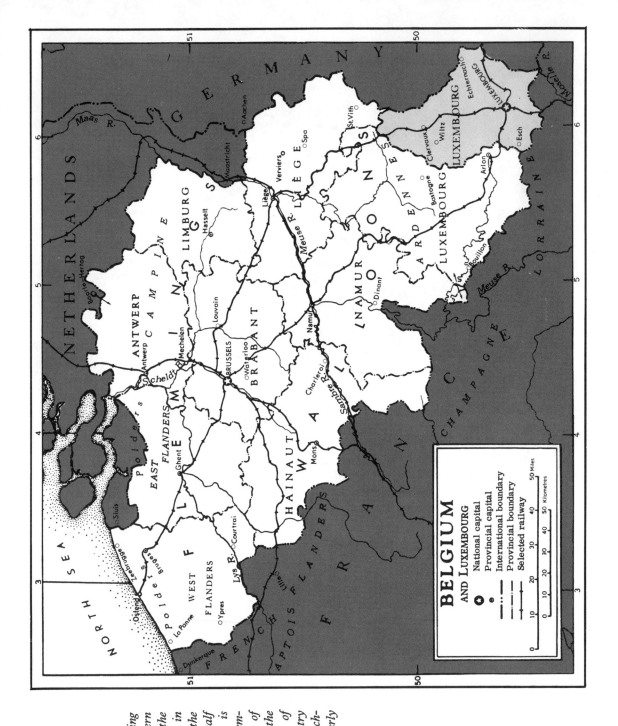

BELGIUM

AND LUXEMBOURG

⊛	National capital
○	Provincial capital
—··—··—	International boundary
—⁺—⁺—	Provincial boundary
——•——	Selected railway

50 Miles

50 Kilometres

The Flemings, or Dutch-speaking Belgians, occupy the 4 northern provinces, as shown on the map; the French-speaking Walloons live in the 4 southern ones. Brabant, in the middle, is half Flemish and half Walloon. Brussels, the capital, is completely bi-lingual. The term Fleming strictly applies to the people of East and West Flanders, and the adjacent strip of France, most of which was annexed to that country by Louis XIV. However, all Dutch-speaking Belgians are now popularly called Flemings.

BELGIUM and LUXEMBOURG

At Poilvache, the Meuse winds past orchards, fields and poplar hedges and splits to form the Ile de Houx, an islet covered with fruit trees. Although the Meuse Valley is the axis of Belgian industry, much of it is still unspoiled.

THE LAND

BELGIUM AND LUXEMBOURG lie in northwestern Europe near the western end of the great North European Plain. Belgium has a short frontage on the North Sea, about 40 miles long; Luxembourg adjoins Belgium on the east and is wholly land-locked. With Holland, which borders Belgium on the north and east, the two nations form a wedge between the large countries of France and West Germany. The three small states of the wedge are often called collectively the Low Countries. Indeed, the name Netherlands, meaning Low Countries, was applied throughout much of Europe's history to all three, although now the term is used officially as the name of Holland only.

Actually, of the three lands, Holland is most accurately described as low, for nearly half of Belgium and much of Luxembourg are hilly rather than flat.

The territory of Belgium contains 11,400

High above the Sûre Valley in Luxembourg, the ruined castle of Bourscheid looks out over the farms and forests of the Ardennes. Built in the 10th century, the fortress housed a long line of Crusader knights. Most of Luxembourg's hundred or more castles were demolished by the French.

square miles and is roughly the size of the states of Maryland and Delaware combined, or one and a half times the size of Wales. From a point near the French port of Dunkirk, the sand dunes of Belgium's short coastline run towards the northeast until they meet the Dutch frontier near Sluis. There, the land boundary with Holland strikes eastward in a jagged line until it encounters the Meuse River running south to north. The river serves as the boundary with Holland for about 30 miles. A little south of the Dutch city of Maastricht the land frontier resumes, proceeding due east for a short distance until, southeast of the German city of Aachen, it plunges southwards, delimiting Belgium from West Germany and Luxembourg, until the French border is reached. From here the frontier follows a meandering line northwestward as far as the North Sea.

Luxembourg is just short of 1,000 square miles in area, or somewhat smaller than the state of Rhode Island, the size of the English county of Derbyshire. The country is not small enough to rank with the "postage-stamp" states of Monaco or San Marino, yet is small indeed for an independent nation. Luxembourg is bounded on the south by France and on the east by West Germany, from which it is separated by the Moselle River and two of its tributaries.

Both countries can be crossed in the course of an afternoon's ride: the greatest distance from northwest to southeast in Belgium is not quite 175 miles, and from north to south, a little over 100 miles.

BOUNDARIES

Except for the natural boundaries mentioned already, the frontiers of both countries are artificial, having been determined over many centuries by war and treaty. One small Belgian community, Baarle-Hertog, is entirely sur-

As the Meuse enters Belgium's Namur Province from France, it twists past impressive heights such as this one at Freyr, which, while far from rivalling Switzerland's, are still impressive for a Low Country and provide opportunities for mountain climbing.

rounded by Holland, cut off from the rest of Belgium by close bargaining at the treaty table. This little exclave, or small outlying territory, is one of several remaining in Europe, and as such is a curiosity. There is still today a piece of Spain surrounded by France. This and two fragments within Switzerland, one Italian, the other German, are, along with Baarle-Hertog, reminders of the European past when countries were often collections of isolated territories brought under a common rule, rather than unbroken expanses inhabited by people sharing a common background and experience, as they are today.

Belgium and Luxembourg lie at the cross-

Carts propelled by sails are a popular sport on Belgium's North Sea coast, as here near the resort town of La Panne in West Flanders, one of the nine provinces of Belgium. East and West Flanders, together with the Department of Nord in France form the old territory called Flanders.

BELGIUM and LUXEMBOURG ■ 479

Vineyards line the Moselle banks. The river, which is an important link in Western Europe's chain of inland waterways, gives its name to the fine white wines produced on its valley slopes.

roads of Europe. They are situated near the heart of the great industrial and population complex stretching from the Seine River in France to the Elbe in West Germany. This location has been of great benefit to the development of their commerce, but it has made them pawns in the power struggles of larger nations. Their carefully delimited boundaries reflect the give and take of centuries of decisive battles fought (more often than not on their soil) to determine not only their fate but that of much of Europe. Belgium has been a major battlefield of the Continent since the days of Julius Caesar.

TOPOGRAPHY

The Sambre River enters Belgium from France at a point midway on the Franco-Belgian frontier. The river flows northeastwards and enters the Meuse, which flows on in the same direction to Liège. The two rivers divide the country into two well-defined regions:

northwest of the line which they form, the land is flat; southeast, it is hilly. The land rises gradually from the North Sea until it reaches a peak of over 2,000 feet in the wild and rocky region of the Ardennes, a plateau whose average elevation exceeds 1,000 feet.

Northern Luxembourg is a continuation of the Ardennes highland, but the southern part of the country is lower, and there rolling hills alternate with broad plains and fertile valleys.

WATERWAYS

Like its fellow Low Country, Holland, Belgium makes considerable use of canals and rivers for inland transport. Well over 1,000 miles of navigable waterways within the country link Belgium with the flourishing canal traffic of West Germany, Holland, and France. Best known of man-made waterways is the mighty Albert Canal which crosses the sandy, fortress-studded marshes of the Campine district, connecting Antwerp with Liège. Although canals are important to Belgium, they, in one instance at least, are yielding to more modern means of transport: the Mons Canal, built under Napoleon, is to be drained and replaced by a modern highway. In a country where space counts heavily, maximum use of the land must be made. Obsolete facilities are not simply abandoned, as is often the case in larger countries.

The principal rivers of Belgium are the Scheldt, which rises in France and flows through the rich fields of the provinces of Hainaut and East Flanders to Antwerp, where the Dutch frontier cuts it off from its estuary; the Meuse, which also rises in France, and like the Scheldt empties into the North Sea in Dutch territory; and the Sambre, remembered as the scene of some of the fiercest fighting of World War I. Apart from the Moselle and its tributary, the Sûre, the chief river of Luxembourg is the Alzette, on which is located the country's capital, the city of Luxembourg. The Sûre has been dammed to create a large lake; but otherwise there are few lakes of any consequence in either Luxembourg or Belgium.

CLIMATE

Belgium and Luxembourg share with the rest of northwestern Europe a generally oceanic climate, that is, one tempered by the moisture-laden air of the Atlantic Ocean, without great extremes of heat and cold. In the low-lying regions towards the North Sea, the climate is milder than in the highland of the Ardennes, where hotter summers and colder winters are

The Moselle rises in the Vosges Mountains of France, flows through Lorraine and then forms part of the eastern frontier of Luxembourg before entering Germany and joining the Rhine. Here, small craft hug the Luxembourg shore. In the background is Germany.

BELGIUM and LUXEMBOURG ■ 481

the rule. Storms on the North Sea can lash the Belgian coast with great severity. Unlike Holland, Belgium has only a small area at sea level where the land must be buttressed by dikes to protect crops and dwellings from the ravages of the waves. In these areas, farming is done on fields reclaimed from marshes, called *polders*, laid out in a chessboard of canals, ditches, and long lines of poplar windbreaks. Here the resemblance to Holland is strongest.

NATURAL RESOURCES

Within the small area of Belgium and Luxembourg, a considerable mineral wealth exists. Original deposits of coal, iron, zinc, lead, and copper, some now depleted, gave Belgium an early advantage in the industrialization of Europe that took place in the 19th century. The rock strata of southern Belgium furnish granite, marble, slate, limestone, and chalk in quantity, both for domestic use and for export. Sand of good quality is an important product of the north, especially the Campine region. Belgian clays are well suited for brick-making; and the Belgian glass industry, a world leader, draws most of its materials from within the country.

While most of Belgium's land is cleared and intensively cultivated or given over to housing and industry, much of the Ardennes highland supports dense forests. These are an important source of wood products, although far from

The rocky fastnesses of the Müllerthal district in eastern Luxembourg served as hideaways in time of war for the ancient Celts, as evidenced by many archæological remains. Today, they are a popular holiday retreat, called familiarly the "Little Switzerland" of Luxembourg.

satisfying the needs of the country's huge chemical, paper, and textile industries.

The park of the Château of Enghien, south of Brussels, is all that remains of a vast and splendid garden laid out by the dukes of Arenberg in the 17th century, and considered in its day a rival of Versailles in France. Even today it is a place of great beauty and tranquillity. Enghien lies just on the language boundary between Flemish and Walloon.

The Château of Val Duchesse in the province of Brabant has a garden distinguished by shrubs trimmed in fanciful shapes. This form of gardening art is called topiary work.

Electric power is derived mainly from low-grade coal burnt in thermal power plants. Water power is of very slight importance. The development of offshore petroleum production in the North Sea, in which Belgium will share, could eventually give the country a domestic source of oil fuel. At present there is none.

The North Sea coast yields very fine shrimps,

Narrow old houses line a narrow street in the heart of the old section of Brussels, within the shadow of the lovely Gothic spire of the Hotel de Ville, or city hall.

sole, and prawns; the Ardennes forests are rich in game: deer, wild boars, pheasants and partridges are numerous. The Meuse, Sûre, and Ourthe rivers furnish excellent trout and crayfish.

LUXEMBOURG RESOURCES

The importance of small Luxembourg in the world economy rests on the country's rich iron deposits. However, there is no domestic coal production, and the booming steel industry depends on imports for its fuel. Sufficient timber exists to support an export trade, and slate is abundant. The gnarled oak trees of the Ardennes have long provided tanbark for the country's flourishing leather industry. The soil and climate of the Moselle Valley are ideal for grape production. The wines of Luxembourg compare to advantage with the more famous Moselle wines of Germany.

CITIES

A land as densely peopled and as heavily industrialized as Belgium (over 780 people to the square mile, a per capita output of steel twice that of France) might well look like one vast factory. Such is not the case. For one thing, there is plenty of open country, some of it, as in the Ardennes, quite untouched. The landscape of Belgium has not been so completely shaped by the hand of man as is the case of Holland, but where it has been, the Belgians have demonstrated as notable a talent for neatness

Luxembourg, capital of the Grand Duchy of the same name, is built upon two bluffs separated by a gorge. This charming city of 77,000 is one of the most picturesque capitals in Europe.

and order as the Dutch. Industrial blight and slum conditions have not been allowed to spread. The inborn sense of proportion of the Belgian people has worked to keep a balance between farm and factory. Fresh paint and cleaning materials are not spared. Gardens are planted everywhere. The result is an ordered landscape in which the architectural treasures of a rich past are set off to advantage, and the old blends happily with the new.

Belgian industry follows the Sambre-Meuse line to a large extent, cutting a broad diagonal across the middle of the country. Brussels, the capital, and the great seaport of Antwerp, lie north of this line, amidst rich farmlands. Here, too, are the splendid cities of Ghent and

A modern skyscraper looms over Brussels' busy Place Rogier. In the lower part of the building is located the Théâtre National, a government-subsidized repertory company.

Ostend is the greatest of Belgium's North Sea resorts and one of Europe's principal playgrounds, with a casino and a race-track as well as bathing beaches. A very 20th-century appearance belies a thousand-year history.

Bruges, famous for art and learning. The humming industrial areas of Mons, Namur, Charleroi, and Liège are on the line. Southeast of it, scattered among the green pastures and woodlands of the Ardennes are attractive small cities such as Arlon, Dinant, and Bastogne.

Brussels is one of Europe's major cities, a true capital, with a distinct charm of its own. Zoning laws protect that charm in the old central part of the city. In the newer districts, however, modern skyscrapers are rising rapidly —for Brussels is the overseas base of hundreds of United States firms. The demand for office space has brought about the construction of a dozen giant buildings, some well over 30 storeys.

Antwerp ranks as the second port of Europe and fourth in the world. Through their two great cities, hubs of world trade and communications, the people of small Belgium are in daily touch with half the world. Ghent and Bruges, cities of the first rank in mediaeval European culture and commerce, are still important for maritime and manufacturing activities. They also house one of the greatest assemblages of architectural and artistic wonders outside Italy, and through them the Belgian people can recall the time five centuries back, when their country emerged as one of the focal points of European civilization.

The clocks and carillon of Antwerp Cathedral's belltower mark the hours for the great seaport's busy people. Here, some of the city's 700,000 Flemish-speaking citizens pause to rest beside the statue of the painter Rubens, himself a long-time resident of their city.

BELGIUM and LUXEMBOURG ■ 485

HISTORY

Grass and wild flowers grow upon the ruins of the once great castle of Bouillon overlooking the Semois Valley in southern Belgium. From these thick walls, Godfrey of Bouillon sallied forth in answer to the call of Peter the Hermit in the 11th century, and led the First Crusade, becoming King of Jerusalem after his conquest of the Holy Land.

AS THE ANCIENT ROMANS ADVANCED into northern Europe, they encountered near the mouths of the Rhine and the Scheldt a tribe of people of mixed Celtic and Germanic stock, the Belgae. The Romans regarded the homeland of these people as part of Gaul, and after a hard-fought campaign, they annexed it and named it Gallia Belgica. Caesar, in his *Commentaries*, praises the Belgae as the bravest of all the Gauls.

The modern nation of Belgium dates only from 1830, yet the history of the country as a definite entity can be traced back through many upheavals to the time of the Roman Empire. Luxembourg as a distinct territory dates from the early Middle Ages, but did not become wholly free of foreign domination until 1866.

The two countries were linked politically for 300 years. Their history until they became independent in the 19th century is outlined in the table which follows.

EARLY TIMES

B.C. 52.   Roman conquest complete. Gallia Belgica, embracing modern Belgium and Luxembourg, as well as parts of Germany, France, and Holland, settles down to 400 years of mostly peaceful development under Roman rule.

A.D. 406. Invasion of Europe by the Huns uproots the Germanic tribes of Central Europe and forces many of them into Roman territory, including Belgium.

A.D. 496. Clovis, ruler of the Salian Franks, accepts Christianity. Belgium now part of the Frankish lands. Its people composed of Frankish converts and already Christianized Belgo-Romans, become a unit of the great West European state that culminates in the Empire of Charlemagne.

A.D. 814. Death of Charlemagne leads to breakdown of the Frankish Empire.

A.D. 843. Treaty of Verdun splits Frankish Empire in three parts. Belgium divided between two of them, France and Lorraine.

MIDDLE AGES

A.D. 900. Rise of feudalism in all parts of former Frankish Empire. Weak rulers of the kingdoms resulting from the partition are unable to impose their will on nobles. Countships, duchies, bishoprics, and principalities come into being, and such local rule largely replaces the authority of the kings. In this period the countship of Luxembourg and the historic provinces of Belgium appear: Flanders, Brabant, Hainaut, Liège, Limburg, etc.

1200 to 1300. The German Emperors attempt to assert control over the principalities of the Low Countries, and are checked by Jean I, Duke of Brabant, at the Battle of Woeringen. However, the struggle of the Counts of Flanders to repel the French kings is less decisive. The Belgian principalities continue to be threatened by France, after losing the Battle of Bouvines in 1214.

1302. French badly beaten at Courtrai in the Battle of the Golden Spurs. The citizen militia of the cities of Flanders play a decisive rôle in the victory. For several cen-

Citizens of Bruges don the chain mail and helmets of their mediaeval forebears as part of the celebrations of the annual Pageant of the Precious Blood. In the 12th century, a Count of Flanders returned from the Holy Land with several drops of what the Brugeois regard as the blood of Christ and installed the relic in a special chapel.

This splendid octagonal tower, worthy of a cathedral, is the belfry of the 13th-century market place in Bruges. The great wealth of the Flemish trading cities was expressed in magnificent public buildings like this one, whose carillon is installed in the 278-foot tower. Its bells, one of which weighs nearly 6 tons, have rung out across the plains of Flanders, bearing messages of war and peace, for 500 years.

turies the towns of Bruges, Ghent, and Ypres, among others, had been advancing in wealth and culture, and have gained a large measure of self-rule. From here on, the pattern of Belgian life is largely influenced by the townspeople.

1308. Henry VII of Luxembourg elected Holy Roman Emperor (i.e., Emperor of Germany). For a century and a half the House of Luxembourg becomes a leading force in the struggle of European rulers for titles and lands.

1443. Decline of the power of Luxembourg leads to its annexation by Burgundy. Burgundy subsequently acquires Belgium and from here on the fortunes of Belgium and Luxembourg are linked.

1467. John the Fearless, Duke of Burgundy, dies. The marriage of his mother, Margaret of Flanders, to his father had brought Flanders under the sway of Burgundy.

1477. Charles the Bold of Burgundy dies, having devoted his reign to the attempt to bridge the gap between his dominions in the Low Countries and Burgundy proper by conquering the intervening lands of Alsace and Lorraine. His ambitions have brought him into conflict with France, and his death leaves his daughter and successor seriously menaced by the French.

The 15th-century castle of Beaufort in Luxembourg was built about the time that Luxembourg ceased to be a separate country and became a possession of Burgundy, Spain, Austria, and France, before gaining independence in the 19th century. ⟶

1477. Mary of Burgundy proclaims the Great Privilege at Ghent, whereby Flanders, Brabant, Holland, and Hainaut are granted the rights they had lost under Burgundian rule. This concession is intended to ensure their support in the face of French intervention.

1477. Mary, still building her defences, marries Maximilian of Habsburg, ruler of Austria, and her principal ally against France. Henceforth, the fate of the Low Countries is linked with that of the Habsburgs.

1482. Mary's son, Philip I, inherits the Burgundian dominions, including Belgium and Luxembourg. He marries the heiress to the Spanish throne, and in 1506 assumes the throne of Spain.

The castle of Septfontaines, in the Middle Ages a stronghold of the knightly order of the Templars, looks down upon the village of the same name and the grain fields of central Luxembourg.

HABSBURG PERIOD

1500. Birth of Charles V of Habsburg, son of Philip, and heir to Austria, Bohemia, Burgundy, Hungary, the Netherlands, Naples, Sicily, and Spain. The destiny of Belgium and Luxembourg is now firmly tied to that of Austria and Spain.

1555. Charles, though born in Ghent, had subordinated the interests of the Low Countries to those of Spain. He abdicates and his realm is divided, the Austrian territories going to his brother, the Spanish to his son, Philip II. Belgium and the rest of the Netherlands sink to the status of outlying provinces of Spain.

1576. The Reformation had left Holland Protestant and Belgium Catholic, but both areas unite in rebellion against Spanish tyranny. But the religious differences prove too great for the two areas to maintain a united front. Holland fights on and gains independence in 1579. Belgium and Luxembourg remain under Spanish rule.

1598. The Spanish Netherlands, as Belgium and Luxembourg are now called, enjoy a temporary autonomy under the rule of Isabella, daughter of Philip II.

1621. Following the deaths of Isabella and her husband without children, the Spanish Netherlands revert to direct Spanish rule. Under the Inquisition, Protestantism is stamped out completely in the ensuing years.

1648. Treaty of Westphalia ends the Thirty Years War, some of whose bloodiest battles were fought in Belgium, and confirms Spanish rule of Belgium and Luxembourg. However, hostilities continue between France and Spain, and France begins to annex piece after piece of the southern frontier of Belgium.

1697. The Treaty of Rijswijk halts the progress of French annexation. Belgium has now served for half a century as the principal battleground between France and Spain, and much of the country is devastated.

1700. Louis XIV of France claims the Spanish Netherlands on the death of Charles II of Spain.

1709. The Battle of Malplaquet checks the renewed French effort to gain Belgium.

In the 17th century, the Bruges goldsmith, Jan Crabbe, made this magnificent reliquary to encase the Precious Blood. Every year the citizens of Bruges parade through the streets of their city carrying the reliquary in affirmation of the Catholic faith of Flanders, unbroken since the Middle Ages.

1713. The Treaty of Utrecht, ending the War of the Spanish Succession, removes Belgium and Luxembourg from Spanish control and awards them to Austria. They are henceforth known as the Austrian Netherlands.

1740. Maria Theresa of Austria ascends the throne. Her policy towards the Austrian Netherlands is enlightened and considerable progress is made in restoring order and prosperity.

1790. Following the outbreak of the French Revolution, the Belgian Provinces, disillusioned by Maria Theresa's successors, attempt to throw off Austrian rule; the United States of Belgium are proclaimed, but the Austrian monarch, Leopold II, puts down the insurrection.

The town of Clervaux in northern Luxembourg was long famed for its great Benedictine abbey and its castle of the noble family of de Lannoi. A member of this family emigrated to America in 1621 and founded the Delano family from which U.S. President Franklin Delano Roosevelt descended. Both abbey and castle were badly damaged during World War II.

UNDER FRANCE AND HOLLAND

1797.   Belgium is invaded by the French, and Austria is forced to cede its Netherlands dominions to France. Belgium and Luxembourg are subsequently annexed outright by France and re-organized as departments of the French state. As such, they continue until the overthrow of Napoleon's French Empire.

1814.   The downfall of Napoleon restores the traditional institutions and political units of Belgium, which had been swept away by the Emperor's reforms.

1815.   Napoleon returns from exile in Elba and is finally defeated at Waterloo, near Brussels. The Congress of Vienna, remaking the map of Europe awards Belgium and Luxembourg to Holland. The districts of Eupen and St. Vith go to Prussia, however.

1815 to 1830.   Under William I, King of the Netherlands, the Belgian provinces are restless and dissatisfied. Their new ruler, regarding them as a lost branch of the Dutch, rather than as the distinct nation which centuries of separate rule had made them, imposes unpopular measures.

1830.   Revolution breaks out against the Dutch. The yellow, black, and red flag of Brabant is raised as the banner of all Belgium, and a provisional government is set up in Brussels. A Dutch army is sent in and driven back. The Dutch sign an armistice.

1830.   At the Conference of London the Great Powers of Europe recognize Belgian independence.

1831.   The Great Powers declare the permanent neutrality of Belgium. Prince Leopold of Saxe-Coburg-Gotha elected

King of the Belgians. The Dutch again invade the country, but are driven out by the French.

1839. Final settlement of Dutch and Belgian hostilities as boundaries are regulated.

The provinces of Limburg and Luxembourg are partitioned, half of Limburg going to Holland, while the Walloon, or French-speaking, area of Luxembourg remains united with Belgium. The Germanic, or *Letzeburgesch*-speaking part of Luxembourg is constituted as a separate state under the rule of the Dutch King, but not annexed to Holland. To further complicate matters, Luxembourg is forced to join the German Confederation, a league of independent German states that preceded the unification of Germany.

MODERN TIMES

The new nation of Belgium prospered under self-rule. Leopold I, who was an uncle of Prince Albert, husband of England's Queen Victoria, ruled Belgium as a constitutional monarch, his powers being severely limited by law. Within the limits imposed on him, he governed wisely and used his influence at home and abroad to further the interests of his adopted country. Under his leadership, the monarchy became a symbol of Belgian unity and the Belgian will to preserve the country's hard-won independence and neutrality. Neither Leopold nor his people wished to see Belgium again become the Battlefield of Europe.

Luxembourg, which had been raised to the status of a grand duchy in 1815, was guaranteed neutrality and full independence in 1866, by the Treaty of London. The Grand Duchy was removed from membership in the German Confederation, but retained the King of Holland as its sovereign. This personal link with Holland ended in 1890 when Wilhelmina ascended the Dutch throne, while the crown of Luxembourg passed to Adolf of Nassau.

LEOPOLD II

The second King of the Belgians ascended the throne in 1865. The dynasty of Saxe-Coburg-Gotha had been established as "Kings of the Belgians," not as "Kings of Belgium," to emphasize the fact that they were the chosen rulers of Belgium's people, not super-landlords as were past sovereigns. The second Leopold was a man of great vision and energy. Although not truly a popular monarch, he served Belgium well. During his reign the economy of the country expanded and developed, and Belgian leaders laid the groundwork for the enormous network of communications, finance, commerce, and industry which today is controlled from Brussels and Antwerp.

Leopold's most spectacular personal exploit

Some parts of the Cathedral of St. Sauveur in Bruges are a thousand years old, but its Romanesque belfry, seen here rising beyond a typical small Flemish inn, is of the 19th century. Bicycles are widely used by young and old to get to work or school.

King Albert I takes the constitutional oath before the assembled Houses of Parliament, on succeeding his uncle, King Leopold II, in 1909.

was the creation of the Congo Free State. In 1876, he invited to Brussels a number of distinguished men to propose to them a plan for the development of Africa. At this time, the powers of Europe were turning their ambitions for territorial expansion towards the "Dark Continent," so called because much of it was still unexplored.

The Belgian people were not disposed to join in a scramble for colonies. Nor was Leopold; his interest lay in bringing Africa into the modern world, and in particular abolishing the slave trade. The proposals made at the Brussels meeting led to the founding of the International African Association. Leopold became president of the Association, which from the outset was largely Belgian in membership.

In 1877, Leopold sent an expedition to Lake Tanganyika. Later, he sent the American explorer Stanley on a three-year trek across the vast uncharted Congo basin from Lake Tanganyika to the Atlantic Ocean. Stanley's discoveries led to the organization of the Congo Free State with Leopold as president.

In time, what had begun as a private exploitation of the Congo's resources became increasingly a matter of Belgian national interest. In 1908, Belgium formally assumed control of the vast mineral and forest resources of the Congo.

ALBERT I

While Belgium and Luxembourg advanced in the arts of peace, protected by the principle of permanent neutrality, the Great Powers came into mounting opposition to one another. The two small countries had no responsibility for the events leading up to the outbreak of World War I in 1914, but when war broke out, Germany violated their neutrality and invaded them in an effort to outflank France. However, the realistic Belgians, with Leopold's successor, Albert I, at their head had sensed the trend of events and were prepared. Luxembourg could offer no resistance, but Belgium did, and the Belgian Army fought on at the side of the British and French, and, later, the forces of the United States, until Germany was defeated in

BELGIUM and LUXEMBOURG ■ **493**

In the costume of 1916, Belgium's King Albert and Queen Elisabeth pose on the terrace of their villa at La Panne, where they lived while Albert led his own armies in a heroic defence against the Germans in World War I. Queen Elisabeth, long a patron of the arts, died in 1965.

1918. The German occupation and the bloody battles fought on Belgian soil had devastated the country and drained its resources. The Treaty of Versailles returned Eupen and St. Vith to Belgium and created a Belgian mandate over two former German possessions in Africa, Ruanda and Urundi. The Belgians resolutely set about rebuilding their country under the leadership of the immensely popular King Albert.

LEOPOLD III

Albert's death in 1934 left a troubled realm to his son, Leopold III. Belgium, which had never fully recovered from World War I, was hard hit by the world-wide economic depression of 1930. On the political front, the rise of Hitler in Germany was a cause of alarm. Europe was again drifting towards a general war. The Belgians had no choice in the face of the tre-

mendous military strength of Hitler's Germany but to rely on strict neutrality and on the guarantees of the Great Powers. When Hitler sent troops into the de-militarized zone of the Rhineland in 1936, England and France issued renewed guarantees of Belgian neutrality. Germany followed suit. When World War II began in 1939, Belgium formally reaffirmed its neutrality, and put its trust in the Great Powers to respect it. England and France did so, but Germany once more violated the frontiers of Belgium and Luxembourg when it launched its attack on France in 1940.

WORLD WAR II

Belgium could offer little resistance. King Leopold surrendered to avoid further bloodshed, and the Belgian Government went into

The Congo Museum at Tervueren in the province of Brabant documents the rôle of Belgium in the development of the Congo Basin in Africa. The vast resources of the Congo have provided raw material for Belgian industry since the 19th century. Even today, after the granting of independence to the Congo, Belgian investment ◄——— there is heavy.

exile in London. Units of the Belgian armed forces joined those of England and its Allies. The people at home in Belgium organized an underground resistance to the Germans, as Germany proceeded to strip their country of money, goods, and manpower. When the Allied armies invaded Europe, the Belgians rose to support them. The retreating Germans launched their last offensive on Belgian soil in December, 1945, when they broke through the Allied lines in the Battle of the Bulge around Bastogne. When the war ended, the task of recovery was complicated by internal dissension in Belgium. Strong criticism of Leopold's surrender prompted the king to abdicate in 1951 in the interests of internal harmony.

BAUDOUIN I

With the accession of Leopold's son, Baudouin I, the leaders of post-war Belgium guided their country towards whole-hearted participation in maintaining peace through international co-operation. Belgium was already a charter member of the United Nations. In the economic field, Belgian leadership in the establishment of the Belgian-Luxembourg Economic Union in 1921, and later in setting up the Benelux organization with Holland and Luxembourg, had laid the groundwork for the European Economic Community (Common Market) in 1957. In these associations, Belgium and Luxembourg each kept its political sovereignty but pooled their commercial, financial, industrial and agricultural resources with France, West Germany, Italy, and Holland.

In 1960, following the example of France and England in setting their African colonies free, Belgium granted independence to the Congo, and in 1962 to Ruanda-Urundi, which became the separate nations of Rwanda and Burundi. In this action, Belgium cast its lot decisively with Europe and with the concept of European unity.

Today, with the damage of World War II repaired and a high degree of prosperity attained, Belgium and Luxembourg stand firmly committed to the peaceful solution of all problems, internal and international.

At Hamm in Luxembourg, U.S. General George Patton is buried, with 5,000 Americans slain in World War II. The soil of Belgium and Luxembourg is drenched with the blood of soldiers from the English-speaking nations. In World War I, a quarter of a million British soldiers died on the fields of Flanders.

BELGIUM and LUXEMBOURG ■ 495

The various foreign rulers of Luxembourg from the 17th century on turned the capital of the country into one of the greatest fortresses in Europe. Much of the fortification of the city is the work of Vauban, the great engineer of Louis XIV of France. Among the most remarkable of the city's defences are the casemates, or vaults, in the rocky cliffs on which the city is built.

The vaults and chambers of the casemates are connected by miles of tunnels cut out of the solid rock.

496 ■ BELGIUM and LUXEMBOURG

In the charming old West Flanders town of Furnes, black-faced sheep crowd past the stepped gables of the houses as they take their place in a harvest parade.

THE PEOPLE

THE PEOPLE of Belgium and Luxembourg are often mistakenly thought of as hybrids, half-Dutch and half-French in the case of the former, Germans with a French veneer, in the case of the latter. This is not true. These people form genuine nations with characteristics that distinguish them from the people of adjacent countries.

The Belgians number about 9,500,000. They consist of two language groups: the Walloons, who speak French, and the Flemings, who speak Dutch. There are cultural distinctions between the two, but it would not be easy to establish any decided racial difference. They

are both descended from the original Romanized Belgae and the later Frankish invaders. Germanic speech prevailed in the Flemish area; Latin survived in the Walloon provinces. A long history of separate development sets them off from both the French and the Dutch. Centuries of united effort to resist foreign rule have given both groups a sense of belonging to the Belgian nation.

In Luxembourg, the people form a single ethnic bloc. For centuries, their country included a larger area of Walloon speech, now the Belgian province of Luxembourg. In this older, larger Luxembourg, French was the

Typical Belgian schoolchildren, one might think. Actually they are the children of French, West German, Italian, and other officials and employees of the European Economic Community, at the European School in Brussels. There are several such schools in Community countries, where the school methods of all the participating countries are blended, and teaching is in four languages: French, Dutch, German, and Italian, the four official languages of the Community.

speech of the court and ruling class. The language of the common people other than Walloons was and is *Letzeburgesch*, an offshoot of German that is now a virtually distinct tongue. Today, French and standard German are both official languages; the native dialect remains the idiom of the home and everyday affairs. The Luxembourgers are, in effect, tri-lingual.

LANGUAGE

Standard French and Dutch are both official languages of Belgium. The word "Fleming" is now applied to all speakers of the southern Dutch idiom of Belgium. Originally it referred only to the inhabitants of Flanders. Dutch as spoken in Belgium is popularly called Flemish. It is much closer to Dutch than the Walloon dialects are to French. Standard French is taught in schools in the Walloon provinces and most Walloons use it in daily life. But a French tourist in the remoter farm regions of the Ardennes might have difficulty understanding the dialect of the people. Even the standard French of Belgium is spoken with a distinctive accent so that a Frenchman can readily identify a Belgian.

Language is often a touchy matter in Belgium. Both Flemings and Walloons are fearful of encroachment by each other's speech. Brussels and its immediate area are bi-lingual, as are the people who live along the line of demarcation between the two tongues. This line runs from east to west across the land; north of it, the people speak Flemish, south of it, Walloon French. It must be admitted that owing to the long use of French as the only official language of Belgium, the Flemings are generally better acquainted with it than the Walloons are with Flemish. It was not until late in the 19th century, some time after Belgian independence was gained, that Flemish discontent finally led the government to recognize Flemish as an official language.

Emile Verhaeren, born at St.-Amand near Antwerp, made much use of the free verse form and of symbolist techniques in his powerful poetry, written in French. ——→

LITERATURE

Belgian writers form three groups: writers in Dutch, writers in French, and writers in Walloon dialect. From the Middle Ages a rich literature in Dutch survives, composed of folk songs, romances, allegories, and mystery plays. The authors of these works are mostly unknown, except for a few like Jacob van Maerlant of Bruges. After the 16th-century Reformation there are few outstanding Flemish writers until the 19th century. Then Flemish literature experienced a revival. The greatest writers of this reawakening were the novelist Hendrik Conscience (1812–1883), whose classic work, *The Lion of Flanders*, did much to revive Flemish as a literary idiom; and Guido Gezelle (1830–1899), a lyric poet of the first rank, and one of the greatest writers in the Dutch language.

Writers in French may be either of Flemish or Walloon background. In general, their works are better known abroad than those of writers in

Flemish. Among them are Charles de Coster (1827–1879), whose novel *La Légende de Uylenspiegel* achieved world fame; Octave Pirmez (1823–1883), author of mystic meditations such as *Les Heures de Philosophie*; Henri Pirenne (1862–1935), author of many historical works; Maurice Maeterlinck (1862–1949) whose symbolist dramas such as *The Blue Bird* and *Pelléas et Mélisande* reached a world audience; the poet Emile Verhaeren (1855–1916), known for powerful, impassioned verse such as *La*

←——
Maurice Maeterlinck, the renowned dramatist, was born in Ghent. In addition to such plays as "Pelléas et Mélisande," he is remembered for his zoological study, "The Life of the Bee."

Georges Simenon, born at Liège, is the world's most prolific novelist—he has written over 420 books—and one of the most successful.

Ville Tentaculaire; and the dramatist Michel de Ghelderode (1899–1962), author of *Fastes d'Enfer* and other macabre dramas that have earned him a place beside Brecht, Beckett, and Ionesco as an innovator in the modern theatre.

Perhaps the best known (and most prolific) Belgian writing in French today is Georges Simenon, creator of the fictional detective, Inspector Maigret.

Writing in Walloon dates from the 12th century. The dialect possesses a rich regional literature noted for its satirical and burlesque qualities. The title of a comedy of 1757 gives some idea of the extent to which Walloon varies from French: *Li Lîdjwè égadji* (*Le Liègeois Engagé*).

Luxembourg has a purely regional literature in all three of its languages. The country's authors are not known outside of their homeland except, perhaps, for Michel Rodange (1827–1867), author of the epic poem, *Reynard the Fox*.

MUSIC

During the late Middle Ages and the early Renaissance period, Belgian musicians were the foremost composers of church music in Europe. In the days before the full emergence of secular, or non-religious, music, Belgian masters taught all over the Continent from Prague to Venice and Madrid. The names of Adriaan Willaert (1480–1562), founder of the Venetian school, stands out, as do those of Philippe de Monte (1521–1603) and Orlando de Lassus (1530–1594), composers of masses, madrigals, and

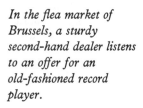

In the flea market of Brussels, a sturdy second-hand dealer listens to an offer for an old-fashioned record player.

The home of Rubens in Antwerp houses a collection of the work of the painter and his pupils. Rubens himself designed the mansion and had it built in 1610.

motets rivalling those of their Italian contemporary, Palestrina.

Belgium continued to produce composers in later centuries, but none so well known as César Franck (1822–1890). Though a native of Liège, Franck became a French citizen and is usually classed with the composers of his adopted country.

ART

The bustling cities of Flanders gave rise to one of the greatest schools of European painting during the Renaissance, as artists turned their attention from strictly religious themes to a broader range of human activity. This period of transition took place between the 14th and 17th centuries. At that time, the cities of Belgium were among the richest in Europe, on a par with those of Italy. Their wealth and stimulating activity inspired in the Flemish school a long line of Europe's greatest painters.

Flemish painting of the 15th century, still strongly religious in character, is represented by the brothers Van Eyck, Hubert (1370–1426) and Jan (1365–1440), whose masterwork is the

The statue of Jan Van Eyck, who, with his brother Hubert, painted some of the most acclaimed works of Western art, stands in Bruges where he spent much of his creative life.

BELGIUM and LUXEMBOURG ■ **501**

altar-piece of the cathedral at Ghent, one of the acclaimed works of Western civilization; by Rogier van der Weyden (1399–1464), painter of the compelling *Descent from the Cross*; and by Hans Memling (1430–1494), whose art struck a note of warmth and serenity as well as strength in works such as *The Last Judgment*.

Quentin Massys (1466–1530), praised for his delicate hues and superior composition, introduced Italian influences into Flemish art. Hieronymus Bosch (1450–1516) rendered traditional religious themes in a strangely modern, almost surrealist, manner. Pieter Breughel (1525–1569) portrayed the daily life of the Flanders of his day with great vivacity. Peter Paul Rubens (1577–1640) was a master of the flowing, emotional style called Baroque, typical of the 17th century. Anthony Van Dyck (1599–

The Municipal Museum of Brussels occupies the splendid Gothic mansion in the Grand' Place known as the Maison du Roi. The Emperor Charles V is reputed to have abdicated in this house, a room of which is shown here.

A painter at work near the entrance to the famous Béguinage of Bruges. The Béguinage is a community of religious women who follow the practices of nuns but do not take binding vows. Each béguinage is a small city of its own within the larger communities of Ghent, Malines, Bruges, and others.

1641), one of the great portraitists of all time, became the court painter of Charles I of England and left a lasting effect on English painting.

With Rubens and Van Dyck, the great age of Flemish painting ended. Of the many Belgian artists since then, two stand out: James Ensor (1860–1949), a master of the modern school of Expressionism, who depicted emotional tensions in daring hues and fanciful subjects; and René Magritte (1899–1967), whose arrangements of realistic details in overall patterns of mystery and seeming confusion place him among the Surrealists.

ARCHITECTURE

Belgium houses examples of all the principal building styles of Western Europe from Romanesque to Modern, but is famous for its profusion of Gothic structures of both civic and religious character. The bishops, nobles, and burghers of the 14th, 15th and 16th centuries expressed the faith and vitality of their age in Gothic town halls, guild halls, mansions, and cathedrals whose soaring vaults and lacy pinnacles still stand in Belgium's cities despite centuries of war. Many of the finest examples have been destroyed or badly damaged. Those

The Institut Royal du Patrimoine Artistique in Brussels is a workshop dedicated to the restoring of old paintings. The art treasures of Belgium are so numerous that the shop is never without work.

The new municipal theatre in Luxembourg city is one of several modern structures built in the ancient capital since World War II.

that survive or have been restored, are still numerous and impart a unique quality to the Belgian landscape. From their belfries the carillons for which Belgium is known still toll their messages of hope and resolution.

MEN OF ACHIEVEMENT

In a sense, all Belgians are men of achievement. Like the Dutch and the Swiss they work hard in an effort to adapt the resources of their small country to the demands of the world market. The present prosperity of Belgium rests in large measure on the ingenuity and perseverance of its technicians and administrators in applying their researches to Belgian trade and industry.

Among Belgians of the past who have furthered human knowledge are: Andreas Vesalius (1514–1564), a pioneer in the study of anatomy; Jan Baptista van Helmont (1577–1644), discoverer of carbon dioxide and first to use the word "gas" as a scientific term; Gerard Kremer, called Mercator (1517–1594), father of

The Théâtre Royal de la Monnaie is Brussels' opera house and home of the famous Ballet du XXième Siècle. The language of the Brussels stage is mainly French.

mapmaking and modern navigation; Simon Stevin (1548–1620), developer of the decimal system; Jan Palfijn (1650–1730), anatomist and inventor of the forceps; Ernest Solvay (1838–1922), the chemist who devised the process for making soda that bears his name; and the chemist Leo Baekeland (1863–1944), who as a naturalized citizen of the United States, invented bakelite, the forerunner of modern plastics.

Luxembourg, with only 335,000 people, may also be termed a nation of unsung heroes. Through a thousand years they have kept their identity. The national motto is "We wish to remain what we are" (in *Letzeburgesch,* "*Mir woelle bleiwe wat mir sin*"). On becoming fully independent in 1866 they turned their tiny country into one of the world's chief producers of iron and steel. The names of individual Luxembourgers may not be very well known abroad, but the name of their country is.

In the Middle Ages, the ruling families of Luxembourg provided kings and emperors for half of Europe. One of these, John, Count of Luxembourg and King of Bohemia (1310–1346), was a man of legendary exploits and is the national hero of his homeland. A president of the United States, Franklin Delano Roosevelt, claimed Luxembourg descent through his Delano ancestors. The distinguished American photographer, Edward Steichen, was born in Luxembourg.

EDUCATION AND RELIGION

Belgium and Luxembourg are almost wholly Roman Catholic, Protestants and Jews being few, yet complete religious tolerance prevails. In Belgium, salaries of ministers, rabbis, and priests alike are paid in part by the government. The Catholic tradition is very deep in both countries and is reflected strongly in daily life and in a full calendar of religious festivals observed publicly throughout the year. The Flemish provinces especially are noted for the piety and intensity of their religious expression.

At present, Belgian children are required by law to attend school until the age of 14. Educational policy calls for the extension of the age requirement to 16 in the next few years.

The Manneken-Pis, near the Grand' Place in Brussels is almost a trademark of the city. The popular Manneken has a very large wardrobe, including everything from Boy Scout uniforms to Oriental costumes, which the citizenry of Brussels have provided for him to wear on special occasions.

Standards are high and the government devotes 19 per cent of its budget to keeping them that way. Belgium has one of the highest educational expenditures in Europe.

A special feature of Belgian education is the existence of public and private schools, both supported by the government. Fifty-seven per cent of the country's students attend privately operated schools, mostly run by religious groups. The private schools must adhere to minimum curriculum standards set by the government to qualify for state support. Tuition at both public and private schools is free.

This double system has grown out of a long conflict dating from the gaining of Belgian independence in 1830. Anti-clericalism, that is, opposition to state-church ties, was an important political force in 19th-century Belgium, and

Tongres, in the province of Limburg, is a city of great antiquity, with traditions going back to the Romans. At the nearby village of Russon, during the feast of St. Evermeire, girls in the guise of angels form an escort for the saint on his special day, May 1.

even today the political scene is not entirely free of this force. The present system is a compromise providing, in effect, a choice for parents to send their children either to non-denominational or religious schools at state expense.

Students who finish secondary school (girls' high schools are called *lycées*, those for boys or for both sexes are called *athénées*) may attend any of the four universities or the numerous special institutes of advanced training. The universities of Ghent and Liège are government-operated; those of Louvain and Brussels are free—that is, if they go beyond the minimum

Students from all over the world attend the University of Brussels. Forty per cent of Belgian students are holders of scholarships. Brussels University is the rallying point of liberal thought in Belgium.

The roads of Belgium and Luxembourg, like those of other Catholic countries, often pass by a wayside "calvaire," or depiction of the death of Christ, as this one in the Ardennes.

courses prescribed by the government they may themselves decide the content of their curricula. Louvain is Catholic; Brussels is liberal and non-denominational. At one time, all the universities taught only in the French language. Now Ghent and Louvain use Flemish mainly; Brussels and Liège, French. In this way, the language balance is maintained.

CRAFTS

A long tradition of fine workmanship exists in Belgium and Luxembourg. Centuries-old crafts survive side by side with modern industry. Belgian lace is highly esteemed both for

The Virgin Mary is believed to have saved the city of Luxembourg from pestilence and siege. As Our Lady of Luxembourg, she is venerated at a special shrine in the cathedral. Here, a procession for her is seen advancing towards the shrine.

BELGIUM and LUXEMBOURG ■ 507

the variety of its patterns and the delicacy of its needlework (or bobbin-work, for some of it is made on spindles). The laces of Malines, Brussels, and Binche are particularly well known, but in many other towns as well, nuns and elderly ladies bend over their needles and bobbins. Very fine lace is made in the *béguinages* of Bruges and Ghent. These unique Belgian institutions are convents of lay nuns, that is, religious women who follow the dress and practices of nuns without taking binding vows.

Both Belgium and Luxembourg produce first-rate leather goods. Their gloves and hand-bags vie with those of Paris for style and quality. Some of Belgium's huge iron output goes into the crafting of fine wrought-iron furniture and ornaments, a highly developed Belgian skill. Fine crystal tableware is another speciality, some of it made by carefully guarded secret methods. The jeweller's art is also traditional in Belgium, and its practitioners have made Antwerp the world capital of diamond-cutting. Custom-made firearms of rare workmanship and precision have made the name of Liège a byword among sportsmen throughout the world.

A lady dressed in lace, perhaps of her own work-manship, manipulates her bobbins as she elaborates one of the delicate patterns for which Bruges is famous.

Belgian crafts reflect aspects of Belgian character: balance, patience, restraint, and consciousness of a rich artistic heritage.

FOOD

The Belgians are a hearty people. They eat well, and need to do so, for they are among the most energetic people in the world. Belgian breakfasts tend to be more substantial than those of nearby France, but the schedule of meals is similar: a long lunch hour to accommodate the main hot meal of the day, and a supper of soup, cold meat, cheese, and salad. Beer is the beverage of the country and the usual accompaniment of a meal. Very little wine is produced, but a great deal is imported from

The Plantin-Moretus Museum is a 16th-century house in Antwerp containing the nearly intact equipment of the greatest family of Antwerp printers. In addition to ancient presses, the museum contains many of Rubens' paintings. Belgium has been a leader in the printing art since 1481.

France, and the fine Moselle wines of Luxembourg find a ready market. The excellent beer of Luxembourg is largely consumed domestically.

In the leading restaurants of Brussels the tourist will find menus that are French in inspiration, featuring many dishes typical of French *haute cuisine*. But the abundant tables of everyday restaurants and private homes are un-French and typically Belgian. There is a great variety of sea fare: tender shrimps, eels— smoked or fresh, a bounty of fish, some of which end up in *waterzooi*, a fish and vegetable stew. Belgium is the home of the endive, and this tasty white vegetable is a standard item of Belgian cookery.

Beef is the usual red meat consumed, and it may appear as a simple steak or in a succulent *carbonnade*, where it is braised in good Flemish beer. There is a great range of sausages and cured meats. The esteemed Belgian hare often appears in a *civet de lièvre à la flamande*, a stew to which prunes are added. Goose is often served, and in season the Ardennes forests provide venison and boar to the butchers of Brussels and Antwerp.

The high standard of living of Luxembourg is also expressed in a plentiful, appetizing menu,

In Belgium, cafés are important in the social and business life of the country. The Belgian is hospitable, friendly, and forthright by nature, but he guards the privacy of his home and does a large part of his entertaining in cafés and restaurants. Here, in Brussels' Grand' Place, Belgians sip coffee against a background of 17th-century houses.

including such delicacies as jellied suckling pig, the fine ham of the Ardennes, and *carré de porc fumé* (a relative of sauerkraut).

RECREATIONS

There is a great zest for living in Belgium. The people work hard and play hard. The North Sea coast is lined with resort towns, some like Ostend, of international repute. Ostend is often thronged with English visitors, but the Belgians themselves make full use of their beaches. The lovely hills and valleys of the Ardennes offer superior hiking, hunting, and fishing, and even

The tradition of handcraft is strong in Luxembourg. Here a skilled potter works on a teapot in one of the Grand Duchy's many small ceramics enterprises.

Tourists relax on a resort terrace at Bévercé, high in the Ardennes. The bracing climate, mineral waters, and rustic beauty of the region have made it a health resort since Roman times. The town of Spa, a few miles away, was so fashionable in the 18th century that it gave its name to similar resorts.

Little Luxembourg has many youth hostels. Among them, perhaps the most romantic is the mediaeval castle of Hollenfels in the lovely Valley of the Seven Castles. Here, young people from all over the world are accommodated.

Young cyclists mass before a youth hostel at Bourglinster in Luxembourg. Youth hostels provide inexpensive accommodations for students on tour, and other young people.

Camping is an increasingly popular recreation in Belgium and Luxembourg. Near the historic Luxembourg city of Echternach, a tent city sprouts on the hillside. Echternach is a pilgrimage site, where thousands congregate to do homage to St. Willibrord, the English missionary who founded the city's famous Benedictine Abbey in the 7th century.

mountain-climbing, for many of the low mountains of the region end in abrupt cliffs. The Ardennes is also full of caves and grottoes for the amusement of speleologists, or cave-explorers.

Cycling and football are the most popular spectator sports. And pigeon racing is a pastime furnishing excitement to all ages throughout the country. *Pelote*, a handball game, is the usual sport of city boys and country youths alike.

The Bird Market in Brussels is located in the historic Grand' Place, the mediaeval heart of Brussels. Pigeons, as shown here, are always in demand, for pigeon-racing is a national pastime.

At Wiltz in Luxembourg on Whit Monday, a spring festival of ancient origin takes place. Because it focuses upon the gathering of armloads of the plant called broom, it is called the Broom Festival.

FESTIVALS AND FOLKWAYS

The long simmering of Germanic and Latin elements in Belgium has resulted in a national character that is cheerful and fun-loving, exuberant even, but basically orderly and respectful of tradition. Around their firm Catholic faith, the people have built up a remarkable range of folk festivals—some, of the greatest religious solemnity; others waggish and light-hearted. Throughout the year, people of both town and farm march in fanciful costumes to commemorate saints, historic events, even legends based in pre-Christian beliefs.

Girls in traditional dress carry wicker wine baskets as they parade through the streets in the course of one of the many wine festivals held in the Moselle Valley of Luxembourg.

512 ■ BELGIUM and LUXEMBOURG

On these occasions little Belgium often becomes a land of giants. A feature of many regional celebrations is a parade of giant figures 10 to 20 feet high. At Binche, brilliant dancers in plumed headdresses and barbaric costumes recall the occasion when the Spanish rulers of Belgium celebrated the conquest of Peru. The cheery uproar of many of these celebrations is balanced by the profound solemnity of others such as the Procession of the Penitents through the Gothic streets of Furnes. Between the two extremes, the famous

Boating on the canals, rivers, and lakes of Belgium and Luxembourg is a popular sport. Here a boat is launched on the banks of the lake formed by damming the Sûre River in Luxembourg.

Larger than life, St. Nicholas parades before the church dedicated to him in the West Flanders town of St. Niklaas (St. Nicholas).

Procession of the Holy Blood at Bruges combines elements of both carnival spirit and religious piety.

Christmas is still very much a religious observance, however; the children celebrate December 6, the feast of St. Nicholas, in a manner similar to that of children in the United States and Great Britain on Christmas Day itself. In Belgium, St. Nicholas arrives on

A citizen of Malines in the province of Antwerp steadies a giant lady of legend as they take part in a folklore parade. Malines is famous for its lace and tapestry. In 1954, the Malines workshops presented the largest tapestry ever made to the United Nations.

BELGIUM and LUXEMBOURG ■ 513

On the North Sea Coast, fishermen and their wives wearing "sabots" (wooden shoes) line up for a parade. The Belgians are very fond of parades, but their parading is very different from that of warlike countries. Parades bring out the earthiness, conviviality, and joy of living found in the Belgian.

his feast day, by tradition in a boat from Spain, but now often by other means of transport. He is accompanied by his assistant, Black Peter, who carries presents for the good children.

Mounted fishermen are an unusual feature of Belgium's coast. Horses wade far out in the shallow coastal waters, dragging shrimp nets behind them.

The blast furnaces of Belgium and Luxembourg are among the world's most productive. Luxembourg has the world's highest per capita production of steel, Belgium the second highest.

BELGIUM AND ITS PARTNER LUXEMBOURG are vitally interested in the question of peaceful economic co-operation among nations. Belgium itself is an example in miniature of what common economic interests can do to overcome differences of language and culture. No Belgian denies that there are strains in the relations between Fleming and Walloon, between urban worker with socialist or anti-clerical views and conservative farmer, between employee and management. The important thing is that Belgium holds together, and does so very well. It is no wonder that Belgians are among the strongest supporters of the European Common Market, that huge scheme which seeks to blend the national economies of Western Europe into a single unit comparable to the economic might of the United States or the Soviet Union.

INDUSTRY

Iron and steel produced in vast mills fuelled to a great extent by Belgium's large coal deposits are the basis of the economy. Iron and additional coal brought into the factories of the Sambre-Meuse Valley at low cost from Belgium's partners in the European Economic Community are used to produce an impressive range of steel products. Sheet steel, wire, ingots, railway equipment, cast steel, tools, machinery and machine tools—everything from fine surgical instruments to floating oil refineries are exported to points round the globe. Belgium, with about 5 per cent of the population of the European Economic Community, produces about 10 per cent of its steel. In non-ferrous metals Belgium ranks first in export of cobalt, second in zinc, third in lead.

BELGIUM and LUXEMBOURG ■ 515

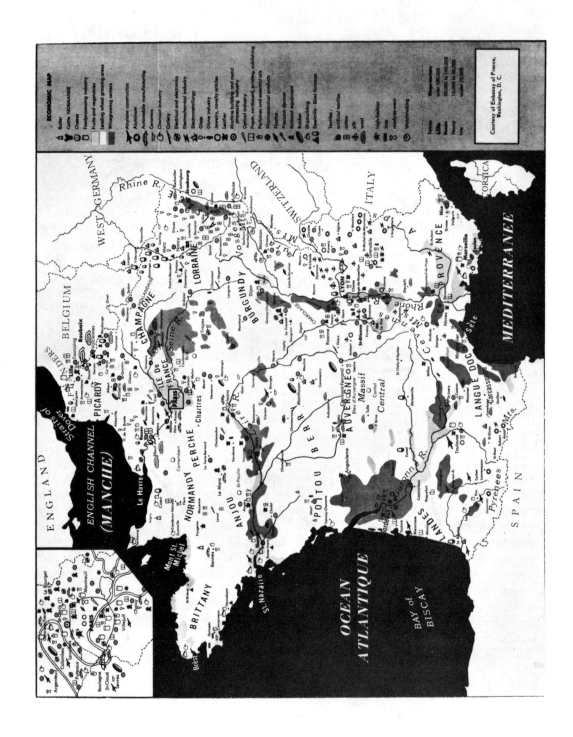

ECONOMIC MAP

Butter
Cattle NORMANDE
Cheese
Food-processing industry
Fruits and vegetables
Leading wheat-growing areas
Wine-growing centers

Airplane construction
Aluminum
Automobile manufacturing
Ceramics
Chemical industry
Coal
Cutlery
Electrical and electronic industry
Electrometallurgy
Glass
Glove industry
Jewelry, novelty articles
Leather
Machine building and metal processing industry
Optical industry
Paper, cardboard, printing, publishing industry
Petrochemical products
Porcelain
Precision devices
Railroad equipment
Rubber
Shipbuilding
Sawmills - Blast furnaces

Textiles - artificial textiles
cotton
silk
wool

High-fashion
Iron
Refining - oil
manufacturing

Towns   under 100,000
          50,000 to 100,000
          50,000 to 100,000
          15,000 to 50,000
          under 15,000

Courtesy of Embassy of France,
Washington, D. C.

WEST GERMANY
Rhine R.
Strasbourg
Mulhouse
Vosges Mts.
SWITZERLAND
Jura Mts.
ITALY
CORSICA
MEDITERRANEE

BELGIUM
FLANDERS
Lille
Roubaix
Tourcoing
PICARDY
CHAMPAGNE
LORRAINE
Metz
Nancy
BURGUNDY
Dijon
Troyes
Seine R.
ILE De
FRANCE
Paris
Chartres
PROVENCE
Nice
Marseille
LYON
St-Etienne
Clermont-Ferrand
AUVERGNE
Massif
Central
Cevennes Mts.
Rhone
Sète
Nîmes
LANGUEDOC
Carcassonne
Toulouse
Garonne R.
Pyrenees
SPAIN
Bordeaux
LANDES
POITOU
BERRY
Loire R.
Orléans
ANJOU
Angoulême
Tours
PERCHE
NORMANDY
Le Mans
Le Havre
Straits of
Dover
ENGLISH CHANNEL
(MANCHE)
ENGLAND
Mont St.
Michel
BRITTANY
Rennes
Brest
St-Nazaire
OCEAN
ATLANTIQUE
BAY of
BISCAY

Amiens

Paris
Argenteuil
Colombes
Le Bourget
Montreuil
St-Cloud
Sèvres
Boulogne
Puteaux
Villejuif
Levallois

The great Benedictine abbey of Mont-Saint-Michel perches atop a rocky islet in the Gulf of Saint-Malo, at the point where Normandy and Brittany meet. According to legend the Archangel Michael commanded the founding of this abbey-fortress, which in the Middle Ages withstood many sieges. In the foreground are lobster traps. Brittany is famous for its fisheries.

France

FRANCE IS A LAND of many faces. Because of its position astride the continent of Europe, France fronts on both the North Sea and the Mediterranean. Its Atlantic ports look upon the sea lanes that carried French ships to all parts of the world in the Age of Discovery, and made France one of the great world empires. To France's Mediterranean shores the ancient Greeks came 2,500 years ago and settled Marseilles, establishing an unbroken contact with the classic lands where Western civilization began. France's land frontiers comprise, in part, two of Western Europe's principal natural features, the Alps and the Rhine. Over the mountains came the ancient Romans; across the river, the Teutonic tribes. These two peoples merged with the Gauls, who preceded them, to form the modern French nation.

This great country has been a focal point in Europe. Historically France has been a guardian of European culture, and at the same time, an innovator. Gothic architecture and impressionist painting, revolutionary in their day, now symbolize France to people the world over. The French Revolution altered the map of Europe, yet did not profoundly alter the fabric of French life. Even today the traditional habits and customs of the French provinces survive. A leader in science and technology and an industrial giant, France is at the same time one of the most rural of the great powers.

France's splendid mountains, rich fields and vineyards, noble rivers and forests, are the background against which the French people carry on skills that have made the quality of their products esteemed throughout the world. In French cities the most modern buildings contrast with the glories of Gothic cathedrals and Romanesque churches.

France is a land of great regional variety and an underlying unity. It is the purpose of this book to describe and depict its diverse characteristics.

From the jagged, naked peaks of Mont Blanc, a vast Alpine glacier, the Mer de Glace, descends towards Chamonix. The summit of Mont Blanc is in France, but the eastern slope of the mountain is in Italy.

518 ■ FRANCE

The rolling terrain of the southwest where the high plateau of the Massif Central meets the coastal plain is the setting for a typical rural manor, the Château de Presque.

THE LAND

FRANCE, WITH AN AREA of 212,659 square miles is the largest country in Europe excluding Russia. Its greatest length from north to south is about 600 miles; its greatest width from east to west, about 550 miles. Shaped roughly like a hexagon, it occupies the western end of the main European land mass, its southern land boundary marked by the solid wall of the Pyrenees Mountains which separate it from the Iberian Peninsula. The remaining sides of the hexagon are formed by the English Channel (La Manche) and the North Sea on the northwest; the frontiers of Belgium, Luxembourg, and the West German states of Saarland and Rhineland-Palatinate, on the northeast; the Rhine River, the Jura Mountains, and the Alps, on the east, dividing it from the West German state of Baden-Wuerttemberg, Switzerland, and Italy; the Mediterranean Sea on the southeast; and on the west, the Bay of Biscay, an arm of the Atlantic Ocean.

France thus looks in many directions. Its

history reflects this position, for France has played a vital rôle in the history of Europe and of the modern world.

The Atlantic coast of France varies from the low, sandy shores of French Flanders on the North Sea to the Spanish border where the massive Pyrenees overlook the sea. Between these extremes are the chalk cliffs of the Channel, corresponding to those of England twenty miles distant at their nearest point; the wild rocky indentations of the Brittany peninsula; and the long sweep of dunes, marshes, and low coastal elevations on the Bay of Biscay. From Hendaye, at the point where France and Spain meet on the Atlantic, the Pyrenees extend for more than 250 miles in a slightly southeasterly line, and once more reach the sea, in this case the Mediterranean, near Perpignan. The coastline veers sharply north from this point, then follows a generally eastward course until it reaches the Italian frontier, where once

Sub-tropical vegetation and abrupt, rocky shores typify the eastern end of France's Mediterranean coast. Here the tiled roofs of Eze overlook the waters off Cap Ferrat, near Nice.

Between the Pyrenees and the Massif Central lies Carcassonne. Restored in the 19th century by the famous architect Viollet-le-Duc, this mediaeval walled city is the most perfect example of its kind in France. In the foreground is part of the modern town.

520 ■ FRANCE

A hunt starts in the forest of Rambouillet, southwest of Paris. France's great forests support deer, boar, and an abundance of small game. In the mountains of the south are found chamois, ibex, and wild sheep. The traditional "cor de chasse" or hunting horn can be seen in the middle foreground.

again great mountains look upon the sea, and the Alps merge with the Appenines.

Unlike Britain, Greece, and Denmark, France has few islands off its coasts, and none of these are of any great size. Corsica, with an area of 3,367 square miles, is politically as much a part of France as Paris; but geographically this large island, the birthplace of Napoleon, is closer to Italy. Along both the Atlantic and Mediterranean coasts are a number of good ports. Those of Marseilles, Toulon, Brest, Sète, St. Nazaire, and Lorient have played an important rôle in

the rise of France as one of the great maritime powers of the world. Of France's total frontier of 3,250 miles, the coastline accounts for 1,760.

Thus five sides of the hexagon are clearly delimited by nature. The sixth, the land frontier on the northeast, is not marked by any natural barrier. Here, where France meets Belgium and Germany, the fields of Flanders and Champagne blend into the great North European Plain, which stretches east to Russia. In this area some of the decisive battles of European history have been fought.

The mountains of Auvergne in south central France include many unusual formations. The chapel of Saint-Michel-d'Aiguilhe surmounts an isolated conical mass of rock.

TOPOGRAPHY

Within the bounds described, the country includes a variety of terrain. Roughly, the southeast and the extreme south are very mountainous, the west and north are low, and in the middle is a plateau rising southward and becoming increasingly mountainous.

The French Alps rise in tiers from the coast near Nice, culminating in Mont Blanc, 15,781

These great cliffs of chalk and limestone at Etretat in the Caux region of Normandy, just north of the great port city of Le Havre on the Channel coast, were originally laid down as sediment on the floor of a prehistoric sea.

feet, the highest peak in Europe outside the Caucasus. The Pyrenees are less spectacular than the Alps, but attain considerable altitudes nonetheless, many peaks rising over 10,000 feet. Apart from these two great mountain systems, the highlands of the country are grouped as follows: the Vosges in Alsace and eastern Lorraine; the Jura in Burgundy and Franche-Comté, extending into Switzerland; and the Cévennes and the mountains of Auvergne and the Massif Central in the south central part of the country. Few of the peaks in these chains exceed 6,000 feet.

While most of these French highlands possess no striking characteristics, the mountains of Auvergne and the Massif Central are of unique formation. The landscape here is studded with isolated needle-like peaks which rise abruptly from the plateau floor, the result of ancient volcanic action.

The plain that occupies the northern and western regions of France is broken by many chains of hills and ridges, such as the Ardennes on the Belgian border; the hills of Brittany and southern Normandy, the latter often called la Suisse Normande (or Norman Switzerland); and the Bocage Poitevin. As the Central Plateau descends westwards to the plains, erosion has cut deep gorges, especially in the picturesque region of the Dordogne. Two great depressions exist in the French lowlands, the Aquitaine Basin in the southwest, and the Paris Basin in the north. The general appearance of northern and

Dense pine forests cover the flat coastal region along the southern reaches of the Bay of Biscay. Discovery of oil in this area, which is called the Landes, is transforming the landscape as derricks rise, such as this one at Parentis.

western France is one of rolling hills and low plateaus; large expanses of very flat terrain are rare except in the extreme north, in Flanders, and in the lower coastal areas of the Bay of Biscay in the region known as the Landes.

Past a typical Breton stone farmhouse near Tredrez, an old woman plods in wooden shoes. "Sabots," as the shoes are called, are still in use in rural France. Traditionally, French children place them near the hearth on Christmas Eve, to be filled with gifts by the Père Noël (Santa Claus or Father Christmas).

On the Left Bank of the Seine in Paris, opposite Notre-Dame, a man leisurely walks his dog along the quai under new spring foliage. Such embankments are an agreeable feature of many French cities.

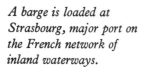

A barge is loaded at Strasbourg, major port on the French network of inland waterways.

These curious cottages at Saintes-Marie-de-la-Mer near the mouth of the Rhône suggest Africa rather than France. They are peculiar to the open, watery region called the Camargue, famous for its herds of black cattle and picturesque mounted herdsmen.

The Pont du Gard, an aqueduct and bridge built by the Romans, casts an 800-foot span across the Gard River in Provence. The dry climate of the region accounts for the fine state of preservation of this and other ancient remains in the area.

WATERWAYS

Through the mountains and hills of France many rivers flow to the sea. Two of the most important of these do not rise in France, but in Switzerland—namely, the Rhine and the Rhône. Indeed, the Rhine properly does not flow through France, but serves as the boundary between France and Germany for 100 miles. However, many French streams are part of the Rhine drainage system, and in this sense the Rhine is more of a French natural feature than it may appear to be. In ancient times the Rhine was regarded as the frontier of Gaul (as France was then called) all the way from the Alps to the mouth of the river in what is now the Netherlands. In the 17th century Louis XIV carried on repeated campaigns to extend his dominions to the Rhine which many Frenchmen called the "natural frontier of France."

The Rhône, as it flows through Switzerland, is a minor stream; in France it becomes a mighty one as it flows southwards to enter the Mediterranean Sea west of Marseilles. Along with the Alps and the Cévennes, which it separates, it is one of the dominant physical features of southeastern France.

The greatest of the rivers which rise and pursue their entire course within France are the Seine, the Loire, and the Garonne. From north to south, in the order named, all of these flow generally westwards from the eastern highlands and empty into the Atlantic. France is a well-watered land for the most part. A 3,000-mile network of canals links the rivers, joining the English Channel to the Mediterranean and linking Paris with Belgium and the Netherlands. Due to the Seine and the canals, Paris is a major inland port. Brightly painted barges from the Low Countries may be seen moored along the Seine embankments in the very heart of the city. These inland waterways play a prominent rôle in French commerce.

The many rivers of France are featured on the map in a way that may not be at first apparent. Since the time of Napoleon, France

The picturesque hill town of Gordes in the lower Rhône valley. Dry and sunny, this part of France resembles Italy in architecture as well as in climate. The area is famous for its fruits and vegetables.

has been divided into governmental units (departments) which bear the name, in all but a few cases, of the principal natural feature within their boundaries. These units, which correspond roughly to the counties of Great Britain or the states of the U.S.A., are in some instances named for mountains—Basses-Alpes, Jura, and Vosges, for example; in others, for arms of the sea, such as Manche, Gironde (an estuary at the mouth of the Garonne), and Pas-

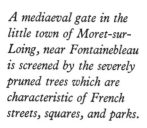

A mediaeval gate in the little town of Moret-sur-Loing, near Fontainebleau is screened by the severely pruned trees which are characteristic of French streets, squares, and parks.

de-Calais (Straits of Dover). By far the greatest number of the names of departments, however, refer to rivers. Some, like Rhône—the department that includes Lyon—Marne, Somme, Oise, Meuse, and Cher, carry the name of a single river. Others refer to more than one, or specify a certain stretch of the river, as Ille-et-Vilaine (Ille-and-Vilaine), Seine-et-Marne, Bouches-du-Rhône (Mouth of the Rhône), Haute-Marne (Upper Marne), and Bas-Rhin (Lower Rhine). It is generally possible for a visitor to France to learn the name of the principal river in the area where he finds himself, if he knows the name of the department.

PROVINCES

The departments were actually created after the upheavals of the French Revolution, to simplify the task of government, and also to replace the traditional regional names. These

Half-timbered houses at Romorantin in the Loire valley recall the age of Rabelais and François Villon. Bicycles are widely used in France as a means of transportation.

France is well supplied with electric power, but here and there old windmills are seen, as this one near the mouth of the Loire. Young folk-dancers don the costumes their ancestors wore when the mills were in use. Bagpipes have provided music for country revels since early times in France.

names were reminders of the feudal system and the monarchy, under which France at the time of the Revolution was divided into 32 provinces. The provinces were of unequal size and often of unwieldy shapes, but the majority of them corresponded to areas with distinctive customs, dialects and traditions. Even today the names of the provinces are in daily use, although they have had no official standing for over 150 years. A native of Seine-Maritime is still a Norman, and people from Côte d'Or are Burgundians. Similarly, products, arts and crafts, and breeds of domestic animals, long typical of a former province, retain the provincial name—Percheron horses (from the province of Perche); Burgundy, Anjou, and Champagne wines; and Quiche Lorraine, a ham and custard pie. In fact, a typical Paris restaurant menu may list half a dozen dishes named for the province whose regional style of cookery they exemplify.

FRANCE ■ 527

Luxury hotels look upon pines and palm trees lining the Boulevard de la Croisette at Cannes, perhaps the most famous of Riviera resort towns. Tourism is a vital occupation here, but the 70,000 Cannois also produce aircraft parts and textiles.

CLIMATE

The climate of France is for the most part oceanic—mild and damp, neither extremely hot nor extremely cold, with frequent rain and long growing seasons. The large peninsula of Brittany is completely oceanic in climate, with almost constant rainfall, normally grey skies and small variation in the year-round temperature, much like the western side of the British Isles.

The Mediterranean coast is dry and sunny. Sheltered from the interior by mountains, it supports an almost sub-tropical vegetation, especially at its eastern end, known to the English-speaking world as the Riviera, and to the French as the Côte d'Azur. Curiously unlike the Riviera in every other respect, Brittany,

due to the Gulf Stream, also tolerates the growth of certain sub-tropical plants. Here and there along its coasts, outlined against the grey sky and rocky shore, palm trees may be found, not growing wild, but planted in a hotel garden or town square.

Elsewhere in France winter and summer are sharply defined, and sunny days, while much less frequent than on the Riviera, are far from rare. In winter, snow falls more heavily in the eastern part of the country than in the west. Great Britain and France share with much of western Europe the moisture-laden Atlantic winds warmed by the Gulf Stream. Spanish and Italian visitors, on the other hand, find in the

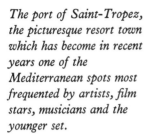

The port of Saint-Tropez, the picturesque resort town which has become in recent years one of the Mediterranean spots most frequented by artists, film stars, musicians and the younger set.

narrow strip of France along the Mediterranean resemblances to their own homelands—avenues of palms and mimosas, almond orchards, orange, lemon, and olive groves, and the cypresses and pines so typical of southern Europe.

NATURAL RESOURCES

France is blessed with the highest percentage

of arable land in Western Europe. Alone among the industrially advanced nations of Western Europe, it can largely feed itself from the produce of its fertile soil. Its mountains and numerous rivers provide France with great sources of hydro-electric power. In recent years the discovery of petroleum in the Landes, and later in other regions, notably the Paris Basin, have put France in the position of being an oil-producing nation. The exploitation of off-shore petroleum deposits in the North Sea is expected to benefit France as well as countries having greater frontage on that body of water.

France is a major world producer of coal. The iron ore deposits in eastern France and the aluminium ore deposits in the central region are so extensive that they make France a leading world producer of both these commodities. Bauxite, the chief ore of aluminium, takes its name from Les Baux in southern France.

France leads Western Europe in the production of uranium, the basic mineral source of

Chartres, most celebrated of Gothic cathedrals, can be seen for miles across the wheat fields of the plain of Beauce. Although the great edifice appears to rise abruptly from the plain, it is surrounded by a city of 40,000 people.

FRANCE ■ 529

Old houses in Quimper, Brittany, overhanging the little Steir River are joined by footbridges. Brittany derives its name and its Celtic language from the ancient Britons, some of whom, driven from their homes by the invading Anglo-Saxons in the 5th century, crossed the English Channel and settled there.

atomic energy. Other minerals found in abundance are rock salt, asphalt, potash, lignite, mineral oils, and pyrites. France is rich in building stone of various kinds, and in chalk and gravel.

The country is well-watered and also well-wooded. Forestry is an important activity in the woodlands found extensively throughout France. An impressive ring of forests still surrounds Paris. In ancient times, when the Romans invaded Gaul, they found the land almost entirely covered with vast forests. Today after 2,000 years of civilization, most of the land is cleared; yet it is still possible to hunt the wild boar in the dense forests of Sologne, just south of Paris. Oak, beech, elm, and chestnut are the characteristic trees of most French woodlands.

CITIES

The countryside of France, except in two areas, has not so far been greatly altered by the growth of great cities and extensive industrial areas. The exceptions are the Paris region and the departments of Nord and Pas-de-Calais, around Lille. The population is much more evenly distributed over the surface of the land than is the case in England or Germany. A much higher percentage of the people live on farms, in small villages, or in small, widely separated cities than in those two countries. Although the northern half of France is more densely populated and more built up than the south, there is no industrialized zone there that corresponds in size and manufacturing activity to the Midlands of England or the Ruhr area of Germany. France has only one city, Paris, with a population in excess of 1,000,000; the city itself contains 2,800,000 people and the metropolitan area claims about 9,000,000. The only other really large cities are Marseilles with 900,000 people and Lyons with 543,000. Many medium-sized cities dot the land—Strasbourg, Nantes, Nancy, Limoges, Toulouse, Bordeaux, St. Etienne, and Dijon are among the many cities in the 100,000 to 500,000 class.

Even today with a rapidly increasing population and the spread of industry and new housing, France is still very much a country of wide-open spaces and scenes of rural peace.

An excellent example of Stone Age art is this painting in the cave of Lascaux in the Dordogne region. The murals here and at nearby Font-de-Gaume are outstanding specimens of prehistoric art. Presumably painted by the light of crude oil lamps, these works show a high degree of artistic sensitivity, a quality abundantly present in the modern population of France. The Lascaux paintings are no longer open to the public, since it was discovered that air from outside the cave was causing the paintings to deteriorate.

HISTORY

IN THE ICE AGE, 25,000 years ago, giant woolly mammoths roamed the snow-covered terrain of France. Their remains and those of prehistoric peoples who came before and after them have been found in parts of the country. Many names used by archaeologists to distinguish Stone Age cultures derive from places in France where traces of these cultures were first discovered: Abbevillian, Aurignacian, Cro-Magnon, to name a few. The arrangements of huge stones at Carnac and the remarkable cave paintings at Lascaux date from prehistoric times.

In 58 B.C. when the Romans under Julius Caesar began their conquest of Gaul, the land was chiefly occupied by Celtic-speaking tribes akin to the ancient Britons. With the defeat of the great Gallic chieftain, Vercingetorix, at Alesia in 52, the Roman conquest was complete.

The Romans organized the country into provinces, built roads and cities, and developed agriculture and commerce. In the next 300 years a high order of culture and prosperity prevailed, and Latin replaced the Gallic dialects as the language of the land.

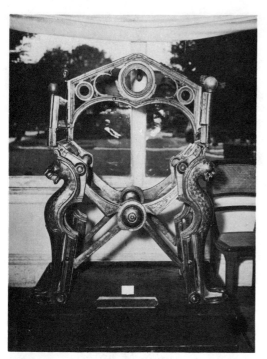

This chair of the Merovingian period is said to have belonged to King Dagobert I. Like Britain's King Cole, this monarch's name is kept alive in a nursery rhyme. French children today sing of "Le Bon Roi Dagobert."

As the Roman Empire declined, large numbers of Teutonic tribes came into Gaul from Central Europe, some as invaders, some as settlers invited by the Romans. A period of upheaval ensued until the arrival of the Huns from Western Asia served to unite Teuton and Gallo-Roman in an effort to repel them. These fierce invaders were turned back in the decisive battle of Chalons in A.D. 450.

In the era that followed, the fate of Gaul was increasingly determined by the Franks, a powerful Teutonic nation living partly in Gaul and partly in Germany. In time they came to rule the whole country. Of the several Frankish tribes, the Salians became dominant. Clovis, their king, accepted Christianity in A.D. 496. From him and his dynasty, the Merovingians, the French trace the beginnings of the Christian nation of France. Clovis is an archaic form of Louis, the name which, above all others, was later to stand for the King of France.

EARLY MIDDLE AGES

For the next 300 years Frankish affairs were in turmoil. The Moorish conquerors of Spain crossed the Pyrenees and advanced as far as Tours, on the Loire. There, in 732, the Frankish leader, Charles Martel, defeated them and stopped forever their advance into Europe.

Charlemagne, his grandson, brought most of Western and Central Europe under his sway. In 800 he assumed the title of Holy Roman Emperor and was crowned in Rome by Pope Leo III. After his death his dominions fell apart, the western ones becoming France, and the eastern ones developing into Germany; the west retained the Latin speech of the Gallo-Romans, now transformed into French, while the east kept the Teutonic tongue of the Franks.

Charlemagne, ruler of Neustria, 8th century Frankish state corresponding to northern France, rode to victory over half of Europe, bringing order and civilization to the northern barbarians. The Holy Roman Empire that he founded lasted until Napoleon swept it away a thousand years later.
This bronze statuette is in the Louvre.

Eudes, Count of Paris, defends the city against the Northmen, A.D. 885. He repulsed them and later became king, but the Viking raids continued until well into the 10th century.

The kings of France descending from Charlemagne, known as the Carolingians, were weak. During their rule the coasts were ravaged by Vikings or Northmen. The area about the mouth of the Seine now called Normandy was ceded to these sea raiders in 912.

Under the Carolingians, a system of vassalage (feudalism) began. Among other things, the king could become the protector of a faithful servant (vassal) and in effect make him the equivalent of a loyal prince. As the power of the king waned, that of these nobles, the vassals, grew. One of the great feudal vassals, Hugh Capet, assumed the throne in 987. The dynasty he founded ruled France under the feudal system characteristic of the Middle Ages without interruption for 800 years—until 1789.

In the feudal period the French kings strove to reduce the power of the great vassals. The actual rule of the king was limited to the region of Paris, called the Ile de France because it was like an island in a sea of vassal states. Philip Augustus (1180–1223) and Louis IX (1226–70, later canonized as St. Louis) were notable in restoring order and reducing the power of the nobles. In their century the great Gothic cathedrals arose and the age of chivalry flowered. Much of what we think of today as typical of the Middle Ages evolved in 13th-century France.

Louis IX was a man of exemplary virtue and wisdom. Later canonized as Saint Louis, he founded the Sorbonne and made Paris a great capital of mediaeval learning. He led the Seventh and Eighth Crusades, dying in Tunis in the course of the latter.

FRANCE ■ 533

LATER MIDDLE AGES

The period that followed was stormy, marked by French quarrels with the Popes, and especially by the harsh struggle—known as the Hundred Years War (1337–1453)—with England and its French vassal allies. The land was despoiled, the peasantry reduced to starvation, violence reigned, and for a time the kingdom seemed doomed. Henry V of England won the battle of Agincourt in 1415, and forced the French king, Charles VI, to give him his daughter in marriage, as well as to agree that the throne of France should pass to her descendants, that is to England. Three events changed the situation: the deaths in 1422 of both Henry and Charles, and the emergence of Joan of Arc, the peasant girl who broke the siege of Orleans in 1429, and inspired the French to resist until the English were at last driven from all of France except the city of Calais.

During the remainder of the 15th century the crown succeeded in crushing the vassal rulers. Burgundy, Brittany, Provence and other great dukedoms and countships were brought under direct rule; and France came out of the Middle Ages a unified country. From here on, French energies were directed outwards to the rest of Europe. In 1494, Charles VIII invaded Italy to enforce a vague claim to the throne of Naples. He failed, and his successor, Louis XII, carried on an even more energetic effort there, with no greater success in the long run. Francis I (1515–46) launched the bitter rivalry with Spain which was to underlie French policy for the next 200 years.

The mighty donjon of the 14th century Château of Vincennes on the eastern rim of Paris, an impressive relic of the feudal period, was begun in 1344. The castle was a fortress residence of the kings of the Valois line. In the Hundred Years War it fell to the English, and in 1422 Henry V of England was stricken with dysentry and died within its walls.

A view of Paris in the 15th century, from an illustration in the chronicles of Jean Froissart, historian of the late Middle Ages. Froissart is seen in his study at the left, while at the right, Isabelle of Bavaria, queen of Charles VI, rides by on a litter.

SIXTEENTH CENTURY

The 16th century brought to France the full surge of the Renaissance, the "revival of learning" that took place in Italy following the decline of feudalism. With a return to Greco-Roman concepts and with a new spirit of inquiry, the fields of science, literature and art took on new dimensions; clothing, furniture, manners, speech, and diet became more elaborate; French ships sailed to Asia and America in the wake of Columbus; and the authority of the Church was questioned, as the Protestant Reformation spread to France.

The form which Protestantism took in France was not the mild one of Luther, but the radical one of Calvin, and the conflict with Catholicism was bitter. A very large number of Frenchmen turned Protestant; some estimates place it as high as one out of every three. Persecution of the Protestants went on relentlessly during the 16th century, reaching a peak in the general massacre on St. Bartholomew's Day in 1574.

THE BOURBONS

The Valois branch of the Capetians sputtered out in a line of weak kings, ending with Henry III (1574–89), whose assassination left the throne vacant. A power struggle followed, from which Henry of Navarre, of the Capetian house of Bourbon, came out the victor. A Protestant, he turned Catholic on ascending the throne as Henry IV. He sought, through the Edict of

Nantes (1598), which granted religious toleration, to unite Catholic and Protestant in a common effort to check the power of Spain. His murder in 1610, left the crown to a boy, Louis XIII, whose reign was dominated by his chief minister, Cardinal Richelieu. Richelieu laid the foundations of the absolute power of the monarchy that reached its peak under Louis XIV. He stifled opposition from every quarter within France—nobles, Protestants, provincial parliaments, members of the royal family. In foreign affairs, he allied himself with the Protestant nations to thwart the great Catholic powers, Spain and Austria, which he regarded as the true enemies of France.

In 1643, Louis XIV, a child of six, assumed the crown. During his childhood the policies of Richelieu were maintained by Mazarin, another cardinal-statesman. Under Mazarin foreign wars were ended, and he quelled the internal dissensions called the Fronde. The Fronde was a widespread rebellion of different groups opposed to the centralization of power in the throne. Louis took full control at Mazarin's death in 1661, and until his own death in 1715,

Henry IV, founder of the Bourbon dynasty, a spirited and energetic ruler, is remembered for his promise of "a chicken in every peasant's pot on Sunday."

The Porte Saint-Denis, Paris, is not truly a gate, but a triumphal arch commemorating the victories of Louis XIV in Germany and Holland. In the reign of this king the walls of Paris were demolished and new edifices such as this were built on what was then the edge of the city.

536 ∎ **FRANCE**

Versailles, the city and the palace, was the crowning monument of the reign of Louis XIV and became the virtual capital of France until the Revolution. The cost of maintaining the king and the court in such grandeur was supported by heavy taxation and was a major cause of the dissatisfaction that culminated in the Revolution.

his long reign was a constant assertion of his belief that "I am the State."

Louis had, in Jean-Baptiste Colbert, a brilliant finance minister who put France on a sound economic footing. But Colbert fell from grace and the resources of the country were severely strained by the extravagance of Louis' style of living. Even more costly was a series of aggressions against Spain and Holland, which led to a general European war. The battle of Blenheim in 1704 was a defeat from which France did not recover and the war was lost. At home Louis did further harm by revoking the Edict of Nantes, thereby causing a mass emigration of Protestants.

(Left) Louis XIV was called the Roi-Soleil, or Sun King, because of the magnificence of his reign. A patron of the arts and a man of taste, although extravagant, he made his court the cultural capital of Europe.

In 1789 French finances were on the brink of ruin. Louis XVI summoned the French parliament for the purpose of initiating fiscal reforms. This body, the States-General, met only at the king's request, and had not sat since 1614. It was composed of three "estates"—the nobility, the clergy, and the commons. The latter, the Third Estate, refused to disband until a constitution was granted. Denied access to their regular hall, they took over the royal tennis court (Jeu de Paume) at Versailles, as depicted here by David.

The Fall of the Bastille, July 14, 1789, is now commemorated as the French National Holiday. A 14th century citadel used as a prison, its capture by the citizens of Paris triggered the Revolution. It was demolished in 1790.

Bagatelle, meaning a mere trifle, was the name bestowed on this exquisite small mansion in the Bois de Boulogne, the great park on the western edge of Paris. A hideaway for members of the royal family, it was built just before the Revolution. It often housed Marie Antoinette, the unlucky queen of Louis XVI, who, with her husband, was beheaded in 1793. The Revolution began as an attempt by moderates of the middle and upper classes to obtain constitutional government, but soon passed out of their control.

EIGHTEENTH CENTURY

While French arts and civilization reached heights of refinement, the government steadily decayed. Under Louis XV (1715–74) abuse of royal power created mounting unrest, while abroad unsuccessful wars resulted in the loss of most of the French possessions in India and America.

Louis XVI (1774–92) tried vainly to meet the demands of his people, but fell victim to the swelling cry for revolution. His attempts at financial reform were largely undone by the heavy burden of the French contribution to the American Revolution. But the democratic ideas of Voltaire and the 18th century French philosophers had gained wide acceptance: revolution was in the air. The First Republic was declared, and the monarch beheaded. The powers of Europe leagued against France. French citizen armies, however, swept into Italy and the Low Countries. Napoleon rose to glory, first as a military leader, then, as the revolutionary government fell apart, as a dictator who unified France against its enemies. A rapid succession of changes in government, from the Republic through the Directory and

Napoleon, shown here in coronation garb, was one of many members of the upper classes who served the Revolution. A man of great organizing genius, he rose to power when the Revolutionary government failed and eventually re-established a monarchy with himself as Emperor.

Talleyrand (1754–1838), nobleman and extraordinary diplomat, served under the Revolution, the Empire, and the Bourbon Restoration. Often involved in intrigue, he nonetheless served France well at the Congress of Vienna after Napoleon's downfall, when the powers of Europe met to carve up the French Empire.

the Consulate, ended in Napoleon being crowned Emperor of the French in 1804.

NINETEENTH CENTURY

The next ten years saw the rise and fall of a great French empire in Europe; France overextended itself and Napoleon was overthrown at the Battle of Waterloo in 1815. However, his rule had effected permanent reforms in all areas of French public life. The Bourbon monarchy was restored, but it was overturned in 1830 after Charles X unwisely tried to increase royal authority. A constitutional monarchy was declared and the crown was given to Louis Philippe, son of a Bourbon prince who had supported the Revolution of 1789. He in turn lost the support of his people through un-

popular policies and was ousted in the Revolution of 1848. The Second Republic was established, with Louis Napoleon, a nephew of the late emperor, as president. He followed the path of his uncle, and shortly succeeded in having himself crowned as Napoleon III. (Napoleon II was a title accorded to the first emperor's son, who never ruled.) A series of wars brought him into collision with the Prussian-dominated Germany of Bismarck. The Franco-Prussian War of 1870 was his downfall; France was badly beaten and lost Alsace-Lorraine. The Second Empire gave way to the Third Republic.

1870-1914

Under the Third Republic, France gained a great new colonial empire in Africa and Indo-China. In Europe, French policy aimed at limiting the growing ambitions of the new German Empire created by Bismarck, an effort that led to alliance with England and Russia. At home, bitter social, religious and political unrest prevailed, overshadowed by the coming of World War I in 1914.

Marie-Louise, second Empress of Napoleon (the first was Josephine, whom he divorced), survived her husband's death in 1821 by many years, living into the age of the camera. This 1847 photograph shows her in "Victorian" dress.

The disasters that befell France from 1870 to 1945 were crippling both morally and materially. In spite of the Allied victory in World War II, a feeling of hopelessness affected many Frenchmen after the war. The ruins of the great inland port of Rouen are typical of the destruction amid which the French resumed peacetime existence. But today Rouen is rebuilt and the country is once more a great world power.

1914-1945

France and its allies defeated Germany in 1918, but the country suffered staggering losses in men and material in the process. Further weakened by the financial depressions of the 1930's and by the failure of the Allied governments to stem the resurging power of Germany, France fell to the armies of Hitler in 1940. In the underground movement and from bases abroad Frenchmen resisted the German occupation. This resistance was led by General Charles de Gaulle. When the Allies smashed the empire of Hitler in 1945, France was left plundered and war-torn, damaged not only by World War II, but feeling the accumulated effect of three generations of strife with Germany.

THE PRESENT

The struggle to rebuild was long and painful, complicated by rebellions in Algeria and Indo-China in the 1950's, and by the inability of the splintered French political parties to provide stable government; but France was aided by the economic co-operation of the Marshall Plan, and European unification schemes initiated by Jean Monnet. In 1959, Charles de Gaulle was elected President under a new constitution. Through his leadership, the Algerian war was ended, the French colonies in Africa gained independence, and the French people united to make France once again a force in world affairs.

The Place de la Concorde in Paris, a superb example of the work of the 18th century architect, Gabriel, was the scene of bloody executions during the Revolution.

Cadets of Saint-Cyr, the French West Point or Sandhurst, parade on Bastille Day. In the distance is the Arch of Triumph. Built to commemorate Napoleon's victories, it has become the chief symbol of French patriotism and national prestige. Beneath its arch lies the tomb of the Unknown Soldier.

The Palais-Bourbon is the seat of the National Assembly. Shown here is a reception room used by the President of the Assembly. It is a fine example of Louis XV period decor. This style is the one most popular among the French themselves.

Police Headquarters in Paris is on the Ile de la Cité, adjoining Notre-Dame. The French police are world-famous for their efficiency and thoroughness. France contributed materially to the development of criminology as a science. All police in France are under the direct control of the Ministry of the Interior in Paris. Sight-seeing boats are called "bateaux-mouches."

The façade of the Palais-Bourbon can be seen from the Place de la Concorde. In the foreground is one of two huge fountains dating from the reign of Louis-Philippe.

GOVERNMENT

FRANCE IS A REPUBLIC governed by a president and a legislature consisting of a Senate and a National Assembly. The Assembly has 482 members, the Senate 274. The present government dates from December 21, 1958, when Charles de Gaulle was elected first president of the Fifth Republic under a new constitution approved by the voters on September 28, 1958. General de Gaulle had become Premier in June, 1958, after a long succession of post-war prime ministers who were unable to unify the differing elements of the French legislature.

Under the Fourth Republic, the Prime Minister had executive power, while the President was a figurehead, and the legislature was enabled to curtail the executive power to a marked degree. De Gaulle's first step was to reform the constitution, giving real power to the President, and limiting his responsibility to the legislature. The people of France rallied once again behind their World War II hero and overwhelmingly voted for the new constitution.

This constitution applies not only to France but to the French Community, formerly called

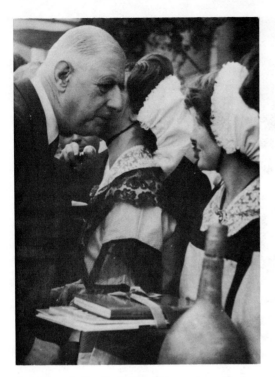

President de Gaulle (1959–69) receives gifts from girls dressed in the traditional costume of southeastern France.

Membership in the Senate is based on the proportion of one senator to 300,000 voters. Senators are chosen by special electors, drawn from the deputies (members of the Assembly) and the councillors of the departments and municipalities. One third of the Senate is replaced every three years.

GOVERNMENTAL UNITS

The deputies represent the 95 governmental units of France (the departments), as well as four overseas departments—Guiana, Guadeloupe, Martinique, and Réunion—and the remaining small widely scattered French colonies. The Overseas Departments are administered as integral parts of France. The colonies, called Overseas Territories, are classed as dependencies of the French Republic, and not as separate members of the Community. These colonies include the Territory of the Afars and Issas (formerly French Somaliland) and the Comoro Islands in Africa; St. Pierre and Miquelon off Newfoundland; French Polynesia and New Caledonia in the South Pacific; and diverse possessions in Antarctica and adjacent waters, which are mostly uninhabited. The

the French Overseas Empire. All but one of the members voted along with France to accept the new constitution. Guinea, in Africa, chose instead to become an independent republic with no ties to France.

By a constitutional amendment in 1960, the territories were allowed to remain autonomous republics within the Community, or to become fully sovereign yet associated with France (in a manner similar to the British Commonwealth). Senegal, Madagascar (renamed Malagasy Republic), Chad, the Congo Republic, Gabon, and the Central African Republic remained within the Community; Dahomey, the Ivory Coast, Upper Volta, Mali (formerly the French Sudan), Niger, and Mauretania chose the looser association. The Presidents of the first six republics form, with the Premier and certain cabinet members of the French Government, a special Executive Council, headed by the President of France. In addition, these six republics are represented in the French Senate by at least three members each.

In the communes or smallest administrative units, the "garde-champêtre," or town crier, makes public announcements.

The city hall of Paris, or Hôtel de Ville, is in the foreground. Behind it are annexes and the church of Saint-Gervais. On the upper right are the Ile Saint-Louis and some of the many graceful bridges that span the Seine.

former French possessions of Tunisia, Morocco, Laos, Cambodia, and Vietnam were given full independence in the 1950's, before the creation of the Community. Algeria, once considered an integral part of France, won complete independence in 1962, following the ending of the civil war there.

The departments of France are divided into 311 arrondissements, which in turn are divided into cantons (3,031) and communes (37,963). A prefect, nominated by the government, heads each department, while sub-prefects are in charge of the arrondissements. A municipal council directly elected by the voters governs each commune.

THE PRESIDENCY

A second constitutional amendment, in October, 1962, changed the method of electing the President. As first ordained by the new constitution, the President was chosen by an electoral college. The amendment provided that he be elected by popular vote. The President serves for seven years. The Premier, who was formerly elected by the Deputies, is now a

presidential appointee. The President is empowered to dissolve the Assembly and order new elections; to call for referendums on special questions of national interest; and in time of national emergency to govern with full authority. The government can only be dissolved by an absolute majority of the Assembly.

CAPITAL

In the capital, Paris, the various branches of the government have their offices—in historic buildings for the most part. The official residence of the President, the Elysée Palace, in the very heart of the city, was once the home of Madame de Pompadour, the mistress of Louis XV. The Palais-Bourbon, across the Seine, is the seat of the National Assembly. The Senate convenes in the historic Luxembourg Palace, built for Queen Marie de Medici, wife of Henry IV.

Paris, a hub of world government like New York, Geneva, and The Hague, has been the headquarters of many international organizations, among them UNESCO, NATO, and the Organization for European Economic Cooperation.

The port of Bordeaux, chief point of export of the French wine trade, is also noted for oil-refining, shipbuilding, and chemical production.

This prize Charolais bull was bred near Nevers. Half of France's livestock total consists of cattle.

This huge plant at Flins produces Renault cars. The automotive industry is located principally in the Paris area.

From nuclear power plants such as this one at Chinon, Indre-et-Loire, France expects to derive half its power from atomic energy by the 1970's.

THE ECONOMY

THE INDUSTRIAL REVOLUTION of the 19th century did not have the same impact on France as on Germany and England. Until well into the present century, French industry comprised a very high percentage of small, often family-run, factories producing a remarkable range of products of high quality. The wars of 1870, 1914, and 1940 drained French manpower and money and checked industrial expansion. The introduction of modern methods of mass production lagged.

Today the economy is booming. Behind this growth are several factors:

First are the basic conditions of geography, access to world markets, mild climate, and natural resources.

Secondly, the great increase in population after a century of low birth and high death rates is creating both a large work force and an ever growing body of consumers.

Thirdly, the organized effort of government and industry to promote industrial development and to make the maximum use of manpower and resources, thus increasing productivity, is a major cause.

The discovery in France in recent years of natural gas, petroleum, and uranium for atomic energy, has sparked the growth of new industries. These new sources of energy, and the increase in hydro-electric power provided by the construction of new dams and generating plants, have doubled France's power output.

Lastly, the participation of France with Italy, West Germany, and the Low Countries in building the Common Market, a tariff-free combine of 185,000,000 people, has created a condition of healthy competition in which French producers must compete with those of other member nations for the business of the French consumer. To do this, they must streamline their production methods and cut costs.

Skilled technicians test jet engines of the Atar class. France ranks fourth in world aircraft production.

INDUSTRY

France produces 67,000,000 metric tons of iron ore a year, ranks third in world output after the United States and the Soviet Union, is the world's third largest exporter of steel, and has the third largest machinery and equipment industry in Europe. Its aircraft industry is fourth in the world. France ranks seventh in world output of electric power, fourth in motor car production, fifth in shipbuilding, fourth in chemical exports, fifth in textiles (fourth in artificial fibres). The worldwide network of French airlines covers 340,000 miles; and the French merchant fleet, the world's eighth largest, counted, in 1962, 783 vessels.

AGRICULTURE

The surface of France is devoted 91.5% to agriculture. More than 50% of the total land area is held by owner-operators. One-third of the land area, but only one-fifth of the total number of farms are held by tenant farmers. Twenty per cent of all farms are operated on a mixed basis, i.e., the farmer owns some land and leases more. Of the rural population of 16 million, over half earn their living directly from the land.

From the time of the French Revolution, agriculture has suffered from a breaking up of farm holdings into small, often scattered, units. Inheritance laws were passed after the Revolution, designed to counteract the established system of primogeniture, i.e., the inheriting of the entire holding by the oldest son. In many farming communities a single farmer may have to work isolated fields as far apart as several miles. The Fourth Plan aims to consolidate farm holdings by inducing farmers to exchange

Steel arriving at the Denain mill is reheated before being put through the hot-steel rolling process.

Agricultural machinery is fast replacing draft horses, such as this fine Percheron mare, on French farms, but France remains a world leader in the breeding of saddle and race horses.

their outlying fields for ones adjoining their main holdings. The increase in farm output from this more efficient use of land is important in French economic planning.

The chief French agricultural products are wheat, barley, corn, oats, rye, fruits and vegetables, potatoes, sugar beets, flax, hemp, oil seeds, and forage. France is famous as the leading producer of wine in the world, both in volume and quality. It is the world's fourth largest producer of both beef and pork, and eighth largest of lamb and mutton. Poultry-raising ranks third among French farm activities. The breeding of draft and saddle horses is also important. Some 270,000 acres of ponds are used to raise carp and other fresh-water fish. Salt-water fisheries are also of considerable economic importance.

Girls label bottles in a winery at Frontignan, Hérault. This region of France produces the greatest volume of ordinary table wine.

A catch arrives at Douarnenez, Brittany. French coastal waters provide some of the finest oyster and lobsters in the world, while from deeper seas the French fishing fleets bring in sardines, anchovies, herring, mackerel, and tunny.

A grey November day in Paris, but the boulevard is thronged, for a street fair is in progress.

THE PEOPLE

THERE ARE, according to a 1970 French Government estimate, 50,000,000 people in France. (In 1946 the population was 40,517,923.)

The French are a nation of individuals, self-reliant, ingenious, inquiring, yet conservative in many respects. They are tolerant of the actions of others, being much more concerned with seeing that their own houses are in order. This tolerance has misled some foreign visitors into thinking that France is a land of gaiety and laxity. More often than not, the visitor has based his conclusions on the acts of other foreigners taking advantage of the French tolerance of exuberance.

By and large the French are frugal, industrious, cautious, and proper. They are less inclined, however, to participate in organized

Bigouden ladies in front of the cathedral at Chartres wear the starched lace headdress of their district. Most bizarre of the many regional "coiffes" of Brittany, this tower of lace has actually grown over the past century from less than half its present height.

The Rue Mouffetard, a narrow, crowded, shopping street, is in one of the oldest quarters of Paris.

schemes for civic betterment than are Anglo-Saxons. What a Frenchman tolerates in another is not necessarily what he approves for himself. Some observers trace the French regard for self-reliance and individual action to the atmosphere of political instability that has prevailed for so long at the top level of government.

As for the physical appearance of the people it is possible to identify certain types as "French." From the long, slow, fusion of many races, some recognizable French types have emerged. But, it is not possible to generalize in terms of complexion, stature, etc. Tall, fair people are quite as common as short, dark ones, and both are greatly outnumbered by people of intermediate pigmentation and height. In general, true blonds are more common in the north, true brunets in the south.

Unlike most other Europeans the French have not emigrated overseas in great numbers. The only sizeable overseas community of French blood (not merely of French language, as in Haiti) is in French Canada; and this is descended from a relatively small number of 17th and 18th century colonists. The French, except for the Huguenots (who were largely absorbed by nearby nations), found little reason to quit their country, as did the millions who

The Canal Saint-Martin is part of a bypass diverting Seine traffic from the middle of Paris. Here, near the Place de la République, the canal goes underground, to emerge again near the Pont d'Austerlitz on the river.

Cafés line the broad pavements of the Champs-Elysées, the principal thoroughfare in Paris. Cafés are an important part of French daily life. Much business and social entertaining is done in them rather than in the home.

fled from harsh living conditions or religious intolerance in Russia, Germany, Ireland, and Italy.

On the contrary, there have been rather large influxes of people to France in recent times. The chronic shortage in the work force due to war losses and a low birth rate earlier in this century brought hundreds of thousands of Italians, Poles, and others, into France. The Russian Revolution contributed thousands of White Russians, and the Spanish Civil War of the 1930's drove tens of thousands of Spaniards to take refuge in the region of Toulouse. Free access to France from Algeria prior to Algerian independence brought over 400,000 Muslims from North Africa into Paris, Lille, and other cities; and the later exodus of the French population of Algeria added a new element, since the Algerian "French" were to a large extent descended from Spanish, Italian, and Maltese colonists.

In addition to such new groups, France has for centuries included within its borders blocs of people of distinctive race and language—Bretons, Flemings, Alsatians, Basques, and Provençals. Several million people still speak non-French tongues in addition to French, although French is the only official language, and the only one taught under the French system of universal compulsory education. The Provençal language, closest to French in origin, has merged into the dominant language, and survives only as a *patois* or dialect. The Breton and Alsatian tongues have held out. In both Brittany and Alsace traditional ways of living have survived markedly. Brittany, indeed, is the only region where peasant women still wear traditional costume in daily life. In all the other historic provinces of France, fanciful local dresses are only worn on festive occasions or for the promotion of tourism.

The "concierge" with her "chat" is a familiar sight along the streets of French cities. The concierge held an important official court position during the Middle Ages—that of custodian of a royal palace.

552 ■ FRANCE

Members of the French Academy in full regalia are seen arriving at the inauguration of the new campus of the University of Caen in 1957.

LANGUAGE AND LITERATURE

The French language is basically Latin in derivation. The ancient Gauls contributed only a few words to the French vocabulary, but it is believed that the influence of Gallic grammar and sentence structure may have been appreciable. The Franks added quite a large number of common words to the vocabulary and are credited with having had a great influence on the pronunciation, for French has a phonetic system distinctly different from Italian and Spanish.

Two Latin dialects developed in France, the *langue d'oil,* or French, in the north; and the *langue d'oc,* or Provençal, in the south. The boundary between them was never sharply delimited, and as the north contained the political core, its speech prevailed. Before sinking to the level of a French dialect, however, Provençal developed an impressive literature of its own.

By the 17th century a uniform standard of educated French speech was established for polite society. The social reforms after 1789 definitively introduced this standard into all levels of society and into all corners of the country.

The French language of the educated classes and of the galaxy of brilliant writers of the 17th and 18th centuries became the medium of refined expression in all the courts of Europe, the language of international diplomacy and of all people who sought to express themselves with elegance, clarity, and subtlety. Frederick the Great of Prussia spoke habitually in French; the Russian aristocracy used it among themselves; even today the passports carried by citizens of remote Asian and African countries are likely to be written in French.

Before the 17th century, the great names in French literature were those of the lyric poet, François Villon; of Joachim du Bellay and Pierre de Ronsard, who led the group known as the *Pleïade*; of François Rabelais, creator of Gargantua and Pantagruel; of Margaret of Navarre, author of the *Heptameron*; and of Michel de Montaigne, brilliant author of the *Essays.*

The 17th century was the age of the great dramatists—Molière, Corneille, and Racine; of La Fontaine and his *Fables*; of the moralists, diarists, and philosophers: Pascal, Descartes, Bossuet, Fénelon, and La Bruyère, and La Rochefoucauld, author of the *Maxims.* In this period the French language took on the precision and polish that have characterized it ever since.

The 18th century, with its rationalist philosophical movement "The Enlightenment," was dominated by the social, political, and philosophical writings of Voltaire, author of *Candide*;

André Malraux, author of the novels "Man's Fate" and "Man's Hope," was appointed Minister of State for Cultural Affairs in 1959. In this rôle he exercises very broad responsibility for government-subsidized activities in the arts.

of Rousseau, who wrote the *Contrat Social,* a work that greatly influenced the leaders of the French Revolution; of Montesquieu, whose *Spirit of the Laws* outlined a system of government based on checks and balances, later adopted

in the Constitution of the United States; and of Diderot, whose *Encyclopedia* expressed the outlook of The Enlightenment and had a far-reaching effect on European thought.

The early 19th century was dominated by Chateaubriand, a leader of the Romantic movement, best known for the *Genius of Christianity,* which spurred a revival of interest in the Middle Ages. Among his contemporaries was Lamartine, author of the *Meditations.* The most complete expression of the 19th century is found in the works of the poet, playwright and novelist, Victor Hugo. Other figures of the time are the novelists, Balzac, Zola, George Sand, and Flaubert; the poets Rimbaud, Baudelaire, and Verlaine; and the great historians Michelet, Guizot, Taine, and Renan.

Prominent among 20th century writers are the poets Paul Valéry, Charles Péguy, and Guillaume Apollinaire; the philosophers Henri Bergson and Jean-Paul Sartre; the dramatists Paul Claudel, Jean Giraudoux, Jules Romains, Jean Anouilh, Eugène Ionesco and Jean Genêt; and the novelists François Mauriac, Romain Rolland, Georges Bernanos, Albert Camus, Marcel Proust and Françoise Sagan.

A unique feature of the French educational scene is the French Academy, a supreme council of 40 eminent men, mostly literary, who are officially responsible, through publication of a dictionary and a grammar, for maintaining the purity of the French language.

Some of the most exciting episodes of Victor Hugo's "Les Misérables" took place in the famous sewers of Paris. Paris has a vast network of subterranean structures, including the Metro, or underground railway system.

These toddlers are in an "école maternelle" (nursery school). Broad reforms in French education will give these children greater educational opportunities than their parents had. Smocks such as that on the little boy at the right are worn by small children at school and play.

EDUCATION AND RELIGION

French education is compulsory and free between the ages of 6 and 16. Before 1789, all education was in the hands of the church. The constitution of 1791 stripped the church of all power in this respect. Napoleon made education a function of the state but re-introduced the authority of the church up to a point. After his downfall, the church attempted to remove education as much as possible from control of the government. In 1833 private schools were allowed by the government, and in 1875 private universities were authorized. However, the Third Republic abandoned the policy of joint state-church control and took stern measures to crush the influence of the church. In 1904, the right to teach in all schools, public and private, was withdrawn from members of religious orders. These harsh restrictions were later relaxed to some extent.

Discipline is strict in French schools, as is obvious from the close attention of these boys in a primary school class in Paris.

A student recites in a first-year class in an experimental lycée or secondary school at Sèvres, near Paris. In.an ordinary lycée boys and girls are not mixed and first-year students are of a higher age group.

Today religious control is no longer a serious issue. The chief problems of education are those of curriculum reform, of making higher education more widely available, and of building more schools to meet population growth. In 1968, violent student disorders, which led to a general strike that paralyzed the nation, prompted the government to announce that sweeping reforms would be made in the near future.

Great emphasis is placed on reforming higher education to provide more complete training in science, technology, business, and finance. An important reform under way is the postponement of the age when a student in primary school must choose between a "terminal" course that will end his formal education, and a course that will prepare him for admission to a lycée, or secondary school. Until now pupils have been obliged to make this decision at the age of 11.

French universities number 21, all state-controlled. The best known is the University of Paris, popularly known as the Sorbonne. The universities are widely scattered, each serving a legally defined area. Though comparatively few

in number, their standards of scholarship are exacting. The lycée is generally comparable in academic level to the American undergraduate college (although accommodating a younger age group) and the better English grammar schools.

The majority of French churchgoers are Roman Catholics. There are about 1,000,000 Protestants, mostly in Paris and the south. While church and state have been completely separate since 1905, the influence of the Catholic Church in everyday life is very great.

Cadets stand to attention during graduation exercises at the Ecole Polytechnique in Paris. Under the jurisdiction of the Ministry of Defence, this world-famous technical institute turns out the future élite of French industry and government.

The Church of the Sorbonne contains the tomb of Cardinal Richelieu, who had it built as a gift to the University of Paris. The Sorbonne is a vast complex of buildings housing the administration of the University.

ART AND MUSIC

France has been a major influence on Western art and is a treasury of Romanesque and Gothic architecture, the latter having originated in France. The exquisite chateaux of the Renaissance and the classic grandeur of Versailles influenced the style of public buildings throughout the world until well into the present century.

France is the cradle of modern painting. Although many first-rate French painters, such as La Tour, flourished before 1800, French painting attained an unprecedented development during the past 150 years. David, Gérôme, Géricault, Ingres, Delacroix, Courbet, Daumier, and Corot ushered in the 19th century. The impressionists Renoir, Degas, Manet, and Monet dominated the 1870's and 1880's, creating a revolution in painting technique that paved the way for the post-impressionists in

This 13th century stained glass at Chartres cathedral is an example of the fine windows found throughout the country. The earliest known school of stained glass in France flourished in the 12th century.

FRANCE ■ 557

The vast museum, the Louvre, of which only a segment of the east façade appears here, was originally a royal palace. Begun by Francis I in 1541, it was extended many times, notably by Louis XIV, Napoleon I, and Napoleon III. Its use as a museum dates from the Revolution.

"Le Moulin de la Galette,"
by Pierre Auguste Renoir,
1876, Louvre, Paris.

The great modern painter, Marc Chagall, points to a sketch of his new ceiling murals in the Paris Opera. Modern in tone, they nevertheless conform with the Second Empire style of the building. France has a special capacity for harmonizing the old and the new.

This is the interior of the magnificent Romanesque abbey church of the Madeleine at Vézelay. Here, amid the green hills of Morvan in Burgundy, Saint Bernard preached the Second Crusade in 1147.

The Romanesque church of Notre-Dame-la-Grande at Poitiers was built during the 11th century. The richly carved façade tells stories from Scripture, a common function of sculpture in an age when illiteracy was prevalent.

France at the turn of the century—Cézanne, Gauguin and Van Gogh, and the giants of modern art who followed—Picasso, Matisse, Léger, Rouault and Braque.

Gothic architecture grew out of Romanesque. Many churches combine features of both styles. Notre-Dame in Paris, begun in 1163, is one of the finest examples of pure Gothic. Bookstalls fastened to the wall of the Seine embankment are typical of Paris.

In the field of music, France has produced an impressive list of composers from Couperin, Rameau, and Lully through Gounod, Berlioz, Bizet, Saint Saëns, Massenet, and Debussy.

MEN OF ACHIEVEMENT

Islands, rivers, and territories the world over bear the names of their French explorers. Canadians and Americans especially are familiar

Charles Gounod (1818–93), composed the opera "Faust" and the oratorio, "La Redemption."

During the celebration of Paris' 2000 years as a city a re-enactment was held of the first balloon ascension by Montgolfier in 1782, one of mankind's first successful attempts at air travel.

with the exploits of Cartier, La Salle, and Champlain. In modern explorations of the ocean depths, the name of Cousteau is pre-eminent.

Through the discoveries of Becquerel, Pierre and Marie Curie, Louis and Maurice de Broglie, among others, the French contribution to our modern atomic age is enormous.

The great naturalists Lamarck, Buffon, and Cuvier; Ampère, in the field of electricity; Claude Bernard in medicine; Alfred Binet in psychology; Lavoisier, Berthelot, and Pasteur in chemistry; Laplace and Lagrange in mathematics and astronomy; Montgolfier and Blériot in aviation; Poincaré in mathematics and physics; Descartes and Pascal, in both philosophy and science; Niepce, Daguerre, and the Lumières in photography and cinematography; all of these and many, many more shaped the world in which we live.

A skilled potter shapes a vase upon his wheel in the famous porcelain factory at Sèvres.

ARTS AND CRAFTS

Reflected in a wide variety of exquisitely made items, French taste has set a world standard. The products of French craft industries are an important factor in the country's export trade.

Fine leather goods (especially gloves), the world's finest perfumes, luxury textiles, and high-fashion clothing spell France and Paris throughout the world. No less esteemed are the porcelain of Limoges and Sèvres, the crystal of

Flowers, musk, and essential oils from all over the world go into the manufacture of the renowned perfumes of France. The industry is located mainly at Grasse on the Riviera, a small town surrounded by fields of flowers that provide much of the raw material. A technician in a distillery is preparing a quantity of perfume from a secret formula.

In a Parisian maison de couture, a high fashion designer pauses to survey his newest creation, while the mannequin patiently holds her pose.

Baccarat and Saint-Louis, Gobelin tapestries, musical instruments, liqueurs, chocolate and confectionery, jewelry, laces, wrought iron, ivory and tortoise-shell goods, and cabinet work. Paris is a world leader in period furniture reproduction and art bookbinding.

FOOD

The French cuisine is the most refined in the world, imitated in better restaurants from Copenhagen to Buenos Aires. Blessed with a variety and abundance of home-grown food-stuffs, the French have made the preparation and serving of them an art.

Limoges is celebrated for its fine china. Here skilled workers polish finished pieces by hand.

The famous Paris restaurant, the Tour d'Argent, typifies the French ideal of carefully prepared meals served in an agreeable setting.

In France, wine is a usual accompaniment of meals. Here representatives of the Marennes district on the Bay of Biscay pair their famous oysters with the delicate white wine of Alsace. The girl wears the traditional Alsatian costume.

Although rich sauces and elaborate decoration are typical of expensive restaurants in France, the essence of French cookery lies in restraint and discrimination. The aim is to bring out the natural essence and texture of the food. Cooking in the home and in ordinary restaurants reflects this principle.

A simple meal of meat, potatoes, salad, fruit, cheese, and crusty bread in a bistro (small local restaurant) can be a delight. A meal of this sort

Truffles, black fungi found in the ground, are highly esteemed as a garnish for certain foods, especially paté de foie gras. Production of the paté from goose liver is a major enterprise in the Périgord district, where pigs and dogs are trained to scent out the precious fungi.

A little girl brings home fresh bread from the local bakery. Local bakeries turn out these crusty loaves two or three times daily so that fresh bread can be served at every meal.

Caen in Normandy is famous for its method of preparing tripe. Here a lady in Norman costume judges one of the entries in a tripe cooking contest.

is much closer to the average Frenchman's usual fare than is the fancier food offered in many tourist restaurants.

Every region of France has its own style of cooking, depending on the nature of the local produce, the character of the local wines, and other factors. Many Paris restaurants specialize in provincial menus. Wine is customarily drunk with meals. In the regions of northern France too cloudy for the grape to ripen, cider and beer are produced, but wine is available everywhere. Breakfast is usually light—coffee and rolls; the main meal is at midday; and the evening meal again is light.

The French eat well, food accounting for quite a large slice of the family budget. One reason for this is consumer reluctance to buy canned or frozen foods. Economic changes now taking place in France may alter this.

France is famous for the production of table delicacies such as truffles, pâté de foie gras, cured ham, preserves, and many other items of gourmet food.

France is a cheese-fancier's paradise. Over 300 distinct kinds are made, every region having its special variety. The dairy section of this French supermarket offers many of the best known cheeses. Self-service stores are relatively new in France.

CUSTOMS

Escorted by guardians, cowboys of the Rhône delta, gypsy pilgrims carry the statue of Sarah, their legendary ancestress, in a ritual procession into the waters of the Mediterranean at Les-Saintes—Maries-de-la-Mer. Every year on May 25, gypsies from all over Europe assemble in this ancient town where Sarah is believed to be buried.

Mardi Gras (Shrove Tuesday) is celebrated in Nice with a great carnival.

The grape harvest at Orschwir in Alsace is a festive occasion. The most esteemed wines in France come from this area and from Champagne, Burgundy, Anjou, and the Bordeaux area, especially the latter.

RECREATIONS

Longchamp, the famous race track in the Bois de Boulogne (the principal park in Paris) is the scene of the annual "Grand Prix de Paris."

The Frenchman values his leisure and knows how to use it. A wide range of sports is afforded by his country's varied climate and terrain. Skiing is a major sport in the numerous mountain areas. The long seacoasts of the Atlantic and the Mediterranean are equipped for every type of water sport. Paris is almost deserted in August—everyone who can has shut up shop and office and gone to seashore or the country. Cycling, hiking, fishing and mountain-climbing have numerous adherents. Soccer, or "le football," is the national spectator sport.

The French are proud of their historical, architectural, and artistic treasures. Sightseeing and museum-going are popular recreations. The ballet, the opera, and the theatre draw patrons from all classes of society.

Traffic congestion is becoming a problem in some cities, but the broad boulevards, river embankments, winding shopping streets, the many parks and public gardens, the café terraces, and charming country roads of France still provide excellent conditions for simple relaxation. A leisurely stroll, coffee at an out-of-doors restaurant table, an hour thumbing through books and prints at a riverside bookseller's stall, or watching children in the park— these are moments of great value to the Frenchman. It is his firm intention to maintain his traditional cultural values as his country draws more and more upon the technological advantages of our times.

At the Parc des Princes stadium in Paris, a French soccer team vies for the ball with a team from Monaco.

"Pelote," national sport of the Basques, has many enthusiasts throughout France. Similar to handball, it may be played with the hand, with a racquet, or, as shown here, with a curved wicker basket, the "chistera" (and it is then sometimes called "jai-alai").

The Tour de France, an annual bicycle race round the whole perimeter of France, is a major sporting event that evokes as much interest as baseball in America or football in England.

Christmas Day on the Promenade des Anglais, the seaside boulevard in the great resort city of Nice. Mild sunny winters make the Riviera a year round vacation area.

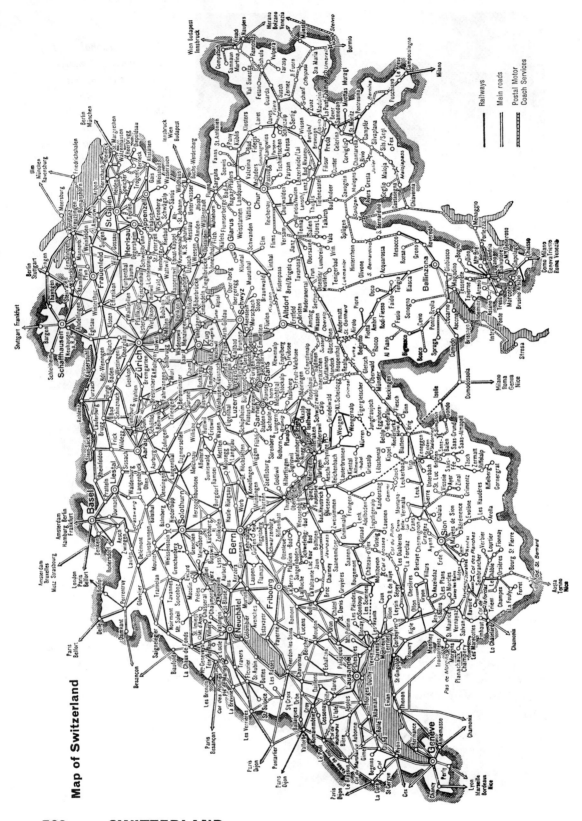

Map of Switzerland

SWITZERLAND

HISTORY

Long ago, before the Christian era, most of the country now known as Switzerland was inhabited by a Celtic people called Helvetii. The country itself was called Helvetia. In 58 B.C. the Helvetii tried to emigrate to that part of Gaul which is France today, but they were met and driven back by Julius Caesar. After this defeat Helvetia remained Roman until about A.D. 450. At that time the Roman Empire was invaded by the barbarians, and the western part of Helvetia was occupied by people called Burgundians; the eastern part was taken over by the Alemans. It was the Alemans who brought a Germanic dialect, which, over the years, became the language now spoken by more than two-thirds of the population. The Burgundians, however, adopted the language of the country, which was Latin. This in time became French. In A.D. 496 Helvetia was incorporated into the Kingdom of the Franks and later became part of the Holy Roman Empire. So much for the early history.

It was in the 13th century that the foundation of today's Switzerland was formed. This happened when three communities—Uri, Schwyz and Unterwalden—were forced to defend themselves against the aggressions of the House of Hapsburg. In 1291 these three mountain states, or cantons, as they are still called, formed an alliance, pledging mutual support against all invaders. The name Switzerland comes from that old community of Schwyz, and the legendary hero and leader of the alliance was William Tell. The Confederation that was formed gradually broke away from the Holy Roman Empire and became an alliance of free peoples who were acquiring a strong tradition of self-government. The "Everlasting League" sworn to by the three states became the foundation stone of the Swiss nation. Soon it was strengthened by other communities which joined it, one by one, as they shook off foreign rule.

The League had to struggle hard for its existence. Yet it continued to expand, and by the 16th century there were thirteen members. Over the centuries the League's solidarity and the courage of its members were put to severe tests by attacks from the outside. First the Hapsburg army, then an army of Austrian knights, and finally the followers of Charles the Bold, Duke of Burgundy, fell victim to Swiss arms. A final clash with the Holy Roman Empire could not be avoided, and came about in 1499. The Swiss were once again victorious. Not until 1648, however, when the Peace of Westphalia ended the Thirty Years' War, was Switzerland's independence from the Empire recognized under international law.

While their great feats of arms might have inspired the Confederates with a feeling of their own strength, the League itself had been formed to protect each of its members and not to increase their power. In addition, the many ethnic groups in the League made it important that the little country stay uninvolved with other countries' foreign policies. This formed the groundwork for the principle of permanent neutrality.

Yet all was far from peaceful. Once again Switzerland was seriously threatened when Napoleon set about changing the face of history. He unified Switzerland, calling it "The Helvetic Republic," and annexed part of its territory to France. The rest he divided into cantons. But this experiment didn't last long. When the Treaty of Paris was signed in 1815, the idea of federation was still strong. The Swiss constitution was adopted in 1848, when the old federation of states was replaced by the Federal state with no internal customs barriers or obstacles to trade. Instead, there were the advantages of a uniform currency and customs duties, a common postal service, and a centralized army. Switzerland was at last a truly unified independent country.

The Swiss assume a more direct responsibility for governing their country than the citizens of any other land. They not only elect representatives for the conduct of public affairs on the cantonal and federal levels; they often participate directly in decisions on the highest level by voting on federal as well as cantonal decisions.

Breaking with its long-standing policy of non-alignment, Switzerland joined the League of Nations in 1920, but reverted to complete neutrality after World War II by refusing to accept membership in the United Nations, since participation in that organization would involve possible military commitments. The Swiss Government does participate, however, in many social and scientific bodies affiliated to the United Nations—the International Labour Organization; World Health Organization; United Nations Educational, Scientific and Cultural Organization (UNESCO); and the Food and Agriculture Organization.

GOVERNMENT

The form of the Confederation has changed since its early days, but its basic principle has remained the same. The Swiss Confederation is a union of 22 states, with a form of government that is very similar to that of the United States. The Federal Assembly is set up like the United States Congress, with two houses, the State Council and the National Council. Instead of all executive authority being vested in a president, however, there is a 7-man board, known as the Federal Council. This Council, in turn, is presided over by one of its members, who is President of the Confederation. A new President is chosen every year. Berne (or Bern), the federal capital of Switzerland, is the seat of government.

Switzerland is still founded on its member states, the cantons, which are sovereign in so far as their rights are not limited by the constitution. In this way the cantons resemble the states in the U.S.A. Their democratic character rests on the solid foundation of the *communes* and the free citizens of the 3095 free communes.

Three of the 22 cantons—Appenzell, Basel and Unterwalden—are divided into half-cantons, which have separate representation in the State Council. These cantons were split because of economic or religious differences among the people. Today there is a movement in the French-speaking western part of the canton of Berne to break away from the German-speakers of the eastern part and form a new half-canton.

Swiss citizenship is primarily communal, and every Swiss has a home commune. It is in the commune that all public activity begins. Here, too, in the local self-government, every citizen takes part in discussion and shares in work.

At the age of 20 each male Swiss becomes an active member of his commune, that is, he obtains the vote in communal, cantonal and federal affairs, and is himself eligible for election. At the same time he becomes liable for military service in the Swiss militia. Women in Switzerland do not have the vote, except on cantonal matters in the cantons of Geneva, Vaud and Neuchâtel.

One of the interesting aspects of the Swiss state is the combination of pure and representative democracy. The citizen has to decide upon questions arising in the communes, especially in those that are practically self-governing. He can be and in many communes *must* be present at the most important assemblies. In a number of cantons the citizens

Self-government has been a Swiss privilege and responsibility since the Confederation was established in the 13th century. Today open-air parliaments convene in the capitals of cantons as they have for centuries. Here the Honour Guard of the State Government of Appenzell gets ready for the parade which will open the parliament.

Since 1505 the Swiss Guards have had the duty of guarding the Vatican, a testimonial to their neutrality and international character. The members of this personal guard to the Pope are recruited from the Catholic cantons of central Switzerland.

A sabre, sword or rifle is an old emblem of the Swiss citizen's status. The Swiss are not only a tradition-bound people; the umbrella is a symbol of their eminently practical nature.

The open-air Landsgemeinde *or Citizens' Asssembly of Trogen, in the canton of Appenzell-Ausser-Rhoden, decides political issues by the ancient hand vote.*

annually gather in a *Landsgemeinde* or folkmoot. Assembling on the public square of the capital of the canton, they take part in discussions, decide by show of hands what laws and financial measures are to be enacted, and elect the members of the government. Even in

those cantons which have outgrown this form of direct democracy, the citizens have the last word.

The history of Switzerland and its governmental structure contribute greatly to the country in which liberty is the staple raw

In Sarnen, drummers precede the open-air parliament. Switzerland, although dedicated to neutrality, is a land of citizen-soldiers. Military training is compulsory and a strong army is trained so that any attempt by a foreign power to take over the territory will be too costly to be tempting. The Swiss Army is purely defensive. The citizens undergo regular periods of military training, including refresher courses and marksmanship tests, and keep their uniforms and equipment at home, ready to use. As a result, Switzerland can mobilize about 350,000 soldiers in a day, although there is no standing army.

For all the picturesqueness of the costumes, election day in Switzerland is more than mere pageantry. ⟶

material. But all this does not give a picture of the republic known as the "Heart of Europe." It is the Swiss people, and the land itself, that have impressed their spirit on the little country. The following chapters will introduce you to the land and its people.

The large, intent crowd indicates the interest and participation of the people in their government. Eight parties are represented in the federal legislature, but the people show considerable independence in their voting, often following their own personal convictions rather than a party line. The Swiss political system, providing direct participation by the people, may be complicated and cumbersome, but the years have proved that this results in solidity and stability.

The landscaped park of the United Nations Building in Geneva is a popular place with visitors.

THE LAND

Switzerland is only 226 miles long, and 127 miles wide at its widest point. Its area, 15,940 square miles, can be crossed in less than a day. Yet within this compact country, there is a wealth of contrast. Every type of climate and scenery is to be found between the giant spur of the Matterhorn, whose summit is the goal of all ambitious Alpine climbers, and the warm waters of the Southern lakes.

Surrounded by Germany on the North, Austria on the East, France on the West and Italy on the South, Switzerland controls some of the major communication routes between those countries, particularly the passes and the tunnels through the Alps. This location has played a large part in determining Switzerland's role of neutrality.

Magnificent peaks rise high above St. Moritz, one of the most famous winter playgrounds in the world.

Nestling at the foot of the mountains, the town of St. Moritz in the canton of Grisons has not only pleasure-bent tourists. Here farmers tend their land as they have been doing for centuries.

PHYSICAL FEATURES

The country is divided into three main regions, two of which are mountainous. The Jura Mountains on the North and West cover one-sixth of the land; the Alps on the East, Southeast and Southwest cover half the territory. Between them are the Midlands. Slightly more than half of Switzerland consists of farm, vineyard and pasture land; a little less than a quarter is forested.

The many rivers and lakes put Switzerland at the watershed of the continent. Several important rivers have their source here: the Rhine, which flows through Germany and Holland to the North Sea; the Rhone, flowing through France to the Mediterranean; the Ticino flowing into the Italian Po and on to the Adriatic.

Snowy slopes and lakeside chalets are typical of Switzerland, where extreme contrasts in scenery are only a few miles apart.

Switzerland has no direct access to the sea, but is bounded by natural frontiers, with the Rhine forming part of its northern and eastern border. The Lake of Constance, the Lake of Geneva, the Alps and Jura Mountains and the Doubs River form other natural boundaries between Switzerland and adjacent nations.

The Lake of Neuchâtel is the largest lake entirely within Swiss territory, followed in size by the Lakes of Lucerne and Zurich. Over 1,000 glaciers feed the many lakes, waterfalls and rushing mountain streams.

The Cima del Largo (10,560 feet) is one of Switzerland's most attractive but also most dangerous peaks. It lies off the beaten track overlooking the lonesome Bondasca Valley, some 50 miles southwest of St. Moritz. Here two bold Alpinists—the tiny specks nearing the top of the mountain—prepare for the final assault.

SWITZERLAND ■ 575

This is the Switzerland known to millions of people who come yearly for an exhilarating winter holiday.

This too is Switzerland—the vineyards of Lavaux, in the Lake Geneva region. Only about three-fourths of Switzerland's land is productive, and of this area one-third is used for pasture, one-third is forested, and the remainder is devoted to vineyards and raising food crops. Even 1,800 feet above sea level Swiss vineyards flourish.

Like a setting for a fairy tale, the Castle of Oberhofen rises next to the lake of Thun in the Bernese Oberland.

The Alps, of course, are the most outstanding geographic feature, and account for the unusual diversity in climate. The highest mountain, Monte Rosa, rises 15,217 feet. (Mont Blanc, the highest peak in the Alps, is not in Switzerland but in France.)

Mount St. Gotthard, the central junction of four mountain chains, unites the main watersheds of Europe, most of which are filled by the large glaciers. Switzerland's most important valleys follow the course of the rivers, yet the rivers within Swiss borders do not provide as good waterways as the many lakes—more than 1,000, with numerous smaller bodies of water.

Surviving from medieval days, this castle of Bottmingen, in the Birsig Valley, is reflected in its surrounding moat.

SWITZERLAND ■ 577

The Hufi Glacier, in the St. Gotthard region, looks bleak and desolate. The Alps themselves were shaped over many thousands of years by the movements of such glaciers, in addition to such forces of nature as climate, avalanches, and mountain streams carrying solid materials to lower lakes.

CLIMATE

Switzerland is divided into different climatic zones by the Alps, and the variation is remarkable in so small a country. In the lake area of southeastern and central Switzerland, it is often very hot in the summer. Winters in the valleys are generally colder than in mountain regions of the same elevation, because the cold air sinks to the foot of the mountains. In the Alpine region, there is dry, clear and usually cool weather all year round.

The Swiss climate is characterized also by various winds. The Alps form a dividing line between equatorial and polar winds. Eastern Switzerland and the upper river valleys of the Rhone and Rhine are the targets in spring, summer and fall of the *foehn*, a warm, moist wind that makes people and animals feel uncomfortable. On the whole, however, the climate of Switzerland is delightful, and if the weather does not suit a visitor, he need only make a short trip to find completely different conditions.

Many Swiss towns are packed with avid skiers during the winter months. Zermatt, at the foot of the Matterhorn, is one of the most popular.

As the land changes from the wild glacier country to the southern mildness of the Rhone valley and the Ticino plain, the conditions of life change too. The type of houses and settlements varies from district to district. In the Alps the wooden chalets cling precariously to steep slopes, while in the Midland farmsteads stand broad and prosperous in their spreading fields. The solid, stone-roofed houses of the Ticino look as if they had been hewn out of the Gotthard rock, but the quaint wooden cottages of Appenzell lend a peculiar charm to the green slopes on which they stand. The towns rise proudly above the rivers or cluster at the ends of the lakes, but none is like the other, and each is stamped with its own individuality. This is Lugano, a romantic and picturesque town in the southern Italian-speaking part of Switzerland.

The great Gothic cathedral of Berne dates from the 15th century. The city of Berne is both the capital of the canton and of the Confederation. Although it is the site of such international agencies as the Universal Postal Union and the International Copyright Union, it is a city of medieval architecture and many arcades and fountains.

Interlaken, in the canton of Berne, is a famed summer resort. The town got its name, meaning "between lakes," because it is situated between the Lake of Brienz and the Lake of Thun. The visitors who stay at the many hotels and inns, stroll down the tree-lined promenade pictured here, and take the clear air as they ride in hansom cabs, far outnumber the permanent residents of the town.

Lucerne, founded in 750, still has its feudal walls and watchtowers, but it has been brought up to date with wide, well-lighted streets traversed by street 'tramways.' Picturesque buildings, scenic beauty and modern efficiency combine to make the city an important tourist sight. The Reuss river flows through the town, accommodating both sailing yachts and swans.

The Pilatus Railway climbs effortlessly up the mountainside.
Switzerland has an efficient, speedy and almost completely electrified railway network, owned and run by the state-operated Swiss Federal Railways. Inter-urban expresses connect with mountain railways, and these meet with funiculars and suspension railways that ascend almost to the rooftop of Europe.

Lugano, the jewel of the Swiss Riviera, owes much to its enchanting landscape. Across the Lake of Lugano, Mount San Salvatore thrusts its rugged peak skyward.

FAUNA

The hunting of animals is severely restricted, and this fact has enabled many species to survive among the rocks and crags near the snowline, as well as in the forests farther down the mountain slopes. Characteristic mammals of the high altitudes are the ibex, which is a wild species of goat with great curved horns; the chamois, a small antelope of extraordinary sure-footedness and agility, once much hunted for its soft pliant hide; and the marmot, a close

When Thomas Gray wrote "Full many a flower is born to blush unseen," he might have had this curious juxtaposition in mind. The great differences in climate and altitude in Switzerland produce a large variety of vegetation, including many plants that grow almost nowhere else. Some Alpine plants grow 7,000 feet above sea level.

Wild animals are at home in the mountainous countryside. The last bear seen in Switzerland was shot at the end of the 19th century, but boar, ibex, chamois, foxes and deer are found. This fox seems not at all bothered by the fly perched on his ear.

relative of the woodchuck. At lower altitudes, large mammals surviving are deer and wild boar, while small ones include hares, squirrels, badgers and foxes.

Hawks, owls, cuckoos, woodpeckers, jays and blackbirds are some of the many bird species found; fish, including trout and salmon, are numerous; and of reptiles, the viper is frequently observed.

FLORA

A few plants grow above the altitude of 7,000 feet, but these are dwarf herbs. Here,

Terraced hills rise from the water in a lovely village in the canton of Ticino, where grain, orchard fruits and grapes grow on the sunny slopes.

In the 16th century, with the arrival of John Calvin in Geneva, the city became the focal point of the Protestant Reformation. The tradition of intellectual leadership was carried on through the 18th century, with Voltaire and Jean Jacques Rousseau among the most prominent residents. Yet for all the activity going on in Geneva today, the city sometimes seems as placid as its lake.

A spacious hall hewn entirely out of the solid ice of the glacier on the Jungfrau is one of the most unusual tourist attractions in the world. Some 65 feet below the surface of the glacier are this booth and wine cask of solid ice. A new entrance to the hall must be cut each year because the glacier is continually moving.

In Basel, the second largest city in Switzerland, an ancient cathedral and a university founded in 1459 give the city a strong historical feeling, yet here too are international financial firms and busy textile and chemical factories. The Rhine divides the old and new parts of town.

where summer lasts little more than a month, a hundred species of tiny flowering plants, including the well-known edelweiss, form brief carpets of bloom while the sun is high overhead. Farther down the slopes is a rich vegetation of low shrubs—rhododendron, heath, dwarf pines and dwarf willows. Above 4,000 feet coniferous trees predominate in the woodlands, while below that level are forests of beech and oak. In the south, along the lakes on the Italian border, Mediterranean plants grow in orchards, parks and gardens: palms, camellias, figs, oranges and almonds.

Ibex, about the size of a large goat, are agile animals with hoofs that can cling easily to rocky surfaces. Ranging the mountain snow line in summer, ibex leap about with a nimbleness mountain climbers envy.

The Council Chamber in the Palace of the League of Nations at Geneva has imposing panels depicting the horrors and futility of war.

Cable cars are frequently found in Switzerland transporting sightseers over rugged slopes for breathtaking mountaintop panoramas.

586 ■ SWITZERLAND

THE PEOPLE

Perhaps the most remarkable thing about the self-contained little country is that its people, numbering more than 6,000,000, belong to several different and distinct ethnic groups, each with its own language. Approximately 72% of the population speaks Swiss-German, 21% French, 6% Italian, and 1% Romansch, a language derived from spoken Latin. Swiss-German is a language of dialects, too, and almost every village has its own variation, although written German is the same.

In other countries where several languages are spoken, it often happens that the German-speaking people are classed as Germans, the French-speaking as French, and so on. Such habits are utterly alien to the Swiss way of thinking, for here no matter what a man's mother tongue may be, he is first and foremost Swiss. Indeed, in each of these languages as it is spoken in Switzerland, there is a genuinely Swiss element which binds the people together and is itself the product of the encounter and mingling of different European cultures in the Federation.

Just as the different languages and the differences in culture are a typical feature of the Swiss national character, the various religions also help to enrich a common national life, and have been a powerful factor in educating the people in tolerance and in instilling a respect for the rights of others. In Switzerland just over half of the people are Protestant, over 45 per cent are Catholic and less than 2 per cent are of other religions.

Also contributing to the variety among the Swiss people is the contrast between town and country, urban and rural areas. Nearly two-thirds of the population lives in rural districts, in villages and towns of less than 10,000 inhabitants, with some 75 per cent settled in

A large part of Switzerland's prosperity has been derived from the watch- and clock-making industry, yet this sundial still serves as the clock on a village church in the canton of Berne.

the Midlands, the rest in the Jura and the Alps. Zurich, the largest city, has less than 500,000 people. Even with the growth of cities in the last decade, the urban element is still decentralized. The industrialization of Switzerland took place without the growth of huge towns, and nowhere in Switzerland are there the gloomy industrial areas which have sprung up elsewhere.

While the Switzerland of officialdom may be sober in the extreme, the Swiss people themselves have always loved the gay pageantry in which their local traditions find expression. In spite of their very modern way of life, there are

A local bull drinks his fill in the trough set in a Grisons square.

Everywhere in the world children use the streets as their playground. Here a cobbled hill in the canton of Ticino absorbs three small girls.

The inhabitants of this lonely house on Mount Pilatus in central Switzerland have a remark-able view of the countryside beneath them, but coming home late at night must present problems.

many local and national events which serve as reminders that the past is not dead and is worthy of meditation and enjoyment. They range from century-old ceremonies commemorating national victories to popular pageants and processions. Each district has its own folklore and its vivid festivals, which differ greatly in character according to whether the population speaks German, French, Italian or Romansch, for despite the great unity, each group cherishes its typical way of life.

Each district, too, has its own traditional costume, many of them costly works of art, and these enhance the unique picturesqueness of the age-old festivals and processions. It is a mistake to suppose that the many fêtes are merely shows staged artificially to attract more visitors. They have a living background, as they evolved from old-time customs and the traditions of an ancient people with a stirring history.

Zurich is Switzerland's largest city, both in number of people and economic importance. Here, too, the old and the new co-exist: silk and cotton, radio and automobile, printing and food production are carried on in the shadows of ancient churches and modern buildings.

A Swiss Alpenhorn trio blows a pastoral serenade in the Säntis area of eastern Switzerland. An instrument known as far back as 1280, the horn was originally used by the men of the high mountain districts as a call to battle, a signal for help against marauders or a warning of fire. Played fortissimo, it can be heard as far away as 8 miles with a carrying wind, and is at its best when played in the mountains where the echoes give the tones a marvellous effect. The horn is handmade entirely of mountain pine which is dried and seasoned for two years and then carved.

590 ■ **SWITZERLAND**

The Swiss take pride in their thriftiness, and this housewife carefully inspects the meat in an outdoor stall in Morges before making her decision.

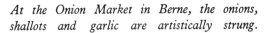

At the Onion Market in Berne, the onions, shallots and garlic are artistically strung.

When the annual autumn fair is held in the canton of Valais, the ladies have a chance to do some shopping. The high-crowned black headgear are as old and traditional in the canton as is the manufacture of fine linens and woollens, which began in Switzerland in the 13th century.

Tile stoves are still the pride of many Swiss homes. This stone-lined medieval stove is a triumph of ceramic skill. The attractive tiles display heraldic designs, prominent people and religious and historic scenes. This stove is still used in the city hall of Chur.

Not everything in Switzerland is old. Modern design has gained great acceptance, especially by the students who lead the avant-garde in every country.

Switzerland's new schools not only educate an ever-growing number of children, but compare well architecturally with modern schools elsewhere.

Doing the laundry is a social affair in the Engadine, where the village trough has served as a community gathering place for many years.

Marketing in front of the town hall of Basel is a lively affair. No matter what the Swiss people may be doing, they are never out of touch with the activities of government.

The Swiss are a deeply religious people, and individual differences are respected in this sphere as in all others. This simple but powerful statue is in Unter-Engadine, in the canton of Grisons.

The boarding schools of Switzerland have an international reputation and are attended by students from all parts of the world. It is only fitting that Swiss schools should provide all the advantages of an excellent education, plus a carefully planned program for physical development and recreation, for Switzerland was the home of Johann Pestalozzi, who laid the foundations of modern elementary education in the 18th century.

MEN OF ACHIEVEMENT

Small Switzerland has fathered many leaders in the arts and sciences, some of whom have lived abroad and become identified with their adopted countries. Two famous Americans were of Swiss birth: Albert Gallatin (1761–1849), diplomat, congressman, and financial genius, who as United States Secretary of the Treasury did much to put the new republic on a

Children's homes have been established in Swiss mountain regions, famous for their excellent climate, for the benefit of delicate youngsters and for the convenience of parents who may have to board their children temporarily.

The University of Lausanne is only one of seven universities noted for high academic standards.

sound financial footing; and Louis Agassiz (1807–73), the great naturalist, who, at Harvard University, advanced the teaching of the natural sciences.

In the Renaissance and Reformation periods two famous and controversial Swiss were the chemist and physician Philippus Aureolus Paracelsus (1493?–1541), whose real contributions to medicine were offset by his dabbling in alchemy and magic; and Ulrich Zwingli (1484–1531), who was instrumental in establishing Protestantism in his country.

The Romantic movement in Western literature owes much to the philospher, Jean-Jacques Rousseau (1712–88), who spent most of his life in France. Modern man's understanding of the

The clocktower in Berne forms the background for two cyclists on a day's outing.

Switzerland has certainly had its share of famous native sons and daughters. Johann Pestalozzi, the founder of modern elementary education, is appropriately pictured with a small boy.

Renaissance was aided by the studies of the historian Jakob Burckhardt (1818–97).

Friedrich Dürrenmatt (1921–   ) is the author of enigmatic modern dramas, such as *The Visit*, which have been staged throughout the world; Arthur Honegger (1892–1955), a leading modern composer domiciled in France, is known for oratorios such as *King David* and symphonic works such as *Pacific 231*. The theologian, Karl Barth (1886–1968) has exerted a profound influence over modern religious thought.

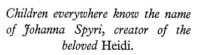

Children everywhere know the name of Johanna Spyri, creator of the beloved Heidi.

THE ECONOMY

Switzerland has practically no raw materials or natural resources except waterpower. With only 16.5% of the working population employed in forestry and agriculture, the country produces only about 30% of the food it needs. The result, then, is that imports far exceed exports. The one natural product Switzerland does have in abundance is stone, and limestone, sandstone, cement and marble are exported.

With the industrial revolution in the 19th century, Switzerland developed into a highly industrialized country, importing all the necessary raw materials and converting them into high-quality finished products for export. It is in this way that the Swiss achieved their high standard of living. Since Switzerland cannot compete with mass production methods, its manufacturers concentrate on quality and perfection as one of the means of meeting foreign competition. Most of the industries are decentralized and consist of small or medium-sized concerns in which the skill and craftsmanship of the individual worker are at a premium. Because of Swiss artisans, the phrase "Made in Switzerland" has come to stand for quality and precision.

Swiss watches, of course, are highly regarded throughout the world. Switzerland also has a highly developed machinery industry whose products range from heavy electrical equipment and diesel engines to textile machines, machine tools and precision instruments.

The greatest number of Swiss workers are employed in the building industry. There is also a thriving textile industry, and high-grade silks, cotton fabrics, embroideries and knitwear are produced. Of even greater importance is the Swiss chemical industry, which manufactures dyestuffs and pharmaceuticals.

Swiss watches are synonymous with accuracy and precision. Watchmaking in Switzerland dates from the 16th century and attained its greatest prosperity after the second World War, when the demand for Swiss watches reached an all-time peak. Today Switzerland exports 95% of the watches it manufactures. Between 40,000 and 70,000 people are employed in the Swiss watchmaking industry, and most of them are highly skilled. It is the intense productive effort of the working force that has compensated for the lack of natural resources, and has transformed a poor country into a rich one.

A visitor to Switzerland can be sure that the souvenirs he buys are authentically handcrafted.

Among the foods, Swiss cheese and other milk products, chocolate and preserves are exported in large quantities, and Swiss wines, produced mostly in the western part of the country, are appreciated by connoisseurs everywhere.

Recently Swiss books, particularly in the fields of art and science, have become an important export.

Contributing to Switzerland's prosperity is the fact that there are no currency restrictions or exchange controls. Swiss currency, with its basic monetary unit the franc, is freely convertible. A sound financial policy, combined with political stability and the absence of upsetting economic factors, has given Switzerland an international reputation for reliability and financial security. These elements have also made Switzerland one of the financial and banking capitals of the world.

Although only one-sixth of the wage-earners are actively involved in agriculture and forestry, the Swiss have by no means abandoned the land. They are, for the most part, a people rooted in the soil and since there are no great urban concentrations, those not engaged in working the land have kept their attachment to it.

After the cheese has set, the curd is removed from the heating vat.

The dividing of the cheese is an ancient and picturesque custom in the Bernese Oberland. Each September the people from the region set out to call for their cheeses, which have been made on the high pastures from the milk of their cows.

The agricultural products are as varied as the land and the soil. Cattle, horses and pigs are raised, and dairy products are important to the economy.

One of the most important sources of national revenue is the tourist industry, with more than 8000 hotels, pensions and inns known the world over. It is the extraordinary concentration of the natural beauty and an excellent transportation network that have made Switzerland an ideal vacationland visited annually by millions of tourists. Some enjoy the picturesque lakes, swimming and sailing or mountain climbing in summer, some visit historic sites and art treasures, others ascend mountains in cog railways or cable cars to see the superb panoramas.

The dairymen in charge of the cattle keep a careful record of the quantity of the milk produced by each cow, and then the owners collect a corresponding quantity of cheese. Under this system, some wealthy farmers may be entitled to a great number of cheeses, while the less fortunate will receive but one or two. Since many will not want the cheeses due to them, the surplus is disposed of by auction.

Fine craftsmanship is highly regarded and encouraged. To safeguard the quality of workmanship on which the Swiss economy depends, there are laws and regulations. Only qualified "masters" who have served their apprenticeship are allowed to go into business for themselves. Here a skilled woodcarver makes small figures that will find their way into homes the world over, while his young daughter watches intently. Some day she may carry on the business.

In recent years the tobacco industry has begun to thrive, with about 125 factories employing some 7,500 workers. The photograph shows a spacious shed for the drying of tobacco.

The Swiss are not only expert skiers—but also expert wood ski makers. After the hickory is sawed, it is carefully seasoned in sheds for several years before being converted. A shortage of acceptable grade hickory has necessitated the importing of some American wood into Switzerland.

Haymaking near Interlaken, with the famous Jungfrau, 13,668 feet high, in the background.

FOREIGN RESIDENTS

It is estimated that during the many European wars before the 18th century a total of 2,000,000 Swiss went abroad to serve in foreign armies. Today the influx of peaceful foreigners to Switzerland in a single year is more than double that number. In addition, there are 700,000 alien residents—about 11 per cent of the population. Some of these are drawn from all over the world, employees of the many international organizations and private firms making their headquarters in Switzerland. But the majority are Italian and German workers employed in Swiss industry.

All through the working day the musicians play, lightening the toil. Perhaps on their way home the sound of yodelling will replace the music. Yodelling, in which the natural voice suddenly shifts to a falsetto, is believed to have evolved from the evening prayers chanted at sunset.

Farming is a family occupation, with children literally pitching in.

At Champéry in the Valais, food provisions for the dairy people summering on the high pastures used to be transported in this manner. The custom survives today at the annual Costume Festival.

Every April the slopes south of Sierre in the Rhone Valley resound with the music of flutes and drums. This is a sign that the peasants of the mountain villages of Chandolin and St. Luc are working in their vineyards. The men march to work in column fashion, the musicians leading, the farmers shouldering shovels and hoes close behind, while children watch and cheer them on.

On the Lake of Neuchâtel, noted for the Fendant and other white wines, the grapes are provisionally pressed right in the vineyards and the casks are filled. Further refining processes are carried on in the wine cellars.

SWITZERLAND ■ 603

Folk dancing is usually part of every festival, and the festivals are many, providing recreation to natives and tourists alike. The Swiss flag, a white cross on a red background, hangs from a balcony; the bull is the heraldic emblem of the canton of Uri. Each wine-growing area has its vintage festival in the autumn; Geneva celebrates its victory over the forces of the Duke of Savoy in 1602; a gay carnival is held in Basel; Zurich hails the arrival of spring with a historic pageant organized by the Guilds, with the grand finale the burning of an effigy of winter. At Neuchâtel an ancient tradition of cross-bow marksmanship is maintained by the "Noble Company of Musketeers" and during a religious celebration in a high valley of the Valais, "God's Grenadiers" parade in century-old uniforms.

Meat is sure to be tender when it's sliced "high off the hog."

The snow-covered Jungfrau rises high above a field of flowers in the Bernese Oberland.
True to tradition, the boy carries an alpenstock, the girl clings to her big sister's skirt.

For the many who are enthusiastic mountain climbers, mountains are not merely to be admired and dreamt of. They make men see a vision and they present a challenge. Both in summer and winter, the Swiss mountains invite access. Chair lifts and mountain huts make the approach to the high slopes relatively easy. Then comes the test of skill and bravery!

TOURISM

As a winter sports resort Switzerland is unexcelled. Around 5,000,000 people spend their holidays in Switzerland every year. They come from all parts of the world, in summer and winter, for a robust sporting holiday or for rest and relaxation amid magnificent scenery.

Superb tourist facilities—excellent hotels and recreation sites, good transportation, and varied natural scenery—make Switzerland an ideal vacation spot all year round. Swiss stress on comfort, efficiency, and proficiency in other languages helps to make the visitor's stay a happy one. For those who are not sports-minded, the country offers shopping for fine Swiss products, sightseeing in medieval towns and villages, visiting the many first-rate museums, and simply

The Swiss are very sports-minded, partly because universal military training makes them aware of the need for physical fitness. Here a rink in St. Moritz is the scene of a game of curling, in which "curling stones" are hurled along a level stretch of ice in an attempt to get close to a mark.

Ice skating is enjoyed in a picture postcard setting.

relaxing in picturesque surroundings. Two dozen spas throughout the country are famous for their mineral waters.

Swiss cuisine offers many regional specialties: *raclette* and *fondue* (melted cheese dishes) are typical of the French-speaking cantons; sausages, ham, air-dried beef (*Bundnerfleisch*) tempt the palate in the German-speaking districts. Swiss wines, especially the white ones, are delicate and best when new; and Swiss brandies such as *Kirsch* and *Pflumli* are strong and aromatic.

Recreational facilities of Switzerland are not limited to the visitor—the Swiss people take full advantage of all their country has to offer, and skiing, mountaineering, skating and sailing are enjoyed by young and old.

No matter how many people come each year to the Alpine slopes, there is room to accommodate them all as they skim over the crisp, dry snow. Skiing in Switzerland is a way of life, with every third Swiss an expert at the slalom and schuss.

When the natural rinks are melted, the Swiss skaters keep in shape on this beautiful ice skating rink at Davos. It is operated all summer long.

The ride to the top of the high ski run offers skiers an exciting view of the white-blanketed countryside.

Switzerland is not all ice and snow. There is much to attract the less energetic, and sight-seers have a wide choice of views. Here is the Castle of Chillon on the Lake of Geneva near Montreux.

"Devil's Bridge," subject of several paintings by J. M. W. Turner early in his career, is too small to handle modern-day traffic and has now been joined by a higher modern bridge.

The "snake" is actually a steep road with hairpin turns leading through the St. Gotthard Pass across a high point in Switzerland's rugged, beautiful Alps.

Known in Switzerland as the Year of the Alps, 1965 was celebrated for the 100th anniversary of the first ascent of the Matterhorn. Mountain climbers take great risks but are rewarded with views like this.

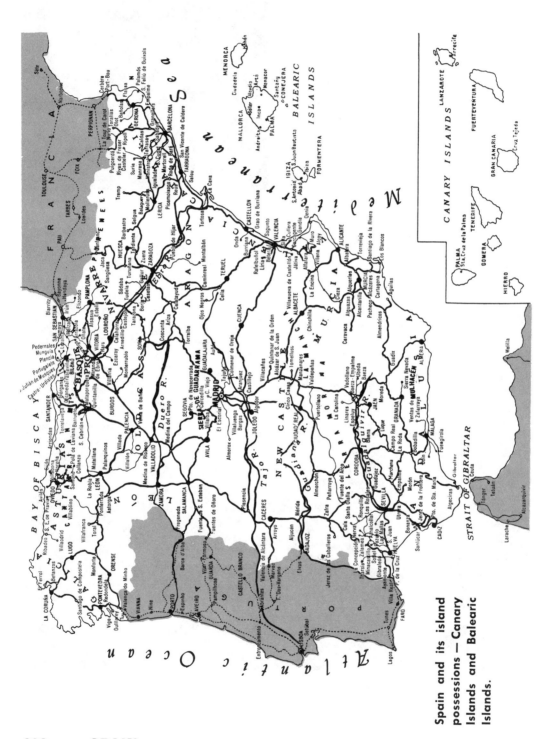

Spain and its island possessions — Canary Islands and Balearic Islands.

SPAIN

THE LAND

SPAIN OCCUPIES about five-sixths of the squarish peninsula attached to southwest Europe. This peninsula, called Iberia, is separated from France by the extremely high Pyrenees Mountains, where the Basques and other mountain peoples live. Off to the west of Spain running north-south along the Atlantic coast, divided from Spain by natural barriers, is the small but important nation of Portugal, a friend with whom Spain has long lived in peace. At the southern tip of Spain is the gigantic Rock of Gibraltar, only 8½ miles across the straits

A scene in Oviedo, a town on a steep hillside in the Cantabrian Mountains. The many mountains of Spain have hindered national unity for centuries by cutting off communication between valleys, causing villagers to live in relative isolation.

The drainage from a lagoon near Avila. Spaniards call any water that flows—no matter how little—rio (river).

from Africa, where in prehistoric times a land-bridge once must have existed.

Spain also owns two groups of islands. One, the Balearics, consists of four islands—Mallorca, Menorca, Ibiza, and Formentera—in the Mediterranean off Spain's east coast. The other group, the Canary Islands (named after the Latin word for dogs—*canis*) are 60 miles off the coast of Morocco, in the Atlantic.

CLIMATE

A land of great variety and contrast, Spain itself averages a mere 500 miles from north to south and slightly less from east to west. Its climate is not always as pleasant as the "sunny Spain" label seems to imply, but it is certainly warmer than most of Europe. Northern Spain lies where winds from the west coming across the Atlantic bring weather (and rainfall) from that direction; the Gulf Stream, too, brushes the Atlantic coast of northern Spain where it merges with the North Atlantic Stream. As a result, Spain's northern provinces have moderate climates, with no great extremes. Southern Spain gets its weather from the Mediterranean, and so has a very short winter and rather hot summer.

The rains are irregular. A few large drops for a few hours of a few days of the year may be all that southern Spain gets. Much of southeast Spain is arid (10 inches annually), but in the north and west along the Bay of Biscay and the Atlantic rainfall may be as heavy as 66 inches. My Fair Lady may tell us, "The rain in Spain stays mainly in the plain," but this is not true.

A view from a villa near Palma in Mallorca. On the hilltop in the background is Bellver Castle, framed by the Mediterranean Ocean. Mallorca is the largest of the Balearic Islands, which are off the mainland's east coast.

PHYSICAL FEATURES

Although the coastline is long (1,350 miles), Spain has relatively few good ports. Ranges of mountains come close to the sea on the Biscay and Mediterranean sides, leaving only narrow strips of land along the coast. The best port is at Cádiz, near Gibraltar, but on the Atlantic side, where there is a broad coastal plain and where the Guadalquivir, Spain's deepest river, empties. The British own the port of Gibraltar, which is not only a fueling station for many ships crossing from the Mediterranean to the Atlantic, but the Rock itself is a strong fortress protecting the narrow channel. The whole Mediterranean coast is rocky except for a low swampy area around the port of Valencia, and a great river delta near the port of Barcelona. Small natural ports along the Galician coast on the Bay of Biscay provide bases for Spain's sardine and anchovy fishing fleets.

The greatest contrasts exist in the surface of the land. There are vast expanses of moorland, desert, rocky slopes, and a broad plateau (called the Meseta) covering the interior half of the Iberian peninsula. To the north and northeast are snow-capped mountains rising with Alpine grandeur (average height greater than the Alps), often with sheltered, rich, and beautiful valleys at their base. In the Basque country and elsewhere there are rolling forest-clad hills. Near these hills are broad plains, some uninhabitable and others irrigated by a network of canals and richly cultivated.

It is said that the Meseta is the true Spain, geologically, geographically, and politically. It is isolated from the coast on all sides by mountains (the Cantabrians and Pyrenees on the north and northeast, the Sierra Morenas on the south), and by the Portuguese border on the west. The Meseta itself slopes gradually from north to south and from west to east; it is not a lowland, but a rocky shelf or plateau about 2,000 feet above sea level. In this area are the provinces of New Castile and Old Castile, Aragon and Navarre; in the very middle is the capital city of Madrid. Since Roman times, roads from the Meseta to Léon and Galicia in the north, and to Cordoba, Sevilla, and Cádiz in the southwest, went through the river valleys. From Madrid to Valencia by road is difficult even today.

Scenically, Spain is a delight. From Madrid can be seen the Sierra de Guadarrama range rising out of the plateau of Old Castile. In these mountains is El Escorial, the summer home and also the burial place of many kings. Spain's highest peak (11,420 feet) is Mulhacén, near Granada, in the Sierra Nevadas (after which the Californian range is named). Along the Bay of Biscay in Galicia are the *rías* or fjords while, along the coast north of Barcelona, is a long sandy beach ending in the Costa Brava ("wild coast"), rugged and picturesque.

Spain's mountains sometimes rise to heights which ensure a perpetual covering of snow. One such group are these in the Pyrenees Mountains.

The region around Santander on the north coast is mountainous. Located here are some of the country's few forests.

In subtropical Andalusia, known as "the frying pan," are beautiful fountains, shaded patios and awning-covered streets.

AGRICULTURE

In spite of generally arid and poor soil, and little mechanization, Spain's agriculture is a mainstay of the nation's economy. In the southern plain of Andalusia, are olive groves, oranges and lemons, and grapes; along the southern coastal plain are date palms, bananas, rice, cotton, almonds, figs, and pomegranates in abundance. In the wooded areas south of Barcelona are the famous cork oaks (Spain provides one-fourth of the world's cork supply); elsewhere the woods contain pine, fir, ash, birch, beech, poplar, oak, and sweet chestnut.

The fabled thick forests that ancient writers mentioned have all but disappeared from Spain, and today less than 5 per cent of the land is wooded. Through the centuries the forests were cut and destroyed, partly because greedy landowners wanted more room for their grazing sheep, and partly because of a mistaken belief by some of Spain's nobility

that the birds living in the trees harmed crop cultivation. Even the birds have gone, except for the hardy sparrow and starling. Without birds, insects are abundant. With the decline of the forest, too, went water, which normally is stored by trees and is needed for irrigation as well as for power. Floods swept away vegetation, caused electricity to be rationed at times, and even caused Spain to import vegetable oils instead of exporting them. In this century, efforts have been made to reforest, but not enough success has yet been achieved to supply Spain's needs for timber in its general rebuilding.

Trees normally help rivers maintain an even flow. Without them, rivers dwindle in the dry season to little more than a trickle; some even disappear to the point where they can be used as roadways. After a brief rain, these rivers swell to raging torrents that sweep everything in their paths. Harnessing the rivers for irrigation and for electric output is not so difficult, and Spain has started developing hydroelectric projects along its longest river, the Ebro, and its tributaries. But for transportation, the rivers which formerly were

A panoramic view of the valley of Riano, a national park in León. This park is noted for its excellent hunting and fishing areas and also for its parador (*a government-operated tourist inn*).

mainstreams of communication are largely unsuitable today. One city, Sevilla, for example, some 40 miles inland but reached by the Guadalquivir River, was once a focal point for much sea-going traffic with Spain's colonies. Galleons unloading their cargoes of gold and silver at Sevilla were frequent sights. But today the river's depth can no longer accommodate ocean-going vessels.

MINERALS

Since ancient times when the Phoenicians occupied Spain, it has been a rich storehouse of mineral wealth, a leading producer of copper, mercury, sulphur, lead, and iron ore. However, in the 20th century, other deposits outside Europe were discovered and exploited, while Spain went through periods of political upset and declined in importance partly because of a lack of capital. Spain was also well known for many centuries for its precious metals—silver and gold—which are still being worked. Deposits of manganese, tin ore, and wolfram have been found, and are important because of their use in armaments.

A scene in Guipuzcoa. Travel by small boat is common in a land criss-crossed by waterways, in which mountainous terrain and poor roadways discourage land travel.

The Alcázar (fortress and castle) in Segovia in central Spain, built in the 11th century by Alfonso VI.

HISTORY

LIKE MANY Mediterranean countries, Spain underwent repeated invasions thousands of years before recorded history. Cave paintings 15,000 years old suggest that Spain's early inhabitants were relatively intelligent and gifted. Other relics, from the Copper Age, indicate that parts of Spain were peopled with peaceful village-dwellers who ground grain, wove linen and hemp, and worked silver and copper.

PRE-ROMAN SPAIN (1100–206 B.C.)

Sea-going Phoenician traders founded Cádiz around 1100 B.C., for trade with the "tin isles" (British Isles). The Phoenicians introduced iron, arts and crafts, and writing. When the Greeks came 500 years later, they brought their own splendid culture, then at its height. They built roads, theatres, aqueducts, and schools. From Africa, the Carthaginians, in the

The aqueduct in Segovia that brings water from a spring 10 miles away is a heritage from Roman times. It was built of chiselled interlocking stones without the aid of mortar and reaches a height of 100 feet.

6th century B.C., were invited to help Cádiz fight off invaders from the north, and they stayed for conquest. These descendants of Phoenicians preceded the Romans in trying to make a single state of Spain and were successful as far north as the Ebro River in Castile.

THE ROMANS (133 B.C.–409 A.D.)

When the Roman legions came, the loyal and independent natives (Celtiberians) fiercely resisted them and forced them to conquer every pass and hamlet separately. The Roman conquest, bloody and cruel, lasted to 133 B.C., but uprisings and revolts continued for two centuries longer.

During the 600 years of occupation, Spain became one of the most thoroughly Romanized of all the provinces. The country was completely transformed in laws, customs, political structure, language, architecture, and eventually in religion. The Roman Church, in fact, worked one of the most important transformations of all, which conditioned Spain's history through the present period.

The Romans built roads, aqueducts, temples, bridges, and arenas. Their walled camps often grew into cities. *Emerita* became Mérida, noted for its amphitheatre and other Roman ruins; *Caesarea Augusta* became Zaragoza; *Asturica Augusta*, Astorga; *Pax Augusta*, Badajóz. At Italica, an important Roman town near Sevilla, are baths, old walls, an aqueduct, and the remains of an amphitheatre that once seated 40,000. Nearby peasant homes boast floors of Roman mosaic, and Roman lamps have been dug up from the fields.

Spain's incorporation into the empire is reflected in Roman culture. Four Roman emperors were either born in Spain or of Spanish ancestry: Hadrian, Trajan, Theodosius, and Marcus Aurelius. Among other Romans of Spanish origin were both of the Senecas, who were born in Cordoba; Martial the poet, and Quintilian the orator.

THE VISIGOTHS (409–711)

When the Roman Empire fell, the peoples of the north overran both Italy and Spain.

The Palace of Charles V in the Alhambra. Not part of the Moorish Palace, this building is neoclassical in design, with plain stone exterior walls around an open courtyard.

This bridge across the Tajo River was built by the Romans. It was later repaired by the Moslems and, in the 14th century, was reconstructed.

After 400 years of peace, Spain put up weak resistance. Once the Visigoths captured Barcelona, they rapidly engulfed all of Spain.

The Visigothic period was one of disorder, except for the stabilizing influence of the church. The vigorous Visigoths were culturally inferior, but partly civilized and nominally Christian. Nonreligious education was nonexistent under the Visigoths, though the scholars were church-sheltered (among them St. Isidore of Sevilla, whose monumental works touched on all branches of knowledge to that time). In the way of material structures, the Visigoths left little, but some of their splendid crowns and jewels may still be seen in the Armería in Madrid. They also left a legal code, which later became the basic Spanish law.

THE MOSLEMS AND THE CHRISTIAN RECONQUEST (711–1492)

The Moslems (usually called Moors) who invaded Spain by way of Gibraltar brought a rich and splendid culture and stayed for 800 years. The Moslem invasion coincided with the decline of Visigoth rule and King Roderic was overthrown.

Spain's Arabian ruler was virtually independent of the rest of the Moslem world, and treated the people well except for heavy taxes and land confiscation. Spaniards were allowed to exercise their own religion; some, called *renegados* by their countrymen, converted to Islam. All Christians in Moslem territory were known as *Mozárabes*.

In Moslem Spain, extensive irrigation systems helped agriculture thrive, and flourishing commerce brought wealth to the people. At a time when other European cities wallowed in poverty and filth, Cordoba was a spacious metropolis rambling along the banks of the Guadalquivir for 10 miles, filled with splendid palaces and many public bathhouses. Education and the arts blossomed. Cordoba's library housed 400,000 volumes; the university, where classes were held in the Great Mosque (*La Mezquita*), attracted students from all over western Europe. Advances were made in medi-

Two views of the monastery at El Escorial. This austere palace-mausoleum of Philip II was built in the 16th century and is the burial vault of many Spanish monarchs. The structure has 16 towers, 86 stairways, 1,110 windows, and 2,800 doors.

cine, law, astronomy, philosophy, mathematics, and geography. The great scholar Maimonides, a Jew who wrote in Arabic, lived during this time.

The Moslems expressed their love of beauty in music, poetry, leatherwork, and architecture. The very word "arabesque" suggests how much their artistic gift ran to decoration. They allowed no images of their deity, but worshipped amidst lavish and sensuous beauty. Many of their buildings remain, though most have undergone adaptation to Christian use, such as the *Mezquita* in Cordoba. Other famous structures are the Alhambra in Granada, the Giralda and the Alcázar of Sevilla, and the Generalife. Moslem music was a highly developed art, using complex rhythms. The Moslems introduced the lute to Europe.

A number of small Christian kingdoms, scarcely more than principalities, persisted across the north of Spain: Galicia, Asturias, León, Navarre, Castile, Aragon, and Catalonia. Although their kings often warred with one another, they knew a centralized rule was needed for the sake of order and to drive out the Moslems. A consolidation process began, making slow progress because the nobles also ruled little sections of their own and were loath to submit to any central authority. In the 11th century, Alfonso VI, king of Castile and León, managed to unite the Christian kings sufficiently to push the Moslems as far south as Toledo and Valencia. His able organizer was Rodrigo Díaz de Vivar, celebrated as Spain's national hero, El Cid. During the next two centuries, succeeding kings pushed the Moslems further south. For the last 250 years of their presence in Spain, the Moslems controlled an ever-shrinking territory.

The stream of development through these medieval centuries focused around two principal struggles. One was between monarch and nobles; the other between the industrial classes in the towns and the great landowners whose interests were vested in agriculture. Consequently, Spain was almost continually torn by civil strife, during which time Castile emerged as Spain's most powerful kingdom.

Toward the end of the 15th century, Castile

This pool in the gardens of the Alhambra is framed by a Moorish structure having massive rose-red towers, small windows, and deep underground rooms.

The house of Cristóbal Colón (Columbus) at Las Palmas on the Grand Canary Islands. Here is where the great discoverer spent his early years. ↓

An ancient windmill surrounded by cacti stands out against the landscape at Las Palmas.

came under the rule of Isabella, succeeding her deceased half-brother, Henry IV. At this time, Isabella was already married to Ferdinand, king of nearby Aragon. Each ruled a separate domain, but this personal union brought a kind of unity to Spain.

These two monarchs insisted that political unity include religious unity. To insure this, they introduced the Inquisition to Spain to wipe out heresy. Its efficient administrator, Tomás de Torquemada, tried and convicted thousands. The monarchs made the Inquisition answerable to them rather than to the bishops. It tried heretics and sent them to the civil arm of the law for punishment and confiscation of their estates.

The two rulers sheared the nobles of voting rights in the Royal Council by having the majority of votes come from the towns. They regularized the tax system and increased the revenues annually for 30 years, set up *audiencias* (royal courts) and clarified the jurisdiction between civil and ecclesiastical courts, and

The waterfront at Cádiz. The city's ancient name was Gadir. It was first settled by the Phoenicians who turned it into a thriving trading post.

reorganized the army. While occupied with driving the Moslems out of Granada, they found time to outfit three small ships for Cristóbal Colón (Columbus). They made it clear that any lands he might occupy would be administered by the crown of Spain. Thus they laid the cornerstone for a great colonial empire.

THE HAPSBURGS (1516–1700)

When Ferdinand died in 1516, his grandson, Charles of Ghent (also grandson of Maximilian of Austria), became king. There followed a period of grandeur, during which Spain became the world's greatest power. Its *Conquistadores* colonized immense areas in the Western Hemisphere from which flowed a steady stream for the mother country of precious metals and profits from trade with the colonies. It was a time of prosperity and glory.

As time went on, however, regulations on economic activity began to restrict trade. The military victories drained Spain's treasury as well as the reservoir of young men. In 1588, the resounding defeat of the Armada that Philip II sent to invade England set the all-around decline in force. By the end of the 16th century, Spain's commerce, agriculture, and manufacturing were suffering, and the population had declined by almost one million. The next hundred years brought more disasters, resulting in the loss of territory and prestige.

Throughout the 16th and 17th centuries, the importance of religion and the church in Spain was great. The Protestant Reformation in Spain made little headway—partly because of the efficiency of the Inquisition. Equally important were the Jesuits, an order founded in 1539 by St. Ignatius of Loyola. Members of this order refused to live in monasteries; they lived and worked among the people, in Spain and in overseas dominions. Wherever the colonizers went, the Jesuits followed.

THE BOURBONS (1700–1814)

Spain's first Bourbon king, Philip V, was the grandson of a Spanish princess. Her marriage to Louis XIV was intended to ensure

A unique feature near the port at Palma de Mallorca. The ancient windmills silhouetted against the sky were primitive means of providing power for irrigation and for other purposes.

Spirals of the unfinished church of the Holy Family (la Sagrada Familia) reach skyward. This structure in Barcelona was created in the late 19th century by the famed architect, Antonio Gaudí.

The altar in the enormous cathedral at Toledo. The sun shines copper-red through the polychrome glass of the upper windows.

perpetual peace between Spain and France. Philip was a mediocre man whose energies were diverted during his 46-year reign by the wars of the Spanish succession. In these, England took Gibraltar and Menorca, and alienated much of Spain's overseas commerce. After Philip came a long era of peace, in which Charles III and his ministers made many wise provisions on behalf of agriculture, trade, military service, education, and religion to the benefit of economic and intellectual life.

Toward the end of the 18th century, however, Charles IV found himself without a throne as Spain was overrun by Napoleon Bonaparte and the French. The Spaniards made every effort to expel them. English forces, led by Arthur Wellesley, who later became Duke of Wellington, helped drive out the French. In the meantime, Spanish colonies in the Americas seized the opportunity to break away, so that only a fragment was left of Spain's once-proud colonial empire.

The liberated Spaniards drew up the new Constitution of 1812, outlining a liberal democracy under a limited monarchy, and invited back Ferdinand VII, son of the abdicated Charles. At first called *Deseado* (the Longed For), Ferdinand very soon made himself disliked. He showed himself to be a staunch Bourbon who would not accept modern concepts. He tore up the constitution and ruled with unlimited power, executing liberals and even calling on the French to help crush an uprising among his own people.

THE MONARCHISTS AND REPUBLICANS (1814–1923)

After his death, more uprisings broke out and again in 1848, 1855, and 1873. Though there was a queen, Isabella II, Spain through the mid-19th century was ruled by the republicans—a succession of generals who imposed army control. This kind of government persisted until the corrupt Isabella II abdicated in 1868.

The question of a new form of government arose in the Cortes (legislature), which voted for a monarchy and invited in a new king from Savoy. He remained only two years; upon his departure, a republic was proclaimed. Unfortunately, not one of the four presidents of Spain's first republic could cope with the complex problems that confronted the nation. The republic collapsed in a little over a year.

The Spanish appeared confounded without royal leadership. They invited back the son of the deposed Isabella, Alfonso XII, who promised a constitutional monarchy. Under the new constitution, the Cortes consisted of two houses. The king was not responsible to it; his decrees, however, had to be signed by a responsible minister.

Alfonso XIII was born after the death of Alfonso XII in 1885. In the interim (until 1902) Spain was governed by a regent, the late king's widow, María Cristina. During these years, Spain fought another war, this time with the United States of America, losing Puerto Rico, Cuba and the Philippines.

When Alfonso XIII was 17, he was declared of age to rule. The country's problems proved beyond his power to resolve. Agrarian difficulties persisted: the *latifundios*, the great estates dating from the Middle Ages and owned by absentee landlords, still existed; many lay idle, while most Spaniards tried to eke a living from the land. There were some efforts at reforestation, and some schools were opened, but not enough of either. Conservative and liberal parties alternated in office, with no noticeable difference in the results, and splinter parties began to form.

MILITARY DICTATORSHIP (1923–1930)

In 1923, a military uprising in Barcelona triumphed without so much as a shot being fired. Primo de Rivera, its leader, became dictator and suspended the constitution. Rivera never instituted a constitutional government but he made some badly needed improvements in the roads and founded a new university city near Madrid. Finally, after seven years, republican sentiment revived and Rivera gave up and fled to Paris.

The king called in two successors, neither of whom remained more than a few months, and disorders multiplied. Some were suppressed,

The Columbus Monument at Barcelona. Columbus returned to this city from his first trans-Atlantic voyage to attend the court here.

A replica of Columbus' flagship, Santa María, is displayed in the bay at Barcelona. Of his three tiny ships, only this one was equipped with a deck.

SPAIN ■ 627

but republican leaders who were jailed went on with their activities from prison. Demonstrations of all kinds took place: against the church, against the monarchy, student uprisings, and strikes. In the elections of 1931, all the large cities turned in republican majorities (although the over-all results gave a monarchist victory). Alfonso XIII departed to avoid bloodshed.

THE SECOND REPUBLIC AND THE CIVIL WAR (1931–1939)

Alcalá-Zamora was proclaimed president of the Second Spanish Republic, and Catalonia, a self-governing republic, was persuaded to remain as part of Spain. Intellectual leaders all over the country participated in the new political life. They adopted a liberal constitution, renouncing war as an instrument of national policy. This constitution set up a unicameral (single chamber) Cortes, elected through universal suffrage, and having a president, a premier, and a cabinet. It separated church and state, took away from the clergy all government support after two years, and outlawed religious orders of certain types, threatening to confiscate their property. Education was to be taken from the clergy; all titles of nobility abolished; and the *latifundios* were to be divided up.

At once, monarchists and others showed dissatisfaction. In the elections held under the new constitution, they elected many members to the new Cortes. A stormy session followed.

Violent opposition arose to this conservative reaction. Rebellion developed in Oviedo, Asturias, where 1,300 people were killed before order could be re-established. The general who accomplished this was Francisco Franco, who led Moslem and Foreign Legion troops from Spanish Africa. The political climate grew stormier until, in 1936, the president dissolved the Cortes and called for new elections. The republicans, socialists, and communists formed a popular front and won.

Under the new republic, violence broke out, even in sections where trouble was unexpected. The republican government failed to quell these riots as well as the military rebellion that began in Spanish Morocco. The army rebellion was at first led by four generals, but General Franco quickly established himself as supreme commander and advanced on the Loyalist government. Franco's insurgents, the Falange, had most of the trained troops on their side—not only those of Spain but also the Fascist troops and matériel of Hitler and Mussolini. The republicans received little support from the Western democracies, which adopted policies of non-intervention. But volunteers from many

This view of the port at Palma shows the island's impressive Gothic cathedral in the background. The enormous and magnificent 14th century masterpiece stands broadly on its high terrace just at the water's edge.

countries went as individuals to fight with the Spanish republicans.

The Civil War raged for three horrible years, with both sides perpetrating fearful atrocities. Casualties were heavy: as high as 4 per cent of the population. Scarcely a family in Spain did not suffer some loss. Spanish refugees poured over the French border, where about 100,000 still remain; others, including many intellectuals, fled to England and the Americas.

The republicans held on to Madrid for more than 28 months, battered by Franco's besieging forces. At last the government retreated to Valencia; Franco split the republican territory by driving a column through it to the Mediterranean, and the government was removed to Barcelona. Premier Juan Negrín tried to hold on until the massive war threatening Europe began. He failed by only a few months.

General Francisco Franco, in 1936, was designated as chief of state and *caudillo* (military leader), and the state he intended to head as "broadly totalitarian" (a one party system). Two years after the fighting ceased, a quarter of a million political prisoners crowded Spain's prisons. In the World War II holocaust that began to engulf the world only a few months after the Civil War ended, exhausted Spain remained neutral.

Statues of the fictional Don Quixote and his henchman, Sancho Panza, stand before the Cervantes Monument in Madrid. In the background of this tribute to the 16th century author is the towering Edificio España.

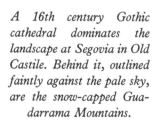

A 16th century Gothic cathedral dominates the landscape at Segovia in Old Castile. Behind it, outlined faintly against the pale sky, are the snow-capped Guadarrama Mountains.

THE GOVERNMENT

FOR PURPOSES of administration, Spain is divided into 52 small provinces under a central authority. Spaniards, often torn by local jealousies and loyalties, have been unable to maintain for long the ability to govern themselves, and their attempts at democratic government have been short-lived.

ADMINISTRATION

Spain's government has almost unlimited power. Although there is a cabinet, its 18 members are responsible only to its chief, Generalissimo Franco. A Cortes (legislature) does exist. Of 563 members, most are elected by an indirect and complicated system; 25, however, are appointed by the *Jefe de Estado* (Chief of State), Franco. The Cortes may enact laws but, to have effect, these must be approved by the chief of state. In place of a constitution, there are a series of "basic laws." In theory, the judicial system is independent, but all members are directly responsible to Franco, and justice is administered in his name.

Franco was chosen Chief of State in 1936 by a Junta or Committee of Generals. Technically, Spain is still in a state of war. The decree issued by the Defence Junta in 1936 is

The Royal Palace in Madrid was built by an Italian architect in the 18th century for French-born King Philip V, a Bourbon. The palace, now a museum, conforms to the cosmopolitan mood of the capital, and lacks provincial design.

still in effect and it gives Franco unlimited power. The United Nations at first refused to recognize the constitutionality of the Franco regime, and excluded Spain from membership until 1955.

Political debate is ineffectual; there is no "loyal opposition" as severe criticism may be regarded as treason. The press is censored by the government, the army, and the church. The only uncensored publication is *Ecclesia*, the organ of Catholic Action.

Political parties do not exist. The Falange was a political party organized along fascist lines in the early 1930's, but now its importance has receded; it is simply "the party," its head being the chief of state. Its purpose is to control all levels of political and economic life. The present governmental organization has been described as a pyramid. At the top is Franco; the bottom spreads out to include every one of Spain's adults. There are no independent trade unions in Spain, only workers' unions within the Falange. The policies of the unions are set up by government, which furnishes their leaders. Although to strike is illegal, the wave of miners' strikes that swept Spain in 1962 indicates the growing unrest of the workers.

In part, the force that holds Franco's dictatorship in power is the people's fear of another civil war or that a foreign power might attempt to resolve their internal affairs through intervention. Another factor is that the Franco régime has made improvements in social welfare: in housing, public health facilities, social insurance, education, and the organization of co-operatives. Social security covers accidents, and provides health and old-age insurance, cost-of-living bonuses, marriage grants, paid vacations, and family allowances. No doubt much of this progress has come about to prevent active revolt.

A private room in Tavera Hospital, Toledo. Medical care in Spain is provided under a government-sponsored national health scheme.

At León, along the Way of St. James, is this exquisite cathedral built of cream-tinted stone, one of the finest examples of Spanish Gothic architecture.

CONSTITUTIONAL CHANGES

In 1966 a series of mild reforms began, tending to relax, but only slightly, the tight control of the government. As a result 104 members of the Cortes are now elected by direct vote of heads of families and married women. A new press law, while maintaining censorship, guaranteed some measure of dissent to the press. In 1967 religious liberty was granted to non-Catholics, but was offset by a stipulation that members of non-Catholic churches be registered with the Ministry of Justice.

These slight reforms were considered to be possible first steps in a general liberalization in Spain, perhaps in response to increased opposition from students, workers, and even clergy; possibly in recognition of an improvement in the country's economy; and very likely to promote national unity as the day nears when age or disability will remove Franco from the

scene. One of the most significant provisions of the new laws is one spelling out (for the first time) the methods by which a successor to Franco will be chosen.

In July, 1969, Franco named his successor. He decreed that Prince Juan Carlos of Bourbon be his heir, granting him the title of "Prince of Spain." According to the new law of succession, the Prince will assume the title of King in the event of Franco's death or incapacitation. The Prince is a grandson of King Alfonso XIII, and a descendant of Queen Victoria of England.

THE CHURCH

The Roman Catholic church has always been a powerful influence in Spanish life. Spain's Roman Catholic leaders are perhaps the world's most conventional. The Spanish clergy has always been partners with government dictators. During the Civil War, for example, the clergy was strongly pro-Franco.

When the Civil War ended, Franco wiped out separation of church from state. His agreement with the Vatican provided: (1) The

An interior view of the cathedral at León. This structure was started in 1199 and completed in 1399.

The cathedral at Santiago de Compostela was built over a 9th-century tomb said to enshrine the body of St. James the Apostle, Spain's patron saint.

At Burgos is this monastery of St. Domingo de Silos, established in the 6th century. It is one of the oldest in Europe, and its Romanesque cloisters are considered among the most beautiful in the world.

been unsuccessful in attempts to encourage Spanish religious leaders to recognize social and economic advances in other countries. Today, however, a young priest's education includes economics, politics, and a survey of the modern world. This tends to align him more with the common people than was formerly the case. In 1956, during the Basque disturbances, many young priests asked their bishop for permission to publicly support the workers. Not only was permission denied, but many priests were shifted to other parishes. Spain's older clergymen, with a few exceptions, were trained in a world in which the church taught the common people obedience to the established order and made small effort to understand their problems and aspirations.

The church in Spain has many artistic treasures (non-income producing) and relatively small holdings in business and property. Thus, it is not as wealthy as the Catholic Church elsewhere.

Protestantism is considered a dividing force in Spain, while Catholicism is considered a source of unity. There are not more than 25,000 Protestants in the entire population of 32,000,000.

church receive a yearly subsidy; all church property be tax-exempt; (2) the educational system of Spain be put into the hands of the clergy; (3) the Roman Catholic religion be made the sole recognized religion of Spain.

The Roman Catholic church in Spain is closely linked with the Franco government; to be anti-Franco is to be anti-church.

For almost five centuries, the Vatican has

Note the names on the elaborate tombs at the Royal Monastery in the Escorial, Madrid. All the Hapsburg kings of Spain and their queens are buried here, with the exception of Philip I.

THE PEOPLE

IN A LAND where the people profess only one religion, Roman Catholicism, one might expect also to find a common language and ancestral tie. In Spain, however, four languages are spoken, and there is much diversity of custom.

LANGUAGE

The standard literary language of Spain is Castilian. It grew out of the vulgar Latin, known as "Romance," that was spoken—not written—in the final centuries of the Roman Empire. Written Spanish first appeared in documents of the 10th and 11th centuries.

The Catalan language grew partly from this tongue too. It is spoken in the eastern provinces, from Catalonia down the Mediterranean coast through Valencia. Since the Civil War, it has been discouraged: it is no longer taught in the

Pilgrims, en route to a shrine, cross the River Quema on their journey from Sevilla to Rocio.

provincial schools, and periodicals in which it had been written are suppressed. In recent years, one Catalan theatre has been permitted. Catalonians are a progressive and industrious people, particularly in trade and commerce. They are of an independent temperament and resist a centralized rule from Madrid.

The three Basque provinces are along the north coast and in the Pyrenees. (Not all the Basques live in Spain; there are four Basque provinces in southern France.) These people speak a language drastically different in structure from other European tongues. It is believed that the Basques and their language descended from the early peoples of the peninsula known as Iberians.

The Basques cling to their traditions, rarely intermarry with outsiders, and maintain a clan organization in which women are dominant.

A girl in typical Mallorcan dress, as worn on festive occasions.

Olive pickers in Ubeda, Jaén. Olives are one of Spain's chief exports and provide 40 per cent of the world's supply.

*Rocky cliffs and blue
Mediterranean waters
surround Tossa del Mar,
on the Costa Brava.*

There is a saying that "every Basque is a nobleman." In practice, this means they have little of the class divisions common elsewhere in Spain, even though differences in wealth exist.

In the northwest, the language—or dialect—most commonly spoken is Galician, which resembles Portuguese. The northwestern provinces were those heavily settled by Celts, having fair complexions, fair hair, and blue eyes.

Castilian—the language spoken by more than 100,000,000 of the world's people—is the language of central Spain (the Meseta). Castilian was widely exported during the time of Spain's colonial expansion. The only Latin-American country where it is not prevalent is Brazil. It is a language pleasant to the ear and lends itself to vivid figures of speech.

In the south of Spain are the dark-skinned Spaniards, descendants of those who inter-

View of Barcelona from El Tibidado Amusement Park.

An ox-cart driver moves his team slowly along the winding roads through the Riano Valley in León.

León woman carrying laundry down to the stream in the small community of Oreja de Sajambre.

Fishermen prepare their nets in La Selva Port at Gerona. Spain's annual catch of 600,000 tons of fish is the third largest in Europe.

married with the Arabic peoples. Many Arabic words were absorbed into the language, as many Moslem ways remain in Andalusian life.

TEMPERAMENT

Spaniards display a high regard for localism, as the mountainous terrain and a low rate of literacy have caused poor communications between people of different localities. Because of this, it is difficult to generalize about the Spanish as "a people."

Among the characteristics that are held in common are: fiery, intense personality; ability to adapt to any prevailing régime without losing individuality; unfailing sense of personal dignity; politeness and courtesy. Yet flashes of barbarism, even cruelty, have been noted. For example, in their idealizing bullfighting, regarding it as an expression of the union of life with death.

Baker preparing doughnuts on an outdoor stove in preparation for the Festivity of San Antonio in Madrid.

A woman washing in her kitchen in Córdoba. The well in the middle of the room provides the water supply, hoisted up in a wooden pail on a pulley suspended from a ceiling beam.

Brilliant sunshine bathes a tranquil street in Sagunto, near Valencia.

Holiday crowds in the summer resort of San Sebastian on the Bay of Biscay near the French border.

This porron *(or giant glass flask) is so heavy that anyone able to lift it to his mouth with one hand may drink his fill. It is a stunt that attracts tourists near Barcelona.*

A forest of shoppers and sight-seers mill about the Flea Market at El Rastro in Madrid.

640 ■ **SPAIN**

A woman strolls down a typical street in the city of Cáceres in the region of Estramadura. The people earn their livelihoods primarily breeding pigs in this area noted for its fine hams.

A Galician farmer employs an ox-cart to move a new hórreo *(family-sized granary).*

A Mallorcan farmer cultivates his field, within an orchard, with a horse-drawn plough.

A procession of townspeople in Murcia. This ox-drawn float pays a symbolic tribute to the corn harvest.

CULTURE

Such names as Cervantes, El Greco, and Segovia suggest the remarkable cultural contributions made by Spaniards to the world.

Literature. One of the earliest literary expressions was the epic poem. Spain's best-known epic is *El Cid*, a 3,700-line work based on the life of Rodrigo Díaz de Bivar, who lived in the 11th century. The hero is the beloved medieval Spaniard—brave, ingenious, honorable, and devoted to his family. This epic is in Castilian. The ballad literary form made its appearance in the Middle Ages. Many of the plots of Spanish ballads persist into our own time as bases for novels and dramas.

Spain's first novel appeared in 1499. *Celestina*, first published anonymously, was written by Fernando de Roja, a converted Jew of Burgos. From his book grew that peculiarly Spanish novel, the *picaresque*, which deals with the life of a *picaro*—a Spaniard who lives by his wits and attaches himself to various masters.

Perhaps Spain's greatest novel is *Don Quixote*, written by Miguel de Cervantes in 1605. Its popularity has survived three centuries. The author lived a life almost as adventurous as his hero and is also noted for his dramas, poetry, and pastoral novels. He is buried in an unmarked grave at a convent in Madrid.

Theatre. Companies of players wandered about Spain in the 16th century, presenting their dramas. During this period Spain had its most active cultural expansion, so much so that the mid-16th to mid-17th century period has been called Spain's Golden Age. During this time the great dramatist Lope de Vega Carpio lived. His *comedias* were in constant demand, for theatre-going was popular. He produced more than 800 full-length plays, and many one-act *autos* (short-religious dramas).

Painting. Spain's Golden Age produced many great paintings. Among the illustrious painters who worked in Spain during that time were El Greco and Diego Velázquez de Silve. El Greco was born in Crete, but worked in Toledo from 1577 until his death in

Salvador Dali, who became famous as a surrealist painter in the mid-20th century.

Pablo Picasso, Spanish-born painter and sculptor, famous for his abstract art.

Juan Ramón Jiménez, modern Spanish blank verse poet, became known as the "poet's poet."

1614. Despite his Greek origin, his work is intensely Spanish, very original, and has strong contrasts of light and shade. Most of his work was done for the church, and a spiritual quality even occurs in his landscapes.

Velázquez, a realistic painter, served Philip IV for nearly 40 years and painted 40 portraits of him. When Pope Innocent X saw one of Velázquez' portraits he said, "Too true." He also painted many religious pictures and interiors. Visitors to the Prado in Madrid can find many of the works of El Greco and Velázquez displayed there.

Bartolomé Esteban Murillo, now regarded as a lesser painter, lived and worked in Sevilla during this time. The most notable painter to follow him was the intensely vital Francisco Goya y Lucientes in the later 18th century. Goya put his tremendous zest for living, roistering, fighting, and loving, into pictorial expression.

The Prado in Madrid contains some of the most valuable art treasures in the world. Shown here is one of the museum's three rooms dedicated to the works of Velázquez.

Science. In the 16th century, while Spaniards were expanding and exploring the New World, their quest for knowledge contributed importantly to the sciences. They improved map-making, naval construction, and navigation, and invented a special maritime compass. Pedro Chacón corrected the Gregorian calendar that had been in use for centuries; Daza de Valdés studied the human eye and developed spectacles; Francisco Hernández described and painted more than 14,000 different plants in the New World. Spaniards of that time also added to the knowledge of mining and metal refining.

Music. Spanish music is rich in rhythm, melody, and harmony. During the Golden Age, more than 100 Spaniards wrote on the theory of music, and many more were well-known performers. In the 17th century, the opera was not yet developed, but its forerunner, the *zarzuela*, flourished. Philip IV converted a hunting lodge near Madrid and called the place *La Zarzuela* (bramble) where he enjoyed short sketches with music and singing, backed by elaborate settings. In the 18th and 19th centuries, these performances became lighter in tone and were devised for popular as well as royal audiences.

More than any other instrument, it is the guitar that has come to be considered peculiarly Spanish. The early guitar was probably introduced into Spain by the Romans, who had found it in Egypt. Composers for the guitar have often been inspired by music written in several melody lines at once and by folk tunes. The style of playing characteristic of this kind of guitar music has been revived by such modern musicians as Andrés Segovia.

Spanish music has become internationally known chiefly through the influence of three modern Spanish composers: Isaac Albéniz, Enrique Granados, and Manuel de Falla. Albéniz was a noted concert pianist as well as

Pablo Casals, renowned Spanish cellist, now living in Puerto Rico.

A lively, rhythmic dance is performed by this Salamancan girl, wearing an embroidered and glittering costume.

composer. His works, *Iberia*, contain a series of "impressions" of Spanish life; many incorporate the rhythms and melodies of Andalusian folk songs and dance music.

Granados drew his major inspiration from the times and the work of Goya. His best-known compositions are in the suite called *Goyescas*.

Falla, a native of Cádiz, died as recently as 1946. His ballet, *The Three-Cornered Hat*, first produced in London in 1919, was directed by the famous Leonide Massine, and costumes for it were designed by the great Spanish-born painter, Pablo Picasso.

Dance. The fame of Spanish dancing dates back to ancient times when dancers from Cádiz were the rage of Rome. Today, the

Teams of Basque oxen compete at hauling heavy stones.

Note how the townspeople have crowded around for a glimpse of the spectacle.

646 ■ SPAIN

flamenco dancing of the south, particularly of Andalusia, is popularly identified as Spanish. Unbelievable speed occurs in the traditional movements of *meneo*, the whirling turn; *zapateado*, the stamping; *taconeo*, heel-tapping; and *cimbrado*, the swaying body-bend. Other popular Spanish dances include the Castilian *bolero*, the *fandango*, the *sequidilla*, and the Cádiz *vito*.

Sports. Bullfighting is the "sport" most often considered Spanish. The *toro bravo* (fighting bull) is especially bred for the arena. The spectacle involves the participation of the *presidente* (a town official who directs the scenes), the *monosabios* (odd-job men in the arena), the *picador* (who rides the horse), the *banderilleros* (cape-handlers), and the *matador* (bullfighter). Gaily decked prancing horses add to the scene.

Other popular Spanish sports include fishing and hunting, *pelota* (*jai alai*), and the *paseo*, a brisk walk or parade held every evening in each community.

Bowling in one of its ancient forms—using nine pins—is a popular diversion for the provincial Spaniard. This scene is in Sotillo, León.

An amateur bullfight in the streets of La Alberea, Salamanca. The streets are blocked off to form a run for the bull while the townsmen alternately chase and flee from the frenzied beast.

THE ECONOMY

ECONOMIC wealth in Spain is unevenly divided: 5 per cent of the very rich receive 38 per cent of the national income, and 83 per cent of Spain's people receive less than 30 per cent. In Madrid, a high-wage area, three-fourths of the people are in a low-income bracket.

The government controls wages, hours, and working conditions. The worker may protest at times for better arrangements, but to strike is illegal. The government is usually sensitive to rumblings of discontent among industrial workers. When disturbances arise (as in the Basque country in 1956 and 1962), they are recognized as danger signs and investigated.

For years there has been a trend toward inflation in Spain. Wage increases often have been offset by prices which rose more than wages improved. At the same time the last 10

New petroleum refineries, such as this one at Escombreras in Murcia, are an important factor in Spain's industrial development.

Bird stalls along Las Ramblas, a picturesque thoroughfare in Barcelona. The small merchant, using the streets for his retail store, still has a place in Spain's economy.

years have seen an unprecedented expansion of industry, with a general rise in the per capita income, and some improvement in living standards.

Spain's industry is handicapped by long economic isolation, and foreign investment has not been encouraged until recently. Government-owned enterprises control or affect the output of most basic industries. There is an elaborate system of controls on foreign trade and foreign exchange which is in the process of being reformed.

Some of the disadvantages of Spanish industry are its high-cost structure, old-fashioned equipment and machinery, lack of modern production knowledge, and scarcity of foreign capital. Some of the railway locomotives are a century old, and railway equipment is out-dated, though there are a few ultra-modern trains. On the whole, the transportation system, including highways and railroads, is not adequate for the country's needs.

Agriculturally, about nine-tenths of the land could be productive, despite the centuries of careless mishandling and neglect. More than half of Spain's people work on the land; the proportion of the national income that goes to

Women picking sugar cane in Granada. Workers wear heavy clothing for protection not only against the tough cane, but also against the dehydrating effect of the Andalusian sun.

A native of the southeastern province of Murcia weaves esparto grass into a tough rope. This grass is also used to make paper, baskets, shoes, and coarse cloth.

Workers in a Valencia textile factory. The spinning of artificial yarn, dating from 1944, has almost supplanted the natural silk industry that was once a mainstay of the Spanish economy.

them, however, is less than 30 per cent. Animals do practically all the draft work on Spanish farms. Only one farm in two hundred possesses a tractor.

The effects of the climate can be overcome with proper irrigation, and measures to cope with this problem are being introduced. Today, about a tenth of the potentially fertile land is irrigated; when more farms can have this benefit, it will greatly increase Spain's agricultural production. The reforestation program now underway will help watershed control.

Spain's agricultural problem is complicated by the system of land-holding. In the north, holdings usually are in *minifundios* (small farms), worked by the peasant who lives on them. But in the south, the land is held mostly in *latifundios* (vast estates) whose wealthy owners often live elsewhere and are unconcerned about the land's optimum productiveness. The *latifundio* system is an institution from feudal times when serfs who worked the land were considered a part of it. Today, not quite a third of all Spanish farmers work their own land; about half are casual low-paid workers. The agricultural worker has not yet gained the

← *A tambourine stand in the Plaza Mayor (main square), Madrid, during the Christmas festival. "Las Fiestas de Navidad" is the most important holiday in Spain, as it is for Christians in all countries.*

A pre-fabricated ship section is lowered into place at the Elcano shipyards at Sevilla.

April festivities in Sevilla. There are few secular (non-religious) holidays in Spain; when there is no church holiday, the people take advantage of any minor occasion to proclaim a celebration.

social status of the industrial worker, nor is he eligible to receive the social services that supplement the pay of the industrial worker.

Apart from textiles, exports are chiefly agricultural products—such as fruits, olive oil, and raw materials for which demand varies.

Thus, income from exports also varies. When a freeze destroys citrus crops or olive trees, Spaniards feel a severe loss of income. At times, moreover, there are not enough native edible crops for Spain's domestic needs, and essentials must be imported.

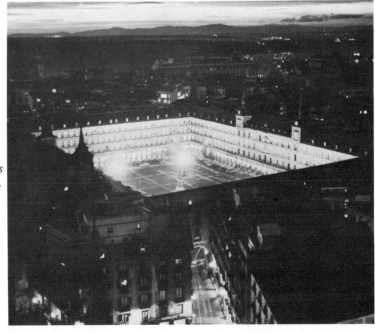

Bull fights and tournaments were once held in Madrid's splendid Plaza Mayor, built in 1619.

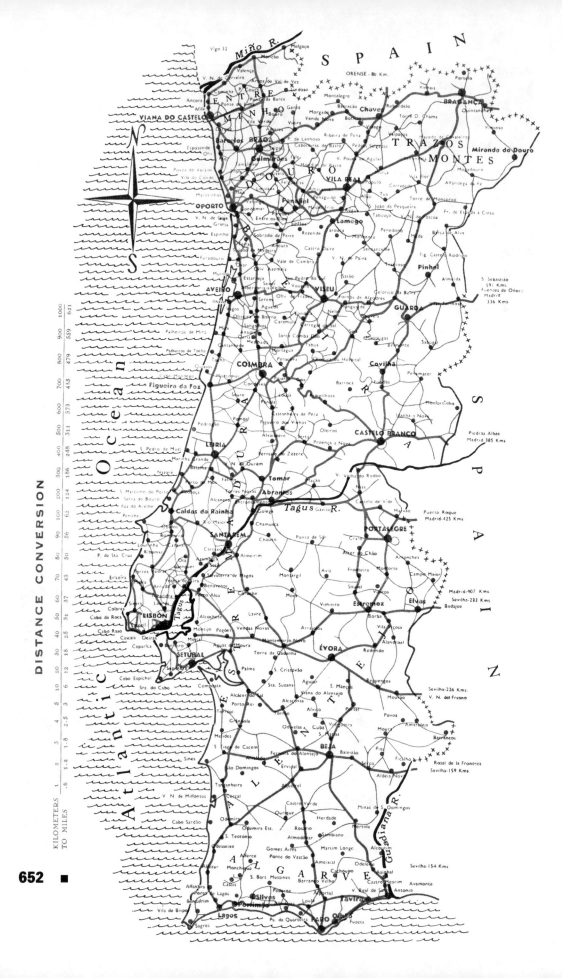

Fireworks arc high in the night sky above the Marshal Carmona Bridge across the Tagus River at Vila Franca de Xira, a town famous for bullfighting.

PORTUGAL

THE LAND

PORTUGAL, situated on the Iberian Peninsula of southern Europe, shares a boundary with only one other country: Spain. Portugal is not a large country; the total land area is only 35,466 square miles—or approximately the same size as the state of Indiana. (England has an area of 50,337 square miles.) Portugal stretches 365 miles from north to south, and the greatest width does not exceed 130 miles.

TOPOGRAPHY

Despite its relatively small size, Portugal is a country of widely differing surface features. In general, the land slopes from northeast to southwest. Highlands, river valleys and coastal plains are all part of the Portuguese landscape.

The hilliest sections of the country are in the north where over half the land has an average elevation of more than 1,000 feet. Long mountain ridges rising in Spain continue into Portugal. Rivers run at the bottoms of the narrow valleys between the ridges. The gorge of the Douro River is of great beauty. Vineyards cling to the steep mountainsides rising above the river. Several peaks in this area are over 5,000 feet in elevation.

In central Portugal is the long ridge of the Serra da Estrêla which includes the highest point in the country, 6,535 feet. Farther to the

Fishing boats litter the beach at Nazaré, a picturesque fishing and resort town on the Atlantic coast north of Lisbon. In the background, a knot of people have gathered about a fishing boat that has just returned from the sea.

south is the broad, fertile valley of the Tagus River. Rice, wheat, vegetables, and fruit are grown on the farms in this region. North and south of Lisbon, the hills form rocky headlands where they meet the Atlantic Ocean.

South of Lisbon, the land is rather flat. However, there are ranges of low hills in the direction of the Spanish border.

RIVERS AND SEACOAST

The largest Portuguese rivers all rise deep in the interior of Spain. From north to south, the most important rivers are the Minho, the Douro (on which Oporto is located), the Tagus (on which Lisbon is located), and the Guadiana.

Because the rivers flow through mountainous regions, they are not navigable for more than a few miles of their length.

Except in the places where the mountains reach the sea, Portugal has a long coastline of sandy beaches famed for their beauty. Easily reached from Lisbon, the beach at Estoril is a popular summer resort for people from the capital and for foreign visitors to Portugal. The total length of the country's seacoast is about 500 miles. Lisbon is Portugal's largest port, thanks to the sunken mouth of the Tagus. When completed in 1966, the suspension bridge built between Lisbon and Almada on the other side of the Tagus became the longest in Europe.

Housewives in Viseu do their washing on the river bank. Across the stream, laundry is drying in the hot Portuguese sun. This is a quaint custom of villagers in some parts of the country.

CLIMATE

Because it is located on the Atlantic coast, Portugal feels the full effect of the North Atlantic Drift—a branch of the Gulf Stream. Warm westerly winds blowing in off the ocean give southern Portugal a subtropical marine climate. In the largest cities—Lisbon, Oporto, and Coimbra—the average annual temperature is about 61° F. There are no extremes of temperature in Lisbon. The heat of summer is eased by a cool evening breeze, and snow falls rarely in winter. However, the Algarve area in southern Portugal experiences rather hot summers. In winter, a carpet of snow blankets the higher mountains.

Near Peniche, a fishing village on Cape Carvoeiro renowned for the making of fine lace, the breaking waves of the Atlantic Ocean have carved the rocky headlands into strange shapes. These cliffs extend as far southward as Cape Roca. The people clambering over the boulders near the water's edge give an idea of the size of the rocks.

A shepherd tends his flock which is grazing beside the Tagus River upstream from Lisbon. Almourol Castle, the supposed scene of many love stories and legends, rises from a rocky island in the middle of the stream. Visitors reach the castle—originally built by the Romans and remodelled in 1171 by a Portuguese noble—by ferry.

Use of modern agricultural machinery is not widespread in Portugal. However, the ingenious Portuguese have devised many methods to make up for this deficiency. Here, a water wheel lifts water to irrigate fields.

FLORA AND FAUNA

Portugal is the home of both temperate and semi-tropical vegetation. Plants from the two zones often grow side by side. Thus, cactus plants are found growing among chestnut and pine trees. The elm, poplar, and oak all grow naturally, but several kinds of trees have been brought to Portugal from foreign countries—and have thrived. The eucalyptus tree of Australia is probably the farthest-travelled "immigrant."

A wide variety of small animals and birds live in the forest regions. Wild boar thrive in the forests of Algarve. Wolves still haunt some of the more remote mountain areas.

NATURAL RESOURCES

Much of Portugal's mineral wealth remains unexploited. The development of new industries may lead to increased mining activity. Instead of having to export her mineral wealth, Portugal may some day be able to use it at home. Deposits of tin, wolfram, iron, copper, and pyrites are all of commercial importance. Mountain rivers are another important resource that can be and are being used to generate hydro-electric power.

The fortifications surrounding Obidos were originally constructed by the Moors, but were rebuilt several times by Portuguese kings beginning in the 12th century. Now merely a tourist attraction, the 45-foot-high walls were a formidable obstacle for would-be attackers in the times before gunpowder came into use as an instrument of war. Obidos itself has changed little over the centuries.

CITIES AND PORTS

Portugal has a small population compared with that of many other European nations. In 1967 there were 9,440,000 Portuguese living in European Portugal. The population continues to increase at a slow rate. Many Portuguese farmers have emigrated to the Overseas Provinces with the assistance of the government. (The total population in the Overseas Provinces in 1960 was 12,949,274.) Portugal's population density of 252 persons per square mile is far less than Britain's 558 but greatly exceeds the United States' 50.

Lisbon, located on the estuary of the Tagus, is Portugal's capital, largest city, and most important port. It has a population of over 800,000. Built on a series of hills, Lisbon is a contrast of the old and new. In the central part of the city, there are wide squares flanked by modern buildings. Streets and avenues run at right angles to one another, a result of plans drawn up after the great earthquake of 1755. However, the steep, winding streets of the old town have changed little over the centuries.

Modern buildings, including an outdoor cafe, flank Oporto's João I Square. The city, Portugal's second largest, is the focal point for the thriving port wine industry. It was in Oporto in 1394, that Prince Henry the Navigator was born.

PORTUGAL ■ 657

There, one can find shops selling antiques and exotic goods from the Overseas Provinces. Many Lisbon pavements are covered with designs made with mosaic tiles.

Oporto, on the banks of the Douro River, is the country's second largest city with a population of over 315,000. Many British wine merchants have businesses in the town, for virtually all port wine for export passes through Oporto. Large merchant ships cannot come up the Douro to the city, but take on their cargo at the mouth of the river 15 miles away. Other important Portuguese towns include Coimbra, Braga, Setúbal, and Funchal (on the island of Madeira).

(Right) Women in Leiria often do their shopping at the town's open-air market. A castle built by Afonso I in 1135 dominates the hilltop. The castle—now restored—was used by the king as a strong point during his campaign to gain control of the southern regions of Portugal.

The Aguas Livres Aqueduct, reminiscent of the great Roman aqueducts, was built between 1728 and 1748 to provide Lisbon with an adequate water supply. Its most interesting section is the 35-arch crossing of the Alcantara Valley, the highest arch being 214 feet above the river. In the foreground, a crowd watches a game of football (soccer).

The Azores Islands are of recent geological origin, and earthquakes and volcanic activity still occur frequently. However, most of the islands are very fertile and are used for agriculture, although, in a section of the valley of Las Furnas, hot springs, small geysers, mud pools, and sulphur vents are common.

MADEIRA AND THE AZORES

Two groups of islands in the Atlantic Ocean are administered as parts of European Portugal. Madeira is located about 535 miles southwest of Lisbon and 360 miles off the coast of Morocco. There are several small islands in the Madeira group and some are uninhabited. The bulk of the population (282,678 in 1960) lives on the main island of Madeira which is 35 miles long and 13 miles across at its widest point. Although Madeira was known to the Romans, the island dropped from the knowledge of European geographers and was not rediscovered until it was sighted by the Portuguese navigator João Gonçalves Zarco in 1418.

Madeira is a lush paradise of jagged volcanic ridges and fertile valleys. At one time much of the island was covered by thick forests, but most of them have now been cut or have been burned. The warm climate makes Madeira ideally suited for the growing of grapes and sugar cane. Madeira wine is especially popular in England, and it was an Englishman who helped improve the Madeira vineyards during the 18th century. Because of its year-round pleasant climate, Madeira is a popular stopping place for cruise ships and tourists.

The Azores, an archipelago of nine major islands and several smaller islets, are located about 750 miles to the west of Lisbon. Many of the inhabitants (1960 population: 336,933) have blond hair and blue eyes, for they are descendants of Flemish knights and ship-wrecked sailors from Brittany. The bulk of the population is engaged in agriculture, the main crops being cereals, vegetables, pineapples, oranges, tea and tobacco. Because of the rich volcanic soil, crops thrive. In recent years the Azores have gained importance as a crossroads of air routes and undersea telegraph cables.

Sailing ships still ply Lisbon's port on the Tagus River; however, an aircraft carrier, one of the modern vessels of all nations that now call at Portugal's capital, rests at anchor in midstream. In bygone days, bold Portuguese explorers sailed from Lisbon on their voyages of discovery to the far corners of the globe. Some ships returned laden with riches; others were never heard from again.

Built between 1717 and 1730 on the orders of King João V, the great convent at Mafra measures nearly 800 feet across its front. During periods of peak construction as many as 45,000 men and 1,000 oxen toiled on the project. A special hospital for workers was built at great cost before the main building was completed.

660 ■ **PORTUGAL**

Sailing ships of many nations came to trade at Lisbon at the time this old French engraving was made. Exotic products from the Far East—spices, coffee, and other goods from Portugal's overseas possessions— attracted merchants from all over Europe.

HISTORY

UNTIL THE 12TH CENTURY A.D., Portugal's history is virtually the same as that of the rest of the Iberian Peninsula. The part of the Peninsula that is now Portugal has been occupied by men for several thousand years, but there is little historical knowledge of them until the coming of the Carthaginians and the Greeks in the 3rd century B.C. The newcomers came to the Iberian Peninsula chiefly for trade and established numerous posts at river mouths to trade with the native tribes. Roman power soon eclipsed the influence of the Greeks and the Carthaginians. During the period 138–72 B.C. the Roman legions overran the Iberian

Peninsula, first seizing the more-developed southern parts and then fanning out to the north to subjugate the wild tribesmen of that region. The invaders met with strong resistance, especially from the Lusitanians, a tribe that inhabited what is now part of northern Portugal. However, the superior military discipline of the legions, aided by acts of treachery, eventually brought victory to the Romans.

Under Roman rule the Iberian Peninsula was divided into three provinces. Most of what is now Portugal was included in the Province of Lusitania. Rome continued its rule over the Iberian Peninsula until the great Germanic invasions of the 5th century A.D. which destroyed much of the Roman Empire. Although the Romans were forced out of the Peninsula, they left their mark on Iberian language and institutions.

MOORISH INVASIONS

The new conquerors of the Peninsula, known as the Alans and the Suevi, were not able to retain their possessions for long. Yet another wave of invaders swept down from the north. These were the Visigoths who by A.D. 585 had overwhelmed the Suevi kingdom which had been established in the north-western part of the Peninsula. But scarcely had the Visigoths consolidated their hold than a new threat arose in the south. In little more than a century, the new Moslem religion spread from its birthplace at Mecca (in Arabia) along the coast of North Africa, across the Straits of Gibraltar, and into the Iberian Peninsula where it was carried by fierce Arab armies. The Moslem invasion began in 711, sweeping over the entire Iberian Peninsula and across the lofty Pyrenees Mountains into France. It was not until 732 that the Arab armies were brought to a halt. In that year Charles Martel and his Frankish army routed the invaders at the battle of Tours in central France and prevented the

Skulls and bones cover the walls and pillars of a chapel of the church of the monastery of St. Francis in Évora, about 70 miles southeast of Lisbon. The church is a blend of Moorish and Gothic architecture. In 712, Évora was conquered by the Moors, who named it Jabura, and remained under Moorish domination until 1166.

Pena Castle crowns a densely-forested mountaintop overlooking Sintra. A blend of several architectural styles—Moorish, Baroque, and Gothic—the castle, built between 1840 and 1850, has a drawbridge, battlements, bastions and a fantastic group of wings.

Arabs from fanning out across Europe. However, the entire Iberian Peninsula remained under Moorish (Arab) control. This did not mean that the entire population was forcibly converted to the Moslem religion. Most people kept their Christian faith, for the Moors were largely content to remain as overlords, and the era of Moorish rule was not nearly as harsh as is popularly believed. The Moors brought with them a new cultural heritage, and this had a strong effect on the Iberian people. Many remained Christians but adopted various Arab customs. There were even instances of Christian priests with Arab names. The Moorish influence on architecture can be seen to this day in the design of many buildings in Spain and Portugal. Far from being barbarian horsemen, the Moors were patrons of the arts, and

Christian, Moslem, and Jewish scholars flourished during the period.

Yet the Christian nobles of the Iberian Peninsula were not content to remain subjects of the Moors. A half-century after the Moorish invasion a Christian kingdom had arisen in Asturias and León which drove the Moors south of the Douro River. The next few centuries witnessed continual fighting between Christian and Moorish armies. Slowly, the Moorish armies were driven farther and farther to the south. By 1097, mention of the "County of Portucale" was being made in documents. The origin of the name comes from the settlement at the mouth of the Douro River, which in Roman times had been known as Portus Cale (Port of Cale) and is now the city of Oporto.

Ceramic tile adorns the sides of the staircase and the adjoining walls which bound a canal, also lined with tile, at the former winter palace of the king at Queluz, a few miles from Lisbon. The palace and grounds are on the grand scale of Versailles and boast watered gardens, orange groves and a fish pond.

INDEPENDENCE

At first, Portugal was part of the larger Kingdom of Galicia (which was in turn part of the Kingdom of Castile and León). Realizing that the County of Portucale could be better ruled by itself than as a part of Galicia, the King of León, Alfonso VI, made the French knight, Henry of Burgundy (husband of the king's daughter, Teresa), Count of Portucale and ruler of the region stretching from the Minho River in the north to the Tagus in the south. Count Henry restored the power of the Roman Catholic church in his domains, and French monks were brought in to rule the dioceses at Braga and Coimbra. Quarrels among other Christian rulers in Iberia helped Henry strengthen his hold on Portugal but did not allow him to become completely independent, although after the death of his father-in-law in 1109 he termed himself "By the Grace of God, Count and Lord of all Portugal."

When Count Henry died about 1112, Portugal passed to his widow Teresa, who carried on friendly relations with the Galicians. Unhappy Portuguese barons led by her son, Prince Afonso, rebelled and defeated her in battle in 1128. Afonso then became Count of Portugal.

Although he no longer owed allegiance to Galicia, Afonso was still a subject of the King of León, Alfonso VI, a situation which Afonso resented. At this time the Moors began attacking from the south, so the two Christian rulers temporarily settled their differences in order to deal with the common enemy. After defeating the Moors at the battle of Ourique, Afonso found himself in a strong position, and he began referring to himself as "King of Portugal" about 1139. At a meeting with the ruler of León in 1143, Afonso received the title of king from Alfonso VI, even though the title was not recognized by the Roman Catholic Popes until 1179.

Portugal was then an independent country, but the Moors remained an ever-present threat to its existence. Battles with the Arabs continued throughout Afonso's reign. In 1147 Lisbon was recaptured with the help of English, French and German crusaders. From time to time Afonso attempted to expand Portuguese territory at the expense of León, then ruled by his son-in-law, but when a serious Moorish attack developed in 1171, Fernando II of León came to Afonso's rescue.

When the aged king died in 1185 he was succeeded by his son, Sancho (1185–1211), who devoted his energies both to fighting the Moors and to encouraging the growth of towns and agriculture. Portugal's first Parliament (Cortes) met at Coimbra in 1211 at the beginning of Afonso II's reign. During Afonso's reign and that of his successor, Sancho II, there was considerable friction between the church and the crown. Sancho was officially deposed by the Pope, and the throne passed to his brother Afonso III, under whom Portuguese European territory was expanded to its present size.

Portugal continued to flourish during the long reign of the scholar-king Dinis (1279–1325). A Concordat was made with the Pope, the first university was founded, and great attention was paid to agriculture and naval construction. Portuguese history during the remainder of the 14th century was punctuated by several wars with Castile. In 1373 Portugal and England signed a treaty of alliance, and the two nations have remained allies until this day.

A NEW DYNASTY

In 1383 King Fernando, last ruler of the Afonsine dynasty, died. A period of anarchy followed, and the king of Castile laid claim to Portugal and invaded the country. At this critical time, the Parliament, meeting at Coimbra, chose as king, João, Master of Avis (1385). In the same year, King João, first of the Avis dynasty, defeated the Castilian army in the battle of Aljubarrota. This ended the threat to Portuguese independence, even though a final peace treaty was not signed until 1411. The alliance with England was further strengthened by the Treaty of Windsor of 1386. In 1387 King João married Philippa, daughter of John of Gaunt, the duke of Lancaster (who was also the father of King Henry IV of England).

An early alliance with England is depicted in this miniature from a manuscript showing the marriage of John of Gaunt's daughter, Philippa of Lancaster, to King João I.

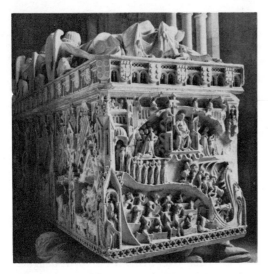

João and Philippa had four sons. The oldest, Duarte, became king (1433-38). However, it was the third son, Henry—later known as Prince Henry the Navigator, who achieved the greatest fame. As a young man of nineteen, Henry displayed outstanding bravery in the capture of the North African Moorish stronghold of Ceuta in 1415. Afterwards, Henry retired to Point Sagres in extreme southwestern Portugal, where he spent the remainder of his life. Henry brought outstanding navigators, chartmakers, and mathematicians to his court with the aim of putting sailing on a scientific basis. He believed it possible for ships to reach India and the Far East by sailing around Africa —a wild notion at the time. Trade with Asia was in the hands of the Arabs and Italians.

The tomb of the Spanish noblewoman Inès de Castro, beautifully decorated with stone carvings, lies in the great Cistercian monastery at Alcobaça close by the tomb of her beloved, King Pedro I. Inès was murdered in 1355 at the behest of King Afonso IV who feared that she and her brothers were exercising too much influence over Pedro, heir apparent to the Portuguese throne.

Discoveries in the East as well as in the New World ushered in a golden age for Portugal. Tremendous profits were realized from the sale of spices imported from the East Indies. The demand for ships kept Portuguese shipyards busy for many decades.

Contrary to popular belief, Prince Henry the Navigator lived a quiet life at Sagres in southern Portugal. However, the prince was the patron of mapmakers, mathematicians, astronomers, and ship designers who played a key rôle in voyages down the west coast of Africa. Portuguese seamen learned to discount stories of monsters and bottomless pits in the oceans and eventually went on to reach India and the Far East.

THE AGE OF DISCOVERIES

From the revenues of Portugal's southern province of Algarve (granted him for his display of bravery at Ceuta), Henry financed his school of navigation and sent Portuguese sailors down the west coast of Africa. Progress was slow at first. By 1445 the Portuguese had reached Cape Verde. Henry died in 1460, but the voyages went on. Finally, in 1488 Bartolomeu Dias rounded the Cape of Good Hope, gateway to the Indian Ocean. Ten years later Vasco da Gama reached India—object of Columbus' "unsuccessful" voyage of 1492. Discovery of the sea route to East Asia was of tremendous importance for Portugal, for it enabled the Portuguese to deal directly with the sources of spices, precious stones, and a host of exotic Oriental products in great demand in Europe, without having to depend on Arab and Italian middlemen.

The 16th century was Portugal's golden age. The country became Europe's leading trading nation and naval power. Meanwhile, Spain concentrated on voyages to the New World. To avoid clashes between the two Catholic powers, Pope Alexander VI drew up an agreement in 1494 by which Spain was granted right to new territories west of a line 370 leagues from the Cape Verde Islands. This permitted the Portuguese to claim Brazil while the remainder of the Americas fell in the Spanish sphere of influence. In the East, the bold Afonso de Albuquerque spread Portuguese influence far and wide. Goa, on the west coast of India was taken in 1510 and made headquarters for Portuguese commercial and missionary activities in Asia. In 1511, Malacca, the great trade emporium on the Malay Peninsula, was

A decade after the voyage of Dias to the Cape of Good Hope, Vasco da Gama, following the same route around southern Africa, continued onward across the Indian Ocean and reached India in 1498, thus accomplishing Prince Henry's dream of reaching the East by sea. In this picture, an Indian prince greets the bold da Gama.

Following a course down the middle of the Atlantic Ocean, Bartolomeu Dias turned eastward and rounded the Cape of Good Hope, the southernmost tip of Africa, in 1488. He claimed the new discovery for Portugal. Here, Portuguese soldiers are erecting a cross with the coat-of-arms of Portugal to establish their nation's claim to the Cape.

The Tower of Belém was built about 1515 to protect Lisbon from naval attack. Vasco da Gama and many other navigators sailed from the spot where the tower stands. Francisco de Arruda, architect of the fortress, was greatly influenced by Moorish designs he had seen during his stay in Morocco. Originally, the Belém Tower was on a small island in the Tagus, but a change in the river's course has made the island part of the mainland.

captured. Agreements were made with rulers of several of the Spice Islands for sale of their products to the Portuguese. One Portuguese who journeyed to the Spice Islands during this period was Ferdinand Magellan. Unfortunately, Magellan had a disagreement with the king and offered his services to Charles V of Spain. Sailing westward through the 370-mile long Strait that now bears his name, ships of Magellan's fleet were the first to circumnavigate the globe, although Magellan himself was killed at a halfway point by natives of Cebu Island in the Philippines in 1521. (Actually Magellan *was* the first man to go completely around the world, for he had already reached the Spice Islands, which are east of Cebu.)

Soon, the acquisition of a great empire began to take its toll. Portugal was a small country with a small population. It took a great number of men and ships to garrison colonies stretching from Brazil in the west to Macau on the China

Many interesting buildings line the streets of Lisbon, but none is more intriguing than the Casa dos Bicos (*The House of Points*). Diamond-shaped stones stud the front wall of this house which once belonged to the family of the famous Afonso d'Albuquerque.

Portuguese exploration and conquest in South America and the East was spurred on by two desires. The first was for trade and riches, the other was a wish to bring Christianity to "pagans" and "infidels." The Jesuit St. Francis Xavier, the foremost missionary in the East during the 16th century, is buried in this elaborate tomb in Goa—a Portuguese Overseas Province until 1961 when it was seized by the Indian government.

coast in the east. Thousands of men died in shipwrecks, from disease, and in battles with natives. The Portuguese desire to spread the Catholic religion far and wide caused antagonism with foreign peoples and harmed trade. In 1578 an expedition to Africa to punish the Moors met with disaster. Nine thousand Portuguese, including King Sebastião, were slaughtered at the battle of Alcazarquivir.

SPANISH DOMINATION

Following the battle, the dead king's uncle, Henry, a cardinal, succeeded to the Portuguese throne. He died in 1580 and there were no direct heirs entitled to the crown. At this point, Philip II of Spain laid claim to Portugal since he was a grandson of King Manuel I. By the end of 1580 Philip had bought and fought his way to power. Under Philip II (whose Invincible Armada was defeated by the English in 1588), Portugal retained its national identity but came under the influence of Spanish foreign policy. After Philip's death in 1598, his successors, Philip III and Philip IV, treated Portugal like a conquered land. Finally, in 1640 a revolution broke out in Lisbon, and the Spaniards were expelled from Portugal. The

From 1580 to 1640 Portugal was forced to endure Spanish rule. However, in the latter year a revolt broke out in Lisbon and the Spanish were expelled. On December 15, 1640, João, Duke of Braganza, was acclaimed king of an independent Portugal by the assembled nobles of the country. Several years of hard fighting were necessary before the Spanish threat was ended.

Duke of Braganza became King João IV. Spanish attacks were repulsed and a peace treaty was signed in 1668.

Sixty years of Spanish occupation had a disastrous effect on Portugal's Eastern trade. The Dutch, who had formerly purchased spices and other Asian goods at Lisbon and distributed them throughout Europe, were fighting Spain for their independence. Banned from trading at Lisbon, the Dutch (and the English) began voyaging to the sources of supply in the East. Many Portuguese ships and possessions were captured, and Portugal was eliminated as an important trading nation in Asia. To this day, the Dutch call their finest porcelain "carrack porcelain" after part of the booty taken from a Portuguese carrack (cargo ship) captured in the East Indies.

After the Spanish occupation had ended, Portugal resumed friendly relations with England. King João IV's daughter, Catherine of Braganza, married King Charles II in 1662. England received Bombay (in India) and Tangier. Portugal received arms to fight Spain.

At the beginning of the 18th century, Portugal became involved in the War of the Spanish Succession. In 1701, Portugal allied itself with France, but two years later the country changed sides and joined England and other members of the Grand Alliance. The Methuen Treaty of 1703 provided for the exchange of English textiles for Portuguese wine and proved beneficial to both nations.

During the reign of João V (1706–1750), Portugal regained much of the prosperity it had enjoyed during the 16th century. This time the source of wealth was in the West rather than the East. Gold was discovered in Brazil in 1692 and diamonds were found in 1728. Brazilian agricultural products—coffee, rice, and sugar—also gave rise to many fortunes. The wealthy built fashionable new homes in Lisbon and other towns. Foreign trade increased. The king used royal revenues to strengthen the army and navy, for public works projects, and for the improvement of religious and educational institutions.

In 1755 Lisbon was struck by a terrible natural disaster. An earthquake levelled the greater part of the city, killing thousands and wiping out great fortunes in a matter of seconds. The city was rebuilt under the direction of the Marquis of Pombal. Pombal was a controversial figure. He tackled Portugal's economic problems with great energy, but his often dictatorial methods gained him numerous enemies. When his protector, King José I died, Pombal was dismissed from office.

PORTUGAL AT WAR

Portugal, like most European countries, was drawn into the wars resulting from the French Revolution of 1789. In 1793 Portugal allied itself with Spain and England against France. Troops and naval vessels were provided by the Portuguese. When Spain and France unexpectedly signed a peace treaty in 1795, Portugal remained at war. In 1801, Spain invaded Portugal and forced the smaller Iberian nation to sign a peace treaty. Portugal had every reason to remain neutral, but peace or war often depended upon the desires of the larger European powers. When the Portuguese refused Napoleon's request to arrest all Englishmen in the country and seize their property, a Franco-Spanish army invaded the country (1807). The

The hall of the coats-of-arms (sometimes called the stag room because of the paintings high on the ceiling) of the royal palace at Sintra dates from the early 16th century. Tiles on the walls depict scenes of hunting, war, and everyday life of the nobility of the period. In a nearby room, King Afonso VI was kept a prisoner until his death in 1683. Worn floor tiles show where the captive monarch paced back and forth during his years of imprisonment.

The Coach Museum in Belém, a suburb of Lisbon, contains one of the world's greatest collections of old coaches. Various types of the vehicles are on display. The oldest, dating from the late 16th century, was used by King Philip II of Spain when he travelled to Portugal. Others on display include small pony-chaises used by royal princesses during the 19th century. The museum itself was built as a riding school during the 18th century.

royal family fled to Brazil. In 1808 a British army commanded by Sir Arthur Wellesley (later the Duke of Wellington) landed in Portugal. After much hard fighting, Wellington's army threw the French back into Spain for the last time in 1811.

After the downfall of Napoleon in 1815, liberal ideas swept Europe. There was unrest and bloodshed in Portugal. When King João VI returned from Brazil in 1821, he was forced to agree to a constitution. More turmoil followed. One of the king's sons was forced into exile; the other, Pedro, became emperor of an independent Brazil in 1825. João VI died in 1826, and a war between the two brothers continued until 1834 when one died and the other was exiled. Pedro's daughter, Maria, became queen and ruled until 1853, but her reign was marred by fierce struggles between opposing political factions.

In the second half of the 19th century domestic political disputes became calmer, and the beginnings of a two-party system of government came into being. Railways were built,

The reign of King Miguel (1828–34) was marred by violence. Miguel was the leader of the conservative faction in Portuguese politics. His brother Pedro, the first Emperor of Brazil, was a leader of the liberals.

progressive laws were passed, and higher education was improved. Abroad, Portuguese and British colonial interests in Africa came into conflict. In 1890, Britain forced Portugal to drop its claims to a large area of southern Africa. Humiliation at the hands of foreign powers, growing economic problems, and unhappiness with the dictatorial regime of João Franco strengthened the hand of the republicans. In 1908 King Carlos was assassinated, and his successor, Manuel II, was forced into exile in 1910—Portugal's last monarch.

The Portuguese Republic was not a success. Every republican had his own plan for governing the country. Some 40 cabinets fell during the 16 years of the republic. Arguments among politicians that could not be settled with words were settled with bullets. In 1926 the army intervened and seized power.

A provisional government was established by the new regime. General António Carmona was elected president in 1928 and re-elected three times—there was no opposition candidate. Carmona died in 1951. António de Oliveira Salazar, a professor at the University of Coimbra, who had been appointed minister of finance in 1928, set about putting Portugal on a firm economic footing. Salazar became prime minister in 1932 and has remained the dominant figure in Portugal's government to this day.

In World War II Portugal remained neutral. (The nation had fought as an ally of Britain, France, and the United States during World War I.) But, when Britain asked for military bases in the Azores to help in the fight against German submarines in the Atlantic (invoking the old Anglo-Portuguese alliance) the request was granted. The United States, as an ally of Britain, was also granted rights in the Azores.

Magnificent tapestries adorn the walls of the hall of the Dukes of Braganza in the royal palace at Vila Viçosa. Portraits of the dukes can be seen on the ceiling. Construction of the palace began in 1501 and was not finished until a century later. The palace was used by Portuguese kings until the overthrow of the monarchy in 1910.

Some homes in small Portuguese villages are not equipped with running water. Instead, housewives use community water wells. Filling water vessels is not without its pleasant side, for women always find the well a good place to exchange gossip.

THE PEOPLE

THE PORTUGUESE PEOPLE carry the blood of many races in their veins, a result of the Iberian Peninsula's turbulent history. Originally, the inhabitants were of Iberian or Basque stock. However, intermarriage resulting from the arrival of different peoples in Iberia has altered many of the characteristics of the native Basque stock. In northern Portugal many persons show traces of northern European features, a result of the invasions by the Suevi and the Visigoths. Several centuries of Moslem rule left an Arab and Berber imprint on the people of central and southern Portugal. There were many Jews in the country before King Manuel I expelled them in 1496 (at the urging of Queen Isabella of Spain); however, a number of Jews converted to Christianity and remained. Portugal's close links with the African continent since 500 years ago also highly influenced the racial composition of its people.

Two students walk through the courtyard of the University at Coimbra garbed in their traditional black capes. In a break with tradition, the University now admits women students. Every June, the students stage great festivities at the time of examinations. Each one casts his distinctive class ribbon on a bonfire to celebrate the end of the academic year, and merriment is the rule throughout the town.

Afonso d'Albuquerque, intrepid explorer of the East, died at sea in 1515. Known variously as "The Great" and "The Portuguese Mars," his papers and journals were published by his son Afonso and serve as an important commentary on his life and time.

LANGUAGE AND LITERATURE

Its language is Portugal's most important heritage from several centuries of Roman rule. The Portuguese language is a member of the Romance group of languages, which also includes Spanish, French, Italian, and Rumanian. Portuguese is similar to but—it must be emphasized—not the same as Spanish. Portuguese- and Spanish-speaking people can usually understand each other without too much difficulty. The Spanish people of Galicia (north of Portugal) speak a dialect of Spanish which is akin to Portuguese. In addition to its use in European Portugal, the Portuguese language is also spoken in the Overseas Provinces and in Brazil, which, with a population of 85,000,000, is the largest Portuguese-speaking nation and the main independent country in Latin America where Spanish is not spoken.

Portugal has a long literary tradition. Epic poems and love songs were written in great

Fados are the traditional songs of the working people of Lisbon. Patrons of a number of Lisbon cafes and restaurants are entertained nightly by the haunting strains of these ballads.

numbers in the period after national independence was gained. Two of Portugal's early kings, Afonso III and Dinis, were accomplished literary figures themselves and attracted a number of outstanding poets of the age to their courts. King Dinis was the founder of Portugal's first university in 1290. The battles with the Moors gave rise to epic poetry celebrating the triumphs of the Christian forces over the Moslems. King Duarte, brother of Prince Henry the Navigator, wrote moral treatises and books on horsemanship. Fernão Lopes achieved fame for his chronicles of the lives and times of Portuguese kings during the late 14th and early 15th centuries. The Age of Discoveries in the 15th and 16th centuries saw the writing of many works by those who knew of or participated in the great period of Portuguese exploration. Modern historians find the *Commentarios de Grande Afonso d'Albuquerque* and similar works to be invaluable when they do research on early European colonization in Africa and Asia. At home Gil Vicente achieved fame as a great playwright, although his comedies later displeased the Inquisition and were suppressed. Other European countries—

Spain, France, Italy, and England—have had a great influence on Portuguese authors. Many of the best Portuguese authors from the 15th to 18th centuries wrote in Spanish rather than Portuguese. It was not until the 19th century that Portuguese literature, under the leadership of Garrett and Herculano, recovered its former stature. Both men were poets; Garrett later turned to writing plays and Herculano wrote a history of Portugal and a history of the Inquisition. Modern Portuguese authors have carried on their country's literary tradition even though turbulent political developments have sometimes interfered.

CUSTOMS

The Portuguese share many traits with other Latin countries. Strangers are usually impressed with the extent of Portuguese hospitality and friendliness. The Portuguese are also a proud people. Insults are not taken lightly, and courage is considered an important virtue. The day in 1578 when 400 Portuguese soldiers attacked and captured a fort held by more than 8,000 Malays and many other heroic incidents

Although the Alfama is a poor district, the residents are friendly and hospitable to strangers. The streets, always alive with interest, are decorated with thousands of lights on important holy days.

Street vendors are sometimes seen along Lisbon thoroughfares.

from the past have not been forgotten. In a similar spirit young Portuguese men risk their lives for fun twice yearly during festivals at Villa Franca de Xira when bulls are released in the streets of the town.

Significant regional differences of custom exist. For instance, in the provinces of Minho and Douro women usually dress in black clothes with floral embroidery. The people of Algarve province have their own traditions including the *vendas* and *ajudadas,* local dances accompanied by the distinctive *corridinho* music. In the province of Ribatejo gay costumes predominate. The most popular dance in that region is the lively *fandango.*

Thousands of faithful Roman Catholics make the pilgrimage to the shrine at Fatima every year. In 1917, three young shepherds reported seeing visions of the Blessed Virgin at the present site of the shrine. Soon after, increasingly larger numbers of the faithful began making the pilgrimage to the spot.

Festivals play an important part in Portuguese life. June, the month with feast days for the country's three most beloved saints—Anthony, John, and Peter—is celebrated with religious processions, bullfights, folk dancing, and firework displays in nearly all the cities and towns of the country. The Portuguese regard these saints as their special friends when they are confronted with personal problems. One of the most spectacular festivals is held only once every three years in Tomar to give thanks for the harvest. The climax of the *Festa*

dos Tabuleiros comes during the parade of offerings through the decorated streets of the town. Girls balancing tall *tabuleiros* (wicker baskets) on their heads wind their way through the throngs of onlookers. The baskets contain offerings of bread carefully displayed and interwoven with poppies.

Religious festivals usually begin with a sermon at the local church, often with an accompaniment of sky-rockets and other fireworks. A procession through town follows. White-robed church wardens carry heavy shrines commemorating local patron saints. (Appropriately, this shrine is being carried in a procession through a fishing village.) Several bands usually participate in each religious procession.

678 ▪ PORTUGAL

Every three years the town of Tomar celebrates the Feast of the Tabuleiros. The highlight of the Feast is a parade of women balancing pyramids of carefully arranged loaves of bread on their heads. Each marcher is accompanied by a man who is there to give aid if the tabuleiro should begin to fall. After the parade, the town holds a gigantic, and free, beef-and-bread feast.

Alcobaça's monastery was founded in 1152 to commemorate the capture of Santarém from the Moors. The huge Cistercian church is the largest in Portugal. Many famous Portuguese princes, including Henry the Navigator, are buried at the monastery.

Most Portuguese are pious Roman Catholics. Every May and October, up to half a million Portuguese make a pilgrimage to the Shrine of Fatima. There, in 1917 three shepherd children saw a vision of the Virgin Mary under an oak tree. Many pilgrims walk from their homes—no matter how distant—to the shrine. On the nights of the 12th of May and the 12th of October, thousands of the faithful walk up the winding road to the shrine, carrying candles to light their way. Mass is said the next morning in the huge square in front of the cathedral (the square is larger than that of St. Peter's in Rome).

Folk dancing always plays an important part in Portuguese festivals. Here, dancers perform on an outdoor stage at Viana do Castelo in Minho province. Each region of the country has its own dances.

PORTUGAL ■ 679

Football (soccer) is Portugal's most popular sport. Large crowds invariably pack stands to watch important games. Portuguese football teams often compete with rivals from other countries.

SPORTS AND RECREATION

The Portuguese engage in a great variety of sports either as participants or spectators. Football (soccer) is as popular in Portugal as it is in other European countries. Thousands of Portuguese pack stadiums in order to watch "their" team fight for victory. Various other sports attract a good deal of attention. Sailing, once the nation's lifeblood during the Age of Discoveries, has many enthusiasts who compete in races in the Atlantic. Horse shows are a natural result of the country's having large numbers of the animal which are used by the *campinos* (cowboys) of Ribatejo province to ride herd on grazing cattle. Car racing has become an established sport, and the annual Grand Prix of Portugal road race always brings out a large crowd of spectators. Road racing is so popular with the Portuguese that a Grand Prix is even held in the Overseas Province of Macau, half-way around the world. Tennis, golf, and basketball are also played in the country.

Portugal's "national" sport is bullfighting. Foreigners often do not realise that Portuguese bullfighting is entirely different from the version of the sport pursued in Spain and Latin America. Whereas in Spain a bullfight always ends with the death of the bull (or, more rarely, the death of the matador), the Portuguese method of bullfighting preserves the skill and grace of the sport without the deadly ending: the bull is never killed. Most bullfighting in Portugal is done on horseback. The finely trained horses, the riders, and the bulls themselves usually come from the "bullfighting" province of Ribatejo, which is on the Tagus River above Lisbon. In Ribatejo nearly every village has its own bullfighting ring.

Portuguese farmers long ago learned that it is easier to shake olives from the tree than to pick them one by one. Fallen olives collect on a large canvas. However, this method is generally used only when harvesting olives for olive oil to be used for cooking and packaging foods. Those intended to be sold whole to olive lovers in Portugal and abroad are carefully picked by hand. About two-thirds of Portugal's olive groves are concentrated in the central provinces.

THE ECONOMY

AGRICULTURE DOMINATES the Portuguese economy. About 60 per cent of the Portuguese people make their living from farming, and some 40 per cent of the country's total land area is cultivated. The most important food crops grown are wheat, oats, rye, barley, rice, maize, and potatoes. Portuguese farming methods have not been modernized to any great extent, and they are basically the same as they were several centuries ago. Most farms are small and lack agricultural machinery. The soil is usually turned with the aid of oxen. As a result, crop yields are not very high, and farmers and their families consume a great deal of what they produce each year. Portugal must import grain from abroad to make up for the difference between demand and supply. One effect of overpopulated farmlands has been the emigration of thousands of Portuguese to the Overseas Provinces and to foreign countries.

The breeding of livestock plays an important rôle in the rural economy. There is extensive cattle-raising in the northern part of the country. However, bulls for the bullfighting ring are bred chiefly in Alentejo in the south. Other animals raised include sheep and goats. Donkeys are often used for transportation in rural areas.

After having been cut with an axe, the cork is pulled from the tree. Mature cork oaks are stripped no oftener than once every nine years. Unlike most oaks, the cork oak does not shed its leaves in the winter.

CORK GROWING

Portugal is the largest producer of cork in the world, the industry dating back to the 12th century. Annual production runs as high as 150,000 long tons—quite a large amount considering that cork weighs very little, since more than half its volume is air (water is four times heavier than cork).

Cork is the outer bark of the cork oak. These trees grow mostly in the southern part of the country, and Portugal's cork oak forests cover more than 1,500,000 acres. In some areas, cork oaks are grown on plantations, but most grow wild.

The cork is actually dead bark and can be stripped from the tree without killing it. It takes at least twenty years of growth before a cork oak is ready for stripping. After the first stripping, cork may be removed legally from a tree only once every nine years. The quality of cork improves with the age of the tree, although

The old man's tales delight these two young boys and their dog. Wires firmly attached to the ground prevent the wind from blowing the cork hut away. The stocking cap and quarterstaff are typical of Alentejo Province.

682 ■ PORTUGAL

Cork is a cargo that oxen do not mind pulling. Here, men load cork collected in the forest on to carts for the trip to the factory. The stripping of the trees takes place during the months of June, July and August.

stripping is usually halted when a tree is about 140 years old. Exceptionally hardy cork oaks may live for centuries, and there may be some that are even older than Portugal.

Once the cork has been stripped from the trees, it is hauled from the forest to a factory, where it is boiled in vats of water and then put out to dry in the warm Portuguese sun. After ten days of drying, the cork is graded, and pieces that are found acceptable are cut into squares for sale to manufacturers in Portugal as well as overseas. The material has a variety of uses. Bottle stoppers are probably the most familiar application of cork, but it is also utilized in life preservers, as insulation, and for soundproofing. Cork scraps are ground up and used to make composition floor tiles and similar products.

The casual observer might think this huge mound at Moita to be a monument of an ancient civilization. A closer look reveals nothing more than a gigantic pile of cork. The "stone" slabs on the sides of the pile protect the cork from the elements. Smokestacks rising in the background are part of a cork-processing factory.

FISHING

One of Portugal's greatest economic assets is the sea. Fishing villages are located at frequent intervals along the coast, especially where there are beaches. Portuguese fishermen put to sea in heavy, high-prowed boats styled after ancient Phoenician galleys. Launching a boat into the Atlantic surf is a difficult task in some places. First, the boat is dragged down to the edge of the water by oxen, with small boys placing logs underneath for the vessel to roll on. When a good wave is about to break on the beach, the boat's master gives a signal. The crew, often up to 40 in number, pushes; the oxen wade into the surf dragging the boat with them. On the beach women tug on a cable attached to the craft in order to keep the bow pointed out to sea during the launching. Perfect co-ordination is essential, for at the proper moment—when the boat is afloat—the women must release the cable they hold, the oxen must be detached from the boat, and the crew must jump over the sides into their vessel and man the oars.

The oars (sweeps) of the boats are so big that each one requires eight to ten men to operate it. Each boat heads straight out into the Atlantic for two or three miles paying out a line whose other end is firmly anchored on shore where the fishermen put to sea. When they have gone far enough, the boat's master gives the order to turn parallel to the coast. A several-mile-long net attached by the line to shore is then slowly dropped overboard. After that, the boat is turned towards the beach and another cable—attached to the other end of the net—is payed out as the boat heads for shore at a point a half-mile or so from the launching point.

After the tricky landing operation—almost the reverse of the launch—oxen begin hauling in the two ends of the net, a job that takes several hours. Finally the net reaches shore with a catch which may be large or small, depending upon the luck of the fishermen.

Fishing is backbreaking work. Atlantic gales make it a dangerous occupation at times. It was the ancestors of these hardy sailors who braved the unknown almost five centuries ago and led Portugal into its golden age of discovery.

Sardines, mackerel, hake, and flounder are

With a hold filled with sardines, everyone has a good reason to smile—even the government revenue collector who will receive 12 per cent of the value of the catch. Much of the fish tax is used for schemes to improve the living conditions of the fishermen.

Teams of oxen strain to pull a returned fishing boat out of reach of the tides on the sandy beach at Nazaré. Fishermen of the town usually wear black stocking caps; ox drivers prefer cloth caps.

some of the various types of fish caught. Other fishermen, those from the province of Algarve, specialise in intercepting the annual run of tuna heading for the Mediterranean. Every year a fleet puts to sea from Lisbon, bound for Newfoundland to fish for cod.

Hundreds of dykes divide the salt marshes near the Aveiro River into scores of rectangular compartments. When the gates to the compartments are closed, the sun evaporates the water, leaving the salt behind for collection and sale.

Windpower is used to grind grain in parts of Portugal. This cluster of windmills is along the road from Bussaco to Penacova. The long poles extending from the roofs are used to turn the cloth sails into the wind.

(Above) In summer many Portuguese hillsides take on a golden hue from the ripening wheat crop. Whole families participate in the harvest which is done by hand with the help of sickles.

(Left) Two peasant women of the Alentejo pause during the harvest for a refreshing drink of water. Broad-brimmed black hats ward off the rays of the hot sun. The Alentejo, which makes up about one-third of Portugal's land area, is a region of rolling plains and occasional low mountains. Cereal-growing and livestock-raising are the chief occupations of the people of the Alentejo.

WINE

Portugal has a world-wide reputation for its excellent port wine which, like the country, takes its name from the region about the city of Oporto. The grapes from which the wine is made are grown on terraces built on the steep hillsides flanking the Douro River. Heavy rains sometimes wash away the walls that have been built over the centuries to keep in place the grapes and the earth in which they grow. The walls must then be painstakingly rebuilt.

Most Portuguese grapes are actually part American. When European vineyards were struck by disease during the 1860's, a disease-resistant strain of American grapes was brought to Europe to prevent disaster. Today, Portuguese stock is still grafted on to American-descended roots to produce a healthy vine.

Every autumn the grape crop is harvested and brought to large stone tanks for fermentation. There, men tread back and forth, barefooted, on the grapes to squeeze out the wine. It is considered that the human foot can do a better job than a machine. When the wine is sufficiently fermented, it is collected in casks and taken down the Douro River to the lodges (warehouses) of the Oporto wine merchants. Expert tasters grade all arriving wine.

It is harvest season along the Douro. Having filled their wicker baskets in the vineyards, the grape pickers trudge down the hills with their loads. Two of the workers provide a musical accompaniment for the marchers on an accordion and a drum. Soon the luscious grapes will be turned into port wine, much of which will be exported to other countries.

A wine merchant rolls a cask of port wine down an aisle in a wine cellar at Vila Nova da Gaia. Aging the wine in wooden vats and casks improves its quality.

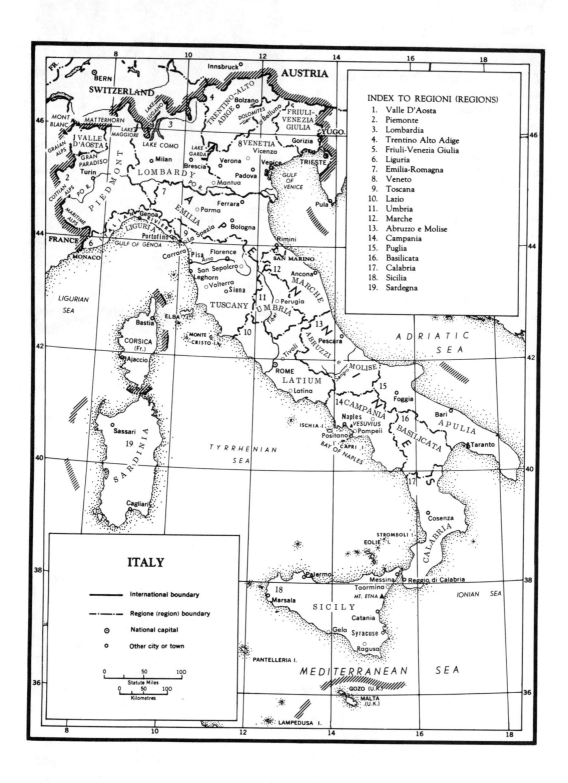

INDEX TO REGIONI (REGIONS)
1. Valle D'Aosta
2. Piemonte
3. Lombardia
4. Trentino Alto Adige
5. Friuli-Venezia Giulia
6. Liguria
7. Emilia-Romagna
8. Veneto
9. Toscana
10. Lazio
11. Umbria
12. Marche
13. Abruzzo e Molise
14. Campania
15. Puglia
16. Basilicata
17. Calabria
18. Sicilia
19. Sardegna

ITALY

International boundary
Regione (region) boundary
National capital
Other city or town

0   50   100
Statute Miles
0   50   100
Kilometres

Portofino on the Riviera is a charming Ligurian fishing port that has become a fashionable resort and yachting spot. Set against cliffs rising sharply from the sea, it is typical of the Eastern Riviera (Riviera di Levante).

THE LAND

GEOGRAPHICAL POSITION

ITALY occupies a central position in southern Europe. Cut off from the rest of the continent by the great mountain chain of the Alps, the country consists of two well-defined regions: a long mountainous peninsula thrusting south-eastward for 700 miles into the Mediterranean Sea; and, between the peninsula and the Alpine chains, a broad, fertile plain.

The outline of the peninsula resembles a high-heeled boot. Near the toe of the boot, the great island of Sicily is aimed like a foot-ball at the shores of North Africa, 90 miles away at the nearest point. To the northwest of Sicily is Sardinia, an island nearly as large as Sicily. These two Italian islands form, with the French-owned island of Corsica, and the

Lake Como, ringed by the foothills of the Alps, is 1,300 feet deep, 30 miles long. Beyond measurement is its breathtaking beauty, resulting from a rare marriage of man-made gardens and villas with mountain, sky, and water.

The great seaport of Trieste, long under Austrian rule, was later a bone of contention between Italy and Yugoslavia. Created a free city in 1947, it was returned to Italy in 1954, but most of the surrounding territory was awarded to Yugoslavia.

The Blue Grotto on the island of Capri is one of the most celebrated of sea caves. Known in Roman times, it was re-discovered in 1826.

Palermo, capital of Sicily, is a unique blend of Saracen, Norman, and Byzantine influences in an incomparable setting between the mountains and the sea. A fine example of an Italian formal garden is La Favorita, laid out for one of the island's Bourbon kings.

west coast of the Italian mainland, a triangle enclosing an arm of the Mediterranean called the Tyrrhenian Sea. The eastern coast of the peninsula flanks the Adriatic Sea, another arm of the Mediterranean, across which lie the steep coasts of Yugoslavia and Albania. The sole and heel of the boot front upon the Ionian Sea, which separates Italy from Greece.

The northern land frontiers of Italy are almost entirely defined by the towering ranges of the Alps. To the west, the Maritime and Graian Alps rise like steps from the blue waters of the Mediterranean, separating Italy from France. Mont Blanc, whose summit is in France, but whose eastern slope is in Italy, is the highest peak in Europe outside of Russia. The highest point wholly within Italy is Gran Paradiso in the Graian range (13,652 feet). Included in the northern section of Italy's great Alpine wall are parts of the Pennine and Central Alpine ranges, forming boundaries with Switzerland and Austria. Switzerland's mighty Matterhorn is actually on the boundary line. The Alps swing eastward in a great arc, meeting the sea again near Trieste at the head of the Adriatic, where they separate Italy from Yugoslavia.

AREA AND COASTLINES

Italy contains 116,372 square miles, of which Sicily accounts for 9,936 square miles and Sardinia 9,292. The distance from the Alps to the tip of the peninsula is about 750 miles.

From east to west the greatest distance is 250 miles across the northern, or continental, land-mass, and 150 miles across the peninsula itself.

Italy's coastline measures more than 2,000 miles. At some points, notably along the Riviera near Genoa, and on the splendid Bay of Naples, mountains rise abruptly from the sea; at others, long stretches of silt and marsh conceal from the eye of the sea-borne visitor the fact that Italy is one of the most mountain-

The snow-clad peak of Mt. Etna looms 10,000 feet above the Sicilian town of Taormina, noted for its architectural and scenic beauty.

The Rialto Bridge over the Grand Canal in Venice was begun in 1588. This city of nearly 400,000, built on islands and shoals by Roman refugees from Teutonic invaders, is today a haven for the pedestrian, for no motor traffic is permitted within it.

ous countries of Europe. Apart from Venice and Trieste, there are few good ports on the Adriatic. On the Ionian Sea, the flourishing port of Taranto, cradled between Apulia (the heel) and Calabria (the toe), possesses excellent natural facilities. The western coasts include several major ports of call—Naples, Genoa, La Spezia, and Leghorn. Sicily is well provided with port facilities, chief of which are Palermo, Catania, Syracuse and Messina. The latter city is located on the narrow straits of the same name, near the point where the mainland of Italy and Sicily are only two miles apart. This spot is where in ancient times were located the rock of Scylla and whirlpool of Charybdis, between which Ulysses had to sail in "The Odyssey." In fact, the name of Scylla (Scilla) still survives on the mainland shore.

There are few islands along the Adriatic coast of Italy. The Tyrrhenian Sea, however, has many small islands scattered about its shores, among which are Elba, Napoleon's first place of exile; Stromboli, with its active volcano; Monte Cristo, known to readers of Alexandre Dumas the Elder; and Ischia and Capri, beloved of tourists, rising like gateposts on either side of the Bay of Naples.

CLIMATE

Peninsular Italy has a generally dry and sunny climate.

It is not, however, a sub-tropical paradise, for the high altitude of most of Italy makes for frequently severe winter weather, although the warming influence of the sea produces sub-tropical effects along the southern coasts and in sheltered areas as far north as the Riviera.

Italy shares in the gradually increasing drought that has affected the entire Medi-

The glaciated limestone blocks of the Dolomite Mountains rise above the Alpine village of Forno di Zoldo near Belluno in northeastern Italy.

terranean area since ancient times. In the days of the ancient Romans, extensive forests covered many sections now stripped bare by two thousand years of land-clearing, sheep-raising, and human settlement. The forces of erosion and drought have made some parts of the South virtual deserts. Low humidity in most of the country makes conditions comfortable

Seen from the Funicular, the houses of Capri cling to the limestone cliffs. The island has been a resort since ancient times, when the Emperors Augustus and Tiberius built villas there.

even in the heat of summer. This is a blessing for the tourist, but often the despair of the farmer. Rainfall is more abundant and regular in the northern plain, but elsewhere seasonal and undependable. In the North, winters are relatively short, but severe. The climate of

Naples, third city of Italy with 1,205,000 people, stretches round its azure bay in the shadow of Mount Vesuvius. As Neapolis (literally New Town), 2,500 years ago it was one of the principal Greek colonies in South Italy.

northern Italy is basically not too different from that of Central Europe. In the peninsular regions, the high altitudes counteract the influence of the Mediterranean and make areas such as the Abruzzi among the coldest in Italy. As in other Mediterranean countries, sudden winds bring sharp changes in the weather. The chill *maestrale* which blasts the date palms and orange groves of the Riviera is the same *mistral* that plagues the adjacent Côte d'Azur of France. The Bora, another bitter wind from the Alps, lashes the northern shore of the Adriatic, and can make Venice seem as cold as Leningrad. The *scirocco* (sirocco in English), a hot, stifling wind blown northward from the Sahara Desert, can make Naples feel like Timbuktoo.

FLORA AND FAUNA

A truly Mediterranean flora is found only in the extreme south, in Sicily, and along the sheltered coast of the Riviera, where there are stunted evergreens and scrub thickets. Dense, coniferous forests occur in the Alps, and a mixed flora, not truly Mediterranean, occurs

Tourists march to the music of 1,500 fountains in the splendid garden of the Villa d'Este at Tivoli. This ancient town on the outskirts of Rome has been the site of splendid residences since the days of Augustus and Hadrian, both of whom sojourned here.

On a country road near Scanno in the Central Apennine Region of Abruzzi e Molise, a cluster of women wear the folk costumes for which they are renowned.

in central Italy. The land of Italy, wherever it has proved even passably arable, has been cleared and shaped by the hand of man for so long that natural landscapes are uncommon. Everywhere the land supports the plants introduced from elsewhere to answer economic needs—the vine, the mulberry (for silk culture), the almond, walnut, olive, and in Liguria and the South, the orange and lemon. Much of Italy looks like a vast garden.

Wildlife is scarce. Among larger forms, bears and deer are the most common, and the great-horned wild sheep, or *mouflon*, is found in Sardinia.

SURFACE FEATURES

The dominant feature of peninsular Italy is the Apennine mountain chain, actually a continuation of the Alps, joining the latter near the French border, thrusting eastward almost to the Adriatic, and then running all the way to the tip of Calabria, like a giant backbone. The Apennines reach their highest point (9,560 feet) in the Gran Sasso halfway down the peninsula, on a line with Rome.

In the North, the great loop formed by the combined Alpine-Apennine system almost encircles the broad plain of the Po Valley, walling it off from both the peninsula proper and the rest of continental Europe. This great plain, the richest agricultural region of Italy, is open only at its Adriatic end.

Sicily and Sardinia are both largely mountainous.

VOLCANOES

Italy lies within a vast earthquake zone, and severe quakes have been frequent throughout Italian history. As recently as 1908, the city of Messina was flattened in a catastrophe that took 200,000 lives in Sicily and Calabria.

Italy is a huge laboratory for the study of

Tiers of vineyards hug the mountain slopes at Caldaro in the Adige Valley near Bolzano. The Italian Tyrol is noted for the variety and quality of its wines, as well as for its bilingual character, for both German and Italian are spoken.

Ruins of the ancient Greek theatre are sunk like a crater amid the intensely cultivated fields near Syracuse in Sicily. Syracuse was once one of the greatest cities of the ancient world and covered a far greater area than it does today.

volcanism or volcanic action. Records of eruptions go back farther than in any other country. In fact, the words "lava" and "volcano" are both Italian, as are many other terms relating to volcanism. At present three volcanoes are considered active—Stromboli; Etna, on Sicily; and Vesuvius, towering over Naples, remembered for its destruction of the ancient cities of Pompeii and Herculaneum in A.D. 79. Visitors to the Naples area today can see vivid details of ancient Roman life which were preserved by the sudden descent of hot ashes from Vesuvius and not excavated until modern times. Much of Italy's soil is volcanic in origin, and very fertile where an adequate water supply exists.

The Archaeological Museum in Palestrina, historic town of Latium, houses objects dating from the 6th century B.C. Under the name of Praeneste, the city was a rival of Rome in the latter's infancy. The composer Palestrina was born here in 1514.

The Flavian Amphitheatre, or Colosseum, was opened to the Roman public in A.D. 80 and for 400 years was the scene of gladiatorial combats and public spectacles. In the Middle Ages it was used as a source of building material, more than half of its original mass being taken for this purpose. What is left is still colossal.

The Basilica of Saint Anthony (San Antonio) in Padua dates from the 13th century. Padua is a great place of pilgrimage, for the church is built over the Saint's tomb.

The Basilica of Saint Peter's in Rome is the largest church in the world and the focal point of Roman Catholicism. With the Vatican (upper left) and other buildings it forms the sovereign territory of Vatican City. Among those who helped build St. Peter's, between 1452 and 1626, were Raphael, Michelangelo, and the architects Bernini and Bramante.

The Ducal Palace in Venice, begun in 1354, was the residence of the Doges, or chief magistrates of the Venetian Republic. The clustered domes of the nearby Basilica of St. Mark (San Marco) appear to rise from the palace roof, their Byzantine form contrasting with the Gothic style of the palace. St. Mark's, begun in A.D. 830 and completed in 1052, is one of the outstanding examples of Byzantine art.

The ancient Tuscan hill town of Volterra, known for its alabaster carvings, was founded by the Etruscans, and contains well-preserved remains from all periods of its long history.

RIVERS AND LAKES

The only large river in Italy is the Po, the principal stream of the North Italian Plain. It rises in the Cottian Alps near the French frontier and flows 400 miles to the Adriatic where it fans out into a broad delta below Venice. It is navigable for 320 miles, and in volume of water it is one of the great rivers of Europe. Its valley is not only the agricultural, but the industrial, heart of Italy, and contains 40 per cent of the country's people.

The rivers of peninsular Italy are short and precipitous. Plunging down from the Apennine crests they carry off much of the soil and deposit it along the shorelines. In this way the coast has been extended even within recorded times. Many towns and cities, now several miles inland, were once thriving ports. Pisa, now 10 miles from the sea, was a mediaeval maritime republic rivalling Venice and Genoa. The silty plains formed in this fashion (such as the Maremma north of Rome) were for centuries

In Rome, the Spanish Steps descend from the Church of Trinità dei Monti to Bernini's Fountain of the Boat in the Piazza di Spagna.

The Leaning Tower of Pisa is actually the campanile (bell tower) of that city's beautiful Romanesque cathedral, one of Italy's greatest architectural monuments. The Tower is currently the subject of extensive studies to prevent its leaning further.

malarial wastelands until reclaimed in modern times. Best known of the peninsular torrents are the Arno, the river of Florence, and the Tiber, Rome's river.

The Alpine slopes of Lombardy are renowned for their beautiful lakes, some of which are shared with Switzerland. Lakes Como, Maggiore, Lugano, and Garda are among the principal tourist attractions of Europe. The protective Alpine foothills give the shores of these lakes an unusually mild climate for northern Italy, and provide a spectacular background for fabulous villas and palaces that line their shores. In central Italy, the crater lakes of the Latium region, especially Lake Bolsena, are set amid a timeless, classical landscape of open fields, olive groves, and stands of chestnut trees.

NATURAL RESOURCES

The country is poor in minerals. Its fuel resources are inadequate. Only sulphur and mercury are found in sufficient quantities to export but some pyrites, manganese, lead, zinc, bauxite, and asphalt are mined. Marble of fine quality is quarried in some areas, notably around Carrara. Mineral resources are concentrated in the Regions of Tuscany, Sicily,

The Region of Apulia is noted for its strange peasant dwellings called "trulli." Alberobello, near the large city of Bari, has more than a thousand of these beehive structures with their conical stone roofs built without mortar.

The Pirelli and Galvani skyscrapers are among the many modern towers of Milan, Italy's second city in population (1,660,000) and its economic capital.

Sardinia, Lombardy, and Piedmont. There has been a great recent development of water-power resources, and the discovery of oil near Ragusa, Gela, and Fontanarossa in Sicily is turning that region into a major European oilfield. These, and natural gas discoveries in the North, are helping Italy to overcome its dependence on fuel imports.

Extensive reforestation schemes are being developed to replace the country's badly depleted woodlands.

The Mediterranean is not as rich in marine life as the Atlantic; therefore, although fisheries are important locally, and furnish a livelihood to many people, the catch of the Italian fishing fleet is far smaller than that of countries on the Atlantic. The seas around Italy chiefly provide tuna, sardines, anchovies, mackerel, and a variety of molluscs and crustaceans.

CITIES

The Italian land cannot be discussed apart from human structures. In Italy these are as much a feature of the land as the mountains and the coasts. The scenic beauty of Italy is based in large measure on a striking harmony between the rocks and peaks bestowed by nature, and the towns, farms, castles, abbeys, fortresses, walls and towers that men have built upon them. Villages cling to craggy coasts and nestle in mountain clefts as though they had grown there. Most views in Italy include notched battlements, watchtowers, and the domes and spires of small cities.

In the cities of Italy, some of them older than the Romans, the Renaissance was born. It was in Italy that the revival of learning marked the beginning of the modern world. Venice, Milan, Bologna, Padua, Parma, Florence, Pisa, Verona, Mantua, Perugia, Siena and Genoa are a few of the cities whose pre-eminence in art, culture, science, and commerce made their names household words throughout Europe in the late Middle Ages. Instead of comparing the shape of Italy to a boot, it might be more apt to liken it to the trunk of a tree, rooted in the Mediterranean, with Western Christendom as its crown of leaves and branches.

The Battle of San Romano, as depicted by Uccello, was fought in 1432 by the city-states of Florence and Siena. The Renaissance was an age of struggle and political disorder as well as one of great artistic and intellectual vitality.

HISTORY

THE HISTORY OF ITALY as a unified modern state goes back only to 1861. For a thousand years before that, the history of the geographic entity of Italy is that of a group of separate states, large and small, often under foreign domination, their borders alternately growing and shrinking, some of brief duration, others quite long-lived. Before that, Italian history is the history of ancient Rome.

ANCIENT HISTORY

The legendary date of the founding of Rome is 753 B.C. At that time, the Italian peninsula was occupied by many different peoples. The vicinity of Rome was populated by the Latins, one of many related Indo-European tribes of peninsular Italy. North of Rome the Etruscans, a people of unknown origin, held sway over a large area. Southward and in Sicily the Greeks were establishing thriving colonies. The Etruscans possessed an advanced culture showing Greek influence. Rome was under the rule of the Etruscans for a long period before emerging as a strong independent state, and owed the beginnings of its distinctive civilization to them. As Rome grew, Etruria declined, and new invaders entered Italy—the Gauls settled in great numbers in the Po Valley, and the Carthaginians, a North African offshoot of the Phoenicians, began to threaten mainland Italy and the growing power of Rome.

The ancient Etruscans were a lively race, if the vibrant and informal quality of their art is an indication. Here the tombstone of a married couple is viewed by former Italian president Einaudi and his wife. The Etruscan language has never been deciphered; scholars hope that its eventual unravelling will throw new light on Roman origins.

B.C.

509   Rome throws off Etruscan yoke and the Republic is established.

390   Gauls sack Rome.

264–146   The Three Punic Wars break the power of Carthage.

148   Rome annexes Greece.

60–49   Julius Caesar emerges and conquers Asia Minor, Spain, and Gaul. Invades Britain.

44   Caesar assassinated after assuming dictatorship.

43   Conquest of Britain begins.

29   Octavius (Augustus) becomes Emperor.

A.D.

54–68   Nero ascends throne. Christian persecutions begin.

98–275   Height of Roman power under Trajan, Hadrian, Marcus Aurelius, and others. Empire embraces most of Mediterranean world and much of Western Europe. Period ends with a line of weak Emperors and the start of the barbarians' invasions.

325   Emperor Constantine recognizes Christianity.

330   Imperial capital moved to Byzantium.

395   Empire divided into Eastern (Byzantine) and Western (Latin) Empires.

410 Rome sacked by Goths. Roman rule of Britain abandoned.

476 Empire of the West dissolved by Odoacer, Herulian chief.

493 All Italy united under Gothic kingdom of Theodoric.

533 Byzantine Empire annexes much of Italy.

568 Lombards conquer Northern Italy, reduce Byzantine power.

756 Franks invade Italy under Pepin and establish the States of the Church, with the Pope as temporal ruler of Central Italy.

800 Charlemagne, ruler of the Franks, crowned Emperor of the Romans.

With the accession of Charlemagne and the creation of the Holy Roman Empire, the Italian peninsula entered an age of power politics between Pope and Emperor, in the course of which two parties arose, the Guelphs (anti-Empire) and the Ghibellines (pro-Empire). The townsmen of Italy organized to defend their own territory, and a host of city-states came into being, some Guelph, some Ghibelline. These cities were granted autonomy by Pope and Empire, and in time some gained complete independence. However, the Guelph-Ghibelline struggle tore Italy apart for hun-

The Greeks so heavily colonized Sicily and southern Italy that the entire area was known in ancient times as Magna Graecia, or Great Greece. Some of the most illustrious of the ancient Greeks lived or taught in splendid cities such as Agrigentum (modern Agrigento), whose temple of Hercules is shown here.

dreds of years. The issues were complicated by struggles between nobleman and townsman, between city and rival city, and between factions within each small state.

827 Saracen conquest of Sicily begins.

877 Feudalism established in Frankish dominions in Italy. Frankish power declines.

962 Otto I crowned as Emperor. The Holy Roman Empire, henceforth based in Germany, has suzerainty over much of Italy.

1031 The Normans conquer Sicily and establish their own rule there.

1077 The Emperor Henry IV, having attempted to wrest control of the Church from the

Adria in northern Italy near the mouth of the Po was founded by the ancient Greeks. Shown here is a Greek vase of the amphora type from the city's Museum of Archaeology.

Twice during the summer, Arezzo in Tuscany stages its annual Joust with the Saracen, a custom that originated at the time of the Crusades and was revived in this century. Mounted citizens in mediaeval dress attack the effigy of the Saracen. The Saracens ruled Sicily from 827 to 1061. Even after they were ousted by the Normans, the long, open coasts of Italy were often threatened by Moslem raiders.

The 3,000 years of civilized life in Italy is well illustrated by the Cathedral of Syracuse, originally the Temple of Athena (6th century B.C.). Converted into a church in the 6th century A.D., the flanking columns of the temple were filled in to make the walls of the church.

Papacy is excommunicated by Pope Gregory VIII, loses all support of his vassals, and is obliged to beg papal forgiveness at Canossa.

1152 Emperor Frederick II (Barbarossa) crowned. Campaign to subdue Guelph cities. Cities form Lombard League to resist him.

1268 French house of Anjou assumes rule of Sicily and Naples. The famous massacre of the French, called the Sicilian Vespers, ends Angevin rule in Sicily.

1282 Aragon annexes Sicily, beginning long period of Spanish domination of southern Italy.

1305–78 Violent conditions in Italy force papacy to move to Avignon, France.

1321 Dante dies. Renaissance movement spreads over Italy in a great burst of artistic and literary activity, reaching its peak in Florence.

1381 Venice, after three wars, finally defeats Genoa and becomes a major naval power.

1434 Cosimo de Medici establishes his family as the rulers of Florence.

1455 The Borgias come to power with the accession of Calixtus III to the papacy.

1494 Italy invaded by Charles VIII of France. Foreign interference in the affairs of the Italian states grows.

1534 Faced with the Protestant Reformation, Pope Paul III launches reform within the Church—the Counter-Reformation.

1559 Treaty of Cateau-Cambrésis leaves Spain the dominant foreign power in Italy.

1632 The Duke of Savoy assumes royal rank and starts gradual expansion of power.

1713 Treaty of Utrecht. Victor Amadeus II of Savoy gains Sicily. Austria awarded Naples.

1720 Victor Amadeus of Savoy trades Sicily for Sardinia, and assumes title of King, in the face of growing Austrian power.

1791 France annexes Nice and French-speaking part of Savoy.

1796 Napoleon invades Italy and overthrows Austrian rule. Puppet republics established. Venice given to Austria and ceases to be an independent state.

1805 French organize Kingdom of Italy (embracing only part of the North) as a unit of Napoleon's empire.

1809 Napoleon annexes the States of the Church.

1815 Congress of Vienna, following Napoleon's downfall. The boundaries of Italy prior to the French Revolution are largely restored.

The Forum, the heart of Ancient Rome, has been largely excavated since 1870, and is today one of the greatest attractions of Italy. Here were transacted affairs that affected the entire Mediterranean world. Rising in the background is the Torre delle Milizie, popularly called Nero's Tower in the belief that from its height the Emperor watched Rome burn. Actually the structure dates from the reign of Pope Innocent III.

MODERN ITALY

After 1815, Italy was divided into the Kingdom of Sardinia, including Piedmont; the Kingdom of Naples; the Grand Duchy of Tuscany; the Duchies of Parma, Lucca, and Modena; the Papal States; and the Austrian dominions of Lombardy and Venetia. But the Italians of all these regions were restless. The ideas of the French Revolution had gained wide acceptance, owing to the French creation of Italian republics in the 1790's. Italians every-

where now wanted a unified nation under a republic. This widespread spirit of nationalism was called the *Risorgimento* (Resurgence), and was directed chiefly against Austria, for the Austrian influence extended beyond the territory actually ruled by Vienna, the thrones of Parma, Modena, and Tuscany being occupied by Hapsburg relatives of the Austrian monarch, and that of Naples by a Hapsburg protégé. Sardinia alone was free of Austrian influence, but its King, Victor Emmanuel I, had little sympathy for liberal reforms in government.

Victor Emmanuel II of Savoy, first king of a united Italy, originally sought to consolidate only northern Italy under his rule. But the tide of events made him the focus of Italian nationalist hopes and carried him to the throne of all Italy.

Yet his dynasty, with its ambition to drive Austria out of Italy and unite the country under the House of Savoy, was eventually to merge its aims with those of Italian patriots everywhere.

The years 1815–1861 were full of uprisings and underground activity, in Sardinia as well as in the lands under Austrian and Papal control.

1820   A revolutionary society, the "Carbonari," instigates rebellions in Piedmont and Naples.

1831   Insurrection breaks out in Parma, Modena, and the Papal States. Austrian troops are brought in to restore order.

1848   The widespread popular revolts in Europe of 1848 frighten the rulers of Tuscany, Naples, and Rome into granting constitutional governments.

1848   The Lombards rise against Austria. Charles Albert, King of Sardinia, invades Lombardy to aid the rebels, but is defeated at Custozza.

1849   Austria invades Sardinia. Charles Albert is defeated at Novara and abdicates, leaving the throne to Victor Emmanuel II. A short-lived republic is established in Rome under Giuseppe Mazzini, founder of the Young Italy Movement but the Pope is restored to power by French intervention. Constitutional rule in most of Italy is revoked as Austria once more regains control.

Giuseppe Mazzini, born in Genoa in 1805, spent much of his life in exile organizing Italian revolutionary activities. A proponent of republican government, he refused to swear allegiance to Victor Emmanuel II when the Kingdom of Italy came into being in 1861.

Giuseppe Garibaldi (1807–82) spent much of his young adult life in America, biding his time for the day when Italy would be ready for revolution. After the unification of his country which took place along lines distasteful to him, he fought for France in the Franco-Prussian War.

CAVOUR AND GARIBALDI

The events leading to Italy's unification were influenced by conflicting desires and ambitions of four men—Count Camillo di Cavour, Prime Minister of Sardinia; King Victor Emmanuel; the Emperor Napoleon III of France; and the revolutionary leader, Giuseppe Garibaldi. Victor Emmanuel was mainly interested in extending the power of Sardinia at Austrian expense. Cavour, while furthering his King's aims, genuinely wished to bring about liberal reforms in Italy. Napoleon III played a double rôle, since he wished to free Italy from Austrian rule, but did not look kindly upon the emergence of a strong new nation ruled by the House of Savoy. Garibaldi was the chief spokesman of all those Italians who wished Italy to be unified as a republic. All had one aim in common: the expulsion of the Austrians. In

achieving this goal, they paved the way for the creation of modern Italy under the Savoy monarchy.

1853   Cavour leads Sardinia into the Crimean War against Russia in order to gain the friendship of England and France.

1856   The National Society is founded with the secret backing of Cavour, its purpose being to unify all Italian nationalists behind the House of Savoy. In joining the society, Garibaldi in effect sacrifices his desire for a republic in the interests of national unity.

1859   Sardinia goes to war with Austria, with the aid of Napoleon III, but the French Emperor soon withdraws and compels Sardinia to make peace out of fear that a decisive Austrian defeat would result in too great an extension of Sardinian power. However, Lombardy is ceded to Sardinia, and Naples, Parma, and Modena overthrow their rulers and request to be annexed to Sardinia. Napoleon III consents to the annexations in return for the territories of Nice and Savoy (which had been reassigned to Sardinia in 1814).

1860   With the secret aid of Victor Emmanuel, Garibaldi leads a volunteer army into Sicily and Naples, while Victor Emmanuel invades the Papal States.

1861   Garibaldi turns his conquests over to Victor Emmanuel, who is proclaimed King of Italy. The Papal States are restored under French occupation, however, and Austria still rules Venetia.

1866   Italy sides with Prussia in the Austro-Prussian War and gains Venetia.

1871   Prussia's defeat of Napoleon III in the Franco-Prussian War leaves Rome without French protection. Italy annexes the Papal States. Pope Pius IX refuses to accede to the annexation and withdraws to self-imposed confinement in the Vatican. Not included in the unification is the tiny city-state of San Marino which survives today as an independent country surrounded by Italy.

1871–1914   King Umberto (1878–1900), the successor to Victor Emmanuel, joined the other European powers in the race to

Napoleon III, Emperor of the French, shown here with his Empress Eugénie, contributed materially to the unification of Italy although this was not his intention.

carve up Africa. Eritrea and Somalia in East Africa were annexed piecemeal, but an attempt to conquer Ethiopia ended disastrously in the Battle of Adowa in 1896. Prior to this, Italian hopes to acquire Tunisia had ended when France established a protectorate there. In 1881, Italy had formed the Triple Alliance with the new German Empire, and an old enemy, Austria. To some extent this alignment was based on resentment towards France; to some extent on a community of interest with Germany, since both countries had acquired national unity late in the game and were seeking to expand, if necessary, at the expense of the established powers. Distrust of Austria continued despite the Alliance. In 1911, Italy went to war with Turkey and acquired Libya.

WORLD WAR I

1914 Austria attacks Serbia and the First World War begins with Germany and Austria against England, France and Russia. Italy refuses to abide by the Triple Alliance, claiming that Austria is the aggressor and the Alliance applies only to a defensive war.

1915 Desire to regain "Italia Irredenta" (Italian-speaking lands still under Austria) leads to Italian entry into the War on side of England and France.

1919 The Treaty of Versailles, ending World War I, awards the South Tyrol and Istria to Italy, but Italian hopes for greater gains at the expense of Austria are crushed. Desired land is included in Yugoslavia and boundary with that new nation is disputed. Italian nationalists blame France for thwarting their country's ambitions and Italy drifts away from its wartime allies.

MUSSOLINI

In 1919, Benito Mussolini founded the Fascist Movement, a blend of nationalism and socialism reflecting Italian discontent. Italy had entered the power struggle late and with serious disadvantages: a fast-growing population living on a depleted soil, and insufficient mineral resources to develop heavy industry. Economic

Benito Mussolini participating in a Fascist Party celebration in 1938.

and social crises caused many Italians to look to the Fascist Movement for help, so Mussolini's rise was rapid.

1922 Mussolini becomes Prime Minister, following virtual seizure of Rome by Fascist marchers.

1924 Mussolini is made Dictator, and assumes the real rulership of Italy, King Victor Emmanuel III becoming a figurehead.

1926 Italy signs a friendship pact with Germany.

1929 Mussolini clarifies the doubtful status of the Papacy by signing the Lateran Treaty with the Pope, creating the independent State of Vatican City. The Pope ceases to be the self-imposed "Prisoner of the Vatican."

1935 In a bid to extend Italy's overseas empire, Mussolini invades and conquers Ethiopia.

1939 Mussolini annexes Albania, confident that no one will oppose him, thanks to his series of pacts with Hitler's Germany, begun in 1936.

WORLD WAR II

1939 Germany invades Poland and World War II begins.

1940 Following German invasion of the Netherlands, Belgium, and France, Italy declares war on Great Britain and France, expecting a German victory.

1941 Italy declares war on the United States.

1943 Britain and U.S. seize Italian island of Pantelleria. Invasion of Italy by the Allies begins. Italian mainland is invaded. Mussolini resigns and withdraws behind German lines. Italy concludes armistice with Allies and officially joins forces with them.

1945 Germans finally expelled from Italy after bitter struggle fought inch by inch up the Italian peninsula. Mussolini put to death by Italian partisans.

1946 King Victor Emmanuel III abdicates. The new king, Umberto II reigns only a few months. House of Savoy is rejected by the Italian people for its collaboration with Mussolini. Republic is proclaimed.

THE PRESENT

Mussolini's Fascism never reached the excesses of Nazism. The Dictator had effected some improvements in the years before World War II—extensive public works and land reclamation projects, and addition of rail facilities, for example. His popularity diminished as the Italians found themselves more and more under the domination of Hitler. After Mussolini's downfall, the Italian government made every effort to co-operate with the Allies. Italy renounced all territories seized by Mussolini and entered the post-war world with a will to undo the damage of the past and build a democratic future. With U.S. foreign aid and in a spirit of full support of international co-operation, the Italians have concentrated in recent years on rebuilding their war-torn country and contributing to world peace and stability. Under the Republic, Italy has taken a firm step towards resolving its age-old problems of economic imbalance and political instability.

Showcase for Italy's products is the great Milan Trade Fair held every year in mid-April and attended by several million visitors.

GOVERNMENT

ITALY IS A REPUBLIC governed by a President and a Parliament composed of a Senate and a Chamber of Deputies.

The seat of government is Rome, historic capital of the Roman Empire, but not the first capital of modern Italy. When the Kingdom of Italy was created in 1861, Turin became the capital, then Florence, and finally in 1870 with the removal of the Pope as ruler of Rome, the Italian Government was permanently located in the great city on the Tiber. Rome has therefore been the capital of its country for a much shorter time than have Paris and London, or even Washington. However, the enormous prestige of Rome as a force in culture and religion for such a long time gave the city the character of a national capital long before the unification of Italy.

Just as Rome is not really a new capital, neither is the republican form of government new to Italy. Indeed the Romans were governed under a republic for 500 years before the Roman Empire came into being in 31 B.C.

During the Middle Ages many Italian states were actually republics, including Venice which was one until 1797. However, the Roman Republic and the various city-states of the Middle Ages and the Renaissance were not truly democratic. In general, the right to vote was limited to the more influential citizens.

The modern Italian Republic, established under the Constitution of 1947, is a true democracy. The Fascist Party is outlawed and titles of nobility are no longer recognized. Male members of the former royal family are even barred from Italian territory.

Since Rome was not the seat of a long line of European kings, it has no great royal palace equivalent to the Louvre in Paris or Buckingham Palace in London. (The Vatican Palace, of course, is in Papal territory.) But the city is full of magnificent residences on a smaller scale—the former homes of great noble families and of members of the Pope's court, dating from the time when Rome was the capital of the Papal States. One of these splendid buildings, the Quirinal Palace, is the residence of the President of Italy. Many more are in use as government offices.

PRESIDENT

The Italians would seem to agree that age brings wisdom, for the President must be at least 50 years old. He serves a longer term, seven years, than does the President of the United States and is not elected directly by the people. Instead he is chosen by the two houses of Parliament meeting together with delegates from the 19 "Regions" into which Italy is divided. He must be elected by a two-thirds majority, but if such a majority is not obtained after three votes, a simple majority is enough. The President has the power to dissolve both houses of Parliament, except during the last six months of his term. He automatically becomes a Senator when his term ends, unless he chooses not to serve.

PARLIAMENT

Members of the Chamber of Deputies, or lower house, are elected for five years by the direct vote of the people, and must be 25 years of age or over.

Each deputy represents about 80,000 voters. The Senators serve for six years and are elected on a regional basis, each Region having at least six Senators (except for tiny Aosta, which has only one), or one for every 200,000 people. The Italian Parliament thus rather resembles

the United States Congress. In addition, the President of the Republic may nominate leaders in the fields of art, science, and social affairs as senators for life.

CONSTITUTIONAL COURT

Another feature of the Italian government that has an American counterpart is the Constitutional Court, similar in purpose to the United States Supreme Court. The Court, created in 1955, has 15 judges, one-third appointed by the President, one-third by the Parliament, and one-third by the highest law court. Its judges decide on the constitutionality of laws and decrees, define the powers of the Government and the Regions, and decide conflicts between the two. The Court may also try the President and his Ministers.

REGIONS

For purposes of government, Italy is divided into Communes, Provinces, and Regions. The Communes are the small local divisions of the Provinces. The latter are roughly the size of counties in the United States or Great Britain, and several of them make up each Region. The Constitution of Italy proposes to make all of the 19 Regions into self-governing units, which would make Italy a federal republic like West Germany or the United States, but this plan has not been put into full effect. At present five Regions have self-government, with their own legislatures and a large amount of control over their local affairs. These are Sicily, Sardinia, Aosta, Trentino-Alto Adige, and Friuli-Venezia Giulia. The reason for creating such a federal system lies in the long history of separate political and cultural development that existed in each Region prior to the unification of Italy.

Three Regions have sizable minority groups speaking languages other than Italian—French in Aosta, German in Trentino, and in Friuli, a Latin-derived language related to the Romansch of Switzerland. The remaining Regions are Piedmont, Lombardy, Liguria, Venetia, Emilia-Romagna, Marche, Umbria, Tuscany, Abruzzi e Molise, Latium, Campania, Calabria, Apulia, and Basilicata.

Italy's booming electrical industry is an important factor in the country's economic progress. New facilities such as the Sabbione Dam in the Alto-Adige Region have helped double Italian hydro-electric power output since World War II.

THE ECONOMY

ITALY has made a remarkable, if somewhat uneven, recovery from the damage of World War II. The country's industry is expanding at a much higher rate than that of the United States, for example. Yet many severe problems remain unsolved, especially in the agricultural Regions of the South.

The bitter struggle between the invading Allies and the retreating Germans devastated much of the country. Everywhere transport and communications were destroyed and millions of people were made homeless. For a country of Italy's limited natural resources, the task of recovery was all but overwhelming, complicated as it was by the spread of Communism. In the years since World War II, the Italian Communist Party has been the largest in any European nation outside the Iron

At Bardonnechia on the French border, special freight trains haul Fiat cars over the Alps to France. Fiat builds 80 per cent of Italian cars, mainly in its vast plants at Turin. Italy ranks fourth in European motor-car production.

Curtain. Yet in spite of this, Italy has had a fairly stable government and outstanding industrial growth.

In 1950 the gigantic task of reconstructing damaged buildings was over, and long-range economic planning began. One of the chief problems facing the planners was the economic backwardness of southern Italy.

CASSA PER IL MEZZOGIORNO

In 1950, the Italian Government created the *Cassa per il Mezzogiorno*, or Fund for the Development of the South. The Italian South (*Mezzogiorno* in Italian) is economically a different world from the bustling modern Italy lying between Rome and the Alps. It is a land of poor peasants working farms ruined by long years of erosion, drought, and mismanagement, with little industry compared to the North. Cut off from the North by centuries of separate political history, the South was largely neglected by the House of Savoy and Mussolini. Famine, unemployment, and dissatisfaction caused millions of southern Italians to emigrate during the last hundred years, mostly to the Americas and to other European countries. Today, new industries are sprouting all over the South, water supply and transport facilities are being improved, and farming methods modernized, but the changes have not been fast enough to stop the trend to emigration. Every year large

The "Michelangelo" and her sister ship the "Raffaello" are among the world's most modern ocean liners. At the end of World War II the Italian mercantile fleet had dropped to one-tenth of its pre-war tonnage. Extensive rebuilding since then has made Italy a leader in world shipping.

numbers of southern Italians leave their homes in Sicily and Apulia to seek a share in the humming industrial life of Milan, Turin, or in countries like France and Germany. Much of southern Italy is still geared to the oxcart, the patient little donkey staggering under his load, and the farm woman daily carrying water from a distant well. Until the economic growth planned by the Cassa per il Mezzogiorno really takes hold, southern Italians will continue to look for opportunity elsewhere.

INDUSTRY

The great cities of northern Italy constitute one of the major industrial areas of Europe. Milan is unique among European cities for its grouped skyscrapers. Turin is Italy's Detroit, hub of the important Italian motor-car industry, fourth in rank in Europe, producing 1,105,291 vehicles in 1963. Genoa, Italy's largest port, is a shipbuilding, aircraft and automotive manufacturing city. The country's vital textile industry, one of the world's largest, has its headquarters in Milan. Cotton is the principal natural yarn produced, followed by jute and wool. On a smaller scale is Italy's renowned silk industry, dating from Byzantine times. In recent years the manufacture of artificial and synthetic yarns has grown into a major industry, surpassing cotton in the total amount produced.

At the Bocchetta Pass in the Alps, work proceeds on the Central Europe Pipeline, one of two major pipelines under construction by ENJ, the Italian national oil combine. The line will eventually carry 12,000,000 tons of crude oil over 6,000-foot heights from Genoa to Germany.

At Avezzano in the Abruzzi Region, students in an agricultural secondary school receive instruction on modern farm management.

An assembly line in the Vespa motor scooter plant. Scooters, largely an Italian development, have become a major industry and a principal means of transportation in Italy.

Throughout the world people have become familiar with finely engineered products of Italy's booming mechanical industries—sleekly styled typewriters and adding machines, motorcars, textile looms, machine tools and sewing machines. Expansion in the chemical industries has made Italy a major producer of sulphuric acid and superphosphate.

FUEL AND POWER

The discovery of large quantities of natural gas in the Po Valley just after World War II is considered a leading cause of Italy's industrial recovery and expansion, since it provided a great new source of fuel. Scarcity of coal within Italy had long hampered the country's economy,

A farmer waters his oxen at the land reclamation project of Orbetello in the Maremma district north of Rome. Under the direction of the Ente Maremma, a government agency, this once desolate and malarial coast is being re-populated.

Near Brolio the grape harvest is loaded upon oxcarts to be hauled off and pressed into wine.

COMMUNICATIONS AND TRANSPORT

Italy's merchant fleet is the world's seventh largest. Italy was a leader in world shipping prior to World War II, but lost most of its fleet in the war. The country's present high place in shipping comes as the result of a huge effort to replace wartime losses. Inland waterways are found largely in the plains of the North, and are a much less important factor in the country's transport situation than in France or the Low Countries. Not only are the canals less numerous, but they are shut off from the waterways of adjoining countries by the Alps.

Railways are a vital factor in hauling goods over Italy's numerous mountains and in maintaining the flow of trade between the country and its partners in the European Economic Community. Nearly two-thirds of Italy's rail network is electrified. In the field of air transport, the state-owned airline, Alitalia, carried 2,854,745 passengers in 1963, making it an important factor in world air transport.

FINANCE AND FOREIGN TRADE

In 1960 the lira, Italy's unit of currency, was devalued and now amounts to about 620 to the

making it unable to compete with coal-rich countries like England and Germany. Italian participation in the European Coal and Steel Community, making Belgian, German, and French iron and coal available to Italy at lower cost, has helped to overcome the shortage.

This, plus the new gas resources, the later discovery of oil in Sicily, and a big jump in hydro-electric power through the building of many new dams and power stations, have made it possible for Italy to produce 10,000,000 tons of steel a year, an impressive output for a country without its own iron deposits.

Italy is also speeding atomic power development and now has three nuclear power plants.

Modern Italian engineering carries on the fine tradition of the Romans and the Renaissance. Italian architects and engineers are engaged in public works and industrial projects all over the world. The Port Authority Bus Terminal at the George Washington Bridge in New York, shown here, is the work of architect Pietro Nervi.

ITALY ■ 719

U.S. dollar and 1,736 to the pound sterling. The prospect of inflation remains a matter of constant concern, however.

The Italian balance of trade has been generally satisfactory. Although normally, imports exceed exports, Italy would be paying more money out than it takes in if it were not for certain factors such as tourism which bring a vast quantity of foreign currency into Italy, and the remittances sent home by millions of Italian emigrants and migratory workers in foreign countries. The country's economy has come to rely heavily on the export of manufactured goods, and vast quantities of raw materials must be imported to supply the factories of Turin, Milan, and Genoa.

Chief imports are coffee, maize (corn), rubber, metals, wood and pulp, cotton and wool, meat, and machinery. Exports are mainly produce and preserves, wine, textiles, chemicals and mechanical products.

NATIONALIZATION

A special feature of the Italian economy is the Institute for Industrial Reconstruction, a government agency created under Mussolini, that controls directly or indirectly a vast com-

The new Mont Blanc Tunnel, opened in 1965, a joint French-Italian project, cuts through the base of the highest mountain in Western Europe, for 7¼ miles. The longest motor-car tunnel yet built, it brings Rome and Paris 125 miles closer by road.

plex of industrial and commercial activities in the fields of shipping, transport, communications, power, banking, and iron and steel production. Yet it is private enterprise that is basically at the core of Italian economic strength. Most of the great industries of Turin and Milan are privately controlled. Many business activities are financed jointly by government and private enterprise.

AGRICULTURE

Wheat for bread and pasta is the chief crop of Italy, although rice is grown in the Po delta, and barley, oats and rye are raised in quantity.

New textile equipment is demonstrated at the Milan Trade Fair. The textile industry is located chiefly in the Milan area, although Pisa and Naples are important for cotton milling.

Maize is raised widely in the North. Grape production, of course, is of great importance in a country that produces as much wine as Italy. Large crops of potatoes and sugar beets are harvested. Olive cultivation is widespread, olive groves being as much a feature of the landscape as vineyards. The tomato is a staple of the Italian diet and its cultivation is an important activity.

Oranges and lemons are an important export crop in Sicily and the country south of Naples, where there is the least chance of frost damage.

In the rich fields of Lombardy and Piedmont dairy cattle are the most important livestock, providing milk for the esteemed cheeses of northern Italy. In the more arid and mountainous South, sheep and goats are raised in great numbers for meat, milk, and hides. Many of Italy's millions of pigs end up as *prosciutto* (Italian ham). Oxen, mules, donkeys, and even water buffaloes are widely used as draught animals, especially in the South, although modern farm machines are increasingly in use in the rich northern plains.

Progress in farming has always been impeded by the existence of large, often absentee, landowners, particularly in Sicily. The Italian

At the Buitoni plant in San Sepolcro, spaghetti is extruded from a modern machine. The food processing industries are located for the most part near Naples and in the northern industrial regions, especially Milan, Modena, Parma, Bologna and Bergamo.

government has caused many of these estates to be broken up, and the land redistributed. The Cassa per il Mezzogiorno is carrying out over 12,000 separate land-reclamation, water-supply, and communications projects in the South in an effort to increase farm production. Government planners are trying to induce the Italian peasant, who is a conservative man by nature and resists change, to shift from wheat-growing to raising more fruit and vegetables, since the latter crops are in great demand by Italy's Economic Community partners.

Women decorate Easter eggs in a Milanese confectionery plant. Italy specializes in the production of very high quality sweets, biscuits, and preserves, for which larger foreign markets are being sought.

Wine-tasting is a serious matter in a country where fine wine is produced on a large scale. In Bolzano experts sample the different vintages to determine their quality.

Sicilians in folk costume gather at Piana degli Albanese near Palermo. The Near Eastern look of their costume derives from Albanian ancestors who fled the Turks in the 15th century and settled in this area.

A fashion show held in the Pitti Palace in Florence draws buyers from all over Europe and America.

In Venice, gondolas massed in the Grand Canal under festoons of lights hold celebrants of the Feast of the Redeemer. This brilliant "festa," held in July, commemorates the city's deliverance from the plague of 1576.

THE PEOPLE

AFTER THE GREEKS, the Italians may well claim to be the oldest civilized community in Europe for their recorded history goes back 2,500 years, and ruins and relics of civilized life go back even farther. The 51,507,000 modern Italians descend from an ancient mixture of many races, for the Romans after conquering half of Europe and the whole Mediterranean shore, brought people from all over their Empire back to Italy, as slaves, soldiers, and merchants.

These people were absorbed by the already mixed Italian population, composed as it was of Romans, Gauls, Etruscans, and Greeks.

The barbarian invasions after Rome's fall brought whole tribes of Teutons. Centuries of Byzantine, Arab, Norman, Spanish, French, and Austrian rule of the diverse Italian states added further to the mixture. The result is a varied population, predominantly brunet, but not predominantly Mediterranean in type.

The family with its personal allegiances, sense of loyalty and pride, and religious ties, has always been the backbone of Italian life whatever the form of government. Misruled for centuries, the Italians are somewhat distrustful of government and skeptical of ideologies and

In a public square at Marostica near Vicenza, a chess match is in progress. The pawns and pieces are living, even to the knight's horse.

movements. They are not easily regimented. Mussolini never really succeeded in whipping them into fascist uniformity. The high percentage of Communist voters in Italy today does not necessarily reflect belief in Communism but, rather, dissatisfaction with existing conditions.

Italians have a great sense of rising to the occasion—they accomplish even the most menial tasks with a flourish. To give the appearance of being light-hearted, even when one is not, is an Italian art. There is much genuine cheerfulness, as well, for the Italian tends to be vivacious in speech, quick to laugh at himself as well as others, disposed to enjoy whatever blessings he has, sing aloud and appreciate beauty whether natural or artistic.

The hordes of tourists who come to Italy (23,000,000 in 1963) are likely to overlook one very important aspect of Italians—a great capacity for hard work. The long Italian lunch hour (or *riposa*) is part of the long Italian working day; two or more hours are set aside for partaking of the day's main meal. To wrest a living from a land not too well-endowed by nature has always been difficult for the Italians. The fact that they accomplish it with grace and cheerfulness does not lessen the backbreaking quality of their toil. Although the Marshall Plan and the European Cooperation movements were instrumental in the Italian recovery from World War II, the diligence and courage of the Italian people were perhaps of greater value.

Equestrians of the Gioco del Calcio, members of a costumed company of citizens, pass through the Piazza della Signoria in Florence. In modern Tuscany the richness of the Renaissance is annually relived, not only in Florence, but in the Pisan festival of the Gioco del Ponte and the famous Palio of Siena. The statue in the background is a full-size replica of Michelangelo's "David."

LANGUAGE AND LITERATURE

Italian was the last of the Romance languages to develop from Latin. The first records of a distinct Italian tongue date from a little before A.D. 1000. Of the many dialects of Italian that arose, Tuscan, owing to the cultural leadership of Florence, became the standard literary form, and is the basis of the educated speech of modern Italy. Italian literature is generally considered to date from the year 1200 with the appearance of lyric and religious poetry and chronicles and tales of literary merit. In the late 13th century there emerged in Dante one of the great poets of all time, and in his age Tuscan literature became dominant. In the 14th century, Petrarch and Boccaccio, also Tuscans, were at the head of the "humanist" movement, the revival of Greco-Roman learning or Renaissance that reached its peak in the 15th century. Under the Medici rulers of Florence the Platonic Academy was founded, devoted to

Christmas, a time of particular charm in Italian cities, is celebrated with street fairs, fireworks, and novenas. Shepherds from the mountains of Abruzzi arrive in pairs, one with a flute, the other with a bagpipe to play traditional Nativity airs in the streets, as here in Rome's Piazza Navona.

the application of the thought of Aristotle and Plato to contemporary life. Ariosto (1474–1532) in his epic poem, *Orlando Furioso*, brought the literary language to a height of polished expression. Niccolo Machiavelli (1469–1527) wrote masterworks of political science, and his *The Prince* is the first realistic study into the means of gaining political power. Outstanding among later writers of the Renaissance was Torquato Tasso (1544–1595), author of the great religious epic, *Jerusalem Delivered*.

The popular theatre of northern Italy of this period, the *Commedia dell' arte*, left a lasting impression on European comedy, and the names of its stock characters—Harlequin, Punchinello, Columbine, and others still survive.

POST-RENAISSANCE PERIOD

The great age of Italian literature was followed by two centuries of decadence, during which many good writers such as the satirist, Salvatore Rosa (1615–1673) were far outnumbered by wordy and imitative ones. Towards the end of the 18th century, the resurgence of national spirit brought new life to Italian writing. Among the authors of this period, the dramatists, Carlo Goldoni (1707–

Dante Alighieri, Italy's greatest poet, was banished from his native Florence in 1302. He found refuge in Verona, where this statue commemorates him.

1793) and Alessandro Manzoni (1785–1873) stand out, along with the lyric poet, Giacomo Leopardi (1798–1837).

MODERN PERIOD

The poets Giosue Carducci (1835–1907) and Gabriele D'Annunzio (1863–1938) mark the transition to the 20th century.

Other modern literary figures are the novelists Alberto Moravia, author of *The Conformist*; Giuseppe di Lampedusa, author of *The Leopard*; Ignazio Silone, author of *Bread and Wine*; the playwright, Luigi Pirandello, author of *Six Characters in Search of an Author*; and the philosopher, Benedetto Croce.

Italy has been the final resting place of many foreigners seeking peace. Here, in the foreign cemetery of Rome, is the grave of the English poet John Keats. Nearby is the grave of Shelley.

The Italian contribution to science and discovery is great. Among the Italian explorers who opened Asia and the Americas to European domination were Marco Polo, who went by the overland caravan routes to China in the 13th century, sparking a renewed interest by Europeans in the worlds beyond their own; Christopher Columbus, who reached America in 1492; Giovanni da Verrazano, who explored the coast of North America and sailed into New York Bay nearly a century before Henry Hudson; Amerigo Vespucci, who established the fact that America consists of two continents, North and South, and whose first name was given by mapmakers to the New World; and John Cabot, on whose explorations England later based her claims to territories in America. For the most part they served the great Atlantic maritime powers of England, France, and Spain, but they were Italians.

All Western science may be said to stem from the development of scientific research in

Luigi Galvani (1737–98), anatomist and physicist, conducted the experiments on the reaction of the leg muscles of a frog to metals that led to the discovery of galvanic electricity.

Count Alessandro Volta (1745–1827), a leader in the development of electricity, invented the voltaic pile, the condenser, and the electroscope.

Guglielmo Marconi (1874–1937) first transmitted long-wave radio signals in 1895. His studies of electro-magnetic waves led to the development of wireless telegraphy.

ITALY ■ **727**

During his reign (1958 until his death in 1963), Pope John XXIII, in addition to being the spiritual head of the Catholic church, was recognized as being a leader in the struggle for peace and unity throughout the world. He deeply affected the lives of many people through his messages concerning world peace, and religious tolerance.

Renaissance Italy. The individual Italians who have contributed materially to Western and world knowledge are Galileo (1564–1642), astronomer and physicist, perhaps the greatest single influence in scientific development; Francesco Redi (1626–1698), naturalist; Alessandro Volta (1745–1827), physicist (for whom the volt is named); Marcello Malpighi (1628–1694), anatomist; Guglielmo Marconi (1874–1937), physicist and pioneer in wireless communication; and Enrico Fermi (1901–1954), one of the chief developers of atomic physics.

EDUCATION AND RELIGION

Education is compulsory between the ages of 6 and 14. Pre-school training is given in public nursery schools. Primary education consists of grades 1 to 5, followed by three years of junior secondary education which may include vocational training. Compulsory attendance at school ends in the 8th year. Senior secondary education is available in three forms —classical, scientific, and technical. It includes agricultural, industrial, commercial, nautical, and teachers' training courses. Higher education

The Pope's personal bodyguards, the famed Swiss Guards, are recruited in the Catholic cantons of Switzerland. Their uniform is of the 16th century, the period when a treaty was first signed between the papacy and the cantons of Zurich and Lucerne establishing the Guard.

The white marble Gothic Cathedral of Milan, studded with pinnacles and heavy with sculpture, is the second largest church in Italy. Gothic architecture is much less common in Italy than in the rest of Western Europe. With the completion of the west front of the cathedral in 1965, the building was finally officially completed, 579 years after the cornerstone was laid.

is available at 29 universities and University Institutes. Universities are state-controlled, the universities of Bologna (A.D. 1200), Padua (1222), Naples (1224), Genoa (1243), Perugia (1276), and Siena (1300) being among the oldest in Europe.

The Italian constitution of 1948 confirmed the treaty between the Catholic Church and Italy of 1929, whereby the Roman Catholic religion is declared the only religion of the State. Other creeds are permitted, however. The Italian government has the right to pass on appointments of bishops and archbishops within Italy. Catholic religious teaching is given in elementary schools. Italy is 95% Catholic; Protestants number about 100,000; Jews, 50,000.

The University of Bologna, the oldest in Italy, was one of the greatest seats of European learning in the Middle Ages. In more recent times, the poet Carducci and the physicist Galvani taught amidst its serene arcades.

The Via Veneto in Rome is lined with smart cafes and shops. In the background is the Porta Pinciana leading to the gardens of the Pincian Hill, famed since ancient times as an agreeable place for Romans to stroll.

FOOD

Pasta or macaroni and spaghetti in its many forms is widely regarded as the basis of the Italian cuisine. This is true only of the South, where such dishes are served with a variety of piquant sauces and seasonings. In the South, also, garlic, olive oil and tomato paste are ingredients of the daily diet. The farther north one dines, the milder the seasoning, and in the North generally, *pasta* is served in small portions as an opening course more often than as the main dish or it is replaced by *polenta* (corn-meal mush) or potatoes. Actually, the Italian menu is quite diversified and each Region has its distinctive style and special dishes. Fresh beef is less frequently served than in Northern Europe. Shellfish, fish, and veal,

ham and sausages, mutton, cheese, and green vegetables are items of everyday fare in the North. The cuisine of the northern city of Bologna is rated the highest in Italy by many gourmets. Unfortunately, the diet of the people in the stricken Regions of the South is far more limited.

In northern Italy, food is cooked in butter rather than in olive oil. In the South such sea creatures as the octopus and the sea urchin are highly esteemed as delicacies. Throughout Italy mealtime is an occasion when the family comes together and shares experiences and hearty food. Meals are leisurely and social in character, events to be enjoyed.

Italian cooking has been carried overseas by Italian emigrants on a large scale. In the United States and other countries with many

Sausages (from Bologna) and cured meats are important in the Italian diet and their production is an Italian art. Parma is renowned for hams, seen here hanging in splendid array in a curing chamber.

Italy accounts for 30 per cent of the cheese produced in the European Economic Community. Parmesan, Gorgonzola, Pecorino (made from ewe's milk), Mozzarella, Bel Paese, Taleggio, are a few of the many varieties. Here at a dairy near Naples, Provolone, made from buffalo milk, is shaped into its distinctive pear-like form.

citizens of Italian origin, some Italian dishes have become regular parts of the menu, such as spaghetti and pizza. Many of the famous dishes of Milan, Parma, and Bologna, such as veal cutlets Bolognese (with ham and cheese) are standard items in fine restaurants from London's Soho quarter to San Francisco.

Italian cheeses are justly famous, ranging from the soft, blue Gorgonzola to the hard, nut-like Parmesan. Italy is one of the great wine-producing countries of the world, and wine is the customary beverage at meals. Italian wines are varied and many are of excellent quality, although few approach the perfection of the best French and German wines. Espresso coffee, strong and black, concludes a meal.

Religion is deeply engrained in the Italians. The full measure of their feeling is expressed in the solemnities of Holy Week. Here, hooded penitents, some carrying crosses, take part in the observance of "la Settimana Santa" in Taranto.

As might be expected in a country celebrated for both roads and motors, auto-racing is an important sport. The Autodrome at Monza near Milan is the scene of the awarding of the Grand Prize of Italy.

RECREATION

On the high mountains of Italy, from the Alps to Etna in Sicily, skiing is a major sport. Excellent bathing facilities exist and few places in peninsular Italy are far from the sea. In addition to such well-known resorts as the Lido near Venice, and the Italian Riviera, there are miles of unfrequented shoreline. Soccer is the national sport, with bicycle-racing a close second. Baseball has a considerable following, as has auto-racing.

Bocce, a form of bowling using heavy balls

An out-of-doors theatrical performance is held in the Roman theatre at Pompeii. This ancient city near Naples was preserved for 1,900 years in the ashes of Vesuvius until excavated in the 19th century.

A bob-sled careens along the run at Cortina d'Ampezzo high in the Dolomites—often the scene of the winter Olympics. Italy's high mountains provide a long season of winter sport. At nearby resorts the skiing season lasts till June.

and sand pits, is a popular pastime of older men in quiet villages and busy towns alike.

Fairs and festivals occur all over Italy throughout the year, and form one of the main amusements of the population, as well as a prime tourist attraction. In these events, the Italian love of pageantry expresses itself in splendid mediaeval costumes, dazzling displays of fireworks, cascades of pennants, lanterns, balloons, flowers, song and dance. Many of the festivals commemorate historic events, many more are religious in character.

The Italians have a great knack for simple, convivial amusements. They entertain one another with singing, conversation, family strolls in the park or countryside. Music is of great importance in Italian life. Opera companies perform throughout the country. On the day of a performance arias from the opera to be presented may be heard in barber shops, cafes and on the street, sung by the ordinary people of the town. Puppet shows are a traditional dramatic entertainment for both adults and children. Entire plays, sometimes employing nearly life-size marionettes, are staged in many parts of Italy, especially Sicily.

The Italian's wit is keen. Although too polite to display it, the average Italian draws much mild amusement from observing the vast throng of foreign tourists, students, and bargain-hunters who tramp through his country

At Petralia Sottana in Sicily, girls in folk costumes hold their tambourines in readiness for the dance. Folklore groups are active throughout Italy and folk dancing is a normal feature of local festivals.

The principal Italian literary award is the Strega prize. Here, in Rome's Villa Giulia, voting takes place for the 1963 award of the prize to Natalia Ginzburg for her novel "Lassico Famigliare."

every year. This kindly amusement, neverthe-less, brings millions into the Italian treasury. And the Italians laugh at one another: satire is an Italian gift, and the Italian turns it upon himself and his foibles as readily as on others.

Lastly, the Italians are not indifferent to the haunting beauty of their own countryside. They find great satisfaction in contemplating the rugged landscape which for 2,500 years they and their ancestors have softened and embel-lished. The many new highways, such as the great *Autostrada del Sole* running down the peninsula, make it increasingly easy for the Italian to see the scenic wonders of his own country.

Bicycle-racing has a devoted following in Italy. The champion racer Presenti is shown here winning the 1,000-metre sprint during the 1956 Olympics at Melbourne, Australia.

The "Last Supper" by Leonardo da Vinci (1452–1519) is a fresco in the church of Santa Maria delle Grazie in Milan. Artist and scientist, Leonardo was the ideal Renaissance man.

THE ARTS

PAINTING AND SCULPTURE

ART IS INSEPARABLE FROM ITALY. The country is a vast gallery of treasures from every age beginning with the Etruscan. No other country of the West has such a long history of artistic achievement. The greatest period in Italian art, and in Western art as well, was the Renaissance, or Revival of Learning, the period roughly between 1300 and 1500. The Renaissance (which means rebirth) was a return to the knowledge of the ancient Greeks and Romans, and an attempt to apply that knowledge to 15th-century Europe. For hundreds of years the artistic and scientific principles of the ancients had remained dormant, as Europe passed through the Dark Ages of barbarism and feudalism, with the Church as the main civilizing influence. Art during that period was mainly religious in nature. Human figures were depicted in stiff and formal attitudes. The Renaissance re-introduced realism in painting and sculpture, and shifted the emphasis from the spiritual to the humanist point of view,

The "Pietà di Palestrina" by Michelangelo (1475–1564) is on display in the Galleria dell' Accademia in Florence. Michelangelo was also a painter, architect, and poet. He spent the last years of his life as chief architect of St. Peter's Basilica in Rome.

that is, to the all-round values represented by ancient art. Religion continued to be the foremost subject of art, but it was treated more as a part of life than as a separate and mysterious thing.

The painters Giotto and Cimabue, prior to 1400, were the first to create life-like scenes markedly different from the stiff, unrealistic style prevailing previously. The initiators of Renaissance art were Brunelleschi, an architect and sculptor who designed the dome of the great cathedral of Florence; Donatello, sculptor of the life-like statues of David and St. John the Baptist; Della Robbia, best known for his exquisite terra-cotta statues; Uccello, who greatly developed the use of perspective in drawing; and Fra Angelico, the painter whose delicate use of pigments can be seen today in the frescoes in St. Mark's Convent in Florence. The Renaissance came to its peak in the late 15th and early 16th centuries. This was the age when Botticelli painted the *Birth of Venus*; Michelangelo did the murals in Rome's Sistine Chapel; and Leonardo da Vinci, the embodiment of the Renaissance ideal of a man capable of many things, not only painted *The Last Supper* on the walls of Milan's Church of Santa Maria delle Grazie, but designed models of aircraft, parachutes, pile-drivers, roller

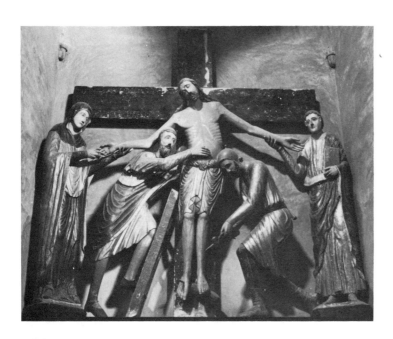

A mediaeval sculpture depicting the Descent from the Cross is one of the many works of art in the Cathedral of Volterra.

Antonio Canova (1757–1822) was one of the great sculptors of recent times. This self-portrait in marble, in the Tempio Canoviano at Possagno, shows the influence of classic Greco-Roman style.

The Vatican Library, a corner of which is shown here, is, along with the Vatican Museum, one of the greatest storehouses of Western culture, sheltering a priceless collection of art and manuscripts. Among its treasures is Tasso's manuscript of "Jerusalem Delivered," mysteriously stolen and recovered in 1965.

bearings, and many other things long before they were perfected and put into general use. Vitality and richness under the control of man's intelligence was the ideal of the age, and Leonardo typified it.

BAROQUE TO MODERN PERIODS

The splendid hues and shades, three-dimensional forms, illusion of movement, and imagination that flourished in Renaissance painting gave way to a style called Baroque in

The portrait of St. Sebastian by Raphael Sanzio (1483–1520) hangs in the Accademia Carrara at Bergamo. It is a good example of the sweetness and tenderness characteristic of Raphael's work.

The Teatro Olimpico designed by the architect Andrea Palladio (1518–80) is one of the marvels of Vicenza. It has a permanent set so perfectly scaled as to give a remarkable illusion of distance. The Palladian style was long regarded as a model of architectural perfection.

which the subject matter became sentimental and the design intricate and fanciful. Notable in the period of transition from Renaissance to Baroque are the painters Correggio, known for his startling use of foreshortening, and Caravaggio, remembered for his effective use of light and shade to create dramatic effects. Baroque painting is best illustrated in the work of Guido Reni (1575–1642) who produced pretty, rosy groupings of figures in trailing garments against backgrounds of clouds and sunbursts. Since the Renaissance, Italy has continued to produce artists of merit, but few have approached the level of the Renaissance masters. Tiepolo, in the 18th century, painted in the Baroque manner, with remarkable technical skill. Two great modern painters of Italy are the late Amadeo Modigliani and Giorgio di Chirico. The former is known for his portraits in outline in a curiously distorted style, the latter for surrealist landscapes.

Since World War II, a great new spurt of creative effort has taken place in Italy, and it is not impossible that Italy may rival France as a leading force in modern art, when the work of the new generation of painters and sculptors has been evaluated.

Within sight of Mount Vesuvius an artisan carves cameos amidst the ruins of the Temple of Apollo in Pompeii.

Arturo Toscanini conducting the orchestra at La Scala, Milan.

Giuseppe Verdi, the son of a peasant inn-keeper, died in 1901 after providing the world with many of the most popular operas of his time—"Rigoletto," "La Traviata," and "Il Trovatore."

MUSIC

Everyone is familiar with such words as piano, concerto, allegro, and many others. Actually, almost the entire technical vocabulary of Western music is Italian in origin. After the full development of polyphony in church music (in which two or more melodies are combined) by Palestrina in the 16th century, Monteverdi introduced harmony in the late Renaissance. This heralded the beginning of European secular (non-church) music. Monteverdi is considered to be the father of opera, the field in which the Italians reached their highest musical achievements in later centuries.

Although Italian composers are chiefly operatic, many of the great sonatas, orchestral concertos and organ compositions of the 17th century came out of Italy. The 19th and early 20th-century operas of Rossini, Donizetti, Verdi, Puccini and Bellini have been presented throughout the civilized world. But it is in Italy itself that they have their most enthusiastic audience. Attendance at the opera is a vital and cherished part of the life of all of the people of Italy.

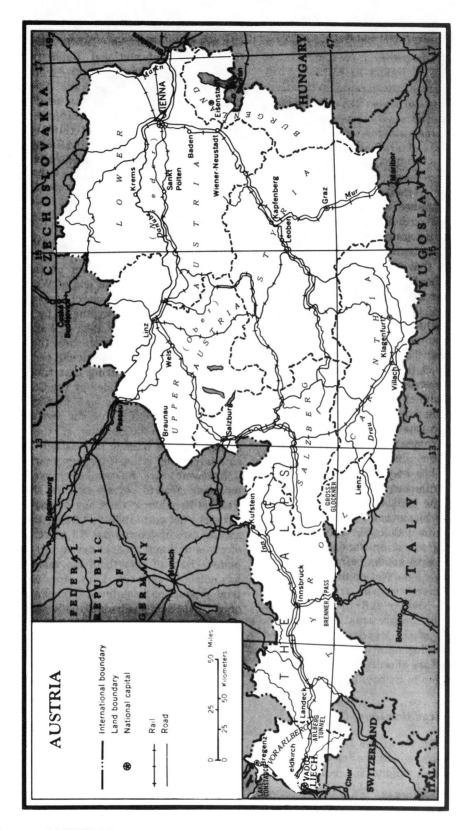

AUSTRIA

International boundary
Land boundary
National capital
Rail
Road

50 Miles
50 Kilometers
25
25
0
0

740 ■ **AUSTRIA**

AUSTRIA

HISTORY

AUSTRIA in modern times personifies the concept that the pen is mightier than the sword. In the past 100 years the country has shrunk from a vast empire, proud and powerful, to a tiny land whose entire population is less than that of London or New York. But its fame depends not on ancient conquests or half-forgotten wealth and grandeur. It exists, above all, in the living music of its composers, past and present, and the living musicians who make Austria today a mecca for the music lovers of the world.

The work of the composer's quill, the monuments to the architect's pencil, the knowledge recorded by pens of Vienna's physicians and psychiatrists, all these endure.

And while the country is small, it is also beautiful. The mountains, too, endure.

THE BEGINNINGS

Austria was inhabited in the beginning of recorded history by Celtic people, akin to those who then inhabited Germany, France and Spain, and whose progeny still live in Brittany, Ireland, Northern Scotland and Wales. Then, as now, its major population must have lived in the valley of the Danube, farming and probably hunting in the nearby hills. Other groups were established in the lesser valleys which grow narrow and wild near their sources in the high Alps. At least one industry was already in full swing before Austria is first mentioned in the chronicles of the Roman Republic: from prehistoric times salt was mined in the province of Salzburg, shipped in primitive boats down the Salzach and the Traun into the Danube and thence, by prehistoric trade routes, to many parts of Europe.

In the second century B.C. the legions of an expanding Rome crossed the Alps through the Brenner Pass in the west and the Semmering Pass farther east, and easily conquered the valley lands. They built fortified camps around which cities grew. The legionnaires who were, according to the Roman custom, stationed more-or-less permanently in the more remote outposts, tended to intermarry with the local population. The Danube basin was eventually

The equipment is up-to-date but the salt mines at Hallein in Salzburg province have been worked for at least 2,000 years. They may be the oldest mines in Europe still in operation. This region of limestone mountains is called the Salzkammergut and spreads into the adjoining provinces of Upper Austria and Styria. Salt was worth its weight in gold during the Bronze Age. Today the world-famous lakes of the area—Wolfgangsee, Mondsee and the others—may be worth more than the salt.

Built in about A.D. *300, Carnuntum (now in Lower Austria) was a Roman military camp and trading post, perhaps a good-sized town. Among the excavations one can find clear remnants of elaborate water supply and drainage systems, lovely mosaic floors, a magnificent amphitheatre. Even on the frontiers the Roman legionnaires wanted comfort, beauty and drama.*

organized into colonies of the republic, Moesia in the west, Pannonia in the area that is now Austria, and Dacia near the mouth of the river. Only in the latter province did Roman power extend north of the Danube, in the country now called (by no accident) Romania. In Austria proper the river formed the northern frontier of Rome. Thus Vindobona, which eventually became known as Vienna, started out as a fortress that served both as trading post and military stronghold, much as Fort Duquesne grew into the city of Pittsburgh nearly two millenia later and half a world away.

The Danube frontier held out for the duration of the Roman Republic and, nominally at least, through the $4\frac{1}{2}$-century epoch of the Roman Empire. The Empire is described as a martial civilization; however, few new territories were added to Roman sway during that period. On the contrary, the emperors were

hard put to defend the boundaries they had inherited, especially along the Danube and the Rhine. During this period the Germanic tribes were moving westward, pushing the Celtic peoples before them, occupying whatever lands in central and southern Europe were not firmly held by the Roman legions. The Danube defences were breached once in the first century A.D. and again in the third century. By the middle of the fifth century not only Austria but Italy itself was overrun and the Roman government was effectively destroyed.

For Austria, as for most of Europe, this was the beginning of the Dark Ages, a period virtually without history. Wave after wave of nomadic herdsmen living in an iron age culture swept into Europe, conquering the civilized peoples and the semi-civilized "barbarians" who had preceded them. Roman roads and aqueducts, buildings and baths, were either destroyed or allowed to fall into decay. Lost, too, in part, were many of the civilizing concepts that had prevailed in the Mediterranean basin for a thousand years, concepts which the Romans had carried with them into central and western Europe: ideas of law and justice, the organization of trade and communication, the search for knowledge in science and history, the study of philosophy and the love of art.

THE BARONS AND THE HAPSBURGS

In about 1189, Richard I, *Coeur de Lion*, King of England, left for the Holy Land on the Third Crusade. More adapted to a life of knight errantry than to his special position as king, "Lionheart" spent the greater part of his reign away from the cares of the court. Returning from high adventures in the East, he was captured by some unknown local baron and held captive for many years. According to the legend, a brave minstrel-knight named Blondel, Richard's friend, searched for him all over Central Europe. He would worm his way as close as he could manage to castle after castle, and there sing songs that only a Norman Englishman would recognize. Receiving no response he would assume that he had not reached the correct place and wander on, unwilling to entertain the thought that the king might no longer be living.

One day, at last, he arrived at a narrow passage of the Danube. High on a steep cliff, accessible only by a narrow path full of hair-

All over Europe, during early mediaeval times, strong men built castles on inaccessible heights overlooking the highroads and rivers. This part of the Danube valley, about 30 miles upstream from Vienna, is called the Wachau. It is one of the few places where the mountains come so close to the banks on both sides; merchants travelling by road or by water had little chance to escape if attacked by brigands. For this reason there were at least six castles belonging to the robber barons of the period within a 10-mile stretch. Dürnstein was one of them.

pin turns and dizzying precipices and escarpments, was a small castle. From the safety of these thick stone walls the lord and his knights descended to conduct their business, retreating when they faced overwhelming forces. The baron was engaged in dangerous affairs from time to time, what we would now call highway robbery. Sometimes his loot would be the goods of merchants, travelling slowly along the rutted riverside highroad or negotiating the rapid waters in boats; sometimes he would return with gold and jewels, lightening the pouches of passing dignitaries of the church; and sometimes his booty would be a captive, a fellow-knight who would provide companionship for long winter evenings—and hopefully a rich ransom, the price of permission to depart.

Blondel won over the peasants in the village below the castle, by means of his sweet songs, and with their help he was able to creep close to the cliffs. There he tuned his lute and raised his fine voice in a song which he and Richard had composed. Scarcely had he finished the first stanza when, to his joy, he heard the tune repeated from above. In Norman French, scarcely blunted by its short contact with the Saxon tongue, came the words of the second stanza. It was, he knew at once, Richard the Lion-hearted, his lord and companion of old.

There the story ends. Negotiations resulted in a ransom being raised and delivered, and Richard is next seen in England rescuing the country from mismanagement at the hands of his brother John. But the legend takes on reality in Austria, for the castle in which the English king whiled away his captivity still stands; it is in ruins, of course, but what is left of Dürnstein is plain to see. Roman remains in Austria are scarce, and the Dark Ages left few enduring monuments in any part of Europe; but evidences of mediaeval times are plentiful, for castles and convents, churches and cathedrals, lend charm to the Austrian landscape.

There were three kinds of baron, in early mediaeval times. There were those like the lord of Dürnstein, Richard's captor, who were essentially robbers, interested in fighting for plunder. And there were those like Richard himself who, combining religious sentiment

The village of Dürnstein is on the north bank. Unlike the castle, it is not a ruin. The biggest inn of the town is called Richard the Lion-Hearted and a café is called The Minstrel Blondel. The section of town wall shown here probably dates from about A.D. *1,000.*

with a love of adventure, were devoted to fighting for glory. The third kind fought for land and power. Such men were the lords of the House of Hapsburg. Sometimes they conquered adjacent principalities, slew their barons and gave the lands to loyal followers who ruled over local affairs but remained vassals of the Hapsburgs. At other times they accepted the existing barons as vassals, receiving their fidelity in exchange for protection from other enemies. Power begot power and broad lands attracted further territories. By the 13th century these Hapsburgs, a Swiss family originally, became the archdukes of Austria. True, no sovereigns in that period ruled over organized nations, in the modern sense, being rather the leaders of semi-independent barons—but the Hapsburgs rapidly grew in power and were among the earliest strong monarchs of mediaeval Europe. Even though more centuries were to pass before the archdukes could control the

The Hofburg in Vienna was the principal home of the Hapsburgs for at least 600 years, during most of which the building grew. As a result, the various parts range in architectural style from Gothic to baroque. The Michael's Gate faces the Inner City. Just inside is a small concert hall used exclusively for the more intimate Mozart operas, such as "The Marriage of Figaro."

last of the robber barons, nevertheless highways were rebuilt and maintained, cities began to grow up, trade was resumed, and the isolated primitive life of the Dark Ages was broken.

Even earlier, in the ninth century, an attempt to unify Europe had been made by the church. Charlemagne, king of the Franks, had conquered France and most of what are now Italy, Belgium, Holland, and Germany, and he was crowned by the Pope as "Emperor of the Romans." His domain was to include virtually all of Christendom except for the Byzantine Empire to the east. He and his successors were to be the secular—and military—arm of the church.

This Holy Roman Empire (which Voltaire was to characterize many centuries later as being "neither holy, nor Roman, nor an empire") turned out to be, essentially, a loose federation of the German-speaking world. It functioned in European history in many ways, but the most important was to guard Christian European culture from the forces of non-Christian Asiatic cultures which continued to press westward from the Caucasus. Then, after several centuries this pressure became concentrated along the Danube basin, and the leadership of the Holy Roman Empire passed from the Frankish and German kings to the Hapsburgs.

The Austrian empire grew steadily. By the middle of the 16th century, through conquest and through royal marriages, the Hapsburgs controlled Austria, Hungary, Bohemia (Czechoslovakia), Holland, Belgium, Spain, and parts of Italy, Poland and Yugoslavia! However, the height of Austrian power coincided with the peak of expansion on the part of the archenemy, the Ottoman Empire. In 1529 the Austrians had stopped the Turks only in the outskirts of Vienna. For 150 years the threat was never far off. In 1682, while the minds of western Europe and its American colonies were on other matters entirely, the Turks again attacked in full force. For over a year Vienna was besieged; the city was reduced virtually to rubble by artillery bombardment from the surrounding hills; but in the end the Turks were defeated once and for all. Consider that Vienna is more than halfway from the Dardanelles to the English Channel—and you will understand that the whole European way of life was preserved by this heroic defence!

During the same century and a half Austria had other things to do. In the beginning of the period, the Reformation had swept over Europe; and Austria, as a leading Catholic country, was among the leaders of the counter-Reformation. One magnificent outcome of this religious development was the great age of architecture in Austria. The baroque style was then evolving in Italy and spread rapidly into Austria. Hundreds of churches and cathedrals, monasteries and convents were being built. The University in Vienna was expanded and new ones were built in other Austrian cities. Today there are still some Roman ruins, many remains of early castles, and a few great Gothic structures. They make Austrian towns historically interesting and the landscape pictur-

esque. But it is the many baroque masterpieces that give these cities their unique grace and lively charm.

The University of Vienna, in good times and evil, turned out scholars, scientists, humanists—but especially doctors, and especially Freud. During most of the past three centuries the city had been world-famous for medicine as well as for music.

Evidence of the destructive power of the Turkish artillery during the siege of 1682-3 can still be seen as one looks over the Inner City today. Only St. Stephen's Cathedral remains of all the tall Gothic structures which we know once stood in the city. Virtually every other building in the picture belongs to the baroque period.

This panorama of Salzburg is in itself a panorama of Austrian history. On the hill is the mediaeval castle. Below are the baroque cathedral built on to a very early Romanesque style church, a Gothic church, and several magnificent late baroque edifices. The foreground represents today—a sunny outdoor café from which one looks out on the eternal mountains and the long sweep of history.

DECLINING POWER
AND THE MOUNTING SOUND OF MUSIC

During the 18th and 19th centuries the Hapsburg court in Vienna was among the most brilliant in Europe, and the Austrian empire remained enormous; yet the height of its power had passed. During the 1700's there were few periods of peace. The wars of that century were not fought between peoples—rather they were like chess games, with small armies fighting under specific rules. The prizes were territories. Austria gained more than it lost, in square miles, but the scene of power had shifted to England and France, with Prussia and Russia growing rapidly to the north and the east of Austrian dominions.

The 19th century opened with defeat by Napoleon, Vienna itself being twice captured. The glitter of the Austrian court shone brightly, after the final overthrow of the "Little Corporal," when the rulers of Europe gathered to sign a treaty at the famous Congress of Vienna (1815) that was to make the world safe for royalty. Austrian territories were broader after the treaties were signed than they had been before the Napoleonic wars; but royalty was actually less safe than ever. Before long, Germany was united; in the course of becoming a nation Germany beat Austria in a humiliating seven weeks' war; Italy was unified on the south; and most threatening of all was the rising tide of nationalism which nearly flooded the empire during the revolutions of 1848. Clearly the Slavic inhabitants of the northern and southern Austrian provinces, the Hungarians to the east and the Italians to the southwest were not long to remain under the rule of the German-speaking Austrians. In fact, this out-of-date arrangement, left over from mediaeval machinations, 600 years of strategic warfare and even more strategic royal marriages, outlasted the 19th century by less than two decades. The Treaty of Versailles which ended the first World War brought the House of Hapsburg

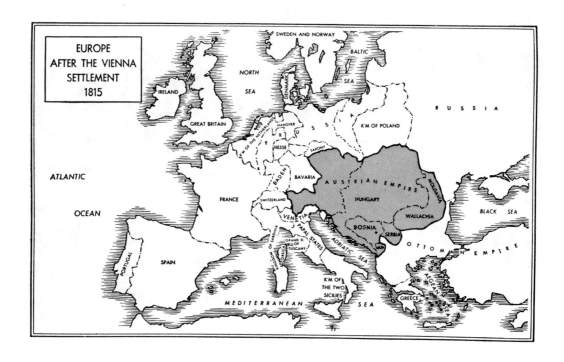

EUROPE
AFTER THE VIENNA
SETTLEMENT
1815

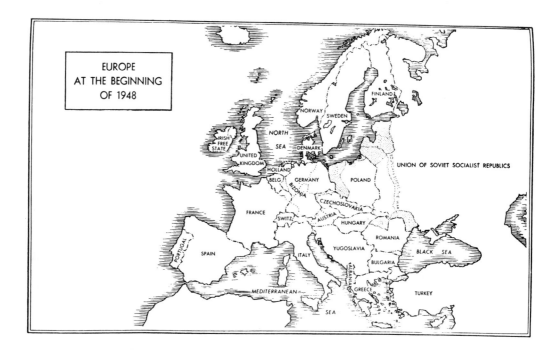

EUROPE
AT THE BEGINNING
OF 1948

Belvedere, the palace of Prince Eugene, was built outside the city walls as a country seat. The city has grown up around it and its enormous expanse of formal garden is today one of central Vienna's countless parks. The palace is in very early and restrained baroque style, almost Renaissance, although it was built in the late baroque period.

and the Austrian empire to their inevitable demise.

But these centuries of pomp without power, land without loyalty, saw the rise of something of far greater value, the music which was to be Austria's enduring gift to the world. In 1732, while Bach was in Germany and Handel in England, there was born near Vienna the founder of the classical style, inventor of the symphony, the string quartet and countless other musical forms: Josef Haydn. Haydn was 24 when Mozart was born in Salzburg. Haydn was 58 when the young Beethoven arrived from Bonn to take up permanent residence in Vienna. Haydn was still hale and productive when Franz Schubert was born in Vienna in 1797. Most of the greatest classical music

A carry-over from the glittering 18th-century court life is the Spanish Riding School in the Hofburg in Vienna. Here white Lipizaner horses, originally raised in Yugoslavia but now in Burgenland, are trained for ceremonial displays.

In this tiny house in Salzburg, Mozart lived for several years. During his brief lifetime (35 years) he composed (starting at age 5) what many critics and music lovers consider to be the epitome of classical music. He died penniless and was buried in an unmarked pauper's grave. It is said that there was only one friend to follow his coffin from the church to the burial ground.

was composed and played in Vienna in the 18th century; there too romantic music was born and perhaps its greatest works produced by Beethoven, Schubert, and others in the 19th century; there 20th century music was developed by composers like Schönberg and Alban Berg. In the future the story of the 700-year reign of the Hapsburgs may grow ever smaller on the receding historical stage— but the music of Austria will ring out undiminished in the concert halls of the world.

THE BRAIN WITHOUT A BODY

The Treaty of Versailles which ended World War I dismembered the Austrian empire. The purpose was not only to reduce the military might of the German-speaking nations, but also to give national sovereignty to the vast non-German areas that had long been under Austrian sway. From being one of the largest countries in Europe, Austria emerged as a small one. Its cities, at that time, had more charm

Beethoven was born in Bonn, Germany, but came to Vienna as a young man and stayed. This is one of many houses in Heiligenstadt where he dwelt (the village was then a suburb but is now part of the city). On the square in front of the house there is an annual outdoor concert of Beethoven's music.

750 ■ AUSTRIA

During the late 19th century and early 20th, two kinds of music were being composed in Vienna. The first was serious, with such notable contributors as Bruckner and Mahler, late romantics; Arnold Schönberg, one of the great innovators of modern music; Alban Berg and others. Simultaneously a lighter vein of music was being developed—waltzes, marches, light opera and other popular pieces. Johann Strauss, the Younger, the Waltz King, composer of "The Blue Danube," "Tales from the Vienna Woods" and

innumerable other beloved tunes, was born in this suitably ivy-clad cottage.

than industry; the countryside, then as now, contained more mountains than farmland. But hardest hit was Vienna in which more than a quarter of the population was concentrated, for this beautiful capital remained, as the inhabitants ruefully complained, the brain of an empire that no longer possessed a body.

Vienna's role had been not only cultural and political, in the affairs of empire, but commercial and financial as well. This was the business capital and the focal point of distribution. It depended upon grain and dairy products from Hungary; textiles, glassware, machinery, shoes, and other manufactured products from Czechoslovakia; timber from Yugoslavia; fruit from northern Italy. From all these areas, it had derived tax revenues. In all these areas, it had found a market for the goods traded by Viennese businesses.

A republic was established, and immediately a curious political situation arose. The city government of Vienna was controlled by a socialist party, while the federal government was traditionally conservative. In Vienna the idea of public housing projects was born, and many of the blocks built during the 1920's are still in use, less comfortable but more attractive to the eye than those built in the present decade.

This thatched-roof cottage, the birthplace of Josef Haydn, is thus the birthplace of the symphony.

Health services and public education flourished. The medical school of the University of Vienna attracted students from all over the world. Sigmund Freud, father of modern

Deep in the Vienna Woods stands Mayerling, a Hapsburg hunting lodge, scene of tragedy in 1889. Rudolph, crown prince and only son of the Emperor Franz Josef, was married to Princess Stephanie of Belgium, but was in love with the "unimportant" Baroness Marie Vetsera. His family attempted to quash this romance, but it ended sooner than they had anticipated when the crown prince, in a suicide pact, shot the baroness and then himself at Mayerling. The young man had been interested in literature, history and science, but not politics, and furthermore, was a free thinker, violently anti-clerical. There has always been some question as to whether he was assassinated or actually a suicide, especially since everyone connected with the affair was sworn to secrecy and the entire file on the subject removed from the state archives and destroyed. Characteristically, the Austrians prefer the romantic love-death story —and anyway, the truth will probably never be known.

psychology, and his followers were completing the groundwork of a new science—psychoanalysis. But there was little food and virtually no money.

Vienna had progress and poverty. The rest of the country had poverty only. The brain without a body is likely to be hungry! In addition, most of Europe was wracked by a depression that seemed as though it would never end. Austria shared in this miserable circumstance, at the same time struggling to organize an entirely new economic basis as a small and self-contained nation.

Perhaps it was because of continuing hardships and the hopelessness of the economic outlook that Austria was unable to resist the rising tides of Fascism to the south and Nazism to the north, during the early 1930's. There was a succession of governments, each more dictatorial than its predecessor; an attempt to form an alliance with Mussolini as the lesser of two evils; a flurry of civil strife during which the Social Democrats of Vienna, the only hope of resistance to Hitler, were disarmed and disenfranchised.

Many times in history a freedom-loving people has tried to avoid a showdown with a totalitarian opponent by imitating the enemy's totalitarianism. It is inevitably futile. In 1938 Austria became part of Hitler's 1000-year

Reich which was to go down in flames less than a decade later. On March 13, 1938, after more than 700 years, Austria ceased to exist. Germany became one large expanse with a dotted line on the map between the German province of Bavaria and the province of Austria.

Many people refer to our times as "the air age" and assume that aviation has made geography obsolete. But this is no more true than to say that automation has made man obsolete. From time before history the Danube has been a major artery of transportation. Today, not only the ever-growing traffic of river boats but the railway lines and super-highways along its banks make it more vital than ever.

During the Second World War, with Germany in control of all that part of Europe lying south of the Carpathians, from Romania to Greece, Vienna was the important transportation hub. This had an unhappy consequence for the Viennese. Once the Allied air forces managed to stop the supposedly invincible Luftwaffe, Allied planes began to attack German industrial cities and transportation hubs just as the German planes had bombarded the cities of Coventry and Rotterdam. Vienna ranked high on the list of essential targets. The destruction represented a smaller percentage of the whole than that perpetrated by the Turkish artillery in the siege of 1682-3—but this was little comfort to the people in 1944 and 1945 as they saw their homes and places of work go up in smoke, and the two chief landmarks of their city (the opera house and the cathedral) gutted.

Following the war, Austria was restored to the map though not to independence. The country was divided into four zones of occupation (French, British, American and Russian) and the city of Vienna was jointly occupied by the four Allied powers. But the aftermath of World War I was not repeated. In the beginning as in 1918-19, the very lives of the Austrians were sustained by outside help, first supplied by UNRRA, later by Marshall Plan funds. But despite the ruin of war and the disintegration of the economy, the occupation years were used to establish a workable government and a sound basis for economic life.

In 1955, ten years after V-E Day, a peace treaty was signed between Austria and the Allied powers, restoring its sovereignty for the first time since 1938. The occupation troops departed. Austria joined the United Nations, resuming a place in the affairs of the world. Its new constitution committed the nation to neutrality, as between the East and the West; but this neutrality is essentially military and to a lesser degree commercial. In spirit Austria is as firmly part of the Western world as during those distant days when it stood embattled against the Ottoman Empire at the Siege of Vienna.

In only one way have Austria's foreign relations been touchy—and that is with regard to Italy's administration of the German-speaking South Tyrol or Alto Adige, as the Italians call it. This area, once Austrian, was given to Italy after World War I. In 1946, after World War II, Italy made an agreement with Austria that it would give more freedom to the people of the area. Until 1969, when Italy finally satisfied Austria's demands, relations between the two countries were often strained.

Municipal housing in Vienna provides a balcony for every apartment and never fails to put a statue on every lawn. Other Austrian towns have recently followed the lead of the capital in sponsoring public housing.

AUSTRIA ■ 753

THE LAND

AUSTRIA may be thought of as two countries. It is a land of the Danube valley and it is a land of Alps. But the valley of the Danube is itself mountainous during most of its Austrian reaches, even though it is broad and level further upstream, in Germany, as well as downstream in Hungary and the lands to the east. Austria is, in fact, a mountain country, comparable to Switzerland, Albania, and Greece in its high proportion of steep rugged terrain. The only considerable area of level land lies on the eastern edge of the country along the Hungarian border.

The Alps, except where they curve down towards the Mediterranean Sea in the extreme western part of the range, tend to form roughly parallel ridges running from west to east. Because this structure prevails throughout Austria, it is hard to cross the country in a north-south direction. There are a number of passes, of course, but they themselves are mostly high and narrow. All but a few north-south highways are impassable in the winter, and the three north-south railway lines operate throughout the year only because the Austrians have the equipment and the know-how to deal with vast accumulations of snow.

In the north-eastern third of the country there is the valley of the Danube itself, from Passau on the German border to Bratislava on the Czechoslovakian line. But in addition, in the middle of the country, there is a kind of intermittent valley from the Arlberg pass near Switzerland to the Semmering pass near Hungary; this route follows the valleys of the Rivers Inn, Selzach, Enns, Mur and Mürz, providing a passage virtually the entire length of the land.

THE NINE PROVINCES

After the first World War when the Austrian empire came to an end, the various parts of the little nation seemed more inclined to fall apart than to pull together. The western region wished to join Switzerland. The central area wanted to join Germany, but as this was expressly forbidden by the Versailles Treaty they preferred to be independent. The eastern part of the country wanted unification under the ancient leadership of Vienna.

Just as in the early history of the United States, the provinces knew that they needed each other but still distrusted one another. A compromise was reached in the form of a federal republic, in which the provinces were to exercise a great deal of self-government; the former English colonies in North America had made such an arrangement under the Articles of Confederation, 1781-89. One immediate problem of federalism is that small provinces have equal voice with large ones, so the voters in the large ones have relatively less influence. In Austria, the western provinces had small populations, so

In the southern part of Upper Austria lie a dozen lakes, world-famous as resorts in every season of the year. This is the Gosausee, or Lake of Gosau. In the background rises Dachstein on whose height the three provinces of Upper Austria, Salzburg and Styria meet. The peak is 10,000 feet above sea level and the snow fields below the summit remain white the year round.

the more densely populated eastern regions were given more power by having the city of Vienna (and a few miles of surrounding hills) established as an independent province; thus the people of Upper Austria, in which Vienna is located, had two votes in the national government, not an unreasonable proportion since over 40% of the Austrians live in this region. The federal plan did not work and the central government rapidly replaced the provinces as the effective ruling power, but Vienna remains a province unto itself—containing less than one two-hundredth of Austrian territory but almost a quarter of its citizens.

The other eight provinces follow a more usual pattern, consisting of countryside, villages and cities, most of them going back to early mediaeval times and occupying more or less the same area. In some cases, the names are so different in their native German from the English form that a person knowing one might be unable to identify the other. A little language lesson goes along with the geography, to overcome this problem.

THE DANUBIAN PROVINCES AND BURGENLAND

In the north-east are the two Danubian provinces called Upper Austria and Lower Austria. To their inhabitants, the names are quite different: *Ober Österreich* and *Nieder Österreich*. The word *ober* is clearly related to the English *over; nieder* is first cousin to our word *nether*, as in the term *Netherlands*. As for *Österreich*, this is simply *Austria* in German, and it means the *eastern nation*.

Upper Austria is bounded on the northwest by the Salzach, the Inn and the Danube Rivers, beyond which lies Germany. On the north it is separated from Czechoslovakia by the height of land which divides the watershed of the Danube from that of the Moldau. These ancient granite hills in places come to the very banks of the Danube, and in at least two places they seem to have slipped across the river in the night, occupying the southern bank as well. In the south this province is Alpine in character and it includes the famous lakes called the Mondsee, the Attersee, the Wolfgangsee, the Traunsee and still others. This is the part of the country in which the salt mines mentioned earlier have been operating since prehistoric times. The rest of the province is high and rolling.

Third in size, according to area, this province has the biggest population of any except Vienna, amounting to more than 1,400,000. Of these, 200,000 live in the provincial capital of Linz, a river port and industrial city.

Lower Austria lies down stream from Upper Austria. All of its rivers flow directly into the Danube and all of them actually rise within Lower Austria as well. The northern and east boundaries follow roughly the course of the River Thaya and then the March into which the Thaya empties. The differences between the course of the Thaya and the actual border have to do with the language spoken by the inhabitants. One aim of the treaties which ended the first World War and divided up the Austrian Empire, was to make boundaries follow linguistic distribution. This principle, called "irredentism," was particularly sponsored by Woodrow Wilson. Where German-speaking people predominated north of the Thaya, the land was given to Austria, and where the Czech language predominated on the south bank, that territory was given to Czechoslovakia.

The southern part of this province is Alpine. The Alps comes so far east and so far north that Schneeberg Mountain, over 6000 feet high, is barely 50 miles from Vienna. The remainder of the province is rolling country with small relatively level areas along the Danube east and west of Vienna and a territory southeast of Vienna leading to Burgenland.

By area, Lower Austria is the biggest of all the provinces, and its population is 1,100,000, not counting Vienna which lies within its boundaries but is politically separate, as was explained above. If Vienna had not been thus removed from its parent state, Lower Austria would count 2,800,000, more than a third of all the people (7,255,000) in the country. Another peculiarity brought about by the separation of Vienna is this: Vienna remains the provincial capital of Lower Austria—of which it is not a part!

In the south-eastern part of the country is Burgenland, spelled alike in English and German. In the south it contains low rolling Alpine foothills; in the north it is part of the Hungarian plain and includes a remarkable

The Traunsee is plied by launches for six months of the year. The boats not only offer vacationists a chance to enjoy the scenery, but are the only means of access to some of the resort hotels along the shores.

Vineyards, low hills, a baroque church, and houses with tile roofs, all characterize Lower Austria.

body of water. Lake Neusiedl is over 20 miles long and averages about 5 miles in width—yet it is said to be so uniformly shallow that a man can wade across at any point. (Pick that point with some care, though, or you may end up wading into Hungary!) The boundary crosses the lake near its southern end. This entire region, both the lake and its marshy shores, forms one of the world's greatest breeding grounds for wild waterfowl. Ornithologists travel from far and wide to study here.

Burgenland is the second smallest of the provinces, both in area and in its population of 300,000. Its rivers all rise farther to the west, either in Styria or Lower Austria, and flow easterly into Hungary where eventually, of course, they empty into the Danube. There are no sizeable cities. The provincial capital is Eisenstadt, more famous musically and historically than for its industry or commerce.

THE ALPINE PROVINCES

No part of Austria is level or low-lying, but the five provinces next to be considered are strictly mountainous. The highest peaks lie to the south and west and the land descends toward the Danube valley in the north and to the Hungarian plain in the extreme east.

Starting in the west, first comes the Vorarlberg, smallest of all the Austrian states. To pronounce this name in German you must say the *v* like an *f* and the *e* like a long *a*, producing something like *for-arl-bairg*. This province, with its population of a mere 200,000, is world renowned among skiers. On both its southern and western borders lies Switzerland, while to the north lies Germany; it is easier to reach the Vorarlberg from either of these countries than from the adjacent province of the Tyrol. Access to the rest of Austria is virtually limited to one route, through the Arlberg pass.

The rivers of the Vorarlberg flow westerly into the Rhine or directly into Lake Constance which is actually part of that river. The chief city of the province is the small but beautiful lake port, Bregenz.

The Tyrol is spelled with an *i* instead of the *y* in German. The proper pronunciation is the same in both languages, with the accent on the second syllable. Its capital is Innsbruck, a handsome city of 100,000 which forms a vital transportation hub. Here the main east-west routes of both highway and railway, which follow the River Inn, intersect the principal north-south line in the country. This latter artery comes from Munich in Germany, enters Austria through the Scharnitzer pass, and continues almost due south until it leaves the country via the Brenner pass to enter Italy. The northern boundary of the Tyrol is along the highest ridge of the Chalk Alps. Across the sky-high southern boundary lie the rugged Dolomite Alps of Italy.

All the rivers of the Tyrol flow into the Inn which, after a long easterly course, runs northeast to the Danube. The half million people of the province, if they do not live in Innsbruck, inhabit the narrow twisting valleys of the many small rivers. They identify themselves by these valleys, saying, "I am an Ötztaler" or "I am a Zillertaler," meaning a native of the valley of the Ötz or of the Zill. Dialect, costume and outlook vary somewhat from one valley to the next, and a village a dozen miles away in an

The valleys are narrow and over the centuries the Tyrolese have pushed their farms as far up the mountainside as reluctant nature allowed. Typical of the Austrian Alps are the crisscross fence and the leather pants of the farmer, while his son is dressed in "ordinary" clothes like a boy in any part of Europe or America.

adjacent valley, as the Alpine crow flies, may be 50 or 60 miles away by road.

One section of this province, called East Tyrol (or *Ost Tirol*, in German) is separated from the rest by a "corridor" of land, partly Italian and partly belonging to Salzburg. Travel between East Tyrol and the remainder of its province is virtually limited to mountain goats as some of the highest peaks in the Alps lie between the two regions.

East of the Tyrol comes the province of Salzburg. Nearly a third of the 350,000 inhabitants of the province live in the capital city which bears the same name.

Most of the rivers of Salzburg flow into the Salzach, which runs east to the village of Schwarzach and then turns north for the rest of its course. Starting a few miles north of the city of Salzburg, the Salzach marks the boundary between Austria and Germany until it empties into the Inn which then takes up the burden of dividing the two countries. The only river in Salzburg which behaves differently is the Mur, which flows eastward into Styria and eventually south-easterly into the Drava whose waters join the Danube hundreds of miles away, north of Belgrade in Yugoslavia.

Provincial boundaries in mountainous land, like national boundaries, frequently follow the height of land along the mountain ridges. It should, then, be no surprise that two of Salzburg's corners are occupied by towering peaks.

Over 12,000 feet above sea level, these hikers in the East Tyrol are comfortable in shirt sleeves, but their knapsacks contain thick winter jackets, mittens and caps. If the clouds, almost indistinguishable from the mountain tops, should happen to cover the sun, or if a wind should rise, the temperature might drop 40 degrees Fahrenheit in five minutes.

Mountains, lake and cattle —the Tyrol at a glance.

Few cities as cosmopolitan and urbane as Innsbruck live so intimately with towering mountains. No overcoats are needed on this sunny spring day on Maria Theresa Street, while overhead the mountains wear their winter mantles.

760 ■ **AUSTRIA**

Where Salzburg, East Tyrol and Carinthia join stands Austria's highest peak, Gross-Glockner. The meeting of Salzburg, Lower Austria and Styria is similarly marked by a giant among giants, the gleaming Dachstein.

The remaining two Alpine provinces have names, already mentioned in passing, which are confusingly different in English from their native forms. These are Styria, lying east of Salzburg, and Carinthia which lies south of the latter two. Styria in German is *Steiermark*. The first part of the word is pronounced like *shire* with a *t* inserted, adding up to *shtire-mark*. The capital is Graz, Austria's second largest but fastest-growing city. A popular saying declares that "Styria has everything Austria is proud of, with the exception of Vienna." The evidence is ample: it has the country's main heavy industry in and around Graz; it has many of the principal mine resources, excellent farming, and considerable timber; and still it manages to rival the western provinces as ski and vacation country.

Everybody knows about Salzburg the city. Few know that Salzburg is the name of the province, too, so mountainous that its entire population is just triple that of its capital. The hiker is standing on a glacier, a slow-moving river of ice, with Gross-Glockner, Austria's highest summit, in the background.

The population of Styria is 1,100,000. About a quarter of a million live in Graz.

Styria has three different river systems. In the north-west part of the province, all streams drain into the Enns which then flows northerly toward the Danube. In the east, all the rivers flow south-easterly into the Raab, which in turn empties into the Danube in Hungary. But

The mountains in Carinthia are so high and so inaccessible that the average inhabitant may live in view of a peak every day of his life and never dream of climbing it. The village of Heiligenblut is shown looking westward to Gross-Glockner, but if the picture looked in any other direction it would show peaks less well-known but almost equally high.

Dividing the ancient Inner City from the rest of Vienna is the series of boulevards called "the Ring," lined with public buildings and public parks. The passenger in the horse-drawn carriage is looking at the main entrance of the Hofburg, the seat of empire for many centuries. To the left and to the right of this building, along the Ring, are large formal gardens.

the main river of Styria is the Mur. This river rises in Salzburg and flows in a north-easterly direction to the town of Bruck where it is joined by the Mürz flowing south-westerly from its source in Lower Austria. Thus reinforced, the Mur turns sharply to the south and flows into Yugoslavia where it eventually meets the Drava.

Carinthia is called *Kärnten* by its inhabitants, the first syllable being pronounced like the English word *cairn*. South of this province lie Italy and Yugoslavia, but the mountains that separate them from Austria are high and craggy. In fact, Carinthia is pretty well cut off from Salzburg and Styria, too, by another spur of the Alps. Year-round highway communication between Klagenfurt, the capital, and the outside

The City Hall and City Hall Park are landmarks along the Ring where the arts of the builder and the landscape gardener combine to make a haven in the middle of the town.

A corner of the Inner City is flanked by two long-time popular restaurants. These buildings are mediaeval in structure but were refurbished with baroque façades some time in the 16th or 17th centuries. The residence for technical students, on the other hand, leaves no doubt as to the century in which it was constructed, inside or out.

world is limited to two highways and two railway lines.

Carinthia is about the same size as the Tyrol and has roughly the same population, about a half million. It is probably the least visited, most remote part of the country—but skiers are increasingly discovering its slopes, while its lakes are beginning to attract adventuresome summer tourists too.

VIENNA

Geographically the province of Vienna is entirely surrounded by Lower Austria, but in every other sense it stands alone. It is not only the capital of Austria but it is one of the great capital cities of Europe. People say of it, as they say of Paris, "It belongs to the world."

Written in its own language the name looks different: *Wien;* but when it is spoken in German the similarity is more apparent. It is pronounced *veen.* The word is obviously a shortening of the original, Vindobona. This is a reasonable place for one final language lesson since Vienna and the Danube are inseparably connected. In Austria and in Germany this river is the *Donau,* pronounced *dough-now* with a slight accent on the first syllable.

Vienna lies largely on the south-west bank of the Danube. Two districts lie on the northeast bank and two more on the island which is formed between the river itself and the Danube Canal. The old part of Vienna, or the Inner City as it is called, forms a semi-circle. Around it once ran the city walls, but these have long since been replaced by a series of boulevards collectively called the Ring. Each section of this magnificent street has its own name, such as Carinthia Ring, Park Ring, etc. Along the Ring are found many of the great public buildings— the opera house, the Hofburg (which was the principal palace of the Hapsburgs), the parliament, the city hall, the university, and two outstanding museums. In addition there are numbers of small parks, handsomely laid out and perfectly tended, and many of the city's famous hotels and cafés.

About a mile beyond the Ring is another boulevard, called the Belt, concentric with the Ring. This is a newer street and serves as the

The Burg Theatre is the showplace of classical drama, Grillparzer and Goethe, Shakespeare and Molière. Neither floodlights nor the new red-white-red flag of the republic lend a modern touch to this landmark on the Ring. Not far away, on Kärntnerstrasse (Carinthia Street), night converts a bit of the Inner City into pure 20th century.

principal traffic artery. The main line of the subway follows the Belt, while the other line runs along the Danube canal. Together with fast trolley (tram) cars—which always have the right of way over other traffic—these trains make up one of the most efficient urban transportation systems in the world.

Several miles beyond the Belt there is another segment of a concentric circle, but this is not a street. It is a ring of hills, reserved for public use as a gigantic park, the Vienna Woods. These hills are very old sandstone formations. They start virtually at the river's edge, north of the city, and continue for more than half of a circle forming a large part of the land boundary of Vienna. They are covered with magnificent forest extending, at some points, as much as 20 miles from the city limits. They serve the Viennese for many kinds of recreation, ranging from a half hour's stroll, followed by coffee in one of the innumerable tiny inns, to major hiking and camping expeditions. The forests are scientifically logged which serves to keep them in prime condition, incidentally providing a source of revenue to the state.

But the Vienna Woods serve in still another

The giant wheel in the Prater amusement park, Vienna.

capacity. Where the woods begin, the city abruptly ends. While virtually every other metropolis of Europe and America spills out of its bounds into ever-spreading suburbs, destroying the countryside and leaving the heart of the city to decay, Vienna remains neatly contained. To the last house on any street leading out of town, it remains utterly urban. Ten paces farther the land is thoroughly rural. Beyond the Woods comes farmland, and country life continues uninterrupted by the proximity of the city. It is not merely the physical geography which produces this delightful situation, however. The hills around Athens and those around San Francisco are less hospitable, yet the outskirts of those cities creep up the mountain sides corrupting the lovely backdrops with which these cities are endowed. But the Vienna Woods are common land, protected by wise and rigid law against sale or desecration, protected now and forever, a green ring in spring and summer, a golden ring in the fall, a white ring in the winter, an ever-perfect setting for the gem that is Vienna.

CLIMATE

The climate in Austria has a wide range. Along the Danube, in the eastern part of Lower Austria and in Burgenland, the climate is similar to most of the Continent. The summers are warm though not very long, the winters are damp with moderate temperature, while spring and fall tend to be long, mild and with considerable rainfall.

The Alpine sections have short hot summers, long cold winters. Precipitation (rain and snow) is moderate and the number of clear bright days per year is exceptionally high. The valleys (and consequently the cities) are prone to be foggy, especially in the winter. One result is that they are colder in the daytime than the higher villages, while these villages, because of their altitude, are much colder at night.

Schönbrunn, summer palace of the Hapsburgs, was once about five miles from the city. Now, of course, the city extends beyond it and its parks, cafés, zoo and the building itself are a popular haunt for Viennese on a sunny Sunday afternoon.

GOVERNMENT AND ECONOMY

THAT AUSTRIA should prosper is something of a miracle. Compounded as it is of intelligent government, and a reasonable balance between private enterprise and public control, encouraging careful exploitation of natural resources, and scientific improvement in agriculture and the extractive industries, with no expensive military establishment, Austria has become prosperous. A miracle it surely is.

After the First World War it seemed unlikely that Austria could operate an effective government, impossible that its economy could produce much more than genteel poverty. The Second World War should have reduced its chances still further. Yet today there is no poverty in Austria, no slums in its cities, no political unrest, no apparent threats to its continued security except for those worldwide pressures which threaten the security of all.

FORM OF GOVERNMENT

Austria is organized as a federal republic. Its president is elected for a six-year term and, as in many European countries, his office is more prestige than executive. He appoints the Chancellor and the cabinet, who form the executive branch of government, but these appointments are in themselves ceremonial; the selection of office-holders is the prerogative of the lower house of parliament.

The lower house is called the National Council or *Nationalrat*. Its 165 members are elected by the population at large, through proportional representation. They serve a term of four years. In addition to selecting the government they are responsible for most legislation and for the allocation of funds.

The upper house is called the Federal Council, or *Bundesrat*. Its 50 members are appointed by the provincial governments for indefinite terms of office. History in Austria has not democratized the election of Federal Councillors; instead it has gradually curtailed the power of this Council.

Since World War II elections have amounted to a continual tie between the two principal parties, the moderately conservative People's Party (which before the war had been the so-called Christian Socialist Party), and the Socialist Party (formerly known as Social Democrats). The remaining parties account for less than a dozen members of the National Council. This tie could have produced inertia, with each party able to block action by the other; instead a co-operative situation has arisen. If the Chancellor is of one party, the principal cabinet posts go to the other party. There is virtually no political patronage, and the balance between the two parties, each of which is able to scrutinize the conduct of the other, works to maintain political honesty. Government action tends to make few headlines. It is quiet, slow, deliberate—and the evidence shows it to be effective.

Civil liberties are better protected in Austria today than at any previous time in its history. The press is free and though it rarely behaves as a watchdog over the public welfare, it will cover controversial situations when they arise. Several years ago, an official claimed that the postal department, which controls all communication media, was shockingly wasteful in the area of television broadcasts. Both the attack and the official reply were freely printed in the newspapers, which freely took sides in the matter. The same material was broadcast on television by the very officials who were being blamed.

The government, like many other moderately socialist regimes in Europe, involves itself with the welfare of its citizens. Public education is universal and painstaking, if somewhat old-fashioned. Residential rents are carefully controlled and public housing, practically a Viennese invention, is continually expanded. Citizens are protected against unemployment, old age and illness. Employment conditions are regulated. In general, not much is left to chance, as far as the evil possibilities of life are concerned; and the opportunity for a citizen to better his lot, financially or professionally, can be found everywhere by those who look.

BUSINESS

The old people say that these are the most prosperous times in Austria since the days of the Emperor Franz Josef. But this is an understatement, concealing the truth. They are far more prosperous today than *ever* before, from the point of view of all the people. For the prosperity of the Empire affected the upper classes and the upper middle class greatly, and perhaps the lower middle class moderately; but the mass of peasants, industrial workers and people in the service trades benefited almost not at all—unless we are to believe the fiction that seeing the gentry well dressed, well fed and well housed brought happiness to the humble soul of the peasant.

Two unfortunate conditions "helped" Austria to its present economic well-being. One was the annexation by Germany; the Nazis, for their own needs, established new industries, increased mine production, and dispersed a good deal of light industry in the militarily safe mountain areas. Many of these improvements remained after the Germans had gone. The other event was the harsh occupation demands of the Russians, following the war. Unlike the Western Allies, the Russians demanded full reparations and dismantled many factories or demanded payment for those they left intact. This had a profitable, long-range effect, however, beyond the obvious disadvantages. During the period between 1946 and 1955, there was a steady flight of capital and industry out of Lower Austria and Vienna into the other provinces which England, France and the United States occupied; the result, here again, was a more even distribution of industry throughout the country. No longer is there an industrial north-eastern section of the country at economic odds with an agricultural majority everywhere else.

Today about one quarter of the working force is engaged in farming and forestry. Food and forage crops have been steadily increased, over the past decade, although it is unlikely that this steep and mountainous land will ever be able to feed itself entirely. At present, it is independent in the production of dairy foods, potatoes, fruits, vegetables, beer, wine and sugar. It must import about half of its supply of grains and a larger part of its meat, chicken and eggs. Since the balance of trade permits, it also imports fruits and vegetables during the winter from the Mediterranean countries to the south, and of course such items as coffee, tea and spices.

Forestry, on the other hand, produces a surplus. This industry, one of the largest in private hands, accounts for a fifth of the entire export budget with timber and paper products. The other major industry that is privately operated is the textile industry which also creates a small surplus for the export market.

Where the postman goes, the buses go. Here the Post Bus is seen on the Gross-Glockner Highway, the highest motor road in Austria. This road is open only from May through October, but the buses operate in every season elsewhere, providing public transportation to almost every village and hamlet in the country.

Schwechat airport serves Vienna. It is the leading international air hub in eastern Europe and the main terminal of the government-run Austrian Airlines.

Even where the land is too steep for a man to stand, a hay crop may be gathered if the farmers are willing to tie themselves like mountain climbers to a rock or a tree up above.

THE PEOPLE

THE PEOPLE of Austria are (generally speaking) Alpine in type, of medium height, with round heads and brown hair. Their physical characteristics are similar to their geographical location in the middle of Europe. They are shorter and darker than the northern Europeans, taller and fairer than the Mediterraneans. Within the country there is a slight variation of physical types, the mountain people to the west being somewhat more rangy, the Danubian and eastern people rather more stocky.

Linguistically, the Austrians are by and large Germanic, but this is naturally not 100 per cent true. There are Austrians who speak Hungarian (and across the border Hungarians who talk German), those whose language is Slovenian, Croatian and Czech, and some Italian-speaking Tyrolese. The latter are outweighed by a larger group of German-speaking Tyrolese in Italy whose presence has caused considerable agitation from time to time in western Austria. However, the non-German-speaking Austrians are few and they form no political language pocket.

The German of Austria is softer and warmer than that spoken farther north. In Vienna it has an interesting French cast, showing largely in a tendency to accent the last syllable of words which Germans would accent near the beginning. The Viennese also are prone to use international words rather than Germanic ones, given the choice. Examples of this are *telefon* rather than *fernsprecher*, *television* as opposed to *fernseher*, *kino* (short for cinema) instead of *lichtspiel*, *auto* instead of *wagen*. In the higher, more remote Alpine valleys the dialect becomes

The men of Upper Austria dance the "Schuhplättler," a folk dance in which the rhythm is marked by the slapping of hands against the soles of the performers' shoes.

difficult for lowland Germans to understand. At the other end of the country, the Viennese cherish a virtually incomprehensible local dialect which is a source of delight to the well-educated Viennese, much as Londoners make sport of the Cockney accent or New Yorkers entertain themselves with Brooklynese.

FRESH MILK AND OLD CUSTOMS

Despite the spread of light industry to some towns, the whole Alpine area is characterized by dairy farming. Village streets in the early morning become rivers of cattle as the creatures are turned out of their barns and head up to the mountain pastures. A vacationer who has arranged to stay at any resort other than a big hotel is likely to find that his good host keeps cows as well as guests. Excellent cheeses and excellent chocolate are among the products of the region.

Partly because the settlements are far from the mainstream of modern life and partly, perhaps, because of the long cold winters which restrict social life for many months each year, the mountain people have tended to preserve their traditional costumes and the festivals and dances that go with them. These special clothes are no longer worn every day, except in a very few instances, but on an appropriate holiday the villagers emerge wearing clothes dating back to the Middle Ages.

In recent years the coming of radio, motion pictures and television has threatened the survival of these ancient rites. It is easier to sit and be entertained than to make your own music and dance your own steps. But the traditions continue; perhaps the fact that they attract tourists will provide an additional motive for their preservation for a long time to come.

Biggest of the parks on the Ring is the City Park, through which the river Wien flows toward the Danube. This statue, one of many, is a monument to Johann Strauss, composer of "The Blue Danube," "Tales from the Vienna Woods," and many other popular light operatic pieces. The park has special areas for young children into which grownups may not go, and sections reserved for old people which children may not enter.

THE RIVER AND THE HILLS

The Danubian provinces have a milder climate than the rest of Austria. Travel is easier all year round and the towns are more accessible to the country folk. Farming and forestry are the predominant occupations with grain, sugar beets and hops as the chief farm products.

Here, as in the Alps, people still like to make their own music and no wedding is complete without the local band. Old costumes are carefully preserved in chests for religious festivals. But the pace is calmer. The temperature does not change so vividly. The population does not rise and fall with the winter inundation of skiers and the summer flood of tourists. (Of course the southern parts of Upper and Lower Austria are Alpine and the lives of people there are more akin to those in Salzburg and Styria.)

Both these provinces produce beer that is among the world's best. It is served in big glasses—the merrier the occasion the bigger

Over the centuries the Danube has shifted its course from time to time. An abandoned stretch of the river forms a series of lakes, providing boating and swimming in summer, ice skating in winter. Looking in most directions, the visitor in Alte Donau Park may have no clue that he is inside the city limits of Vienna.

Just across the Danube Canal from the Inner City is the huge Prater. The near end of this park is devoted to Coney Island kinds of amusements, including the giant ferris wheel which is almost a symbol of Vienna. But the greater part is gentle woodland with mile upon mile of bridle path. This was once the private hunting preserve of the Hapsburgs, artificially stocked with game from all parts of the empire.

the glass. In village inns whole groups sit together and pass around a two-litre (more than two-quart) stein. In Lower Austria the wine country begins, and the grapes generally increase in quality and quantity to the east. Here in addition to the religious feasts there are great celebrations of the grape harvest.

THE MERRY WIDOW—VIENNA

Austrians are noted for their love of music, their pleasure in fine food and drink, their enjoyment of nature, their easy-going optimistic way of life. All these characteristics, triply distilled, describe the Viennese. The Viennese work hard, but their hours of work are not too long, due to strong trade unions and a protective government. So there is leisure, plenty of it, and the Viennese need no help from unions, government or anyone else in knowing how to enjoy it.

Social life is based on the coffee house and the wine shop. Over one tiny cup of strong coffee one may sit for hours in a café, reading newspapers and magazines supplied by the management, talking, watching the world go by outside the huge plate-glass windows. In good times, you may order *Schlagobers*, a great dollop of whipped cream, on your coffee. Or perhaps a piece of rich Vienna pastry. For a real

celebration you can add pastry with *Schlagobers* too!

What the café is by day, the *Heurige* or wine shop is by night. The regional vintage, a fragrant white wine which does not age and which is drunk within the year, is served in the *Heurige*. The word itself means *this year's* and applies to the wine, and only by extension to the tavern where the wine is sold.

The people of Vienna meet in another place too—in their parks. There are few cities where parks are so plentiful and so essentially part of the city life. If the Vienna Woods, which is more like a national forest than an urban park, is included, Vienna must have a larger percentage of its area devoted to nature than any city of comparable size.

But the greatest single factor of Viennese life is music, and it can be found in almost any corner of the town. Often the café has music, perhaps a chamber group playing quietly in a corner. In the *Heurige*, music is essential. There are concerts in the parks, too. But the real music takes place in the State Opera House (which ranks with La Scala), in the People's Opera House where light opera and the famous Viennese operettas are performed (*The Bat, The Merry Widow, The Gypsy Baron* and all); in two large concert halls and a dozen small

The "Musikvereinsaal," or Music Association Hall, is one of the dozen important Viennese concert halls. The interior is a baroque masterpiece, elaborately decorated with caryatids and statues glowing with gilt and vivid overhead frescoes. Here the Vienna Philharmonic plays to a full house every performance of the year; getting a ticket requires early morning rising, a long wait on line, and extra good luck.

ones. This is the living heart of Vienna, the city of less than 2,000,000 which has produced a good half of the great music of the Western world.

THE LOOK OF THE FUTURE

The look of Austria's future is a reflection of its geography. Austria is the meeting ground of east and west in Europe today, just as in the past. About half of its boundary touches communist countries (Czechoslovakia, Hungary and Yugoslavia) and half abuts non-communist lands (Italy, Switzerland and West Germany). Culturally, it has always related to the west, having especially strong ties with Italy, France and Germany. Economically, it has always been involved with the east; Prague and Budapest for hundreds of years ranked just below Vienna as the capitals of the Austrian empire.

Should relations between east and west become more hostile, Austria will serve as a meeting place—a neutral ground—on which both sides may seek means for co-existence. If relations continue to improve, the prosperity and importance of Austria will continue to grow as statesmen and businessmen, students and tourists from east and west come together in its cities, in its mountains, on its ski slopes and in its concert halls, in an effort to make the world whole.

Since its completion, the Wallsee-Mitterkirchen power plant on the Danube is helping Austria to expand its industry.

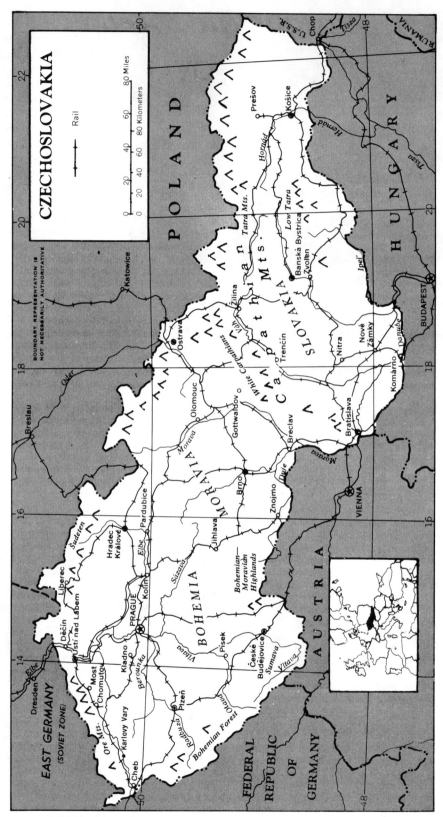

The historical citadel of Bratislava, capital of Slovakia, stands high above the Danube. Begun in the 9th century, the stronghold was rebuilt in the 13th.

CZECHOSLOVAKIA

IN THE WESTERN PART of Bohemia, not far from the town of Cheb, is a stone marker designating the spot as the precise midpoint of the European continent. Czechoslovakia can therefore justifiably claim that it lies in the heart of Europe.

This geographical distinction is at the same time a massive burden, for Czechoslovakia is small and unable to defend itself against conquerors from other nations who wish to secure its strategic location—most of its history was spent as a captive state of other nations, but after hundreds of years Czechoslovakia finally achieved nationhood at the end of World War I.

The new country merged the destinies of two peoples—the Czechs and Slovaks. Though they had lived in proximity for centuries and shared a common Slavic background, in many ways these people were quite different. Slovakia until recently was primarily agricultural, Bohemia and Moravia—the Czech lands—have an industrial heritage. Traditionally, Slovakia, which had been part of Hungary for nearly 1,000 years, looked to the East; the Czechs looked West. Even their languages are different, although so close that anyone who knows one can understand the other.

Despite their differences, the nation which these two peoples forged has been a success.

Ten centuries old, Prague is an unplanned, but picturesque maze to anyone unfamiliar with it.

THE LAND

LOCATED IN THE VERY HEART of the European continent, Czechoslovakia is a land-locked nation about the size of New York State or of England alone. Lack of seaports and small size have not, however, lessened the country's attractiveness to visitors or conquerors. Bordered by six nations—the German Democratic Republic (East Germany), the German Federal Republic (West Germany), Austria, Hungary, the Soviet Union and Poland—Czechoslovakia has known both the military disadvantages of a small nation and the cultural stimulus of its position at the crossroads.

The 49,381 square miles of Czechoslovakia are shoe-shaped, the toe of the shoe kicking eastward. The nation is divided into three sections—Bohemia, the westernmost sector, the square heel of the shoe; Moravia, the central region, or "instep"; and the easternmost section, Slovakia, the narrowing "toe." Bohemia and Moravia are the historic homelands of the Czechs; Slovakia is the home of the Slovaks. Though these two peoples now share a common state and government, their histories have often been different.

TOPOGRAPHY

For the most part a fertile land of green fields, dense forests and rolling hills, Czechoslovakia also contains numerous urban industrial sites—mostly in Bohemia—and two major mountain ranges. Dominating the northern border of the nation are the Tatra Mountains of Slovakia, a part of the Carpathians sometimes called the Alps of Eastern Europe, and the Krkonose (Giant) Mountains of Bohemia. Mt. Gerlach, at 8,737 feet the highest peak in Czechoslovakia, is located in the Tatras.

Another mountain range, the Sumava, forms a densely wooded wall between Bavaria, in Germany, and the southern portion of Bohemia. Several hundred years ago, only a few passes and mountain trails cut through this range, which formed a line of defence for the Bohemian heartland. Along these trails, how-

The old section of Bratislava, Slovakia's capital, has a romantic aspect that is vaguely Spanish in feeling.

Known as the "City of 100 Spires," Prague actually has more than 140.

CZECHOSLOVAKIA ■ 777

A natural bridge in northern Bohemia, called the Pravcice Gate, is one of Czechoslovakia's loveliest spots.

ever, trade was possible and towns began to spring up. Later, gold mining and the growth of the timber industry contributed to the wealth of the region. The town of Susice for example, became famous throughout the world for its manufacture of "Solo" brand matches.

The wild, romantic beauty of the Sumava blends easily into a gentler, lower range known as Cesky Les (Bohemian Forest). During the early Middle Ages, Bohemian rulers assigned the people of this section the task of guarding the frontier. The men walked—*chodit* in Czech—through these hills and upon sighting an enemy lighted signal fires to warn of approaching danger. The Chods, as these people were known, were rewarded for their service by the Bohemian kings who freed them from being

Sulovske Skaly in Slovakia is famous for its oddly shaped towers, pinnacles and ridges and features a unique cliff amphitheatre called Skalne Mesto (the Rock Town).

serfs of the local nobility. Domazlice, the main town in the area, was the site of a castle in which were kept the royal documents granting this privilege.

West of the Giant Mountains, in the northwestern corner of the nation, are the Krusne Hory (Ore Mountains). As the name itself indicates, this is a mining region. Vast deposits of low-grade brown coal (lignite) may be found here and it was near the town of Jachymov that the French scientist, Marie Curie obtained the radium for her experiments.

The typical Bohemian countryside is one of low, wood-covered hills, their slopes a patchwork of cultivated fields. In the valleys, scattered among the many orchards are numerous small villages with clusters of white houses crowned with red slate roofs.

Moravia, in contrast, in the central and southern regions at least, is mainly a fertile flatlands area. In the east, not far from the regional capital of Brno, is the Moravian Karst —a karst is a limestone region with an underground drainage system. Beneath green-clad hills, carved out of limestone deep below the

The military history of Bohemia is apparent even in this pastoral setting. In the background are the ruins of Trosky fortress, whose two towers are still called the Virgin and the Old Woman, although the folk tale that gave them those names has long since been forgotten.

A popular pastime for Czechoslovak citizens, as well as foreign tourists, is skiing. Excellent resorts have been constructed in the Tatras and the Krkonose Mountains.

earth's surface, are vast caves and chambers of breathtaking beauty, decorated with thousands of glistening stalactites and stalagmites and connected by a labyrinth of tunnels. At the bottom of the 455-foot-deep Macocha Abyss is a small underground stream called the Punkva which joins two small lakes. These caverns are illuminated and each year thousands of tourists enjoy underground boat rides on the Punkva.

The major rivers of Czechoslovakia, the Vltava (Moldau) and the Elbe, flow through Bohemia to Germany, and the Danube, which marks the nation's southern border, separates Slovakia from Hungary. For a thousand years, Slovakia had indeed been a part of Hungary and was joined to the modern nation of Czechoslovakia only in 1918. Slovakia's terrain is one of fertile plains in the southern region, rising suddenly in the north to the austere heights of the Tatras.

CLIMATE

Czechoslovakia has a mixed climate, representing a transition from the milder climate of

Western Europe to the more severe one of Eastern Europe—the Czech lands of Bohemia and Moravia have milder winters than Slovakia. The warmest places are the Danubian lowlands, the southern basin of Moravia and the Elbe River Valley, where the annual mean temperature is 50 degrees F.

The coolest regions, as might be expected, are in the mountains along the border, from the Sumava to the Krkonose (Giant) ridge, and in the Tatras. The lowest annual mean temperature is experienced on Mt. Lomnicky, nearly 8,700 feet high, in the High Tatras; here the thermometer averages 25.7 degrees F. Prague, the capital, in central Bohemia, has an annual mean temperature of about 49 degrees F., some 5 degrees lower than New York City.

Rainfall is most prevalent in June, July and August, particularly in the mountainous regions. Snowfall is common in winter and winter sports are enjoyed throughout the nation. In 1970 the world ski championships will be held on the slopes of the Tatras.

Wild mountain flowers add beauty to the Tatra Mountains in Slovakia, inspiring bright and multi-hued native folk costumes.

Czechoslovakia is one of the few countries in the world where one can find chamois, mountain antelope of extraordinary agility.

*Wildlife is abundant in the forests of Czechoslo-
vakia and hunters come to the country from all
over the world. The Italian Count Cinzano, scion
of the wealthy vermouth-producing family, is a
frequent visitor.*

FLORA AND FAUNA

One-third of all of Czechoslovakia is covered
by forests. An important raw material, as well
as an adornment, the timberland is protected
by government limits on cutting. Yearly output
is approximately 43,000,000 solid cubic yards
of lumber, coniferous timber constituting 80
per cent and broadleaf timber 20 per cent of the
total yield.

Beech is plentiful in the hills of eastern
Moravia, where the modern wood-bending
industry got its start more than 100 years ago.
Czechoslovak bentwood furniture is still
famous throughout the world and millions of
pieces are sold annually.

Wildlife is abundant throughout the country
and for hunters some kind of game is in season
12 months a year. Big game includes several

*Not all of the animals are in the woods. These two
bear cubs play in a zoo at the Tatra Mountains
National Park.*

varieties of deer; bears; the chamois, a type of
European antelope; the wild boar; and the
moufflon, a wild mountain sheep characterized
by massive, curved horns. Small game include
pheasant, wild duck and hare.

With its round tower reminiscent of castles in fairy tales, Krivoklat, just 36 miles from Prague, is an attraction for tourists. The castle, built in the 13th century, is now a museum.

HISTORY

WHILE THE NATION of Czechoslovakia is a child of the 20th century, barely 50 years old today, the Slavs, from whom present-day Czechs and Slovaks are descended, are old inhabitants of Europe—it is believed that they were in central and eastern Europe as early as the 7th century B.C.

Beginning a history of conquest that was to engulf the tiny nation right up to the present, Celtic tribes invaded the region and settled there in the 5th century B.C. An advanced group, these tribes left an imprint on the population and the land before they were in turn vanquished by the Teutonic Marcommani and

Quadi shortly before the advent of Christianity. It was from one of the Celtic tribes—the Boii—that Bohemia got its name and the adjacent German state of Bavaria as well (Bayern in German).

With the downfall of the Teutonic conquerors and their commander, King Marbod, at the close of the 1st century A.D., the region came into contact with the Roman Empire. The next wave of invaders were the Avars, a tribe of Asian origin, which first took the Danube plain and then began raiding into the Czech lands. The Slav tribes banded together to face the common enemy, choosing Samo, a Frankish merchant, to lead them. Samo reigned for 35 years, from A.D. 623–658, over a territory comprising Bohemia, Moravia and part of present-day Austria. On his death, his realm crumbled and a 100-year blank appears in the history of the territory.

THE COMING OF CHRISTIANITY

In the early part of the 9th century, the Czech princely house of Mojmir I seized the town of Nitra, seat of a nearby state located on present-day Slovak soil, and established the foundation of the Great Moravian Empire. Prince Rotislav, who followed Mojmir, extended the empire further to the east and was successful in warding off two attempts at conquest by the Franks. At one point, the Great Moravian Empire was one of Europe's largest states, covering a vast area of the central and eastern parts of the continent.

But Rotislav's place in history is assured not by his military feats, but because he was the ruler who asked first Rome, and then Constantinople, to send Christian missionaries to Central Europe. The Byzantine missionaries— Constantine (later called Cyril) and Methodius —were cultured brother priests who not only carried the word of Christianity to the Slavs, but also created for them a characteristic alphabet, Cyrillic, using it to translate various liturgical texts into old Slavonic. Thus was founded a written Slavic language.

After 900, political power shifted from Moravia to Bohemia, where a new state had been formed under the Premyslid princes. It is claimed that Borivoj, the first Bohemian prince, was converted to Christianity by Methodius himself. His grandson, Prince Vaclav, celebrated even today as the "Good King Wenceslas" of the English Christmas carol, was an ardent Christian, (later made a saint) and a highly-cultured monarch who had mastered Church Slavonic, Latin and Greek.

Under Vaclav's successors, Boleslav I and Boleslav II, the Czech tribes, who called their Bohemian homeland Cechy, became increasingly strong and prosperous, its leaders were made dukes of the Holy Roman Empire, thus beginning an association with the Germanic

lands to the west that profoundly affected Czech history.

Travellers to Bohemia described an advanced system of farming and cattle-breeding in use there. Ibrahim Ibn Jacob, an Arabian-Jewish merchant, wrote in the middle of the 10th century: "The town of Prague is built of stone and lime, and in trade it is the richest of all (Slavic) towns."

In 1025, Moravia, and slightly later, Silesia, were incorporated into the Czech nation. Slovakia, however, became part of the Magyar state, whose fate it shared until the 20th century. Under Premysl Otaker II, in the 13th century, Czech rule was extended southward with the conquest of Austria, Styria, Corinthia and Carniola. At this time the Czech rulers assumed the title of king. Otaker was defeated in battle in 1278, however, and his conquests were cut short. In the *Divine Comedy* Dante sings the praises of Otaker II. He was followed by Vaclav III, an unfortunate ruler who was

This excavation at Mikulcice unearthed the foundation of a church dating from the time of the Great Moravian Empire (9th century) as well as many objects of the same period.

The Great Moravian Empire, which flourished in the 9th century A.D., left many archaeological remains, notably the basilica at Mikulcice and the fortress at Kourim, where these exquisitely worked ornaments of hammered silver were found.

deposed by assassination in 1305. By 1310 the battling competitors for the throne conceded to the House of Luxembourg, and a new dynasty acquired the Czech kingdom.

THE LUXEMBOURG DYNASTY

The first sovereign of this house, John of Luxembourg, left governing to his nobles and sought his fame on the battlefield and his amusement at the French court—he rarely visited Prague. In 1345, now blind, King John fell at the Battle of Crécy, defending the King of France against Richard III of England. In recognition of his bravery, the British royal family to this day includes the three ostrich feathers from King John's crown in its coat-of-arms.

Karlstejn Castle, not far from Prague, was once the repository of Bohemia's crown jewels.

John's son, Charles IV, was not only a Bohemian King, but was also elected Holy Roman Emperor. He brought the nation to the level of a great feudal power. The constant memorials throughout the country bearing his name—many built during his reign—today give evidence of his outstanding achievements. A statesman and wise leader, Charles established the Prague Archbishopric, and in 1348 he founded Prague University, the first institution of higher learning in Central Europe. He completely rebuilt the capital city of Prague and supported both trade and art. As the imperial city of Bohemia, Prague became one of the focal points of European politics.

When Charles died in 1378, his son, Vaclav IV, proved incapable of managing this vast inheritance. He was deposed as emperor and many conflicts, formerly held in check by the firm hand of his father, burst into the open.

THE HUSSITE MOVEMENT

Seeds of discontent were sprouting throughout Europe. In Flanders there had been a revolt of weavers and peasants, and in England Wat Tyler and John Ball had led rebellions of the poor. Church corruption became a source of heated controversy. Among the advocates of reform were a group of University professors, including Jan Hus (1371–1415), Rector of the University and pastor of Prague's Bethlehem Chapel congregation, where sermons were delivered in the Czech language. These sermons were filled with doctrines inspired by the writings of the English reformer, John Wycliffe.

Attacked for his criticisms of Church administrators, including the Pope, Hus was banished from Prague in 1412 after he had denounced the sale of indulgences. From Kozi

Charles IV, King of Bohemia and Holy Roman Emperor, gave his name to many of Czechoslovakia's most important sites—for example, Karlstejn, Karlovy Vary (Carlsbad), and Charles Bridge.

After Jan Hus was burned and his ashes scattered, his ideas continued to inspire men and for two decades, battles raged between the Hussites and the crown. The Hussites even developed their own songs and tapestries.

Jan Zizka of Trocnov, known as the blind squire, was an iron hand in the Hussite community, holding together its feuding factions—the conservative Ultraquists and his own Taborites.

Hradek, in southern Bohemia, Hus continued his preaching and his writing. In 1414, he was summoned to Constance where a council of the Church had been called to settle the Great Schism—a dispute in the Church, whereby two popes had been elected, each by a different party. Armed with the promise of safe conduct from Emperor Sigismund, he had scarcely reached Constance when he was seized and put on trial for heresy. When all attempts to make him recant had failed, he was burned at the stake in July, 1415.

The death of Hus stirred the Czech lands profoundly. His followers, known as Hussites, established their own fortified towns in the region of southern Bohemia where he himself had sought refuge. To their new homes they gave such biblical names as Tabor, Oreb and Mount of Olives.

On July 30, 1419, open warfare broke out between the Hussites and the forces of officialdom. Signal for the outbreak was the defenestration of several Prague town counselors by an angry group of Praguers. Defenestration, the throwing of an enemy from a window, thus made its first appearance in Czechoslovakia.

In 1420, the Pope proclaimed a crusade against the Hussites, who made Tabor their headquarters and Jan Zizka their general. Using ingenious tactics and benefiting from high morale, the Hussites repeatedly repulsed attacks by Sigismund's army, although their weapons were adapted farm implements and they fought against knights clad from head to foot in mail.

Rifts began to develop within the Hussite community, however, and in 1424 Zizka died. Under his successor, Prokop the Great, the rebels twice again beat back attacks upon their stronghold and in the late 1420's, they took the offensive, raiding several times into Germany and once even reaching the Baltic Sea.

In 1434, not quite 20 years after the martyrdom of their leader, internal dissension in the Hussite camp flared into bloodshed. Prokop fell at the Battle of Lipany on May 20, 1434. What tens of thousands of crusading soldiers were powerless to achieve, was accomplished in one fratricidal contest. A century later, Martin Luther was to acknowledge Hus as his "great predecessor."

Hussite moderates made their peace with the imperial power after Lipany and the breakup of the rebel armies. Wealthy from their successful years of raiding, the Hussite nobles transformed the Bohemian state into a monarchy with an elected ruler, Jiri (George) of Podebrad, himself a Hussite.

The first hint that Czechs and Slovaks could live united came when the Jagellon kings, who succeeded Jiri, merged Hungary into the Bohemian kingdom. Poland was the homeland of the Jagellons, so that the new state was large and diverse, and the power of the nobles grew to rival the king's.

UNDER HAPSBURG RULE

The death of King Louis, last of the Jagellons, in the battle against the Turks at Móhacs in 1526 left the throne vacant and the nobles offered the throne to Ferdinand of Hapsburg, whose brother was the German Emperor. Hapsburg rule was to last for nearly 400 years until Czechoslovakia was declared a republic in 1918.

Among the early Hapsburgs was Rudolf II, who chose Prague as his capital. Rudolf was an eccentric, who collected works of art and worthless trinkets, a patron of alchemists and astronomers. A scholar working in Prague under Rudolf's domination was Jan Jessenius, a Slovak, who was the first man to dissect a human body.

In 1618, when Catholic-Protestant hostility flared again, several Protestant nobles threw

two of the king's governors from a window of Prague Castle in what was to become known as the Prague Defenestration. Thus began the Czech War of 1618–1620, forerunner of the Thirty Years' War which was to engulf Europe. The Protestant nobles formed a provisional government of 30 directors, hired mercenaries and rode to battle. At White Mountain near Prague, on November 8, 1620, the forces of Ferdinand, the Emperor, vanquished the dissidents in just two hours. Participants in the uprising lost over three-fourths of their lands and 27 of their leaders were beheaded on June 21, 1621, in the Old Town Square of Prague.

Following the Battle of White Mountain in 1620, Protestants fled Czechoslovakia; more than 150,000 persons, including more than 80 per cent of the nobility, went into exile within six years. One of the exiles, the great educator Jan Amos Komensky (Comenius) wrote, ". . . after the tempest of God's wrath shall have passed, the rule of thy country will again return unto thee, O Czech people."

In 1627, when all the traces of opposition had been eradicated, the throne decreed that the rule of Bohemia had been taken from the nobles and made hereditary within the Hapsburg line. Catholicism was proclaimed the only religion. The German language was elevated to higher status than the Czech. Lands were confiscated, nobles exiled and foreign influences were introduced throughout the country. Resistance continued, but only sporadically. In Domazlice, the Chods rebelled and lost their rights as freemen. In Slovakia, bands of brigands roamed the hills; one of their leaders, Juraj Janosik is celebrated as a Central European Robin Hood who stole from the rich to give to the poor.

THE BEGINNING OF REVIVAL

Towards the end of the 17th century, manufacturing began to appear in the Czech lands. Linen, and later cotton goods, developed as important products for export. Workers were no longer bound by feudal customs, but could earn wages. Division of work was introduced, and simple machinery came into use. A tech-

nical school was opened in Prague, and in 1784 the Czech Royal Society of Learning was created. Emperor Joseph II, son of Maria Theresa and a monarch of enlightened viewpoint, abolished serfdom in 1781. Schools were established, national identification and development were emphasized, and in 1848 the contagious revolutionary fever sweeping Europe reached Bohemia and Slovakia.

The emperor acceded to demands that the Czech language be restored to equality with the German and that a Bohemian Diet would be convoked with full legislative power. The desire for national identity continued to grow until the First World War.

THE CZECHOSLOVAK REPUBLIC

Shortly after the outbreak of war, Professor Thomas Garrigue Masaryk went abroad to seek support from the Allies for an independent Czech and Slovak nation. During the war, the people of the Czech lands became masters at passive resistance in order not to aid the Austrian war effort. In the manner of the fictional

An abortive attempt to rid Czechoslovakia of its Hapsburg rulers was highlighted in 1618 by the so-called defenestration of two Prague vice-regents of the emperor—they were hurled unceremoniously from a window—and this led to the Thirty Years War.

Crowds thronged Wenceslas Square in Prague on October 28, 1918, when the country was proclaimed a sovereign republic.

Good Soldier Schweik, who is recognized now as a national folk hero, they proceeded resolutely toward the front, but somehow always wound up moving in the wrong direction. Indeed, many Czechs and Slovaks residing abroad, as well as some who deserted from the Austrian army, formed a Czechoslovak legion which fought on the Allied side.

In June 1918, the members of several American Czech and Slovak societies met in Pittsburgh in the presence of Masaryk and affirmed their agreement with his aim of developing a unified Czechoslovakia. On October 28, 1918, with the active assistance of United States' President Woodrow Wilson, Czechoslovakia was at last proclaimed a republic. The long resistance of the Czechs and Slovaks against the Hapsburgs finally had triumphed, inspired by the movements for national independence and social reform prevalent in Europe.

A progressive and prosperous nation until the economic depression of 1929, Czechoslo-

vakia nevertheless suffered in some ways from having too diverse a population, about 7,500,000 Czechs, 2,500,000 Slovaks, 3,000,000 Germans, 750,000 Magyars, 500,000 Ruthenians and smaller numbers of Jews, Poles and other groups.

Thomas Masaryk, once a blacksmith, was a founder and first president of Czechoslovakia.

On May 27, 1942, Czechoslovak partisans assassinated the Nazi governor, Reichsprotector Reinhard Heydrich, as he drove through a section of Prague.

MUNICH AND NAZI OCCUPATION

The rise of Hitler in Germany gave active voice to a Sudeten German Home Front in the western portion of Bohemia. In March, 1938, the Nazi Fuehrer, taking advantage of the indifference of the Western powers and the weakness of the League of Nations, annexed Austria and prepared his attack on Czechoslovakia. Hitler demanded the surrender to Germany of the Sudetenland. Prime Minister Neville Chamberlain of Great Britain, with the acquiescence of France, signed the infamous Munich Pact granting the cession on September 30, 1938, and announced that this guaranteed "peace in our time." On October 1, the Germans occupied and annexed parts of Czechoslovakia. On October 5, Eduard Benes, second president of the republic, resigned and retired to London to set up a government in exile. A month later, 4,000 square miles of Czechoslovak territory were ceded to Hungary. Other parts of the nation were sliced off to benefit Poland.

On March 14, 1939, Hitler dissolved Czechoslovakia entirely and made protectorates of Bohemia and Moravia, meanwhile establishing Slovakia as an autonomous state, with Joseph

This is the way the town of Lidice appeared after the Nazis destroyed it in retaliation for the assassination of Reinhard Heydrich, Nazi "Protector" of Bohemia and Moravia.

In 1944 the Slovaks rose against Nazi domination, and materially aided the Soviet forces in expelling the Germans from Slovakia. Here hastily armed men of the Slovak underground assemble at a rallying point.

On the walls of the Pinkas Synagogue (Prague's Jewish Museum), students have inscribed the names of 77,297 Jews who perished at the hands of the Nazis.

Tiso as president. Strong resistance movements sprang up, and in May, 1942, during World War II, Czech underground members assassinated the German governor, Reinhard Heydrich. In retaliation, the Nazis leveled the village of Lidice, shot all of its men, interned the women in concentration camps and scattered the children throughout Germany.

During the war, nearly 80,000 Czech and Slovak Jews were imprisoned and later killed.

Czechoslovakia finally was liberated by the Allies in May, 1945, the Russians marching victoriously into Prague and American troops penetrating to Plzen, in western Bohemia.

According to the Allied agreement at Potsdam after the war, the Germans from the Sudeten border regions, except for those who were considered to be anti-Nazi, were evacuated to Germany.

The period immediately following the war was one of economic hardship and political struggle to determine the course of future development.

COMMUNISTS COME TO POWER

In this quarrelsome climate, the Communists, who had been numerically strong and politically

Soviet tanks entering Prague as liberators in 1945 were welcomed warmly.

active before the war, increased in numbers until they gained control of the National Assembly in 1946. President Benes followed tradition and named Klement Gottwald, leader of the victorious Communist Party, as the nation's prime minister.

In October, 1945, key industries, natural resources, banks and insurance companies, and foreign trade operations were nationalized. The land belonging to big estate owners and Nazi collaborators was confiscated and distributed among peasants and small farmers gradually. By February, 1948, nationalization was complete. On May 9, which is celebrated as Liberation Day, a new constitution was adopted, and on May 30 the first elections were held under this

Throngs again formed in Wenceslas Square when the Communists won the elections of 1948, thus placing the nation among the allies of the Soviet Union.

Ludvik Svoboda, World War II hero, became president of Czechoslovakia in 1968, replacing Antonin Novotny.

constitution. Benes resigned as President on June 7, and a week later Gottwald became President. Gottwald ruled until his death in 1953. Antonin Zapotocky became the second Communist president of Czechoslovakia and carried on the policies established by Gottwald.

His successor, in 1956, was Antonin Novotny, who had a reputation of being disinclined to adapt policy to changing circumstances. In the past few years, however, pressure for change was growing in Czechoslovakia and the Communist Party; artists, writers and film-makers were seeking new freedom of expression and students echoed them. And a growing economic crisis led planners to ask for more leeway in which to get things done. In 1966, new emphasis was placed on making profits, not merely meeting quotas.

Politically, the winds of change blew across Prague on January 5, 1968, when Alexander Dubcek, a reform-minded Slovak, replaced Novotny as Czechoslovak Communist Party chief. In March, the government lifted censorship of the press. In April, a new and more liberal cabinet was formed and a manifesto was issued assuring the people of fuller civil rights. Novotny was replaced as president, a position which he also held, by war hero Ludvik Svoboda (whose name in Czech means freedom).

As the months passed, the new Czechoslovak leadership won the devoted loyalty of the people.

However, questions arose in the minds of Czechoslovakia's allies, and in July, 1968, Soviet and Czechoslovak leaders met at Cierna, a small town in Slovakia. After three days, the two nations re-affirmed their continuing friendship in public demonstrations.

But on August 21 troops of the Soviet Union, Bulgaria, East Germany, Hungary and Poland, crossed the borders of Czechoslovakia. Although most of the foreign troops were later withdrawn, their entry caused difficulties in Czechoslovakia's external relations. Czechoslovak leadership has shown a determination to overcome these difficulties and to carry forward the basic elements of the course set in January, 1968.

In January, 1969, the aspirations of Slovak Nationalists were realized, when a new Constitution established Czechoslovakia as a Federal Republic composed of two equal member states, the Czech Republic and the Slovak Republic.

The lakes of eastern Slovakia are ideal for weekend camping.

THE PEOPLE

THE PEOPLE OF CZECHOSLOVAKIA reflect the often changing currents of their national history. In appearance, they bear resemblance to Germanic and Hungarian, as well as to Slavic, ancestors; in music, literature, theatre, and indeed, in their daily customs they show the influences of a varied cultural background. The Czechs number 10,000,000, and the Slovaks, 4,000,000.

A proud people, they celebrate their heritage with festivals, songs and traditions—indeed, music is second nature to the people of Czechoslovakia. Franz Liszt was taught by the famous Czech musician, Rejcha, a professor at the Paris Conservatoire. Beethoven, Weber, Gluck and Mozart all worked and lived in Prague. In fact, Mozart's "Don Giovanni," is still per-

One of Czechoslovakia's most famous composers was Antonin Dvorak (1841–1904), who lived for many years in the United States and whose most famous work is the "New World Symphony."

formed at Prague's Tyl Theatre, the very opera house in which it received its world première. Twentieth-century Czechoslovak composers, such as Dvorak, Smetana and Janacek, are well known to people around the world.

The pulsing mood of contemporary music has not eluded this musical nation. It is intriguing to listen to songs of the Beatles and the Rolling Stones being sung in Czech. Louis Armstrong, the American jazz idol, was accorded one of the greatest receptions of his career during a recent visit to Prague. Jazz, in fact, is now so much a part of the Czechoslovak scene that each autumn for the past five years, Prague has been the site of an International Jazz Festival.

LITERATURE AND LANGUAGE

Czech and Slovak are Slavic languages very close in nature and both can be understood by anyone who speaks one or the other. Unfortunately, neither is well-known in the Western

Jaroslav Hasek (1883–1923) gained world fame for satirizing war and the military life in his novel "The Good Soldier Schweik."

Author of adult satire and charming children's tales, Karel Capek is acclaimed throughout Czechoslovakia.

world and the great body of Czechoslovak literature is therefore lost to us except through translation—and only a few Czech and Slovak authors have been translated widely.

Unquestionably, the Czechoslovak writers best known in English-speaking countries are Franz Kafka (who wrote in German), Jaroslav Hasek and Karel Capek.

Kafka was a brooding genius who created books of great, imaginative horror. His *Metamorphosis* is the story of Gregor Samsa, who awakes to find himself transformed into a giant cockroach. *The Trial* is about a man who is accused of a crime, but never told its nature, so that he finds it impossible to defend himself. *The Castle* deemed by many to be Kafka's finest work, was inspired by the massive profile of Hradcany (Prague Castle), which towers over the Prague skyline.

Working women usually get about 26 weeks of paid maternity leave, after which they can leave their children at day care nurseries for a modest fee.

DAILY LIFE

Most Czechoslovak men marry at about 23 to 26 years of age, usually to a girl 3 to 5 years younger. Often, because of housing shortages in some areas, newlyweds will live with the parents of one partner.

Special nursery schools and child care facilities are provided so that women may pursue employment after marriage. An allowance is provided for each child and leaves of absence for maternity often permit a woman to continue receiving the greater part of salary. The family is the basic factor in the education and guidance

Czechoslovak vacationers, like people everywhere, make a bee-line for the sun.

Since the core of Prague is dominated by beautiful old buildings which deserve preservation, new housing complexes must rise on available land at the outskirts of the city.

of children, although the government assumes all responsibility for medical and dental care, social security and formal education.

Young adults and teen-agers in Czechoslovakia are generally idealistic and outspoken. They have much the same fondness for new clothing and hair styles as in the United States and England. And they enjoy cinema, music, sports and parties as do the young in the West. Many young people, too, are proud of their traditions, kept alive often by grandparents still living in their homes.

Housing demands are being increasingly accommodated through the construction of high-rise apartments. Steel jungles of television antennas cover roof tops, and automobiles are becoming increasingly available, though their cost is quite high for a Czechoslovak worker, and there usually is a two-year wait for delivery. Supermarkets are springing up across the country, though often the housewife still shops daily for her needs.

A family group enjoys an evening out, in surroundings of richly decorated wooden panelling.

Czechoslovak medical technicians prepare to administer treatment using a machine that functions as an artificial liver.

The bracing air of the Slovakian mountains attracts many victims of respiratory diseases to sanitariums such as this one at Novy Smokovec,

FOOD

If the French are the gourmets of Europe, then the people of Czechoslovakia may be considered its *gourmands,* those who eat very heartily. Roast pork with dumplings and sauerkraut is the national dish and platters are invariably heaped high. Among other popular dishes of Czechoslovakia are goulash soup made with diced beef, paprika, garlic and spices; and pork chop à la Lucenec in which the chop is stuffed with a mixture of spinach, cream and egg yolk.

Breakfast usually consists of pastries or pan-

This elderly woman is comfortably installed in a home for the aged in Prague.

Shopping in Czechoslovakia is much the same as it is in the West. Fruits, particularly lemons and bananas, are especially popular and tend to disappear quickly from the stands.

cakes and strongly brewed coffee. Lunch, the main meal of the day for most, is usually a dish of meat and dumplings, possibly preceded by a thick, hearty soup and washed down with Czech beer. Supper very often is similar to lunch, but with perhaps slightly smaller servings. In addition to the three main meals of the day, Czechs and Slovaks usually have two snacks each day at about 10 in the morning and 4 in the afternoon.

FESTIVALS

The major Czechoslovak folk festivals are held each year in the heart of the nation, the central province of Moravia. Straznice, a tiny town in South Moravia, is the locale for the premier festival of all, celebrated each July. For the two days of song and dance, the population of the town swells from scarcely 5,500 to more than 75,000. The leading folk music performers

in the land—professional and amateur—are all on hand.

Some visitors, a serious few, come as students of native folklore. But most are casual tourists, there to see the area's gaily painted houses and to enjoy the flashing hues of native costumes, the living dancing and the singing. No one watches clocks at Straznice; when darkness falls over the three stadiums of the Castle Park, fires are lighted as they might have been by shepherds of old. And in the firelight the singing continues. Finally, when it is late, the visitors ride leisurely back to their hotel or walk to their campsites. On the way they may be hailed by Straznice's native villagers, vintners by trade, who invite the visitors into their houses for just one more song and a glass of one of the region's wines—either the ruby red Frankova or Skalicky Rubin.

Znojmo, also in Moravia, not far from the regional capital of Brno, is the site of another of Czechoslovakia's important folk festivals, this one in September. Summoned in the dewy late summer dawn by buglers perched in the tower of the town hall, the townsfolk of Znojmo pour forth in festive medieval costume to open the annual Znojmo Vintage Harvest. Special trains bear tourists and visitors to the revelry and tradition of this 48-hour-long celebration.

The climax of the Znojmo Festival occurs when a two-wheeled chariot hurtles down the road behind four fiery steeds, calling the crowds to attention. "The King is coming," sounds throughout the crowds lining the avenue. Preceded by three royal flag bearers with "His Majesty's banner," and accompanied by attendants in full regalia, and by a court jester resplendently garbed in gold and jewels, the chariot bears a townsman chosen to impersonate John of Luxembourg, King of Bohemia (1310–46). The "royal" procession moves on with its church dignitaries, wine guild members, dancing children and knights in coats of mail. Finally, into sight come three wagons—the first carries a huge wine cask, the second an oversized wine jug, the third and largest of all, carries the figure of Bacchus, Greek god of wine.

Nearly 650 years ago, the King, John of Luxembourg, gave the townspeople of Znojmo licence to make and sell wine. The proclamation also stipulated that all "cheaters and dishonest tavernkeepers" would be punished by being dipped into the town well. Somehow a legend has grown from these beginnings. Today, tradition decrees that during the two-day festival no one drinks from the town well, for that is said to constitute an admission of dishonesty.

Czechoslovakia's best known and most picturesque folk music festival is held each June at Straznice, Moravia.

To display its achievements to the world and to stimulate international trade, Czechoslovakia has created a massive exposition complex at Brno, the capital of Moravia. Two important trade fairs take place here each year—one for consumer goods and one for industrial equipment.

INDUSTRY

CZECHOSLOVAKIA RANKS as a highly industrialized country. Since 1948 emphasis has been laid on heavy industry and also on engineering and chemical production. The post-war years changed the formerly agrarian Slovakia to a highly industrialized country with a good living standard.

Czechoslovakia is far from being self-sufficient in raw materials. It is dependent on Russia for nearly all of its oil, 80 per cent of its iron ore, 50 per cent of its cotton and 70 per cent of its non-ferrous metals. International economic relations are based on trade and co-operation with the Soviet Union and other members of the Council of Mutual Economic Assistance (Comecon) organized in 1949. The Comecon includes the Soviet Union, Poland, East Germany, Czechoslovakia, Hungary, Rumania, Bulgaria and, since the early 1960's, Mongolia. Czechoslovakia is also actively seeking further expansion of trade and economic co-operation with the West, especially with Western Europe.

Inspection of the Czechoslovak economy would show industry as the dominant factor, employing some 34 per cent of all workers and accounting for nearly 65 per cent of national income.

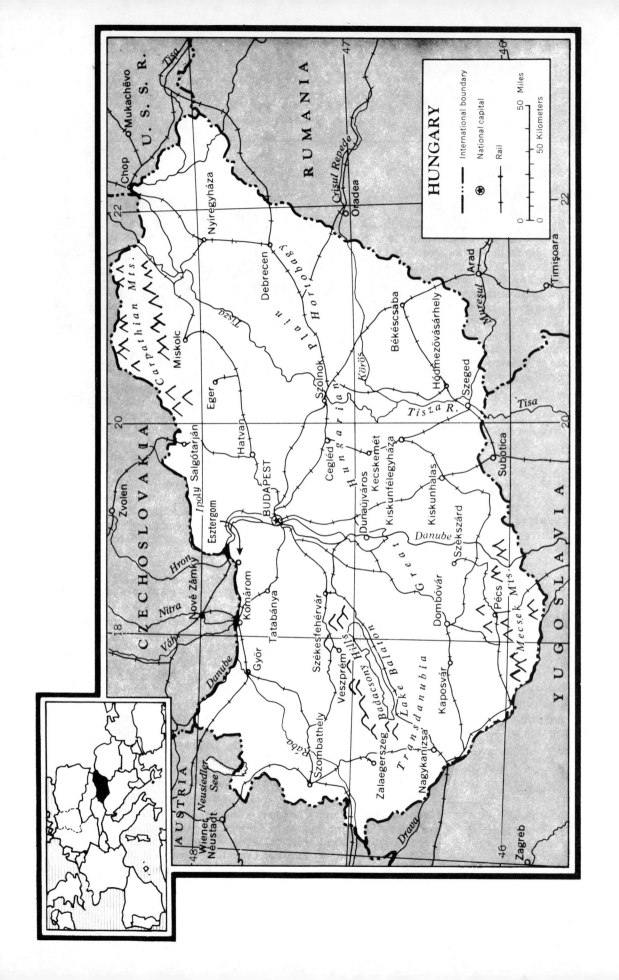

One of the most familiar of Budapest panoramas is the view from Gellert Hill. St. Gellert was a martyred bishop of the 11th century, whose body was flung into the river in a barrel from the rocks where his statue now stands.

HUNGARY

THE LAND

HUNGARY OCCUPIES THE BASIN of the Carpathians, a semi-circular mountain range linking the Alps in the west to the Balkans in the east. This is the heart of Europe in an almost geometrical sense: it is 1,500 miles from the Atlantic sea coast of Portugal to the west, and the same distance to the crest of the Ural Mountains to the east. The country is entirely land-locked: it is surrounded by Austria, Czechoslovakia, the Soviet Union, Rumania and Yugoslavia. In area it is approximately 35,000 square miles, about the size of Indiana, or of Scotland and Northern Ireland together. The Danube, which flows into the country in an easterly direction from Austria, makes a right-angle turn 40 miles north of Budapest and divides the land into three regions—hilly Transdanubia in the west, the foothills of the Carpathians in the north, and the Great Hungarian Plain in the middle and in the east. The three regions converge on Budapest (formerly the twin cities of Buda and Pest), hilly on the Buda side of the river and flat on the Pest side.

The graceful spire of the Coronation Church in Buda Castle is outlined against one of the hills of Buda, Szabadsaghegy.

804 ■ **HUNGARY**

THE GREAT HUNGARIAN PLAIN

Although comparatively sparsely populated, the Great Plain remains to most Hungarians the essential Hungary. It is entirely flat, barely rising 400 feet above sea level, a land of vast vistas which yet escapes monotony. During the Turkish period, most of its population took shelter in a few towns; and to this day these remain large straggling villages rather than cities in the Western sense. When the people moved back into the countryside they created the characteristic Hungarian rural settlements, the "tanyas." These are hamlets consisting of a few farmhouses, stables and granaries, without a church, school or village shop of their own. Often the buildings cluster round a tall well whose gracefully nodding silhouette can be glimpsed from many miles away as it rises above the acacia trees.

Despite recent industrialization in the main towns and the discovery of oil and natural gas deposits, the Great Plain remains predominantly agricultural, one of the richest wheat-growing regions in Europe. The central area, which has sandy soil, was virtually a desert until about a hundred years ago. Landless peasants, migrating from other parts of the country, then took possession of it and planted fruit trees. Today it is covered with orchards (mainly apricots and apples) and vineyards.

The focal point of this region is Kecskemet, a small urban town surrounded by a residential area and, beyond, hundreds of isolated tanyas. Much of the locally produced fruit is processed here into jams and preserves. The apricot brandy distilled in the city has a world-wide reputation.

As one travels south or southwest from Kecskemet, the orchards give way to a sea of golden grain, an unforgettable sight. Towns and even villages are few and far between until the River Tisza is reached. Here, in a sharp bend of the river, lies Szeged, until recently Hungary's second largest city. Although an ancient settlement, it acquired its present appearance when it was rebuilt after a ruinous flood in 1879. Its fine central square is domi-

A herdsman of the Great Plain tends his horses.

nated by the Votive Church, the scene of Hungary's oldest open-air summer festival of music and opera. Once a purely agricultural "village-town," Szeged now has a university and growing textile and food industries.

The country east of Szeged was for centuries known as Hungary's "storm corner," an allusion not to climatic conditions but to peasant uprisings. Until 1945, this was a region of vast semi-feudal estates and of landless peasantry. Today it is famous for growing some of Hungary's best vegetables and livestock.

THE HORTOBAGY

Perhaps the most impressive and celebrated— if also the most "touristy"— part of the Great Plain is the Hortobagy. Covering some 300 square miles east of the River Tisza, it is like a transplanted chunk of the Siberian steppes— sparse, flat grazing land, whose fauna (both wild and domestic) remains unique in Europe. Large herds of cattle with forked horns (of Asiatic origin) are tended by mounted shepherds armed with long crackling whips, and by two ancient breeds of Hungarian sheepdog, the "puli" and the "kuvasz." This is the true Hungary, or "puszta," whose customs, folklore and almost nomadic way of life have hardly changed since the ancestors of the Magyars left Central Asia to populate Hungary.

A mounted herdsman wears his traditional cloak.

Travelling from Budapest, the main road to the Hortobagy leads on to Debrecen, until recently one of the typical giant villages of the Plain. It now has a university, some excellent schools and agricultural industry. A large and handsome church in the main square proclaims it the "Calvinist Rome," the stronghold of Hungarian Protestantism.

This bridge with nine arches is a landmark of the Hortobagy region.

Typical of Transdanubia's old cities, Veszprem, one of the ten bishoprics founded by St. Stephen, is now the home of a new university.

TRANSDANUBIA

The varied, often intimate, scenery of Transdanubia offers a striking change after the flat, distant horizons of the Great Plain. The rolling mellow countryside seems to be the natural expression of an ancient and unbroken civilization. A thousand years before the Magyars broke camp in Central Asia this region was already a flourishing Roman province, Pannonia. In the 16th century the western parts of it escaped being demolished under Turkish rule.

Apart from the immediate environs of Budapest, Transdanubia is also industrially the most developed part of Hungary, but nowhere (except perhaps in the coal-mining district around Dorog) is industry dominant. Indeed, it is the rural charm of the region which may first captivate the visitor from the West.

The villages here are still of a type less often found on the western side of the Austrian frontier, with low, long, whitewashed peasant houses, thatched roofs, and storks nesting on the chimney tops. An 18th-century church usually marks the middle of the village, its bulbous spire recalling Austrian Baroque architecture. Half-hidden in a park of chestnut trees, there may be an elegant 18th-century manor house.

Although even the secondary roads are generally good, the motorist must share them with gaggles of geese and flocks of darting chickens. His speed in the late afternoon may be set by the measured tread of home-going cattle or the clatter of ox-carts transporting mountains of hay or grain.

LAKE BALATON

Lake Balaton lies at the geographical midpoint of Transdanubia. A vast expanse of shallow water (the largest in Central Europe), it is deceptively calm most of the time, but when a storm breaks, the lake rises in sudden fury. The southern shore, with its gently sloping sandy beaches, is a bathers' paradise; it is, in

Most Hungarians treasure summer holidays on Lake Balaton as their happiest childhood memories—and they come again with their children to recapture the magic. The vineyard-covered Badacsony hills rise from the opposite shore.

Steamers dock at a resort on Lake Balaton.

The 18th-century Benedictine monastery of Tihany commands one of the finest views over Lake Balaton.

fact, dotted from one end to the other with summer resorts, camping sites and holiday settlements.

Those less intent on bathing may find the rocky northern shore more attractive. From here, the Peninsula of Tihany juts out into the lake, its 18th-century Benedictine monastery (now a museum) occupying a commanding hilltop position. Only a few miles from Tihany is Hungary's oldest and most celebrated spa, Balatonfured. Although it is surrounded today with camping sites and modern summer hotels, the town retains much of the calm elegance of the past. The healing properties of its medicinal springs are now supplemented by the country's largest hospital specializing in heart ailments.

Further to the south the curiously formed Badacsony region is one of Hungary's best vine-growing districts and the haunt of painters and poets. Part of a picturesque mountain range which extends northwards for some 50 miles, its hills are densely wooded. Now and again stark volcanic rock formations rise up in bizarre shapes, many with the ruins of a medieval castle perched on top. About 100 miles south of the lake another cluster of hills, the Mecsek Mountains, provide a green back-

drop to the ancient and attractive university town of Pecs.

HAYDN COUNTRY

The western part of Transdanubia is intensely cultivated rolling country of great, if modest, charm. Little of this is visible from the

The 13th-century façade of the Cathedral of Pecs has recently been restored.

One of the greatest 18th-century musicians, Joseph Haydn, spent much of his working life in the service of the Princes Eszterhazy in their magnificent country seat, Fertod. The composer's quarters were in the servants' wing where he ranked over the grooms, but not over the cook!

main arterial motorways which lead from Vienna and the southwest towards the capital. Only the extensive marshland around Lake Ferto (the Neusiedler See, to Austrians) has remained uncultivated: an oddly enclosed world of its own, it now shelters an aquatic bird sanctuary.

To music lovers, the whole border area, along with Burgenland on the other side of the Austrian frontier, is Haydn country. Not only did the great composer spend most of his working life in one or other Eszterhazy chateau of the region, but his music seems the very expression of this land of gentle contrasts and radiant harmonies. The Eszterhazys were a family of powerful nobles, and the grandest of their residences, Eszterhaza (now renamed Fertod), has been dubbed the Hungarian Versailles. The château now houses an agricul-

tural research institute, a school and a museum, and is the setting of an annual music festival.

Further north along the banks of the Danube, the lesser Hungarian Plain is a flat, highly developed agricultural region, spreading out from the town of Gyor.

ESZTERGOM

Many of the towns of Transdanubia have great interest and character. Esztergom on the Danube, only 25 miles northwest from Budapest, has been for centuries the seat of Hungary's Roman Catholic cardinals and boasts a suitably imposing 19th-century cathedral.

Some 50 years ago a citizen of the town, strolling in his back yard at the foot of Cathedral Hill, was nearly crushed by a stone which had become detached from the ramparts supporting the archbishop's palace. It seems that in those days Hungarians still relished long and involved lawsuits. In the course of investigating the cause of the mishap, the offending stone was identified as part of an elaborately carved Romanesque arch. The discovery led to the complete unearthing of the medieval palace of Bela III, one of the Arpad kings. Even some of the paintwork had been preserved.

The city's Christian Museum, an elaborate storehouse of medieval and Renaissance art, the remarkable red marble Bakocz chapel (now part of the cathedral), and the excavations together form a remarkable memorial to Hungary's past.

OTHER LANDMARKS

Some 20 miles south of Esztergom, off the main road to Vienna, in Tata is one of the most elegant of Baroque châteaux in the country (also a former Eszterhazy residence), as well as the ruins of a medieval castle. In the 18th century the town was the home of Hungary's pottery industry. Its faïence rivalled in fame and merit the products of the great factories of France and Holland. Fittingly, the castle museum now houses a representative collection of local ceramics. The pottery tradition is now carried on at the famous porcelain factory of Herend, about 100 miles farther south.

Near the country's western border several towns—Szombathely, Koszeg and above all, Sopron—have whole streets and squares of unspoilt Baroque architecture. Nestling among the wooded foothills of the Alps, they have preserved much of the unhurried atmosphere of a graceful age. Keszthely at the southern tip of Lake Balaton has a palace which houses the country's oldest library.

Hungary's oldest pharmacy is in Sopron, Transdanubia. Like several other towns in western Hungary, Sopron has an unspoilt Baroque atmosphere of great charm.

THE NORTH

The Matra and Bukk Mountains, the south-ernmost range of the Carpathians, are all that remain since World War I of "historic" Hungary's extensive mountain possessions. Their highest peak, Mount Kekes, rises to 3,000 feet above sea level and is a popular skiing resort. The southern slopes are fertile and their orchards and vineyards provide an enchanting setting to one of Hungary's best-loved cities, Eger. Some of the reasons for the special place of affection the city enjoys are historic. Founded as a bishopric by St. Stephen in the 11th century, its defence by Istvan Dobo in 1562 against an overwhelming Turkish force, is one of the episodes in Hungary's long struggle against foreign invaders which still stirs the hearts and minds of the people. The epic novel, "The Stars of Eger," which tells the story of the siege, is probably the most popular book in the language. Its author, Geza Gardonyi, now lies buried among his heroes on the ramparts of the castle. But many of the attractions of Eger are still there. Its Baroque churches, rococo chapter houses, old colleges and the ruins of the castle attract many thousands of visitors every year.

The caves of Aggtelek in northern Hungary are famous for their stalactites.

One of the few architectural remains of Turkish rule, this minaret towers above the historic town of Eger.

TOKAY AND BEYOND

Standing on one of the eastern bastions of the castle of Eger, on a clear day one can just glimpse the outlines of the Tokay hills. This is the region which has given its name to one of the world's great wines—the sweet, golden juice of the Tokay grape. King Edward VII, of England, a good judge both of wine and his fellow monarchs, described it as the wine of kings and the king of wines.

Further north the city of Miskolc and its sister town, Diosgyor, are the focal points of a thriving industrial region. Reflecting Hungary's transformation from an almost purely agricul-tural to an industrial country, Miskolc has now replaced Szeged of the Great Plain as the country's second most populous city. In sharp contrast to the steel mills of Miskolc, the town and environs of Mezokovesd have long been celebrated for their folk art, especially for their beautiful embroidery. Farther east, near the eastern Carpathians and the Soviet frontier, the

At Sarospatak in northeast Hungary are the ruins of an ancient castle, along with one of the country's oldest and most famous colleges.

city of Sarospatak is the home of one of Hungary's oldest and most famous colleges.

BUDAPEST

Many European capitals outstrip Budapest in political importance, artistic merit or historical interest, but few can rival its natural beauty. The Danube, a majestic river, divides it into bustling, commercial Pest on the left (or west) bank and hilly Buda on the right. Among many splendid panoramic views the one from the top of Mount Gellert is perhaps the most

memorable: it embraces Castle Hill with its part-medieval and part-Baroque Royal Palace, the spire of the Coronation Church, the distant hills of Buda, six Danube bridges, the neo-Gothic bulk of Parliament, a row of hotels and public buildings along the Pest embankment, the cupola of St. Stephen's basilica, and the green parkland of St. Margaret's Island. Mount Gellert itself has been extensively fortified by successive Hapsburg emperors. The walls and bastions now serve as a popular restaurant and café. Above them rises the huge Liberation Monument.

This open-air swimming pool is on Margaret Island in the Danube at Budapest.

Almost fully restored after the ravages of World War II, the Royal Palace on Castle Hill again commands the river and the twin cities of Buda and Pest. Some of the medieval and Renaissance battlements which have recently been fully excavated were first revealed by wartime shells.

HISTORY

WITH A LOVE for legend, Hungarians hold dear the myth of the Golden Stag. This fabulous creature is supposed to have lured two princely hunters across the Ural Mountains and the great rivers and plains of Siberia to a land flowing with milk and honey. Here, in a clearing of a dense forest, the stag dissolved into two beautiful maidens. Hunor, the elder of the two brothers, lifted one of the maidens into his saddle and rode away with her. Their descend-

ants became the Huns; and, with the appearance of Attila, this part of the legend merges into history.

Roman and medieval chroniclers have called Attila the "Scourge of God." Slaughter and devastation marked the trail of Attila's horsemen, the first of the great nomadic hordes which put an end to centuries of Roman peace and civilization in Europe. Attila himself died in 453 A.D., preparing a final assault on Rome itself. Hungarians have never lost their sense of kinship with the Huns, despite their evil reputation in the West, and Hungarian literature is probably the only setting in which Attila appears as something of a hero, rather than a monster. Hungarian boys are still named after him.

The other princely hunter, Magyar, settled with his bride in Central Asia. This remained the home of their descendants for centuries. Then, around the year 800 A.D., seven Magyar tribes set out in the footsteps of their legendary Hun kinsmen.

THE HOUSE OF ARPAD

After crossing the historic Pass of Verecke in the Carpathian Mountains, the chiefs of the seven tribes entered into a "blood contract" and elected Arpad as their major leader. The event was commemorated a thousand years later by the "Millenary Monument," a splendid memorial and one of the sights of modern Budapest.

Under Arpad's leadership, the seven tribes took more-or-less peaceful possession of the fertile but sparsely populated plain which stretched from two great rivers, the Danube and the Tisza, to the mountain range of the Carpathians. But for another century the

The Millenary Monument in Budapest is like a history lesson in stone and bronze. The figure of Arpad stands high on the column above a group of the tribal chiefs who led the Magyar conquest of the country a thousand years ago. Behind the Chiefs is a colonnade containing a number of statues (barely discernible) of Hungary's greatest kings and national leaders, from St. Stephen to Kossuth.

A Roman settlement has been excavated near Szekesfehervar in Transdanubia. Transdanubia is the only part of the country which was included in the Roman Empire.

Magyars continued their wanderings. Moving on their horses with a speed that overawed and terrified their enemies, they roamed the length and breadth of Europe. In the west the prayer was born: "From the Black Death and from the Magyars, oh God preserve us." This "Age of Adventures" (as it was to be called by later Hungarian historians) came to an end with the defeat of the raiding Magyars by the German Emperor, Otto I in 946 A.D. It forced the Magyars to turn their attention and energy to the land which, until then, had been merely their home base.

STEPHEN

Half a century after their defeat in Germany, the ruling prince, a direct descendant of Arpad, bowed to Christianity and received the name of Stephen in baptism. He was also presented with

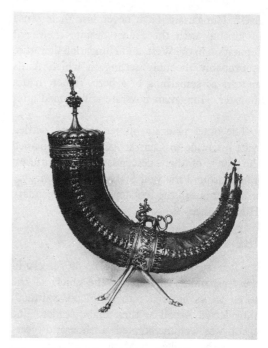

King Sigismond's drinking horn dates from the 15th century.

St. Stephen's Crown was the symbol of Hungary's freedom for 900 years. The upper part of the crown came to Stephen as a gift from Pope Sylvester II in 997 A.D. The lower part is of somewhat later Byzantine origin. Replicas of the Crown Jewels are exhibited in Buda Castle.

a richly bejewelled golden crown by Pope Sylvester II. With this he had himself crowned as first "Apostolic King" of Hungary (1001 A.D.). During his 40-year reign Stephen transformed his loosely organized tribal lands into a powerful unit of a state. Stephen was canonized after his death, and his feast day (August 20th) is still celebrated. For centuries his "Holy Crown" remained a symbol both of Hungarian independence and of the country's links with Western Christianity.

For 300 years after Stephen, the House of Arpad continued to provide Hungary with some of its greatest kings, saints and scholars. In 1222, King Endre signed the "Golden Bull," the Hungarian Magna Charta. His son, Bela IV, restored the country after an invasion by the Mongols and founded many of Hungary's cities as a defence against future invaders. His daughter, Margaret (another future saint), gave her name to the beautiful island on the Danube (between present-day Buda and Pest) where she spent her life in prayer. Another Arpad King, Coloman Beauclerk, was the first to forbid the branding and burning of witches.

THE HOUSE OF ANJOU

In 1301, the male line of the House of Arpad ended and St. Stephen's crown passed to descendants in the female line. Two kings of the House of Anjou, Robert (1309–40) and Louis (1340–80) raised the prestige and power of the Hungarian monarchy. They subdued their warring barons and carried Hungarian arms victoriously into the Balkans, into Italy and as far north as the Baltic. Among the many schools and monasteries which they founded was the first Hungarian University. The long and troubled reign of Louis' successor, Sigismond of Luxembourg, was remembered best for the emergence of Janos Hunyadi.

FROM HUNYADI TO THE HAPSBURGS

The origin of the Hunyadi family is obscure: some historians believe that Janos was an illegitimate son of King Sigismond. Whatever the truth, his rise to power at court was rapid, and his generalship became a legend even in his lifetime. The great English historian, Edward Gibbon, regarded him as the leading military genius of his age.

A national leader of his ability was badly needed. By the beginning of the 15th century the Turks were advancing across the Balkans. The once powerful Christian kingdoms of Serbia, Bulgaria, and Albania crumbled under the Turks' attack and what still remained of the Byzantine Empire offered little resistance. Western Europe, was, as usual, fully occupied with internal quarrels—both political and religious—and there seemed no way to save it from another Mohammedan invasion. In a series of brilliant campaigns and by the defence of the key fortress of Belgrade, Hunyadi stemmed the tide and preserved his own country from Turkish rule for another century.

Janos Hunyadi's elder son, Laszlo (the hero of Hungary's best-loved national opera) fell victim to the treachery of his fellow nobles. But the younger son, Matyas, was carried to the

Janos Hunyadi leads his troops in defence of Belgrade against the Turks in 1456. His victory saved Hungary from Turkish rule for another century. The picture, one of many representations of the battle, is by the 19th-century artist, Anton Bogner.

HUNGARY ■ 817

Buda is seen in a contemporary engraving of King Matyas's palace, one of the wonders of Renaissance Europe. Hardly any of the palace survived 150 years of Turkish occupation.

throne on what modern commentators would describe as an irresistible wave of popular enthusiasm. As a ruler (1458–90) he proved himself the ideal Renaissance prince: he was handsome, brave, ambitious, ruthless and intelligent. His small regular army became one of the most efficient fighting forces of Europe, and he used it to discipline his own nobles as well as to defend his kingdom. To his subjects he was known as "Matyas the Just." Foreign travellers spoke with wonder about the magnificence of his court. The few surviving volumes from his famous library (called "Corvina" after the family emblem, the raven, embossed on the covers) are among the highest achievements of Renaissance art. Recent excavations in Buda and Visegrad give a glimpse of the magnificence of his palaces.

Matyas failed in only one respect: when he died, still comparatively young, he had done nothing to ward off the Turkish advance. The threat grew under his weak successors. In 1514, a peasant revolt under the petty noble, Gyorgy Dozsa, was put down with blood-curdling ferocity, and the country was left "an open

Visitors inspect a restored section of another of King Matyas's residences, the Palace of Visegrad on the Danube, 20 miles north of Budapest.

grave." It took less than 10 years for the nation to tumble into it.

In 1526, a Turkish army of 200,000 led by Sultan Soliman II, met the Hungarian army on the field of Mohacs in southwest Hungary. The young Hungarian king, Lajos II, had barely been able to raise 20,000 men, and even these he lacked the authority and experience to command effectively. The battle lasted less than six hours, but it finished Hungary as an in-

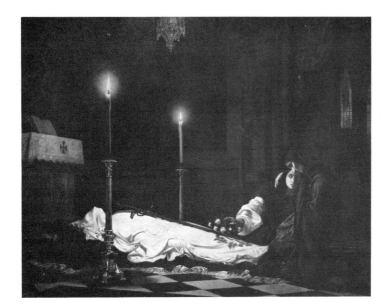

At the bier of Laszlo Hunyadi, are his mother, Janos Hunyadi's widow, and his younger brother, the future King Matyas. The picture is the best known work of the 19th-century artist, Viktor Madarasz.

dependent military power. The king himself perished on the battlefield.

After Mohacs, the country remained divided into three parts for nearly 200 years. The eastern, mountainous region became the semi-independent princedom of Transylvania, and for a few decades, under the Protestant Prince, Gabor Bethlen, it even enjoyed a measure of prosperity. The western fringes became little more than an outlying province of the Austrian monarchy, the House of Hapsburg. The central plain, with Matyas's capital city, Buda, lay under the yoke of Turkey. The Turks' policy was one of total exploitation which left large areas of the country depopulated. From the cultural and artistic point of view, the Turks had little influence. Apart from a few minarets in provincial cities and public baths in Budapest, perhaps their only legacy is the Hungarian passion for drinking hot sweet coffee at all

The body of King Lajos II is recovered after Hungary's disastrous defeat by the Turks on the Field of Mohacs in 1526. This is a painting by Bertalan Szekely.

hours of the day and night. There is some truth in the Hungarian contention that they alone stopped the Turks from advancing farther west.

HAPSBURG RULE AND THE WAR OF INDEPENDENCE

After the middle of the 17th century, the Turkish forces were gradually pushed back beyond the southern frontiers of Hungary and the country became reunited under the rule of the Hapsburg kings of Austria. Theoretically the Hapsburgs were "elected" as kings of an independent Hungary. In practice, most of the Hapsburgs regarded Hungary as a newly-won dominion, a remote and backward province to be administered in the interest of their German-speaking subjects. For more than 200 years their persistent efforts to Germanize the

language and customs of Hungary were fiercely resisted.

Between 1703 and 1711, Prince Ferenc Rakoczi II led the first great armed rebellion against Hapsburg rule, but, after some initial successes, his "kuruc" (crusader) state collapsed. Under the Hapsburg Empress Maria Theresa (1740–80) relations between the people and the ruling house improved. The Empress was threatened early in her reign by the combined forces of Prussia and France, who challenged her claim to the throne and sought to dismember the Hapsburg Empire. So she appealed to the loyalty of her Hungarian subjects. Won over by her personal appearance before the Diet of Nobles (Parliament), the Hungarians offered her their "lives and blood" (but no taxes). They were as good as their word, and it was during the reign of Maria Theresa

The leader of Hungary's first great rebellion against Hapsburg rule (1704–11) was Prince Ferenc Rakoczi II. This portrait is by Adam Manyoki, an itinerant painter of the early 18th century who followed his defeated prince into exile.

The Rakoczi Museum is housed in the former stronghold of the Prince, the Castle of Sarospatak.

The "kuruc" soldiers of Rakoczi's army derived their name from the Hungarian form of "crusader."

that the "huszar," the Hungarian mounted soldier, won his lasting reputation.

The second half of the 18th century was a period of comparative calm and cultural advance. The Germanizing efforts of the Hapsburgs now led to the settling of large colonies of German-speaking people the "Svabs" (Swabians), in the still sparsely populated rural areas and in the few towns which had survived Turkish occupation. The Svabs were a skilful and industrious folk, and in the towns they were soon absorbed. In rural districts, however, they retained their German language and culture.

The Napoleonic wars touched Hungary only indirectly. But, in Hungary, as elsewhere in

This 18th-century engraving reflects the comparative calm during the reign of Empress Maria Theresa (1740-80). But soldiers were still part of everyday life.

Lajos Kossuth, leader of Hungary's War of Independence, addresses the country's first independent National Assembly.

822 ■ HUNGARY

The poet Alexander Petofi recites his poem, "Arise Hungarians," on the steps of the National Museum in Budapest on March 15th, 1848. The event sparked off Hungary's two-year War of Independence.

Europe, in the decades that followed Napoleon's defeat at Waterloo, a great upsurge of nationalism took place. The arts and literature flourished and, with Franz Liszt, Hungarian music made its first appearance on the European stage. The political scene was dominated by two giant figures whose outlook and political teaching are still live forces in Hungary today. The first was Count Istvan Szechenyi, acclaimed as "The Greatest Hungarian" by his most bitter opponent, Lajos Kossuth. The second was Lajos Kossuth himself.

SZECHENYI

A member of one of Hungary's oldest families, Szechenyi embodied many remarkable qualities not only of his class but also of his people. He had a brooding, mystical spirit which, over the years, had developed into a burning love of everything Magyar. His outlook

and inspiration were essentially religious. His concern with the material advancement of his country was but an expression of his concern with the "soul of Hungary." His entry into politics was characteristic. Convinced that "the soul of a people resides in its language," he electrified the Diet of 1825 by offering a year's income from his vast estates towards the foundation of a National Academy for the improvement of the Hungarian language. Although he wanted above all a moral rebirth of Hungary, his approach to the task was severely practical, and so he was uniquely effective. He told his fellow nobles that the real reason for their country's backwardness and poverty lay with their own selfishness, that exempting the nobility from taxation had prevented public funds from accumulating. With great clarity of vision he called attention to the outmoded peasant-landowner relationship that kept the

Buda Castle is seen in a mid-19th-century print. The Szechenyi chain bridge, the first to span the Danube between Buda and Pest, became the symbol of Hungary's "Reform Age."

farmers poor. At the same time he was instinctively loyal (an ex-officer of the huszars and a magnate of the realm). He was convinced that Hungary's advance depended on closer co-operation with the Hapsburg monarchy rather than on the pursuit of an adventurous course of political independence.

KOSSUTH

Szechenyi's great rival, Lajos Kossuth, was no less a patriot and his patriotism was no less characteristically Hungarian. Yet the two men could not have been more different. Kossuth regarded political liberty as the main goal. Once political freedom had been won—and only then—would cultural, economic, and social advancement follow. As Szechenyi embodied the curious mixture of the mystical and practical in the Hungarian character, Kossuth embodied both its romantic and its uncompromising streak. Partly out of genuine love for his countrymen, partly to strengthen Hungarian nationalism against outsiders, Kossuth wished "not to abolish noble liberties but to extend them to the whole people." In this way, he

came to advocate the abolition of serfdom (slavery), freedom of the press, and many other political and social reforms.

The wakening of nationalistic feelings, and increasing social and economic activity made the harsh regime of Prince Metternich, the Austrian chancellor under the Hapsburgs, more and more distasteful. By 1848 (a year of revolution throughout Europe) the youth of Hungary were in a ferment. At first a peaceful settlement seemed possible, and laws were passed by the Diet in April, 1848, which incorporated most of the peaceful aspirations of the preceding "Reform Age." These were duly signed by the Emperor, Ferdinand. Soon, however, Austria reacted to Hungary's independent course of action and prepared to fight. Kossuth, now the undisputed leader of his country, authorized the formation of a people's army. Officers and men deserted the Hapsburg armies by the thousands to create this new force, the "honved." For the first time in their country's modern history, Hungarians of all classes rallied under the national flag.

For over a year the outcome of the war

against Austria hung in the balance. The operations on the Hungarian side were conducted with great skill, and by April, 1849, the Austrians were in full retreat everywhere. The new Emperor, Francis Joseph (who a few months earlier had succeeded the incompetent Ferdinand), then appealed to his fellow monarch, the Russian Czar. Help was given willingly, since Czar Nicholas feared that the Hungarian revolt might be initiated by his own subjects. A Russian army of 250,000 men invaded Hungary, and after several months of bitter fighting the Hungarian army was forced to surrender. On October 13, 1849, the Russian commander, Marshal Paskievicz, reported to the Czar: "Hungary lies at the feet of Your Majesty." Kossuth himself went into exile, where, for another 30 years, he remained the leader of an uncompromising resistance at home.

FROM 1849 TO THE PRESENT

Independent Hungary's first prime minister, the high-minded Count Lajos Batthyany, and 13 generals of the defeated national army were executed, and thousands of others were carried off to Austrian prisons or forced into the imperial army. Hungary was now administered by officials drawn from the Czech and German districts of the Empire and they were backed by a newly-established semi-military force, or gendarmerie.

The regime was particularly ruinous to the lesser nobles, but there were few people of any class who did not suffer. Yet this last attempt at harsh Hapsburg rule in Hungary was doomed, not only by the sullen resistance of the people, but also by a succession of reverses which the House of Hapsburg suffered in other parts of its empire. After a major defeat of the Austrian army by the military kingdom of Prussia, and a humiliating expulsion of Hapsburgs from Italy, it became clear that the Hapsburg dynasty

could not survive without the support of its Hungarian subjects.

Lengthy negotiations between the emperor, Francis Joseph, and Hungarian national leaders, Ferenc Deak, Gyula Andrassy, and Jozsef Eotvos, eventually led to the compromise of 1867. Hungary recovered its independence in internal affairs; foreign affairs, defence, and finance were declared to be questions common to Austria and Hungary, and were placed under a "common" minister, responsible to both national parliaments. As part of the deal, the Emperor was crowned King of Hungary with St. Stephen's crown amid great pomp (to the strains of Liszt's specially commissioned Coronation Mass), and the Dual Monarchy of Austria-Hungary was born. It lasted for fifty-one years (1867–1918).

Like the Victorian Age in England, the years between 1867 and 1914 were a period of great prosperity. For the first time, industry and commerce took roots in what had been an almost exclusively agricultural country, a network of railways was built, and Budapest became a capital city in appearance as well as in

The rampart of the grim Hapsburg fortress, the Citadel, on Gellert Hill is now an open-air café. The huge Liberation Statue in the background can be seen from most parts of the city.

HUNGARY ■ **825**

This typical Hungarian manor house is in Dormand in northeast Hungary. Many manor houses were destroyed in World War II, others are now used for village social or cultural activities.

name. (It did not, in fact, acquire its name until 1871 when the twin cities of Buda and Pest were united.) Yet pride in these achievements could not disguise the fact that the system failed to solve many problems, some inherited, some new. The land, Hungary's primary source of wealth, remained in the hands of powerful noblemen whose political power and wealth had increased at the expense of the ruined lesser nobility. At the other extreme, the condition of the agricultural workers, their number swollen by thousands of ruined small farmers, continued to decline. In 1897, following years of mounting unrest, the agricultural workers struck just before the harvest. But the uprising was sadly organized and was put down. Severe new laws, to be enforced by the gendarmerie, caused almost 1,000,000 of the peasantry to leave the country to seek their fortune—or at least a living—in the New World. The new and numerically small industrial working class fared no better, and housing conditions in Budapest were said to be worse than in any other large European city.

Even more fatefully for the future, Hungarian rule proved to be as backward and intolerant of minorities as Austrian rule had been over Magyars in the past. Hungary at this time extended over parts of what is now Yugoslavia, Rumania and Czechoslovakia. Even the local administration of the non-Magyar regions was conducted by officials who identified themselves with Magyardom. Office-seekers had to qualify as Magyars to be allowed to enter state service. This policy was ineffective and short-sighted. Forcible Magyarization no more changed the racial character of the country than forcible Germanization in the past had succeeded in stamping out the Magyars. It merely caused bitter hostility among the various peoples of the Danube Valley.

To a large extent, the Dual Monarchy was held together by the person of the monarch. Francis Joseph was in many ways an autocrat of the old school, but he was not without shrewd common sense in practical politics, and his position seemed as solid as was Queen Victoria's in England. His only son, Crown Prince Rudolf, committed suicide at Mayerling. More fatefully, his heir, the Archduke Franz Ferdinand, was assassinated by a Serbian patriot. Francis Joseph was approaching 80 when, in the 64th year of his reign, he signed the ultimatum to Serbia which was to spark off World War I, with Austria-Hungary allied with Germany.

Military reverses and wartime shortages exposed the weaknesses of the patchwork monarchy. Charles IV, who succeeded Francis Joseph at the turning point of the war (1916), made a few half-hearted attempts to sue for separate peace, but his powerful and more determined German allies carried him and his Empire on to destruction. In October, 1918, in the face of revolution at home and defeat at the front, he gave up the throne and the 600-year-old Hapsburg Empire fell apart. In Hungary, a short-lived Social-Democratic government under Count Mihaly Karolyi was followed by a Communist government and this in turn was supplanted by counter-revolutionary forces led by a former naval officer of the Dual Monarchy, Admiral Horthy.

Soon after Horthy took power, he was forced to sign the Peace Treaty of Trianon which reduced "historic" Hungary to a third of its former size. Hungary had much in common with defeated Germany, although at first neither the régime nor the country as a whole showed much sympathy for German Nazism, when it sprang up in the 1930's. With the outbreak of World War II, German pressure became irresistible, and Hungary declared war on Russia. Subsequent attempts to abandon the

German alliance merely provoked the German military occupation of the country in 1944. With the Russian armies advancing across Hungary's frontiers, Horthy made a last attempt to extricate himself and Hungary from the war, but his ill-organized effort was foiled by the German occupying army and he was replaced by Nazis. In this way, the war in Hungary became a prolonged agony of bloodshed and destruction.

While the German army and their Hungarian Nazi followers were fighting a desperate rear-guard action, the new Hungary was born in the provincial town of Debrecen: a coalition government of all anti-Nazi parties. This government gave way in 1947 to a Communist government and the Hungarian People's Republic became part of the Communist Eastern Bloc, where it has remained, in spite of opposition by many Hungarians. In 1956, this opposition expressed itself in a brief but violent rebellion, which was put down with the aid of Russian troops.

Budapest was badly damaged after four months of bitter house-to-house fighting in 1945. All the Danube bridges were destroyed by the retreating Germans.

The vast neo-Gothic pile of Parliament House on the Pest side of the Danube has become as much a part of the river landscape of Budapest as the Houses of Parliament (also dating from the 19th century) have become part of the London scene.

GOVERNMENT

THE SOVEREIGNTY of the Hungarian People's Republic was recognized by the peace treaty of Paris in 1947 and enacted by the Hungarian National Assembly. The country was admitted to full membership of the United Nations in 1955. Hungary is also a member of the Warsaw Pact and an ally of Soviet Russia. The system of government differs in several aspects from republics and other constitutional forms familiar in the West. The most important difference lies in the balance of power between the leaders of the Communist Party. In the West, political parties formulate platforms, organize and fight elections, and support or oppose governments, but their power is always subordinate to the power of the state. The secretary or the chairman of the party in power may be an influential figure, but he is not as powerful as a president, a premier, or even a cabinet minister. In people's republic the position is reversed—the party secretary is the key figure, and the party *is* the state.

It is January and there is snow on the ground, but two chess enthusiasts relax in Budapest's open-air Szabadsag Bath. The heated pool is visited by an average of 1,000 people a day even in the coldest weather.

THE PEOPLE

HUNGARY'S POPULATION IS nearly 11,000,000, with about one-fifth of the people living in the capital, Budapest, or in its immediate vicinity, and a further 25 per cent in other cities. Nearly all are of Hungarian stock—Hungary has practically no minorities today, and everybody speaks the Magyar language.

LANGUAGE

Until the 18th century the Hungarian language remained an oddity, for it appeared to be in no way related either to Latin or to German, Rumanian, Turkish, Russian, or indeed to any other known European tongue. In 1769, an astronomer by the name of Sajnovich travelled to Lapland in northern Scandinavia, and was so impressed by the unexpected similarities between the language spoken by the Lapps and his own that he forgot all about his astronomy and wrote a book (in Latin) noting the close resemblances between the two tongues. Since then many more facts have come to light supporting his discovery and establishing Magyar as a member of the Ugric branch of the Finno-Ugrian linguistic family.

While the discovery remains of great interest

to language experts, it does nothing to make it easier for most non-Hungarians to master or even to understand the language. To mention just one of its peculiarities, the precise meaning of verbs and nouns is governed by affixes or suffixes—i.e., by letters and syllables tucked on to the end of words. The single word "apamert," for example, means "for my father," the letter "m" standing for "my" and the syllable "ert" meaning "for." "Ver" means "he beat," "verhet" means "he can beat," "vereget" means "he often beats," and "veret" means "he causes to beat." A copious vocabulary exists in Magyar, with few points of reference in any other language.

LITERATURE

Despite the isolation their tongue has imposed on them, Hungarians have always been devoted to their language, and the literature represents the finest flowering of their creative genius. Among the great 19th-century lyric poets whose work is, in small part at least, available in both German and English translation, Alexander Petofi and Janos Arany stand supreme.

This old house in Badacsony was the home of the 18th-century man of letters, Sandor Kisfaludy. The vineyard-covered hills on the northern shore of the lake still attract painters, poets and writers.

The printing press on which the revolutionary Manifesto of 1848 was printed stands next to a picture of the Manifesto's author, the poet Alexander Petofi.

A gypsy orchestra wears traditional costume. The stringed "cimbalom" (dulcimer) is as much part of the band as the leader's violin.

Dancers in Hungary's internationally famous Folk Dance Ensemble whirl into action.

MUSIC

The origin of true Hungarian folk music reaches back to Central Asia. The discovery of these remote origins alone would ensure Hungary's two great composers, Bela Bartok and Zoltan Kodaly, a permanent place in musical history, but, of course, their contribution to music has been far greater.

Until a few years ago, Bartok was too much of a pioneer genius to assess his real stature. Today he is regarded as one of the greatest creative musicians of the century. Despite his close personal friendship with Kodaly and their common devotion to folk art (not just Hungarian folk art), the two were far apart both temperamentally and in their musical idiom. Bartok wrote one short opera and some beautiful songs, but he was essentially an instrumental composer, at his greatest in piano and chamber music. Indeed, his "revolutionary" innovations may one day be regarded as the culmination of traditional European instrumental sound.

The Hungarian women's fencing team won a silver medal at the Olympic Games in Mexico City, 1968. Fencing is one of Hungary's national sports.

SPORTS

Though football far outstrips other games in popularity, Hungarians have always done well in other sports, coming in third or fourth in all post-war Olympics. International fencing tournaments, in particular, have provided an opportunity for Hungarians to excel. In boxing, Laszlo Papp has won a gold medal at three successive Olympic Games, in 1948–52–56. Water polo and table tennis are other sports at which Hungarians excel. Riding, track and field, swimming, and tennis are immensely popular.

FOLKLORE

The immense riches and variety of Hungarian folklore, reflecting a thousand years of Turkish, Slav and German influence, as well as the native Magyar genius, almost defies description. Ancient customs and folk art have been best preserved on the Great Plain, the heart of rural and pastoral Hungary. The mounted shepherds of the "puszta" (plain) still wear what is perhaps the most splendid and characteristic of

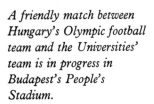

A friendly match between Hungary's Olympic football team and the Universities' team is in progress in Budapest's People's Stadium.

Wall-painting has been performed in the district of Kalocsa for centuries.

national costumes, the "cifraszür," a long, thick cloak, richly decorated with stitched and "inlaid" pieces of felt. The making of this garment has been a special craft for centuries and is still far from extinct.

Pottery is another craft which still flourishes —indeed it is showing signs of renewed life.

The use of unglazed black pottery with "sgraffito," or scratched-on decoration, which allows the natural tint of the clay to shine through, goes back many centuries. Painted and glazed earthenware is more recent and is produced in hundreds of small potteries, especially in and around the town of Hod-

Felt stitching, one of the traditional crafts of Hungary, is used mainly for shepherds' cloaks.

HUNGARY ■ 833

An inspector examines sausages and paprika salamis in the smoking unit of a new meat-dressing plant.

834 ∎ **HUNGARY**

mezovasarhely. The "Miska-kancso," literally Michael Jug, is the Hungarian equivalent of the English Toby jug, the place of Toby being taken by a shepherd, wearing an outsize cloak.

A unique form of folk art has survived in the region of Kalocsa on the Danube where whole houses and rooms are decorated with a carpet-like pattern of many-hued floral painting. Kalocsa is also famous for its dances. Many of these reflect the nomadic way of life of the shepherd of the plain. They are performed with a shepherd's staff or cracking whip wielded with great agility. Such dances should properly be accompanied by simple and traditional instruments, such as the zither or bagpipe.

The north and northeast contain two regions whose folklore is unique—the Paloc region on the southern slopes of the Matra mountain and further east, the Matyo region. The Paloc land has produced and still produces some of the finest folk embroidery in Europe. Every village in the region has its own distinctive style, instantly recognized by the experts, but all have certain common characteristics—the use of small geometrical patterns and the combination of blue and red on a white background. The Matyo region consists of three villages only, but their art is unlike any other in the country or indeed anywhere else in Europe. Stylized floral motifs in vivid and contrasting greens, red, blue and yellows recall Turkish and Persian art.

Transdanubia is best known for its carving, both in wood and in bone. Again, each region has its technique: some do carving alone, others combine it with painting and metalwork. In many villages the craft has been handed down from father to son, the so-called "carver-dynasties," for many generations. The "kanasz-tancz" or swineherd's dance of this region requires almost acrobatic skill.

The state has done much in recent years to foster folk art in all its manifestations. Even the smallest town and many villages have their local museum where examples of the regional craft are exhibited and great love and care is generally devoted to their display. Among the public too, folk art has become popular and shops selling folk pottery and embroidery are numerous in all the main cities.

A life-time collection of earthenware plates adorns the home of this resident of the small town of Bekescsaba on the Great Plain. Some of the plates are several centuries old. Included are masterpieces of Hungarian earthenware and porcelain from such famous workshops and factories as Hollohaza and Herend.

FOOD

The name of at least one Hungarian national dish, goulash, spelled "gulyás" in Hungarian, has passed into almost every language, and many other dishes are well known to gourmets. In cooking, as in many other spheres, Hungary has benefited from cross-currents of Austrian, Mediterranean and Slav influence. The most popular meats are pork, beef and veal, and pork is also the basis of an endless variety of sausages and salamis. Meats tend to be highly seasoned, ground-up "paprika" or mild red pepper lending them a characteristic Hungarian taste.

Most dishes are accompanied either by an innumerable variety of potatoes or by "galuska," a Hungarian form of pasta. Bread is also eaten with every meal and is excellent, as might be expected in a traditional wheat-growing country. Poultry is popular for festive occasions—"Chicken Paprikas" is an internationally liked dish—and the region of Lake Balaton is famous for its hot fish soups.

Harvesting machines sweep across a wheat field.

THE ECONOMY

THE PRESENT STATE and recent achievements of the Hungarian economy must be judged in the light of two historical facts. First, until World War I the country was one of the most backward in Europe, in many ways comparable to Czarist Russia. Second, at least 40 per cent of its national resources were destroyed during World War II. Against this background the country's economic progress during the past 20 years has been remarkable.

INDUSTRY

Industrialization remains the keynote of Hungary's economic policy, a revolutionary break with tradition. Partly for reasons of climate and geography, and partly as a result of historical and social development, Hungary has been for many centuries a purely agricultural state. In particular, during its long association with the Hapsburg Empire its two-fold rôle has been to provide Austrian industry with agricultural raw material and to act as a free market for Austrian manufactured products. Industry did not start to take root in Hungary until the end of the 19th century. Even by 1938 it contributed less than 40 per cent to the total national income. By 1968, despite the ravages of World War II, the figure had risen to 67 per cent and is still rising.

Both the planning and the execution of industrialization are in the hands of the State. The policy is carried out within the framework

The machine tool factory in Esztergom, Transdanubia, exports its products to 44 countries.

This is one of the new artificial fertilizer plants in northern Hungary.

of 5-year plans, the current plan having started in 1966. It envisages an overall industrial growth rate of 4 to 5 per cent a year.

Although Hungary's raw materials make up a long and varied list, none are available in large quantities. Moreover, at least until recently, the country's natural sources of fuel and power have been severely limited. Mainly for these two reasons, there has been a tendency to promote those industries which depend for success primarily on high standards of skill, technical knowledge, laboratory research, and the quality of their finished products.

In this context, the chemical industry can be

This new chemical factory in northern Hungary is separated from the town by "a green belt."

singled out. Its most important products are fertilizers—until 1965, mainly nitrogen-based, but in recent years phosphate-based as well. The industry has pioneered a number of important manufacturing processes, and for some years now its output has been increasing at a rate of over 10 per cent annually. Another branch of the chemical industry, the manufacture of pharmaceutical products, cannot compare with fertilizers in volume of output, but in terms of quality it represents Hungarian science-based industry at its best.

Light engineering, too, has benefited from a policy of linking factories with research facilities and technical universities. Hungarian medical instruments, in particular, have won a world-wide reputation for excellence. Progress in the field of telecommunications and the manufacture of other precision instruments has been no less impressive.

The growth of other industries, including the food industry, the cotton-print industry and the synthetic textile industry, has been less spectacular but steady. Steel production now exceeds 300,000 tons a year. It is confidently predicted that the rich natural gas deposits of the Great Plain will eventually solve one of industry's main problems, the shortage of energy. Natural gas should also make it

Yarn for folk-art embroidery is produced in the weaving room of a folk-art workshop in Deos.

possible to exploit the country's rich mineral resources (especially uranium, manganese, and bauxite deposits) more economically and profitably than at present.

Apart from the promise held out by natural gas, two other developments have undoubtedly contributed to industrial advance. During recent years, there has been a progressive relaxation of political pressure at the technical level, along with a growing realization that standing in the Communist Party is no substitute for industrial skill. Also, during the past few years, competition between branches of industry and between individual plants and factories has been deliberately stimulated by a system of financial and other rewards for efficiency.

Harvesting onions is now mechanized—here an onion-lifter goes into action

Cattle throng a pasture in Transdanubia.

AGRICULTURE

Hungarian agriculture, no less than industry, has undergone profound changes in the last two decades. In the past, Hungary was predominantly wheat-growing, agricultural policy being determined by vast and often under-capitalized feudal estates. The dominant forms of agricultural units today are state or co-operative farms. Only about 3 per cent of the land is privately owned, mostly in very small plots. A no less radical departure from tradition has been the increase in the production of fodder cereals and sugar beets in regions which, for centuries, have been exclusively wheat-growing.

Hungarian agriculture today is extremely varied. Apart from cereals (oats, maize, barley and rye, as well as wheat), the country produces tobacco and a great variety of choice fruits and vegetables—melons, apricots, apples, cherries, onions, tomatoes, peaches, as well as the famous mild red pepper (paprika) of Szeged. Hungarian wine, celebrated for centuries, is gradually regaining its high international reputation.

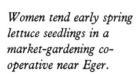

Women tend early spring lettuce seedlings in a market-gardening co-operative near Eger.

A wine-taster samples the world-famous produce of the Tokay Hills—the golden, sweet "aszu" wine.

Much of it is again being exported to the West. As in industry, research on experimental farms is closely integrated with bulk production.

Hungary's livestock now consists mainly of pigs, cattle, sheep and poultry. The number of horses has inevitably declined owing to mechanization. Nevertheless, horse-breeding, especially of the famous Lipizaner, continues on several state stud farms. The country's rivers and lakes abound in fish, the "fogas" or pike-perch of Balaton being particularly renowned.

FOREIGN TRADE

Some 40 State companies, established for this particular purpose, handle all trading with other countries. About 90 per cent of Hungary's exports go to the Continent of Europe, the 13 countries of the Communist Bloc, including Russia, accounting for more than 65 per cent. The latter group is linked economically through the Council for Mutual Economic Assistance (Comecon); and accounts between them are settled in roubles on a multilateral basis. The Hungarian Chamber of Commerce is responsible for promoting expansion of foreign trade, and it sponsors and organizes the Budapest International Trade Fair held in Budapest in May of every year.

PRIVATE ENTERPRISE

Although the State plays an overwhelmingly important rôle in all economic activities, the Constitution guarantees private property acquired through work and accepts the right of private inheritance. A high proportion of professional people—doctors, dentists, lawyers —engage in part-time private practice. A

Horses of the famous Lipizaner breed are raised on the state stud farm at Babolna, Transdanubia.

The fishing season on Lake Balaton begins in the autumn, when the drop in water temperature starts the fish migrating in large schools.

limited "private sector" operates in commerce and the craft industries. Owner-occupation of houses and flats is encouraged by the State.

STANDARD OF LIVING

There is no real poverty in Hungary today: the country's industrial slums and agricultural depressed areas (formerly among the worst in Europe) have disappeared. Welfare services—health, child care, paid holidays, cultural amenities—are probably among the most advanced in the world. On the other hand, by Western standards, Hungary remains a poor country and the standard of living of professional people remains comparatively low. This is particularly noticeable in housing: a university professor or the director of a large state enterprise and his family rarely have a "reception room" to spare. Many blocks of houses in Budapest still look like war-scarred cities.

These sea-going ships are moored in a Budapest shipyard. When the ice disappears, they will sail down to the Black Sea and then to their final destination.

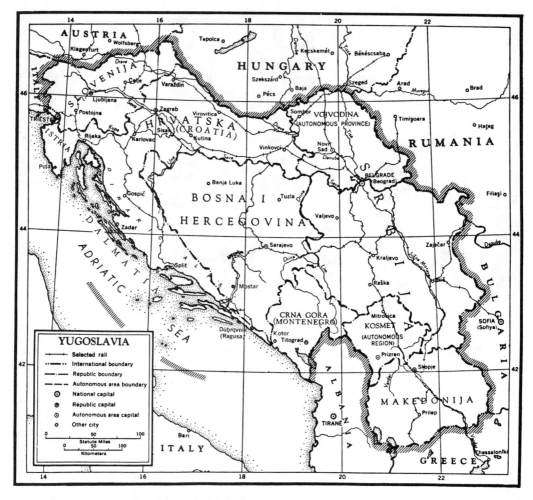

Lights burn late into the night in a modern Zagreb office building.

A sect known as Bogomils arose in Bosnia-Herzegovina some time before the Turkish invasion and conquest. The Bogomils buried their dead in necropolises (death cities) ornamented with strange carved tombstones. Although their faith showed some Christian influences, the Bogomils were Manichaeans, a group whose religious beliefs were derived from ancient Persia.

Yugoslavia

HISTORY

Invasions of one sort or another have been the most distinguishing feature of Yugoslavia's history through the years. In what is today Yugoslavia, the first inhabitants we know about were called Illyrians. Merchants of ancient Greece carried on a limited trade with the Illyrians and founded several cities along the Adriatic seacoast, notably the town of Trogir which still exists. The Illyrians fought hard to retain their national independence, but well-trained Roman legions were too strong to be defeated and Illyria became a province of Rome in 168 B.C.

After a few brief struggles for independence, the Illyrian people gradually became absorbed into the Roman Empire. Diocletian, an Illyrian peasant boy from Dalmatia, joined the Roman army, rose through the ranks because of his bravery in battle, and eventually became Emperor of the entire Roman Empire. After a worthy reign of 21 years, Diocletian retired from public life and built himself a magnificent palace on the shores of the Adriatic. Later, the Yugoslavian city of Split grew up around Diocletian's palace. Another Illyrian was Constantine, who became the first Roman Emperor to accept Christianity. Constantine moved the capital of the Roman Empire to Byzantium on the shores of the Bosporus (now Turkey) in A.D. 330, and the city was renamed Constantinople after him.

THE MIDDLE AGES

Europe was invaded several times in the early Middle Ages by Asian tribes, such as the Huns under Attila, but these barbarians were eventually defeated. After they vanished from Europe, during the 6th and 7th centuries, large numbers of Slavs began invading the Balkan Peninsula from their ancestral homeland in central Europe. Actually, the Slav "invasion" was really just a large-scale migration southward of scattered tribes and families which continued until Yugoslavia became saturated with Slavs. Most of the Illyrians gradually became absorbed into the more numerous Slav population.

Until the 20th century, the Yugoslavs ("South Slavs") were never united into a single nation. Instead, they lived for centuries in separate groups in different parts of the country. These are the present-day "nationalities": Serbs, Macedonians, Montenegrins, Croats, and Slovenes. All Yugoslavs gave up their former pagan religion for Christianity not long after they had settled down in the Balkans. The Croats and Slovenes were converted by missionaries from Rome; the Serbs, Macedonians, and Montenegrins by missionaries from Constantinople, then capital of the Byzantine Empire. Independent Slav states sprang up briefly in Slovenia and Croatia, but soon fell under the control of more powerful surrounding countries: Austria, Hungary, and the Republic of Venice.

However, in the east the Serbs took advantage of the weakness of the Byzantine Empire to set up a powerful local kingdom founded by Stevan Nemanja in the 12th century. The Serb Kingdom expanded to cover a large part of the Balkans. This happened mainly because the Byzantines, whose capital at Constantinople had been sacked and pillaged by fellow Christians from the West in 1204, were too weak to offer any opposition. The Emperor Dušan (1331-55) was the greatest of all the rulers of the Nemanja dynasty of Serb kings. He extended the influence of the Serb Kingdom on all sides and introduced a famous law code (known as Dušan's Code) to govern his subjects. The medieval Serb Kingdom also flourished culturally and economically. Many churches and monasteries were built and

Considering its advanced age, the Pula amphitheatre is in remarkably good condition. Unfortunately, many other fine examples of Roman architecture were destroyed by Attila and his Hun invaders when they ravaged the Dalmatian coast during the fifth century A.D.

were decorated with beautiful (and today priceless) frescoes. Agriculture was important, but copper, tin, gold, and silver made Serbia even richer.

The Serb Kingdom began to decline in power after the reign of Dušan. At the same time a new threat to the security of all the nations of Europe arose. Out of Asia Minor came the Ottoman Turks. Unlike some of the earlier conquering hordes from the east, the Turks were very well organized and used efficient administrative techniques in the areas they ruled. The Turkish advance was slow but steady. Turks crossed into Europe in the 1350's and began subduing the Balkan nations one by one. Serbia's turn came on June 28, 1389 when the Turks defeated the Serbs in the battle of Kossovo. The last traces of Serbian liberty, however, did not vanish for another 70 years. In 1453, the Turks captured Constantinople putting a permanent end to the Byzantine Empire which could trace its history back to Augustus,

Sheep graze peacefully below crags of volcanic rock. Marko Kraljević, a 14th century prince, used these jagged Macedonian rocks as a foundation for his medieval fortress.

the first Roman Emperor. Soon after, the areas of Bosnia and Herzegovina fell to the Turks. Nor were the powerful rulers of Europe safe from attack. As late as 1683, a Turkish army besieged Vienna, capital of the Austrian Empire.

OTTOMAN DOMINATION

Turkish rule, which in some parts of Yugoslavia lasted as late as 1912, was very harsh. The Ottoman conquerors were Moslems and did not treat their Christian subjects any too kindly. Many churches were turned into mosques, frescoes covered over with plaster, and Christian children taken from their parents to serve in the administration of the Ottoman Empire. *Janissaries*, the Turkish professional soldier corps, were stationed in the Balkans and became notorious for cruelties inflicted on the enslaved populations. Yugoslavs living under the Christian Hapsburg house of Austria and Hungarian nobles were not much better off. A large-scale peasant revolt in Croatia led by Matija Gubec broke out in 1573, and was suppressed only after a great deal of bloodshed.

Only two places in Yugoslavia maintained their independence. In Montenegro, the combination of rugged mountains and a population fiercely devoted to freedom kept the Turks out.

Beginning in 1697, Montenegro was ruled by hereditary prince-bishops. The other outpost of South Slav liberty was the city-state of Ragusa (now called Dubrovnik) on the Adriatic Sea. Ragusa was a republic and managed to remain independent by skilful diplomacy with the stronger nations of the area. Ocean-borne commerce was the mainstay of Ragusa's prosperous economy; in fact the word "argosy" (meaning a large merchant vessel) is a corruption of the name of the city. Napoleon's armies put an end to Ragusa's independence in 1806, and after the downfall of the French conqueror, Ragusa became part of the Austro-Hungarian Empire.

The 19th century was to see the beginning of the end for the Turks. At the same time a desire arose among Croats, Serbs, and Slovenes for some form of national unity for all the South Slavs. In 1804, the Serbs, under the leadership of Karadjordje Petrovic revolted against the Turks. The first uprising was not entirely successful, but a second revolt led by Miloš Obrenović obtained official recognition from the Turkish Sultan. In 1830 Miloš became prince of a semi-independent Serbia. The country remained a Turkish tributary and Turkish soldiers remained on Serbian soil, but Serbia was permitted self-government. Ottoman power continued to decline. Turkey, the former terror of Europe, became known as the "sick man" of

Europe. All Turkish soldiers left Serbia in 1867, and in 1878, as a result of the Congress of Berlin among the European powers, Serbia attained full independence.

SEEDS OF WAR

While the Croats managed to wring some slight concessions from Austria-Hungary, several differing groups of South Slavs were making plans for a united Yugoslavia. Serb nationalists desired a Yugoslavia under Serb control, a re-creation of the glorious days of the 12th century Nemanja dynasty. Others asked for a Yugoslavia in which all South Slav groups would have an equal voice. The Croatian extremists wanted nothing to do with the Orthodox Serbs. To complicate the picture still further, the great powers in Europe, including Austria-Hungary, Britain, and Russia, all took a very keen interest in Balkan political developments. Each hoped to gain something from the confused situation.

With the coming of the 20th century, the pace speeded up.

The Pasha (Turkish ruler) of Niš built a gruesome tower with the skulls of Serbs killed during an unsuccessful uprising in 1809. Built as a warning to discourage further attempts to overthrow Turkish rule, the tower of skulls only made the Serbs more determined than ever to rid themselves of the Turks.

Pula, nestled on the southern tip of the Istrian Peninsula, is the site of impressive Roman ruins. Outdoor motion picture festivals are held in the same 23,000-seat amphitheatre where gladiators fought and early Christians were sacrificed to lions many centuries ago.

In 1903, nationalist Serbian army officers murdered King Alexander Obrenović and placed on the throne Peter Karadjordjevic, a descendant of the leader of the Serb uprising against the Turks in 1804. In 1908, Austria-Hungary annexed Bosnia and Herzegovina to its empire, to the annoyance of Serbia. Each power was interested in someone else's land, especially if the other country was weak and unable to defend itself. The first Balkan War broke out in 1912, pitting Serbia, Montenegro, Bulgaria and Greece against Turkey. The Balkan allies soon defeated the Turks and reduced the Ottoman Empire's European land holdings to a small area around Istanbul (Constantinople).

The dead had hardly been buried when the "allies" began quarrelling over the spoils left behind by the defeated Turks. The argument focused on Macedonia, to which Serbia, Greece and Bulgaria all had conflicting claims. Shooting broke out in the summer of 1913. This time Serbia, Montenegro, Greece and Rumania fought and defeated Bulgaria. Turkey took advantage of the situation, at the expense of the Bulgars, to reclaim some of the Ottoman Empire's lost possessions.

The Balkan Wars of 1912 and 1913 turned out to be only preliminary events, for worse was to follow in 1914. Europe's great powers were divided into rival military alliances, some secret and some well known. The entire continent was like a powder keg with an unlit fuse. Gavrilo Princip, a 19-year-old Serb member of the "Young Bosnia" movement lit the fuse by assassinating Archduke Franz Ferdinand, heir to the throne of Austria-Hungary at Sarajevo, the capital of Bosnia and Herzegovina, on June 28, 1914. For Austria-Hungary the assassination was a ready-made excuse to wipe out Serbia, which stood in the way of Austro-Hungarian expansion in the Balkans. Austria-Hungary accused the Serbs of planning the assassination of the Archduke and delivered a humiliating ultimatum to the Serbian Government. The Serbs suggested a peaceful settlement of outstanding problems between the two nations, but the Austro-Hungarians declared war. Russia hurried to back Serbia, while Germany entered the war on Austria-Hungary's side. Soon, most of the leading nations of the world were engaged in what was to be known as World War I.

A NEW NATION

The outcome of this war was victory for the Western Allies and defeat for Austria-Hungary and its partners. The Austro-Hungarian Empire which had declared war on Serbia was broken up into many independent nations. Serbia, the planned "victim" of Austria-Hungary, became the foundation of the first unified South Slav state in history. King Alexander of Serbia became the first king of the new Kingdom of Serbs, Croats, and Slovenes (renamed the Kingdom of Yugoslavia in 1929).

Total peace was not the lot of the new Yugoslavia in the period between the two World Wars. A major problem was the domination of the Government by Serbs at the expense of the Croats, Slovenes, and Macedonians. The Government was strong in police state tactics and weak in democratic principles. The murder of a leading political figure on the floor of Parliament in 1928 caused King Alexander to

A column of Croat Partisans on patrol. The cascade connects two of the 16 Plitvice lakes, all of which are at different altitudes.

declare a royal dictatorship. Outlawed right- and left-wing organizations, such as the Communists and the Ustashi, a Croatian fascist group, went underground and continued operations. Corruption in government and the great economic depression of the 1930's added to the discontent of the Yugoslav people. Right-wing groups assassinated King Alexander during a visit to France in 1934. This left the Government in the hands of Prince Paul, the dead King's cousin, since Alexander's son, Peter, was only eleven years old at the time. Prince Paul attempted to settle the Croatian problem by giving a limited amount of self-government, but this only annoyed the Serbs and Slovenes.

Meanwhile, the dark shadow of Adolf Hitler's Nazi Germany began stretching across Europe. By early 1941, Germany and its ally, Italy, controlled all the countries bordering Yugoslavia except Greece, which was at the time repelling an invasion by Mussolini's Italians. In the face of such danger, Prince Paul gave in to German pressures and agreed to a treaty making Yugoslavia a vassal of the Nazis. The treaty was signed on March 25, 1941. Two days later, patriotic Air Force officers led a revolt that overthrew Prince Paul's government. Thousands of people turned out in Belgrade's streets chanting: "Better war than pact—better grave than slave." Prince Paul left the country and Peter was crowned King of Yugoslavia.

UNDER THE NAZIS

Adolf Hitler was enraged by the sudden turn of events in Yugoslavia. The Nazi dictator put off his planned attack on the Soviet Union for a month in order to deal with the troublesome Yugoslavs. On Palm Sunday, 1941, German bombers struck Belgrade, leaving the city in

During World War II, village after village was destroyed as fighting raged across the countryside. Many villages were burned to the ground by the Germans and their local fascist allies because the inhabitants had provided help to Tito's Partisans.

flames and more than 17,000 people dead in the ruins. Nazi land armies smashed the Yugoslav army in a few days and occupied the entire country. King Peter and other Government officials fled and set up a "Government-in-exile" in London for the remainder of the war.

The Germans divided conquered Yugoslavia with their fascist allies. Croatia was given to the Ustashi terrorists, who for the remainder of World War II specialized in butchering opponents of the regime—usually innocent Serbs, Jews, and anti-fascist Croats—with techniques similar to those of their German protectors.

The Yugoslav Communists saw the war as both an opportunity to save Yugoslavia from the Nazis and to advance the cause of Communism. Many Nazi-occupied countries had underground movements; Yugoslavia insurgents conducted a full-fledged war. Under the leadership of Josip Broz (known as Marshal Tito), the Communist party chief, a National Liberation Army (the Partisans) was formed to fight the Germans, Italians, and other fascist armies. Tito attracted many non-Communists to his cause and carried on a long and bitter campaign against the enemy. Time after time the Germans attempted to surround and destroy the Partisan armies which controlled large areas in the Yugoslav mountains. But the Partisans fought their way out of German traps every time. German brutality in the cities and villages caused more and more Yugoslavs to join or support Tito's army. The Partisans succeeded in tying up several hundred thousand German soldiers whom Hitler would have liked to use elsewhere. During the latter part of the war, the United States and Great Britain provided military aid to Tito.

THE NEW YUGOSLAVIA

The end of World War II found Tito and his Yugoslav Communists in full control. Yugoslavia became a Communist republic and an apparently loyal satellite of the Soviet Union. The pre-war problem of Serbian domination of the Government was solved by dividing the country into six equal republics: Serbia, Croatia,

The case of Andrija Artukovic (second from left, giving the fascist salute to visiting German Nazis at a 1942 meeting in Zagreb) has been a source of friction between Yugoslavia and the United States. Artukovic helped plan the 1934 assassination of King Alexander of Yugoslavia. During World War II, he helped organize the ruthless extermination of hundreds of thousands of Serbs, Jews, and Croats in his position as Minister of the Interior in the Nazi-supported "Independent State of Croatia." Artukovic now lives in California, claiming to be an anti-Communist "family man." The Yugoslav Government has been trying, so far unsuccessfully, to have Artukovic sent back to his homeland to stand trial for his crimes.

Slovenia, Montenegro, Macedonia, and Bosnia-Herzegovina.

On June 28, 1948, Yugoslavia was suddenly expelled from the Communist bloc, to the surprise of the West. The date was the anniversary of the battle of Kossovo in 1389 in which the Serbs were defeated by the Turks. This time the Yugoslavs were not defeated. Yugoslav Communist leaders had fought their way through the war and into power without Soviet help—to the annoyance of Stalin who liked to run Communist satellites as he pleased. Despite the shock of the break with the Soviet Union, Tito managed to hold the Yugoslav Communists together, in the face of Russian political and

economic pressures. Yugoslavia turned to the West for economic and military aid to help it remain independent.

Yugoslavia did not change overnight from being a typical Communist police state into being the most liberal of all Communist nations. The change has been gradual, but those people who predicted that Yugoslavia would knuckle under to either East or West in the cold war have been proven wrong. June 28, 1948 is celebrated as the day Yugoslavia regained its national independence. It has taken many more years to make sure independence is a fact, especially since Nikita Khrushchev admitted to the Yugoslavs in 1955 that the Soviet Union had "made a mistake" in dealing so harshly with Yugoslavia in 1948.

As leader of the Partisan army, Tito was in the midst of heavy fighting throughout most of the war. German attempts to surround and destroy the Partisan forces failed every time, but fierce fighting took a heavy toll of lives on both sides. Tito, posing at the mouth of a cave during a lull in the fighting, was injured in the arm by an exploding German bomb.

(Below) Soon after Yugoslavia freed itself from Soviet control, economic and military aid began pouring in from the Western powers who wanted to make sure Yugoslavia remained independent of Russia. Here, a surplus tank made in the United States is being swung over the side of a Yugoslav freighter.

What better way could there be to spend a spring weekend than exploring old ruins or hiking in the mountains? An inn serves as a convenient place for rest and refreshment for this group of college students.

THE PEOPLE

With a population exceeding 20,000,000, Yugoslavia does not yet have to worry about overcrowding. Compared to crowded Holland, which has an average population density of 918 per square mile, Yugoslavia is a country with elbow-room to spare with a population density of 188 inhabitants per square mile. The population is about evenly divided between rural areas and cities and towns, although, as new industries spring up in the cities, more and more people are leaving the farming regions to take jobs in factories. Rapidly-growing Belgrade, the capital, is also the nation's largest city with a population of over 550,000. The other leading cities are Zagreb (population 470,000), Sarajevo —scene of the assassination that touched off

World War I—(183,000), Skopje (167,000), and Ljubljana (159,000).

About 82 per cent of the Yugoslav people are descendants of the Slavs who migrated to the Balkans during the 6th and 7th centuries. The Slavic population can be broken down into various nationalities in much the same way that the people of Great Britain can be divided into English, Welsh, and Scots. The Serbs, accounting for 41.7 per cent of the total population of Yugoslavia, are the largest Slavic group, followed by the Croats (23.5 per cent), the Slovenes (8.8 per cent), the Macedonians (5.3 per cent), and the hardy inhabitants of Montenegro (2.8 per cent). To confuse matters still further, it should be noted that the Montenegrins are really Serbs, but have developed a national identity of their own while living in their mountain stronghold over the centuries. Hungarians and Albanians form the largest portion of the non-Slavic population of Yugoslavia, but there are also small minorities of Turks, Germans, Bulgarians, Italians, and others.

THREE CULTURES

For a small country, Yugoslavia is a nation with more variety among its people than many larger states. Most of the differences can be traced back through the nation's turbulent history to their original sources. Three great cultures have left their mark on modern Yugoslavia.

From the west came the influence—political and cultural—of Austria and Italy. The Croats and Slovenes, inhabitants of the two western-most Republics of present-day Yugoslavia, are Roman Catholics. Cities and towns in Croatia and Slovenia look very similar to those in central Europe. Dress, customs, and just about every other facet of life in these regions has been influenced to a greater or lesser degree by long years of contact with Austria, Italy and western Europe.

In the same way that western parts of Yugoslavia looked toward Vienna, Rome, and Venice, eastern and southern Yugoslavia took its cultural lead from Constantinople, capital of the Byzantine Empire. Orthodox Christianity and the Cyrillic alphabet both came to Serbia, Montenegro, and Macedonia by way of Constantinople.

The third great cultural force to affect Yugoslavia did not come peacefully, but in the wake of Turkish military conquest. The Turks disappeared from the Yugoslav scene at the beginning of the 20th century, but they have left behind a legacy of Middle Eastern architecture, in addition to more than 2,000,000 converts to the Moslem religion.

The ebb and flow of different cultures has played strange tricks. For instance, a visitor to Mostar in Bosnia-Herzegovina might think himself somewhere in Turkey after seeing the town's mosques, minarets, and Turkish baths. Yet barely 50 miles away on the Adriatic coast

Many years tending sheep through the chilling winds of winter and hot sun of summer have left their mark on the face of this aged, but still spry, Serbian shepherd.

is the ancient city of Dubrovnik (about 20,000 population), a treasure chest of Renaissance architecture where not a mosque is to be seen.

It would be rash to try to give a catch-all description of the Yugoslav character, especially since the most common thing about the inhabitants is that they are different in different parts of Yugoslavia. However, there seem to be at least a few similarities between the Slovenian peasant in his Austrian-like folk costume and a Serb wearing baggy pants and slippers with curled toes. All Yugoslavs invariably are hospitable to foreigners and frequently go out of their way to help some one from another country. On the other hand, Croats, Serbs, Slovenes, Macedonians, and Montenegrins quite often feel very cool towards one another. In general, the Yugoslav seems to be rather easy-going. That is not meant to indicate Yugoslavs are lazy. On the contrary, a Yugoslav is usually a good worker, but resents being "bossed" by someone else. Perhaps, this quality is best reflected in Yugoslavia's unique brand of Communism which places more emphasis on the happiness of the individual than on creating an unstoppable Communist steamroller, using men as mere cogs in the machine.

MODERN INFLUENCES

The 20th century influences of Western Europe and North America have come to Yugoslavia to stay. Motion pictures, nightclubs, and lipstick are now an every-day part of Yugoslav life—at least in the cities. In rural areas, peasants tend to be more conservative than their city cousins, but with more and more people moving to the cities, life in the countryside is bound to be affected sooner or later. The status of women has improved greatly in recent years and it is only among the Moslem peasants of Macedonia and Bosnia-Herzegovina that women are still regarded as inferior.

Despite all the modern innovations of the 20th century, Yugoslavs remain "incurable" romantics, proud of the history of their country. Yugoslavs also possess a remarkable ability to

(Above) Working in a volunteer youth brigade is a good way to develop strong arm muscles and a healthy suntan while helping Yugoslavia's economy by building new highways, factories, and railways. Not all work is done by hand, for bulldozers and other machines are faster and more efficient.

smile. In the past, this must have been a useful trait for a people made into an international punching bag by the armies of surrounding countries. In present-day Yugoslavia, a ready wit is essential during any coffee-house discussions about shortages in housing and consumer goods or about the latest happening in international political affairs.

Finely-embroidered peasant costumes are fast disappearing from the rural scene—except on holidays. Each part of the country has its own distinctive style of traditional dress.

Five cupolas grace the roof of the church at Serbia's Gračanica Monastery. The design of the early 14th century church is a mixture of Byzantine and native Serbian styles. Frescoes, including portraits of King Milutin of Serbia, benefactor of the monastery, cover the interior walls.

RELIGION

Despite Communist rule since World War II, Yugoslavia is still a very religious country. For several years after the war, the Government directed a campaign against religion with very unsatisfactory results—as far as the Government was concerned. In fact, one of the undesirable effects of the anti-religion campaign was to encourage religious intolerance among the different nationalities of the country. For instance, a propaganda film claiming to show "proof" of Cardinal Stepinac's alleged collaboration with fascists during the war was a total failure in Roman Catholic Croatia, but the film proved rather popular among the Orthodox population of Serbia.

The greatest number of Yugoslavs (about 48 per cent) belong to the Serbian Orthodox Church, which is independent and is ruled by a Patriarch and a Holy Synod founded in 1346. A long-standing disagreement between the Byzantines in Constantinople and the Popes in Rome caused the schism in 1054 which created a separate Orthodox Church. Yugoslavia is the westernmost nation with a large Orthodox population.

About 36 per cent of Yugoslavia's population (almost all in Croatia and Slovenia) are Roman

(Below) When the Turks conquered Serbia during the 15th century, they turned many churches into mosques. The Moslem Turks covered up hundreds of Christian wall frescoes at the Church of Our Lady of Ljeviška with a coat of plaster, and the frescoes remained buried and unseen for 400 years. Restoration work begun in 1950 has uncovered many of the frescoes; however, damage from previous mistreatment is considerable.

Catholics. The most violent anti-religious activity of the Government is directed at the Catholic Church because of the Church's connection with the Vatican.

Yugoslavia's Moslem population (about 14 per cent of the total) is concentrated in Bosnia-Herzegovina, southern Serbia, and Macedonia. Excepting Turkey, Yugoslavia has the greatest number of Moslems in all Europe. With the departure of the Turks, the Moslem religion no longer has the same force it once had, and the cry of the muezzin calling the faithful to prayer is no longer heard from many minarets. Veils have been outlawed for Moslem women. Small minorities of Protestants and Jews round out the remainder of the Yugoslav population.

Under the Yugoslav constitution, church and state are strictly separated, although governments of the Republics are allowed to give financial assistance to the various religions. Freedom of worship is guaranteed, but religion must not be used for political purposes.

(*Above*) *From the heights of the rocket-shaped minaret, a* muezzin *will call faithful Moslems to prayer. At street level, shoppers make their round in an open-air fruit and vegetable market. Most towns now have modern, Western-style supermarkets operating in competition with outdoor markets.*

(*Below*) *Macedonia's St. Jovan Bigorski Monastery is noted for its quaint wooden architecture and delicate wood carvings. The present buildings date only from 1743, for the Turks destroyed a previous monastery built on the same site.*

(*Above*) *The altar of the Morača Monastery shows the highly-developed art forms of independent, pre-Turkish Serbia. For many centuries the art treasures of Serbian and Macedonian monasteries remained virtually unknown in Western Europe.*

LANGUAGE AND LITERATURE

Most European nations have a single language. A few have two. Yugoslav has three. Fortunately, Serbo-Croat, Slovene, and Macedonian are all closely related in the Slavonic family of languages. Serbo-Croat is the most widely spoken of the three, being the mother tongue of over two-thirds of all Yugoslavs. The Slovene language is not too different from Serbo-Croat; however, Macedonian, spoken in the southernmost republic, is more akin to Bulgarian, another of the South Slavonic languages.

As if having three main languages and several dialects were not enough of a problem, Yugoslavia also has two different alphabets. This is a result of the nation's turbulent history. The eastern part of the country, closer to Byzantium, uses the Cyrillic, the same alphabet as Russian. People in the western part of Yugoslavia use the familiar (to us) Roman letters.

Yugoslavia has a long literary tradition. In Serbia, literature began in the 9th century. Most of the early works were of a religious nature. Dedicated monks translated and composed religious tracts and toiled for endless hours to produce beautiful hand-drawn, illuminated manuscripts, some of which have survived to this day. Biographers and other writers flourished in Serbia and Croatia during the Middle Ages. Unfortunately, the Turkish invasion practically extinguished literary activity in Serbia for several hundred years while the original Croatian writing styles suffered under Italian and Austro-Hungarian rule.

Literature continued to flourish in the independent city of Dubrovnik and at other locations along the Dalmatian coast. These areas remained relatively free of the oppressive influences which stifled literary development elsewhere in Yugoslavia. Several notable poets and playwrights were active during this period in Dalmatia.

During the 18th century, something of a revival occurred throughout the country. One of the best-known authors from this era is Dimitrije Obradović (1740-1811), a well-travelled Serb and sometime monk. Obradović was the master of several writing styles, and was equally at home when writing about his

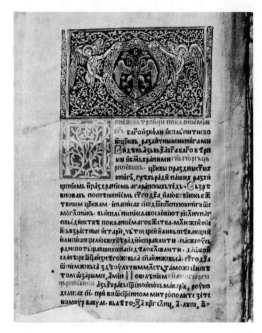

A page from Yugoslavia's first printed book which was produced at Cetinje, Montenegro, in 1494 on a printing press imported from Venice. Like almost all books of the period, it is a religious work and is printed in the Cyrillic alphabet.

adventures in foreign lands or on ethics. Many traditional epic ballads, work songs, and other poems were collected and published in the 19th century. Of these, many tell tales of Yugoslav heroism in the face of the cruel Turkish conquerors. The modern novel made its appearance in Yugoslavia during the second half of the 19th century. Among the leaders in this new field were Jakov Ignjatović, Ljubomir Nenadović, and Stevan Sremac.

Yugoslav literature continues to prosper in the mid-twentieth century. World-wide attention was focused on Yugoslav literary achievements when the 1961 Nobel Prize for Literature was awarded to Ivo Andrić, one of the nation's leading authors. Andrić, a Yugoslav diplomat before World War II, is best known for his novels: *Bridge on the Drina, Bosnian Story*, and *Miss*, which tell of the hard life of the Bosnian people during the turbulent political developments of the 19th century. All his novels have attained international popularity; for example,

The plays of Shakespeare have been translated into almost as many languages as the Bible. Belgrade audiences enjoy listening to Lady Macbeth and her husband discuss their evil plans in Serbo-Croat.

Bridge on the Drina has been translated into well over a score of foreign languages.

Many accomplished Yugoslav authors are virtually unknown beyond the borders of their country. This is largely the consequence of writing in a language which is not spoken outside of Yugoslavia. Thus, with the exception of a few translations of some of the more famous books, the works of Yugoslav writers are not familiar to the reading public in Western Europe and North America. The most famous of Yugoslavia's "unknown" authors is Miroslav Krleža, whose versatile pen has been creating a rich storehouse of novels, poems, plays, and short stories for a half-century.

The Yugoslav Government allows a much greater degree of freedom to the nation's authors and other artists than can be found in any other Communist country. This, coupled with the nation's past literary heritage, has been responsible for a post-war upsurge in creative writing of all types.

One Yugoslav author, widely read in the Western world, has not been popular with the Yugoslav Government. He is Milovan Djilas, war hero, intellectual, and formerly a dedicated Communist and Vice-President of Yugoslavia. Djilas became disillusioned with the bureaucracy and controls of the Communist Party. He made no secret of his beliefs and in late 1953 began a series of increasingly critical articles which appeared, of all places, in the official newspaper of the Yugoslav Communist Party. Resigning from the Party, Djilas continued his writing, using American and other foreign magazines and newspapers as a forum for his views. For these writings he was jailed by the Yugoslav Government. In 1957, his prison term was lengthened with the publication in the United States of *The New Class*, an indictment of the failure of Communism to attain its professed goals. Released from prison, Djilas soon found himself back in jail for publishing a new book, *Conversations with Stalin*, describing his dealings with the Soviet dictator while Djilas was still a trusted member of the Yugoslav Communist hierarchy. Although he has turned against Communism, Djilas has remained loyal to his native land and has preferred to remain in Yugoslavia and face the consequences of his writings. He was set free again in 1967.

Ivo Andric, leading Yugoslav author and recipient of the 1961 Nobel Prize for literature.

Not too long ago, in Montenegro and other mountainous areas, pistols and swords were part of a man's everyday dress. Such sidearms were frequently put to use to kill Turks or members of rival clans. Now that the Turks are gone, the blood feuds between clans have ended, and the weapons themselves are outdated, so friendly shooting competitions are about the only use for old swords and pistols.

RECREATION

The long ski jumps at Planica in Slovenia are the scene of international meets in which jumpers from all parts of Europe compete every winter. A leap of close to 400 feet is the record distance for the Planica jump.

Sturdy, intelligent "Lipicaner" horses are bred at a farm on the Istrian Peninsula not far from the little town of Lipica. The original farm was founded by the Emperor of Austria in 1580 and provided trained horses for Vienna's famed Spanish Riding School. When the Austro-Hungarian Empire was dissolved after World War I, the Austrians started a new "Lipizaner" farm in their own country. Lipicaners are born with dark hair which turns white when the horse is between 3 and 7 years of age.

The numerous mountainous areas and the Adriatic Sea provide ready-made opportunities for outdoor recreation. In the summer the mountains are filled with hikers and campers of all ages. Winter snows bring out skiers and the more audacious ski jumpers, who usually attract large audiences to their competitions. Tourists throng the sunny Adriatic coast resorts during the summer season. This region with its picturesque towns, friendly people, and spectacular scenery attracts many foreign visitors. Students and other young people often spend their vacations in youth camps along the Adriatic.

(Right) In a moment the heavy shot will be flying through the air. Yugoslav women are active in sports organizations, and the nation usually fields a strong women's Olympic team.

Besides crossing the Neretva River at Mostar in Bosnia-Herzegovina, these two bridges span 400 years of history. The modern bridge being traversed by the double-decker bus was built only a few years ago, while the arched bridge in the background was constructed by the Turks in 1556. Many of Mostar's inhabitants are still Moslems.

THE LAND

Like most other European countries, Yugoslavia is not very large. Its total land area is 98,766 square miles, which is about the same size as the state of Wyoming or all of Great Britain and Northern Ireland. Yugoslavia occupies the northwestern portion of the Balkan Peninsula, the most prominent land feature of southeastern Europe.

Yugoslavia's neutralist foreign policy fits in well with the variety of political systems in the countries surrounding her. Greece, to the south, and Italy, adjoining to the west, are both countries firmly allied to the United States, Great Britain, and other Western nations through the North Atlantic Treaty Organization (NATO). Albania, which has closer ties with Communist China than with the Soviet Union, adjoins Yugoslavia on its southwest corner. Neutral Austria and three Communist nations allied to the Soviet Union—Hungary, Rumania, and Bulgaria—occupy the northern and eastern flanks, while the Adriatic Sea forms the greater part of the western boundary.

TOPOGRAPHY

Despite its relatively small size, Yugoslavia contains an amazing number of different landscapes within its borders. The country can be roughly divided into five natural regions.

Slovenia, the Republic in the northwest corner of Yugoslavia, is in a mountainous area known as the Julian Alps, a direct continuation of the Alpine system of mountains which extends from Italy, Austria, Switzerland, and France. Mt. Triglav, the highest peak in Yugoslavia (9,393 feet), is located in the Julian Alps. Picturesque alpine lakes backed by snow-capped mountains make Slovenia one of the most scenic parts of Yugoslavia.

Dalmatia is a narrow strip of land extending the length of the Adriatic coast from the Istrian Peninsula in the north to Montenegro in the south. Steep limestone mountains are never far back from the coast and in some parts of Dalmatia the mountains rise directly from the sea. Because of the lack of flat land along the coast there is no agriculture on a large scale

(*Above*) *Life in Montenegro's isolated mountain villages goes on the same way it has for centuries. The name of the Republic, Montenegro ("Black Mountain"), comes from the appearance of its forested mountains, which, when viewed from a distance, seem to be almost black.*

(*Left*) *People who do not enjoy climbing steep hills should not plan to visit the Macedonian town of Galičnik. However, visitors who do make the trip will be able to relax their weary muscles at a nearby spa.*

YUGOSLAVIA ■ 861

except for the growing of grapes in vineyards which cling to the steep hillsides. Just offshore in the Adriatic are about 600 (mainly uninhabited) islands, the remnants of a sunken mountain range whose peaks rise above the waters of the sea.

Extending southward from the Julian Alps and parallel to the Adriatic coast are the Dinaric Alps, a system of limestone mountains and plateaus reaching far into the interior of Yugoslavia. This is the Karst, a region of rugged limestone hills. Since water dissolves limestone, most streams have cut deep chasms and tunnels through the rock, leaving the surface of the land broken and dry. However, agriculture does flourish in *poljen*, depressions in the Karst where fertile soil has washed down from the hills and collected over the centuries.

The great Pannonian Lowland reaches across the northern part of Yugoslavia in the Republics of Croatia and Serbia. At one time, millions of years ago, the Pannonian Lowland was the bed of a great lake which drained away only when the Danube River, which now flows through the northern part of Serbia, cut a spectacular gorge, known today as the Iron Gates, through

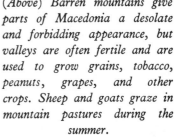

(*Above*) *Barren mountains give parts of Macedonia a desolate and forbidding appearance, but valleys are often fertile and are used to grow grains, tobacco, peanuts, grapes, and other crops. Sheep and goats graze in mountain pastures during the summer.*

(*Left*) *Giant goosenecks in Serbia's Morava River are the result of hundreds of centuries of erosion. Several old monasteries containing frescoes painted during the golden age of medieval Serbia are situated on the steep slopes overlooking the river. People seeking relief from aches and pains are attracted to the region by the many springs of hot mineral water which bubble from the ground.*

Zagreb, capital of Croatia and second largest city in Yugoslavia, is a great industrial and cultural hub for the country. The Turks never set foot in the city, and consequently Zagreb developed under the influence of Austria, which explains the town's Central European appearance. Zagreb's diversity of cultural wealth surpasses Belgrade's. The city is the home of the Solisti di Zagreb, *one of Europe's outstanding chamber orchestras, as well as the home of the motion picture studio which produced the award-winning animated cartoon,* The Substitute.

the surrounding mountains. Yugoslavia's best farmland, the Vojvodina plain, is part of the Pannonian Lowland. The Sava, longest river in the country, descends from the Julian Alps in Slovenia, flows past the Croatian capital of Zagreb, across the Pannonian Lowland before emptying into the Danube at Belgrade, some 583 miles from its source.

The fifth region lies in the southern part of Yugoslavia. Here, high mountains alternate with fertile valleys suitable for farming and livestock raising. Two major rivers drain the area. The Morava flows north and eventually joins the Danube, while the Vardar flows south past the Macedonian capital of Skopje and on into Greece, before finally discharging its waters into the Aegean Sea. The most im-portant lines of north-south communication—roads and railways—follow the valleys of the Vardar and the Morava from Belgrade almost to the Greek border.

CLIMATE

Because of its different surface features and length, Yugoslavia has three general types of climate. Along the Dalmatian coast, hot, dry summers and mild, damp winters are the rule. During the summer months, temperatures on the Adriatic sometimes rise as high as 100° F, but no one really minds since the humidity is low and a refreshing swim can always be had in the nearby sea. Great multitudes of tourists are attracted to Dalmatia every year by the pleasant climate, beaches, and many historic monuments.

Clever diplomacy rather than formidable-looking battlements kept the Adriatic city of Dubrovnik independent while the remainder of Yugoslavia (except for the mountain strongholds of Montenegro) was overrun by stronger foreign powers. Once, the city (then called Ragusa) was a leading commercial port in the Mediterranean Sea area. Now, visitors come to gaze at the town's beautiful Renaissance buildings and to bask in the sun at nearby beaches.

In the mountainous areas of Yugoslavia, short, cool summers and long, cold winters predominate. The mountains, because of their high altitudes, intercept a great deal of moisture —in the form of rain and snow—and are the wettest places in the country. In fact, a weather station located in the Dinaric Alps above the Norwegian-like Kotor Fiord in Montenegro is the dampest spot in all of Europe, with an annual rainfall of over 16 feet! The heavy precipitation in the mountains gives rise to many fast-flowing rivers which are excellent sources for hydro-electric power.

(Right) The mighty Danube River begins in Germany's Black Forest and empties into the Black Sea 1,770 miles away, touching eight countries on the way. The section of the river forming the boundary between Yugoslavia and Rumania is known as the Iron Gates because of the steep cliffs rising on both sides of the Danube. Swirling water in the narrow river channel makes navigation difficult for boats. Now plans are being drawn up for a hydro-electric dam across the gorge which will create a large lake reaching almost to Belgrade.

864 ■ YUGOSLAVIA

The Pannonian Lowland has a climate not unlike that of the midwestern United States. In summer, the long hours of sunlight turn the Lowland into a vast oven; however, in winter, the Dinaric Alps block out the warming influence of the Adriatic Sea and leave the area open to the *bura*, an icy wind from the northeast. Belgrade, in the Lowland, has an average temperature during January of a chilly 30° F. Average annual precipitation in the Yugoslav capital amounts to 24.4 inches (less than New York City's 42 inches).

The extreme southern portion of the Vardar River Valley has a subtropical climate similar to Dalmatia's, because of the nearby Aegean Sea, which is responsible for the moderate winter temperatures. This small region is warm enough for the growing of rice and cotton.

FLORA AND FAUNA

About 30 per cent of Yugoslavia's area, chiefly in mountainous regions, is still forested. Fine stands of oak, beech, chestnut, and evergreens support modest lumbering industries in the Julian and Dinaric Alps. The forests support a great variety of wildlife, too. The black bear and lynx, now very rare in heavily-populated Western Europe, can still be found in the Yugoslav mountains. Many types of birds can be seen, especially in Dalmatia, which is on a major

The Julian Alps of northwest Slovenia form a massive backdrop for beautiful Lake Bled. The little island in the middle is the site of a Catholic church—now a museum—and a restaurant.

migration route for birds flying between Central Europe and North Africa.

The underground streams of the Postonja caves in Slovenia are the home of a strange animal known as the *Proteus anguineus* (cave salamander) which has no eyes, swims like a fish, but has feet looking something like a man's.

Many of Yugoslavia's larger rivers, such as the Sava and Danube, are used for transporting freight. Here, massive grain elevators tower over anchored barges from Belgrade (spelled in Cyrillic letters on the sterns), only a few miles upstream on the banks of the Danube.

THE ECONOMY

Before World War II, Yugoslavia had a very backward economy compared to other countries in Europe. Most of Yugoslavia's people—more than three-quarters—lived and worked on farms, a condition common in countries we refer today as being "under-developed." Where the land was good, peasants were able to live reasonably well, eating what they grew and selling the surplus. Where the land was poor, farmers were not so fortunate. In fact, poverty of the worst sort existed among most Yugoslav peasants. In the thousands of small farm villages, disease and illiteracy were widespread. Yet in the few big cities, such as Belgrade and Zagreb, both the rich and the middle class (small groups) lived lives of comparative luxury. Foreign visitors who stopped only in the larger

cities often received the false impression that the country as a whole was prosperous.

There were several reasons for Yugoslavia's unfortunate economic situation. In the first place, the country had few manufacturing industries and a poor communications network—railways, roads, telephones, etc. In today's world, manufacturing and modern communications are recognized as the backbone of national prosperity. Although blessed with abundant natural resources—minerals, water and forests, among others—the Yugoslavs lacked the money necessary to develop them. What industrial development there was, was mainly controlled by wealthy investors from other countries, especially France and Great Britain.

Montenegro's steep mountain pastures are ideal for raising sheep. These same mountains gave shelter to the proud and courageous people of Montenegro during their successful efforts to avoid enslavement by the Turks who had conquered all the surrounding areas.

This weird-looking mechanical monster is removing soil from a canal which connects the Danube and Tisa rivers. The canal was built to drain excess water from the wheat fields of Vojvodina during the rainy season and to provide water for irrigating the same fields during periods of drought.

1959 was a year of bumper harvests throughout Yugoslavia, especially in Vojvodina, breadbasket of the nation. Since that time droughts have reduced crop yields, forcing Yugoslavia to purchase wheat from the United States.

REBUILDING

As soon as the Yugoslav Communists were able to consolidate their control over the country after the conclusion of the war, they began a drastic overhaul of the nation's economy along Communist lines. The Yugoslav Communists moved with great speed, almost as if they were trying to impress their Soviet "friends" with Yugoslav loyalty to the Communist cause. All types of industrial concerns were nationalized including foreign-owned mines and ore smelters. Private enterprise was abolished, save for agriculture and crafts. The Government seized all large land-holdings of landlords, churches, and banks. Wealthy people with large bank deposits suddenly found themselves penniless.

In 1947, Communist economic planners announced a grandiose Five Year Plan to be completed by 1951. Industrial output was to be greatly expanded and farming was to be "collectivized." The Government was to direct the entire plan at every level. Unfortunately, as so often happens in Communist countries, the planners proved to be better at setting goals than at increasing production to meet them.

Yugoslavia's developing industry has been greatly aided by the construction of new hydro-electric power plants, such as this one at the Jablanica Dam.

There were also grave problems in the agricultural sector of the economy. The peasants did not appreciate being forced into collective farms or being made to sell crop surpluses to the State at the low prices established by the Government. The peasants resented Government interference in agriculture, and farm production slumped.

Factory workers take time off from their jobs to nominate candidates for their workers' council. When elected, the council will hire experts skilled at factory management to direct the everyday details of production. However, the workers' council still has the final say, and retains the right to dismiss the factory manager.

Meanwhile, political events which were to affect the destiny of the Yugoslav economy took place. Of greatest importance was the political and economic break with the Soviet Union in 1948. Yugoslavia found itself truly independent and no longer a mere Russian satellite receiving orders from Moscow. The Yugoslav Communists were left free to run the economy of the country without foreign interference.

In the Soviet Union and other Communist countries, the Government directly supervises the entire economy. Even details of seemingly minor importance must be approved by "the bureaucracy," the term for the inevitably oversized collection of officials and Government departments in charge of directing the economy. In general, the more a bureacracy grows the more inefficient it becomes, until a point is reached where there are more officials taking care of each other than there are directing the work. Yugoslavia decided that it had had its fill of bureaucratic administration of the economy. Yugoslavia is still a Communist state, but has borrowed many ideas from Western capitalism.

WORKERS' COUNCILS

At the heart of Yugoslavia's new industrial economy are the workers' councils. Since 1950, economic enterprises have been managed by the workers themselves in the name of the Yugoslav people, for all means of production—factories, communications, power plants, etc.—are considered to be community property. A workers' council is composed of men and women elected by fellow workers. The council elects a board of management, which in turn selects a trained director to handle the details of day-to-day operation and carry out the plans of the workers' council. Workers in an enterprise have the right (through the workers' council and the board of management) to dismiss a director if they feel he is not running the business properly. They occasionally make use of this privilege.

BUSINESS

Commercial affairs follow a pattern of "socialist free enterprise." Competition is keen among rival firms. An enterprise which fails to

A workers' council controls production and management at this motor factory. The council also does as it sees fit with any profits the factory may make from sales of its product. Profits may be given directly to the workers or invested in factory improvements. Perhaps, that is why this group of men is so interested in the blackboard showing daily production figures.

show a profit must either go out of business or try to merge with a more successful rival, just as in Great Britain, the United States and other Western nations. Even advertising, formerly denounced as a form of capitalist "trickery," is being used more and more to promote sales. Any group of people desiring to start an enterprise are free to do so. However, there is a catch. The banks which finance such businesses are controlled by the Government. Banks lend money only to those enterprises which are likely to prove beneficial to Yugoslavia's over-all economic growth.

More recently the Zastava Automobile Works floated an issue of bonds—the first instance of this "capitalist" financing method in

In a plant near Belgrade, workers test a new antitubercular drug. The Yugoslav working force includes an ever greater number of women.

Molten steel glows through the door of an open hearth furnace in Bosnia-Herzegovina. Before the war, the mining and smelting of minerals were among the few types of heavy industry in the country. Today, instead of exporting most of its raw materials to foreign countries, Yugoslavia keeps them for use in domestic industries and exports manufactured goods instead.

communist Yugoslavia. Another change took place in 1968 when, for the first time, Western industrial firms were permitted to establish offices in Yugoslavia.

The new Yugoslav economic system has helped make the nation's industries far more efficient than they are in other Communist nations. But there are also problems. Although giant strides have been taken, Yugoslavia is still a long way from being a world industrial leader.

For economic growth to continue, profits must be re-invested in industry. Obviously, this does not happen when workers' councils vote away profits to build themselves Olympic-size swimming pools (as has happened). Yugoslavia cannot afford symbols of luxury at the present time. The Government discourages rash investment by levying heavy taxes on ill-used profits and by discreetly applying its various financial powers.

Today, Yugoslav industries produce an array

Soon happy Yugoslavs will be racing these motorcycles down some of the new roads built by the volunteer youth brigades. Automobiles are being assembled on the other side of the plant.

A few carefully-placed strokes with a paint brush and another jug or pitcher will be finished at a porcelain factory in Macedonia. The Government has paid special attention to backward Macedonia since the war, and many new manufacturing plants have been built.

By 1960 Yugoslav production of crude oil was about 500 times more than in 1939. Pipes must be welded together to carry the flow of oil to storage tanks.

of manufactured goods undreamt of before the war. Yugoslavia no longer has to import aluminium items; they are now manufactured at home using bauxite mined in Yugoslavia. New plants produce everything from television sets to electric turbines. Already the number of people engaged in agriculture has dropped from

75 per cent to 50 per cent, as hundreds of thousands of workers give up jobs in the field for places on assembly lines.

The former policy of forcing the peasants into collective farms has been totally abandoned. At the present time, membership in collective farms is voluntary.

Men have used traps as long as they have fished. These fishermen are scooping fish from the trap into small skiffs.

The life of a fisherman is not easy, for there are always jobs to be done. Nets and boats must be kept in good condition.

Jajce, perched on a hillside overlooking a 100-foot waterfall, has more than once found itself in the forefront of Yugoslav history. Here the Turks executed the last king of independent Bosnia in 1461. The conquerors turned the local church and its tall belfry into a mosque and minaret. Nearly 500 years later, in 1943, Tito and other Partisan leaders met in Jajce to draw up plans for Yugoslavia's postwar future.

874 ■ GREECE

Dinner in a Greek taverna is filled with music and likely to be at a late hour, generally between 9:30 and 11:30. The afternoon siesta, usually from 2 to 5, provides a big break in the working day.

GREECE

Modern-day Greece is an exciting country. The land itself is lovely, with its jagged, steep mountains, many of which are capped with snow the year round; its low-lying fertile plains; and thousands of islands, each picturesque in its own way. This scenic beauty is made even more dramatic by the many ancient temples and theatres which dot the countryside and are a constant reminder of the fascinating history of Greece.

Greece began to develop around the year 6000 B.C.! In the 5th century before Christ, ancient Greece built a civilization which the world still admires. Even more remarkable is the fact that this civilization continued to develop even though Greece was conquered by several other nations— Macedonia, Rome, and in Christian times, by the Turks. Even though democracy was born in Athens in the 5th century B.C., the Greeks were ruled by Turkey for four centuries. Their history is one of war and revolution, long periods of economic depression and political unrest.

Greece is the cultural ancestor of all Europe, the birthplace not only of democracy but of countless other human achievements in commerce, art, science and all branches of learning. Although most of Greece's immeasurable accomplishments took place in the 5th century B.C., they provided a foundation on which the Greeks have never stopped building. Even today Greek education begins with study of the classics. Greece was the first Christian country, too. It was in Corinth that St. Paul founded the first church in A.D. 51.

In Greece ancient achievements and contemporary customs blend together as in few other countries to produce a way of life that is simultaneously relaxed and productive, traditional and original, individualistic and yet unified by the people's strong pride in their history.

The national bird of Greece is the Phoenix, which was highly important in mythology and was later taken over by the early Christians in memory of the fact that Christ rose from the dead. The story of the Phoenix tells that after burning itself out and going up in flames, it would rise again from its own ashes and be reborn to a new life. The legendary bird is a perfect symbol of Greece, a nation whose people have never been afraid to start over again. Their courage in winning independence from Turkey in 1827 captured the sympathy of Europe. And in recent times the world has applauded the way in which the Greeks rebuilt their country after much of it was destroyed by the Axis occupation during World War II.

Atop the precipitous granite slopes of Meteora in Thessaly nestle several monasteries which date back to the 14th century. Visitors can reach Meteora by car from nearby Kalambaka. Long ago people were lifted to the summit in nets raised by a windlass, but now there are carved stairways in the rock. The monasteries contain excellent frescoes.

876 ■ GREECE

THE LAND

A wild rocky coast, orchards and vineyards, steep snow-peaked mountains, mild blue seas glittering with islands—these describe Greece.

Occupying the southernmost part of the Balkan Peninsula, the Greek mainland is cut up by numerous mountain chains (covering three-fourths of the land); it has a long indented coast providing many ports and is bounded by three seas. On the southwest is the Ionian; directly south, the Mediterranean; to the southeast lies the Aegean. Included in the Kingdom of Hellas (Greece's official name) are more than 4,000 islands—with 2,000 in the Aegean group alone!

The geography of Greece has influenced its history and culture profoundly since ancient times. The abundance of islands and excellent ports has made Greece a maritime nation, a trade base for all the great Mediterranean civilizations and still a major shipping power. The main ports are Piraeus, which services Athens; Alexandroúpolis near the Turkish border; and Greece's third-largest city, Salonika, near the mouth of the Vardar River in Thessaly.

The diversified land falls into six sections. *Thrace* and *Macedonia* in the north of the peninsula are crisscrossed by Greece's four major rivers (the Vardar, Strymon, Nestos and Maritza) and although none is navigable, cereals, tobacco and many types of fruit are grown on the rich plains at the river mouths. Thrace and Macedonia are further divided and subdivided by mountain ranges extending into Albania, Yugoslavia and Bulgaria. Here, between Macedonia and Thessaly, is historic Mt. Olympus. Only very experienced climbers dare scale 9,754-foot Olympus. It is still as formidable as when it was believed to be the home of Zeus and Hera and the other gods of Greek antiquity. The accessible lower slopes of Olympus provide panoramic views of the plains below and the Aegean Islands.

Epirus is in the western part of the mainland, south of Albania on the Ionian Sea. It is extremely isolated, for it is separated from the rest of Greece by the steep Pindus Mountains. Sheep-raising is the major occupation. The inhabitants of *Thessaly*, east of Epirus on the Aegean Sea, are far luckier than the dwellers in the hilly region to the west. Most of Thessaly is a vast fertile plain. It is Greece's most important agricultural region. Large farms produce cereals and cotton for export.

Central Greece is south of Thessaly and north of the Gulf of Corinth, which separates it from the Peloponnesus. Athens is located here. From 500 B.C. until the fall of Rome, this city was the focus of art and all branches of learning in the Mediterranean world as well as the first democratic state. Appropriately, Athens is the capital of modern Greece. Nearby Piraeus is the nation's most active port and its major industrial hub. Typical Mediterranean crops are grown in central Greece—olives, cereals and vines.

In central Greece, too, is Mt. Parnassus, the mythical home of the Muses. These were nine sisters, each of whom was believed responsible for a specific art. Over 7,000 feet tall, Parnassus is only five hours from Athens by car. At the foot of this stately once-sacred peak is the village of Delphi where in ancient times a famous priestess had her temple. Near

Most Greek cities have an "acropolis." Originally the word meant the high part of any city, but recently it has been associated solely with the splendid Acropolis at Athens. The Acropolis of Greece's capital rests on a butte 500 feet above sea level and forms an uneven plain about 500 by 1,000 feet. The rocky peak on the right is Mt. Lycabettus.

Delphi is the Castalian Spring, sacred to the Muses, and the Corycian Cave which was dedicated to Pan, mischievous god of woods and forests.

Until 1893 the *Peloponnesus* was a peninsula, linked to the mainland by a narrow piece of land, but after the Corinth Canal was built in 1893, it became a large island. On the Peloponnesus, currants are raised and exported from the city of Patras. Figs, oranges, lemons, dates, olives and grapes are also grown, but the stony thin-soiled eastern region is suited to little except sheep- and goat-raising.

Of Greece's thousands of islands, *Crete* is the most famous as well as the largest (130 miles long). Mt. Ida where Zeus is said to have been born is located on Crete, as are the ruins at Knossos and Phaestos of Europe's oldest civilization, the Minoan. Crete is extra-ordinarily lovely. Steep mountains descend into the sea and are crowned with snow the year round. In spring the lower slopes burst into bloom with flowering anemones, cyclamen and hundreds of wildflowers. *Patmos* is famous, too, for here St. John wrote the Book of Revelation.

The *Ionian Islands* off Greece's southwestern coast are densely populated by sailors, merchants and farmers. The mild Mediterranean climate produces grapes for wine and citrus fruits. However, the inhabitants of the various *Aegean island groups* are not so fortunate as those of the Ionian. On Euboea, the Cyclades, the Northern Sporades and the Dodecanese, agriculture is poor. Fishing and sponge-diving provide a living for some people, but there is much emigration from these islands to the mainland or to other countries.

The waters around the mainland and the islands, too, are full of life. There are more than 246 species, and these include some which are highly prized for eating: lobster, shrimp, crab, oysters and mussels. But the most fascinating type of marine life to be seen are the dolphins. These graceful creatures love to play, and in many parts of Greece they can be seen leaping through the air and tumbling about quite close to shore.

The land produces many kinds of trees—slender white poplars, cypresses, chestnut, briar, pine, fir and, of course, lovely olive trees which are noted for their graceful way of growing. In spring Greece's mountains blaze with color, for both cultivated and wildflowers spring up in great abundance. Many of Greece's flowers are mentioned in classical poetry and mythology, but the most famous are probably narcissus, water lilies, primrose and camomile.

Everywhere in Greece the visitor will come across goats. A rare white goat called an *agrimi*, is an unusual variety found only on the island of Crete. The agrimi is a domestic animal, but another interesting feature of Greece is the large number of wild animals

(Above) Gemlike Corfu, the second-largest Ionian Island, was settled in the 8th century B.C. Historians think it may be the site of "Scheria," the home of the Phaeacians in Homer's Odyssey.

(Below) Seen from the street near a thickly wooded park against everyday activities, Athens' Acropolis seems to be something envisioned in a dream. The temple on the lower slope is the Erechtheum, the higher one is the Parthenon.

Awe-inspiring Mt. Olympus rises toward the sky between Thessaly and Macedonia. The abode of the gods is actually a range of ten peaks set apart by deep, desolate ravines. It isn't surprising that Olympus was considered sacred, for the range has a supernatural quality. Often the peaks are clouded by mist and seem to hang suspended between heaven and earth.

(Below) Although much of Greece's land is not suitable for farming, 60 per cent of Greeks make their living from agriculture.

which roam its mountains and woods. There are wild boars, bears, wild cats, deer, wolves, badgers, martens and weasels. As for birds, Greece has 358 species, including birds of prey (eagles, hawks, vultures and falcons), pelicans, pheasants, partridge, nightingales, wild geese, ducks, storks and turtledoves.

With its rugged mountain scenery, sleepy villages dotted with the ruins of ancient temples, rich plains and bustling cities, Greece is a country of exciting variety. The diversity of the terrain explains why the Greeks, living in isolated communities, are highly individualistic, why they have had to struggle for national unity and why their form of government changed frequently from the earliest pre-Christian settlements until after World War II.

(*Above*) *Everywhere in Greece nature seems to rival the achievements of man. Cosmopolitan Athens is dwarfed by the bulk of Mt. Lycabettus. On its summit is the Ayios Yeoryios Chapel.*

(*Right*) *Typical of Greece are smooth, shady roads winding through fertile plains. Typical, too, are the rocky slopes in the background, furnishing endless scenic contrasts.*

All Mikonos' buildings are snowy white. Among the island's 365 churches is this asymmetrical, almost rambling structure in Byzantine style. Mikonos owes its many churches to seafarers who built them in gratitude for having escaped death at sea.

(Below)   The sun-baked port fortifications of Crete curve outward from a wall built by the Venetians in the 16th century when they held the island. In this quarter is the tomb of Eleutherios Venizelos, Greece's great 20th-century patriot, and in the distance is snow-capped Mt. Ida, legendary birthplace of Zeus.

The palace at Knossos on the island of Crete was the first structure of its kind in the Western world. Built around 2100 B.C., it is said to have belonged to King Minos, legendary founder of the first Mediterranean maritime empire. The columns shown here are actually bright reddish-orange set off by blue capitals and strips of blue at their bases.

HISTORY

ANCIENT GREECE

The first Greeks about whom very much is known are the *Hellenes*, or classical Greeks. About 3500 B.C. these light-haired people invaded Greece from the north near the Danube River, overrunning the peninsula as far south as the Gulf of Corinth. The invaders conquered the Aegeans who were already living in Greece, took over their cities and set up a crude sort of feudal life. Each of many local kings was a war lord and plundered adjacent kingdoms at will. Homer's *Iliad* and *Odyssey* picture this lawless period, which is sometimes called the "Homeric Age."

Minoan Civilization: 6000-1400 B.C.

While the Hellenes were becoming established on the mainland, the highly advanced Minoan civilization flourished on the island of Crete. The Aegeans who lived there came in ships from the south around 6000 B.C. Cretan life was organized around beautiful cities dominated by palace-temples and ruled by priest-kings. The greatest of these cities was at

Decorating the palace at Knossos are many geometric designs and this fresco showing flying dolphins. The Cretans loved bright colors, and they were highly artistic in everything they did.

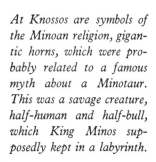

At Knossos are symbols of the Minoan religion, gigantic horns, which were probably related to a famous myth about a Minotaur. This was a savage creature, half-human and half-bull, which King Minos supposedly kept in a labyrinth.

Knossos, and the ruins of its palace contain actual bathrooms with modern drainage systems as well as brightly colored, decorative wall frescoes.

King Minos is said to have ruled Crete at its peak, and to have established the first maritime empire in the Aegean. Scraps of Cretan pottery have been found in lands as far distant from Crete as Spain. But Cretan civilization was destroyed by the cruder peoples on the mainland. In 1400 B.C. the palace at Knossos was sacked, and not long afterward conquering barbarians destroyed this remarkable island kingdom.

Mycenaean Age: 1400-1200 B.C.

As a result of the fall of Crete and the consequent transfer of sea power to the mainland, Greece superseded Crete as a power in the Mediterranean area. For a while there was considerable economic growth. Colonies were established on Cyprus and the coast of Asia Minor. But in 1200 B.C. this civilization, too, disappeared under another great wave of invaders from the north.

(*Above*) *The Lion Gate at Mycenae not far from Corinth was built by Aegeans whose civilization, reaching its peak in the 14th century B.C., was similar to that of Crete though somewhat less advanced.*

(*Below*) *Excavations begun at Mycenae in 1876 uncovered a massive fortress-palace and numerous tombs including this one, reputed to hold the remains of Clytemnestra, the wife and murderer of Agamemnon in Aeschylus' tragedy.*

Dominating Athens' Acropolis is the Parthenon, built about 447 B.C. to extol Athena. This Doric-style temple is the outstanding masterpiece of Greek architecture. On the west side, shown here, the relief sculpture of the frieze showed the contest between Athena and Poseidon for the protection of Athens.

An interior view of the Parthenon shows how the columns were constructed in layers, or drums, set on top of one another and decreasing in circumference toward the top to give the impression of tapering upward. This temple once housed the 40-foot Athena Parthenos, *a statue of the goddess of wisdom.*

One of the two principal temples on Athens' Acropolis is the Erechtheum, built around 420 B.C. in Pentelic marble. Its Ionic columns are the finest of their type. During Justinian's reign (A.D. 527-565) the Erechtheum was used as a church, and under Turkish rule it housed a harem. The temple was heavily damaged during the Greek revolution of 1827.

City-State Civilization: 1200-338 B.C.

At first the invaders lived on isolated farms and each family or tribe raised its own food and made its own clothing, but gradually they came together in villages and towns. The social scale which developed between 1200 and 800 B.C. remained almost unchanged throughout the Classical Period, or 5th century B.C. At the top were land-owning aristocrats, next came free farmers, landless merchants, craftsmen and agricultural workers and, last, slaves and serfs.

The city-state was a politically independent city which chose its own form of government regardless of how adjacent cities were organized. This way of organizing community life, and the idea of democracy came from the tribal customs of the barbarians. Although the Aegean peoples who built the earlier civilizations at Crete and Mycenae believed that the city belonged to the king, the Nordic invaders believed that it belonged to all its citizens together and that they were responsible for the state.

From 800 to 500 B.C. Greece's agricultural economy changed to a commercial one. The growth of commerce meant that merchants and bankers began to rival the landed aristocracy for power. Because of this, several types of government appeared in the various city-states. Some were ruled by aristocracies (groups of rich landowners), some by "oligarchies" (in which landowners and businessmen shared power); others were democracies, and still others dictatorships. This variety affected Greece up until the 20th century.

By 480 B.C. Greece was the strongest country in the Mediterranean area. That year it defeated the Persians (who had conquered much of Greece in 546 B.C.) as well as the Phoenicians. Because of its superior fleet, Athens became head of the Delian League (a protective maritime federation which included 200 cities) and the most influential Greek city.

The 5th century B.C. is the great age of Athenian democracy. Its founders are Solon, who provided a legal code, and Cleisthenes,

(*Above*) The Theatre of Dionysus graces the southern slope of Athens' Acropolis. Ancient tragedies are still performed here much as they were five centuries before Christ to extol the god of fertility, wine, song and drama. Dionysus, who did not belong to the Olympian family, was the chief god of the Eleusinian mystery cults.

(*Right*) The Temple of the Olympian Zeus is in Athens' lower city. Its Corinthian capitals are decorated with acanthus leaves, its columns more slender than the earlier Ionic type. The Corinthian order reached its height in the middle of the 4th century B.C., and this is the first great Corinthian temple.

At Delphi is a strangely beautiful, circular temple which was sacred to Athena. It fits so well into its wild natural surroundings that it is difficult to imagine Delphi crowded with people. But in ancient times it was a meeting place for pilgrims from all parts of Greece.

who drafted a democratic constitution. Athens distributed democratic constitutions among many of the cities in the Delian League.

Sometimes called the "Golden Age of Greece" or the "Age of Pericles," the 5th century B.C. was a time of great achievement in every field of human activity—government, philosophy, history, mathematics, medicine, mechanics, sculpture, drama and architecture. Pericles, who was in power from 461 to 429 B.C., was the century's most important leader, and under his political guidance all branches of learning and art flourished.

Nevertheless, the 5th century ended violently with the Peloponnesian War (431-404 B.C.). Athens was defeated by its jealous rival Sparta. Internal disunity and the disastrous effects of war made Greece powerless against an outside invader, Macedonia. In 338 B.C. Greece was conquered by Philip II of Macedonia, the father of Alexander the Great, and remained politically dependent until the fall of Rome in A.D. 330.

The Greeks made periodic attempts to seize independence, and when Rome attacked Macedonia in 200 B.C., Athens, Sparta and Rhodes supported Rome. They succeeded only in exchanging one master for another.

Roman Domination: 200 B.C.-A.D. 330

For more than a century and a half Rome permitted Greece a large measure of freedom, but in 27 B.C. the Emperor Augustus reversed this policy and declared all of Greece a Roman province called Achaea. Rome deliberately kept Greece isolated to prevent economic competition, so Greece remained a poor country without any chance to build up her trade. Although Rome provided money for the construction of public buildings in Greece, athletics, all forms of culture and the University of Athens, Greece's only real commodity under

GREECE ■ 889

(*Above*) *A row of roaring marble lions guards the west shore of the Sacred Lake at Delos, smallest island of the Cyclades, former headquarters of the Delian League and once a flourishing religious base. The twins Apollo and Artemis were believed to have been born under the Sacred Lake. However, it is now dry.*

(*Below*) *At Lindos on the east coast of Rhodes stands a Doric temple which was dedicated to Athena. Nearby is the spot where St. Paul landed during his mission to Christianize Greece.*

On Cape Sounion on the coast not far from Athens stand the sun-bleached pillars of this temple which was dedicated to Poseidon. He was the god of the sea, in charge of all bodies of water, and is usually represented with the three-pronged trident or spear which he used to cause storms.

(Below) On the west of the Altis, or sacred grove, at Olympia stands the Palaistra, part of what was originally a group of buildings erected for the Olympic Games. Although they were local at first, the games became Pan-Hellenic in 527 B.C. They were held in a stadium east of the Altis.

Roman domination was education. Students from all parts of the Mediterranean world flocked to Athens.

As part of the Roman Empire, Greece again fell victim to invading barbarians from the north. When the Goths captured Athens in the 3rd century A.D., Rome was too weak to send help. By the 4th century the only cities still standing were Corinth and what remained of devastated Athens.

In A.D. 330 Rome collapsed under the pressure of the barbarian invasions and the empire was transferred to Byzantium (present-day Turkey).

MEDIEVAL GREECE AND TURKISH RULE

Byzantine Civilization: 330-1453

The Byzantine Empire was a continuation of the Roman Empire and its history is thought of as Greece's medieval period. The citizens of the empire spoke Greek and were Christianized under Constantine the Great who ruled from A.D. 324-337. Guided by a series of wise emperors, Byzantine life was internally stable and provided good conditions for the continued development of learning and art. Although Byzantine civilization was essentially Greek, Greece itself was overrun by barbarians during this period.

The Byzantine Empire, too, was constantly under attack. During the 13th century much of Greece proper was captured by Venice, then a powerful maritime city-state. What remained

The graceful design of this church at Salonika illustrates the Byzantine architectural style. The plan is based on a Greek cross; unlike the Roman cross, the vertical arm of the Greek type is the same length as the horizontal, creating a square. Characteristic of the Byzantine plan are the four domes at each corner and the larger elevated dome in the middle.

was taken by the Turks. After repeated raids, the Turks finally seized Byzantium in 1453. This marks the end of the old Roman Empire, of the Byzantine Empire, and the start of a long period of oppression for the Greeks.

Turkish Domination: 1453-1827

Economic depression and frequent wars and revolutions typify this period. To escape forced conversion to the Moslem religion and heavy taxation, many Greeks fled to other countries. Those who remained organized frequent revolts, often supporting Venice, who was at war with Turkey off and on until the Adriatic power was decisively defeated in 1669.

During the 18th century increasing corruption within the Turkish Empire and wars which damaged the rest of Europe commercially, enabled Greece to grow in economic power. Its merchant marine became first in the Black Sea. Its people became unified by their desire for freedom and a feeling of strong patriotism arose. Inspired by the ideals of the French Revolution, Greece attacked Turkey and won control of the Peloponnesus, many Aegean islands and Athens and Thebes.

The issue of Greek independence involved much of Europe. In 1827 Britain, France and Russia (the Great Powers) successfully intervened on Greece's side. The London Protocol of March, 1829, declared Greece independent, established new national boundaries and set up a monarchy under Prince Otto of Bavaria.

THE EMERGENCE OF MODERN GREECE

The monarchy set up by the Great Powers did not please the Greeks, for they wanted to rule themselves. While King Otto was away from Athens in 1843 a revolutionary group deposed him and set up a provisional government. Unfortunately, this government did not act soon enough, and again the Great Powers selected a king. This time he was George I from the royal house of Denmark. To win acceptance he brought the formerly British-held Ionian Islands back into the Greek kingdom. Under George I Greece had a constitutional monarchy with a parliament elected by male suffrage.

A major problem during the 19th and early 20th centuries was the *Megalé Idea*, or the desire for territorial unity. At the time of independence there were still 3 million Greeks living under the Turkish Empire, and these people wanted to be united with Greece. Although the Greeks felt entitled to Thessaly, Crete, Epirus and parts of Macedonia, all they achieved until 1913 was the Thessalian plain and a small portion of Epirus.

At the beginning of the 20th century Greece's typical internal political disunity continued to

Not too far from Sparta in the southern Peloponnesus stands Mystra, which contains the ruins of a complete Byzantine city. One of the best-preserved of several churches built between the 13th and the 15th centuries is Pantanassa, *which is now a convent.*

Blue and white—these are the colors of Greece's islands. A tiny, snow-white church on the island of Ios is a peaceful sight against the sea.

prevent it from unifying against an unwanted monarch. In 1909 a group of army officers ousted King George's two sons from crucial military posts and called on a popular Cretan politician, Eleutherios Venizelos, to help them establish a new government. Elections were held and Venizelos' party was overwhelmingly victorious. In 1911 the newly elected Assembly passed major constitutional revisions.

But even with a relatively stable government Greece was unable to settle down to peace and economic progress. After the tiny state of Montenegro declared war on Turkey in 1912, Greece, Serbia and Bulgaria (the Balkan League) joined Montenegro and quickly forced Turkey out of Europe. Greece at last achieved the *Megalé Idea*, for it won Crete, the remainder of Epirus and Macedonia. Later, as a result of fighting with the Allies in World War I (1914-1923), Greece obtained still more territory.

Modern Greece: 1923-the Present

War-weary and consequently conservative in their political attitudes, the Greeks did not re-elect Venizelos and his Liberal Party after World War I. Instead, King Constantine, whom the Allies had deposed in 1917, was returned to

power. He started an offensive war against Turkey and was badly defeated. As a result, he was forced to abdicate in 1921, though he was succeeded by his son, George II. In the settlement of Constantine's rash war, Greece lost much of the territory it had gained at the end of World War I.

With the monarchy very unpopular, Venizelos again became active. Although he believed a constitutional monarchy would be the best form of government, the reaction against King Constantine made the Greeks reject Venizelos' proposal and form a republic. As Venizelos had feared, the republic did not survive. It was replaced by a dictatorship which, in turn, lasted only briefly.

In 1928 Venizelos succeeded in overthrowing the dictatorship, and his party was returned to power. During his four-year administration Greece enjoyed excellent foreign relations; but an economic depression caused Venizelos to be defeated in 1932. After an attempt on his life, he fled from the country he had tried so earnestly to lead toward a stable government.

In 1935 further political chaos enabled a second dictator to seize control of the govern-

(Below) On Santorini, one of the southernmost of the Cyclades Islands, is this simple Greek Orthodox church with its typical central dome. The island owes its name to its protectress, Saint Irene, but in ancient times it was called "Thera."

A round white tower is the identifying feature of Salonika, formerly called Thessalonika. Greece's third-largest city has changed hands many times and was severely damaged during World War II. The city is located on the Gulf of Salonika, a peaceful inlet of the Aegean Sea.

ment. Until the Axis occupation in 1941, General Ioannes Metaxas ruled Greece with the methods typical of a dictator. Although he was always unpopular, the Greeks were unable to unite effectively against him.

The Greeks fought boldly and courageously during World War II. Greece held the attacker, Fascist Italy, to a stalemate, but was conquered when Germany joined Italy. Until liberated by Britain in 1944, Greece was occupied by German, Bulgarian and Italian troops. Its victories against numerically superior Fascist forces and its continuous fierce resistance during occupation won world-wide admiration.

After the war Greece was threatened from a new source—Communism. Although in 1946 a majority of the voters wanted to re-establish a constitutional monarchy under King George II, guerrilla bands protested violently. There

seems little question that the agitators were Communist-led; in addition, poor economic conditions all over Greece provided a motive for revolt against any government in power. At first, Britain provided assistance for forces fighting the rebels, but as a war-torn country, it was forced to withdraw aid. The United States assumed Britain's role, but even with United States help, three years passed before the government was able to gain firm control. Marshal Tito of Yugoslavia played an important role in this conflict, for after his split with Soviet Russia, he closed the Yugoslav border to Soviet-inspired guerrilla bands.

By the 1960's Greece had achieved a stable government, in form a constitutional monarchy. Legislative power resided in a freely elected parliament. Greece had made astonishing economic progress, too. After four centuries of

Looking as though they stepped out of the past, these women display their local costume— elaborate headdresses decorated with flowers and many-layered dresses, heavily embroidered. They wear hand-worked woolen slippers.

foreign oppression and 150 years marked by wars and revolutions, Greece seemed near its goals—fulfilment of the *Megalé Idea* and a strong constitutional government.

Then, following a series of parliamentary crises in 1967, a military junta seized power and suspended parliamentary rule, claiming these measures were necessary to prevent a leftist take-over, and possible abolition of the monarchy. Later in the year, King Constantine went into exile in Rome after an unsuccessful attempt to oust the junta.

During the summer, concerts are often held in the open-air Roman Odeon of Herod Atticus beneath Athens' Acropolis. Notice the architectural use of the arch; it is typically Roman and quite different from the column-type construction perfected by the Greeks.

THE PEOPLE

The individualistic Greeks differ greatly from one region to another and yet are strongly united in their love of freedom and pride in their country's history. Their racial ancestors are the Aegeans and, to a much greater extent, the invading Nordic tribes who were the Greeks of antiquity. The Russian Revolution of 1917 brought large numbers of Russians to Greece, and after the Greco-Turkish War of 1921, there was an influx of over a million refugees from Turkey. Since Turks make up Greece's largest population minority, the Moslem religion is the second-largest, Turkish the language most spoken after Greek.

RELIGION

Nearly all Greeks belong to the Greek Orthodox Church, which in 1054 separated from the Roman Catholic Church. Under the regulations of the Greek Church, priests and bishops are elected by the people, and there is no counterpart of the Roman Catholic Pope.

and the arts, Apollo was especially beloved by the ancients. The adventures of these and other gods provided a vast entertaining mythology which inspired not only the art of Greece's Classical Period but also that of the Italian Renaissance.

Greek mythology did not have set beliefs or rituals, but many ancient Greeks belonged to the Eleusinian mystery cults, which were ritualistic and promised purification from sin as well as personal immortality. These mystery cults sprang from nature-worship and their chief gods were Dionysius and Demeter, who were believed responsible for the fertility of the land and its crops. While mythology enriched the arts and provided a unified cultural tradition, the mystery cults provided an outlet for the expression of religious feeling.

EDUCATION

Pride in their magnificent cultural heritage and the desire to preserve it make Greeks keenly interested in education. The constitution of 1911 provided for free compulsory schooling. Today attendance is required between the ages of 7 and 12. The University of Athens

The Aegean island of Paros, one of the Cyclades, is calm and sunny. Shown outside one of Paros' lovely churches is a bearded Greek Orthodox priest in typical attire, a tall black hat and a street-length black robe.

Mount Athos in southeastern Macedonia is the focus of monastic life; here several orders of monks live just as their predecessors did in the 12th century. The constitution provides for religious freedom; Moslems, Roman Catholics, Protestants and Jews worship as they like in Greece.

Although Greeks are proud of the fact that theirs was the first Christian country, they are also proud of their rich classical mythology. The ancient gods were believed to have human forms, but they were superior to mortals in power and beauty. Zeus, who ruled from Mt. Olympus, was the king of the gods, but he often behaved as foolishly as a human. There are many humorous stories about his quarrels with his wife Hera. The most important gods in the Olympian family were Athena, goddess of wisdom; Aphrodite, the goddess of love; and Apollo. As the god of light, healing, music

This might be Venice—but is not! The apartment buildings shown here line Seaside Avenue in Salonika. For an ocean voyage, the city's citizens need only step outside their front doors.

Syntagma Square in Athens glitters at night. Paris may be more famous for its open-air cafes, but Athens has them, too.

is one of the oldest and most highly respected in Europe, for it has its roots in Plato's Academy which was founded in the 4th century B.C. In the 1st century A.D. the Roman Emperor Marcus Aurelius established professorships in rhetoric and philosophy at Athens.

Today there are about 12,000 students at this distinguished university, and another 2,000 study at the University of Salonika, which was endowed in 1925. Athens also has a Polytechnic Institute, a school for the fine arts, one for economic and commercial studies and a college for advanced industrial study. Among the many foreign schools in Athens is the American School of Classical Studies for post-graduate students of Greek literature and archaeology.

WAY OF LIFE

In Athens, Greeks and visitors alike can choose among a wide range of entertainments: Museums display a host of treasures;

charming open-air cafés rival those of Paris, and *bouzoukia* night spots feature lively Greek music. During the summer there are outdoor symphony concerts, ballets, operas and beautifully produced presentations of classical dramas.

The fun-loving Greeks enjoy good food and before going, perhaps to the Theatre of Herod Atticus for a concert, the average Greek will want to linger over a fine meal. The appetizer may be *dolmades* (grape leaves filled with spiced meat) and the entrée *mousaka* (a casserole containing layers of eggplant and ground meat separated by a tasty sauce), or perhaps *ghiuvarlakia* (highly seasoned meatballs). There will be a salad, of course—perhaps tossed with vinegar and matchless Greek olive oil. For dessert there is *baklava*, a flaky pastry drenched in honey. As an aperitif he may have *ouzo*, Greece's famous anise liqueur.

In their festivals the Greeks combine a love of merriment with pride in their country's past. During the exciting Athens Festival in August

GREECE ■ 899

and September the National Theatre produces the masterpieces of Aeschylus, Sophocles, Euripides and Aristophanes. Each play is presented in English, French and Greek. Concerts, ballets and operas are given in the open-air Theatre of Herod Atticus. Just as exciting as the Athens Festival is the Sound and Light Pageant held in April. Spectators sit opposite the Acropolis and are swept back into antiquity by watching dramatizations of historical events. Another interesting celebration is the Epidavros Festival, which is held in June to commemorate Asclepius. He was the god of medicine and healing, and Epidavros is his legendary birthplace.

CULTURE

From the days of Homer through Athens' "Golden" 5th century and continuing through modern times, Greece has had a rich and varied culture. Although little is known about Homer, the blind poet who gave Europe the *Iliad* and the *Odyssey*, his epics have never been surpassed for strength and heroic beauty. Less well-known than Homer, but also extremely important in the development of European poetry is Sappho. She was the first lyric poet, and her works, which were written in the 6th century B.C., are still enjoyed by many people.

Art and learning reached a peak during the 5th century B.C. The Greeks' tremendous achievements during this period have never been equalled. On the foundations laid in philosophy, science, architecture, drama, sculpture, poetry, medicine, mathematics, physics and other fields, European culture was built. As the English philosopher John Stuart Mill said, "The Greeks were the beginners of nearly everything."

Greek temples were beautifully proportioned, rectangular structures which contained a large central room, or *cella*, and a porch with columns along the front and sometimes both sides. These magnificent temples were decorated with graceful statues. The balance and harmony found in Greek temples is typical of everything from Greece's Classical Period. Phidias, who designed the continuous frieze and the pediments of the Parthenon in Athens,

is the 5th century's most famous sculptor. He was followed in the 4th century B.C. by Praxiteles. Although no classical painting has survived, it was highly advanced. Apollodorus, who lived during the second half of the 5th century B.C., is the first painter who used light and shade effectively.

The poetry of the 5th century was usually topical; that is, it was written to commemorate an important event, as for example, the victory of a popular athlete. Pindar stands out among the many excellent poets of this period; he devised the Pindaric Ode, a lyric form which is still in use. There were wonderful prose works, too; Herodotus and Thucydides wrote the first histories.

The supreme achievement of Greek literature is the drama. It originated at Athens in religious festivals at which songs and dances

A woman from Marathon would never dream of dressing like the women of Mikonos or of Crete. She much prefers her own regional dress—a dark skirt covered by an intricately embroidered apron and a richly ornamented jacket.

In a sleepy courtyard tucked away in Athens, potted plants and a patch of sunlight make city life pleasantly rural. An ingenious housewife has left a bit of washing to dry on the branch of a tree.

were performed by people dressed in animal costumes. Aeschylus started the drama as we know it by adding an actor to these religious rituals. He wrote 90 plays, but we have only seven of them! Sophocles, Aeschylus' younger rival, increased the number of actors still more and refined the idea of drama. He gave us the famous character of Oedipus. Ancient Greece's third great tragic playwright is Euripides. Although he was not popular during his life, Euripides was later recognized as a genius equal to Aeschylus and Sophocles. There were many writers of comedy, but only 12 of their works survived—one by Menander (only discovered in 1957), and 11 of the 44 known to have been written by Aristophanes.

During the 5th century B.C. Greek philosophers had two major interests. One was the nature of the universe; Leucippus and Demo-critus developed atomic theories of matter, while Hippocrates brought a scientific approach to medicine. With minor revisions, the Hippocratic Oath is still used for doctors today. The second great interest of philosophers was the study of man and his social institutions. It was Socrates, the inventor of the question-and-answer method of teaching, who turned man's attention inward to questions about the soul and immortality.

Socrates' famous student, Plato, is best-known for his political ideas, which are presented in *The Republic*. In 385 B.C. he founded the Platonic Academy where young men were educated for public life. An equally famous school was the Lyceum, established by Aristotle in 335 B.C. Aristotle was more interested in practical matters than was Plato. Aristotle gave the world the scientific method of studying the universe, and his system of logic is the basis for all subsequent study of logic in the Western world. Versatile Aristotle himself lectured on logic, metaphysics, psychology, ethics, politics, rhetoric, poetry, mathematics, astronomy, physics, geography, zoology and botany. He represents the classical Greek spirit which boldly inquired into all areas of life. The modern-day separation between science and art did not exist for the ancient Greeks.

Although the 5th century B.C. represents the supreme achievements of Greek civilization, Greek culture never stopped developing. It was so superior that the nations which conquered Greece adopted it as their own. The Romans admired and imitated everything that was Greek, and under Roman domination the Greeks continued to advance. In the 3rd century B.C. there was Euclid, the founder of geometry; Archimedes, who made some of the first discoveries in mechanics; and Hipparchus, famed for his work in the science of exact measurement.

When the seat of the empire was moved from Rome to Byzantium in A.D. 330, Greek civilization continued to dominate the Mediterranean world. Greek was the language of all educated men, and Greek art forms persisted even though they became increasingly emotional and individualistic. Except for minor changes, Greek culture continued unbroken throughout the Turkish period and into the modern national era.

Today folk music and dancing and handicrafts are still a major part of Greek life. Brightly colored, handwoven and embroidered clothing and accessories such as handbags are made and sold all over Greece. Her people still take pride in their fine handicrafts, and they pass many pleasurable hours making hand-painted earthenware, carved rustic furniture, and household articles and jewels made of brass and silver. Since they love color, the Greeks use it lavishly in their own clothing as well as in the handsome items they make for sale.

Festivals are a merry, vigorous part of life in all parts of Greece, and a popular pastime for Greeks as well as visitors. They provide an opportunity for folk dances, some of which are so ancient they go back to the days of Homer. Especially colorful are the *sousta* and the *pentozali*, which the people of Crete dance with great skill. The folk songs of Greece are ancient, too, and they suit the Greek character in their simplicity and strong emotional nature. The themes are basic; folk songs tell of love, marriage, death and heroism. They are well-known and loved by all Greeks, young or old, city-dwellers or farmers.

During the 20th century there has been a great deal of activity in Greek literature. Angelos Sikelianos, whose collected works, *Lyric Life*, is well known, was active politically as well as creatively. He tried to revive Delphi as a cultural base, and in the late 1920's he organized two festivals there to promote world peace. But Nikos Kazantzakis, who died in 1957, is Greece's best known modern writer. He is the author of several novels, including

Folk dancing can be strenuous as well as graceful! Greek men take pride in their ability to execute difficult steps and impossible leaps. Dances like the one shown here require the utmost in athletic ability.

(Right) Athens' "flea market" is a goldmine for anyone who loves a good bargain. Although this cart is loaded with kitchen utensils, others display authentic antiques — amphoras, goblets, statuettes, antique coins and jewels.

(Below) Greeks love to wear their local dress—almost as much as they enjoy their folk dances, some of which go back to the days when Homer was a wandering poet.

Many people on Crete still wear the dress of days gone by, and it would not be surprising to see a dagger at this young man's belt. His fringed turban betrays a love of finery; even the horse wears a tasselled harness.

Zorba the Greek and *The Greek Passion* which have been translated into English, and of *The Odyssey*, an epic poem which is a continuation of Homer's great work. Konstantinos Kavaphis is another Greek poet whose work is becoming increasingly popular with English-speaking readers.

GOVERNMENT

Present-day Greece is governed by a revised version of the 1911 constitution drafted by Eleutherios Venizelos. This document provides for a constitutional monarch and for a prime minister. Both the prime minister and his cabinet are responsible to a parliament elected by secret ballot. Since 1951 women as well as men have been permitted to vote. With its numerous parties, the political system of Greece resembles that of France.

Although Greece is a democracy, its royal family is respected and loved. The Greek Monarchy has more than fulfilled the nation's royal motto: "My strength lies in the love of the people."

Following the coup d'état of 1967, the leaders of the junta stated that it would be at least a year before parliamentary rule was restored,

although the King, in public statements, expressed the hope that it would be sooner. By 1968, the King was in exile, following an abortive attempt to overthrow the junta, and a return to democratic rule seemed remote.

(Below) There are as many varieties of dress in Greece as there are towns, and this man's features also reflect the individualism which is typically Greek.

(Right) A tanned peasant girl holds the sticks on which wool is carded or wound into smooth strands for spinning.

(Below) Hydra's people throng the port late in the afternoon for a chat with friends. Hydra belongs to the Argola island group across the Saronikos Gulf from Athens.

(Above) Greece's festivals evoke the past with perfection. The classic purity of their hair styles, draped gowns and sandals make these girls living embodiments of history as they perform an ancient dance amidst the ruins at Delphi.

(Right) Women on the Aegean island of Skyros around a corner fireplace. The walls are lined with tastefully displayed hand-painted dishes, and the floor is covered with another of Greece's fine handicrafts, a gaily patterned rug.

ART

(*Above*) *Remains of the Temple of Apollo in old Corinth show the Doric column with its massive fluted shaft and simple rounded capital. The Doric order is simpler than the Ionic and Corinthian, which were developed later. It appeared around the 7th century B.C. and was perfected during Athens' cultural peak, the 5th century B.C.*

(*Left*) *The Doric order reached perfection in the Parthenon at Athens. Shown here is the area between the columns and the walls inside. In the 6th century the Parthenon was used as a church, still later as a mosque (a minaret was actually added!), and in the 17th century the Turks used it to store their gunpowder. Not until the 18th century was the beauty of the Parthenon recognized.*

(Above) Supreme examples of Greek architectural sculpture are these 7½-foot caryatids (*figures which serve as pillars*) on the Porch of the Maidens on the Erechtheum's southern side. They are the outstanding feature of this Ionic temple. The Erechtheum was constructed of white marble with black friezes on which there originally appeared relief sculpture in white marble.

(Below) Running all the way around the Parthenon between the columns and the sloping roof was a frieze 525 feet long. The relief sculpture was supervised by Athens' 5th-century master, Phidias, and it pictured a procession regularly held to extol the goddess Athena. In 1806 the Parthenon frieze and parts of the Erechtheum were taken to England by the Earl of Elgin, and they are now in the British Museum.

(*Above*) At the palace of Knossos on Crete is this fresco called the "Ladies in Blue." Sophisticated and highly stylized, this wall painting was done about 1500 year B.C.

(*Left*) In the museum at Olympia are many of the most admired works of ancient Greek sculpture, including this statue of a young girl. Notice that although the details are extremely realistic, the total effect is idealistic.

(*Above*) Pottery-making, Greece's oldest art, began about 900 B.C. At first the designs were mathematical and abstract, but gradually became more realistic. Many vase paintings represent scenes from everyday life or mythology.

(*Below*) Among the antique treasures housed in the museum at Heraklion, Crete, are these vases. Cretan potters still produce handsome earthenware plates and vases.

(*Above*) Cast in bronze, this statue of a charioteer was found at Delphi.

910 ■ GREECE

An aerial view of Athens' port city of Piraeus shows how densely populated is this base of Greek shipping and industry. Today, as in ancient times, Athens and Piraeus serve as a commercial link between East and West.

THE ECONOMY

Although the Greeks have always been expert merchants and sailors, their economy has never been consistently strong. The major reason for this is that only one-fourth of the land is suitable for farming (a smaller proportion than in any other European country). Over 60 per cent of Greece's 8½ million people are dependent on the land! The frequency of war during ancient as well as modern times is a second reason for prolonged periods of depression. Industry has been slow to develop because Greece has a small domestic market and is heavily indebted to other nations. A high birthrate and large influxes of refugees from Russia and Turkey, particularly in the early 1920's, have further aggravated a poor economic situation. Finally, since Greece's major exports are luxury items (wines and tobaccos), the nation's export income is dependent on the prosperity of its customers.

Low wages, the lack of jobs and frequent political upheavals have resulted in a high rate of emigration. During the 18th and 19th centuries large numbers of Greeks settled in Russia, Roumania, Hungary and Egypt. Between 1901 and 1920 a tenth of the Greek population emigrated to the United States!

AGRICULTURE

Added to the lack of good farming land are these problems—inadequate rainfall, depleted soil, and in some areas, outdated farming techniques. Nevertheless, agriculture has developed rapidly since the 19th century when most farmers were entirely dependent for food on what they could raise. Many farmers in mountain areas and on the small islands still live only on what they grow themselves, but specialized farming is carried on in the raisin-growing areas of Crete and the Peloponnesus, in the tobacco regions of Macedonia and Thrace, in Lesbos and Corfu where olives are grown in great quantities, and in the wine-producing

There is one thing about Greek farming that has not changed—women still work in the fields beside their husbands.

regions of Samos and Leukas. Tobacco and cotton, which are equal to the best varieties

Cotton is a major export item in the nation's economy. Modern farming techniques make it possible to water vast cotton fields automatically.

(*Above*) *Since World War II Greece has built several large hydro-electric installations. Gigantic dams such as this one at Lauros are bringing electricity to many isolated communities and are providing stimulus for the country's industry.*

produced anywhere in the world, are Greece's best commercial crops. The resin obtained from pine trees is used in the manufacture of turpentine and as a scent for a popular wine, *retsina*. Greece also exports citrus fruits, figs, fresh fruits (apples, pears, apricots), cereals, almonds, pistachios and walnuts.

NATURAL RESOURCES

During Greece's Classical Period, the Laurium ores (silver, lead and zinc) contributed to Athens' prosperity. Although mining was neglected during the four centuries of Turkish rule, it was resumed when the Greeks won their independence in 1827. Chromium, bauxite, lead, zinc, magnesium, sulphur and manganese are mined today. Superior Greek marble is in great demand. There are workable oilfields in Greece, but so far they have not been extensively developed.

Greece's greatest resource, waterpower, is not yet completely harnessed. Flooding, silting and soil erosion are still problems, but they are being eliminated as the country's vast water resources are brought under control. After World War II the Food and Agricultural Organization of the United Nations estimated Greece's hydro-electric potential at 5 billion kilowatt-hours per year. Recently, thermal and hydro-electric power plants have been constructed throughout Greece, bringing electricity to rural areas and enabling industry to develop much more rapidly than in the past.

INDUSTRY

Concentrated in the Athens-Piraeus and Salonika areas, Greek industry has been developing steadily but slowly since the end of World War I. The Axis occupation during World War II caused a serious setback. Damage to buildings, machinery and raw materials came to $110 (£39) million. With assistance

The seacoast city of Salonika, third largest in Greece, is a hub of shipping and industry, but a far cry from what most people think of as an "industrial" town.

(Below) He won't miss the vase ! Dock workers on all the Greek islands are experts at catching freight, even fragile, hand-painted earthenware.

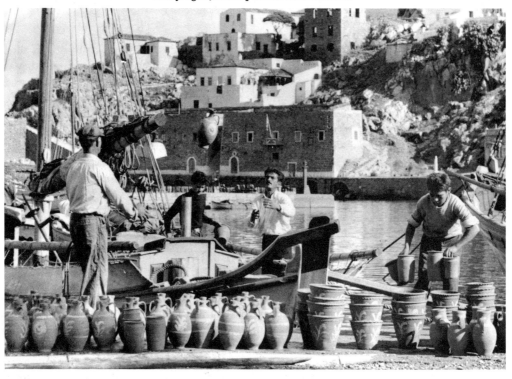

914 ■ GREECE

from the United Nations, Economic Co-operation Administration and the United States Army Corps of Engineers, Greek industry began a rapid recovery after the war.

In spite of Greece's postwar economic advances, agricultural exports remain its most profitable trade item. As always, sea transportation provides work for thousands of Greeks. In 1967 the Greek merchant marine ranked fifth in the world in terms of tonnage under the Greek flag, but third if Greek-owned ships under other flags are included. Greek ship-owners include some of the world's richest men, like Aristotle Onassis, who made news in 1968 by marrying Jacqueline Kennedy.

Postwar Greece is steadily achieving a position of prestige in the modern world. After centuries of triumph as a major Mediterranean power commercially and militarily and, later, as the dominant cultural force, Greece passed through a national eclipse. Under foreign oppression, it became the pawn of more powerful nations. After a long

At sunrise and sunset the sea is peaceful, but during the day it is full of small boats similar to the one shown here. Thousands of Greeks make their living from the sea.

and violent struggle, it achieved independence —only to face another century of political disunity and war. Today Greece is at last a strong, economically sound nation, able to build anew on the greatest cultural achievements known in the Western world.

(Below) All year round the Hellenic Shipyard bustles with activity. A ship in drydock is surrounded by cranes and scaffolds.

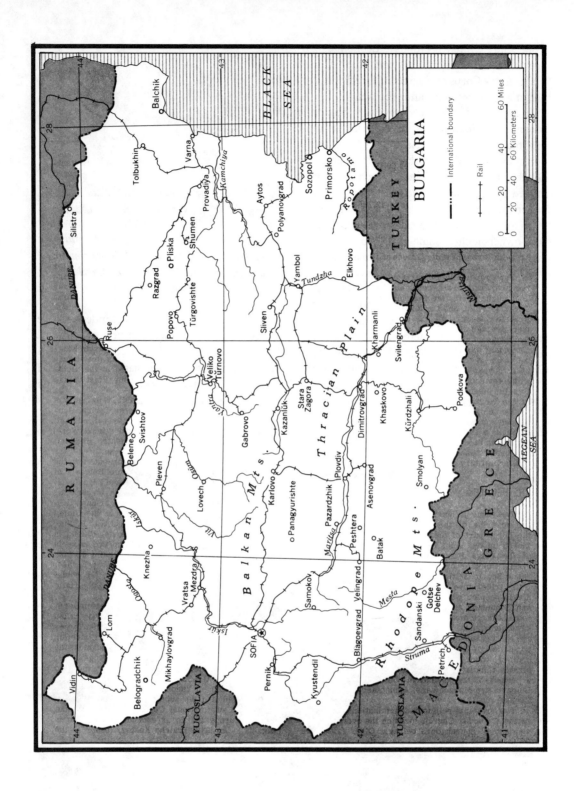

BULGARIA

International boundary
Rail

60 Miles
60 Kilometers

BLACK SEA

TURKEY

RUMANIA

YUGOSLAVIA

GREECE

AEGEAN SEA

MACEDONIA

Balchik
Tolbukhin
Varna
Silistra
Provadiya
Shumen
Pliska
Razgrad
Türgovishte
Popovo
Ruse
Svishtov
Beleneo
Pleven
Knezha
Vratsa
Mezdra
Lom
Mikhaylovgrad
Belogradchik
Vidin
Veliko Türnovo
Gabrovo
Lovech
Panagyurishte
Samokov
Velingrad
SOFIA
Pernik
Kyustendil
Blagoevgrad
Sandanski
Gotse Delchev
Petrich
Kazanlŭk
Stara Zagora
Sliven
Karlovo
Plovdiv
Pazardzhik
Peshtera
Batak
Asenovgrad
Smolyan
Dimitrovgrad
Khaskovo
Kürdzhali
Podkova
Kharmanli
Svilengrad
Elkhovo
Yambol
Polyanovgrad
Aytos
Sozopol
Primorsko

Kamchiya
Tundzha
Thracian Plain
Ropotam
Balkan Mts.
Rhodope Mts.
Yantra
Osŭm
Vit
Iskŭr
Marítsa
Mesta
Struma
Ogosta
DANUBE

Iskur Dam, north of Sofia, is part of a hydro-electric project on the Iskur River, the only river in Bulgaria that cuts through the Balkan range to the Danube River.

THE LAND

BULGARIA, IN THE SOUTHEAST corner of Europe, is one of the smaller European countries. With an area of 43,000 square miles, it is about the size of Tennessee, or half the size of Great Britain. Bulgaria shares borders with Rumania, Yugoslavia, Greece and Turkey. To its east is the Black Sea, which provides access by ship to the Soviet Union on the opposite shore. Through the strait of the Bosporus and the Dardanelles at the southwestern corner of the Black Sea, ships can sail from Bulgaria to the Mediterranean and out upon all the seas of the world.

TOPOGRAPHY

This photogenic land offers visitors a variety of scenery, for high mountains alternate with wooded hills, broad plains, pasture lands and dense forests. The country can be divided into several main areas—the Danube River Basin, the Balkan Mountains, the Rhodope Upland and the Thracian Plain.

The Danube forms all but a small part of the frontier with Rumania. The Danube Basin is a tableland sloping northward until the land drops abruptly in steep cliffs 600 feet down to

In back of these houses at Belogradchik in north-western Bulgaria are bluffs where the Danubian Basin drops into the river valley. Composed of loess, a deposit of loam-like earth, the cliffs are similar to the bluffs along the Missouri River in the United States.

the river. The Rumanian shore of the river, by contrast, is very low.

South of the Danube Basin and running from west to east across the entire country are the Balkan Mountains, which give Bulgaria

the strongest claim to be called a Balkan country. Bulgarians call this range the *Stara Planina* (old mountains). The Balkan Mountains are an extension of the Alps that stretch from France through Switzerland, Italy and

Golden Bridges, on the slope of Mt. Vitosha near Sofia, is a river of rocks left by a glacier. The sun hitting the rocks sometimes gives them a golden hue, which explains the name given to the formation.

Girls in the Valley of Roses pick blossoms that supply almost all of the world's perfumes with one of their essential ingredients— attar of roses.

Austria into Yugoslavia. Although fairly easy to cross, the Balkan Mountains have offered protection from attack through the ages.

Pliska, site of the First Bulgarian Kingdom, is tucked away in these mountains, as is Turnovo, capital of the Second Kingdom. Even in this century, the Balkans were one of the focal points of resistance during World War II.

South of the main Balkan Range and running parallel to it, is the Sredna Gora, or central range. Between the two ranges is the fragrant Valley of Roses, which produces attar of roses, the scented extract for which Bulgaria has long been famous. Kazanluk is the principal city of the valley.

The rugged Rhodope, Rila and Pirin Mountains, collectively called the Rhodope Upland, with their deep gorges and high waterfalls, stand in the southwest of the country. Mount Moussala, in the Rilas, is 9,564 feet

Borovets is a year-round resort in the foothills of the Rila Mountains. From here tourists climb to Mount Moussala, the highest point on the Balkan Peninsula. Winter sports at Borovets include skating, skiing, tobogganing and ice hockey.

BULGARIA ■ 919

Limestone rocks near the fortress at Belogradchik form a petrified forest of weird shapes. So it is no surprise that townspeople have names for certain rocks such as "The Bear," "The Horseman" and "The Cuckoo."

high, and is the highest mountain in the Balkan Peninsula. Icy ravines and swift streams tumbling down their slopes give the Rilas a primitive beauty and make them an especially memorable sight for the visitor.

The rest of the south is occupied by the Thracian Plain, a land known for its fruitfulness since the time of the ancient Greeks. The Maritsa River and its tributaries flow through the Plain, draining into the Aegean Sea, through Turkey and Greece.

CLIMATE

Bulgaria has a variety of climates. North of the Balkans, the climate is like that of central Europe. Summer temperatures hover between 70 and 80 degrees, while winters can get quite cold, especially along the Danube when a cold wind comes whipping down from Asia.

South of the Balkans, the climate is milder, halfway between that of the Mediterranean and

Water pumped from an artificial lake (in the background) is used to irrigate this field near Sofia. Although rich soil is one of Bulgaria's greatest resources, a lack of rain requires large-scale irrigation.

central European regions. Summers are warm and dry, with mild winters.

In the mountainous areas, short, cool summers and cold winters are the rule, with a higher rainfall than the rest of the country. The Black Sea coast is warmer than the interior, and summer temperatures vary between 64 and 80 degrees. Summers in Sofia are hot, but not unbearable, with cool nights.

Rainfall in Bulgaria is light, for the most part, except in the mountains. This is why irrigation has been necessary in the two great farming areas of the Danube Basin and the Thracian Plain, in spite of their rich soils.

PORTS AND WATERWAYS

The Danube River is the mightiest in Europe after the Volga River in Russia. The river is navigable from Ulm, Germany, all the way to the Black Sea, yet its commercial shipping is less than the Rhine. The Danube, after rising in West Germany, is fed by 300 or more smaller streams carrying water from the

Mt. Vitosha provides residents of Sofia with a ready-made resort area, and breathtaking natural scenery. An excellent road leads up the side, with both a ski lift and funicular railway for the more venturesome.

A stream feeding the Ropotamo River flows through a lush growth of oaks, elms, ash trees, willows and ivy, which gives the landscape an almost jungle-like appearance.

Alps, the Carpathians and the Balkans. In the spring, floods on the Bulgarian stretch of the Danube are not uncommon, as the snows melt on the mountain ranges. In severe winters, the river may freeze over.

Bulgaria shares control of Danube commerce with other nations through which the river passes, under the terms of an agreement setting up an international commission. The chief Danube River ports in Bulgaria are Ruse, Svistov and Vidin.

Of rivers within Bulgaria, the largest are the Iskur, which rises in the Rila range, and flows into the Danube, and the Maritsa. Others are the Struma and the Tundzha.

The 236-mile Black Sea coast is mostly lowlying and there are few good natural ports. Marshes and lagoons are common along much of the coast.

NATURAL RESOURCES

Bulgaria suffers from a shortage of certain minerals—especially coal—needed for a nation to grow industrially. To help solve the problem,

Fishing boats rest on a strip of beach by the Black Sea, close to Nessebur. About 180 species of fish, including bass, mackerel, bonito, sole and bluefish, make their home in the Black Sea.

American children are off on a donkey ride at a Black Sea resort. New hotels form clusters, with plenty of space between them, in which old buildings and features of the natural landscape can survive.

scientists have gone out to discover new resources and have had some success. Uranium and new deposits of lignite (brown coal) have been discovered near Sofia, as well as petroleum and natural gas deposits near the Rumanian border, on the Black Sea.

Although still burning coal for some electric power, Bulgarians are now putting their rivers to work to produce hydro-electric power. Hydro-electric power stations use falling water from dammed rivers as the source of energy to make electricity, and do not cause pollution, since they do not send smoke and gases into the air.

There are enough deposits of copper, manganese, lead and zinc to sustain mining operations.

FLORA AND FAUNA

Almost everywhere the land has been cleared so crops can be grown, and much of the natural vegetation has disappeared. However, areas with wild plants similar to those found in central Europe can be seen at the mouth of the Ropotamo River, in the mountains, and on some islands in the Danube. Along the Turkish and Greek borders, typical Mediterranean plants, like citrus fruits, figs and rhododendrons grow.

There are large forests of pines, particularly in the high mountains of the Rila, Pirin and western Rhodope ranges. Oak, beech, hornbeam, elm, ash, lime and hazel trees are found in the Balkan Mountains, and young firs are being planted there also as part of the government's conservation scheme.

With the clearing of the land, some of the

Catch a fish in this mountain stream at Borovets and the chef of your hotel will cook it for you.

Camel-riding at Black Sea resorts is great fun for tourists.

deer and even jackals. For hunters there are partridge, pheasant and grouse in abundance. Cave dwellers, including bats, are numerous, and lepidopterists visiting Bulgaria can have a field day, for there are 1,100 kinds of butterflies and moths to track down!

SOFIA

Sofia, the capital of Bulgaria, dates back over 2,000 years. Through the centuries it was known as Serdica by the Thracians and Romans, and Sredets (meaning middle) by the Slavs. It became Sofia in the 14th century, named for the Orthodox Church of St. Sofia in the city.

Between peaceful eras the city was devastated by the Goths and Huns, Petchenegs, Crusaders and, finally, the Turks. By the 1800's, Sofia had the look of a small Turkish town, with a population of only 20,000, as late as 1878.

Today, there are 800,000 people in Sofia, and it is the nation's industrial, cultural and governmental capital. The city's oldest monument is St. George's Church built in the second or third century A.D. as a pagan temple. When Roman Emperor Constantine ruled Sofia, he converted the temple into a church. Next to the church is a well-preserved Roman road with grass growing between the stones, and foundations of Roman buildings along the sides.

wild life has been depleted, also. Still, many species, some of which are extinct in other European countries, roam freely in the forests: bears, wolves, boars, foxes, badgers, lynxes,

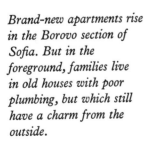

Brand-new apartments rise in the Borovo section of Sofia. But in the foreground, families live in old houses with poor plumbing, but which still have a charm from the outside.

Vine-covered fishermen's cottages line the narrow streets of Sozopol, on the Black Sea. Founded by the Greeks in 610 B.C., Sozopol was first known as Apollonia because of a 42-foot statue of Apollo which stood in a temple dedicated to the god. Today Sozopol has a thriving fishing industry, and many artists come there to paint.

THE COMING OF THE SLAVS

The Western Roman Empire, as well as Byzantium, was invaded by barbarian tribes from Asia including the Huns under Attila. These Asian tribes forced the Indo-European Germans and Slavs to migrate, in most instances into the Roman Empire. Among the tribes who first came to fight, and later settle in Moesia, now Bulgaria, were Slavs originally from central Europe. Today the Slavs make up most of the population of Russia, Bulgaria, Yugoslavia, Czechoslovakia and Poland.

In 679, the Slavs in Moesia were conquered by the Bulgars, tribes of horsemen originally from central Asia. The Bulgars slowly took on the Slavs' language and way of life. The Moesian Slavs and the Bulgars merged to form

This tomb in Kazanluk with remains of unknown Thracian chieftain dates back to the 3rd century, B.C. The open ante-chamber of the tomb leads through a short stone corridor to the burial chamber. The entire wall surface of both corridor and chamber is covered with murals, some showing soldiers in battle.

These walls around Hissar, a mixture of stone and brick, are 10 feet thick in some places, and rise ?0 feet. They were built by the Romans in A.D. 251 as protection after the town (then called Augusta) had been attacked by the Goths. The Turks gave the town its present name of Hissar, meaning fortress.

the state of Bulgaria, with its capital at Pliska. For the next 350 years, Bulgaria and Byzantium were to engage in bloody battle.

THE BULGARIAN KINGDOM

In 681, the boundaries of the First Kingdom were the Danube River, the Black Sea, the Balkan Range and the Iskur River. Bulgaria, like the rest of Europe, was organized under the feudal system. The common people were bound to the lord of the manor, in return for a plot of land. Ruling over the lords were higher nobles, and over them was the khan, or prince. Later rulers took the title or *tsar* or king, actually a Slavic version of the Roman *Caesar*, German *Kaiser*, and Russian *Tsar*.

The south gate at Hissar, called the "Camel" because of the humps on the top, is part of a thick Roman wall still remarkably intact. Since Thracian times, different peoples have lived or visited here, bathing in and drinking the mineral water for which the town is famous. The Romans built marble baths, paved streets, and installed a water supply system fed by an aqueduct.

Veliko Turnovo is an amazing city built on the sides of steep cliffs, with the Yantra River at the bottom. Between 1185 and 1396 it was the capital of the Second Bulgarian Empire. Art and literature flourished there, and writers of the time referred to the city as "second after Constantinople." Merchants carried on brisk trade with other European cities. Gradually, feuding among medieval lords, and later the Turkish invasion, destroyed the kingdom.

Gradually Bulgaria extended its borders. Khan Krum (802?–814) after defeating the Avar horsemen in the west, fought the army of the Byzantine Empire and seized Sofia, then called by its Latin name of Serdica.

In 857, Tsar Boris I took the throne of what had become a powerful state. He wanted to bring Christianity to Bulgaria, and thus further his prestige in the medieval world. He was torn between aligning himself with the Holy Roman Empire, ruled by the heirs of Charlemagne which would have meant accepting the Roman Catholicism and the papacy; or with the Eastern Roman Empire, which meant the Eastern Orthodox faith and the authority of the Byzantine Emperor. The Eastern Empire won out, and the Bulgarians were given greater freedom in running their church. The Byzantine patriarch in Bulgaria claimed no political power, so Boris could strengthen his position.

Among the missionaries who came to Bulgaria to spread the faith were the brothers Cyril and Methodius from Greece. They knew the Bulgarian language and invented an alphabet which made it possible to record it. In its modern form this Cyrillic alphabet (named for Cyril) is used by several other Slavic languages, as well as Bulgarian. At first only religious works were written, but later secular or non-religious books appeared, as Bulgaria grew more independent of Byzantium.

TURKISH RULE

The Turks eventually conquered most of the eastern Mediterranean area, including all of Byzantium and the Balkan countries.

There was some opposition to the rulers by guerrilla groups living in the mountains, but the Turks were able to put down each uprising and inflict new cruelties. After many years as part of the Ottoman Empire, the world, and many Bulgarians, forgot that Bulgaria as a nation had ever existed. The Greek Orthodox

St. Nedelya Cathedral faces Lenin Square in the heart of Sofia. During Roman times, when the city was called Serdica, this site was at the junction of its two main streets. Excavations under the cathedral show the remains of a Roman public building and ruins of a number of small churches built here during the early Bulgarian period when nobles had chapels for their private use. The present church was built in the late 1800's after the style of Russian churches. It was here in April, 1925, that an attempt was made to kill Tsar Boris with a bomb.

Church, whose headquarters were in Constantinople, dominated the religious life of the people. The Bulgarian litergy was suppressed and the Bulgarian language was written in Greek characters.

NATIONALIST MOVEMENT

In the 1860's, a revolutionary movement sprang up with headquarters in Rumania (which had gained its independence in 1861) and little underground groups in Bulgaria. Some of its leaders led an uprising based in Plovdiv in 1876, which was put down with renewed cruelty. This aroused Russia to action, and Russian troops came to Bulgaria's aid. In a stunning victory the Turks were defeated in

1878, with Bulgarian and Rumanian volunteers fighting bravely with the Russians and winning victories at Pleven, Stara Zagora and Shipka Pass.

The Treaty of San Stefano, signed in March, 1878, provided that the Sultan should surrender nearly all of Turkey's territory in Europe except Constantinople. But at this point, the great powers stepped in to prevent Russian influence spreading to the Balkan Peninsula.

Three months later the Treaty was revised at the Congress of Berlin and most of the conquered territory was returned to Turkey. Northern and central Bulgaria gained independence as a new principality technically under the authority of the Sultan. Southern Bulgaria, under the name of Eastern Rumelia, became a partly self-governing Turkish province.

The Congress called for Bulgarian leaders to meet at Turnovo, draw up a constitution, and elect a prince for the new principality of Bulgaria. The Liberals at the meeting outnumbered the Conservatives, and a very far-sighted and democratic constitution was drawn up. It permitted freedom of speech, of the press, and of assembly—quite enlightened for a country in that part of the world at that time. A problem arose when Prince Alexander of Battenberg was elected as the first prince in 1879. He was a nephew of Czar Alexander II of Russia, and he gave preference to Russian over Bulgarian interests.

After Czar Alexander's death, Prince Alexander's sympathies swung away from the pro-Russian elements, or he was forced to switch loyalties. He restored the constitution in 1883 and formed a more moderate government of both Liberals and Conservatives. In 1885 the union of Bulgaria and Eastern Rumelia was declared. Alexander braced himself for a Turkish invasion, but none came.

Any further strengthening of Bulgaria was regarded by Russia as against its interests. The ink was scarcely dry on the Treaty when Prince Alexander was kidnapped and a pro-Russian government was put in power. This faction, in turn, was overthrown by a movement led by Stefan Stambulov, President of the National Assembly. Alexander was brought back, but did not have the support to remain in power.

A new leader, Prince Ferdinand of Saxe-Coburg-Gotha, was chosen who, it was hoped, would unite all factions and gain the support of the world powers. He was eventually successful and able to proclaim complete Bulgarian independence from the Turks in 1908, assuming the title of king.

WORLD WAR I AND AFTER

The immediate cause of World War I was the assassination of an Archduke of Austria-Hungary by a young Serbian. For Austria-Hungary, the murder was a good excuse to wipe out Serbia, which stood in the way of its expansion in the Balkans. Russia backed Serbia, while Germany came into the war on Austria-Hungary's side. After long hesitation, Bulgaria entered the war on Germany's side, hoping to even the score with Serbia, and again was the loser. The Treaty of Neuilly in 1919, forced Bulgaria to give up its land on the Aegean to Greece, western Macedonia to Yugoslavia, and land in the north to Rumania. Toward the end of the war Ferdinand's army was rebelling, and he abdicated. His son Boris became king.

After being shattered by its participation in World War I, Bulgaria was in a state of chaos. Unemployment, poverty and hunger gave rise to a new movement among the working class, and the Communist Party came into existence in Bulgaria.

In 1934, Boris suspended the constitution and the freedoms which it outlined, and banned all political parties.

WORLD WAR II

In spite of protests by Bulgarian intellectuals in the opening months of World War II, the government rejected a Soviet proposal in 1940 for a non-aggression and mutual assistance pact between the two countries. In March, 1941, Bulgaria accepted the Vienna Pact of Hitler, and German tanks rolled into Sofia without a struggle.

However, a resistance movement of Bulgarian partisans opposed to Hitler was forming under the name of the Fatherland Front.

Hero of the 19th century, Vasil Levski helped unite the country against the Turkish oppressors and worked for a federation of the Balkan peoples. His birthplace in Karlovo is now a museum.

After the German defeat at Stalingrad, Bulgarian partisans became more bold and actively resisted the Germans. In August, 1944, some of them met with the Americans and British in Cairo, Egypt, to see how they might ease themselves out of the war. On September 5, while these talks were underway, the Soviet Union declared war on Bulgaria. Operating with partisans and military units that had deserted from the regular army, the Russians took the country in five days.

The Communist-dominated Fatherland Front of Bulgaria was put in power and replaced the unsuccessful government that had been formed to arrange an armistice with the Allies. Later, Bulgarian forces fought alongside Soviet troops against the Germans in Yugoslavia, Hungary and Austria. At the Conference of Paris, Bulgaria gained back land in the north given to Rumania after World War I.

This is one of 100 statues in Pleven commemorating the Russian and Rumanian soldiers who helped the Bulgarians in 1878. In this work an old Bulgarian soldier is reminding a young Russian soldier of their countries' historic ties.

THE PEOPLE'S REPUBLIC

Communist power was strengthened in the next two years, and a People's Republic under a Communist government was set up on September 15, 1946. Georgi Dimitrov became prime minister of the country, and the new constitution, fashioned after the Soviet constitution, bore his name.

Dimitrov was trained from youth as a revolutionary, and had organized unions within the printing industry in which he worked. During World War II he was active in Russian politics and lived in Moscow. While head of Bulgaria he was the most important leader in the Balkan countries, and their ministers came to him for advice. He was often hailed at demonstrations, with the crowds chanting "Dee Mee Trov."

Dimitrov died in 1949 and was succeeded by Vasil Kolarov, and then by Dimitrov's brother-in-law, Vulko Chervenkov. Chervenkov was a supporter of Stalin's policies and reflected Russia's tightening hold on Communist-bloc nations after Yugoslavia was thrown out of the Cominform in 1948. The Cominform, dissolved in

1956, was an international Socialist organization formed by Russia to combat the American Marshall Plan for West European nations.

In 1954, following Stalin's death, Chervenkov yielded the post of party head to Todor Zhivkov. Zhivkov immediately blamed Chervenkov for all the Stalinist persecutions in Bulgaria, and replaced those men in the government who were loyal to the Stalinist régime, with moderates. Chervenkov was finally ousted from leadership in November, 1961. But the final "de-Stalinization" of Bulgaria did not come until a year later when several other high officials were taken from power.

After Zhivkov assumed full power in 1962 he strengthened ties with Russia. In 1969, he launched a campaign against Western influences in Bulgaria's arts and culture, and warned against anti-Soviet "revisionist" nationalism. Nonetheless, his régime has shown a recent wish for closer relations with the West in such areas as trade and tourism.

Dancers and an accordionist perform in a Plovdiv street. These houses have interesting paintings and carvings for decorations.

THE PEOPLE

ABOUT 85 PER CENT of Bulgaria's 8,400,000 people are descendants of the Slav and Bulgar tribes that came together to form Bulgaria in the 7th century. The second largest group (8 per cent) are Turks, living mainly in the eastern Rhodope Mountains as farmers. The balance of the population are gypsies, Armenians, Russians, Greeks and Jews.

Bulgarians as a whole are friendly and hospitable. One visiting Italian commented that in this country the greeting "good morning" really means "good morning." When meeting guests at an airport or rail station, the Bulgarian arrives with bouquets of flowers.

The country takes pride in the beauty of its women, and one folk song describes the Bulgarian girls as having "the slender body of a nymph, a creamy complexion, a mouth like a rose, and eyes like black cherries." The men are tall and sturdy, able to do hard work. Although fair-haired Bulgarians are found, most have dark hair and brown eyes.

These swimmers take a dip in the Danube near the medieval fortress at Vidin. This city in the northwest corner of Bulgaria has had to fight away oppressors ever since it was occupied by the Celts in the 3rd century B.C.

BULGARIAN WOMEN

The Bulgarian woman is much respected by men, and no job is closed to her because of her sex. Although many women work and run a household as well, others are helped out by the grandmother who lives in the home. It is not uncommon to see grandmothers walking their grandchildren, doing the shopping, or chatting on park benches.

Women are found in all types of work from politics to teaching. As in many European countries, they also hold strenuous jobs as street cleaners, streetcar conductors, heavy-machine operators, farm workers, or miners. There are many stories of how Bulgarian women—with or without guns—performed feats of heroism against the Nazis in World War II. March 8th is set aside as a holiday, to pay tribute to the nation's women.

COUNTRY LIFE

Bulgaria is still a land of many small villages, with quaint one-storey houses of wood and bricks. In the past, many of the houses lacked indoor plumbing. Today, an effort is being made to modernize them, and to provide electricity, water and sewage systems for each village.

In the middle of the typical town are buildings housing the local People's Council, grocery, reading club, post office, inn, and public bakery. These bakeries save women the job of making the bread for the family. The heat from the bakeries often provides warm water for public baths nearby.

Small factories and businesses are being started in many farm towns, bringing new prosperity. Young people who would have gone to the city for a better job a generation ago now can stay and work to improve their communities.

CITY LIFE

As with most countries in the 1970's, Bulgaria faces a bad housing shortage in urban areas and has built many new apartment buildings to meet the mounting need. These buildings often have only four floors, so that elevators are unnecessary. Each apartment has a balcony decorated with plants climbing up to the balcony above it, forming a leafy curtain. Red pepper pods are hung out to dry, and then ground into paprika to season spicy dishes.

City life is fairly pleasant, with many parks in the big cities, not too much traffic, and the countryside within an easy bus ride. For entertainment there are the cinema, ballet, opera, museums and sports events.

FOOD

Like his Russian cousin, the Bulgarian eats heartily, filling up with plenty of potatoes. Breakfast and lunch are big meals, with supper a light snack.

Lamb and veal are the basis for most main dishes. The national speciality is *kebaptschetas*, grilled patties of ground veal and lamb, spiced with black pepper, paprika and onions. The

Fish dry outside the windows of this Bulgarian home.

patties are usually served with fried potatoes and a salad. *Moussaka*, ground veal topped with goat cheese and baked, reflects the Turkish influence. Another popular dish is *pecheno sirene*, white cheese with butter and paprika, heated in rolls of paper. At the evening meal, eggs, tomatoes, onions, green peppers and cheese are fried together to make a dish whose English translation is mish-mash. For dessert there is *banitsa*, a sweet and sticky cheese-filled pastry eaten with fruit.

Wine and mineral water are served with meals. But Bulgarians like a choice of beverages, so it is not unusual also to find fruit juices, cola drinks, Turkish coffee, tea made with dried lime leaves, lemonade, or other drinks at the table. The national drink is a thick, grey brew of fermented sesame seeds called *boza*.

Mention should also be made of Bulgaria's yogurt, fermented sheep or goat's milk made thick and creamy by bacterial action. Bulgarians

eat it with the main course, and are convinced of its healthful qualities. They attribute the long lives of their farmers and the vitality of their opera singers to yogurt. In 1969, a sales team from Bulgaria set out to market their kind of yogurt in Western countries, with Bulgarian scientists supplying the know-how and bacterial cultures for the project.

One of the most popular dishes in Bulgaria is "kebaptscheta," made of ground lamb and veal grilled over a fire.

Folk dancers wearing embroidered vests take spectacular leaps in the air. Folk dancing is a national pastime, and dances many have their roots in the Turkish, gypsy or Slavic cultures that have touched Bulgaria.

MUSIC

Bulgaria is a land of singers, and through the centuries music has provided some relief from the dreary life under oppressors. There is a large body of folk songs about everyday activities (songs of the ploughman and the shepherd), those for special occasions, and those about national heroes. Thousands of these songs have been collected by Bulgaria's Institute of Music.

Instruction by trained music teachers is compulsory for young people. Adults enjoy playing in little amateur symphony orchestras, or listening to the popular music from the West that manages to find its way into the country. Bulgarian opera singers have gained international fame, singing at Milan's La Scala, London's Covent Garden, and New York's Metropolitan.

Vera Korova and May Dachevske are Bulgaria's two top ballet stars.

934 ■ BULGARIA

Houses of Veliko Turnovo are reflected in the Yantra River. Once dependent on a small craft industry, the city today manufactures textiles, furniture, canned goods, and a number of other products.

ECONOMY

A generation ago, three-quarters of the national production came from farming, and one-fourth from industry. Now, the nation is proud that, with total output increased, the proportions are reversed. More women work now—one in three workers are now female, particularly in medicine and education.

In the future, computers will come to the aid of government economic planning. For years, economists have been debating the lack of equality in the price system. Some prices are felt to be too high, and some, like railway fares, too low. To unravel some of the confusion of artificial prices and learn how productivity can be raised, economic planning is being computerized, probably on a broader scale than in any Eastern European country.

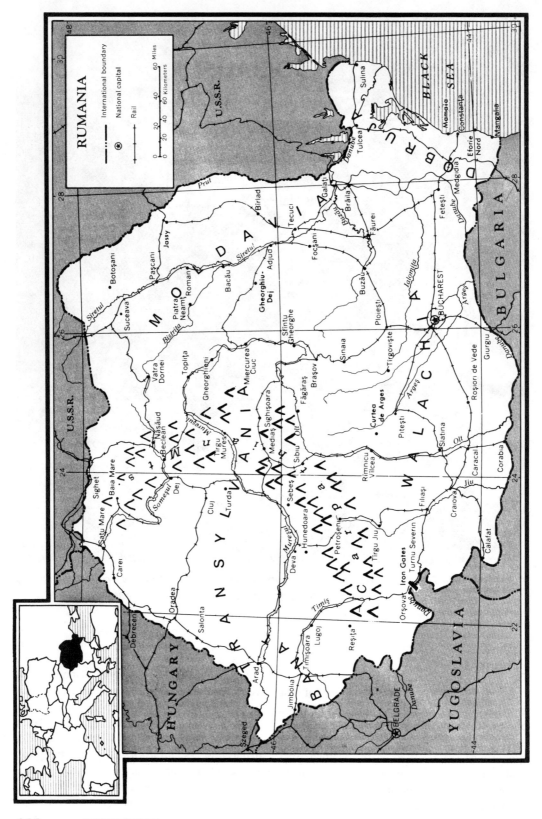

RUMANIA

International boundary
⊛ National capital
Rail

0   20   40   60 Miles
0 20 40 60 Kilometers

U.S.S.R.

BLACK SEA

Sulina

Momaia
Constanța

Eforie
Nord

Medgidia

Mangalia

D O B R U D J A

Tulcea

Danube

Galați

Brăila

Buzău

Fetești

Danube

BULGARIA

Prut

Bîrlad

Tecuci

Focșani

Ialomița

Argeș

BUCHAREST

Giurgiu

Danube

Botoșani

Pașcani

Jassy

Siretul

M O L D A V I A

Suceava

Roman

Bacău

Gheorghiu-
Dej

Adjud

Buzău

Ploiești

Sinaia

Tîrgoviște

Roșiori de Vede

Slatina

Piatra
Neamț

Bistrița

Vatra
Dornei

Toplița

Gheorgheni

Mercurea
Ciuc

Sfîntu
Gheorghe

Brașov

Făgăraș

Curtea
de Argeș

Pitești

W A L L A C H I A

Năsăud
Beclean

Sighișoara

Mediaș

Sibiu

Rîmnicu
Vîlcea

Olt

Olt

Jiu

Corabia

Caracal

Mureșul

Tîrgu
Mureș

T R A N S Y L V A N I A

Sebeș

Filiași

Sighet

Baia Mare

Dej

Someșul

Cluj

Turda

Hunedoara

Petroșeni

Tîrgu Jiu

Craiova

Satu Mare

Carei

Deva

Mureș

Iron Gates

Turnu Severin

Calafat

Orșova

Danube

Oradea

B A N A T

Timiș

Lugoj

Reșița

HUNGARY

Salonta

Arad

Jimbolia

Timișoara

YUGOSLAVIA

Debrecen

Szeged

BELGRADE

Danube

RUMANIA

The Olt River cuts through the southern Carpathian Mountains, with a string of spas and monasteries along its banks. Before the river flows into the Danube, the land around it flattens out. The Olt overflows its banks in the spring, and in the summer the flooded land supports a rich crop of grain.

THE LAND

RUMANIA, IN THE southeast corner of Europe, is a bit smaller than Great Britain, and about the size of Oregon, U.S.A. Its population of almost 20,000,000 is ten times greater than Oregon's, but considerably smaller than Great Britain's 55,000,000. Rumania is at the crossroads of ancient trade routes between Asia and Europe, and even today its position is ideal for trading with both Western Europe, and the Soviet Union, with which it shares a long boundary. Through the Strait of Bosporus, on the Black Sea, Rumania's ships can reach countries bordering on the Mediterranean. Hungary lies to the west, Yugoslavia to the southwest, and Bulgaria to the south.

TOPOGRAPHY

The geography of the country varies widely—lofty mountains and broad plateaus, rolling foothills dotted with orchards, fertile plains and a sunny seacoast. Spread over this landscape are caverns, lakes and forests.

Hunedoara Castle existed as a fortress in the 14th century and was gradually transformed into a residence. Damaged by fire in 1854, the castle is now under restoration. It successfully combines architectural styles that have been popular in Rumania through the ages. Once a town of furriers and tanners, Hunedoara now has two open hearth furnaces that produce tons of steel each year.

Encircled within the Carpathians is Transylvania, a plateau whose untouched beauty makes it a delight for visitors. Bram Stoker, author of the *Dracula* books, describes the castle of the terrible Count Dracula in Transylvania as "on the wall of a terrible precipice. A stone falling from the window would fall a thousand feet without touching anything. As far as the eye can reach is a sea of green tree-tops, with occasionally a deep rift where there is a chasm." There are indeed castles in Transylvania (Bran and Hunedoara are two famous ones), but they are quite free of mystery compared with Dracula's.

The Carpathian Mountains of Central Europe run through part of Czechoslovakia, Poland and the Soviet Union's Ukraine before ending in Rumania. As can be seen on the map, they make a semi-circle through the heart of the country.

There are many rivers and passes that make it easy to cross through the mountains. Among the most scenic are the Bicaz River, which cuts its way through limestone cliffs, and the Predeal Pass. Most of the rivers start in the Carpathians and drain eventually into the Danube, which runs along most of the southern border. The Somesul River in the north links the country with the eastern plain of Hungary, while the Muresul River links the interior with the plains in the western part of Rumania.

Jassy, the former capital of Moldavia, is at a crossroads of ancient trade routes. In the 1800's the city was a headquarters for the movement to unite the states that today form Rumania. Industry in Jassy includes furniture and antibiotics factories, ironworks, and textile mills. The city is proud of its many scientific and cultural institutes.

Busteni, with a health resort and paper mill, is nestled in the Prahova River near Sinaia. The steep mountains near the town are great for climbing.

Mamaia, on the Black Sea, hugs a narrow strip of land between a lake and the open sea. The secret of its mild summer climate is that water evaporating from the lake creates enough moisture to protect the town from the typical heat of the Dobruja region.

Between the Carpathians and the Prut River, in the northeast, lies Moldavia. The western part is mountainous, while the east, between the Siretul and Prut Rivers, is a plain or steppe, good for growing grains. Northern Moldavia is famous for its painted churches whose outside walls illustrate Biblical or historic scenes. Some of these show cruel Turks and were intended as propaganda to arouse hatred for the invader. The principal towns of Moldavia are Jassy, its former capital, and Galati, which has one of the largest steel plants in Europe.

In the central part of the south is the plain of Walachia. Bucharest, with a population of 1,500,000 people, is the former capital of Walachia and now capital of the entire country. North of Bucharest is Ploesti, with its famous oil fields, and beyond these industrial areas is rural Walachia, where farmland, vineyards and orchards lie in hollow valleys.

In the southeast is the Dobruja, where the Danube swings north, branching out into three arms of water and flowing into the Black Sea. Where the river divides the Danube Delta begins. At one time the Black Sea was lower, and the Delta was a wide plain through which the Danube flowed to the Black Sea. Then

The narrow Dambovita River slices through Bucharest, with most of the business district on one side, and parks and lakes on the other. According to legend, the name Bucharest comes from a shepherd named Bucur who was attracted by the beauty of the Dambovita and settled in the area.

Constanta, on the Black Sea, is one of Rumania's oldest cities. It is built over the ruins of the ancient Greek colony of Tomis, founded more than 2,500 years ago. It was to Constanta that the Roman poet Ovid came in 8 A.D., driven into exile by Emperor Augustus after being involved in a scandal. Crooked streets and the Oriental look of mosques add quaintness to the modern city. For amateur archeologists there is a museum, an open-air archeological exhibit, and a Roman ruin noted for its mosaics.

through the centuries the sea became higher than it is today, and flooded the Delta. Now the water is slowly receding and the Delta is in the process of another change. The Delta's scenery is breath-taking, with all sorts of plants and animals that find nourishment in the water.

Along the Black Sea, the Dobruja is well populated with resort towns and the seaport of Constanta. Elsewhere there are fewer people since rains wash away so much of the topsoil that the land is not suitable for farming.

Although the climate of Rumania is generally like that of continental Europe, there are variations. The colder climate in the high mountains has an average summer temperature of 40 degrees, and an average winter temperature of 18 degrees. A warmer climate with a greater

range is found in the basins and plateaus, with hot summers averaging 70 degrees and cold winters averaging 21 degrees. In the plains and lowlands there are hot summers averaging 73 degrees and cold winters of about 23 degrees average.

Rainfall varies, the lowest being recorded on the Black Sea coast, the highest in the mountains. There are heavy rains in the spring, less in summer and autumn. Flooding of the Danube can cause great damage, as demonstrated in the spring of 1970.

The assortment of plants and animals is as varied as the regions of the country. The mountains are the hide-out of the bearded vulture and the chamois, a small goatlike antelope. Deer, bears, wolves, boars, lynxes, squirrels and

A flock of pelicans take wing over the Delta marshes.

martens (like large weasels) are also found. Trout are plentiful in the mountain steams. Fir and spruce forests cover the mountains.

In the steppes or plains, short and tall grasses grow where the land has not been cultivated. The tall grasses are high enough to conceal a man on horseback. Where civilization has not driven them out, rodents, hares, and birds such as the bustard (a heavy, long-legged game bird) are found.

The Danube Delta is a paradise for birds, especially in spring and autumn, when five major bird migrations pass over it. Nightingales, egrets, spoonbills, cormorants, geese, northern ducks, eagles and ospreys live in the Delta in different seasons. On the east bank of one channel is a reservation where the only large pelican colony of Europe nests. White willows or black poplars grow along the banks in sediment deposited by yearly floods. Floating plants such as water lilies and crowfoot lie on the surface of the pools. Reeds in the Delta are harvested in November, when birds have gone to their winter homes.

Lumbering out of the forest is a brown bear, some of which weigh as much as 700 pounds. Bears attack cattle or sheep brought up to graze on the Rumanian mountain ranges during the summer, and are a threat to shepherds.

In Adamclisi, 40 miles from Constanta, stand the ruins of a monument by Roman Emperor Trajan to celebrate his victory over the people of Scythia Minor, the present day Dobruja. In front is a model of what the monument might have looked like.

HISTORY

About 2000 B.C., Indo-European tribes, the Thracians from the west, drifted into the region, ranging over large areas from the Aegean and Adriatic Seas to the western shores of Asian Turkey. One group of these tribes, the Dacians, lived in the region that is now Rumania. They established contact with several slave-owning Greek colonies along the Black Sea—Histria, Callatis and Tomis. The kings of Dacia protected these cities for centuries.

By the 3rd century B.C. the Dacians were organized into a strong state with a high level of civilization. In the 1st century B.C., a great king, Burbista, ruled an empire that stretched across a large section of southeast Europe and managed to defend his kingdom against Julius Caesar. But by 106 A.D. Dacia was conquered by the Romans, led by Trajan, and was to remain a province of the Roman Empire until 271.

From the 3rd century on, the Romans could no longer defend Dacia against the barbarian tribes that were overrunning Europe. Avars, Goths, Slavs and Bulgars swept across what is now Rumania. Surviving in the mountains were the Latin-speaking peasants who had stayed on after the Roman withdrawal. Even today there are pockets of people (Vlachs) in Bulgaria and Yugoslavia speaking dialects of Rumanian. Under the Bulgars, a return to government took form, and when Bulgaria's King Boris was converted to Christianity, he brought this religion to the Vlachs as well as to his own country.

About the 10th century, Transylvania was taken over by the Magyars, or Hungarians, a group of tribes originally from Central Asia. Then under Hungarian leadership, Germans, called Saxons, began to establish a number of

Michael the Brave, ruler of Walachia from 1593 to 1601, won brilliant victories against the Turks and Tatars. To gain further strength against the aggressors, he conquered Transylvania and Moldavia, bringing the three states for the first time under one rule.

Ottomans made Constantinople, capital of the Byzantine Empire, their capital. Today Constantinople is Istanbul.

Walachia got help from Transylvania in fighting the Turks, but the two were defeated in 1396. Although Mircea later returned to the throne, Walachia was forced to yield to Turkey.

The state of Moldavia was founded slightly after Walachia, taking shape in 1359 under Bogdan I. One of the early princes was Petru Musat, a relative of the Basarab family of Walachia. He held the state in the interest of his leader, Mircea the Old. Petru married the sister of the King of Poland, forming a tie with that nation—ever after there would be shifting alliances with Poland. At times Moldavia would turn to Poland for help against the Turks, and then when stronger Poland would dominate, the two states would fight one another. A similar pattern of on-and-off friendship existed between Hungary and Walachia.

The Hungarians, who had held Transylvania for 400 years, suffered a crushing defeat from the Turks at the battle of Mohacs in 1526. By the middle of the 1500's, the Turks had a strong foothold throughout Moldavia, Walachia and Transylvania. But they reckoned without Michael the Brave, Prince of Walachia, who came to the throne in 1593. He obtained a loan of 400,000 ducats, paid off the Turkish ruler, and took the throne from Alexander, the reigning prince. Then he brashly massacred Turkish guards, and with the Prince of Moldavia invaded the lands south of the Danube. He won brilliant victories against the Turks, and defeated the armies of the prince of Transylvania, Andrei Bathory. Michael proclaimed himself ruler of Moldavia, Transylvania and Walachia. He is a great folk hero in Rumania today, since the Vlachs of all three states were united for the first time.

fortified cities such as Cluj, Sibiu, and Sighisoara, in Transylvania.

With the coming of the Hungarians, some Rumanians, or Vlachs, were driven south out of the Carpathians. One group settled in the area later forming Walachia, which gets its name from the Vlachs. The other went into what was to become Moldavia. The Vlachs mingled with Slavs and Tatars already in these areas. Not until 1859 were Moldavia and Walachia to become united as Rumania.

Walachia was first set up as a state under the thumb of Transylvania in the 13th century. But one of its princes, Basarab, defeated the Hungarian King Charles I Robert in 1330 and gained independence for the new state. In the early days, the Hungarians were the enemies, but during the reign of Mircea the Old (1386–1418) the Turks became the main aggressors. The Turkish, or Ottoman, Empire was gradually taking over countries to the south— Serbia (now part of Yugoslavia), Bulgaria, and the Byzantine or Eastern Roman Empire. The

The union of the three states was short-lived, since Hungary moved back into Transylvania and drove Michael's army out. Poland invaded Moldavia and put a friendly prince back on the throne, only to have the Turks take over again in 1618. Turkey took over Walachia and put a puppet prince on the throne.

In the early 1600's the capital of Walachia was moved from Tirgoviste to Bucharest, at a safe distance from Hungarian Transylvania, from which attacks were a constant threat. Turkey began taking a bigger part in choosing the princes of Walachia and Moldavia. The Turkish choices were often of Greek origin. The first important Greek prince was Serban Cantacuzino, Prince of Walachia, who helped the Turks in their unsuccessful penetration of

Hapsburg's Austrian Empire. Defeated at the gates of Vienna in 1683, the Turks began to lose their possessions in Europe. At the height of their power the Turks had penetrated as far as Hungary, and held all the land of present-day Rumania.

CREATION OF RUMANIA

At the Congress of Paris in 1856, Moldavia and Walachia were made independent principalities within the Ottoman Empire. Soon after they were united under Alexander Cuza, and

In the early Middle Ages, Saxons settled in Sibiu, in Transylvania, which even today has a well-preserved medieval section. In the 15th century the town surrounded itself with new walls thick enough to keep out the invading Turks. Today the Germanic influence survives in the neat tiled houses, Lutheran faith, and old Saxon dialect. The most interesting spot for visitors is the Brukenthal Museum, named after an 18th-century governor of Transylvania, whose collection of historic and art objects is displayed in his former house.

The Palace of the Republic (older building in the middle), built in 1930 and used until 1937 as a royal palace, now houses several museums. The National Gallery section has works by Rumanian artists such as Nicolae Grigoresco, as well as icons, manuscripts, carved furniture and sculpture. In the Gallery of World Art are works by European artists. Attached to the Palace is Congress Hall (middle foreground).

used the name of Rumania for the first time, but still within the Ottoman Empire. Cuza brought in a series of land reforms, angering the boyars and clergy by making them break up their lands. He could not please the peasants either, who felt the reforms did not go far enough. So Carol of Hohenzollern, a German prince, took the throne in 1866 and served until 1914.

Not that all was calm under his rule. In 1878, Rumania fought with Russia against Turkey and finally shed itself completely of Turkish domination.

When King Carol died in 1914 his son, Ferdinand, took power, marrying Princess Marie of Edinburgh, a granddaughter of England's Queen Victoria. When World War I broke out, Rumania again tried to stay neutral.

However, it was only a question of time before the country got involved on the side of England and France. At the peace table, Rumania gained Transylvania and Banat, which had been held by Austria-Hungary. Bessarabia was taken from Russia, which had been defeated by Germany and was in a state of civil war.

The death of King Ferdinand in 1927 created a crisis in the monarchy. His 5-year-old grandson Michael I became king, since his father Carol II had given up rights to the throne in 1925. But Carol renewed his claim and finally took over in 1930.

The government of the 1930's was dominated by the terrorist tactics of the Fascist, anti-Semitic Iron Guard, whose members wanted to align the country with Germany and Italy.

The Iron Guard took Rumania into World

946 ■ RUMANIA

War II on the side of Germany. In June, 1940, the Germans insisted that Bessarabia be returned to Russia and two months later the Germans made Rumania return northern Transylvania to Hungary. After the German attack on Russia, Rumania suffered severe defeats from 1943 on, with people at home starving.

King Michael who had succeeded his father Carol, after Carol's death in exile, led a coup and booted out the Iron Guard dictatorship, on August 23, 1944. He signed an armistice with the Allies and confirmed the return of Bessarabia to Russia, gaining back northern Transylvania.

THE PEOPLE'S REPUBLIC

An Allied Control Council, with a Russian as chairman, was sent to Rumania to help run the country until the Peace Treaty was signed in February, 1947. With the added factor of the Russian Army in the country, it was natural that the Communists won elections and took over easily. In December, 1947, King Michael stepped down and the Communists proclaimed Rumania a People's Republic. A constitution like Russia's was adopted in 1948.

RUMANIA TODAY

By 1952 the government had replaced Communists whose loyalties were to Rumania with pro-Soviet Communists. Gheorghe Gheorghiu-Dej became premier in 1952 and a new constitution was put in effect emphasizing Rumania's independence of the Soviet Union.

Since late 1961, Rumanian Communism has become less dependent on Moscow. Along with this has come a more moderate Communism without Stalinist pressure. Nearly all political prisoners were released in the 1960's, and the government has tried to strengthen its position in the country by attracting different groups such as the intellectuals and farmers who were previously against Communism. Party membership has grown.

Leadership since the late 1950's has been stable. When Gheorghiu-Dej died in 1965,

Bucharest's Arch of Triumph was built in the 1930's along the lines of the more famous Paris arch. In the distance is the government printing house, where editorial offices of the main newspapers and magazines and the Rumanian Press Agency are located. The printing house was built after World War II in a heavy style nicknamed "Stalin Gothic," of which one finds examples in Warsaw and Moscow. Presses at the printing house turn out some 2,000,000 copies of newspapers and magazines each day.

Nicolae Ceausescu gradually assumed power, starting as party chief and becoming chief of state in December, 1967.

In 1967, Rumanian Prime Minister Ion Maurer visited President Johnson in the United States. This was followed by a successful visit of President Nixon to Bucharest in 1969, the first time an American president had visited an East European Communist nation in 25 years. He and Ceausescu discussed the possibility of opening a United States-to-Rumania civil air link.

Symbol of Rumania, the Atheneum in Bucharest is a concert hall and headquarters of the George Enesco State Philharmonic Orchestra. The snowy white outside of the building resembles a Greek temple with a heavy Baroque dome.

THE PEOPLE

OF THE 20,000,000 PEOPLE living in Rumania, 87 per cent are ethnic Rumanians. Of the minority groups remaining, 8 per cent are Hungarians, 2 per cent are Germans, and the rest are Jews, Ukrainians, Greeks, Turks and gypsies.

Those of Rumanian stock proudly trace their ancestors back to the Romans, reliving battles fought 20 centuries ago between the Dacians and Romans. They prefer the spelling "Romania" to "Rumania" or the compromise "Roumania," which both point up the Western influence. The Rumanian's link with a Latin past is evident in his dark eyes and features which make him look almost Italian.

The Hungarians live in Transylvania, numbering three-fourths of the local population in some towns. They are a politically significant group and are given some self-government.

Jews first came to Rumania in the late 15th century. Other Jews from Poland and Russia came during the 19th century, introducing some modern financial institutions. Many Jews have emigrated to Israel in recent years.

Women in Bucharest stock up on groceries in this modern store. Fresh meat and vegetables are more often sold in separate shops.

LANGUAGE

Rumanian is a Romance language similar to Latin, but with many Slavic, German and Greek words. Rumanian was long written in the Cyrillic alphabet used in the Slavic languages. Then, in the 1800's a move developed in Transylvania to use the Latin alphabet instead, emphasizing the Roman origins of the nation. It is written with this alphabet today.

German or Hungarian is spoken by small pockets of people in Transylvania. French is heard frequently in the cities, going back to a period of close business and political ties with France before World War II.

LIVING CONDITIONS

Most Rumanians would say that life under Communism is better than under any previous government. Food is available, but lines are long in food shops and it can take two hours a day to collect an ordinary family's food needs. The biggest complaint is the shortage of clothes, appliances and cars. Moreover, quality is sometimes poor since the better goods are sold abroad. Rumanians realize that in a developing country, industrialization is more important than providing consumer goods, but they still resent having to go without certain things.

A crest of peacock feathers adorns the hat of this young man in folk costume.

FOOD

The Rumanians have an interesting style of cooking—rich, but with subtle seasonings. Some dishes have been borrowed from the Slavic, Hungarian and Turkish cultures.

Breakfast is on the light side and may include rolls, butter and jam, along with tea, milk or coffee. Boiled eggs, ham, cheese or sausage are available for a more hearty meal.

Dinner, served about 2 P.M., is the principal meal and is accompanied by wines, or *tuica*, the Rumanian plum brandy. The first course of soup has a base of meat, vegetables or noodles. It may be a *borshch* like its Russian cousin, but with more vegetables, or it may be *ciorba de perisoare*, meatball soup.

Next is the main course—quite likely garnished veal with boiled, fried or mashed potatoes. Other specialities are boiled beef, and broiled or spit-roasted chicken. A national dish, and real staple of the farmer, is *mamaliga*, a boiled cornmeal served either as a bread

substitute, with stuffed cabbage or vine leaves (*sarmale*), or with poached eggs. Hot or cold, *mamaliga* is delicious in melted butter or yoghurt, garnished with salted herring and cottage cheese.

All the above are accompanied by salads and vegetables such as eggplant, sharp peppers, or gherkins.

For dessert there are several popular dishes: *placinte*, turnovers with various fillings; *baclava*, a Turkish cake in syrup; delicious ice cream or the pâtisserie typical of Transylvania. Fresh watermelon, cherries, apples, grapes or peaches may be served as well. Turkish coffee completes the meal.

Rumania is rich in game and fish of all kinds. In the mountains, brook trout and venison are popular, while Danube Delta cooks roast carp on spits, and make a delicious fish soup. Supper, with a basic course of grilled beef, pork or chicken, is served about 8 P.M., again with wines and brandy. The highly seasoned grilled meat balls—*mititei*—are famous at home and abroad.

A fisherman pulls in his net among the tall rushes of the Danube Delta.

"The Table of Silence" is one of Brancusi's large-scale works at Tirgu Jiu, near where he grew up. Perhaps the "table" top is a millstone, and the 12 "seats" around it represent the 12 numbers on the face of a clock, suggesting that time grinds all things down.

ART

Rumanians are an artistic people whose creativity has found expression in every century, even when under the thumb of a foreign ruler. One example of their early art is the black pottery created by the ancient Dacians and reproduced today. It is decorated in a luminous gray, or a range of shades from gray to black.

BRANCUSI

Constantin Brancusi (1876–1957) stands out as the most impressive sculptor the country has produced. As a shepherd boy, he worked in the

surrounding hills and came to know the moods of nature. Serving as an apprentice with a carpenter, he later studied at the Bucharest Academy of Fine Arts. His first nude was so realistic that it was used at the medical school in Bucharest as an anatomical model.

FOLK ART

Through the centuries, folk art has taken many forms—from the Arges pottery decorated with bone pen and wire brush, to the peasants' homes with their quaint garden fences and entrance gates. The peasant measures his wealth in the number of hand-crafted objects and materials in his home, and a girl's dowry is made up of handmade linen and embroidery.

In demand are the Oltenian carpets, with their red and blue floral and animal designs, and the Moldavian carpets, with dark tints and a tree-of-life design. Rumanian painting on glass, of which the most famous are the glass icons of Transylvania, show striking realism and skill.

Many rural Rumanian homes have been moved piece by piece from different sections of the country to make up the charming Village Museum in Bucharest. The houses in this restoration are furnished with authentic utensils, furniture, carpets and decorations—many have looms in them. Besides the houses, visitors can wander through little country churches and see reconstructed windmills. There is even a gold sluice, where gold mined in the mountains was once processed.

This sturdy old peasant may be reflecting on the many changes that are taking place in Rumania.

Folk costumes vary from region to region, but all excel in the variety of their styles, with highly decorative embroidery worked in gold and silver thread, and trimmed with spangles and tiny beads of tinted glass.

The women wear embroidered blouses, apron skirts worn over white underskirts, and either an embroidered veil of raw silk or cap ornamented with pearls. The men wear a shirt, and trousers of coarse wool held up by a belt of cloth or leather. In winter the men embroider sheepskin vests for themselves or for sale.

RELIGION

For some years after the Communists came to power religion was curtailed, even though freedom of worship is guaranteed to all citizens. Many churches were closed, church lands seized, and priests accused of subversive activities.

In the 1960's the government adopted a more tolerant attitude and spent money to restore churches and monasteries. Although this was done mainly to make them tourist attractions, it also drew some Rumanians back to a religious life. The Rumanian Church joined the World Council of Churches in 1961.

About 80 per cent of the people belong to the Rumanian Orthodox Church, an extremely active branch of the Orthodox group, with an extensive monastic network. The Greek Catholic or Uniate Church, which recognized the authority of the Pope, and to which 10 per cent of the people belonged, was forced by the Communists to break with the Vatican in 1948 and join the Orthodox Church.

Today Roman Catholics, largely Hungarian, make up about 9 per cent of the population; the rest are Calvinists, Jews and Lutherans.

A celebration is in progress within the historic walls of Sucevita Monastery.

The August 23rd Steel Works (in foreground) in Bucharest is one of the largest plants in the country. Beyond the plant is a broad zone of new housing.

THE ECONOMY

As WITH THE surrounding countries, Rumania was once a rural, backward land. For centuries under Turkish rule, peasants lived off the food grown on a plot of land, and their sons divided it to make even smaller plots. In the 1800's the country painfully moved from a type of late feudalism into capitalism. Factories and mines were built with foreign investments—mostly English and French. The foreigners preferred to ship the minerals and raw materials back to their own countries and then sell the Rumanians the expensive finished products. Still, there were now some opportunities for the farmers to leave the land and get better paying jobs.

This situation existed until World War II, when all industries were taken over by the Germans. After the war, the Russians and Rumanians jointly took them over, drastically overhauling the nation's economy along Communist lines. All factories, mines, banks and transportation networks were nationalized—run by the government. Private enterprise was done away with except for small farms and craft operations. Many wealthy people suddenly found themselves without a penny because their bank accounts were seized.

Several joint Soviet-Rumanian companies were set up with names like Sovrompetrol

At this shop in Bucharest, the customer has a wide choice of textiles, many produced in Rumania.

(petroleum prospecting and processing), and Sovromtransport (shipping). These ventures gave the Soviet Union trade advantages over other countries in developing Rumania's natural resources.

In 1954 these joint companies were abolished, as Rumania rid itself of Russian influence and now operated them itself. In 1964, Rumania boldly rejected the Soviet plan for East European economic integration and insisted on the right to its own domestic and foreign policy. It did not want to be a supplier of raw materials and produce to more developed Communist nations, and thus have to depend on buying finished products back from them. Rumania still belongs to the Council for Mutual Economic Assistance (COMECON) of Eastern Europe, but is an inactive member.

FLOODS OF 1970

The floods of early 1970 struck a hard blow to the economy, and especially the Galati mill on the Danube. They were caused by heavy rains, and a heat wave that melted snow on the mountains. Dikes built to protect the mill and factories in Galati were fairly effective, but there was much damage throughout the country. Close to 200 people were killed, many farm animals were lost, as well as homes and factories.

This sprawling state farm raises pigs under the most modern conditions.

Albanians don folk costume for a celebration. Proud and clannish, they have kept their identity in the face of many invasions.

ALBANIA

SHQIPERIA IS THE NAME the Albanians give their small country (10,629 square miles) on the Balkan peninsula, on the Adriatic Sea between Greece and Yugoslavia. The Dinaric Alps make most of the country difficult of access, but there is a wider strip of low land along the coast than in either Greece or Yugoslavia. Much of the coast is marshy, unhealthy, and sparsely inhabited.

The Alps rise to heights of more than 9,000 feet. Rainfall is heavy and the lower slopes of the mountains are densely forested. Between the mountain ranges are fertile valleys, and there most of the people live. By far the most common

trees in the southern mountains are evergreen oaks. In the north are mixed forests of beech, pine and fir. The vegetation of the coastal lowland is Mediterranean, chiefly scrub of the type known as *maquis*. The climate is typically Mediterranean only in the lowland region and in the southern mountains. The climate of the northern highlands is much cooler than in the other regions of the country. Animal life shows a mixture of Mediterranean types—wild goats, porcupines, voles, cuckoos and warblers—as well as Central European forms—chamois, moles, lynxes, wolves, foxes, chaffinches and thrushes. Natural resources include petroleum, brown coal, iron, chromium, copper and asphalt.

The country is largely agricultural, industry being still largely undeveloped. Trade is more than half with Communist China.

HISTORY

Albania has a very long history of foreign rule, yet its people have preserved their original Thraco-Illyrian language, although with heavy borrowings from Latin, Turkish and Slavic. Albania, part of Illyria until conquered by the Romans, passed to the Byzantine Empire after the division of the Roman Empire, then to the Goths in the 5th century A.D.; again came under the Byzantines; passed to the Serbs and then the Bulgarians and back again to the Byzantines and to the Kingdom of Epirus. From 1271 to 1368, the central part of the country was ruled by the Kingdom of Sicily. Finally the Turks invaded Albania, and the country remained under their rule until 1912, when independence was regained. Created a kingdom at that time, the nation became a republic in 1925. In 1928, the President, Ahmed Zogu, was declared King Zog I and the restored monarchy survived until 1939, when Italy invaded and annexed Albania. After World War II, a Communist Republic was established, under Russian influence. After Stalin's death, Albania made news by pushing the Russians out and becoming the only European satellite of Communist China.

GOVERNMENT

The country is officially a People's Republic, but is in fact a dictatorship under the rule of Enver Hoxha, who has led the nation since 1946, and whose title is First Secretary of the Communist Party. The head of state is officially the chairman of the presidium of the People's Assembly.

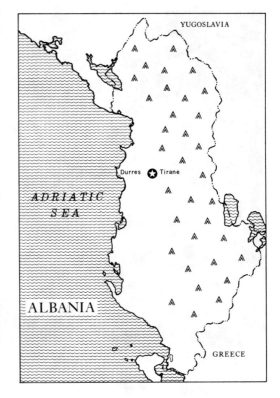

THE PEOPLE

The 2,000,000 Albanians are nearly 70 per cent Moslem, 20 per cent Orthodox Christian and 10 per cent Roman Catholic. There are two ethnic groups—the Tosks, the more advanced, in the south, and the Ghegs, northern mountaineers, with a primitive and complicated code of revenge and blood feuds. In both groups, the traditional style of dress, customs and diet show Turkish influence.

The capital, and largest city, is Tirane (161,000) and the principal seaport is Durres (48,000), long known by its Italian name, Durazzo.

The Valleys of Andorra, one of which is seen here, are all more than 3,000 feet above sea level.

ANDORRA

HIGH IN THE Pyrenees Mountains between France and Spain, Andorra is a tiny nation of 179 square miles, including a number of upland valleys—which give the country its official name of the Valleys of Andorra. The highest point is Pla del'Estany (9,678 feet), and the chief river is the Valira. Technically a principality with two co-princes—the Spanish Bishop of Urgel and the head of the French government—Andorra is run like a small republic, comparable to the cantons of Switzerland.

Andorra's independence is traditionally supposed to have been granted by Charlemagne in the days when the country was part of the Frankish Empire. In A.D. 954, Andorra passed to the Bishop of Urgel, and in 1208, the Count of Foix was made co-sovereign with the Bishop. When Foix became part of France, the joint-sovereignty passed to the French head of state.

The 18,000 Andorrans are Roman Catholics and speak Catalan, the language of northeastern Spain and part of southern France. About 3,000 of them live in the capital, Andorra la Vella. Most Andorrans make their living from agriculture (tobacco, livestock, cereals, potatoes, vegetables) and tourism. Andorra has no sales taxes or customs duties and tourists (1,000,000 a year) flock to Andorra for bargains, as well as for pure mountain air and beautiful scenery.

Set amid snowy Alpine peaks, the Castle of Vaduz looks down upon the capital of Liechtenstein, which bears its name.

LIECHTENSTEIN

THIS BEAUTIFUL Alpine principality nestles in a bend of the Rhine between Switzerland and Austria. Its 17,000 people are German-speaking Roman Catholics engaged mainly in agriculture and light industry (precision instruments, textiles). Tourism and the issuing of postage stamps are also large sources of revenue. Very liberal tax laws have led hundreds of foreign business firms to establish their headquarters in Liechtenstein. A little over 60 square miles in area, the country reaches its highest altitude in the peak called Grauspitze (8,526 feet).

The capital, Vaduz (population 3,500) was the nucleus of the present state, having been constituted a countship in 1342. In 1719 the present principality was created. Although a German state, Liechtenstein escaped absorption into either the Austrian or German Empires. In modern times it has followed a course of close collaboration with Switzerland. A constitutional monarch, the prince governs with the aid of a prime minister and a unicameral parliament. The principality is divided into 11 communes, each with a measure of self-government.

MALTA

MALTA, 58 MILES from Sicily and 180 miles from Africa, has been a focal point in the Mediterranean since Phoenician times. The island group, consisting of Malta (95 square miles), Gozo (26 square miles) and Comino (1 square mile) was ruled by the Carthaginians, Romans, Arabs and Normans among others, and finally passed to a military-religious order, the Knights of St. John, who were given the islands by the Holy Roman Emperor in 1530. Napoleon took Malta in 1800, but lost it to the British. Malta and its people lived through one of the most heroic sieges of World War II, as Nazi planes battered it daily. In 1964, the little island nation became independent, as a Commonwealth member, with Queen Elizabeth II represented by a Governor-General, and the actual executive power in the hands of a Prime Minister.

The islands are bleak, windswept, with poor soil and insufficient water—yet they produce crops of vegetables, fruit and grain, and support over 300,000 people. The main industry is ship repairing, but there are other light industries also.

Valletta (17,000) is the capital. Most of the people are Roman Catholics, and are the only Europeans who speak a Semitic language. In addition to Maltese, English is an official language, and Italian is widely understood.

Valletta lies between two of the best natural ports in the Mediterranean, making little Malta important in world shipping.

MONACO

THE SMALLEST STATE in Europe (excluding Vatican City), Monaco would fit into New York City's Central Park, with room to spare— 369.9 acres! The principality is situated on the Mediterranean Sea, surrounded by France on three sides. It comprises three communes— Monaco-Ville, the capital (2,000 people), La

Tiny Monaco was once much larger, including not only the cliff in the background (now French territory) but much of what is now the French Riviera.

Condamine (11,000) and Monte Carlo (9,000), the latter famous the world over for its casino.

Monaco, located on the magnificent French Riviera, with the Maritime Alps rising behind it, and the blue Mediterranean spread out before it, is a natural playground—and tourism is the chief support of the 23,000 people. Only half the people are Monegasque citizens, the other half being mainly French. French is the language and Roman Catholicism the religion of most residents.

The principality, which dates from c. 968 A.D., passed to the House of Grimaldi in 1297. The Grimaldis still rule, their ranks having been increased by the marriage of American film queen Grace Kelly to the reigning prince, Rainier III.

SAN MARINO

High in the Apennines, San Marino looks out upon the Italian city of Rimini and the Adriatic Sea.

THIS 23-SQUARE-MILE republic, high in the Apennine Mountains of northeastern Italy, appears to have been founded about A.D. 350. The little state has remained independent through all the intervening centuries, when one political upheaval after another took place in Italy, either due to warring Italian dynasties or foreign invaders.

The 18,000 citizens of the republic are mainly farmers, herdsmen and artisans. Wheat, wine, cement, and textiles are the chief products. Tourism and the sale of postage stamps are important sources of revenue. The language is Italian and the religion Roman Catholic.